BLACK SONG:

The Forge and the Flame

Stained-glass window in the chapel at Tuskegee Institute.
POLK'S STUDIO, TUSKEGEE INSTITUTE, ALA.

BLACK SONG:
THE FORGE
AND THE FLAME

*The Story of How
the Afro-American Spiritual
Was Hammered Out*

JOHN LOVELL, JR.

Paragon House Publishers
New York

Published in the United States by

Paragon House Publishers
90 Fifth Avenue
New York, NY 10011

First U.S. Paperback Edition 1986

The edition is reprinted by arrangement with
Macmillan Publishing Company, a division of
Macmillan, Inc.

Library of Congress Cataloging-in-Publication Data

Lovell, John, 1907-
  Black Song.

  Reprint. Originally published: New York : Macmillan,
1972.
  Bibliography:
  Includes indexes.
  1. Spirituals (Songs)—History and criticism.
2. Afro-Americans—Music—History and criticism.
3. Folk music—United States—History and criticism.
4. Folk-songs, English—United States—History and
criticism.   I.Title.
ML3556.L69   1986   783.6'7'09   86-18699
ISBN 0-913729-53-1
10 9 8 7 6 5 4 3 2

MEMORIALLY DEDICATED TO MY PARENTS,

John and Zula Lovell,

WHO LOVED THESE SONGS,
SANG THEM,
TAUGHT THEM TO THOUSANDS OF PEOPLE,
AND LIVED, FOR NINE DECADES EACH,
IN THEIR SPIRIT

Contents

. .
.

PART TWO / THE SLAVE SINGS FREE

PART THREE / THE FLAME

Preface

. .
.

I F A folk song ever grew to epic stature, it is the American Negro spiritual. The thousands of black creators and the irrepressible groups who picked up the songs and kept them alive and moving were certainly perpetually busy. They were spread all over the slave land for hundreds of years. The few thousand songs extant are thus hardly more than a tiny fraction of the total output.

To review the evidence on how the songs were made is to believe, easily, that in the great days of their creation the sky and the air were filled with them. But as in any music-hearted folk community over a long period of time, for definable reasons and for no reason, vast numbers of songs disappear. With keen sadness one must concede that thousands of full-bodied specimens as vital as "Swing Low," "Didn't My Lord Deliver Daniel," "I Know Moonrise," and "Oh, Freedom" vanished into the cold, unpoetic atmosphere. The proper nurture of the relative handful which remains is the best the lover of beautiful songs can now do.

If the past foretells the future, the prognosis for this small drop of respect is not good. With many of its describers and evaluators the black spiritual has lived a Cinderella life, full of belittlement and confusion. Only the world's people, whose ears have been captivated by the melodies and whose hearts and minds have thrilled to the poetry, have paid due homage. The most widely accepted interpretations of this black folk music, when brought together, are far from reasonable, let alone in accordance with the best evidence.

If folk song were a mere gewgaw of social history, this misrepresentation would be bad enough. That folk song is one of the most reliable indexes of growing humanity introduces a really critical note. While we today search for true meanings in racial difference and racial conflict, and true prospects of ultimate racial cooperation, we cannot afford such misrepresentation or the absence of the true revelations in the songs—not for another minute!

For these urgent reasons, this author has set out to present with care the available evidence on the spiritual, the foundation stone of black song and black poetry in this century. In the first section, "The Forge," he offers an authentic and connected story of how the songs were hammered out. In Part Two, "The Slave Sings Free," he identifies the folk community that gave rise to the songs and the creators who actually "framed" them (in the Blakean sense). He then interprets the songs as philosophy and literature. In addition to his own insights he will utilize those of hundreds of all-but-neglected, sensitive interpreters from many parts of the world.

Very rarely is a folk song taken to heart by more than a handful of appreciators outside its original folk. Never in history has this happened when the folk were despised slaves. But the black spiritual has outlasted, by more than a century, its original creators in the minds of Americans, without sign of losing strength. It has also built large new communities in a great many parts of the world. It has been adopted by millions as freedom song and as multipurposed anthem of the human spirit. For innumerable and sometimes strange reasons, it has inspired writers and singing groups to new expression. It has evoked and affected a number of folk and art pieces, secular as well as religious, in a variety of surprising and striking ways. This wide and deep dispersal, still going on, deserves a special section. The title of this special section, third in the book, is "The Flame."

The question of bibliography has been most seriously considered. It is obvious that many areas had to be investigated in order to establish various essential truths about the subject. Key works covering such areas are generally mentioned in the text. It was finally decided that the most useful service to scholars and other curious persons could be performed through a system of source notes. These notes appear in the back of the book and are arranged, in alphabetical order, according to applicable chapters. The first time a source is listed, a full bibliographical note is given. Thereafter, such source is referred to by author's last name and title. Every factual item, or critical opinion not belonging to the author, is covered by a source note.

We turn now back to the smithy where these unique and enduring black songs were fashioned. The fact that a whole group of spirituals envision the hammering process, though in a variety of connections, should point our imaginations in the right direction.

JOHN LOVELL, JR.

Washington, D.C.
1970

◆❀

Acknowledgments

. .
.

ALONG time ago, as a Rockefeller Foundation fellow at Berkeley, I studied American literature with the late T. K. Whipple, a great teacher and a superlative man. One big thing I learned was that the main business of literature was not to peddle philosophical secrets, but to reveal the beautiful and impressive insides of people, as individuals and groups. While doing a thesis on champions of the workers, I found a whole new universe of literary excitements.

When I got back home, with a shiny new doctoral degree, I vowed to put my new knowledge to work. My first big job was to cut open the Negro spiritual for its social implications. After publishing two articles on my findings, I wrote a third called "The Fighting Spiritual." Somehow, it totally disappeared. The lure of the drama and of other literary puzzles, some black, carried me away from the spiritual for many years.

When I came back to it about four years ago, partly egged on by J. Walter Fisher, program chairman of the Association for the Study of Negro Life and History, I decided to pursue it all the way. I soon learned that this was a fantastic decision. I began to spend an average of a hundred hours a week in libraries or sorting my excavations from libraries. I was carried into literature, music, dance, ethnomusicology, folklore, anthropology, theology, philosophy, history, psychology, and a dozen other fields. I had to travel all over the United States to comb regular and special libraries, to talk to people with unique viewpoints, to run down leads. Because of the need for certainty about the backgrounds, I had to visit nine African countries. Because of the intertwining of African influences in the New World, South and North, I had to visit Brazil and Guyana, Trinidad and Tobago, Jamaica, and the Bahamas. These were a minimum for background. And because the Europeans have become major interpreters of the songs, I had to visit five European countries, where I conferred with more than thirty scholars, musicians, and writers, and was disappointed because I could not visit four others.

Thus, my thank you list is very long. These are people who gave me leads, who helped me run down leads, who wrote me valuable letters, who plainly spelled out for me appropriate facts of life, who cleared the way for me to see and read and talk and understand, who established original viewpoints, who reacted to enigmas, who typed and copied, who sang with me and prayed for me.

My deep, deep thanks go to the Chapelbrook Foundation of Boston for awarding me a grant to run a project office and to travel to Europe, Africa, and South America. My thanks go also to Howard University for a research grant that enabled me to complete the project, to pay for dozens of translations, to get the manuscripts typed, to get pictures, and to meet the thousand expenses that always gang up at the end of anything. In the latter grant, Vice President Andrew Billingsley and Colonel James Robinson were extremely helpful.

Julia Ann Byrd Middlebrooks (known and loved by thousands as "Judy") was heaven-sent. She ran the office of the spiritual project (especially when I was out of town or out of the country), made arrangements, corrected me uproariously when she thought I was wrong, and did a lot of wonderful and necessary things behind my back. Joseph Hickerson of the Folk Archive Room of the Library of Congress was indispensable; he helped me find books and articles that I know would have remained forever hidden from me without him. And Toni Morrison, whom I taught English at Howard, turned out to be my key editorial counselor.

Before it was all over, I had three thousand references and nearly six thousand songs. One day soon I hope to publish the whole bibliography in some kind of organized form, especially the sources of songs and interpretations, and the precise historical backgrounds. As things stand, I have referred to key sources in the text so that interested persons can begin to satisfy their curiosity. I also hope to publish the song titles and first lines in a categorical list. To do so would worry me, though, since so many of the beautiful and philosophical verses are neither titles nor first lines.

So, here is my list of helpers. They are broken down as follows: U.S.A., Europe, Africa, South America, West Indies. Helpers, accept my fondest and undying gratitude.

And a special vote of thanks to my Jury of Interpreters, the twenty-nine superior people described on pages 481–84.

U.S.A.

District of Columbia: The late Marian Giles Lovell, Charlotte K. Brooks, Frances Churchill, Barney and Jewel Coleman, Mercer Cook, Rae Corson,

William DeMyer, Henry A. Dunlap, Ethel M. V. Ellis, E. V. Francis, Jean Graham, Priscilla Hall, Myria Hammonds, Alan Jabbour, James P. Johnson, Elsie Joseph, Gordon McDonald, Norma McRae, Patricia Markland, Viera P. Morse, Laura McDaniel Murphy, Eunice Newton, Vilma Harvey Nicholson, Sueli Okata, Dorothy Porter, Peggy Quince, Gladys W. Royal, Ida Hayes Smith, Virginia Spencer, Cornelia Stokes, J. Charles Washington, Charles H. Wesley, Jerry Wright. *Hampton, Virginia:* Lucy B. Campbell, Margaret B. Davis. *Fisk University, Tennessee:* James Lawson, Gracie R. Porter, Ann Allen Shockley, Jessie Carney Smith. *Tuskegee Institute, Alabama:* William L. Dawson, Luther H. Foster, C. Edouard Ward, Daniel T. Williams. *Jackson, Mississippi:* Margaret Walker Alexander, Fred and Taunya Banks, Mrs. Jack Young, Sr. *Piney Woods, Mississippi:* Laurence C. Jones, Eula Kelly Moman, Claude W. Phifer, William Sullivan. *New York:* B. A. Botkin, Marc Connelly, the late Bernard Katz, William Loren Katz, Robert Markel, Pat and Alex Morisey, Marguerite Prioleau, Jane Scott. *Chicago, Illinois:* Dena Epstein, Aurelia and John Hope Franklin. *California:* Byron Arnold, Jester Hairston, James Leisy, Howard Thurman, Don Lee White. *Old Greenwich, Connecticut:* Berenice Norwood Napper. *Northampton, Massachusetts:* Stanley M. Elkins. *Philadelphia, Pennsylvania:* Christa and Stephen Dixon. *Bloomington, Indiana:* William Cagle, Richard Dorson. *Terre Haute, Indiana:* John F. Bayliss. *Detroit, Michigan:* Geraldine Frenette.

Europe

Frankfurt: Janheinz Jahn, Paridam von dem Knesebeck, Osborn T. Smallwood. *Göttingen:* Alfons M. Dauer. *Munich:* Michael and Eva Hesse O'Donnell. *Cologne:* Hans Gerig, Heinz Korn, Alf Schwegeler, Hans Wiedenfeld. *Schlüchtern:* Walter Blankenburg. *Berlin:* William Coleman, Brewster Morris, Ross E. Petzing, Clifford Sealey. *Hamburg:* Fritz Bose, Kurt H. Hansen, Siegfried Schmidt-Joos. *Hannover:* Bishop Hans Lilje. *Freiburg:* Wolfgang Suppan. *Baden-Baden:* Joachim E. Berendt. *London:* Paul Breman, Robert M. W. Dixon, A. M. Jones, Paul Oliver, Rosey Pool, Tony Russell. *Sheffield:* Peter Smith. *Edinburgh:* Christopher Fyfe. *Paris:* Sim Copans, Father Guy de Fatto, Howard Hardy, Simone Haski, John Littleton. *Lyon:* Louis Achille, Jacqueline Coivous, members of the Park Glee Club. *Grenoble:* Jean Wagner. *St. Niklaas:* Hector Waterschoot. *Amsterdam:* H. R. Rookmaaker. *Troyes:* Father A. Z. Serrand. *Budapest:* János Gonda, Forrai Miklos.

Africa

In Washington, the embassies of the following countries: Malagasy Republic, Kenya, Tanzania, Republic of the Congo, especially Monique Akerell,

Ghana, Liberia, Sierra Leone, especially John Akar, Senegal, especially Samba Ba.

Tananarive: Zoëlisca Andrianony, Rabesehola Gaby, Olga Randrianatoavina, Rotmohonano Yorbat. *Nairobi:* Francis L. Karanja, Kathy Mbathi, Sarale A. Owens, R. M. Wambugu. *Kampala:* John Twitty, Cosma Warugaba. *Kinshasa:* Albert Botumbe, Frederic J. Gaynor, Philippe Kanza, Charles E. Robinson, and ten students of Louvanium University who congregated at the home of Professor Heiderschott. *Accra:* Saka Acquaye, Stella E. Davis. *Legon:* J. H. Kwabena Nketia. *Monrovia:* Horace G. Dawson, Bai T. Moore, Samuel Westerfield. *Freetown:* Dorothy von Amsterdam, John Bunting-Graden, Mack Fry, Eldred Jones, Sheku Ya-foday Lansana Koroma, A. Lenner, Logie Wright. *Dakar:* Mary Diagne, Mahamadou Kane, Rob and Mimi Mortimer, President Léopold Sédar Senghor, Leon Slawecki. *South Africa:* Hugh Tracey.

South America

The officials of the Guyanese Embassy in Washington.

Rio de Janeiro: Renato Almeida, José Mozart de Araujo, Josephine M. Barroso, Edison Carneiro, Mrs. Hallee, Sir David and Lady Iro Hunt, Radjino Lisbon, Antônio Olinto, Zora Seljan (Mrs. Olinto), Regina H. Tavares. *Georgetown:* P. A. Brathwaite, Serena Brathwaite, E. Kwayana, Wordsworth McAndrew.

West Indies

The officials of the embassies of Jamaica and Trinidad and Tobago in Washington.

Port of Spain: M. P. Alladin, Carlton Comma, J. D. Elder, C. Victor Niemeyer, G. Anthony Prospect, Gordon Rohlehr, Nina Squires. *Kingston:* Louise Bennett Coverly, Lloyd Hall, Olive Lewin. *Nassau:* E. Clement Bethel, Charles Herbert Fisher, Albert L. Halff, Erna Massiah, Edward Moxey, George Moxey, John (Peanuts) Taylor.

PART I / The Forge

> *You hear the hammers ringing—*
> *Hammering!*
> *You hear the hammers ringing—*
> *Hammering!*
> *You hear the hammers ringing—*
> *Hammering!*
> *You hear the hammers ringing—*
> *Hammering!*
> From a famous Afro-American spiritual

◇❀❀

CHAPTER ONE

Is There an Afro-American Spiritual?

. .
.

To OPEN an investigation by asking if the subject really exists would normally be most peculiar. But not so if one had just finished reading three thousand plus references on the so-called Negro spiritual and its backgrounds. At times, it has seemed that dozens of the describers and interpreters were hardly talking or thinking about the same thing, or even about one thing or any one of twenty things. As one reviews the reading, one grows sure that any number of these writers, who have a range of three hundred years and many countries, did have a host of different subjects in mind. Little wonder! They were writing about the very unusual and persistently famous songs of some talented black musicians and poets who had always been thought of as nothing but slaves.

At the opposite pole, some would say the question is disarmingly simple. Most people who profess the least knowledge of music or folklore or Africanism or American Negro history or anthropology would immediately answer "yes" or "no" depending on their upbringing. On each side there would be all kinds of curious and heavily documented reasons why.

From a 360-degree perspective of mountains of comment several things are clear: (1) Much has been written by self-styled interpreters who were only partially supplied with reliable evidence. (2) From any consistent viewpoint the basic *African* and *American* elements have been confused and misread. (3) Vested interests on all sides, because of the high value placed on the songs, have fomented claims and conclusions that no reasonable analysis can justify.

The crux of the question, really, is in another question. Did the African slave make his spiritual from his own ingredients, culled from Africa and/or America, or did he make it from a ready-made white spiritual or hymn?

The question sounds quite simple and has been treated so. Many people consider it solved and disposed of long ago.

This seemingly simple question, however, is most complex. Would-be detectives in the case have ignored or unconscionably brushed aside some decisive matters. To begin with is the large consideration that the so-called Negro spiritual has certain unmistakable properties by virtue of its two generic natures: as *song* and as *folklore*.

To capture the answer to the big question, then, a logical first step is to get a full-bodied understanding of the nature of song. Though far more comprehensive, it is much easier to define than our spiritual. Some of its essential parts, which are often ignored, point toward a precise characterization of the spiritual.

The second step is to repeat the process with folklore. Like song, it has basic properties, often ignored, upon which any intelligent evaluation or identification of a so-called folk spiritual must rest.

After these two brief researches we will know, as well as we can, how to examine a folk song for its true meanings and for its revealing markings. We will also have the measurements for determining whether and to what extent a given song (or song tradition) is original or imitative; on the surface, or deeply, religious; a congregational chant; a wild, individual cry; or a critique of society.

The study of song is first because song is the elder of the two generic systems.

❀◇

CHAPTER TWO

What Is Song?

. .
.

USIC, says Romain Goldron, writing in 1968, is traceable to the Paleolithic Age. Most primitive peoples were familiar with the concept that "sound forms the basis of reality in the universe." Through music, man, since his beginning, has striven to emulate his gods and to evoke, again and again, the moment of creation for present benefits.

Within this framework Curt Sachs tells us that in primitive man "music began with singing." Song flows all through the life of earliest man. It conveys his poetry. It diverts him in rest and peaceful work. It elates and lulls. It gives hypnotic trance to those who heal the sick and strive for luck and fortune in magic incantation. Like some powerful, invisible drug, it keeps awake the dancers' yielding muscles; it intoxicates fighting men; it hypnotically leads the eternal squaw to the bed of ecstasy.

Song is sound shaped into beautiful form by the desires of the heart and the artful workings of the mind. As Howard Hanson says, it begins in the imagination of an inspired man. "Translated into the glories of sonority," Hanson continues, "it becomes of itself a powerful instrument in the awakening of the spirits of man." It is even a measure of the wealth of ages and nations. Hanson goes on, "The musical progress of a people must be judged, not by its orchestras or by its opera houses, but by the music which arises spontaneously from the creative spirit existing among that people."

The roots of variety in song (and in other music), says John Blacking,

> are to be found in culture and not in music, and in the human organization of sound rather than in its natural qualities. Thus the student of a musical tradition must first know something about the culture which affects the lives and personalities of the humans who organize the sound, in order that he may know better what they set out to do when they perform, and why they do it in a variety of ways.

Song always expands the man who creates it and, through him, the men he inspires. Without song through the ages men would be dwarfs, working at their best only to fulfill tasks at hand. Song enables man to explore his undiscovered world within and brings that world under his active command. Rabindranath Tagore says that song speaks of the intense yearning of the heart for the divine in Man; a single song is a hymn to the Ever Young.

Many historians, such as Rutland Boughton, have emphasized the diversity and transforming power of music, and particularly of song. Boughton stresses the comprehensiveness of this power. It accompanies man's every action: growing, feasting, worship, dancing, sexual passion. It is, therefore, the language of man's essential religion, laying the basis for satisfactory relations within himself and with his fellows on the one hand and with the world of spirits on the other. Sacred primitive songs, says Bowra, are nearly always dramatic, concentrating on the passion of the occasion, not on the occasion itself or its lesson. Through this broad view of religion, nonsecular song becomes man's general psychology, sociology, mathematics, and magic all in one. It covers him from cradle to coffin. Perhaps Boughton's strongest point is that the emotional background of this kind of life is none the less real because it seems mystical.

In Aleksandr Blok's *Spirit of Music*, the transformation caused by song takes another tack. The creative artist here wants to rebuild everything anew so that our lying, dirty, boring monstrous life becomes a just and clean, a gay and beautiful life. The primitive singer is consumed with his own problems and is often immersed in gloom. He still sings of a re-created universe and believes in the perpetual breaking through of the light.

Perhaps the best short statement of the nature of song, from the perspective of earliest times downward, is found in Marius Schneider's sketch on "Primitive Music" (chapter I in *Ancient and Oriental Music*, edited by Egon Wellesz, *New Oxford History of Music*, *1* (London, Oxford University Press, 1957). Professor Schneider reiterates the scope of earliest music in man's life—psychological, sociological, religious, symbolic, linguistic. Since different meanings derive from the way songs are sung, direct contact with singers and their surroundings is indispensable to getting these meanings.

Primitive man sings, we learn, only when he has something definite to express. In this spontaneous expression, song and speech are often intermingled. When a foreign song is introduced, the singer wants first to know what the song is all about. He refuses to sing as a mere convention or to sing in pure imitation another man's song. For him thoughts are at least as important as melody. Even his instrumental melodies and whistling are expressions of definite ideas. As the song develops, tentative ideas become more and more definite. Supposedly nonsensical syllables put to certain melodies assume a magic significance. In such patterns melody is not a chance combination of notes, but an organic and dynamic whole, a form more than the simple sum of its notes and loaded with special communications.

On the theory that music has the power to renew life (people believed that their divine ancestors called forth matter purely by "shining songs and war-dances"), the singer in worship is repeating on his plane the act of creation. This belief helps to account for repetition of words and phrases in traditional songs. Acceptable song texts often turn out to be the repetition of a few significant and sonorous phrases, emotionally sustained by appropriate rhythms, and understood only by the initiated. But the notion goes much further. Professor Schneider writes,

> Singing allows innumerable repetitions of the same words, repetitions which, apart from magical utterances, seem meaningless or clumsy in ordinary speech; it also enables things to be said or hinted at which it would be difficult to express in sober speech. To the uninitiated the words of such songs are for the most part completely unintelligible; but the aboriginal knows exactly what the few, apparently quite disconnected words mean in association with a particular melody.

As we have learned, early man has taught later man that the functions of singing are legion. Loving, playing, mocking, greeting, sorrowing, giving thanks, amusing oneself while at work, engaging in worship, medicine, or magic, easing birth, lullabying the new child, giving him activity as he grows, dominating wars, public ceremonies, weather, and hunting—these are only a few of a very long list of functions. Primitive man has also taught his successors that it is easier to sing than to speak of love; easier to sing abuse than to deliver direct scorn. Hugh Tracey has taken this maxim from the Chopi: "You can say publicly in songs what you cannot say privately to a man's face, and so this is one of the ways African society takes to maintain a spiritually healthy community."

The judges of the ancient communities allowed people to sing their pleas in court, even in divorce cases. Man believed, and he had the right, that music made him superhuman and gave him special powers of self-discovery. In the songs of his all-pervasive religion, heaven and earth were analogous. The would-be interpreter of the spiritual we discuss here should carry this fact in his memory.

Whenever early man borrowed, the native and the foreign forms existed side by side. But early man did not borrow as often as generally supposed. He spent most of his singing time examining and revealing himself and his world—bodies and spirits alike. The sounds of his songs were full of significant symbols.

And so John S. Dwight in 1857, Natalie Curtis Burlin in 1917, and Alan Lomax in 1959 are each correct when they stress the point that singing as expression is the language of the heart. And Alan Lomax adds, "Hearts burned clean of pretense." As the song spreads from the individual to the folk crowd, carrying secret messages of hope, peace, brotherhood, free-dom, and love, Lomax continues, it transforms the crowd into a unified chorus. Percy Grainger tells how the primitive musician never stops mak-ing new songs by weaving fresh combinations of more or less familiar phrases. And Josiah Combs shows how folk songs in Scotland, England, and America have invented and improvised meanings not found in regular use, speech, or poetry.

This improvisation is the essence of creative artistry, just as Grainger has said. In sophisticated circles, he insists, life encroaches on art; in the primitive community, the reverse is true. The primitive singer feels that he personally owns his songs. By investing thought, imagination, and heart in his study of nature, society, and events of which he is a vibrant part, he is also making songs that are new, attractive to people, and explosive with in-sights. In this sense, also, he never imitates; he is too much in love with his role as creator.

No better statement of long-range values in the artistic expression of primitive peoples can be found than that in Alan P. Merriam's *The Anthro-pology of Music* (1964). It is notable that these peoples set the tone of the basic cultures. In his chapter on "Social Behavior: The Musician," Mer-riam establishes the place of the individual, especially the individual cre-ator, in basic society. He shows how the role and status of the individual creator is determined by the consensus of the society of which he is a part. Conversely, the nonconformist (note the "sinner man" in our spiritual) ran considerable risks. In one famous passage, a summons was issued to all women to abide the judgment of the group, as follows: "Women who will not come out in this place, let millipede go into sex organs, let earthworm go into her sex organs."

Though considered less important than music by some folk interpreters, the song text gains high rating from Merriam's findings:

> This expression of general cultural values revealed in song texts can be carried further to a study of the underlying psychological set or "ethos" of a particular culture. . . . Even in those texts in which authority is com-mented upon, the comments take the form of protest against a job, boasts of powers held; in general, excesses of authority or power form the basic line of comment.

The song text, therefore, is the key to how the folk community feels about its most intense concerns. Reinforcing this view, Merriam says,

> We are drawn closer and closer here to the point of view that song texts clearly reflect the culture of which they are a part. . . . An important func-tion of gatherings for community singing was to emphasize the values stressed by the culture. . . . Such songs constituted something very like a legal sanction through public opinion.

Besides being an expression of deep-seated values, song texts, says Merriam, are an expression of thoughts and ideas not permissibly verbalized in other contexts. In this type of expression, protest by the subjugated is fundamental.

Through revelations produced by anthropology, it thus becomes clear that the words of a folk song cannot be read with simple literalness. The song creator is aware that his folk have irrepressible drives and deep feelings that words can signify but not fully declare. He does his best to find the phrases and the poetic organization that will go as far as words can go in the chosen direction, and will suggest the remainder of the way. The folk understand and are grateful for this artistic fulfillment of that portion of their souls that needs airing. It naturally follows that if an interpreter wishes to know this folk, the words of their folk songs are an incomparable indicator. But, following Merriam, he must search in the roots of the people. When he has traced every tiny thread of song to its psychological origin, he knows the people very well.

It is significant that Alan Lomax's monumental study on *Folk Song Style and Culture,* published in 1968 by the American Association for the Advancement of Science, Washington, D.C., supports Merriam emphatically. In chapter 13, "Folk Song Texts As Culture Indicators," Lomax and Joan Halifax say that "it seems obvious that the texts of songs will be limited to those matters, attitudes, concerns, and feelings on which the community is in maximal accord." They continue with a normal deduction, "If this is not the case, a song is not likely to hold its audience and it probably will not pass into oral tradition, where acceptance means that consensus has taken place over and over again through time."

In an article on "The Music of Africa," published in 1960, J. H. Kwabena Nketia writes that African music is at once social, recreational, and functional; it is thus regarded as one aspect of individual and social behavior as well as art. Alan Lomax broadens this view to include all singing. In his striking article, "The Good and the Beautiful in Folksong" (*Journal of American Folklore*, 1967), Lomax demonstrates that as an act of communication, singing can be studied as behavior. He says, "Since a folksong is transmitted orally by all or most members of a culture, generation after generation, it represents an extremely high consensus about patterns of meaning and behavior of cultural rather than individual significance."

This truth seems to have been unknown or forgotten by many analysts of the American black spiritual. They have written of this large body of songs as though each singer were speaking quietly and literally for himself alone. Lomax adds that song is essentially louder and more arresting than speech, that it may be rated by the degree of redundancy, and that it serves to organize group behavior and group response in public situations. The ramifications of the behavior and persistent motives of the group who dictated and perpetuated the spirituals have occupied very few of the enormous number of pages given to the interpretation of these songs.

Song for workers has a special meaning. Like everyone else, the worker in a folk group sings always over the whole range of his life, not just in the apparent limited area of a given song. But, as Elie Siegmeister has shown, a worker's song strikes deep as well as wide: "It can depict the reality and intensity of the suffering, the oppression, the struggle, the hope, the joy and determination of the people; it can inspire courage and fire to action to remove the causes of that suffering."

A word about the meaning of *primitive* in the term *primitive song*. Of course, it relates to people who have retained certain primary forms and mores of civilization. But the idea of barbarism is absent. The cultures of the areas from which the African slaves came were millenniums old and well matured when the slaves were captured. Basil Davidson insists that the preeminent arts of Africa, including drumming and dancing, "had ceased to be 'simple,' let alone 'primitive,' in form and content or in meaning and performance at least by the time of the European Middle Ages, and probably long before." The fact that most contributions to song were retained by the folk for generations and centuries because of satisfying effects is evidence of their value to a more and more sophisticated society. We shall give indication of these influences later in the present chapter and in succeeding chapters.

Antonín Dvořák has spoken to the issue of an advanced culture effectively employing primary songs. In a *Harper's* article in 1895 he explained why he had suggested that inspiration for truly national (American) music might be derived from Negro melodies or Indian chants:

> The most potent as well as the most beautiful (among American songs) . . . according to my estimation are certain of the so-called plantation melodies and slave songs, all of which are distinguished by unusual and subtle harmonies, the like of which I have found in no other song but those of old Scotland and Ireland. . . . The music of the people is like a rare and lovely flower growing amidst encroaching weeds. Thousands pass it, while others trample it under foot, and thus the chances are that it will perish before it is seen by the one discriminating spirit who will prize it above all else. The fact that no one has as yet arisen to make the most of it does not prove that nothing is there.

It is a pleasure to report that ever since Dvořák's challenge was issued, many Americans have accepted it in many abundant ways.

✿◇

CHAPTER THREE

What Is Folklore?

. .
.

I N A recent book called *Our Living Traditions* (New York, 1968), Francis Utley reminds us all that folklore is not merely "literature transmitted orally." It includes "arts and crafts, beliefs and customs of people in lumber camps, city evangelical storefront churches, back-alley dives, farmers' festivals and fairs, . . . chain gangs and penitentiaries, . . . or the remote African jungle from which they [some songs] come." Writing in *Hausa Superstitions and Customs* (London, 1913), Major Tremearne demonstrates that folklore often enunciates folk law. Dan G. Hoffman adds that, since folk art portrays the emotional and aesthetic nature of the group where it arises, it offers a fertile field for analysis. As late as 1968 Gunther Schuller has observed, "Folklore, music, dance, sculpture, and painting operate as a total generic unit, serving not only religion but all phases of daily life, encompassing birth, death, work, and play." Other writers have discussed the processes by which folklore digs out and puts into a folk bank or reservoir the essential and realistic truths of the unique group.

Not many additional authorities are needed to establish the basic qualities of folklore if one will read and absorb Ruth Benedict's article on the subject in the *Encyclopedia of the Social Sciences* (1931). The term, she says, was first used in the middle of the nineteenth century to denote folk traditions, festivals, songs, and superstitions. For anthropologists the chief sources of folklore material have been the rural populations of the civilized world.

Folklore, Miss Benedict specifically states, is literature. Like any art, it has traditional regional styles and forms, and may be intensively studied. But Miss Benedict has found the academic study of folklore uninspiring.

It has "labored under the incubus of theories" and has ignored "the uncon-fined role of the human imagination in the creation of mythology."

Explaining herself more fully, she has written,

> The play of imagination, fundamental in folklore, is given direction by the great opportunity for wish fulfillment. More than in any form of art there is the possibility of pleasurable identification and whatever is thought of as most desirable in personal experience in any region finds free expres-sion.

It is sad to have to report that much of the folklore "analysis" since 1931 has suffered from the same incubus of theories and the same ignoring of the impact of human imagination.

As she goes on, Miss Benedict gives something of the method of folk transfers and something of the function of folklore as social criticism:

> Negro folklore varies comparatively little whenever it is found in North America and in the West Indies. A considerable portion of it seems to have received its present form in the New World, but it is all fundamentally re-lated to West African mythologies which are in turn genetically related to West European folk tales. However, all of it has been remodeled to serve as a vehicle for comment on the conditions that surround the Negro in his new environment. Brer Rabbit and Anansi are opportunities for slave com-ment and the Massa stories are often direct transcriptions of slave life.

On the basis of researches completed since Miss Benedict wrote this ar-ticle, it is possible that she has overemphasized the West African origins. But her insistence on folklore as a comment on environment has been more than confirmed. This fact has great bearing upon the question of black bor-rowing coldly and woodenly from white.

⟦ Folk Music: Definitions

As an outstanding branch of folklore, folk music requires precise defini-tion. One may begin with the definition adopted by the International Folk Music Council at its Conference in São Paulo, Brazil, in 1954:

> Folk music is the product of a musical tradition that has been evolved through the process of oral transmission. The factors that shape the tradi-tion are: (i) continuity which links the present with the past; (ii) variation which springs from the creative individual or the group; and (iii) selection by the community, which determines the form or forms in which the music survives.

In 1907, Cecil Sharp, disturbed by the great confusion over the true na-ture of folk song, addressed himself to a clear definition. In chapter 1 of

English Folk Song he sets down the cardinal points. He stresses first those singers who make much out of purely natural instinct. The spontaneous music of these unspoiled, unlettered classes is folk song.

The phrase is a German compound, adopted by the English. It should apply exclusively to peasant songs and not to all popular songs. By the *Century Dictionary* of 1889 it is described as "a song of the people . . . the words and generally the music of which have originated among the common people, and are extensively used by them." Sharp would eliminate the word *generally*. "*Common people*" refers to those whose "mental development has been due not to any formal system of training or education, but solely to environment, communal association, and direct contact with the ups and downs of life." These people are not uneducated; the unfolding of their consciousness has been merely the result of realistic process. The primitive African, for example, according to the demonstration of Diedrich Westermann, was definitely not uneducated.

Folk music, Sharp continues, reflects feelings and tastes that are communal rather than personal. Always in solution, its creation is never completed; "at every moment in history, it exists not in one form but in many."

The music of these common people, says Sharp, is always genuine and true, "for instinct is their only guide and the desire for self-expression their only motive." But the fact that their music is unconsciously produced does not prevent its being "good" music. It is scientific because it is constructed on "well defined, intelligible principles." In folk music, the individual invents; the community selects. The racial character of a song, therefore, is due to communal choice, not communal invention.

In the highly appreciative definitions of Henry Edward Krehbiel, "folk-songs are echoes of the heartbeats of the vast folk, and in them are preserved feelings, beliefs and habits of antiquity." "The folksong composes itself," says Grimm. It is written, says Krehbiel, by an individual who is a folk product: "His idioms are taken off the tongue of the people; his subjects are the things which make for the joy and sorrow of the people." Since the creator's potentiality is racial or national, and not personal, his work is enduring, not ephemeral.

Ralph Vaughan Williams has added some useful distinctions. Stressing the point that folk song grows straight out of the needs of the people, he writes that the people find a fit and perfect form for satisfying those needs. The folk singer is bound by no prejudices or musical etiquette. In his rhythmical figures he is free. There is no original in traditional art; no virtue in the "earliest known version." Later versions are developments, not corruptions.

This last declaration by the great composer is of utmost importance. Those who speak of the desecration or corruption of the spirituals by free members of the folk community are talking from a position of personal taste alone.

([*Application of Definitions to the So-Called Negro Spiritual*

At this point it is desirable to clarify the definitions of song and folklore by applying two sample phases to the so-called Negro spiritual. The first phase has to do with essential religion; the second, with attitude toward music as a form of group expression.

AS TO RELIGION

Nothing has obscured the true study of this spiritual as folk song so much as the tendency to misinterpret its religious role. Of course many of the songs use religious terminology; but what of that? Religion to the traditional African and to many other primitive singers was all-encompassing, not compartmentalized as it is to us. There is not the least doubt that the essence of these songs goes far beyond the narrow and conventional religious views which shortsighted people have read into the phraseology.

It is even somewhat silly to separate the religious from the secular. If the black folk who created these songs had the universal view—and they most certainly did—of what significance is the fact that sometimes they used "religious" phraseology and sometimes not. Many unquestioned spirituals have no religious phraseology; many so-called secular slave songs have deep "religious" import. The distinction is usually without value in getting at the heart and the true meaning and structure of the songs.

Every folk song is religious in the sense that it is concerned about the origins, ends, and deepest manifestations of life, as experienced by some more or less unified community. It tends to probe, usually without nailing down definite answers, the puzzles of life at their roots. The real issue, for example, in the Jesse James song-legend is not that a "dirty, little coward" shot Jesse when he was defenseless; it is to ask the question why it is allowable that a thing like this can happen, especially to a man with a loving wife and three brave children. The fact that Jesse had killed defenseless people while robbing banks and trains is not part of the song-legend's ethical system, although such facts are reviewed. In essence, the only point to be settled at this particular juncture is, What kind of a world will permit the rank injustice of Jesse's death by obvious cowards? At heart, it is a religious question.

The deeply moral queries, expressed and implied, in the riddles and bloody narratives of the English and Scottish popular ballads are religious in the same sense. Tests of chastity or fidelity in love, excessive grief, visions of paradise, the power of the harp, penances, punishments, poisonings, talismans, tears that destroy the peace of the dead, tasks and problems, difficult and impossible, the fact that Robin Hood will not take Jesus, Peter, Paul, or John as security for a loan but accepts the Virgin at once— all these things are sung about, obviously not for their own sakes, but as sparks in a gigantic ring of fire which open up, if you could only find the magical combination, the ultimate meanings of life from the most ancient past to the most distant future.

In John Greenway's *Literature Among the Primitives* we are told that myth is narrative associated with religion, but also that it is literature "and therefore a matter of aesthetic experience and imagination." Likewise, songs embodying curses, love stories, gambling incidents, reactions to work; songs of contention and ridicule, dirges and proverbs imply a curiosity about the nature of things far, far down that allows the tragic distortions to happen to people. The American Indian (as Charles Hofmann has recently demonstrated) essays to induce rainfall on the desert by singing special words while he dances a snake dance; or attempts to cure sickness with special words recited over dry paintings; or believes that he drives out the evil spirit of a disease by rubbing smoke from sacred fire over his body as he sings,

> Impervious to pain, may I walk. . . .
>
> Happily abundant showers I desire.
> Happily abundant vegetation I desire.
> May it be happy before me.
> May it be happy behind me.
> May it be happy below me.
> May it be happy above me.
>
> With it happy all around me, May I walk.
> It is finished in beauty.
> It is finished in beauty.

In Ghana the confrontation with death arouses in each individual and group a mortal religious question. What can I rely upon, each asks himself, when the great killer appears before me or in my community? As a man of valor he is ready to fight. His conqueror of kings, however, has been eliminated by death and he is left without a leader. He sings (as we read in Nketia's folk song collection),

> Death is carrying us all away. . . .
>
> Alas, father! Alas, mother! . . .
>
> He has shaved our heads bare
> Death has shaved our heads bare.

Death is not an abstract spirit. He is anthropomorphic, and something has got to be done about him. But what?

Every folk song, then, is essentially religious; but not in the narrow sense of creed and ritual and church-going. It is religious, and unique, in the broad sense that every human being and every group must have something to believe in, to live by. This something is too big to understand all at once, particularly as we whirl through the kaleidoscope of everyday life. Ironically, though, our everyday experience drives us to search for the root meanings of this tantalizing thing to which we are devoted, but which we can never fully understand. Our religion is measured by the depth and determination of our search.

It is a pity that the so-called Negro spiritual was ever called a religious song, because always the narrow concept of religion intervenes. Since it has been so accepted, it is imperative that its religious element be defined and differentiated before anything else can be said about it.

Whatever portion of the spiritual can be proved to be African or American, one fact is incontrovertible: The originators of the Negro spiritual were African in their attitudes toward religion and music. Religion to the ancestral group from whom these Africans were sprung did not splinter into social, political, and philosophical subdivisions. It spoke of the social, the political, and the philosophical with one voice born of the overriding desire to fathom the workings of the universe. In every way it trained the individual to adapt himself to these workings for his own good and hope of prosperity and security.

It is, therefore, strongly differentiated from a religion which preaches one thing and invariably practices another. It is not a faith which piously worships on Sunday and ignores the teachings of its professed prophet as soon as the benediction is pronounced. It is not a faith which, behind the mask of a God of humility and compassion, conquers and oppresses large masses of people for economic gain. In the record of American slavery is courtroom evidence that some of the most brutal beatings and maimings of slaves were inflicted by ministers of the gospel and by men and women owners, overseers, and drivers who were pillars of the church. Without engaging in an appropriate condemnation, we have as our purpose here to differentiate brands of religion which affect the writing of folk songs. Pursuing this purpose, we can reiterate that the spiritual was not written under the inspiration of a schizophrenic pattern of religion such as that described above.

Nor was it written in the religious attitude of the whites who attended camp meetings. Although many of these were lower- and lower middle-class folk, as distinguished from the slave owning upper and upper middle classes, religion to them was still a segment of life and not the whole of life. Granted that for many of them the camp meeting fulfilled an emotional need and satisfied a hunger caused by the emptiness of their everyday lives, the incidence of the camp meeting was just a compartment, and these people returned to their regular socioeconomic existences without much carry-over from the meetings. Their songs were thus incidental phases. The lack of depth in the words of the songs reflects this lack of moving power from a comprehensive inspiration. The lack of impact of these songs over the years and in places far beyond their local communities, as compared with the lasting and growing impact of the Afro-American spiritual all over the world, reflects the lack of depth and well-roundedness. Anyone comparing the white spiritual with the black spiritual should keep in mind the enormous difference in religious attitude and inspiration which underlay the two.

AS TO MUSIC

The attitude toward music of the originators and developers of the spiritual is consonant with that toward religion. The musicologist Bruno Nettl has accurately described those phases of the African approach to music out of which our spiritual arises:

> It cannot be denied that Africans, on the whole, do participate in musical life much more—and more actively, singing, playing, composing, dancing—than do members of Western civilization. . . . music in Africa can be said to have a greater or more important role than it does in Western civilization. . . .
>
> The use of music for political purposes of various sorts should be noted. Evidently in some of the African tribes it is easier to indicate discontent with employers or with government if the discontent is sung than if it is spoken. We therefore find many songs expressing criticism of authority, but also songs composed especially to praise chiefs and wealthy men. Songs are used to spread current events of interest and gossip, and to perpetuate knowledge of these events, much in the way that broadside ballads functioned as newspapers in eighteenth-century England and America. Work songs . . . are prominent in Africa.

The spiritual employs all the above purposes, as well as others like them. It does so without confining itself to limited objectives, but rather in fulfillment of its ultimate searching goals.

The most important point about the religious and musical origins of the spiritual with which we are dealing, however, is not negative or argumentative, but positive. As the later chapters of this book will demonstrate, it needs no argument to reveal that this spiritual, as a group of songs, dealt with all manifestations of life from the all-encompassing religious position of the African ancestral group. They were not religious songs in the sense of a compartment of life, nor religious in the sense of the theology of the camp meeting, nor religious because they often used Biblical symbols, nor religious because the hope of heaven was substituted to solve the problems of earth, nor religious for any other such reason. They were religious and spiritual because they tried, with inspired artistry, to pose the root questions of life, of before life, and of beyond life, and to react to these questions as the aroused human being and the bestirred folk have done since the rosy dawn of literature.

✿◊

CHAPTER FOUR

What Are the Number and Range of the Spirituals?

. .
.

P ROFESSOR George Pullen Jackson is probably the outstanding
writer who denies that there is an Afro-American spiritual. He
accepts the term *Negro spiritual*, but only in the sense of a black-
ened version of what he calls a *white spiritual*. In several large
books he has presented his evidence. Relying on his evidence and conclusions, many self-styled evaluators of the spiritual have circulated his view
and have elaborated upon it. Due attention will be given to his key propositions as this story unfolds. At this point it is advisable to record his testimony as to the number and range of the songs on which his theory is
based.

In chapter 14 of *White and Negro Spirituals: Their Life Span and
Kinship* (New York, 1943), he declares that thirteen collections, all published by 1940, comprise the sum total of his sources for his Negro spiritual.
In these collections he found 1,413 song titles, but far fewer unduplicated
songs; perhaps only 500 or 600. His comparison is made with 550 tunes and
texts of white spirituals, which he has found in two major collections.

Professor Jackson admits that he has found a score of Negro songs in
small collections and journals. Most importantly, however, he clearly suggests that these are all the available Negro spirituals. If his few hundred
samples are the sum total—or even were so in 1943—then certain aspects of
his case are strengthened. If they are not and if it can be shown that there
were many thousands of Negro spiritual texts of considerable variety, published not only in regular collections, but also in sincere literary works of
many kinds by a large group of writers whose authenticity in the field of
the material is unquestioned, then this fact puts a new complexion on the
whole issue Professor Jackson has raised.

Let us call a collection any book or magazine article which has published one or more spiritual texts with the intention of adding to the appreciation of these songs or of underlining their value or beauty. To exclude biographies, social histories, general anthologies, sketches on Southern life, foreign explanations of American life, and a dozen other types is to give a false picture and to eliminate many authentic spirituals which were snatched from possible oblivion with great energy and care.

Some of the people who published spiritual texts before 1940 were regular collectors like Allen, Arnold, Bantock, Bolton, Botkin, Burlin, Courlander, Fenner, Higginson, James Weldon and Rosamund Johnson, Hall Johnson, the Lomaxes, Ludlow, Jeannette Murphy, Parrish, Sandburg, and Scarborough. Some were singers, choir conductors, and composers like Lawrence Brown, Coleridge-Taylor, Dett, Gaul, Goodell, Grissom, Hairston, Handy, Hayes, Marylou Jackson, Eva Jessye, R. E. Kennedy, The Southernaires, and three Works. Some were ardent and diligent amateur diggers who, since the 1880s, have displayed their precious treasures in the showcases of the *Journal of American Folklore* and in the journals of other relevant societies. Whereas some collected fewer than ten Negro spirituals, others have contributed two hundred per source.

Over half of the more than five hundred collections assembled by the present writer were published before 1940. Breaking down the pre-1940 collections into four groups, one sees that they emerged in the following time periods:

Time Period	Number of Collections
Before 1889	27
1890–1909	23
1910–1929	101
1930–1940	56

From the original five hundred collections about six thousand independent spirituals have already been catalogued; and the list is not complete. Since the discovery and publication of slave spirituals has slowed down in the past generation, it can be estimated that three-fourths of these were already available in the two hundred collections before 1940. It is true that in the second and third stanzas there has been much cannibalizing. But the basic first lines, secondary stanzas, and refrains, held together by a unified theme, establish a reasonable independence for at least this number. Something will be said later—in the discussion of conditions under which the songs were created—of the possible total number of spirituals created by Afro-American slaves in the two and a quarter centuries during which the creation was going on.

The reasons for Professor Jackson's failure to include in his study clearly

available Negro spirituals are somewhat hard to avoid. His flat omission of
the Johnsons' *Book of American Negro Spirituals* (1925), *Second Book of
American Negro Spirituals* (1926), and the two published together (1940),
each with elaborate introductions, is almost beyond belief. These collections were the most popular and the most highly praised in the field for at
least a generation, and are probably so today. It is true that some critics
have called them sentimental and patriotic. Their 122 songs are, nevertheless, a representative grouping; and their arrangements, both as to words
and music, are the result of patient scholarship, informed insight, and good
taste.

One might argue that Professor Jackson's guess as to the number of
extant Negro spirituals is in line with other published estimates. But, as
early as 1931, Lucile Price Turner had declared that six hundred Negro
spirituals were already written down and that the subject was not exhausted. In 1937 the Cleveland Public Library published an *Index of Negro
Spirituals*. The index was based on twenty-six collections and, though incomplete, listed twelve hundred songs. It is possible that Professor Jackson
wanted to rely entirely on his own initiatives, but these reliable investigators might at least have piqued his curiosity.

The matter of Professor Jackson's thoroughness and selectivity might be
insignificant if he had not considered the number a critical issue (see part
two of his *White and Negro Spirituals*, entitled "The Whole Story of
American Folk Song as the Negroes Sang It" and his chapter 14 in part
two, entitled "The Body of Published Negro Religious Folk Song Is
Briefly Surveyed") and if he had not been quoted as gospel by historians,
anthropologists, musicologists, anthologists of American literature, ency-
clopedists, and others who have set the opinions of Americans and some
foreigners about this Negro spiritual. Even an article on "Spirituals" by
Irving Lowens in *Die Musik in Geschichte und Gegenwart*, a music encyclopedia published in Kassel, Germany, in 1965, draws generously on
Professor Jackson's "findings." (These "findings" will be appropriately
examined shortly, but it is essential that the question of number and range
be clarified at once.)

Aside from the Southern white-oriented evidence based on a limited
number of selected spirituals, the question of the number and range of the
spirituals under examination is highly significant. If the number is small,
and if the small group is homogeneous, the possible answer to the overall
question is seriously affected. The argument that these songs are a few
chips from a basic white block is strengthened by a small number of songs
with easily identifiable religious traits. If the number is large, and if the
songs are varied, going beyond the obvious religious patterns, then other
explanations must be found.

✿◈

CHAPTER FIVE

How Does Imitation Work in Folk Song and Literature?

. .
.

To ESTABLISH a borrowing in folk song or literature, one must first perform the following steps connectedly: (1) Show that the supposed source possesses certain characteristics which are germane to the borrowing. (2) Show that the supposed borrower had motive and opportunity for these particular borrowings and that, under the circumstances, he could not have developed the critical characteristics himself and could not have acquired them earlier from another source.

These two steps would prove that a borrowing is suspected, but on the basis of creative activity—what Miss Benedict calls "the play of imagination, fundamental in folklore"—they are not enough. All the great Greek classical playwrights borrowed openly and frankly from legendary material (and rarely from history) which was well known to the people as a whole. In more than thirty plays Shakespeare never used an original plot; he borrowed from history, legend, popular storybooks, popular plays, early and contemporary poets, even from local ceremonials. He often did not reach the primary source: His Roman plays, for example, were based on North's translation of Amyot's Plutarch. The same type of borrowing is true of great musicians and other artists.

Today only a few scholars know or care about the sources of these supreme artists. Sensitive people care only about what magic the borrower worked with his material. Thus, to complete the creative side of artistic borrowing, one must demonstrate that the finished product of the borrower was either a wooden imitation (that is, a dead steal) or a hopelessly inferior copy. If the borrower—a William Shakespeare, for instance—is far above his source creatively, he gets all the credit for accomplishment. He has breathed life and fire into something that was either dead or only indifferently alive.

If an investigator establishes only that two folk groups used similar materials in the creation of songs which appeared simultaneously, he has not established a borrowing. This is particularly true when a common source (for example, the Bible or earlier hymns) apparently exists for both sets of songs. He is compelled to show that the borrowing group went directly to the lending group and not to the earlier source. He must nail down the time factor to prove, for certain, that the lender was fully in the field before the borrower came along. When the alleged borrower relies entirely upon vocal device (that is, never publishes songs) and the alleged lender uses both vocal and written device (namely, publishes after a period of vocal creation or transmission), the investigator's job is enormously complicated. But unless the laws of proving borrowings, in use over many years of scholarly study, are to be abrogated or declared meaningless and the whole business of source and influence turned over to guesswork, the investigator must prove his case all the way or give up his claim.

The question of which group is socially or educationally inferior is quite beside the point unless special evidence is introduced to make it germane. The lesser group educationally or socially—even defining these terms in the somewhat casual American senses—may well be the superior group creatively. The socially advanced group with lower creative quotient may readily, or sometimes unscrupulously, borrow from the less advanced group that has keener and sounder creative traditions and skills.

That so many self-styled scholars have accepted a chain of borrowing largely because one group was less sophisticated, and presumably inferior, when the evidence showed only that certain songs from each group were being sung simultaneously, is testimony to Miss Benedict's "incubus of theories." One might go further and say it was a desire on the part of the supposedly superior to reduce to "rightful" status the supposedly inferior and simultaneously to capture the glory bestowed upon the latter, all without definitive evidence. The supposedly superior fell completely out of patience with the exorbitant praise showered upon the art of those he looked down upon, particularly when he heard no note of interest lifted on behalf of his own art. They pretended not to hear such advice as they received from the editor of the *Evangelist*, a Presbyterian organ, in 1856: Be not ashamed, he exhorted, to imitate your poor bondmen; "if slaves can pour out their hearts in melody, how ought freemen to sing!" As one of the most quoted critics in the African field, Erich M. von Hornbostel, declared in 1926, some will not credit a race they consider inferior with so much creative power as these songs clearly demonstrate. We may not fully support the approach to Southern cultural concerns taken in 1917 by H. L. Mencken, himself a native of a former slaveholding state; but, because it has been widely circulated and debated, our record would be incomplete if we failed to mention it.

In that whole region, an area three times as large as France or Germany, there is not a single orchestra capable of playing Beethoven's C Minor symphony, or a single painting worth looking at, or a single public building or monument of genuine distinction, or a single factory devoted to the making of beautiful things, or a single poet, novelist, historian, musician, painter or sculptor, whose reputation extends beyond his own country. Between the Mason and Dixon line and the mouth of the Mississippi, there is but one opera-house, and that one was built by a Frenchman, and is now, I believe, closed. The only domestic art this huge and opulent empire knows is in the hands of Mexican greasers; its only native music it owes to the despised negro; its only genuine poet was permitted to die up an alley like a stray dog.

On the positive side, the whole population might well be tested in two famous composers. In 1892 a great composer and teacher, Antonín Dvořák, came to America from Bohemia. He comprehensively studied all the music around him, including Americanized versions of European folk songs, hymns, white spirituals, Negro spirituals, and Indian chants. He arrived at his own decision objectively without pressure from any source. According to his biographer, Paul Stefan-Gruenfeldt, he arrived by himself at the conclusion that the Negro spiritual was the only genuine folk music in America upon which a national music could be developed. A generation later, another great composer, Frederick Delius, coming from England and living in Florida among white Southerners, arrived at a similar conclusion. Both composers used the Negro music, not the white music from which it was supposedly derived. With full opportunity for investigation and with the passion for original music of every kind, why did two great composers, from different countries, without collaboration, deliberately and objectively choose the "imitation" over the original?

Other significant factors in the matter of imitation have already been introduced. We have already learned that the basic folk singer creates song only when he has something definite to express. He examines a foreign song before he borrows from it to be sure that its meanings are adaptable to his needs for creative expression. He owns his song and sings from his heart alone; he consistently eschews mere convention. Of course he improvises on materials outside his life, but only to make critical comment on his own environment. If the Negro slave singer borrowed from the white spiritual in any substantial way, it must be shown that he viewed the universe (earth and heaven being analogous) approximately in the same way as the maker of the white spiritual. Not just religion, but the world of work, society, family relations, cares, trouble, and aspiration, and the hope of heaven, would have to be shown in almost identical views.

CHAPTER SIX

✿◈

How Much of Africa?

. .
.

❨ *Basic Topics and Procedure*

CENTRAL to an enlightened decision on the origins of the so-called American Negro spiritual is the precise definition and bounding of the African backgrounds. Opinions range from an overwhelming African element in the songs with just a thin coating of Americanism to the exact converse. Since music pervades the African character, the problem of definition is quite complex. We have decided to approach it in the following way: (1) Point out and characterize the basic African folk from whom the American slaves derived; (2) study their attitude toward music and related folk forms, their uses of music, their motives and methods, and the impact of music upon them; (3) show, through the word of close examiners, what of their musical attitude, technique, and effects was transferred to the New World, and specifically to the United States of America.

In discussing these transfers, other sections of the New World than the United States of America must be considered. There are many reasons why. The slaves brought to America came from all over Africa and were distributed indiscriminately (without regard to point of origin) throughout the New World. Often, they were taken to the West Indies and later to North America. Sometimes the destination of a slave cargo was changed en route. Quite true there were heavy concentrations of slaves from particular African areas in particular American areas. But, generally speaking, the slave, widely gathered from Africa, was widely spread on both American continents and in the Caribbean. To know him at any one place in his new environment, therefore, one must first know him in that environment as a whole.

Although certain musical characteristics varied from one section of Africa to another, the basic music of Africa was reasonably uniform. This means that fundamental changes in the music from one American area to another are generally the result of local conditions. It also means that basic elements verified in the original Africa and verified again in other areas of Afro-America, cannot be attributed to local conditions in a given area. For example, if basic elements appear in Africa and in Trinidad, they cannot be attributed to local conditions in the United States of America. Also, if African musical traits prevailed against the great variety of life circumstances in other American countries, it will be hard to prove that they died in the United States of America alone.

In the past few years, the panorama of African history has widened greatly. Thus, the character of the African folk is much easier to define than it would have been a few years ago. Considering the range of the field, we would be foolish to try to make a bold spread of this character. It is therefore determined that the character of the African folk will be defined only to the extent necessary to understand the essential music and its transference. Although many authorities have been consulted, special reliance will be given to George P. Murdock, Elizabeth Donnan, Basil Davidson, Melville J. Herskovits, and W. E. B. Du Bois and his German sources. Appropriate references will be given in the Source Notes at the end of the chapter. Where facts or opinions are not so covered in text or notes, it will be understood that the author is relying upon personal interview with the individual in question, during his research tour in Africa.

The fact that for many years, and persistently through the years, a large body of materials has built up bearing upon the African folk tradition and its transference in all directions reduces the justification and excuse for the inaccurate statements and bad guesses that have been published, some quite recently. Bibliographies such as Varley's in 1936, Funkhouser's 1936–39, Haywood's in 1951 and 1961, Thieme's in 1960 and 1964, Gaskin's in 1965, and Suppan's in 1967 should have pointed the way for the serious scholar. Individual works such as those by Waterman, Hare, Murphy, Ballanta Taylor, Nketia, Tracey, and most of all Lomax and his study group at Columbia University should have helped to eradicate some of the more elaborate misunderstandings and misrepresentations. But the latter somehow survive, both in print and in the minds of careless workmen. It is essential that their false impressions be demolished or at least held up to the light of sound scholarship.

❲ *The African Folk*

George Peter Murdock and other historians and anthropologists have stated the clear probability that human life started in Africa. Murdock says, "Africa was probably the cradle of mankind." L. S. B. Leakey declares that man probably evolved from lower animals on the African continent. From various sources we learn that the 4 mother tongues and

125,000 people of 50,000 years ago in Africa grew to 730 languages and 150,000,000 people by A.D. 1900.

African people were not just multiplying, they were building civilizations. Acknowledging such deviations as the blood rituals and the cannibalism, explainable by local circumstances, one cannot deny the prevailing cultural drives in a number of productive directions. Murdock, for example, aligns the West African Negroes as one of mankind's leading creative benefactors in the field of agriculture. Von Franzius credits the African Negro as the original tamer of house cattle. In his *History of Mankind* Ratzel unequivocally declares, "Among all the great groups of the 'natural' races, the Negroes are the best and keenest tillers of the ground."

In the field of manufacture and industry the black Africans have been preeminent for hundreds of years. They have manufactured and woven cotton since deep in the immemorial past. Long before cotton weaving was a British industry, Du Bois demonstrates, the West African and the Sudanese were supplying a large part of the world with cotton cloth. The Hottentot was well versed in the manufacture of cotton clothing, weapons, utensils, in the dressing of skins and furs, the plaiting of cords, and the weaving of mats. Soap was manufactured in the Baushi district of Nigeria; glass was made and colored by the Nupe peoples of Nigeria. The Ibo manufactured cottons, earthenware, ornaments, and instruments of war and husbandry.

On good authority the African black probably originated iron smelting and passed it on to the Egyptians who passed it to the modern Europeans. Boas disqualifies the ancient European, the ancient West Asian, and the ancient Chinese for this invention, and leaves the field open to the black African. Von Luschan joins him in this opinion. Whether or not he was the inventor of the process, he became the supreme master. Gabriel de Mortillet says the African Negroes were the only iron users among primitive peoples. Andrée insists that they developed their own "Iron Kingdom." In showing the significance of their inventing and perfecting iron smelting, Boas makes the point that true advancement in industrial life does not begin until hard iron is discovered. One should also note that expert blacksmithing is a trade practiced for centuries in every part of Africa.

Along with iron, the African Negro stood high in the manufacture and distribution of items in brass, copper, bone, ivory, wood, silver, and gold. Mungo Park reports on marvels in the last three among the Mandingo. Lenz and DuChaillu found expert workers in iron, bone, and ivory in sections of equatorial West Africa. Livingstone found tribes no whites had ever visited who were masters in copper. Excellent wood carvers were uncovered among the Bongo, the Ovambo, and the Makololo, ranging from the Sudan to South and Southwest Africa. The world famous Benin art was based upon original processes in brass, bronze, and ivory. These involved complicated methods of casting that required superior imagination and skill. Smiths in Gambia, described by Jobson in *The Golden Trade* and by many other firsthand observers, have been called "wonderfully adroit." Their products ranged from tobacco pipes and boiling pots to bridles, saddles, and barbed darts and arrows.

Turning to African art, the Benin art of southern Nigeria is an ideal sample. It was practiced without interruption for centuries. In his *Verhandlungen der berliner Gesellschaft für Anthropologie*, Von Luschan describes Benin art as of extraordinary significance. By the sixteenth and seventeenth centuries, he said, it equaled European art and developed a technique of the highest accomplishment.

Frobenius was impressed by the highest development in the art of weaving. Always combining beauty and utilitarianism, the African patiently and proudly achieved distinction in industrial arts and skills. The people of the Congo worked in wood, iron, and ivory, besides their woven materials. Their cups, stools, throwing knives, canes, raffia and grass mats are still objects of interest and value; the spears, drums, ointment boxes, statues, ceremonial head caps, and musical instruments, likewise.

Among the Vai people of Liberia, George W. Ellis found a substantial contribution in art: knives, swords, spears; leather cases, fur covered and grass bags (for carrying money, medicine, and trinkets); wooden spoons, plates, and bowls; inks and dyes made from leaves and barks; and trays for games.

In his chapter on "The Matter and Form of Yoruba Art," G. J. Afolabi Ojo speaks both of art in relation to materials used and to secular art. As to wood carving, he quotes K. Carroll to the effect that the Yoruba were "probably the most flourishing and prolific producers of carvings not only in Africa but in the whole world." Calabash carving was also a fine art among the Yoruba. Much of Yoruba art was dependent upon animal raw materials—the ivory tusks of elephants and the skins of various species of game, goats, and sheep. Mineral art was also expressive—decorative pottery, terra-cotta, brass casting, called the acme of Yoruba art, and stone sculpture.

Sweeney remarks that religion with African Negroes, as with other races, was the chief stimulus for art: the broadest variety of artistic expression is in the ritual masks. Sweeney's report on African art includes textiles of coco palm fiber from the Congo and works in tin, copper, gold, and ivory from all over Africa. Pieces of unusual imagination were an antelope lying down, a pendant in the form of a ram's head, four weights for measuring gold dust, a gong hammer, a mask with red granules, various polychrome masks, and a scepter with the head of a woman.

Carter Woodson reminds us that all African architecture is not Islamic; some of it is definitely Negroid. He also refers to the well-developed histrionic arts of the black African. Although he had no drama in the European sense, his dance around the village fire often contained a comedy staged to divert those needing recreation after the day's toil. Storytelling, involving marvelous stories of ancestors and spirits of the forest, was also elevated to the status of high art, and so maintained for centuries.

According to Desmond Clark, some art among African Negroes is traceable to the Middle Stone Age, 10,000 to 8,000 B.C. Frobenius has described with great enthusiasm the technical summit of Yoruban civilization in the terra-cotta industry, which goes back to the far past, perhaps 900 B.C. Frank Willett has written a memorable article about the Ife entitled "Two Thousand Years of Sculpture." Pursuing the subject of African sculpture, Guillaume and Munro assure the reader that sculpture flourished in central West Africa for innumerable generations before the last century. Certain tribes are listed as having shown a special aptitude in art: Baule, Bobo, Agni, Mossi, Guro, Dan in the northwest; M'Fang and M'Pongwe in Gabon; Bushongo, Baluba, Sibiti, Sangha, Bambalu, Gwembi, Bakelele, Yungu, and Bangongo in the south and east.

More comprehensive and intensive discussions of African art are found in G. Elisofon, *The Sculpture of Africa* (London, 1958); R. S. Rattray, *Religion and Art in Ashanti* (Oxford, 1927); M. E. Sadler, *Arts of West Africa* (London, 1935); W. Schmalenbach, *African Art* (New York, 1954); M. Trowell, *Classical African Sculpture* (London, 1953); L. Underwood, *Figures in Wood of West Africa* (London, 1947); and P. S. Wingert, *The Sculpture of Negro Africa* (New York, 1950).

African religions and religious systems have been much written about. In many places fetishism is a philosophy of life. One informed observer says, "Religion is life, and fetish an expression of the practical recognition of the dominant natural forces that surround the Negro." In many places, also, polytheism is prevalent.

The reliance of the African upon spirit possession is one of the key background factors in the study of the Afro-American spiritual. Even in this factor, however, the picture is uneven. As M. G. Smith has shown, spirit possession, though definitely and supremely African, was not universal in Africa.

A wide reading in the history of religions is not necessary for the reader to know that spirit possession is a common belief all over the world. The earliest manifestation of possession by the spirits of ancestors goes almost beyond the dawn of history in Africa, Asia, and Polynesia. The ancient Greeks believed that the oracles spoke with the voices of the gods. Zarathustra and Mohammed prophesied as the result of being possessed with divine spirits, as did the prophets of ancient Israel.

In the long Christian tradition a human being can be possessed by good or evil spirits. Jesus Christ cast out devils and gave his disciples power to do so. Despite many cases of psychopathological origin, spirit possession is still deeply imbedded in the doctrine and the faith of both Catholic and Protestant. Thus, the use of drums, contortions, and orgiastic dancing by

Africans and by their descendants in voodoo ceremonies in places like Haiti is a mere variation from beliefs and practices revered and practiced by religions of every race and of many nations.

Among Protestant hymns honoring the theme of spirit possession are Isaac Watts' "Come, Holy Spirit, Heavenly Dove," Samuel Longfellow's "Holy Spirit, Truth Divine," and George Croly's "Spirit of God, Descend upon My Heart." But the possession theme in the Negro spiritual of North America seems a good deal closer to the vigorous, dramatic concepts of the Africans. These songs do not describe a pale exercise. When the spirit captures an individual, according to the song, it is a memorable event. The spirit endows the individual with great powers; it transforms him physically and mentally. Expanding his whole role in life and death, the spirit gives the individual new strength, new direction, new motives, and occupations, new capacity for wrestling with life, and above all a new sense of grandeur. The spirit sees to it that the natural world cooperates in all these new grand endeavors and performances.

The titles of a few of the many spirituals reflecting the nature, workings, and effects of spirit possession are found in the following list:

"Ain't No Grave Can Hold My Body Down"
"Balm in Gilead"
"Come Down Angel and Trouble the Water"
"Cry Holy"
"Dese Bones Gwine to Rise Again"
"Don't Care Where You Bury My Body"
"Ev'ry Time I Feel de Spirit"
    (or "Long as I Can Feel the Spirit")
"Gimme That Ole Time Religion"
"I Know He Is a Rock"
"I'm Jes' frum de Founting"
"I Saw the Beam in My Sister's Eye"
"Lord, I Want to Be a Christian in My Heart"
"My Soul's Been Anchored in de Lord"
"O I Know de Lord, I Know de Lord, I Know de Lord Has Laid His Hands
    on Me"
"O No Man, No Man, No Man Can Hinder Me"
"O the Religion that My Lord Gave Me Shines Like a Mornin' Star"
"O My Little Soul's Gwine Shine"
"Religion So Sweet"
"Somebody's Knockin' at Yo' Do' "
"Wade in de Water, God's A-Gonna Trouble de Water"
"Witness"
"You Got a Right, I Got a Right, We All Got a Right to de Tree of Life"
"You Must Be Pure and Holy"

European and American whites have been unduly supercilious about their religious beliefs as compared with those in other parts of the world.

When things are added up, the Christian religion, as taught in the West, contains many elements as strange and peculiar as anything in African religious thought. The Virgin Birth, the miracles of the New Testament (such as feeding five thousand people with five small loaves and two fishes), and other cardinal elements of Christian faith are far more unrelated to the natural world than many of the so-called pagan beliefs. Religion should be judged by the needs of people, their deepest interrelationship with nature and their senses of the meaning of life; not by the divergences from a standard pattern. Concerning African superstitions, Lord Bryce has said,

> Considering, however, that nearly all the ancient world held similar beliefs and that a large part of the modern world, even in Europe, still clings to them, the persistence of these interesting superstitions need excite no surprise, nor are they productive of much practical ill now that the witch-doctor is no longer permitted to do men to death.

The transition of Afro-Americans from African religious beliefs to American is, therefore, a lateral, not a forward, pass. In America, the African often intermixed the two, retaining the more practical and inspiring elements of his African faith.

For our study, besides spirit possession, the most significant phases of African religions are the belief in one God, the influence of the priest, the promotion of slavery by Christianity, and the evidence that the Christian Bible was well known over a wide area. Davidson refers to many studies providing Africans "fully conversant with the notion of a High God who created the world in a time of happiness, before the coming of Death and Work." Africans also believe in a filial divine savior, such as Nummo, son of the High God Mawa, who owed nothing to Christianity.

From her close association with Africans, Natalie Curtis Burlin reports on Malule, the Supreme Being, and Mulungu, the spirit who created all. According to Equiano (Gustavus Vassa), the Supreme God of the Ibos was Chukwu, belief in one creator was general, although there was none in eternity. Joseph Kyagambiddwa is the authority for the fact that the Buganda people worshipped one Supreme Being, Katonda, and that cults of false gods had little effect on this worship. Osifekunde of Ijebu in Nigeria told of his people's single God, superior to all the rest, called *Obba Oloroun*, "king of heaven."

Mungo Park is the authority for the summary statement that the Mandingoes universally believed in one God. Gonzales adds that they saw him in the clouds and heard him on the wind. These kinds of beliefs and the songs clustered about them had been African standards for centuries. In her visit to America in the early 1850s, Fredrika Bremer noted that in both Africa and America the African often believed that the good would go to God who made them, and the bad, out on the wind.

Thus, it is not hard to accredit Theodore P. Ford who writes that these people believed themselves unquestionably to be the children of the gods. From such a literal faith comes such American spiritual terminology as "All of God's Chillun Got A. . . ."

The widespread acceptance of one God in Africa, long before the white man came, is highly significant. This fact pulls down another pillar of white American mythology that "Christian" America supplanted dozens of pagan deities with a single God. Without doubt a variety of gods was acceptable to many groups of Africans, but the concept of one God was firmly established throughout Africa and particularly in West Africa.

After careful research Du Bois declares the widespread influence of the priest in Africa a fundamental piece of evidence in Afro-American survival. Centuries of reliance upon and respect for priests were not wiped out by American slavery. These prerogatives were merely transferred to the American preacher in their midst. This fact helps to explain not only the leadership of many slave revolts by black religious leaders (Nat Turner, Denmark Vesey, and others) but also certain essential developments of the Afro-American spiritual, as later evidence will show.

The attitude of the African folk toward Christianity is a fundamental question on both sides of the Atlantic. Naïve writers state that the black slave in America swallowed Christianity merely because his master taught it to him. Such a view is decidedly fictional from its very roots. Du Bois shows that Christianity was well established in North Africa as early as the fourth century A.D.; it was doubtless known elsewhere in Africa. On the authority of Mommsen we are told that, through Africa, Christianity became the religion of the world. The cross, says Du Bois, preceded the crescent (Islam) on African soil. But Christianity also promoted slavery, a trend of which the slave-elect and the slave Afro-American were well aware. One would have to expect some resistance on the part of some Afro-American slaves to a religion which dubbed the black African as a barbarian and a heathen and pulled open or kept open the door for him to be enslaved for his body's and his soul's health.

If the American white man fancies that he was the first to teach the Bible to his black slave, he is quite mistaken. A number of the African travelers have testified to African acquaintance with the Christian Bible. Jobson, for example, writes of the knowledge by Gambian natives in the early seventeenth century of Adam and Eve, whom they called "Adam and Evahaha," Noah's flood, and Moses. Ellis reports that the Vai priests traditionally possessed copies of the New Testament in Arabic; they knew the life of Christ and the principles of the Christian faith. Osifekunde of Ijebu (Nigeria) wrote that European Christianity had already penetrated the land of the Ijebu by the early eighteenth century. Philip Quaque of Cape Coast had tried to convert people to Christianity in the third quarter of the eighteenth century. He was aided by the fact that the traditional religion included a Supreme Being. Mungo Park, as affirmed by Marion

L. Starkey, found that Fantooma, the Kaffir schoolmaster, had Arabic versions of the Pentateuch, the Psalms of David, and the Book of Isaiah. The unlettered Mandingoes entertained him with stories of Joseph and his brethren, Moses, David, and Solomon. They gave out the stories as part of their own folklore and were much surprised to learn that white men had heard them. If many slaves already knew a great deal of the Bible, the whole pattern of the origin and development of the backgrounds of the spiritual in America will have to be reconsidered.

In addition to complex and highly adaptable religious systems the African was alert in legal systems and in their applications through government. Herskovits has written that African cultures were more complex in government, art, and industry than any other nonliterate culture. The great empires of Ghana, Melle, and Songhay, over a period of at least a thousand years, were examples of extraordinary organizational genius. The city of Jenne (Guinea) controlled seven thousand villages within close range of each other. The Zambesi and Congo peoples built empires and republics which had complex governmental machinery. The emperor of Songhay, Sonni Ali, put together a navy and used it on the Niger to evolve his empire.

In *A Caution and Warning to Great Britain and Her Colonies* (Phildelphia, 1766), Anthony Benezet refutes the notion that the African Negro is insensible to liberty and that living in America is a favor to them. Equiano supports this view by proving the great concern of the individual African with freedom. While on a slaver between Africa and America, Equiano envied the fish their freedom. He speaks of working madly for freedom and rhapsodizes when he finally wins it.

Thousands of Africans over the whole continent felt exactly as Equiano did. Long before the question of foreign slavery came up, they had worked for democratic institutions and processes in government. In spite of various forms of despotism, Murdock declares that primitive democracy was the "first and simplest, as well as the most widespread, type of political system in Africa." Where there were monarchs and despots, some of them were black queens. Among the Ba-Lolo, women took part in public assemblies where all-important questions were discussed.

Many writers have referred to the great gift of the black African exhibited in the fields of trade. For a thousand years beyond 400 A.D. the trading genius accounted for the rise and fall of such great empires as Ghana, Melle, and Songhay. It was part of the state system of the Ashanti to encourage trade. Local and long-distance, inland and ocean trade were the foundation for social and political development. For the Ekpe tribesmen, says Davidson, trading was their lifeblood. The men of Arochuku developed a great trade in house-to-house buying and then established four-day fairs at twenty-four-day intervals, attended by thousands of traders from all over the countryside. Trading nurtured leaders, both in individuals and in groups. The Negroes of Africa were born traders from whom even the Jews and Armenians could learn.

One of the lesser-known fields in which African Negroes have distinguished themselves for a very long time is that of medicine. The Vai tribe long held a reputation for knowledge of hygiene, physiology, and medicine. In their past were memories of surgeons who had done such things as extract bullets and set bones. A highly respected Nigerian psychiatrist, according to Basil Davidson, declared that he and his fellow scientists compared their results with those of the traditional healers (witch doctors). He concluded, "We discovered that actually they were scoring almost sixty per cent success in their treatment of neurosis. And we were scoring forty per cent—in fact, less than forty per cent."

The gentility of the slave was not something he learned from his white master; it had been in his blood for centuries. Among writers of considerable stature and variety, Du Bois has illustrated the ceremony and courtesy which marked Negro life in Africa. Delafosse reports that African Negroes, reputed to be among the most uncivilized, were generally very strict in etiquette and politeness. Livingstone speaks of "true African dignity" as evidenced by every gesture and every fold of clothing.

Nor was the black African living for centuries in blatant ignorance. Delafosse declares that the ignorance of many Negro populations was not noticeably more accentuated than that of many rural populations in Europe; from the standpoint of intellectual development, the same differences separated urban and peasant in Africa as in Europe. The Vai of the Guinea Coast and the Bamoun of the Central Cameroons, and possibly other groups, invented their own systems of writing. East of the Krumen were groups remarkably intellectual, meticulously clean in body, and possessed of a worldly and complicated etiquette.

A word more about cleanliness. Many whites belonging to the Southern slave tradition have commented on the inveterate dirtiness of the African and his corresponding odor. If this is indeed true, it must have arisen in America. Innumerable writers speak of cleanliness as part of the traditional everyday education of the black African, back through many generations. Equiano, for example, told of the family's washing hands before eating, which he described as a ritual. He added that cleanliness on all occasions is extreme.

Although writing was not widespread in black Africa in most places over the centuries, education proceeded in a great variety of ways. One of these was training within an elaborate system of apprenticeships in trades and crafts. Another was the use of what Delafosse calls "*griots*"— individuals with remarkable memories who traveled from place to place reciting things they had memorized. *Griots* were expert, among other things, in music, poetry, storytelling, genealogies, annals, political and social customs, and religious beliefs.

The scope of learning and beliefs among the Yoruba people has been spelled out by Afolabi Ojo in a chapter entitled "The Content of Yoruba Philosophy" in his book *Yoruba Culture*. Concerning Yoruba geosophy,* Afolabi Ojo says: "The Yoruba have their own distinct, systematic and rationalised ideas about the origin of the earth, its extent, shape and boundaries; also about the heavenly bodies, time and seasons." One of these beliefs was that the earth and sky were equal in size. Besides geosophy, the Yoruba educated their people in an understanding of flora and fauna, in linguistic philosophy (words of wisdom, proverbs, riddles), and in the nature of "life affirming," whether in rocks, soil, plants, animals, or human beings.

Another approach to education greatly prized and advanced by the black African was from the point of view of moral sense. Woodson mentions that approach and its development in *The African Background Outlined*. In so doing, he emphasizes the African's three great friends in the world, courage, sense, and insight.

Near the pinnacle of the African education of the past were the universities of the great empires, especially these at Gao, Walata, Jenne, Timbuktu, and Sankore. Among numerous writers swept up by Timbuktu was Alfred Lord Tennyson, England's poet laureate. His poem "Timbuctoo," written when he was eighteen, won the Chancellor's Medal for him as an undergraduate at Cambridge. Inspired by the splendor of this ancient kingdom, he wrote of its pyramids in diamond light "as far surpassing earth's/ As heaven than earth is fairer." He tells of the great glory of the place, of its "pillar'd front of burnish'd gold, interminably high," "if gold it were/ Or metal more etherial." He describes the "multitudes of multitudes" who minister around it. The Spirit who unfolds the kingdom to him speaks of Timbuctoo as an example of "shadowing forth the Unattainable"—

> And step by step to scale the mighty stair
> Whose landing-place is wrapt about with clouds
> Of glory of heaven.

The Spirit also gets down to some remarkable details which reflect Tennyson's exalted vision:

> Child of man,
> See'st thou yon river, whose translucent wave,
> Forth issuing from the darkness, windeth through
> The argent streets o' th' city, imaging
> The soft inversion of her tremulous domes,
> Her gardens frequent with the stately palm,
> Her pagods hung with music of sweet bells,
> Her obelisks of ranged chrysolite,
> Minarets and towers.

* Afolabi Ojo quotes J. K. Wright in defining geosophy as the study of geo- graphical knowledge from any or all points of view.

Lady Lugard's praise of Timbuktu was also lavish. She shows how the learned of Spain, Morocco, and Arabia came many miles to share the wisdom of the natives of the Sudan; how professors came from over the known world to teach in the departments of science, literature, art, grammar, geography, and surgery. Ellis adds rhetoric, logic, eloquence, diction, arithmetic, hygiene, prosody, philosophy, ethnography, music, and astronomy. Du Bois describes the swarm of black Sudanese students. Ellis says that the black students often surpassed the Arabians.

Timbuktu has been described by reliable writers as a model of ancient civilization as rare in diversity and as advanced in ways of life as any civilization of its time. For education the Songhay Empire was also highly considered.

One significant touch of the African folk was the way they handled the question of slavery. The slave in Africa was a recognized member of the family. In the home and in the fields his labor was not hard. The slave was allowed to rise to high position in the tribe depending on his merit, and often did so. Equiano describes the neat slave houses in his native Africa, spread out like a village. Children of slaves could not be sold and were often freed. If the treatment of slaves is a measure of civilization, Europe and America suffered terribly by comparison with the black African.

The ability of the African to develop great personalities has likewise been demonstrated by many writers. As long ago as 1810, Henri Gregoire, constitutional bishop of Blois, wrote *An Enquiry Concerning the Intellectual and Moral Faculties and Literature of Negroes*. Concentrating on fifteen Negroes who distinguished themselves in science, the arts, trades, and politics, Bishop Gregoire dedicated his book to those who have had the courage to plead the cause of the unhappy blacks and mulattoes in writing or public discussion. A century later (in 1915) in his book on *The Negro*, Du Bois made a very large addition to Bishop Gregoire's list.

Although the great majority of the fifteen million slaves brought to the American continents doubtless came from what is loosely called central West Africa—20 degrees west to 15 degrees east longitude and 20 degrees to 5 degrees north latitude—other regions made considerable contributions. Many thousands of the slaves came from Angola. According to Cadornega, a million were taken from the Congo in the seventeenth century alone. Carleton Beals says the conscript labor army was "taken from all parts of Africa," including Madagascar, Ethiopia, and the homes of Hottentots and Bushmen.

Far more came from East Africa than some Afro-American historians are willing to admit. In Elizabeth Donnan's *Documents Illustrative of the History of the Slave Trade to America* (New York, 1965), it is recorded that regular deliveries of slaves were made from Madagascar and Mozambique to New York, Charleston, and other North American (as well as

South American) ports. Hundreds of slaves were deposited on each delivery.

On July 12, 1804, for example, the M'Clures, driving their own boat, the *Horizon*, brought into Charleston 243 Mozambique slaves. The *Horizon* had left Mozambique with 543 slaves, but 300 of these had died as a result of hijacking by a French vessel. Announcement was made in Charleston that sale of the cargo would commence on July 18. Among other details of the announcement was the following: "The character of the slaves from the East Coast of Africa is now so well known that it is unnecessary to mention the decided preference they have over all other Negroes."

Although musical and religious traits of Africans were uniform in essential respects, there were some variations according to location. To ignore the broad spread of geographical and tribal origins is, therefore, to commit the serious error of oversimplification.

The African folk were competitive in almost any scale of civilization. They were not the miserable barbarians that the American slaveholder and his religious advisers pretended, as justification for holding the black man in slavery. Coming to America was not the blessing as advertised for the African slave. In many respects, considering the insecure, struggling, and often uncultured peoples of the American South, it was a decided stepdown.

⟨ Music in the African Tradition

McKinney has established the fact that African Negro culture, by recorded evidence, goes back five thousand years. The first African music, asserts Dan G. Hoffman, was vocal; it was painstakingly developed over centuries. Oluwole Alakija, an African native trained at Oxford, says that Africans learned early that the human voice can produce more notes than any existing musical instrument.

Despite a good many years of his life spent marshaling evidence to prove blacks basically inferior to whites, Count Joseph Arthur Gobineau (1816–82) at length affirmed, "The source from which the arts have sprung is concealed in the blood of the blacks."* One reason for this well-confirmed

---

* In Rene Maran's "Contribution of the Black Race to European Art" (*Phylon*, X, 1949, translated by Mercer Cook) is a further statement from Gobineau, from Chapter 2 of *Essay on the Inequality of the Human Races:* "The black element is indispensable for developing the artistic genius of a race, because we have seen what a profusion of fire, flames, sparks, enthusiasm, spontaneity, lies in its essence, and to what extent the imagination—that reflection of sensuality—and all the physical appetites, make the Negro fitted to undergo the impressions produced by the arts, to a degree unknown in other human families. This is my point of departure, and if there were nothing to be added, certainly the Negro would appear as the lyric poet, the musician, the sculptor par excellence."

belief is the fact that the arts, particularly music, like religion, are everywhere in the African soul. Music is intimately connected with African custom and practice. It is the foremost Negro social art, the right hand, says Hichens, of the native's physiology. He is born, named, initiated into manhood, warriored, armed, housed, betrothed, wedded, buried—to music. After he dies, his spirit is invoked or appeased through music. We are almost a nation of dancers, musicians, and poets, said the Ibo Equiano.

The African has music even for his chores—sawing wood and harvesting, for example—and for his sports—hunting, fishing, and the like. In the West, says Weman, music is considered the expression of an art, a response to the need for relaxation and recreation; in Africa, music-making is the concern of every human being. The African rarely plays *for* someone as Westerners do; he usually plays *with* someone. An inactive audience to a musical performance simply does not exist. Song is the bond of fellowship between men and tribes; music is the essential part of the African's inmost being. It has the power to liberate him fully. In music and dance, concludes Weman, "the African can best be himself." Summing up his researches, Finkelstein declares that the great lesson of African music is human brotherhood.

MOTIVE IN AFRICAN MUSIC

In tracing motive, method, and related topics of African music, we rely upon two main sets of sources: the testimony of a host of authorities from Europe, Africa, and the Americas, and the results of personal visits by the author to nine African countries. Persons consulted on the personal visits included government authorities in the fields of the traditional arts, heads of musical schools, directors and members of musical groups, writers using and evaluating folk material, university students from the villages, knowledgeable old-timers, and other such reliable sources. The countries visited were the Malagasy Republic (Madagascar), Kenya, Uganda, the Republic of the Congo, Nigeria, Ghana, Liberia, Sierra Leone, and Senegal.

For the African Negro, we are told in the *Historical Atlas of Music*, music is a direct manifestation of the vital energy of the people. An interest in music is therefore a direct route to the heart of the people. African music, says A. M. Jones, goes along with social conditions but is not altered by them. Tillinghast lists three objects in African music: the stimulation of religious sentiment, of military spirit, and of sexual passion.

R. D. Wambugu, inspector of music for the Ministry of Education in Kenya, says that music is the most common method of expression there. It is available in all forms of community activity; from the smallest child up, the individual works into the music. Inspector Wambugu emphasizes the fact that dance and voice express involvement in life, rather than reaction to it. From Eldred Jones of Sierra Leone comes the reminder that often the need of the people for entertainment is as strong as that for religious expression.

The occasions for instrumentalizing, dancing, and singing—usually in that order—are numerous and striking. The foundation of the song is generally laid by instruments and dancing. To open the subject, we may set down the list given by Siegmeister in *Music and Society:* songs by young men to influence young women; songs of courtship, challenge, scorn; songs used by mothers to calm and educate their children, including lullabies, play songs, song games; songs used by older men to prepare adolescent boys for manhood: initiation songs, legends to perpetuate the history and tradition of the community, epics, ballads of famous ancestors; songs used by religious and hierarchical heads to keep the community under control: ritual songs to inspire mystery, solemnity, awe, submissiveness; community songs to arouse common emotions and sense of joint participation; songs used by warriors to arouse courage in battle and to instill fear in the enemy: battle songs, ballads commemorating past victories, legends of dead heroes; songs used by priests and doctors to influence nature: medicine songs, rain songs, bewitching songs, evil songs to hurt and kill an enemy, good songs to make friends, arouse love, heal disease; songs by workers to make the task easier: work songs according to the rhythm of labor, group songs to synchronize collectively executed work, team songs in challenge and satire; songs for social occasions: weddings, childbirths, funerals, memorial services, seasonal holidays, each in its own distinct pattern.

In the respective countries, music for the following motives was emphasized: Malagasy Republic—bringing the community together and commentary on life (at the Kianja Mitafo Isotry, the dances and singers would move around the center and point their fingers successively at each audience group); Kenya—expressing the unity and diversity of the community; Uganda—spontaneous expression of individual groups (at each meeting the opening was composed of singing and dancing; in the Mbarara festival every group performed a traditional song from his neighborhood); Congo —birth of twins, great happy wedding, annual celebrations of the chief, the big man under the chief, the first wife of the chief, all people, circumcision, death of a respected man (sometimes after a postponement), death of a hated man (in full irony); Ghana—music correlated with events and with special types of people; Liberia—dancing a means of cooperation, of bringing diverse groups or diverse elements in a group together; Sierra Leone—death or crowning of chief, VIP visit, VIP death, festive occasion, holiday, harvest rites, initiation ceremonies (circumcision, puberty, going into the bush, coming out); Senegal—expression of peculiar characteristics of a local area or tribe.

In 1963, Willard Rhodes showed that even in this generation African folk songs are songs of protest. He entitled his article, "Music as an Agent of Political Expression."

Along with the motive and purpose of musical expression in Africa goes continuity. Women sing and dance with such enthusiasm that babies sleeping on their mothers' backs are bound to be affected. Every child perpetually sings. A. M. Jones says that the tiniest toddler comes into contact with music and has his chance to learn drumming on a tiny drum made by his larger brother from a calabash or an empty wine bottle. Villages still have traditional music, says Philippe Kanza, director of the Conservatoire National de Musique et d'Art Dramatique, in Kinshasa, Congo. The Congolese culture still brings people up through the ranks. In Ghana, Saka Acquaye, director of the Arts Center, provides opportunities for traditional music to be played and danced to. So does Bai T. Moore, under secretary for culture in Liberia, by giving the very young a chance to perform dances they learned at home. Dorothy Van Amsterdam, director of the Sierra Leone Museum, assures us that chants and songs have been handed down for generations through the bush schools and in other ways. Also, she says, traditional dances are passed along to the public on New Year's Day, Boxing Day, at other celebrational days by "devils" who come out and dance in the streets for fun. Since all these things have been going on for centuries, it is perfectly normal and no wonder, as Nketia assures us, that the African carried his music wherever he went—to North America, to South America, to the West Indies, or wherever.

METHODS OF MUSICAL EXPRESSION

The three predominant methods of musical expression are instruments, dances, and songs. The primary instrument is, of course, the drum; but there are many others. Even to this day a notable characteristic of African instrumentalizing is that nearly all instruments are made by the people for a given musical occasion. This creative urge, in response to a creative demand, is fundamental in the African mind.

A normal dance, says A. M. Jones, has three drums and is as artistic as an opera. The drums by fighting against each other—the master drum sets the pace—create a counterpoint that guides the dancing and the singing.

The African dance is far more than fun or relaxation. It is a releasing of the inner forces, which the human body has imprisoned, according to an artistic drive. It builds to climaxes which are sometimes beyond the power of the dancers to control. Although everyone enjoys dancing and participates in the dance, the man selected as the dancer is a thing apart. Both in group dancing and in individual dancing, says Eldred Jones, the integrity of the African dance is amazing.

Not stopping with the fulfillment of its original purpose, the African dance reaches far out into the community. It is a means of cooperation, of bringing groups together. Dance cycles have been responsible for digging soil and planting. Dance clubs have built roads and made farms. Through such activities, tribes have passed laws that a man must never build a house by himself.

The dancing of a major dance organization like the Sierra Leone National Dance Troupe is overwhelming as art, but highly significant in other ways as well. The members of the troupe are from regular tribes; their dances are authentic. Thus, while "entertaining" the public in many parts of the world, they unleash the internal religious and social powers of the African dance. Their costumes and instruments are almost as dramatic as their movements.

For centuries, and even today, the African dance has been a medium of education. Judith Lynne Hanna shows how this happens. The dance, she says, helps to assimilate members of a society to prevailing knowledge, role differentiation, institutionalized emotion, goals, and appropriate means of achieving goals. It also reinforces earlier education. With the young, dance education begins as soon as the child can stand. Through dances the child is taught the importance of fertility in plants and people; proper roles of specific people in the social system; conformity to traditional patterns; and politics, including leadership, government, and the place of war. When the child reaches sexual maturity, the dance unfolds fertility rites. Some dances stress responsibility and self-restraint; others, group cooperation and harmony. The individual's sexual attractiveness and dance skills, says Mrs. Hanna, are interrelated.

Singing includes both chanting and regular singing. Lomax calls it "danced speech." Although it may be started by a group, it often engulfs a whole congregation. In Africa, communal singing is universal. Local songs nearly always have a thrust or punch line with which insiders in the audience identify. These lines are often critical of the establishment or of life in general. Some songs are historical; nearly all are set deep in the social backgrounds of the people.

African singing, though sometimes spontaneous, is often quite complicated. Nketia says that the African emphasis is upon vocal music. In the experience of Rose Brandel (who writes of "Music of the Giants and the Pygmies of the Belgian Congo"), the singing style is full of emphatic gusto because of the accompanying drumming and dancing. The music, she says, is essentially antiphonal: male choruses answer each other in distinct musical phrases. Gorer says that the African singer often improvises; from this improvisation the chorus takes up a refrain, and sometimes two choruses challenge and answer one another. From Doris McGinty we learn that, among the Bantu, the singing ranges from the unaccompanied solo of free, chantlike, unmeasured rhythm or metrical rhythm to group singing (including both sexes) to songs sung responsorially with leader and chorus. The chorus may supply refrain or nonsense interjections, may echo the leader, may answer questions, complete a phrase, or repeat a phrase with variations. When the leader improvises, the chorus supplies a steady, identifying refrain. Songs can thus build up powerful emotional crescendos. All these characteristics, unique to or emphatic in Africa, appear over and over in the spiritual we are now studying.

The subject matter of these songs follows the patterns described above in the discussion of the nature of song. It stems from heartfelt community reaction to people, events, animals, things—the significant symbols of the community's life and the meanings derived from or suggested by these symbols. Mungo Park says that the singing men sang extemporaneous songs and recited historical events; they sang and created devout hymns and performed religious services, all orally. Entering new towns, the singing men at the head of the caravan would sing flattery to the inhabitants to insure the maximum hospitality.

The fact that songs are known by whole populaces over wide areas and handed down through generations shows that memory, also, was cultivated universally.

A form of instrument well established in Africa and vital to an appreciation of the Afro-American spiritual is handclapping. It is closely related to drumming, as A. M. Jones declares. At the Kianja Mitafo Isotry in Tananarive, there were many instruments—drums, violins, accordions, and others. On several occasions a group began its singing and dance movements to the accompaniment of drums and one or more other instruments. Almost unobtrusively handclapping was underlaid. Suddenly, all other instruments stopped and, for the rest of the time, the group relied for its accompaniment entirely upon handclapping.

Weman refers to "rhythmic hand-clapping and graceful body movements" as part of the musical background of people in South Africa, Southern Rhodesia, and Tanganyika. He says that handclapping never occurs where the listener would wish accent, but it is always delivered with metronomic precision. In describing the music of the Venda, Blacking refers to singers who indicate metrical patterns by clapping their hands. This they do with gusto. Doris McGinty cites handclapping as one of the four major sources of African rhythmic complexity; the other three being accents of singers (or of the melody instrument), movement of the dancers, and beating of the drums. Two French observers insist that in Africa handclapping was essential to singing.

Music in Africa has been defined and summed up by Hugh Tracey, director of the International Library of African Music, and his workers in the music codification project. Near the beginning of his codification book, he decries those whose prejudice has created the impression that African music is backward and unworthy of serious consideration. He states his purpose of bringing African music "into the field of African education in its broadest sense." He recognizes three clear divisions of music: vocal participation, the physical manipulation of instruments, and the rhythmic or dance movement associated with music.

The preparation book warns the codifiers that music composed or used for one occasion may frequently be used for another: A dance tune may be used for a lullaby, religious music may be played in a secular context, music stemming from solemn ceremonies may be adapted for the pure pleasure it evokes. This warning should be carried over to evaluators of the spiritual who have tried, quite unsuccessfully, to characterize the spiritual entirely within the narrow confines they have set for religious music.

In another part of the codifier's manual is reference to the intricacies of the African dance. Besides the dance itself and the music accompanying it, is a form of body movement, not necessarily a regular dance, which is stimulated by and stimulates the music. Dancers join the instrumentalists in providing accompaniment, which is an important part of the music. This accompaniment includes singing, clapping, stamping, and using the costume to produce sound. Through such rhythmic movements, the dancing body becomes a musical instrument.

Exhibiting intelligence born of keen insight and long experience, Tracey and his group remain aware of the levels of appreciation of music (which they borrow in part from Jung, the psychologist): (1) the actual artistry of the musical performance; (2) "the unconscious level of sharing common values, of being at ease with them and with other people who also share them, thus forming and ensuring part of the continuity and evolution of tradition"; and (3) "the profound level of common humanity, as universally displayed in the artistic and emotional characteristics of mankind." All three levels are applicable to the proper appreciation of the spiritual in America.

CHIEF CHARACTERISTICS OF AFRICAN SONG

What, then, are the traditional peculiarities of African singing? We have seen a few already: The inevitable links with dance and instrument even when the singer himself had to simulate these (Paul DuChaillu, the French African explorer, observes that African languages are wedded to tunes and dance steps); the natural tendency to sing; the integrating of every action and thought into song, and of song into every thought and action, both as individuals and as communities; the use of song as evaluation and criticism of life and nature; the expression in song of their close familiarity with the powers of the universe, particularly with ancestral gods or with one God.

Rhythm is often set down as the prime characteristic of African music. In his "West African Music and American Popular Culture," Marshall Stearns says that the African Negro's sense of rhythm is not instinctive. It is rather an unconscious pattern handed down from generation to generation by examples, attitudes, and points of view.

To the above can be added polyphony and polyrhythm, antiphony, overlap, repetition of short phrases for the purpose of arousing ecstasy, call-and-response, part singing, recurrent incremental lines and the principle of incremental repetition, and more often than not, syncopation. All these characteristics have been carefully developed by dozens of musical writers and anthropologists, but perhaps nowhere better than by Alan P. Merriam and Alan Lomax.

If one wanted to save time, he could accept at once the minutely developed evidences of Lomax's *Folk Song Style and Culture,* already introduced. With a large staff of experts and with many mechanics and tables, Lomax has demonstrated a great many characteristics and parallels regarding musical patterns all over the world. Lomax and his staff place Afro-America, including Afro-United States, under the large style region *Africa* just as they place Anglo-America under the large style region *Europe* They find the closest similarities between Afro-American and African music. The similarities even deepen when Afro-American is compared with the Guinea Coast and Equatorial Bantu, whence the majority of American slaves were carried away by slavers. Overlap, alternation, and polyphony, for example, appear in Afro-American music precisely as they do in the native African.

Recently, Lomax has added some important footnotes. He now declares, to the shocked dismay of dozens of writers who have made the Africans long on rhythm and short on harmony, that counterpoint was probably invented by black Africa. He says that polyrhythm (two or more different meters moving simultaneously) is a uniquely African trait, used everywhere in Africa, and very, very old. By many charts and computations he has concluded that black Africa is the most homogeneous and the richest style area in the world.

Much of his latest research on African tradition in song has turned upon sociopolitical implications. Overlap and interlock, involving such tendencies as singing a stretch of verse and beginning a chorus before the verse is finished, and doing the same before the chorus is finished, he claims to be the heart of African music. They are symbolic, he says, of the cohesiveness of gregarious societies such as the African tropical garden village. Black Africa, he continues, leads all continents in vocal harmony and in the simultaneous presence of high and low parts. This kind of thing, again, symbolizes the gregarious society where women are 50 percent or more of the food-producers and are forward in social movement. Similarly, a certain voice tension appears in black African song; it is indicative of a society where the premarital sex relation in the female is severely punished. In black Africa, tribal life makes fertility a central value; young men and women are trained in sexual values.

IMPACT OF AFRICAN EXPRESSION IN MUSIC

A fundamental element of African music, and one that can be used to distinguish its influence, is its impact. In the music of a number of other ethnic, national, and local groups, singing and instrumentalizing can be done in peace and quiet. Often music is an agency for restoring or establishing peace and quiet. In Africa things are quite different.

Alfons Michael Dauer, an anthropologist who lives in Göttingen, Germany, but who has spent much of his time in recent years studying African and Afro-American musical expression, leads off our discussion. In a number of places, but particularly in an article called "Kinesis und Katharsis," published late in 1969, Dauer has discussed this impact.

European rhythm, he begins, is mainly an element of time which is extremely important to our culture. The African is not bound to a temporal conception. His rhythm consists of a physical-sensual perception of accent impulses and their transformation into movement. African rhythm, Dauer therefore maintains, is a physical experience, a power with a definite, regulated effect, a "modal" power which is able greatly to increase human vitality.

Differences between the European and the African are not so great as they might seem. If certain features of the European are intensified, they can come closer to the feeling of African music. It is a question of feeling music with the body, of carrying the appreciation of the music into the realm of motive experience.

One can pick up these motive impulses either by hearing or by imagining them inwardly. If the European can produce in himself a course of even accent impulses and be carried along by their flowing and fluent character to the point where they "touch the marrow," then he can move into the African experience.

But the African characteristically transforms acoustically or sensually received impulses into kinetic energy, that is, movement or motion. This ability is spoken of as having a "metronome sense." When this "metronome sense" is turned on, nothing in the world can disturb it. The "gyro-compass" in the insides of the African musician is of such absolute exactness that it cannot be touched by outside influences.

To sum all this up, Dauer is saying that African music inevitably arouses bodily movement. It aims to do so, and it succeeds.

In another article called "Stil und Technik im afrikanischen Tanz," Dauer comments on the relationship between African music and the African dance. Referring to Helmut Günther's article, "The Dances of Africa," he reminds his reader of the European habit of treating his body in the dances as a stiff linear unit in space. The African, on the other hand, does not seek the movement of his body in space, but rather just the experience of moving the body itself. In contrast to the monocentric dance-body of the European, is the polycentric dance-body of the African. Such polycentric movement corresponds to the laws of the polymetrics and polyrhythmics of African music. It realizes different, simultaneous, rhythmic courses of movement through kinetic transformations of movement which are either released actively by various body centers or intensified systematically to frenzies or ecstasies. All over Africa are areas of agreement in dance style and in movement models, stretching throughout all cultural zones, demonstrating dance forms of the same function and natural tendency. But there are also a number of areas of difference. Dauer discusses differences in form and meaning in the dance styles of Central Africa, East Africa, the Sahara region, the Sudan, the Wadai, and West Africa.

Nor is Dauer the only observer who has noted such spectacular uses of movement among Africans. Tracey, whom we recently quoted, refers to the body movements which are the inevitable effect of the music from the very start. Doris McGinty mentions these movements, which have their own pattern, pace, and accent, not coincidental with those of the melody, the clapping, and the drumming. She specifically warns that this concept of movement must not be underestimated. In Weman's account is the description of the wholehearted participation of the singing group, evidenced by free-flowing and unrestrained body movements.

Another strong note of impact is the ecstasy. As A. M. Jones tells it, the rising of the drums makes the dancers go mad. In Blacking's account the people play, sing, dance with gusto or not at all. The function of the music, he says, is to raise both performers and audience far above routine emotion. The sick feel better; the elderly throw away their sticks and dance.

The principle of ecstasy as the result of musical stimulation is hardly an expression of wild, senseless emotion. It is rather a form of full and deep involvement in life. The ecstatic expressions of the whites in the earliest camp meetings was a casual detour; the similar expression of the blacks there was a normal reaction to intense emotional awareness. It is highly likely that the amateurs were learning from the professionals.

In any case African music is characterized by these elements of well-developed body movement and ecstasy. Afro-American music, before, during, and since the time of the widespread creation of the spiritual, is similarly characterized as an inheritance. This undoubted fact is a powerful reagent in determining the original course of the spiritual.

USE OF MASK AND SYMBOL IN AFRICAN MUSIC

We have seen that the earliest primitive music used mask and symbol extensively. It was not just for the purpose of concealing its criticism of rulers and established ways. Mask and symbol represent artistic ways of getting at the roots of life. The Orientals and the ancient Greeks used masks in their drama to prevent preoccupation with insignificant objective details and to reserve the dramatic action for the deepest implications. They also wished to control the channels of thought and feeling among spectators. So did the Africans in their dance and singing.

Herskovits has indicated that the African savored double entendre no less than other people. In speaking of African purpose in music, Nketia has written, "African music lays particular stress on vocal music, for the song may be used for a dual purpose." Historical songs, he continues, are laced with topical allusions. There are also songs of insult, proverbial songs, and humorous references with double edges.

In personal conversation Nketia stressed the wide use of mask and irony among the Africans in revealing human values and human dimensions. The dance celebrating the death of the hated man of the community, described by the students of Louvanium University in Kinshasa, Congo, was a subtle form of irony elaborated through a community celebration. The masked dances of the Jobai Dancing Club of Liberia and of the Sierra Leone National Dance Troupe were not just in the nature of conventions; the masks and the dances coordinated to produce meanings unavailable to each separately.

That African and Afro-American music is loaded with mask and symbol cannot be denied. If the interpreter of the spiritual that grew up in America overlooks the mask and symbol, he is displaying remarkable ignorance and indulging in inexcusable inaccuracy.

OTHER FORMS OF AFRICAN EXPRESSION RELATED TO MUSIC

Hugh Tracey, among other experts in African music, has more than once pointed to the close interrelationship between music, poetry, stories, and other popular forms of expression. President Léopold Sédar Senghor told this writer that he was impressed by the so-called Negro spirituals when he first heard them as a young man in France, partly because they reminded him of revered poems from his childhood in Senegal. The latter poems he translated into French and published. In Babalola's *Ijala Poetry*, reports Eldred Jones of Sierra Leone, are numerous poems comprising the same traditional elements as the spirituals. And it is well known that the African story is blood brother of the African song. Often through the repeated story were the songs preserved.

In and near Freetown, where the tribalized life still goes on, the telling of folk stories is still attractive. Comedians can still get and hold an audience by reciting proverbs as they have done for centuries. In Limba stories (note Ruth Finnegan's *Limba Stories and Story-Telling*), the respondent to the storyteller is designated in advance.

Mohamadou Kane, of the University of Dakar in Senegal, has published many of these stories, particularly those of d'Amadou Coumba. Kane insists that the storyteller is often both dancer and drummer. Like African music, he and his story create movement; they cause people to clap their hands. Although the Arabs brought in some of these stories, the basic elements are Negro African. Although the story may have a religious introduction, it soon gets down to everyday life. The story is sometimes sung.

It nearly always describes the original African feeling, often deriving its philosophy from animism. Usually it reveals the peculiar characteristics of a local area or tribe.

As to popular art forms, it is notable that dancers often appear in African art, as witness the art pieces on display in the Palais de la Reine, in Tananarive, Madagascar.

The fondness of the African for stories and poems is reflected in dozens of spirituals of pronounced narrative and dramatic character. The intimate relationships between the Uncle Remus stories, decidedly African in origin, and the American spiritual have never been properly spelled out.

PRESENT CULTIVATION OF TRADITIONAL ARTS IN AFRICA*

Before turning to the transference of African music to American soil, we must pause a moment on the continuing concern of African countries for the presentation of their traditional arts. Without the maintenance of these arts, much of the background of the spiritual and of other Afro-American monuments will be irretrievably lost.

In the Malagasy Republic, at Tananarive, is a governmental Department of Traditional Arts. Members of this department, particularly Rabesehola Gaby and Rotmohonano Yorbat, are working to preserve the evidences of traditional expression and to expand public interest in it. The department has sound films of traditional dances from all over the nation—such dances as the *Rauolana Fenomenana*, the *Ambovombe*, the *Marovoay*, the *Sakaraha*, the *Nosybe*, the *Brickaville*, the *Salegy*, and others. In the Department of Tourism, Mrs. Zoëlisca Andrianony directs interested visitors to the Kianja Mitafo Isotry, where every Sunday, through most of the day, there is folk dancing involving many and varied groups.

The government has also published, in French and in English, for distribution such informative documents as, Hélène Bonnerberger-Rouillon, "De La Musique Malgache Authentique," "Le Folklore Malgache," and Michael Razakandraina, "Le Folklore Musical Malgache."

In Nairobi, R. D. Wambugu, inspector of music for the Ministry of Education of Kenya, has set as one of the objectives of his department to bring out the essential music of the community. His sponsorship of musical festivals, bringing together singers from all over the country, is only one of his activities in pursuit of his objectives. In the festivals each group is at lib-

* UNESCO published in 1970 (with a Paris dateline) an important contribution to this topic: *Films on Traditional Music and Dance*, a first international catalogue. The countries covered are Angola, Central African Republic, Chad, Republic of the Congo, Democratic Republic of the Congo, Dahomey, Ethiopia, Gabon, Ghana, Guinea, Ivory Coast, Liberia, Madagascar, Malawi, Mali, Namibia, Niger, Nigeria, Portuguese Guinea, Rwanda, Senegal, Sierra Leone, Tanzania, Togo, Uganda, Upper Volta, and Zambia.

erty to choose what songs it will sing. So far, a number of groups have chosen and sung American Negro spirituals.

In Kampala, Cosma Warugaba, head of programs, National Service, Radio Uganda, besides sponsoring much traditional music for public consumption, has written and produced a folk opera, called *Omuhügo* (The great hunt). Efforts are being made to export this opera to the West, where it would serve both as original entertainment and as a revelation of a whole new world of art.

Philippe Kanza, director, Conservatoire National de Musique et Art Dramatique, of Kinshasa, Congo, guides his students in composing music based on the traditional cultures. He has announced that he will strive in this way, among others, to produce a true Congolese music. For the benefit of interested visitors he had several students in his school perform, in full costume and to the accompaniment of native drums, a traditional circumcision dance.

Saka Acquaye, director of the Arts Centre in Accra, Ghana, states as his main objective the development of the various ethnic and traditional values of the eight regions of the nation. One of his dance troupes is composed of dancers from the various tribes. Every Saturday afternoon the public is invited to perform in its own way and to sit as audience. One of these performances revealed a great scope in dancers, singers, and instrumentalists, especially drummers. Acquaye is especially busy in collecting material on funeral rites, childbearing rites, and marriage costumes. For two years he has performed at intervals a folk opera (in English, heavily sandwiched with vernacular), entitled *The Last Fisherman.* One of his goals is to develop audiences with appreciation for the traditional.

Bai T. Moore, of Liberia, Logie Wright, of Freetown, Sierra Leone, and Mohamadou Kane, of Senegal, have similar purposes in awakening their respective peoples to an appreciation of traditional music and literature, and to building upon these for the evolution of further arts. In Liberia, as far back as 1957, the Department of the Interior, Bureau of Folkways, published *Traditional History and Folklore of the Glebo Tribe.*

AFRICAN FOLK AND AFRICAN MUSICAL APTITUDE

From overwhelming evidence, therefore, the nature of the unique elements of the African folk is clear. The peculiar musical character of the African is equally clear. If the characteristics described above are found in pure state or only slightly adapted in the New World, the transfer of African character is proved. These characteristics are forthright, easily identified, easily traced. In most instances they differ from European and other non-African characteristics so boldly that weasel arguments against them are ineffective. Only those who refuse to face their existence in Africa or America would any longer attempt such arguments.

After stating unqualifiedly that the music of the American Negro had its beginning in Africa, Jerome Dowd made a comment on the difficulties of transference. He asserted that the folk music of the native African was difficult to reproduce "for the reason that it cannot be written so as to preserve its emotional color and timbre." The original poetry of African folk music, he said, was lost, but the emotional tone and rhythm were transferred to new compositions, partly original and partly imitative of American white hymns.

If the African characteristics predominate in the spiritual, then the spiritual is an African form. If the African characteristics prove very minor and the American elements predominate, then the spiritual is an American form with a very few foreign strains. If African and American blend in a strong compound, or if the mixture retains clear and definite manifestations of each with some new elements resulting from the blend, then the spiritual is unquestionably Afro-American. It must be one of these three.

❴ African Musical Transfers to South America and the West Indies

Our next job is to show what, if any, African elements the slave imposed upon his American surroundings. We will look first at South America and the West Indies, and then at North America. We take this part of America first because Africans came first to these shores—more than a century before they arrived in the North American colonies. Our examination of this transfer, if there was a transfer, must necessarily be brief,

The earliest recorded reference to African singing in the New World is 1707. Sir Hans Sloane, in *A Voyage to the Islands Madera, Barbados, Nieves, S. Christophers and Jamaica* . . . , tells of dancing and singing on feast days. Reckoning the slaves from Guinea the best, he describes their religion as well as their music. He says that the Negroes from some countries think that when they die they return to their own country—thus, they fear death little, believing it a change from a life of slavery to one of freedom; for this reason, they sometimes cut their own throats. Similar commentary appeared again in the eighteenth century in Monk Lewis's *Journal of a Residence among the Negroes in the West Indies* (compiled 1795).

Singing and dancing in the West Indian colonies were already well established long before the early eighteenth century. The clear indicator is that the singing and dancing never stopped. Even on the slavers in the Middle Passage, whenever conditions were humane enough to permit it, spontaneous singing and dancing took place. The evidence of Theophile Conneau (Captain Canot), George Francis Dow, and Frank Tannenbaum, among many others on the same subject, is convincing.

The fact of continuous singing and dancing by the African from his home to shipboard to a new home an ocean away proves one thing: The African never stops such activities any more than he stops breathing. The matter of a shift in language is utterly insignificant. For centuries African tribesmen have been bilingual and trilingual and surrounded by numerous languages other than their own. Du Bois notes 264 Sudanic languages from the Atlantic to Abyssinia, 42 languages lying between Semitic and other African languages, and 182 Bantu languages. Those who put great emphasis upon the loss of the memory of traditional things because the slave had to go from his native language to English or French or Spanish or Portuguese are utterly ignorant of the inveterate and necessary language facility of the native African.

To the African, singing and dancing are the breath of the soul. No matter where he goes or what kind of life he is forced to live, these two things he will do; and basically in an African way.

The literature of the past three hundred years is filled with expositions, descriptions, narrations, and dramatizations of the ways in which the African imposed his singing, his dancing, and his instrumentalizing upon the peoples of the New World. According to this literature, in most instances it was sheer imposition. Very few peoples matched the African in his high estimate of music as a weapon for living. Very few peoples approach the African in the vigor and dynamics of his music. Thus, when he went into a new area, even when he was dragged into it, his musical domination was in great contrast to his social and political subserviency. He may have been dubbed a slave, but against people of weaker musical aptitudes, he was a master.

The spread of his musical influence is far too great for a comprehensive display in the present volume. Representative samples, however, can be presented; they are indeed quite essential to any proper study of the Afro-American music to the north. We will therefore make a small chart of representative samples by countries and give a somewhat more expanded statement of areas recently investigated through personal visits. The breakdown will be first by South American countries (Mexico and Honduras will be added to these) and second by West Indian countries.

Some outstanding bibliographies need to be mentioned at the outset so that the curious reader can find his way around. The first of these is Douglas H. Varley, *African Native Music* (1936), which, under "African Survivals in the New World," has elaborate subchapters on "Negro Music in the West Indies" and "Negro Music in South America." The second and third are by Gilbert Chase, his *Bibliography of Latin American Folk Music* (Washington, 1942) and his monumental *Guide to the Music of Latin America* (Washington, 1962). (References will be given as "Chase," followed by the page number[s].) The fourth and fifth are products of the Centro Latinamericano de Investigaciones en Ciencias Sociales of Rio de Janeiro: Rémy Bastien (of Mexico), "Introducción a la Bibliografía Sobre Influencias Culturales Africanas en La America Latina" and Regina H.

Tavares and Radjino Lisbon, "Influencias Africanas en America Latina" with a "Presentacion" by Manuel Diégues Junior.

Representative Books and Articles Dealing with Influences of African Music upon South American and West Indian Cultures

GENERAL

Emilio Ballagas, *Antología de la poesía negra hispanoamericana* (Madrid, 1935)

Roger Bastide, *Les Amériques noires: Les Civilizations africains dans le nouveau monde* (Paris, 1967)

Gonzalo Aguirre Beltran, "African Influences in the Development of Regional Cultures in the New World," *Plantation Systems of the New World* (Washington, 1959)

Ralph Steele Boggs, "South American Folklore Regions and Their Study," *Southern Folklore Quarterly*, V (1941)

Ernest Borneman, "The Anthropologist Looks at Jazz," *The Record Changer* (1944), and *A Critic Looks at Jazz* (London, 1946)

Ruth Creed, "African Influence on Latin American Music" (n.d.)

T. Van Dam, "The Influence of the West African Songs of Derision in the New World," *The Record Changer* (1944)

Madeleine Doré, "Bibliographie Américaniste," *Journal de la Société des Américanistes* (1958)

Films on Traditional Music and Dance (published by UNESCO): includes listings of Brazil, Cuba, Haiti, Martinique, and Trinidad and Tobago

Albert Friedenthal, *Musik, Tanz und Dichtung beiden Kreolen Amerikas* (Berlin-Wilmersdorf, 1913)

Melville J. Herskovits, "El estudio de la música negra en el hemisferio occidental," *Boletin Latino Americano Música* (1941)

Harold Nason, "Folk Songs of the West Indies," in Van Campen Heilner, *Beneath the Southern Cross* (Boston, 1930)

Elena Paz, comp. and ed., *Favorite Spanish Folksongs* (New York, 1965)

George Pinckard, *Notes on the West Indies* (London, 1816)

W. Rhodes, "La Musique noire dans le nouveau monde," *La Musique dans la vie*, II (1969)

Martin Sable, *A Guide to Latin American Studies, 2* (Los Angeles, 1967)

André Schaeffner, "La Musique noire d'un continent à un autre," *La Musique dans la vie*, II (1969)

Nicolas Slonimsky, *Music of Latin America* (New York, 1945)

Richard Alan Waterman, "African Influence on the Music of the Americas," in Sol Tax, ed., *Acculturation in the Americas* (New York, 1952, 1967)

SOUTH AMERICA

Argentina

José Juan Arrom, *Certidumbre de America* (La Habana, 1959)

Chase, 83, Afro-American section

Ricardo Rodrigues Molas, "La música y la danza de los negros en el Buenos Aires de los siglos XVIII y XIX," *Historie* (Buenos Aires, 1957)

Brazil

F. Acquarone, *Historia da Música Brasileira* (Rio de Janeiro, 194–)

Mario de Andrade, *Folk Music and Folk Song in Brazil* (São Paulo, 1936)

——, *Música de Feitiçaria no Brasil* (São Paulo, 1963)

——, *Pequena Historia de Música* (São Paulo, 1963)

Nair Andrade, *Novos Estudios Afro-Brasileiros* (1937)

Laura Boulton, *The Music Hunter* (Garden City, 1969)

Edison Carneiro, "Elementos africanos na música o na dança brasileira," *Cadernos Brasileiros, 4* (1962)

——, *Religiões Negras* (Rio de Janeiro, 1936)

Chase, 138–40, Afro-Brazilian section

Luís Heitor Correa de Azevedo, *Bibliografía Musical Brasileira, 1820–1950* (Rio de Janeiro, 1952)

——, *Dois Pequenos Estudios de Folklore Musical* (Rio de Janeiro, 1938)

Luciano Gallet, "O negro na música brasileira," *Estudios de Folklore* (Rio de Janeiro, 1934)

Rex Gorham, *The Folkways of Brazil: A Bibliography*, ed. by Karl Brown (New York, 1944)

Reginaldo Guimaraes, "A divinização da música negro-brasileira," *Seiva* (Bahia, 1939)

H. J. Hansen, ed., *European Folk Art in Europe and the Americas* (London and New York, 1968)

Melville J. Herskovits, "Drums and Drummers in Afro-Brazilian Cult Life," *Musical Quarterly* (1944)

——, and R. A. Waterman, "Música de culto afro-bahiana," *Revista do Estudios Musicales* (1949)

Beatrice Landeck, *Echoes of Africa in Folk Songs of the Americas* (New York, 1961)

Aires de Mata Machado Filho, *O Negro e o Garimpo em Minas Gerais* (Rio de Janeiro, 1943)

Raymundo Nina Rodrigues, *Os Africanos no Brasil* (São Paulo, 1932)

——, "A raca negra na America Porugueza . . . ," *Revista do Brasil*, XIX (1922)

F.-J. de Santa-Anna Nery, *Folk-Lore Brésilien* (Paris, 1889)

Antônio Olinto, "The Negro Writer and the Negro Influence in Brazilian Literature," *African Forum* (1967)

Arthur Ramos, *As Culturas Negras no Novo Mundo* (Rio de Janeiro, 1937)

——, *O Folclore Negro de Brasil* (Rio de Janeiro, 1934)

——, *O Negro Brasileiro* (1934); trans., R. Pattee, *The Negro in Brazil* (1939)

Raymond S. Sayers, *The Negro in Brazilian Literature* (New York, 1956)

Zora Seljan, "Negro Popular Poetry in Brazil," *African Forum* (1967)

Clarival do Prado Valladares, "A Iconologia Africana no Brasil," *Revista Brasileira de Cultura* (1969)

Colombia

José Juan Arrom, *Certidumbre de America*
Chase, 195
H. J. Hansen, ed., *European Folk Art in Europe and the Americas*

Ecuador

José Juan Arrom, *Certidumbre de America*
Chase, 229

Guyana (British Guiana)

P. A. Brathwaite, comp., and Serena Brathwaite, ed., *Folk Songs of Guyana*
 (1970)
———, *Folk Songs of Guyana: Republic Celebrations Issue* (with music) (1970)
———, *Folk Songs of Guyana: Words Only* (1964)
———, *Guyanese Proverbs and Stories* (1967)
———, *Musical Traditions* (1962)
Chase, 158

Honduras

Chase, 245

Mexico

José Juan Arrom, *Certidumbre de America*
Chase, 273–304
Vicente T. Mendoza, *Algo del folklore negro en Mexico* . . . in *Miscelánea de estudios dedicados a Fernando Ortiz* (La Habana, 1956)
Jim Morse, collector, *Folk Songs of the Caribbean* (New York, 1958)

Peru

Chase, 331–42

Suriname (Dutch Guiana)

Chase, 225
Melville J. and Frances S. Herskovits, *Suriname Folk-Lore* (New York, 1936),
 includes N. Kolinski, *Suriname Music*

Uruguay

Lauro Ayestarán, *La Música en el Uruguay* (Montevideo, 1953)
Chase, 363–64

Venezuela

Miguel Acosta Saignes, *Estudios de Folklore Venezolano* (Caracas, 1962)
———, *Vida de los esclavos negros en Venezuela* (Caracas, 1967)

José Juan Arrom, *Certidumbre de America*
Chase, 371–82
H. J. Hansen, ed., *European Folk Art in Europe and the Americas*
Jim Morse, *Folk Songs of the Caribbean*
Luís Felipe Ramon y Rivera, "Los estribillos en la poesía cantada del negro vene-
    zolano," *Folklore Americano* (Lima, 1965)

THE WEST INDIES

The Bahamas

Major H. MacLachlan Bell, *Bahamas: Isles of June* (1934)
Chase, 99
M. Clavel, "Items of Folk-Lore from Bahama Negroes," *Journal of American
    Folklore*, XVII (1904)
Amelia Defries, *The Fortunate Islands* (London, 1929)
Charles L. Edwards, *Bahama Songs and Stories* (Boston, 1895)
James Fitz-James, *Bahamian Folk-Lore* (Montreal, 1906)
A. L. Lloyd, *Folk Songs of the Americas* (New York, 1966)
Daniel McKinnon, *Tour through the British West Indies, in the Years 1802 and
    1803, Giving a Particular Account of the Bahama Islands* (London, 1804)
Jim Morse, *Folk Songs of the Caribbean*
Elsie Clews Parsons, "Spirituals and Other Folklore from the Bahamas," *Journal
    of American Folklore*, XLI (Oct.–Dec. 1928)
N. Clark Smith, *Bahama Negro Folk Songs* (Chicago, 1923)
"Tradition, Creativity, and Values in Bahamian Folklore," *Actas y Memorias*
    (Mexico City, 1964)

Barbados

Jim Morse, *Folk Songs of the Caribbean*
Sir Hans Sloane, *A Voyage to the Islands Madera, Barbados, Nieves, S. Chris-
    tophers and Jamaica* ... (London, 1707)

Cuba

José Juan Arrom, *Certidumbre de America*
William R. Bascom, "Yoruba Acculturation in Cuba," *Les Afro-Américains*
    (Dakar, 1959)
Chase, 211–16, Afro-Cuban section
Melville J. Herskovits, "Social History of the Negro," in Carl Murchison, ed.,
    A Handbook of Social Psychology (New York, 1935, 1967)
Jim Morse, *Folk Songs of the Caribbean*
Fernando Ortiz, *La Africanía de la Música Folklórica de Cuba* (La Habana,
    1950)
Adolfo Salazar, "El Movimiento Africanista en la Música de Arte Cubana," *Es-
    tudios Afrocubanos*, II (1938)

Guadeloupe

Jim Morse, *Folk Songs of the Caribbean*

Grenada

Andrew Pearse, "Aspects of Change in Caribbean Folk Music," *Journal of the International Folk Music Council*, III (1955)

Haiti

Laura Boulton, *The Music Hunter*
Chase, 242–44
Harold Courlander, *The Drum and the Hoe: Life and Lore of the Haitian People* (Berkeley, 1960)
——, *Haiti Singing* (Chapel Hill, 1939)
Lorimer Denis, *Quelques Aspects de Notre Folklore Musical* (Port au Prince, 1950)
Melville J. Herskovits, *Life in a Haitian Valley* (New York, 1937)
——, "Social History of the Negro," in Carl Murchison, ed., *A Handbook of Social Psychology*
Werner A. Jaegerhuber, *Chansons Folkloriques d'Haiti* (Port au Prince, 1945)
James G. Leyburn, *The Haitian People* (New Haven, 1941)
Jim Morse, *Folk Songs of the Caribbean*
Jean Price-Mars, "Les Survivances Dans La Communauté Haitienne," *Les Afro-Américains*

Jamaica

Laura Boulton, *The Music Hunter*
Chase, 247
Walter Jekyll, *Jamaican Song and Story* (London, 1907, 1966)
Olive Lewin, "Authentic Jamaican Folksongs" and "From the Grass Roots of Jamaica" (recordings, with notes, n.d.)
Jim Morse, *Folk Songs of the Caribbean*
Tom Murray, ed. and arr., *Folk Songs of Jamaica* (London, 1951)
Alma Norman, *Ballads of Jamaica* (London, 1967)
Helen H. Roberts, "Possible Survivals of African Song in Jamaica," *Musical Quarterly*, XII (1926)
Sir Hans Sloane, *A Voyage to the Islands Madera, Barbados, Nieves, S. Christophers and Jamaica* . . .

Martinique

Chase, 384
Jim Morse, *Folk Songs of the Caribbean*

Puerto Rico

Chase, 346–47
Ruth Allen Fouché, *Canciones Puertorriqueños* (1958)
Jim Morse, *Folk Songs of the Caribbean*

Santo Domingo

José Juan Arrom, *Certidumbre de America*
Elsie Clews Parsons, "Spirituals from the 'American' Colony of Samana Bay, Santo Domingo," *Journal of American Folklore*, XLI (Oct.–Dec. 1928)
Pierre de Vaissière, *Saint-Domingue* (Paris, 1909)

Trinidad and Tobago

M. P. Alladin (director of culture for Trinidad and Tobago), *The Folk Arts of Trinidad and Tobago* (n.d.)
——, *Folk Chants and Refrains of Trinidad and Tobago* (1969)
——, *Folk Stories and Legends of Trinidad* (1968)
——, *Notes on Carnival* (1968)
Chase, 384
Edric Connor, collector and ed., *Songs from Trinidad* (London, 1958)
Jacob D. Elder (Institute of Social and Economic Research), "Color, Music, and Conflict: A Study of Aggression in Trinidad with Reference to the Role of Traditional Music," *Ethnomusicology*, VIII (1964)
——, "Correlation between Social Status and Communicative Phenomena in Trinidad: Functional and Formal Variation in Linguistic Categories" (St. Augustine, 1969–70)
——, "The Integration of Linguistics and Peasant Culture Research in the Caribbean" (St. Augustine, 1970)
——, "The Yoruba Ancestor Cult in Gasparillo" (St. Augustine, 1969)
Charles S. Espinet and Harry Pitts, *Land of the Calypso* (Port-of-Spain, 1944)
Melville J. Herskovits, "Social History of the Negro," in Carl Murchison, ed., *A Handbook of Social Psychology*
Krister Malm, "Writings on Ethnic Music and Mesomusic in the Lesser Antilles" (unpublished mimeographed bibliography, 1969)
George Eaton Simpson, "The Shango Cult in Nigeria and in Trinidad," *American Anthropologist*, LXIV (Dec. 1932)
Richard Alan Waterman, "African Patterns in Trinidad Negro Music" (unpublished doctoral thesis in anthropology, Northwestern University, Evanston, 1943)

Virgin Islands

Krister Malm, "Writings on Ethnic Music and Mesomusic in the Lesser Antilles" (unpublished mimeographed bibliography)
Jim Morse, *Folk Songs of the Caribbean*

References on the West Indies that follow are taken both from personal notes and from documents. When they are taken from documents, the listing will have been given in "Representative Books and Articles," above.

Brazil is, of course, the most powerful South American example of the African impact in the New World. Of its ninety million people, Brazil has about one-third Negroes and mulattoes. Despite the laws officially eliminating racial differences, Brazil has today many highly Africanized communities. In his book *Religões Negras* (Negro religions), Edison Carneiro records that the slave traffic situated the Bantu Negroes, originating from Angola, the Congo, and Mozambique, in Maranhão, Pernambuco, and Rio de Janeiro in large numbers; in smaller numbers, they migrated to Alagôas, the coast of Para, Minas Gerais, the state of Rio, and São Paulo. The Sudanese Negroes, coming from the Niger zone of West Africa, including Yorubas, Ewes, and Hausas, were settled in Bahia and dispersed over the vast and fertile farming regions nearby. The practice of native African religions and the corresponding music, especially singing, is still prevalent in these areas.

In some instances the African and the Catholic have been blended. Machado Filho's *O Negro e o Garimpo em Minas Gerais* (The Negro and mining in Minas Gerais) gives a fair picture of the blend. Prayers of penitence against drought combine an Angolese custom and a Catholic language:

Pelas vossas chagas,	Through your wounds,
Pela vossa cruz	Through your cross
Livrai nos da peste	Free us from the drought
Senhor Bom Jesus	Good Lord Jesus

Antônio Olinto, presently associated with the Brazilian Embassy in London and the longtime writer on African influences in Brazil, has noted that in the United States of America, the Yorubas were separated; in Brazil they were kept together. Some villages even brought their own kings. Slave owners would allow such kings to be king for a day. Festivals were held and songs were perpetuated or evolved. Xongó gods are still alive in Brazil today; their believers maintain a mythology which challenges that of the ancient Greeks.

Dr. Olinto's wife, who uses the pen name Zora Seljan, has also written on Afro-Brazilian subjects. She notes that African influences, so alive in Brazilian folklore, are used by white, mulatto, and Negro authors and are often intermingled with the Indian and the European. Afro-Brazilian religious sects have mixed the songs of various African nations with verses in Portuguese containing Indian or African words. In her essay on "Negro Popular Poetry in Brazil" she tells of the *Congos* and *Congados*, dramatic dances originating in the Congolese tradition, and of the *Maracuta*, a similar dance in the Sudanese tradition. All of these and many others gave rise to singing, almost purely African or Afro-Brazilian.

The scope of the listings above under Brazil is a fair indication of the importance of Brazil in the African tradition. Antônio Olinto and Zora Seljan have shown that the winds have blown in both directions; there is now a strong colony of Afro-Brazilians in Porto Novo, Dahomey. Dr. Olinto has written a book about them—*Brasileiros na Africa* (Brazilians in Africa).

Moving up to northern South America, the African world is still very much alive in Guyana. Miss Vesta Lowe has published a small book of Guyanese songs clearly showing African relics. P. A. Brathwaite, with editorial help from his daughter, Serena Brathwaite, has published five such volumes. Among the songs presented are the Afro-Guyanese *Queh-Queh* songs, such as "Wha Mek You Brazen So," "Bux 'on Gal," and "Ooman is a Hebby Load"; Afro-Guyanese *Shantos*, like "See Me Li'l Brown Boy" and "The Soojie Moojie"; and Afro-Guyanese plantation songs, like "Maarnin', Mr. Crasbie," "Bettiah from Berbice," and "Manja Cane Piece"; and Afro-Guyanese chanteys, like "Me Mudda Nevva Mek Me Foh a Boatman" and "Draw' Way."

In his book on *Musical Traditions,* P. A. Brathwaite has depicted the African as a pioneer in Guyanese music. He has traced African traditions among the Guyanese people, both in the musical instruments and dances and in the rituals (e.g. the *Cumfa* ritual involving the drums of Kabango and ceremonies of moon worship). Of African tribes still functioning in the country he lists the Congos, the Ashanti, the Angolas, the Kromanti, the Yoruba, the Oku, and the Mazumbo. He also shows how the African led the way to intermixture with the Portuguese, English, Scottish, Dutch, French, and Spanish. Besides the predominant African are touches of East Indian, American Indian, and other race groups in the Guyanese folk song. Two interesting developments are the songs of the "pork knockers," the diggers after gold, and the songs of the Guyanese jungle.

Several other experts in Guyanese folklore were interviewed. E. Kwayana informs us that despite the outlawing of African religious societies by Christian missionaries, a number of samples of African songs, plus African drumming, had survived. Folk songs now appear in meetings and on the radio. Coromantic and Congo relics are notable. African-derived songs are still in festivities the night before a wedding, in songs for wakes, and at funerals. In a drum funeral, with drums only, all tears have disappeared! The Policemen's Voice Choir has recorded some of these Afro-Guyanese folk songs.

Although "society" looks down upon it, the African tradition, says Wordsworth McAndrew, of the Ministry of Information, is still very much alive. In the program he formerly ran over Radio Demarara he used many examples of it. He interviewed old "pork knockers," and brought in drums, dances, and songs. The African ritualistic song still thrives, he says. The drums survive in the village districts and to some extent in the cities. The African Sports Club of Manchester operates a friendly burial society; they will play drums for you if you get married, have a christening, or die.

Going just off the coast of South America to the West Indian islands of Trinidad and Tobago, one finds a proud and lively African tradition. As long ago as 1943 it was thoroughly researched in the doctoral thesis (in anthropology) of Richard Alan Waterman, under the direction of Melville

J. Herskovits. Waterman's thesis is entitled "African Patterns in Trinidad Negro Music."

Early in his thesis Waterman notes that the same Africanisms that appear in the North American spirituals appear in Trinidadian music. Relating this fact to the arguments that the former derived from so-called white spirituals, he writes,

> The conclusion that the white spirituals are merely distorted local variants of widespread patterns of Negro song, is thus given support by scientific musicological analysis no less than by the historical facts. For, in any event, it is highly improbable that the Negroes of Trinidad were greatly influenced by the people of the Southern uplands.

Later, he states that Trinidad music ranges from that used in worship of African gods to spirituals and Baptist hymns. Since correspondences in pattern have been illustrated between Negro music in the United States and in West Africa, then, if it is true that these correspondences are the result of survivals in the New World of West African musical patterns, the Negro music of Trinidad, partly in the same tradition as that of the Negroes in the United States, should exhibit even greater correspondence with African patterns.

This is his problem: His findings are that, although some European characteristics have intervened, they have been Africanized; that European and African musical styles differ less than is commonly supposed; that Trinidad Negro music departs from African musical traditions more definitely, on the whole, than any other New World Negro style considered, with the exception of that of the Negroes of the United States; and that it is reasonable to assume that patterns of West African music which may be expected to be found in the songs of Negroes in the United States will take forms of African modes, rhythms, tonal ranges, and traits of melodic ornament.

Interviews with Trinidadian students of folklore presented wide and substantial variety. There was first M. P. Alladin, director of culture, in charge of the National Museum and Art Gallery. He pointed out that the Calypso (at least two hundred years old), the Limbo, and the steel band had developed African backgrounds in Trinidad; because they have become popular around the world, they have carried the African touch with them. He indicated also that Trinidad joined the Guyanese in supporting *Shango* dances. The *Kalinda* (stick fight dance) also showed African traces. Director Alladin's *Notes on Carnival* points up African characteristics in the famous Trinidadian Carnival. In the Museum and Art Gallery, where his office is located, are paintings which carry out the points and suggestions of the interview.

G. Anthony Prospect, superintendent of the Trinidad Police Band, has written a history of steel band music and has traced its developments over fifty years. Intermixed with the African in Trinidad music, says Superintendent Prospect, are influences from the French, the Spanish, and the Dutch. As a composer, Superintendent Prospect has based a number of his pieces upon Trinidadian folk song. He directed his band in the rendition of one such piece, his "Folk Song Rhapsody" (composed 1965), as well as in two Calypsos, whose backgrounds he described.

Jacob D. Elder is professor and research fellow in the Institute of Social and Economic Research of the University of the West Indies, St. Augustine, Trinidad. His bibliographies, studies, and publications are paramount in the appreciation of Trinidadian folklore. He has gone into the villages and the back country and come out with remarkable tapes. He is an authority on tales, legends, myths, riddles, and religious ceremonies, besides songs.

His sense of the African background is comprehensive. He has done a scholarly study on "The Yoruba Ancestor Cult in Gasparillo: Its Structure, Organization and Social Function in Community Life." In Trinidad, he says, are striking relics of the Hausas, the Yorubas (through *Shango* elements), the Congos (through levitation by corncobs and magical escapes), and the Mandingoes. His publications of *Song Games* from Trinidad is revelatory of some of these items. He has worked with Alan Lomax in collecting them.

Besides songs, says Dr. Elder, African cultural habits in Trinidad are found in the preparation of food, ritual dancing, drum making and drumming, rainmaking exercises, and language. The religious music still makes commentary upon the actions of gods. Overlap and other African elements are still present in the singing.

While conducting his classes at the University of the West Indies at St. Augustine, Gordon Rohlehr, of the Department of English, still studies Trinidadian folk backgrounds. In April 1967 he did a paper for the Caribbean Artists Movement on Calypso—what it reflects of satire, mentality, and psychology of the West Indies. He has also studied *Shango* chants. He is interested in creating a sense of folk in Trinidad. Calypso, he says, has always been associated with the Carnival and probably always with the city. Although African in origin, it reflects cynicism, the pushing of comedy to the borders of experience (with weird, twisted irony), and the refusal to accept the tragic experience.

In Jamaica, Mrs. Louise Bennett Coverley still discusses folklore on her radio programs as she has done for a number of years. She is well aware of the African backgrounds in the Jamaica community.

Miss Olive Lewin of the Jamaica School of Music, however, was appointed in 1966 by the Jamaican Government to assemble and disseminate the folklore of the nation in recognition of the heritage of the people. She begins by telling you that the roots of Jamaican music are African and Anglo-American. She has collected fourteen hundred songs, one-fourth of which belong to an African-inspired set of revival cults called *Pukkumina*.

Though very strict in moral codes, the people of these cults create music with a rhythm similar to that found in the music of dancing people. The Africanism of their music is reflected in part through movement—the body must participate (note Alfons Dauer, above). The singer soars without physical rhythm. Four bars of song cover five bars of thumping. One aim of *Pukkumina* is to put the audience in a trance. A chant often ends with one or more members speaking in unknown tongues.

Besides *Pukkumina* there is other cult music, chiefly African inspired. There is *Kumina* (from the Congolese), *Rastifarian* (inspired by Haile Selassie and the Ethiopians), *Goombay* (with its approach to spirits), *Ettu*, and *Tambo*. There is also music derived from the Baptist, the Anglican, and the Sankey groups. And there are spirituals and work songs. Miss Lewin says that the work songs started when the slaves wanted to communicate and were not allowed to speak.

The Jamaican Folksingers, under Miss Lewin's direction, travel about—sometimes in the United States—and make records. Two of their record albums are "From the Grass Roots of Jamaica" and "Authentic Jamaican Folksongs." The songs are arranged by Miss Lewin. One of them is "Slave Lament," also sung by slaves in the United States of America with slightly different words. Another is "Yerri Me," a *Pukkumina* chorus. Still others are "Bad Madan Law" and "Guinea War," both *Kumina* songs. Included also are several revival choruses and a song of the Maroons (fugitive slaves who ran away to live free in the wilds) of Jamaica.

The last stop on the Western Hemisphere tour was the Bahama Islands. In Nassau the first folklore expert was a famous drummer, Peanuts Taylor of the Drumbeat Club. Peanuts said that the *Goombay*, an African-Cuban style of music, was an important African development in the Bahamas but that most of the African themes there came from Haiti. In his opinion the Bahamas and Haiti had more African culture than any of the other West Indian islands. He said also that spirituals are still sung in churches and at wakes.

Edward Moxey, parliamentary secretary to the prime minister, responsible for community development, is in the business of resurrecting traditional music, most of it African. More than a year ago he founded the Coconut Grove Choral group, forty-five voices, for which he is director and arranger. They produced in 1969 a tribute called "Forefathers in Song." Much of the program comprised spirituals from the U.S.A. (with slightly different arrangements), such as "Go Down, Moses," "Swing Low, Sweet Chariot," and "Nobody Knows the Trouble I See." He expects to develop *Goombay* music, which he says is native to and original with the Bahamians. He also expects to encourage performances of the old traditional dances.

Two impressive old-timers were interviewed together. One, the father of Secretary Moxey, George Moxey, is secretary of the Musicians Union;

the other, his friend of many years, Charles Herbert Fisher, is president of the Musicians Union and choirmaster of the St. Barnabas Anglican Church.

Mr. Fisher located African influences in the harmony of the people and in the songs sung in churches, especially the spirituals. He traced the *Goombay* definitely to the Ashantis who came to the islands many years ago. Mr. Moxey seconded him, adding that the *Goombay* beat is a definite type of rhythm, different from other West Indian types. Both insisted that the spirituals did not originate in the Bahamas, but were brought in from the United States.

Mr. Moxey says that most of the slaves were Yorubas, Congos, and Ashantis. From them, besides singing, came drumming, which has slowed down in recent years. Near the end of the interview, Mr. Fisher remembered that *Goombay* harmonies were to some extent influenced by the spirituals.

Miss Erna Massiah (born in Barbados) is also a choir director. Recently her choir has gone into Bahamian folk songs. Besides singing them, they are doing research on them. The smaller churches, she says, still sing spirituals, or songs closely related, but inject color by using electric guitars, tambourines, and other live instruments. Noisemaking changes the rhythmic pattern of the music. The pathos has been thickened, and some of the lengthy phrases have been shortened. Natural music-makers have taken some of these musical phrases and have stirred them up with *Goombay* and modern dance beats.

The Carnival and the *Jonkanoo* are definitely African, says Miss Massiah. On Boxing Day and New Year's Day the masses of the people bring out their African drums and cowbells. Dancing to appropriate revelry tunes is the order of the day and the night.

In the Bahamas, Miss Massiah assures us, there is lots of gospel singing. Mahalia Jackson and James Cleveland are very popular people indeed.

The final and crowning interview was with Clement Bethel, education officer for music and drama of the Bahamian Government. His prime goal, he says, is to do research in the indigenous music of the country. He plans to collect songs and closely connected stories. He supplied the interviewer with an elaborate bibliography of folk stuff of the Bahama Islands.

As an education officer, he is naturally interested in using his collected materials for textbooks in the schools so that the folk ideals of the Bahamas can grow up with the children. His textbooks would be used all the way up, beginning with the primary children. It is the drummers, especially, that he hopes to bring into the schools. The drums, most African, are the most important. Andros Island, he says, is almost purely African.

Besides his thoughtful and imaginative program, Clement Bethel is a composer. He has written ring-play (nonsense) songs, and he has composed music for Blind Blake, a famous singer at the Nassau airport. He has also set to music a legend of Cat Island under the title of "Belinda."

The existence and length of time of the spirituals in the Bahamas is a separate story with strong bearing upon the history of the spirituals in the United States of America. In Charles Edwards's *Bahama Songs and Stories* is evidence that some of the first slaves were brought to the Bahamas in the 1770s by Loyalists fleeing the colonies before the gathering storm of the Revolutionary War. By far the majority of Negroes in the Bahamas are direct descendants of native Africans. It is clear that these Africans could not have brought the spirituals. But these spirituals, the same as those in the United States, have been in the Bahamas since the Loyalists arrived. Thus, these spirituals were carried to the Bahamas by Loyalist slaves in the 1770s. Again, the spirituals in question were created in the United States before the 1770s, to be available for export. These calculations are supported in full by Lydia Parrish in "The Plantation Songs of Our Old Negro Slaves" (*Country Life*, December 1935).

It should be remembered that the camp meeting tradition originated about 1800. Growing out of this tradition were the white spirituals that started fifteen or twenty years later. More will be said on this time factor later.

《 *African Musical Transfers to the United States of America*

Just as the African, under every possible condition in the West Indies and South America maintained his musical identity and impressed it upon the existing culture, so he did in North America. Principles and practices, ingrained thought, totalized religion, exerted daily, generation after generation, for hundreds of years could not be forgotten. Wherever this African went, his soul was going to express itself in dance and song. As W. L. Hubbard said in his *History of American Music* (Toledo, 1908), in spite of continued contact with American whites, Negro melodies retained their exotic traits. Verna Arvey and William Grant Still have added that the African heritage is always in American Negro music no matter how well educated the Negro may be.

The African music was brought to America by the slaves. What can be more convincing? One can establish the traits in Africa; one can identify the carrier who moved by the millions of people from Africa to North America; one can identify the precise African traits in the United States of America. The case is incontrovertible.

One writer has said that the African Negro, unlike the biblical Jew, could and did sing the songs of the Lord in a strange land. Endowed by African skills and attitudes, he took his misery and grief, his brutal treatment and towering obstacles, and wove them into new songs and melodies.

The confusion about the African element in America has been developed and perpetuated by those who have refused to study the African background or to acquaint themselves with the nature of the slave. As long ago as 1941 Herskovits showed the pointlessness of arguing with those who said the Negro spiritual came from the whites, as long as the latter refused to acquaint themselves with African music. The confusion, thanks to a host of hard research and perceptive interpretation, is now lifting. C. L. R. James, for example, in his brilliant article on "The Atlantic Slave Trade and Slavery" (*Amistad* 1, New York, 1970) has at last given a clear personality sketch of the slave who made the musical transfers.

> For the slave brought himself; he brought with him the content of his mind, his memory. He thought in the logic and the language of his people. He recognized as socially significant that which he had been taught to see and comprehend; he gestured and laughed, cried, and held his facial muscles in ways that had been taught him from childhood. He valued that which his previous life had taught him to value; he feared that which he had feared in Africa; his very motions were those of his people and he passed all of this on to his children. He faced this contradictory situation in a context into which he was thrown among people of different African backgrounds. All Africans were slaves, slaves were supposed to act in a specific way. But what was this way? There was no model to follow, only one to build.

> The slave from Africa was denied the right to act out the contents of his mind and memory—and yet he *had* to do this. How was this contradiction resolved? What were the new forms created in the context of slavery?

> A new community was formed; it took its form in the slave quarters of the plantations and the black sections of the cities. In the United States, this community developed its own Christian church, one designed to meet the needs of slaves and Afro-American freedmen in the New World. It had its own system of communication based on the reality of the plantation. It had its own value system, reflective of the attitudes of African peasants, but at the same time owing its allegiance to dominant American modes. It had its own language patterns, because of the isolation of the plantation system from steady European linguistic influences. West African words and speech patterns were combined with the speech of the eighteenth-century Scotch-Irish.

> This black community was the center of life for the slaves; it gave them an independent basis for life. The slaves did not suffer from rootlessness—they belonged to the slave community, and even if they were sold down the river they would find themselves on new plantations. Here, people who shared a common destiny would help them find a life in the new environment.

As James has demonstrated, the slave made his own community. As music in Africa was chiefly a community enterprise, the creation of the new community in America was a perfect cradle for the musical transfer. Far from giving up his music, he merely went into business at a new stand. In his long history of moving about, he had done this kind of thing dozens of times before.

The evidence of his transfers in the literature of reliable scholars is specific and overwhelming. Herskovits pointed it out in a number of places, but particularly in "Patterns of Negro Music" and "Social History of the Negro." He traces directly the universal African conventions from Africa to America—such as the theme by leader repeated by chorus or choral phrase balanced as refrain against the longer melodic line of the soloist, as found in North American spirituals. He establishes the place of the spirituals and rituals in the American Negro church and proves them markedly non-European. He identifies the Charleston as an African dance. Summing it all up, he concludes that the spiritual has both American and African elements with the latter predominating.

The extensive research of Lomax and his associates has supported all these claims of Herskovits. The Afro-American music is similar to African music from all over the continent, says Lomax, but agrees most strongly with that of the Guinea Coast and the Equatorial Bantu, from which the majority of the slaves came to what became the United States.

In Frederick Hall's account is definite proof of the traceability of spiritual tunes to Africa. He cites the peculiar use of pentatonic, hexatonic, and heptatonic scales; of lowered thirds, raised sixths, and lowered sevenths. He reviews the "perpetual motion" activity of the rhythm. He notes that the rhythm is the servant of feeling rather than accurately measured accent. He notes, also, that scale conforms to song rather than song to scale.

Even foreign researchers, with no reason to be less than objective, have adopted these evaluations. Swami Parampanthi, writing in an Indian folk music journal, declares that the African showed in the spiritual a natural skill for rhythm, melody, and dance. In an impressive speech delivered in 1961, entitled "Some Remarks on the Development of Musical Creation Among African Peoples," J. Stanislav, the Czechoslovakian Orientalist, says that more and more we turn to Africa to understand the bases which made Negro music a center of the world's attention. After playing selections from Congo and Dahomean music, he shows how the pentatonic arrangements and the periodicity of the African song go into the world of the Negro spiritual. Geoffrey Gorer, an Englishman, traces a dance he saw in Harlem to its original in a dance of women in Senegal. Joseph Kyagambiddwa, a native African, in his book, *African Music from the Source of the Nile*, offers evidence that roots the American Negro spiritual in African folk music.

In the considered judgment of some students, the matter and the method of certain American Negro spirituals are almost exactly the same as those found in specific African songs. William Arms Fisher cites such a Rhodesian ancestor for "Swing Low, Sweet Chariot"; Marion Bauer and Ethel R. Peyser show that "Swing Low" uses the same response and refrain as a

Bantu song, "The Story of Tangalimlibo"; A. M. Chirgwin, writing in the *Edinburgh Review* of 1928, says that most of the songs in Odum and Johnson, *The Negro and His Songs* and *Negro Workaday Songs*, Scarborough, *On the Trail of Negro Folk-Song*, and the Johnsons, *The Books of American Negro Spirituals*, are from Bantu models; Hermine Barz's research leads her to a close parallelism between the spiritual "Oh, Wasn't Dat a Wide Ribber?" and the Bantu folktale "Sihamba Ngenyanga"; and Benjamin Brawley designates "See Fo' and Twenty Elders on Deir Knees" as straight from the heart of the African wilderness.

Gilbert Chase finds much meat in Kolinski's comparative studies of spirituals and West African songs. Kolinski, it is remembered, wrote "Suriname Music," which became Part III of Herskovits, *Suriname Folk-Lore* (New York, 1936). In his transcriptions and analyses thirty-six spirituals were found to be identical or closely related in tonal structure to West African songs. "Cyan' Ride" was shown to have an exact Nigerian counterpart; "No More Auction Block," an Ashanti double. The rhythms of thirty-four spirituals were proved almost exactly like those of songs of Dahomey and the Gold Coast. Fifty other spirituals were discovered to have identical formal structures of certain West African songs. To these quite scientific analyses one might add certain tracings by Maud Cuney Hare. "Wrestlin' Jacob" she found, for example, to be based on one of the Bula Tales of the Cameroons. She says it is one of many spirituals rooted in old African myths. Other close correlations of Negro spirituals in America with their African sources have been made by John W. Work in his chapter on "Origins" in *American Negro Songs* (New York, Howell, Soskin & Co., 1940).

Closely related are the respective subject matters of these songs and other folklore. The rabbit of Harris's Uncle Remus tales is directly in the stream of the hare in Africa, as Miss Benedict has stated. In Ambrose Gonzales's books this ancient figure of African, West Indian, and the North American Negro folk is well described—living by astute trickery, a rascal and a deceiver, but always a thriving citizen. The human persona of the spiritual, forced by circumstances to maneuver in order to survive, is not rascal-deceiver, but is aware of the need for mask and irony. Small and lacking in overt physical power, like Jacob, David, Moses, Daniel, and other Biblical figures he borrowed for his purpose, he wrestles with gigantic enemies and triumphs over them. The rabbit himself is not peculiar to Africa (he can be found in European, East Indian, and Teutonic—cf. Easter bunny—folklores), but the method of African development is peculiar. The hare's rival in the famous race is also in African tradition. Robert T. Kerlin quotes an African proverb quite appropriate to the understanding of pure African songs and some African Negro spirituals alike, "We weep in our hearts like the tortoise."

The capacity of the slave to adapt, while retaining the fundamental qualities of his music, is a theme for a number of close observers of Afro-American music. Borneman, for instance, reflects that African songs with no American relationship died out; they were replaced by a new Afro-American music. Oscar Seagle, a highly respected concert singer of the first quarter of the twentieth century (born in the South), says that the native African and his descendants contributed to America a love for music and a rhythmic sense. In his estimation (in 1917) the black slave had contributed the only American folk music.

Although not speaking of the spiritual, John Rublowsky (in *Music in America*) notes the influence of African music in America as early as 1753. He quotes from a story appearing in the *Virginia Gazette* of that year and telling of two African-originated musicians, flutists, from the household of Baron Botetourt, the late governor general of Virginia, and their African-style concerts.

Dorothy Scarborough was a Texas white woman who went about the South collecting Negro songs. Because of natural skill, professional training, and an ingratiating personality she was quite successful. She reports the following "African Counting Song" from Uncle Israel, age ninety-one, in Louisiana:

> Ninni nonno simungi
> Ninni nonno simungi
> Ninni nonno sidubi sabadute simungi

Uncle Israel told her that when you say the above stanza twice, that's ten. He had learned the song from his mother who had learned it from her native Africa. It was one of many songs so learned that Uncle Israel had carried about with him and sung to people for upwards of seven to eight decades.

Miss Scarborough also told of a chant she had picked up from an old black woman in Waco, Texas. Like Uncle Israel, this woman had learned the piece in childhood. She had gotten it from her grandmother, who had in turn received it from an old man brought from Africa as a slave. To Miss Scarborough the air recalled the beating of tom-toms, but there was something English in it, too.

The method of delivery of songs is a definite part of the African tradition. From many descriptions it is established that, before the African introduced his invigorating presence into American music, singing was rare and, when it happened, dull and perfunctory. Perry Bradford, who won a considerable reputation as blues singer, is one of many writers who elaborates the change. From his grandparents and others he was able to reconstruct the singing of spiritual songs brought from Africa. This singing was done with zest and spirit by singers who swayed their bodies, nodded their heads, and clapped their hands in rhythmic movements.

While recognizing the African techniques of delivery, one composer decries the perpetuation of the songs through the larger community with the same methods. Harry T. Burleigh recommends that the songs be sung impressively. He urges attention to the fact that, in the songs, cadences of sorrow invariably turn to joy. He welcomes all singers to these songs which breathe hope and faith in ultimate justice and brotherhood and in the ultimate reign of freedom. But he says that there should be no attempt to imitate the Negro through swaying body, handclapping, or peculiar inflections. He was probably recognizing the inability of non-Africans to be sincerely motivated in intricate and powerful physical terms.

In the American North as early as 1856, an editorial writer characterized the African Negro nature as "full of poetry and song." In 1923, R. Emmet Kennedy wrote of "The Poetic and Melodic Gifts of the Negro," stressing his sense of musical sounds in words, his gift for euphony, his fluency in making liaison, and his skill in summing up literary values. Describing "The Plantation Songs of Our Old Negro Slaves" for *Country Life* in 1935, Lydia Parrish, who studied meticulously the very African communities of the Georgia Sea Islands, states flatly that the musical gift and religious nature of the African Negro were such that no white man has ever composed a similar song to be classed with authentic Negro spirituals. The climax in the field of religious Negro songs is a quotation from the *Letters* ... of the Reverend Samuel Davies, an outstanding religious leader in eighteenth-century Virginia. The quotation is dated 1757. It reads, "The *Negroes* above all of the human species that ever I knew, have an ear for Music, and a kind of extatic delight in Psalmody." In a later letter, referring to Negro singing, he says that "a torrent of sacred harmony ... carried my mind away to Heaven."

Africans like Ballanta Taylor and Alakija insist that many of the spirituals still heard in the American South may be heard—the identical melody —in the jungles of Africa.* On the authority of Percival Kirby, who spent many years in South Africa, the song parallels between the American slave and the South African black are numerous. Because African music was dying out in South Africa in 1951, Alexander Sandilands selected and published 120 American Negro spirituals to provide African idiom for teachers, pupils, ministers, and people in Basutoland. He noted strong similarities between Bantu and West African music, which he says fathered the Negro spiritual, though the two areas of origin are geographically far apart.

* Ballanta Taylor, a native of Sierra Leone, made a special report on this subject in *The New York Age* for July 24, 1926 (see interview entitled "Ballanta Taylor Returns to Tell U.S. Result of 2 Years' Research Work in Native Music on West Coast of Africa"). He had traveled 7,000 miles and had researched the music in tribal communities in Senegal, Gambia, Portuguese and French Guinea, Sierra Leone, Ghana, and Nigeria. He was now more convinced than ever that the American Negro spiritual was fundamentally allied to the primitive melodies of native Africans. In his view the songs had been brought over bodily and sung to different words.

All told, the African tradition is clearly characterizable. It is and was deep-seated in the African and the African-derived peoples. No wonder Professor Lorenzo Turner (in 1958), contradicting his fellow Afro-American Professor E. Franklin Frazier, was able to prove that American slaves retained much African culture; and of the retentions, he insisted language, folk literature, religion, art, dance, and music were the most tenacious.

The significance of African transfers is sometimes reduced in size through a serious historical misunderstanding. In numerous books and in many minds the fact that laws were passed making the African slave trade illegal after 1807 means that the African slave was no longer brought into the United States or that his importation, as contraband and piracy, became a trickle. If this had been true, the African influence in the nineteenth century might have been on the decline. There would have been a great dilution, since Africa would have been remembered only through the children and grandchildren of original Africans.

But after 1807 the importation of African slaves did not stop, not by any means. There are some historians who say that it increased. With characteristic disregard for the law when it interferes with good business, the American capitalist and entrepreneur, fully supported by the planter, continued to bring in slaves in very large numbers. In his *Suppression of the African Slave-Trade to the United States of America, 1638–1870* (New York, 1896) and his "Enforcement of the Slave-Trade Laws," W. E. B. Du Bois shows that slaves were imported from Africa until well after the Civil War. They were not only imported, they were sold and distributed throughout the South. Not until Lincoln's administration was a serious effort made to halt this enormous contrabandage.

Du Bois quotes Stephen A. Douglas as saying in 1860 that more African slaves were imported into the Southern states during the preceding year than ever in any one year when the slave trade was legal. He gives the number for 1859 as at least fifteen thousand, but indicates that the actual number was a great deal above that figure. Herskovits estimates the number of African slaves brought in between 1808 and 1860 as two and one-half million.

Philip D. Curtin's *Atlantic Slave Trade: A Census* (Madison, 1969) tries to play down the contraband business. In the first place, he does not even list in his bibliography Du Bois's "Enforcement of the Slave-Trade Laws," which is far more heavily documented for the subject than any source upon which he relies. He estimates fifty-four thousand contraband slaves for the period 1808–61 (excluding Louisiana in the French and Spanish periods). This figure sublimely ignores the evidence of Stephen A. Douglas and many other excellent witnesses Du Bois and others call to the stand. Professor Curtin seems to be making a prejudiced and incompetent apology for Southern dealers in contraband human flesh. At the very least he arouses innumerable questions. Douglas, for example, estimates fifteen thousand contraband slaves for the one year 1859. Why would a pro-Southerner like Douglas exaggerate in such a matter? It is conceded that the number of contraband slaves brought in will have to be determined by guesswork. If anyone examines the full evidence, however, he would have to agree that the guesses of Du Bois, Deerr, and even of Herskovits are much better supplied with sound factual support than the guess of Professor Curtin.

It is apparent, therefore, that not only was there no decline in African musical influences during the nineteenth century, but an actual rise. The African who was reshaping the American musical tradition was being heavily reinforced daily. His power lay not only in the dynamics, vigor, whole-souledness, and attractiveness of his musical style, but also in sheer numbers.

❀◇

CHAPTER SEVEN

What Part Had Religion in the Spiritual Tradition?

. .
.

NEARLY all the commentators on the various American spirituals have assumed two things: (1) That the African tradition was completely blotted out from the mind and practice of the transplanted slave, as Professor Frazier has stated, but not proved; and (2) that the camp meeting was the only source of the Negro spiritual and its shouting accompaniment. Through these assumptions, which later readers and investigators have meekly accepted without the tough examination of true scholarship, the case has been pushed through for a Negro spiritual overwhelmingly American with hardly any African fiber at all.

The witnesses cited in the preceding section, especially native Africans and whites who have lived in and thoroughly examined both the Western and the African cultures, have clearly demonstrated the falsity of the above assumptions. Alan Lomax, Melville Herskovits, and Lorenzo Turner have further buried the assumptions with documents so deep and comprehensive as cannot be controverted. These witnesses show that the singing and rhythmical body movement peculiar to the slave spiritual have been inseparable partners in the African for thousands of years. This kind of custom and practice was not at all affected by American slavery. On the other hand, the Presbyterians, Methodists, and Baptists who developed the camp meeting had nothing like these sing-shout practices before they got to the frontier. These practices were missing from such people in Europe as well as in the coastal colonies where they first made inroads into America. From this important coign of vantage the African tradition is far more likely as an origin for the slave songs than the camp meeting tradition.

The above assumptions have fathered a great deal of dubious history. Bruce Jackson, an otherwise reliable writer, says in an article entitled "The

Glory Songs of the Land" (1968) that the "spiritual song" was in use as early as the middle of the sixteenth century, that the white spiritual was the oldest of the regular spirituals, and the religious roots of the Negro spiritual go back to John Wesley and his followers. The term "spiritual song" originally referred to formal hymns and had no reference to popular or folk songs, black or white. To say that the white spiritual is the oldest is to make an extremely precarious statement which cannot even be classed as an educated guess. The African had been making songs all along about the conditions of his life and religion. He composed and sang original songs in his native land for centuries and on the slave ships all the time he was carried around the world. Never forget that the Portuguese were struck by his remarkable songs as early as 1444, an event reported by Dena Epstein. When the African arrived in America, he undoubtedly continued these practices. Herskovits is impressed by Hornbostel's declaration that "had the Negro slaves been taken, to China instead of to America, they would have developed folk-songs in Chinese style." Not their imitativeness nor even their capacity for adaptation is the main point here; the stress is on the relentless urge of these creative people to sing wherever they go and on their gift for mixing inherent and local ingredients to fulfill that urge.

As soon as he made the transition from Africa to America and from his native language to his adopted language, the black creator naturally continued what he had been doing all along—making songs about his life and his religion. The language mixture was natural, to wit the variations from Virginia to South Carolina to Georgia, particularly the island sections of the two latter states.

On this basis, the Negro spiritual, by the best available evidence, started in the seventeenth century. The so-called white spiritual could not have started before the first quarter of the nineteenth century.

Bruce Jackson certainly knows that many of the songs in the first large collection of Negro spirituals—Allen, Ware, and Garrison's *Slave Songs of the United States*—had nothing to do with religion, camp meeting or otherwise. They were reactions to work, to individuals, to conditions, and to other miscellaneous things. There is no connection whatsoever between them and camp meetings. Hundreds of Negro spirituals, discovered and published later, are in the same category.

Except that it is necessary to show how false gossip gets around, we would not mention Bruce Jackson's references to John Wesley. The staid old high churchman, who never left the Anglican faith, would have been horrified had he gone to the American frontier and seen a camp meeting, more horrified than Frances M. Trollope, who expressed her horror in chapter 15 of *Domestic Manners of the Americans*, written as the result of her long visit to America (1827–30). Besides, the first camp meeting on record was a Presbyterian gathering in 1799; John Wesley was gathered to his fathers in 1791. He was in America only once—in Georgia from 1735 to 1737, and his permanent Methodist societies were not founded until two years later. While here, he did show deep distress over the religious neglect of Negroes, and he did say that these Negroes liked Watts and the Psalms and were above all others in ear for music. But he did not initiate Methodism here, and most assuredly he did not initiate or have anything to do with the frontier camp meeting.

In his history of *The English Hymn,* Louis F. Benson discusses the steps in John Wesley's development of his hymn. According to Benson, the Moravians on board ship converted Wesley to the fervid type of hymn singing. In 1761 he issued the following directions for singing: Learn the tunes; sing exactly as printed; sing all; sing lustily; sing modestly; sing in time. Methodist spontaneity developed, followed by exuberance of noise and then by deadly formality, especially with choirs engaged in slow singing.

Benson emphasizes the fact that in America, although it was called Wesleyan singing, hymn singing departed radically from the Wesleyan manner. Camp meeting singing went even farther afield from the Wesleyan plan. The tunes of camp meeting hymns, says Benson, demanded only contagiousness and effectiveness. They were adapted to popular melodies, remembered songs, tunes previously used on the circuit, and simple melodies composed on the spot.

Seventy years after Wesley left, when the Methodists did get around to frontier revivalism, their purpose was to reinvigorate the religious process by purifying the heart. Asbury and other new-style Methodists in America used the camp meeting to capture unchurched frontiersmen and to meet the competition of Baptists and Presbyterians bent on the same purpose. The singing they used was definitely not Wesleyan. Though continuing the error of associating the spirituals with Wesley, Ernest Borneman stresses the Afro-American transformation through syncopation.

On the more positive side, astute foreign observers make a strong case for the effectiveness of religion in arousing the African to the fullest use of his most uncommon musical abilities. Without clear and irrefutable evidence, some persons assume that the slave sang as a result of getting religion. This system of cause and effect may have been used by some slaves. On the best evidence it is far more likely that the slave was always looking for opportunities to sing. At times he was allowed to sing at work, at times not. At times he was permitted to go to church, most times not. When so permitted, at times, he was allowed to sing at church. When this happened, he considered himself fortunate because the religious atmosphere gave him the fullest opportunity for singing with least restriction. If he sang the same songs in the woods unsupervised, he stood an excellent chance of being beaten, as Harris Barrett pointed out in 1912. Barrett attributed the determination to sing in the woods, despite the danger, to steadfastness. Knowing the African nature, one must believe that the basic motivation was the irrepressible desire to sing from the heart.

It should never be forgotten that religious singing among the whites was a sideline, a Sunday business. The white singer was not oppressed either by religious principles and practices during the week, or by very much singing at all. On the other hand, the African, for thousands of years, had considered his religious faith and feeling as well as his urge to sing as indispensable to living as breath itself. Ruth Gillum probably did not realize how right she was when (in 1943) she wrote that for the African slave in America God became the reality and slavery the illusion. The weakness of her statement is in her implication that such an insight happened as the result of the slave's identification with American religion. If she had said that in the African, God always was the reality (though the African did not precisely define God in the same terms as the American), and everything not related with the deepest religious drive was illusion, she would have been speaking unimpeachably. She did make another statement which was unimpeachable: It was that the Negro as people realize that the end of all being is expression. To say the same another way, if you have true twenty-four-hour-a-day, seven-day-a-week religious faith, you insist upon exploding or exuding it into song every time you can.

An interesting report on singing under pressure and singing freely is found in *Memorable Days in America*, written by William Faux, a self-styled English farmer. Faux kept a journal of his visit to America (1818–20) and published it in 1823. He described the singing of the galley slaves as regulated by the motion of their oars: this music, he says, was barbarously harmonious. But the text of their songs abounded in praise and satire, depending on whether their masters were kind or unkind. The following year Faux had the chance to hear singing in a black church where the minister, like the congregation, was black. This singing was merry; like the African singing, which sometimes continued uninterruptedly for days, this singing went on all day and far into the night. At times, it was bedlam, accompanied by much clapping of hands and shouting. At the close, Faux reports, one female worshipper, striking the breast of two male friends, said, "We had a happy time of it."

❀◇

CHAPTER EIGHT

How Much of White America?

. .
.

RELIABLE reporters of the white American tradition in song and religion show the white man to be less than enthusiastic and competent in both departments. As already stated, religion was a kind of mask the white man in America wore, not a deep, perpetual commitment. Rich or poor, the white man arose from his knees, where he prayed loudly to a God who commands charity and love toward all people, and hated, despised, and physically hammered his black brother in creation. He rarely permitted his religious professions to interfere with his material or emotional drives. Under these reservations he sang his songs.

He did not sing them memorably or even well. For melody as well as text, his songs were undistinguished. In spite of the claims that the black slave learned his spirituals in Methodist camp meetings, Frank Tannenbaum provides authority in his *Slave and Citizen* that the white church proved incompetent to preach the gospel to the great masses of African slaves. In spite of the great reputation of the Methodists for evangelizing (they were the most active evangelical church during the nineteenth century), in the state of Georgia by 1860, the Methodists had converted only 25,859 of the available 462,189 Negro slaves. Not all of these, quite naturally, stayed converted. Tannenbaum declares slavery unquestionably cruel and brutal. This fact, plus the lukewarmness and fears of masters of having their slaves converted, helped to prevent conversion. (Note that Fanny Kemble reports a plantation owner who forbade his slaves to go to church because religious teaching was "a mighty dangerous thing." "How right he was!" added Miss Kemble.) If the slave were only sparsely identified with the white man's church, how could he have created so many hundreds of songs out of the white man's melodies and words?

A much more negative answer arises from the white man's singing ability. Some observers say that it was nil or, very skimpy at best. We have already quoted the editor of the *Evangelist* in 1856 who chastised his white countrymen, even the women, for being woefully inferior to the blacks in song. Miss Kemble, once more, in 1838–39 emphasizes the pleasantness and melody in the slave songs and the lack of them among white voices. An accomplished and famous English actress, Miss Kemble was surely competent to judge. Years later, in 1932, a white Southerner (John Jacob Niles) accounts for the lack of profundity in Southern white singing in two words—"easy living."

The present students of the so-called white spiritual do not have to take the word of distant observers, however competent, for the song-making capacity of the religious bands of American whites. For the melodies, Alan Lomax and the Folk Archive Room of the Library of Congress possess many samples which record the ways the makers of the white spiritual sang their songs: these records can be played and replayed by interested parties. For the words, Professor George Pullen Jackson and others have published and republished hundreds of song samples as well as reprints of *The Sacred Harp* and other song collections of the middle of the nineteenth century. Melody and text, these songs are characterized by a monotony, a lack of imagination and variety, an absence of relationship of everyday life, and a general absence of deep physical and emotional involvement, even with the life of the spirit, that would make them forbidding to any outside the small groups who created them. Besides, as everyone concerned admits, they deviate in no essential ways, except quality, from the hymns of Watts and others, from which they are admittedly taken.

Some of the best evidence of incompetency in singing and song-making by American whites is found in *Dwight's Journal of Music*. This journal was founded in Boston in 1852 by John S. Dwight; it was a weekly reminder, issued every Saturday, of all things musical, even reprinting significant musical items from musical and general sources throughout America and other countries.

As early as 1855, Dwight reprints an article from the *New York Tribune* which tells of the expulsion of a Quaker from the Friends' communion because he refused to take a pianoforte out of his house and otherwise expressed love for music. Through enforcement of this rule, the Friends lost forty members by resignation. For a number of issues, beginning on June 16, 1855, Dwight and his readers discussed "Musical Talent of the Americans," as exemplified chiefly by the paucity and poverty of congregational singing. The editor reports that three-fourths of church members in America *"are not singers,"* and further that *"the Americans are NOT a musical people . . . do not delight in song, appreciate it or feel strongly about it"* [italics and solid capitals are the editor's]. He says that, although the Methodists started with religious fervor which motivated and colored their songs, "now . . . with few exceptions, they have fallen away from their first love."

To digress momentarily from Dwight and his musical record, one can find confirmation of the weak effects of white hymnody of the early period. H. L. Mencken says that his researches on the subject prove that Methodist hymns lacked rhythm, which the Negro spirituals had. The Negro, he asserts, improved on the Methodist hymns as to rhythm and harmony. If the Negro song-maker was so far ahead of the model, the Methodist hymn, a strong suspicion is raised that he was even farther ahead of the white spiritual which was a particularly undistinguished imitation of the model.

During 1856 *Dwight's Journal* complains of the manufacture and multiplication of new psalm tunes which it found to be "feeble, prosy, sentimental, doctrinal, didactic," written by poetasters, destitute (nine-tenths of them) of all soul of melody and all principle of music, painfully bent, twisted in rhyme, in short, "uninspired."

On the contrary, early in 1861, the *Journal* (reprinting from the *Boston Evening Transcript*) reports favorably the singing of black congregations in Richmond, Virginia; later in the year it is enthusiastic about the singing of black contrabands in South Carolina; it asserts that the words of the Negro songs, sung by Hampton singers in 1873, are as curious as the music, sometimes approximating poetical genius and sometimes descending to mere nonsense. It calls attention to the wide use of repetition, but repetition in primary folk songs has been characterized in earlier pages of this discussion.

Let us sum up the evidence for the two traditions in religion and song. The Africans are inveterate and highly accomplished song-makers in words and melodies for centuries back. The American whites who created the so-called white spiritual were a small group of semi-independents from the established hymn tradition. The Africans were deeply and perpetually religious, using religion and religious song as a motive for being and expression along many lines. For the American whites religion was a Sunday or Wednesday night release from problems; as soon as the service was over, the church-goer reverted to his normal practice, which in many respects was diametrically opposed to his religious professions. Proof has been offered of the coexistence of the white and the Negro religious songs, but none of the preexistence of the white song or of direct and wooden borrowing by the Negroes. There is solid evidence that the African slave never stopped singing, but merely changed languages as he had done on innumerable occasions in the past, and that, therefore, his songs are established before the end of the seventeenth century. The camp meeting tradition, which spawned the white spiritual, did not get started until the opening of the nineteenth century, and the so-called white spiritual is definitely a mid-nineteenth-century product.

And yet, in spite of all this evidence on both sides, we are asked to believe that a musically inferior and casually religious, small offshoot of a large American religious tradition taught a fully competent, continuously religious, large folk group how to make songs! Worse still, thousands have so believed and, without the modesty or shame to keep such unreason to themselves, have printed their beliefs.

❀◇

CHAPTER NINE

What About the Camp Meeting and Black Song?

. .

WE HAVE already shown that the Wesleyan way of song, as spelled out by John Wesley, was not used in the camp meeting or, even, to any considerable extent in America. We have shown that the normal white American song was listless and monotonous. In physical and emotional involvement it was utterly lacking throughout the eighteenth and nineteenth centuries. The camp meeting, a phenomenon of temporary proportions, made no change in this method. Only the Afro-American, before, during, and after the camp meeting episode, used physical and emotional involvement in his singing. Combined with his African ancestors, the black man had been doing this for centuries on the broad religious basis that included the whole of life.

What was the camp meeting anyway? What effect did it have upon singing, white and black? How have so many alleged historians attributed to the camp meeting the greatest spur to the white spiritual and the fatherhood of the black spiritual?

Before getting down to the historical details of the camp meeting, one should note a fundamental distinction. Robert L. Shurter proves the camp meeting to be a special feature of American frontier life. It gave, he emphasizes, society to lonely people; it enabled them to have emotional development. This was certainly true, but note that it applied only to white people. Loneliness was not generally a problem of slaves. If the slave needed anything less than he needed emotional development, that thing is hard to remember. The slave, then, had to have other reasons for joining in the meeting.

From James McGready and John McGee we learn of the great revival in Kentucky and Tennessee which gave rise to the camp meeting tradition. McGready's three congregations in Red River, Muddy River, and Gasper

River, all located in Logan County in southwestern Kentucky, were the starting point. Up to 1798 he admits to a "deadness and stupidity" in the religious community. In September 1798 was a general awakening, followed by another deadness. On the fourth Sunday in July 1799, says McGready, "God returned" and aroused the people at Red River,

> Little children, young men and women, and old gray headed people, persons of every description, white and black, were to be found in every part of the multitude . . . crying out for mercy in the most extreme distress. . . . Boys and girls, 9, 10, and 12, some younger, lying prostrate, weeping, praying, crying out for mercy like condemned criminals.

This kind of experience swept southwestern Kentucky and adjacent Tennessee for two years. McGready was a Presbyterian minister, but soon the Methodists and the Baptists joined with him. McGee was a Methodist minister. He writes that people fell before the word like corn before a storm. There was much groaning in the woods and groves. Women laid sleeping children at the roots of trees. Hundreds of all ages, sexes, and colors were stretched out on the ground in the agonies of conviction, as dead people; and thousands, day and night, were crowding around them and passing to and fro, but nobody was hurt.

It is obvious that the Great Revival was merely an emotional incident in the lives of people whose everyday lives had begun to depress them. Charles A. Johnson says they were tradesmen, yeomen, and farmers—poor whites. The camp meeting movement which arose from it—Charles A. Johnson dates its period of influence from 1805 to 1840—was a continuation of the search for release in this group of the white disinherited. In spite of the fact that several writers use the phrase "black and white," all signs point to the fact that the number of blacks was very small.

It is true that the leaders of the Great Revival in the first decade of the nineteenth century were antislavery in sentiment. Their influence resulted, says Catharine C. Cleveland, in a 150 percent increase in missionaries over the previous decade. But this liberalistic spirit was short-lived. Clement Eaton shows that the revival movement quickly became antiliberal. Besides losing its antislavery verve, it began concentrating on intolerance in its attitude toward the people. It began fighting card playing, dancing, drinking, fancy clothes, and other customs which the people found enjoyable.

As to singing, the variations perpetrated by these people upon the Wesleyan type hymns are hardly worthy of the name of music. In their narrowness of theme, their verse diction, and their method of delivery, they were stodgy and uninspired in the lowest degree. Substantially what happened was that they were incapable of handling the poetic verses of the Wesleys and similar hymn writers. Their songwriters captured the general ideas of these verses, threw them into a form more digestible for the white illiterates, and lined them out for the groups to sing. These so-called white spirituals are utterly lacking in musical distinctiveness or peculiarity of any sort. They have no folk character and are rightfully not included in the catalogue of folk songs. To set them down side by side with true folk songs, like Negro spirituals, is to bring out quite clearly their lack of character and distinctiveness. It is also to demonstrate the fundamental reasons why these fragmented hymns had life only among a handful of religionists for a few years, while the spiritual created by the slaves has spread its influence all over America and around the world for generations.

The role of the blacks in the camp meetings has been clearly portrayed by eyewitnesses and careful researchers. In the first place, to repeat, there were just a few blacks in these meetings. The average slaveowner did not permit his slaves to attend religious services; he was certainly going to make sure that they did not patronize something so unregulated as these meetings.

The few who did go unquestionably had a good time. In Charles Johnson's view they not only got social and psychological release, but also received the opportunity, denied elsewhere, of expressing the higher life. John D. Long says that some masters forced their slaves to attend, but there is no supporting evidence. One writer has said that a few believed religious services kept their workers servile and obedient. This view was clearly discredited later when evidences of revolution were found in these religious congregations.

Once at meeting, the slaves pounded their chests, cried out, and performed holy dances forbidden by the preachers. They sang with melodious, burning sighs and vigorous bodily movements. They shouted unrestrainedly. Their preachers, said Frances Trollope, sprang high from the ground and clapped hands over their heads. They had such a good time and made such a contribution to the meetings that Benjamin Lakin objected to cutting off the Sunday services because black people would then be excluded.

The fact that the slaves had been physically and emotionally vigorous in their music, and especially in their singing, long before the camp meetings started leads to the conclusion that their presence was desirable, especially by the leaders. John Fanning Watson is quoted (in 1819) as saying that the emotional excitement of the camp meeting "began in Virginia among the blacks." He adds that the existence of the camp meeting was justified only under raw, turbulent conditions.

On the basis of this conclusion, the whites most assuredly got from the blacks whatever temporary vigor they were able to muster in their singing. We call it temporary because the evidence shows that they soon reverted to their old, dull, draggy ways.

In the second place, the camp meeting was a segregated outfit. Describing the arrangements, Charles Johnson writes,

In both slaveholding and nonslaveholding regions, the Negroes were allowed to set up their own camps behind the preacher's rostrum. Because of
the close proximity, their services often merged with those of the whites,
adding no little to the general confusion and emotional excitement. The
Negro housing area, with its crazy-quilt tents after the fashion of Joseph's
coat, was a picturesque affair. As the camp meeting matured, the Negro
camp section was sometimes separated from that of the whites by a plank
partition. This barrier was torn down on the final meeting day where the
two peoples joined together in a song festival and "marching ceremony."

Of all the reporters and eyewitnesses of camp meetings, Johnson is the
only one who saw the two groups together. Frances Trollope says flatly,
"One tent was exclusively occupied by Negroes." Catharine Cleveland
quotes an eyewitness from Kainridge in Bourbon County, Kentucky, "and
about 150 yards in a fourth course from the house an assembly of black
people, hearing the exhortation of the blacks, some of whom appeared
deeply convicted and others converted." Elizabeth K. Nottingham says
that the working out of a relationship with Negro converts was "a difficult
problem."

Several things begin to come clear. Whether or not there was an occasional mixture of black and white groups, the pattern of the camp meeting was to keep the blacks and whites separated. Since this is true, there
was no ample opportunity for the blacks to learn the thousands of spirituals
they sang over the entire South from whites at camp meetings.

Even had there been the opportunity, why would people like blacks,
who for years had been in the habit of putting real music, vigor, emotional
excitement, and imagination into their singing *want* to or be induced to
imitate people who sang with little life or excitement at all? Sheer common
sense designates the whole idea as ridiculous.

What undoubtedly happened at the camp meeting was that the black
group went ahead with its usual habit of vigorous singing and shouting.
The noise they made attracted the white groups, who sent spies to visit
them. Observing the good times they were having, the spies went back to
their groups and engaged them in trying to imitate the blacks. This is the
only explanation that fits all the circumstances.

Support for this view is recorded in the recent work of music historian,
H. Wiley Hitchcock. From John F. Watson Hitchcock learns that in "the
blacks' quarter" of the camp ground, the "colored people" sang together
for hours. They sang short scraps of "disjoined affirmations," pledges, and
prayers, "lengthened out with repetition choruses." More characteristically
they sang in the chorus-manner of the Southern harvest-field, or "the husk-
ing-frolic method" of slave blacks. Hitchcock does not disagree with Watson's conclusion that "the repetitive choral refrains of the new type of
hymn" of camp meeting revivalism (obviously referring to the so-called
white spiritual) "derived from the Negro."

Whatever the clearest explanation, the circumstances rule out entirely motive or opportunity for blacks to imitate whites in singing at camp meetings. The so-called (and miscalled) white spiritual and the African (or black) spiritual are two entirely different types of song. They were created under different conditions and for different reasons. They were delivered in different ways. Those who have credited the white spiritual with being the model for the black spiritual have taken their views on faith and certainly not from a firsthand examination of the evidence.

Even if the black singers did get some ideas for songs from the camp meeting, the Afro-American spiritual was well established long before 1800. No doubt the people in the black tents at the camp meetings were singing these spirituals as a regular thing, songs which they and their fellow slaves had been singing for many years.

From Edwards and Parrish above, we have shown that these spirituals were carried to the Bahamas by the slaves of British Loyalists in the early years of the American Revolution. Harvey Gaul has written that these songs were in existence at the time of the Revolution. Miles Mark Fisher (in *Negro Slave Songs in the United States*) has established the fact that they were sung and used throughout the eighteenth century in the South, and probably earlier.

In the face of such evidence from such indestructible witnesses, whoever in the future speaks of Negro spirituals arising either from white spirituals or from the camp meeting tradition should stop and explain what he means. He will have considerable explaining to do.

CHAPTER TEN

●◇●

What About the Blend of African and American Elements?

. .
.

T
O DEMONSTRATE from "best evidence" that the Afro-American spiritual is most unlikely to be a borrowing from the so-called white spiritual is not to say that there is no blend of African and American elements. The blend is a fair compound of equal elements, not a strong superior mixed with a weak inferior. It is as Aggrey, the great African, once declared (as quoted by Herbert A. Chambers on the title page of his *Treasury of Negro Spirituals*): "You can play a tune of sorts on the white keys and you can play a tune of sorts on the black keys, but for harmony you must use the white and the black."

Borrowing is, and always has been, a natural part of artistic creation. The best borrowers are the best improvers of the breed of the art. If they did not borrow, if they relied absolutely upon their native or familiar element, they would be heavily handicapped in creation. As we have shown, the basic issue is in how the borrowing is made. The key factor in this basic issue is the original purpose of the creator. If he begins with a creative design to express, depict, criticize, or exalt his own life, he is entitled, as Shakespeare did, to use any available realistic or legendary material.

The main objection to the set of explanations which tie the black spiritual to the white spiritual is the denial of a creative purpose on the part of the black song-maker, the acceptance of a creative purpose by the maker of the white spiritual (vis-à-vis the established hymns), and the failure of evidence to prove any more than the existence of the two songs contemporaneously. In these matters the present writer is unconcerned about the racial identification of the respective song-maker. He is concerned only by the lack of evidence for the prevailing position and the preponderance of evidence for the creative position of the Afro-American song-makers.

It is now necessary to establish as far as evidence directs the extent of the blend of African and American elements in the so-called Negro spiritual. Although accepting most of the opinions about the Negro spiritual stemming from the white, T. J. Woofter in *Black Yeomanry* (New York, 1930), concerning life on St. Helena Island (South Carolina), says of the black spirituals, "Regardless of any 'white man in the woodpile' in days past, these songs have come to represent in a real way the religious feeling and artistic expression of the American Negro. They are his own."

It is hard to tell exactly what recipe Mr. Woofter is working from. His generosity of spirit is hardly evidence of originality or the lack of it. Even so, his suggestion of the blend is supported by much other evidence. As long ago as 1892, Johann Tonsor pointed to the blend of African jungle music and the American major scale. He credits the great power of the Afro-American for improvisation. A few years later, May West Owen, admittedly engaged in tracing origins of the Negro spiritual, quotes Baltzell's evidence that stresses the mixture of African origin and American environmental influences. Similarly, Robert D. Bass, writing in the *Journal of American Folklore* about Negro songs from the Pedee country, calls the blend of African and white man's music "the irrepressible heritage of the race." And Dorothy Conley insists (as late as 1962) that no Negro spiritual could have been written without the ingredient of Christianity in the mind and heart of the creator, partly because it was sheer spiritual force that transposed African chants into spirituals. She adds, however, "The Spirituals are purely and solely the creation of the American Negro." Like many others, she offers no evidence.

Intensive investigation of the Afro-American blend by industrious scholars has expectedly raised the issue of the extent and direction of borrowing in this special context. John Mason Brown, a Southerner, who in 1868 wrote the first comprehensive evaluation of Negro spirituals, does not mention the white spiritual by name at all. He does strike the inevitable comparison between the spiritual and Negro minstrelsy. He says that Christy, Bryant, Newcomb, and other minstrel-makers are not true interpreters of the Negro and that Negro minstrelsy generally is not reflective of the Negro slave. Remembering that the spirituals are strictly oral, he reflects that only a few are borrowed from whites.

Sidney Finkelstein declares that many spirituals reflect a product of absorption by a stream of music originating in Africa of religious hymns found on American shores. That two such seemingly disparate bodies could combine to form a fresh, homogeneous and vital art hints, in his estimation, at common roots to all folk music—European, African, and Asian. The conditions of the creation of the Afro-American spirituals, he continues, are those of the people themselves, moving and striving for progress, using every means at their command. His theory is quite reasonable. There is hardly any doubt that the Afro-American song-maker borrowed from the hymns he heard and from the Biblical stories he picked up. In putting them into his African-like setting he created something quite new, with obvious characteristics of both original traditions.

The composer William Grant Still and his wife, Verna Arvey, have also spoken to the perpetual creativity of this song-maker. They have pointed out that each section of the country where the slave was found had its own peculiar spiritual. In this peculiar element is reflected the language and the thought idiom of the slave in that section. In the same general area Paul Oliver has noticed that African survivals are conditioned by their appropriateness to a strange country.

Though seriously in error about the influence of whites on the African type spirituals, Anne G. Gilchrist is certainly right when she declares that the American Negroes carried the hymn-making process beyond the early Methodists and fitted their religious songs into the framework of their own African songs of labor. Likewise, there is both truth and dubiousness in Roger Bastide's "Les Trois Folklores." He says that black Americans exhibit three distinct folklores,

African, pure and faithfully preserved

Creole, born in America, as expression of sentiments of blacks in the face of whites, as a technique of evangelization of masses of color

White, which the blacks in their desire for advancement and assimilation have borrowed

Botkin's statement that folk art is social in impulse and inception cannot be reiterated too often. The Afro-American singer was motivated by impulses far stronger than the mere expression of narrow American concepts of religion. He was uniting his past and his present and his hoped-for future in one great artistic manifestation. And as happened in other countries, his folk song, through its blend, became a kind of national music. He was justifying Sydney Grew's conclusion that blended differences within a country make music national in character.

A reviewer of the Allen et al. edition of slave songs, writing in the *Nation* in the fall of 1867, goes the full distance in reversing the common verdict. He offers evidence to show that whites attended Negro camp meetings and spent much time listening to the remarkable music floating up from the Negro quarters on the plantation. In answering the question of where camp meeting songs in general came from, he suggests that there is reason to believe that they emanate from black as well as white worshippers. He strengthens the implication with the recollection that the Negro songs were musically richer than the white, especially in illustrative variety.

Don Yoder has collected information on the influence of the Negro upon camp meeting spirituals. He cites William Colbert (1764–1833), a Methodist circuit rider, who, in his 1804 journal, describes the imprint of black peoples' singing. According to Yoder, the earliest active ascription of Negro influence upon spirituals comes from John F. Watson, a Pennsylvania Methodist and the author of *Methodist Error, Or, Friendly, Christian Advice, To Those Methodists, Who indulge in extravagant religious emotions and bodily exercises* (1819). The fact that Watson was condemning his brother Methodists for borrowing both the songs and the method of singing of illiterate blacks makes his comments all the more impressive. Apparently, his chief objection was that the black music was too much like dance music. He said that the blacks would sink one or the other leg with every word they sang.

Perhaps some would call W. E. B. Du Bois a biased witness, but no one can deny his scholarship or his interpretive genius. Writing in 1932, a full generation after his inimitable "The Sorrow Songs" in *The Souls of Black Folk* (1903), he declares,

> The slaves originated this curious and beautiful volume of song that has come down through centuries as a never-to-be-forgotten contribution to the world's music. From it has developed the "gospel" hymns of the whites, the syncopated rhythm and jazz of the world of art and a wealth of material for great composers like Gilbert and Dvořák.

H. L. Mencken went a step farther. He said that Beethoven would have delighted in Negro spirituals. Brahms, he said, would have borrowed them as Dvořák did.

To tie together the whole blend, one can read Oscar Brand: "Much of our early music was 'square,' " he admits. "But nobody really jumped until the African arrived with his syncopations, his polyrhythms, and his blue notes. Because the African learned to speak English, there was much traffic in song on the Southern plantations. The African could balance the ritual sound of fifty log drums all beating in separate patterns."

Brand winds up, "The slave singers, in other words, liberated our Anglo-shackled music, and provided us with spirituals, work-hollers, patting-games, cakewalks, and a foot-tapping foundation for our popular song."

There is one final thing that the various descriptions of the performance of slaves at the camp meetings prove. This phenomenon was arrested and described at the camp meeting, but it was generally true wherever spirituals were created. Perhaps it was not true for every single spiritual; not, for instance, for these composed in the work fields. But it was so widely apparent as to be almost the rule. Only through this phenomenon can the full character of the songs be accounted for.

This phenomenon is that the spiritual followed the African system of combining dance, instrument, and song. Père Lavat was probably right in saying that the dance was the transplanted African's favorite passion. The dance is reflected in the rhythmic body movements, nearly always present where true Afro-Americans sing; the instrument is the handclapping; the song grows out of the other two. As to the dance part, Julia Peterkin goes so far as to insist that spirituals "are always sung for the shouting." Hand-clapping, as I have previously shown, often combined with drumming; and, when the drumming stopped, the handclapping carried alone the burden of setting, varying, and expounding the rhythm. When the slaves in the United States were deprived of their drums, they resorted to hand-clapping alone. And they were not completely deprived of African drums as Joseph H. Howard proves in his *Drums in the Americas*.

The Afro-American spiritual, then, is merely the song part of a normal, combined, African musical expression, adapted to the American scene.

✿◐

CHAPTER ELEVEN

What Are the Chief Arguments for White-to-Negro Spirituals?

· ·
·

U P TO now, at various points in the examination of the big question, Is there an Afro-American spiritual? we have mentioned the chief architects of the theory that no such independent song cycle exists. We have also brought in their arguments at appropriate places. It is time now to confront them and their arguments head-on.

Not because he is an Afro-American, but because he deals with a root phase of the question, Professor E. Franklin Frazier is a logical place to begin. His well-earned reputation as an important American sociologist is highly respected by this writer. It is notable, however, that his writings do not contain evidence of his views on the present subject—only opinions. His opinions are chiefly expressed in three works: an article in the *Journal of Negro History* in 1930 on "The Negro Slave Family"; his monumental book, *The Negro Family in the United States*, first published in 1939; and one of the last books he wrote, *The Negro Church in America* (1963).

His main points on our subject can be summed up this way: There are very few African traces among American slave Negroes. The only applicable traces are in such places as the Sea Islands off the coast of South Carolina and Georgia, where slaves were most isolated and where some spirituals reveal continuity with African backgrounds. The sacred folk songs or spirituals of these slaves are essentially religious in sentiment and "otherworldly in outlook."

Evidence for the failure of the first two points has already been offered from a variety of effective scholars—literary and social historians like Lorenzo Turner and John Hope Franklin, also Afro-Americans; anthropologists like Melville Herskovits; a good many observers who saw slavery at firsthand; and others, like Ballanta Taylor, who knew intimately both the African and the American sides of the coin. We will deal with Professor Frazier's third point very soon, when we offer conclusive evidence that the slave in question sang of his whole life, not just of a religious compartment, exactly as his African forebears had been doing for centuries.

This much can be said now. The white man reneged even on the otherworldliness. If one reads the sermons preached to slaves by white ministers or those prepared by white ministers to be delivered by masters and mistresses, one notes certain salient features. The preacher stresses the point that the master and mistress are God's agents for the slave and that in God's name they have the best interests of the slave at heart. There is clear indication, often express declaration, that if the slave gives his owner trouble he will never see heaven. Also, many white preachers were so bold as to state that racial segregation would be continued in heaven and slaves had best not think in terms of revolutionary changes after death or of riding roughshod around the golden highways. Why, then, would a slave yearn or strive for a heaven in which the general setup was just about the same as what he was so anxious to leave?

One other thing: The ideas of the happiness of the slave on earth and of his passionate reaching for another world cannot coexist. Either slavery was unbearable and the slave wanted out, even by way of death, or slavery was delightful and he wanted to stay and enjoy it as long as possible, postponing the flight to other worlds where such bliss was not guaranteed. Only abject misery in his slave life could impel the slave to dwell persistently and enthusiastically upon release and happiness elsewhere, either in heaven, the Northern United States, Canada, or some nearby swamp. And if the slave were so miserable as all that, he did not need a white man's watered down religion to stir him up. All he needed was to remind himself of his local situation.

Frazier's views are "supported" by two of his students. One of these, Gold Refined Wilson, wrote a thesis for a bachelor of divinity degree at the University of Chicago in 1921 entitled "The Religion of the American Negro Slave: His Attitude toward Life and Death." Although quoting from fifty-eight spirituals, Wilson demonstrates a deep ignorance of African music, of African transfers, and of the everyday life of the slave. The other, *A Comparative Study of Religious Cult Behavior among Negroes with Special Reference to Emotional Group Conditioning Factors*, by Raymond Julius Jones, reiterates the theory that African religious manifestations were wiped out by Americanization.

Arthur Huff Fauset has answered Frazier, Robert Park, Frazier's teacher, and Frazier's students. Fauset writes,

> Common sense requires us to believe that everything cultural which the Negro brought over with him from Africa could not have been eradicated from his heritage, despite the centuries since he left Africa, the thousands

of miles which have separated him from the ancestral homeland, and the eroding influences of an overwhelming and inescapable super-culture.

He offers Herskovits's irrefutable evidence in support.

In 1893 Richard Wallaschek published in London a volume on *Primitive Music*. Many of his conclusions have been invalidated by later scholarship, both because of evidence industriously accumulated by later scholarship and because Mr. Wallaschek has been proved to have started with a personal bias against the Africans he was writing about. It is heartening, however, to report that he did not fall into the error of some American writers who have tried to demonstrate that the African singer was simple and naïve because he had much rhythm and no harmony. Wallaschek credits Africans (some of whom were ancestors of the American slaves) with harmony and rhythm of high quality. He also confirms other characteristics of African music, such as the union of song, of dance, and of music with physical exertion and great psychical excitement. Since these latter factors are part of the process of the American slave spiritual, even Mr. Wallaschek becomes another witness against Professor Frazier's theory.

Without citing evidence, not even giving the song sources or the scope of songs investigated, Mr. Wallaschek proclaims the American Negro spirituals mere imitations of European compositions with slight variations. He declares them "not primitive," but says that their feeling for harmony is well developed. Effective rebuttal, closer to utter demolition of Mr. Wallaschek's total theory in this regard, was delivered by an outstanding German-American music critic, Alfred Krehbiel, in a somewhat memorable book entitled *Afro-American Folksongs* (New York, 1914). Further rebuttal on the point of "simplicity and humbleness" of African and African-derived subject matter has been given in this document (via Professor Schneider and others) and will be specifically taken up in later chapters of this book.

A sample of biased scholarship from an undoubted scholar (seemingly motivated by racial considerations) is found in *Modern Language Notes* for November 1918, shortly after the publication of Krehbiel's book. It is a note advanced by Professor Louise Pound. She complains that "Weeping Mary," offered by Mr. Krehbiel as a Negro spiritual, was not so for the following "reasons": Her mother sang the song, having brought it from Nebraska to New York; her mother learned "Weeping Mary" in a Methodist revival between 1826 and 1830, "a period long antecedent to its recovery from the Negroes." On the basis of this evidence alone, Professor Pound concludes that Krehbiel's evaluation of the whole body of Negro spirituals was wrong and Wallaschek's was correct.

It is doubtless unfair to linger over this observation of a scholar and teacher who made many fine contributions to American literary and folk studies. It is necessary to do so only because of the fact that, of such stuff has the prevailing opinion of Negro borrowing from white spirituals been concocted. It is necessary, therefore, to point out the following remarkable errors in Professor Pound's thesis: Samuel Davies, Miles Mark Fisher, Dena Epstein, and many foreign and native contemporary observers (a number of them already quoted here) have demonstrated that the Negro spiritual far antedates the 1826–30 period and even the whole camp meeting tradition; since Mr. Wallaschek offered no songs in evidence and Mr. Krehbiel offered many, in addition to much overwhelming technical evidence, a fair-minded reader will have difficulty accepting Mr. Wallaschek's opinion as scholarly theory at all; and, even should one concede that "Weeping Mary" was stolen from the whites by the Negroes, considering the fact that hundreds of songs were involved on both sides and that no one had then, or has up to now, established the time primacy of the white spiritual, it is most unscholarly to discredit a well-documented theory and to credit an undocumented one on the strength of a single piece of evidence.

We must not ignore the generosity bestowed by Miss Pound upon the white Charleston, South Carolina, group calling itself the Society for the Preservation of Spirituals. This society had no truck with white spirituals. On the other hand, all members of the race which the society celebrated as creators of their songs were rigorously excluded from membership. Miss Pound praises the society for showing love for their old servants, for their interest in Negro folklore, and for their appreciation of the beautiful religious songs sung by their Negroes. She called their singing "authentic interpretations" of the Negro spiritual, including the shouting, and hand-clapping, the feet-patting, and the rhythmic swaying of bodies. Of their 120 Negro spirituals already collected, only a few, she announced, had been heard on the professional concert stage. She thought their contribution very significant since it was aimed toward postponing the day when these wonderful old Negro folk songs would die out or be forgotten.

We turn now to face the big guns of the white spiritual theory. They are three Southern-born gentlemen-professors, George Pullen Jackson, Newman I. White, and Guy B. Johnson. Professor Jackson, having produced the largest volume of work on the subject, is considered first.

It is only fair to witnesses of such stature that they be precisely introduced. The Southern white gentleman is uniformly proud of his background, upbringing, and attitudes. The symbols of race and religion, which contribute most to his sense of security, call forth his most energetic efforts. Even when his scholarship is profound, it never overrides his fundamental allegiance to his versions of such symbols.

It is notable that these chief architects for the theory that the Negro spiritual was only a burnt-cork imitation of the white spiritual made their discoveries after the Negro spiritual had become enormously popular, both in America and abroad. To make their interpretations, each had to profess and believe that he had a deep understanding of the slave mind. The inability or refusal of the Southern white man, saturated in a slaveholding psychology, to penetrate the slave mind, let alone to follow it through devious routes, is a truism. Among other incisive scholars Professor Schneider (quoted above) called attention to the misunderstandings arising when the uninitiated and those not in direct contact attempt to fathom the song of the basic folk.

It would not be just to disqualify honest scholars for being among the uninitiated and among those incapable of understanding on the basis of theories alone, however sound the theories. Let us turn to demonstrable facts. It is true that these gentlemen searched for songs among the direct inheritors of the American Negro slaves. Alas, it is equally true that they entered these areas with a predetermined bias. No Southern Negro would have failed to see through them in a moment. In an article on "Racial Traits in the Negro Song" in the *Sewanee Review* of July 1920, Professor White refers to his subject as "that buoyant and invincibly likeable person, the illiterate Southern 'darky.' " In his major work, *American Negro Folk-Songs* (Cambridge, 1928), he calls the Southern Negro naïve, unanalytically minded, thoughtless, careless, unidealistic, fond of boasting—among other things. Professor Jackson even suggests that the African slave lacked musical strength in his traditions; an almost incredible belief in light of historical scholarship, and understandable only in terms of the rigid faith of the unreconstructed Southerner, particularly one with a self-announced tinge of liberality.

The ancestors of such Southern gentlemen as these had listened to the Negro religious songs for a century and a half or two centuries before 1867, when the songs received their first wide publication. There is almost no evidence that during this time any white Southerner spoke of them except in burlesque or contempt. Only two or three white Southerners are known to have mentioned them at all.

What is remarkable about this fact is that it has been recorded by a variety of observers and scholars. I mention two representative samples: First, Oscar Commettant, a Frenchman, who spent three years in the United States in the 1850s, published his results in Paris in 1857. In *Trois Ans Aux États-Unis* he spoke of how the Negro music, not without poetry and charm, had been disdained and ridiculed by the whites. Nearly a hundred years later (in 1951) Hermine Barz, writing a doctoral thesis on North American Negro poetry for a university in Mainz, Germany, said categorically that Southerners did not concern themselves with the Negro spiritual. Although making no direct animadversion to Southern neglect of one of its strongest claims to fame, Joseph Hutchinson Smith, then a professor at the College of William and Mary in Virginia, commented in 1924 on the late arrival of interest in Negro song.

Despite the ignoring by and the contempt of Southern whites with regard to these memorable songs, many famous visitors and travelers from the

Northern United States and from Europe praised the black spirituals
highly. Former slaves, like Frederick Douglass and Booker T. Washington,
spoke and wrote of them thoughtfully and feelingly.

As far back as June 1932, in the *American Mercury*, Professor Jackson
opened his campaign with an article, "The Genesis of the Negro Spiritual."
Later, Professor Jackson began tying together white and Negro spirituals
as a body of camp meeting songs; from this coordination he evolved his
theory of the borrowing of Negro from white. As shown before, Professor
Jackson does not at any point establish the time precedence of the white
spiritual. He merely makes the obvious assumption of a white supremacist
that if two songs appeared simultaneously, one white and one black, the
white inevitably led and the black inevitably followed. The assumption is
bad and unscholarly on its face. In addition, there is strong evidence, which
we have given, that destroys it completely.

Following this brief testing of the water with his toe, Professor Jackson
plunged fully in. His chief strategy was to try to establish that spiritual
folk songs had maintained a reasonably long tradition in America. First, the
white spirituals grew out of this tradition shortly after camp meetings
started around 1800. Then the Negro spirituals developed, not from the
overall tradition of hymns and religious folklore, such as Biblical incidents
and lessons, but exclusively from white spirituals. Pursuing this strategy
took some doing since traditions generally are as broad as air and sky and
rarely engage in such narrow grooves and sharp selectioning. Professor
Jackson nevertheless pursued his strategy in three "masterworks": *White
Spirituals in the Southern Uplands* (Chapel Hill, 1933); *Spiritual Folk-Song
of Early America* (Locust Valley, N.Y., 1937, 1953); and *White and Negro Spirituals: Their Life Span and Kinship* (New York, 1943).

Shortly after Professor Jackson's first major work was published and discussed, a loud negative response came from very near by. Professor Jackson was severely taken to task by John W. Work, a black professor, choral
director, and folk arranger at Fisk University. In his article in the *Fischer
Edition News* (January–March 1935), he acknowledged Professor Jackson as a fellow citizen and a close friend. He declared his friend wrong
on the following counts: First, form; two-thirds of the Negro spirituals,
Work said, were call and response. He defied Jackson or Newman White
to find one white spiritual in this form. Second, scale; he demonstrated that
the two groups of songs differed radically in the employment of musical
scales. Third, figures of speech; while conceding a common source (the
Bible) and some similarities in words, he insisted that the figures of speech
in the black spirituals were unique. Summing up, Work declared that, to
say as Jackson did that six or seven hundred songs were imitations because
fifteen or twenty bore resemblances to other songs, was just not satisfactory.

In point of time, Professor Newman I. White has precedence over Professor Jackson. Following the completion of a doctoral thesis at Harvard University on the subject, Professor White published in 1928, under the imprimatur of the Harvard University Press, *American Negro Folk-Songs*. But Professor White did not iterate and reiterate his thesis as Professor Jackson did. He therefore yielded the place of preeminence.

The reader must be reminded of facts already mentioned that undoubtedly served as a prod to these two scholars: Between 1910 and 1929, over one hundred collections of American Negro spirituals appeared; for more than forty years, since the Fisk and Hampton singers had made the Negro spiritual international, musicians, literary critics, and other evaluators of culture had acclaimed it in boisterous superlatives; they had declared it America's only original music and indeed America's only cultural contribution; if any drop of recognition or praise had fallen upon the white spiritual, or if indeed it had been introduced to the *haut monde* of national and international culture, the matter had been kept a great secret. It was far past time for daring young Confederates in dashing gray to ride to its rescue and to shoot down its black adversary who was literally rolling in glory.

Reduced to its rudiments, this is what Professor Jackson tries to do: (1) He reviews the fact that the hymnody of Watts, the Wesleys, and other evangelical Englishmen was established in America from the late eighteenth century on. (2) He essays to show how these hymns were corrupted through various styles of singing by frontier and common folk into what were called spirituals (although the hymns themselves were first known as "spiritual songs"—note Isaac Watts, *Hymns and Spiritual Songs*, 1709). (3) He recognizes that the whites who sang and supposedly created those songs were generally illiterate and relied primarily upon oral transmission; he notes, however, that after a few years of oral usage, these songs began to get into print through such songbooks as the *Kentucky Harmony* (1815), *Missouri Harmony* (1820), *Christian Lyre* (1831–32), *Millennial Harp* (1843), *The Sacred Harp* (1844), and *The Social Harp* (1855) (it is interesting that the second, third, fourth, and sixth of these songbooks were published in Cincinnati, New York, Boston, and Philadelphia, respectively, certainly not camp meeting or frontier towns). (4) He carefully selects Negro spirituals which seem to have the same themes and similarities in melody and style, ignoring meanwhile the far greater number which are quite different. (5) He assumes that because a few Negroes attended the camp meetings where the white songs were adapted from hymns (most Negro slaves, it is reiterated, were effectively prevented by their owners and managers from attending any sort of gathering, religious or otherwise), these few were the creators of the Negro spirituals and undoubtedly adapted them from the white spirituals, in direct imitation of their fellow illiterates, instead of adapting them from the hymns as their fellow illiterates had done. (6) He places white and Negro spirituals side by side to demonstrate parallelisms which are mostly inconclusive and which often demonstrate the opposite; at no time does he prove a direct influence, making his case purely on assumption. (7) He clearly reflects a belief that the African tradition in song, instead of being of high quality, was nonexistent. Finally, after tossing together such odds and ends of scholarship, he draws the definitive conclusion that Africa had nothing to do with the American Negro spiritual, which grew up entirely—melody and text—from a casual association by a handful of slaves with a body of white illiterates in camp meetings. All the wonderful music and poetry which for generations has stopped the breath of listeners and readers over the world was now reduced to so simplistic, so unproved, and so utterly improbable an origin!

One very unfair thing about the thesis of Professor Jackson and of those whom he has misled is the implication that the white spiritual is a basic form of song capable of being imitated. Even Professor Jackson admits that these songs are based on hymns. Often they are merely garbled accounts of hymns. If someone is doing imitations, how can he model his song on something which is at the outset nothing more than a weak imitation? Let us go back a step even behind the hymns. Anne C. Gilchrist and Lucy Broadwood traced fifty hymns in early English and American hymnals to origin in folk songs. Yet, little is said of these imitations. The conversation radiates around one set of imitations only, obviously because of racial bias.

A number of critics have been unimpressed by Professor Jackson's "parallels." I mention three. I have already referred to Hermine Barz's comment that his textual similarities are strained. Gilbert Chase is more explicit:

> What these investigators (Jackson and his school) have done . . . is to establish an incontrovertible correspondence or analogy between the white and Negro spirituals, but they have proved nothing as regards the *direction* of the influences. The fact that the white spirituals were *printed* before the Negro spirituals is not proof that they existed earlier in the oral tradition.

Sidney Finkelstein says flatly that Jackson's comparisons argue the opposite of his arguments.

The immediate issue cannot be more clearly disposed of than in that manner. We have already shown that the slaves belonged to a singing tradition that was centuries old and that they had often adapted to changes in language, setting, and theme as dictated by new circumstances. When one recalls that the Negro spiritual was present and was continuously created, in areas where there were no camp meetings, in addition to those areas where they were denied the privilege of attending, one can easily see that Professor Jackson's effort to establish the white spiritual is a vain, forlorn hope—if one is willing to decide on the facts.

Two other very important things: The black spiritual is a folk song; the white spiritual is not. The Afro-American slave belonged to a continuous folk tradition, stretching from the far past and still in existence in the present day; for example, the funeral singing celebrating the death of Martin Luther King. The singers of the white spiritual were merely attenders at church, as were innumerable Americans, from settled areas to the frontier, from New England to Kentucky, Tennessee, and Georgia. They had in common only membership in a religious faith, which they sang and talked about but which they practiced indifferently. Many of them were illiterate and poor, hoping for a better world after death and for entrance through the salvation gate. Such common characteristics in people do not by themselves create a folk. On the other hand, for example, they were joined by many opposite members—the well-to-do planter, the cynical individual who used religion for social status, business purposes, or for insurance—just in case the stories about reward and punishment after death were true.

Thus, the creators of the white spiritual are a folk group only in a very loose and unrestricted sense. The Methodist Church worldwide or an ecumenical conference or an international labor union is a folk group in the same kind of general way. The creators of the black spiritual were a folk group in every essential sense; they created folk songs accordingly. Not so with the creators of the white spiritual.

Every reader is invited to compare the long lists of parallels Professor Jackson presents and to draw his own conclusions. Without question, he will often be puzzled at exactly what the key to a given parallel is. This writer is willing to concede the common sources of the two spirituals (hymns, the Bible, the folklore of American frontier religion). He will even concede that some small borrowing may have moved in both directions. He insists, however, that for the many reasons given (and to be given) the black spiritual as a body of songs did not stem from the white. He insists further that the creator of the black spiritual is a greater artist than the white creator, with a keener sense of poetry, of philosophy, and of social analysis. He offers Professor Jackson's own parallels as proof (from *White Spirituals in the Southern Uplands*):

White	*Negro*
Not a word he spoke.	An' he never said a mumblin' word.
They rushed the spear in his side.	Were you there when they pierced him in the side?
Ah, poor sinner, you run from the rock When the moon goes down in blood To hide yourself in the mountaintop To hide yourself from God.	O de rocks and de mountains Will all flee away, an' you shall have a new hidin' place dat day. Went down to the rocks to hide my face, The rock cried out no hiding place.

To turn to Professor Newman I. White is to be both uplifted and depressed. Professor White is a genuine scholar and works like one. The main thing wrong with his work is its basic assumptions. These he has apparently been born with and never questions, regardless of the fact that a full scholar must question all assumptions, including those he is born with.

Professor White opens *American Negro Folk-Songs* with the statement that Negro song is more influenced by white song than current writers realize. For this statement he presents no evidence except the same kinds of parallels Professor Jackson offers. He continues with a series of entirely unjustified social assumptions, such as the following: (1) The whole life of the Negro is conditioned upon his acceptance and partial imitation of the white man's ideas of life; (2) the Negro has always shown a compliant and imitative tendency; (3) the Negro is possessed of a "very limited English vocabulary, an invincible racial indifference to the meaning of words and verbal structure in songs as compared with the meaning of rhythm and melody." All these assumptions have been disproved by competent evidence already presented in our earlier pages or to be presented later.

Besides assumptions, he bases his case on several significant misstatements of fact. Let us investigate three: (1) There is little or no record of Negro singing in America in the eighteenth century. Dena Epstein's article on "Slave Music in the United States Before 1860" lists many such references. Notable examples, from which we have already quoted, include the Reverend Samuel Davies. We can add here William Bartram, who wrote of Negroes singing "songs of their own composition" in Georgia in 1776. R. A. Waterman has shown that Trinidad had spirituals going back to very early years and very similar to those in the United States. Hans Sloane should be included here because he was writing in 1707 of Afro-American music in the West Indies, establishing that this music, which produced the West Indian spiritual, was definitely a part of the tradition which produced the North American spiritual.

(2) The Negro spiritual arose from missionary activities of Methodists and Baptists; it is in origin a product of exploitation. We have shown that the missionary activities referred to were extremely limited largely because the slave owner was fearful of lending his slaves to gatherings. In any case, neither Professor White nor anyone else has proved any such eventuality.

(3) To the Negro, Professor White points out in *American Negro Folk-Songs*, life was only a pilgrimage to eternity. He was too pagan for this idea to be more than a convention. We have shown that the tradition from which the African slave came was not predominantly pagan. Even if he had been originally pagan, he was so highly adaptable, especially in his folk expression, that he would have quickly adjusted to the point where he would unhesitatingly use the life around him for his "wish fulfillment," as Miss Benedict said. As to life being only a pilgrimage to eternity in the mind of the slave, this view is another Southern white superstition. The historians, Franklin, Stampp, and others; the records of slave revolts; the records of the Underground Railroad; even the Southern newspapers, which rarely published an issue without advertisements of runaway slaves, have long since shattered this canard. We will shatter it further with evidence from the spirituals.

Despite these false premises and shaky foundations, Professor White has contributed an intensive analysis of American slave songs. He has shown the close relationship between so-called religious and so-called secular songs (those he categorized as "Social Songs," "Rural Labor," "General and Miscellaneous Labor," "Recent Events," "Race Consciousness," "The Seamier Side"). One day the whole wall of distinction between religious and secular folk songs will have to be pulled down. The African tradition does not honor such a wall. Besides Dena Epstein, many other writers have shown that the African slave in America inseparably joined the religious and the secular, the song-dance-instrument routines, the sitting and the shouting folk song, and all other folk types. Harvey Gaul, for instance, shows that the religious songs, especially the salvation song, are all intertwined with fiddle, devil, corn, and love songs, even with ribald songs. When we come to full appreciation of these folk contributions, we will bring them all under one tent as artistic expression and evaluation of a comprehensive individual and social life, whether in various parts of Africa, various parts of America, the West Indies, or Suriname. To divide them into minute sections and subsections is to impose distinctions not inherent in the folk art itself.

In the final analysis Professor White's basic artistic sense overcomes at least a portion of his racial biases. At length he writes:

> Originals for the better-known Negro spirituals have never yet been discovered in the white man's songs. If they are, they will probably be of the nature of those I have suggested for "Swing Low" and "Steal Away," mere starting-points from which the Negro had developed the most impressive religious folk-songs in our language. Originally the Negro spiritual was a sincerely intended, if erratic, imitation, but the white man would be both stupid and prejudiced if he failed to see that the Negro has long since made it his own.

Most of Professor Guy Johnson's conclusions are in line with those already reviewed, and most are based on his study of folk culture on St. Helena Island, South Carolina. With Professor Howard W. Odum he published in 1925 a very thorough study entitled *The Negro and His Songs*. It contains valuable information and insight but is cursed by the same predigested assumptions about the origins of Afro-American singing which we have described above. Like the others, Professor Johnson offers assumptions and parallels as evidence; like them, he proves no direct borrowings; like them, he fails to show how the Negro singer could have created so many hundreds of original songs on very limited experience with the uninspiring white spirituals. He quotes lines from the white spiritual songbook, *Millennial Harp*, with such fervor as to suggest that the slaves read it avidly and copied their own spirituals from it with trembling hands. He affirms that when the Negro spiritual spoke of freedom, it meant freedom from sin; thus in "Go Down, Moses," the Pharaoh who was ordered to free the people was a symbol of sin, and the Israelite oppression was of a destructive moral slavery.

Not so generous as Professor White, Professor Johnson insists that, if the records were complete, they would show a much larger number of white songs taken over by Negroes. He also says that Negro spirituals were a mere simplification of white phraseology. If one reads the text of the white spirituals, one would wonder how they could ever be simplified, especially with such lines as

> Didn't my Lord deliver Daniel, Daniel, Daniel,
> Didn't my Lord deliver Daniel,
> And why not every man!

In 1968, Professor Johnson's book on folk culture on St. Helena Island was republished. The new edition was reviewed by Dena Epstein of the University of Chicago. This review expresses astonishment that an author, so confident of his theories in 1930, should today have so little knowledge of African language and music. Of Professor Johnson, Mrs. Epstein said:

> In his thinking, the existence of similar or parallel speech forms in archaic English and Gullah was sufficient evidence of cause and effect. No investigation of alternative explanations seemed necessary or desirable.

Mrs. Epstein also noted that his scholarship tended to overlook material which would complicate his picture.

Professor Johnson is indeed somewhat of a surprise. Three years before writing the above unsupported statements about borrowings, he had published in the *Journal of Abnormal and Social Psychology* an article on "Double Meaning in the Popular Negro Blues." What he refused to the spiritual, he graciously granted to the blues. Could he perhaps imagine that they belonged to different or conflicting traditions?

In one of his articles Alain Locke inquires in this manner. Suppose we do laboriously prove the white spiritual to be the father of the black, we still do not counter or counteract the uniqueness of style of the Negro spiritual, either as folk poetry or as folk music. The acid test, he contends, is the continued spontaneity and fresh creativeness of the black strain as compared with the sterility and stereotyped characters of the white. One hardly moved its own; the other has been creatively potent at all musical levels and has moved the whole world.

The whole Frazier-Jackson-White-Johnson case has been summed up (though inadvertently) in Frederick Hall's article on "The Negro Spiritual" in the *Midwest Journal* (Summer 1949). As Professor Hall says there, it is contrary to all reason to imagine that the slave singer in whose life song had functioned so largely would close mouth, heart, and soul and wait to hear singing from others before singing himself. It is reasonable to believe that the African began singing soon after he was settled in the new land.

To that, a thousand amens! The quartet above have set their sights two hundred years behind the great singing event.

✿◇

CHAPTER TWELVE

Where Is the Preponderance
of the Evidence?

· ·
·

ALTHOUGH it is clear by now in what direction the strong wind blows, it is desirable to determine the preponderance of the evidence, chiefly from the works of insightful historians, critics, and scholars. The present writer is not the only one who has been impressed by the great difficulties encountered when the Southern white analyst, however honest, attempts to evaluate black song. Carl Van Vechten refers to the unusual frankness on this point of Professor Newbell Niles Puckett in his *Folk Beliefs of the Southern Negro* (Chapel Hill, 1926). Van Vechten adds:

> My peep behind the curtain has destroyed for me the fable that "the Southern white man thoroughly understands the Negro," and has opened my eyes to the importance of objective study as a means of establishing more cordial relationships. . . . Regarding the feelings, emotions and the spiritual life of the Negro the average white man knows little.

In an earlier review, of Odum and Johnson, *The Negro and His Songs*, Van Vechten had said that Odum and Johnson had done well, but since it is utterly impossible for the white man to comprehend the Negro's point of view, the final word had to be given by Negroes. The same sort of comment might apply to Richard Waterman when he declared that the hierarchical polytheism of the African had to be repudiated before any part of the Protestant religious dogma could be accepted. We have already shown that in some parts of Africa from which slaves were exported there had been for centuries a belief in one God. Furthermore, there is no such thing as "the African," meaning that every black African had uniform ideas about religion or anything else.

Since the issue is germane to the interpretation of spirituals as well as to

many racial problems of the late twentieth century, let us pause a moment
to consider it. It is equally wrong to say that no white man can ever understand the black man's point of view as to say that only white men can view
black men objectively. The core of the issue is in the determination to become involved or the necessity of having been involved. The Afro-American in America has perforce been involved in the total world of whites as
well as in his own concerns. The white man has usually approached the
Afro-American world with some kind of reservation, a sense of superiority,
contempt, need for compelling him to work or behave himself, missionary
spirit, hypocritical benevolence, scholarly or unscholarly curiosity, pure
sexual gratification without strings, or arm's-length cooperation. All of
these attitudes are destructive of a spirit of genuine involvement and, therefore, of a spirit of true understanding.

Proof that the white man can become involved to a worthwhile extent if
he wishes is found in the continuing popularity of the songs we are discussing. The songs have attracted white audiences in unprecedented numbers,
both because they express unique feelings on the part of a sincere folk, as
Dvořák pointed out, and because their cry was so penetrating as to strike
universal human depths. If a white man wishes really to become involved
and to work at it on an equal human basis, he can understand the black
man's point of view.

He probably cannot identify completely, because there may be nothing
in his arsenal of reaction to compare with the assaults on the human spirit
brought on by rank injustice, unfulfilled promises of democracy, laceration
of delicate feelings, physical and mental torture, and daily chipping away
at his self-respect and justifiable pride. But the fact that, in recent years, he
has bought in large quantities and read with care such works as James Baldwin's *The Fire Next Time* and King's "Letter from a Birmingham Jail"
proves something. If he is willing to show enough sincerity to win the
black confidence and then to go as far as he can toward identification, he
can acquire a strong semblance of the black viewpoint, and in so doing can
incalculably enrich his own.

The smallness of the number of whites who have succeeded in this noble
endeavor is no argument against the possibility. The chief argument is
raised against those who wish to observe from a distance under, say, one of
the reservations mentioned above; whose point of view is, therefore, palpably unidentified with the subject, but who write and talk as though they
had been and are fully identified.

If the critic, white or black, identifies to any appreciable degree with the
slave singer, he will know that this singer approaches life, singing, and religion entirely differently from the creator of the white spiritual. The first
serious difference might be the absence in the Negro singer of any tendency toward ambivalence or hypocrisy in religious values. It is obvious that
the white religionist behind the song read only those parts of the Bible

which did not conflict with his social and political theories on earth. The Negro religionist, though concentrating in certain areas, did not arbitrarily exclude any part of the Christian doctrine. As Waldo B. Phillips has said, the Negro spiritual was not hypocritical; it could absorb the militant and freedom-seeking attitudes without injuring the religious makeup of the slave singer. On the other hand, as we learn from Joel Chandler Harris, in the Negro song not only virtue, but weakness and apparent helplessness, exemplified in the rabbit fables, have ways of triumphing over bear, wolf, and fox.

Perhaps the strongest argument for difference is in the uniqueness of the human consciousness possessed by the creative slave. Sister Mary Hilarion refers to this in her essay in the *Catholic World* (April 1936). She declares that the spirituals are not motley piecework. They reflect a genuine spiritual image, clothed in melancholy beauty and barbaric color and passion, and indisputably the Negro's own. Edward Shillito, seven years before, quoted (and supported) Countee Cullen in his belief that the Negro spirituals were spontaneous cries from the soul of a people—no man, but a people. At this time (and to a lesser extent, now) evidence for this view was available in the old-time meetings.

The approach to the singing was different. The white spiritual was sung with sincerity, but without drama or poetic grace and lilt. The black spiritual was sung with the highest poetic and dramatic effects, even with dance effects in the shout. Beatrice Landeck has spelled out the latter effects in her *Echoes of Africa in Folk Songs of the Americas* (New York, 1961). In reading her work and that of other writers who have developed the subject, one can clearly see that not only were the black spirituals merely transplanted African songs but that they were also an entirely different type of song from the so-called white spiritual, in purpose and fulfillment.

Evidence of differences in religious approach has been spelled out to some extent, but there is a great deal more such evidence. Laurence Buermeyer, a white expert in aesthetics, writing on "The Negro Spirituals and American Art," stated flatly as early as 1926 that whatever American religion the slave adopted, it had nothing in common with the hardheaded, prudent, legalistic Calvinism (which characterized the Presbyterians and the Baptists, and to some extent the Methodists). Like Catholicism, the Negro's religion was ritualistic, but it comprised a drama in which all could participate. It expressed the whole personality, as orthodox Christianity never did for whites. Mr. Buermeyer demonstrates the folly of such writers as Johann Tonsor, who in 1892 said that the spirituals were remnants of former idolatry before shrines of fetishes in dark African jungles. The latter view was held by many people whose superstitions about Africa—fully disproved now by Franklin, Herskovits and others—were more fantastic than the African superstitions they pretended to describe.

The actual religion of the slave creator was not one of tension and des-

peration about salvation as was the religion of the creator of the white spiritual. It was chiefly one of energetic and practical assurance. An example
of this quality is found in an anecdote reported by a South Carolina corre-
spondent, Laura M. Towne. The master had asked slave Marcus if he
thought Christ was going to take "damned black niggers into heaven";
Marcus replied that he felt sure of one thing: they would be where Christ
was, and even if in hell, it would be heaven. Many black spirituals reflect
such assurance.

From the thinking and writing of John Jacob Niles, a white Southerner
who made a genuine effort to think black, we acquire the insight that the
Negro creator, as realist and individualist, insisted on seeing God with his
own eyes, on walking step by step with blessed Jesus. And James Redpath,
a Northern journalist who toured the South in the 1850s, reports that the
happy-looking faces of the Negroes in church coincide with heavy hearts
and raw backs. In the African church, he overheard one Negro whisper to
another, when the white preacher reiterated the Negro's religious duty to
submit: "He be d--d! God am not sich a fool."

Once more the main point of this whole story is not to affirm that there
were absolutely no borrowings white-to-black or black-to-white. Such
borrowings, on a limited scale, could hardly have been avoided where two
religious groups occupying the same general geographical area were juxta-
posed. The main point is artistic outlook—what each creator was trying to
create from an artistic standpoint. Thus far it is obvious that the white creator had only a simple religious intention, only a narrow social tradition,
and very little musical skill. The black creator, it is evident, had a broad religious motive for singing, drew from a powerful African musical tradition
as well as an American social tradition, and enjoyed a musical talent unsurpassed in quality and originality anywhere in the cultural world.

Summary evidence of the above point is found in many places. Harvey
Gaul, who studied the spirituals for a very long time, asserts that the American Negro got little help in folk song creation from his white brothers. He
declares the American Negro much richer in folk songs than the Indian,
the Hawaiian, or the mountain whites.

Pursuing his subject with keen awareness of both scientific and artistic
points, Paul F. Laubenstein emphasizes a stronger-than-imitative thrust in
the music he analyzes. The Negro's strong individuality, says Laubenstein,
caused him to pass all in religion, poetry, language, and music. Chirgwin
praises the Negro for being a born improviser, but says he goes farther than
improvisation. From the standpoint of the impact and worth of the Negro
songs, Alan Lomax observes that it is only of academic interest that some
of those songs may be based on white hymns. The Negro creator never
gave up the basic musical approach of his African ancestors. John F. Szwed,
writing in 1968, sums things up: There is no question that this music is
completely Afro-American, since there is no precedent for it anywhere.

Besides the differences in nature, purpose, and approach, there are notable differences in conditions of creation. Criticizing Greenway (in *American Folk Songs of Protest*) for accepting portions of Professor Jackson's thesis, Irwin Silber points out that the Negro spiritual was often a song of social protest, whereas the white spiritual never was. The present writer will more than support this statement at a later time.

The white spiritual was created entirely in church and under very restricted religious conditions. The Negro spiritual was created under every possible condition of human experience. A number of writers have cited the "death spiritual" in its great variety as a lineal descendant of the African wake music. The spiritual was born, also, at home and in the plantation fields; in the kitchen and at the loom; on Mississippi wharves and in Baltimore canning factories; in the cabin at night; at camp meeting, yes, but also at private slave revivals and other meetings forbidden to the slave by his master. This broad scope is traced by A. E. Perkins in a brilliant article, appearing in the *Journal of American Folklore* in 1922, and entitled "Negro Spirituals from the Far South." Perkins adds that slave spirituals were inspired by a great variety of events—a death, hardness or cruelty of a master, the selling of friends or relatives, the resultant heartrending separations, the sadness and loneliness of old age, the bursting of a comet, and an unlimited number of other causes.

Krehbiel's evidence (in *Afro-American Folksongs*) that the Negro spiritual is unique, rooted in Africa, and entirely different from any other folk songs, still stands. Many writers have complained about Krehbiel. Some have attacked him on isolated issues. No one, however, has destroyed his fundamental arguments with respect either to melody or words. No one of his stature as a musical analyst has addressed himself so systematically as he to basic questions of melody and words. His opposition has generally been of the character of Miss Pound's note (mentioned above, pp. 91–92), chiefly emotional, sentimental, and full of racial bias.

One other collection of pieces of evidence helps to demonstrate that the black spiritual and the white spiritual belong in entirely different categories. The latter was bound to a limited set of religious doctrines aiming chiefly at salvation beyond the grave. The former not only dealt with everyday life on earth, but with salvation on earth, as well as after death, the injustices of slavery, and the need for personal freedom to set things right. Christianity was meaningful to slaves only in these senses. We will examine later the supporting evidence in the black songs. Right now, in this formative stage, let us look at original hymns created for former slaves who had managed to get free, but who retained their religious faith.

Three of these gentlemen poets were quite remarkable. The first, in point of time, was the Reverend Richard Allen (1760–1831), founder of the African Methodist Episcopal Church, which today has 1.2 million communicants. From about 1800, Richard Allen published books of every sort

for his parishioners, including hymn books. Some of the hymns he personally wrote. Some of his "spiritual songs" are quite conventional, in the tradition of the white spiritual. Others devote themselves to admonitions to
improve the flock. For example, Richard Allen did not like shouting Methodists; he thus had his congregation sing,

> Such groaning and shouting, it sets me to doubting,
> I fear such religion is only a dream;
> The preachers are stamping, the people were jumping,
> And screaming so loud that I neither could hear,
> Either praying or preaching, such horrible screaching,
> 'Twas truly offensive to all that were there.

The significant factor is that the hymn is directed toward the personal and
group behavior of the people.

Though not so well known as Richard Allen, the Reverend Thomas
Cooper (ca. 1775–ca. 1823), who had dozens of trying experiences with
slave stealers after he broke free, was more militant in his hymn writing.
He preached in the Northern United States, in England, and in Africa. His
book, *The African Pilgrim's Hymns* (1820), partly composed and partly
collected, contained 372 hymns; many of them are reminiscent of the most
radical of the spirituals. He made the collection for the use of congregations in London and Africa.

In one hymn, called "The Negro's Complaint," set to the air of "Old
Hundred," he has his congregations sing,

> Great God dost thou from heav'n above
> View all mankind with equal love?
> Why dost thou hide thy face from slaves,
> Confin'd by fate to serve the knaves?
>
> When stole and bought from Africa,
> Transported to America,
> Like the brute beast in market sold,
> To stand the heat and feel the cold.
>
> To stand the lash and feel the pain,
> Expos'd to stormy snow and rain.
> To work all day and half the night,
> And rise before the morning light! . . .
>
> Although our skin be black as jet,
> Our hair be friz'd and noses flat,
> Shall we for that no freedom have,
> Until we find it in the grave.
>
> Hath heav'n decreed that Negroes must,
> By wicked men be ever curs'd
> Nor e'er enjoy our lives like men,
> But ever drag the gauling chain.

> When will Jehovah hear our cries,
> When will the sons of freedom rise,
> When will for us a Moses stand,
> And free us from a Pharaoh's land.

Others of Cooper's hymns, like the black spirituals, use the battle of Jericho, and the characters of such as Gideon and David with pointed and telling effect in singing the need to "fight on."

The *Narrative of William W.(ells) Brown, A Fugitive Slave*, written by himself and published in 1847, contains spiritual songs which Brown says were composed and sung by slaves. Sample stanzas are,

> See these poor souls from Africa
> Transported to America;
> We are stolen, and sold to Georgia,
> Will you go along with me? . . .
>
> See the wives and husbands sold apart,
> Their children's screams will break my heart;—
> There's a better day a coming,
> Will you go along with me
> There's a better day a coming,
> Go sound the jubilee.

In the 1850s Miss Bremer heard free Negroes sing in an African Methodist Church in Cincinnati. Enchanted and delighted, she calls their music a "melodious torrent . . . exquisitely pure," full of life. These worshippers sang *a capella*. Their songs were devout spirituals heavily endowed with realism, like this one, first published in 1853:

> What ship is this that's landed at the shore?
> Oh, glory hallelujah!
> It's the old ship of Zion, hallelujah, (repeat)
> Is the mast all sure, and the timber all sound?
>
> She's built of gospel timber, hallelujah. . . .
>
> What kind of men does she have on board? . . .
>
> They are all true-hearted soldiers, hallelujah. . . .
>
> What kind of Captain does she have on board? . . .
>
> King Jesus is the Captain, hallelujah. . . .
>
> Do you think she will be able to land us on the shore?
> Oh, glory hallelujah!
> I think she will be able, hallelujah, . . .
>
> She has landed over thousands, and can land as many more,
> Oh, glory hallelujah!

The peculiar qualities of harmony and rhythm in the black spiritual help to establish a preponderance of the evidence on the questions raised. They argue against borrowing from any non-African source or from any type of song with the properties of the so-called white spiritual. From native Africans, Germans, English, and Americans, from musicologists, anthropologists, social historians, and firsthand listeners to the songs, and from critics and analysts who wrote from 1856 to 1968, the evidence has been accumulated.

The usual contention of those who claim the black spiritual borrowed from the white is that the black spiritual and its original singers were lacking in harmony. The theory underlying this contention is that the Negro singer-creator was simpleminded. Singing always in unison, he had no knowledge of harmonies. He imitated what he heard and nothing else. Lacking religious and musical tradition, he embraced entirely the religion and the religious expression of the white camp meeting singers.

First, it should be noted that should all this be true, there is no evidence that lack of harmony is proof of simplemindedness. Harmony is a natural attribute of some singing groups, not requiring cultivation. Unison singing is used in the most sophisticated music—hymns, anthems, and otherwise. Often it is employed for direct or contrasting effect. Considering the large number of places where the spiritual was created and could have been heard, one would have great difficulty determining style and effects at any given point. Thus, the most reliable evidence would have to come from those who had studied the songs from a variety of circumstances and on the basis of a large number of firsthand witnesses and participants. Such are most of those who testify here.

Cosmo Warugaba, musical specialist of Kampala, Uganda, told this writer that in some parts of black Africa part singing is a natural thing; in others, it is not. Even in unison singing there may be several octaves between singers, with a certain number of singers on each octave. The naturalness of the singing is probably the best criterion for judging harmony or the lack of it.

Of nineteen witnesses, all but three declare the Afro-American singer to have used harmony in his songs, including the spiritual. To name them in alphabetical order, one refers to Oluwole Alakija, Mary D. Arrowood (and Thomas Hoffman Hamilton), Verna Arvey, W. A. Barret, Phillips Barry, Fredrika Bremer, Natalie Burlin, A. M. Chirgwin, Nathaniel Dett, Harvey Gaul, Walter Goldstein, Percival Kirby, Alan Lomax, H. L. Mencken, H. K. Moderwell, Frederick Olmsted, Henry Russell, Carl Van Vechten, and W. E. Ward.

Arvey, Goldstein, and Kirby had reservations: The first was that harmonization of spirituals occurs seldom; but, that when harmonized, the song follows inherent racial qualities, shows little Caucasian influence, and does not sound at all like Anglo-Saxon hymns; the second, that the harmony is uninteresting despite many references to it by early travelers; the third, that spiritual harmonies derive from the European harmonic system.

Oluwole Alakija, W. A. Barret, and Harvey Gaul say that the Negro spiritual has little or no harmony. Gaul stresses its reliance on unison singing, but adds that it upsets the laws of melody writing, going up when it should go down. Barret, writing in a London magazine in 1872, says there is no part singing in the Negro spiritual. In the interpretation of the African-born, English-trained Alakija, the European needs counterpoint because his inner musical soul lacks expression; the African does not because he can produce fine music at the dictates of his soul. He also demands that African music be judged by African standards, not by those of the European or of the European derivative.

The other thirteen witnesses are emphatic that the harmonies of the Negro spiritual are original and superior. Writing in the *Gold Coast Review,* W. E. Ward says the African is as musical as any race in Europe, and probably more musical than any. Music, he says, is the most alive of the African arts. H. K. Moderwell supports Ward by declaring the American Negro spiritual a "well-rounded folk music," not just rhythmic.

Olmsted heard the slave singers many times. He contradicts Cartwright's view that Negroes do not understand harmony. Of Negro steamboat dockhands who could not count, Olmsted says that their part singing had great spirit and independence. They sang, Olmsted said, "in perfect harmony, as I never heard singers, who had not been considerably educated at the North." Fredrika Bremer also heard them sing innumerable times, and listened intently. Of their river music she says that "chaotic confusion dissolved itself into the most beautiful harmony." Russell did not hear slaves, but he heard their immediate descendants. He credits them with a great transforming power. Likewise Mrs. Arrowood (and Hamilton), writing in the *Journal of American Folklore* in 1928, says the Negro singers (descendants of slaves) sang in parts, without instruments, and were never discordant. Speaking of a group of former slaves who settled in Maine at the instance of General Howard, Phillips Barry says that these Negroes sang their spirituals six to eight parts at once, all in harmony.

Chirgwin calls the Negro spiritual unusual among folk songs because it was sung in harmony rather than in unison. Dett goes further: He says it is unique in that it sprang into being already harmonized. Natalie Curtis Burlin reports a visit of a young German musician to Hampton Institute in 1918. Here, he heard nine hundred students singing naturally, spontaneously, in parts, not even segregated by part groups (sopranos, tenors, etc.). When told that they had had no training, the foreign visitor was incredulous. Mencken says the American Negro is more harmonist than melodist; without training, he is capable of giving any tune new dignity and interest with strange and entrancing harmonies and "in the midst of harsh discords, they produce effects of extraordinary beauty." Van Vechten agrees with

Chirgwin and Dett that the Negro spiritual swings in harmony and that the Negro folk harmonize instinctively.

In similar ways the rhythm of the Afro-American spirituals is defined as distinctive and original. Quoting from Kenneth Richmond's book, *Poetry and People*, Hermine Barz underlines the fact that oppression cannot destroy a people's love for rhythm and cites the English peasantry and the American slave as examples. In a personal interview, J. H. K. Nketia told the present writer that Afro-Americans develop harmony without being taught. Syncopation in the Negro spiritual, says Goldstein, is deeply racial, a heritage from the remote past. Goldstein quotes Kipling to the effect that the Negro "quivers with rhythm." From Barret's researches one learns that the rhythmic tunes of the spiritual are well adapted for dancing. This fact bridges the Negro's past to his unique American method of getting religion.

It is, therefore, clear that on the basis of harmony and rhythm, the black spiritual is rooted in African tradition. Its American elements stem from the unique experiences of its folk singing group. The fact that some observers say the songs were purely in unison speaks only to a limited observation. The broadest evidence designates them as harmonic, basically original, and musically complete.

There is no better summary for the preponderance of the evidence than two short statements by two Southern white women, the first delivered by Jeannette R. Murphy in 1899, the second by Lydia Parrish in 1935. The first reads: "The white man does not live who can write a genuine negro song." The second is equally emphatic: "No white man has ever composed a Negro song to be classed with authentic Negro spirituals." In other words, the white spiritual and the black spiritual are similar in name only; in every other way, they belong in different worlds.

❀◇

CHAPTER THIRTEEN

The Answer to the First Big Question Is "Yes"

. .
.

I T IS now emphatically clear that for a century or more before 1867 there was an Afro-American spiritual. It was and is an independent folk song, born of the union of African tradition and American socioreligious elements. It was affected to a limited extent by the American Christian evangelical tradition and the Anglo-American hymn, but not at all by the so-called white spiritual. Its creators were religious folk in the broad sense of the African, not in the narrow sense of the white spiritual creator. They settled upon Christianity as a source for ideas and models only because Christianity was the nearest available, least suspect, and most stimulative system for expressing their concepts of freedom, justice, right, and aspiration. The one God of Christianity was not new to their centuries-old tradition; in their creative hands, however, he became a close associate. As one writer said, a God of loving familiarity, "nearer to them than to most people."

The uniqueness of the theology of the Afro-American spiritual has been meticulously developed by Theo Lehmann in his monumental study, *Negro Spirituals: Geschichte und Theologie* (Berlin, 1965). This brilliant author drew upon 515 sources (from the United States, Germany, England, France, and other countries) which he listed in his "Literaturverzeichnis" at the end of his book. At appropriate places in succeeding chapters we will present Professor Lehmann's evidence and views. At this point it is significant that his thorough investigation adds one more strong foundation to our support of the unique Afro-American spiritual.

From the fountainhead of the Afro-American spiritual, thousands of songs poured forth. Many of them used Biblical characters and events to dramatize their concepts; most of them grew from roots of everyday life.

They sang, as the African blood has always sung, of the varied aspects of that life, stressing the realistic and the drive for something better.

This Afro-American spiritual was perpetually threatened by the rules of the plantation and the necessities of preventing any sort of union or common ground among the slave masses. It had a great number of unique and practical purposes: One of its most consistent was to prevent disunion among slaves, to encourage solidarity in the face of hardship, to bring spiritual hope out of material hopelessness, to make the individual slave believe that some day, before he died, he would be physically free and fulfilling his destiny in a free country on one side or the other of the Atlantic. Although those creators used death as a figure of speech (as their ancestors had done), they were young men and women who thought very little about literal dying. No literal death could have been worse to them than slavery. (Remember John Wesley's letter to William Wilberforce, one week before he died, begging Wilberforce to step up his fight against all slavery? Of American slavery Wesley said, "it is the vilest that ever saw the sun.") To wear the mask of death, as, once more, their singing ancestors had often done, was to open a free sky to plan, without penalty from the oppressor, the secret ways to become free, and more important, to do something constructive with their lives.

Proof of the free and independent Afro-American spiritual just described has been given through the evaluation of available external factors. Internal evidence, in further support, will be given in later chapters, as it has come from hundreds of Afro-American spirituals themselves.

Something should be said of the extent to which the Afro-American spiritual was a "back-to-Africa" song. The case for this conclusion has been elaborately and brilliantly displayed by the Reverend Doctor Miles Mark Fisher in *Negro Slave Songs in the United States* (1935). This book has been praised by critics and historians (Professor Ray Billington, for one) who prefer to believe that the spiritual, if it has any social meaning, was pointing the black man back to his home of origin and out of the American white man's hair. These critics were overjoyed that the documentation was prepared and the conclusions reached by an intelligent Negro author.

In some respects, however, all concerned have led themselves into a trap. If the Negro spiritual was a flat imitation of the white spiritual, then it could have no social connotation whatsoever. If it was a back-to-Africa song, then it had social connotation; and if it had social connotation, the import might as readily be physical freedom in the North as the same in Africa. Generally speaking, the proponents of the white spiritual theory turn thumbs down on the notion that the spiritual calls for physical freedom in the North. To be logical, then, they would have to rule out the back-to-Africa idea, since it opens a dangerous door.

Dr. Fisher, not one of the above strict constructionists, is entirely honest, and he is eloquent. His main trouble is the facts about African colonization.

If thousands of spirituals were written by Afro-American slaves about their yearning to get to Africa, this alone would be indicative of a passionate movement. All such a movement would have required was opportunity for the slave people concerned to fulfill the motive of their songs. The slave people had such opportunity on a large scale, both from private sources (many white slave owners put provisions in their wills for their slaves to be free if they would accept moving to Africa) and from large organizations, like national and state colonization societies. In P. J. Staudenraus, *The African Colonization Movement, 1816–1865*, is voluminous evidence for the answer to the whole question. It can be summed up in the fact that over a period of eighty years, the American Colonization Society alone, not including state groups, collected $2,762,467.87 for the sole purpose of returning freed slaves to Africa. During this total period only 15,386 colonists were transported; between 1817 and 1860, only 10,518 colonists went to Africa. This is far fewer than the acknowledged numbers of slaves who ran away to freedom in the Northern United States and Canada during the same period. Moreover, African transplantation was free and open, while American was hazardous, involving crushing sanctions and the loss of one's life.

Thus, Dr. Fisher's view cannot stand unless we close our eyes to the historical facts and figures. This author, for one, however, is willing to believe that some spirituals carried a return-to-Africa connotation. Among millions of slaves you will find a great variety of opinions. Our concern, however, is with predominant opinions and those supported by incontrovertible evidence.

At this point a further brief comment on opinions and evidence is in order. We have complained that the Afro-American spiritual has not received a fair interpretation because people have accepted as evidence parallel columns of white and black spiritual texts when the text in the white column is never shown to have time precedence and when the two texts, even to a casual observer, are quite dissimilar. We now extend our complaint to include the failure and refusal of the same people to examine the carefully developed evidence of dozens of writers who have clarified pieces of the mosaic of interpretation one at a time. As we proceed to establish, unquestionably, the Afro-American spiritual, we again offer conclusions from writers whose patient and insightful research on spirituals has been ignored.

❲ *Freedom as a Passion in the Afro-American Spiritual*

There is hardly a better way to nail down the Afro-American spiritual than to describe the central passion of it and its creators—a thing called freedom. Actual proof of freedom in the songs will follow. Just now, the job is to show the spirit of freedom, earthly freedom, in the hearts and minds of the Afro-American creators. No such passion could or did exist in the hearts and minds of the creators of the white spiritual.

From the standpoint of inheritance, this passion is described by Professor Allison Davis as early as 1928, when he links the spirit of freedom and religious discipline. He begins by describing the men and women who, flogged to death, died smiling and saying, "Soon we shall be free," and those on the Middle Passage who, leaping overboard, waved exultant farewells to friends rejoicing in their escape. From this ancestral attitude he moves down to the slaves themselves who used religious discipline, and taught their children to use it, to generate "the determination to survive and to wrest a home and education for their children from a hostile environment."

In *An African Treasury*, edited by Langston Hughes (New York, 1960), present-day black African writers from Kenya, Ghana, South Africa, and other states show how, for centuries, concepts of viable freedom and poetic consciousness have been inextricably linked in the black African personality. Thus it is not surprising that Roland Hayes, the great tenor who intelligently and artistically interpreted spirituals throughout the world for nearly a half century, found through research that liberty and freedom were to the slave creator "realities of their earth, not far removed from celestial promises found in their Bible."

In his essay, "Understanding the Spiritual," accompanying spiritual arrangements which made him famous, R. Nathaniel Dett accounts for the superiority of the slave spiritual by reason of an exuberance all the more terrific because the slave's impulses and emotions had been suppressed. This was especially true in the slaves' own meetings—generally secret. Craving freedom, says Dett, the slave saw in the American religion his only hope of emancipation; for example, the freeing of Israel from Egypt and of Jesus from the grave.

If a passion like this can be communicated to sympathetic observers, it certainly was in the case of the black American slave. At least, the observers have testified that it was. In 1739 when the New Inverness petition was submitted by Scottish whites in South Georgia, one of their reasons for requesting the replacement of slaves by working whites was the shock "to human nature that any race of mankind, and their posterity, should be sentenced to perpetual slavery." They continued on the note that freedom was as dear to slave as to them and that to postpone the slaves' freedom was to extend unnecessarily a horrible and bloody scene. This type of petition must have arisen in part from the petitioners' observation of the slaves' yearning for freedom.

Nearly two hundred years later, Moderwell, calling the spirituals "The Epic of the Black Man," declares that the slave creator's racial enemy was the white man "and his racial desire freedom."

Much of James Redpath's book, *The Roving Editor: Or, Talks with*

Slaves in the Southern States (1859), is reportage of interviews with slaves. Like Uncle Tom when he was well treated, Virginia slaves who had been treated kindly still wanted their liberty. A North Carolina slave testified: "*All the colored people of my acquaintance* (and I know them all here), *would* gladly be free if they *could get their liberty*." If there had been a slave plebiscite, the result would have been a nearly unanimous and resounding shout for liberty.

From the earliest times, writes Dorothy B. Porter in "Early American Negro Writings: A Bibliographical Study," the freedom theme is predominant in the literature produced by American Negroes of all categories. The Abolitionists may have published the autobiographies of ex-slaves who freed themselves at the risk of their lives—Linda Brent, William Wells Brown, Lewis and Milton Clarke, Frederick Douglass, J. D. Green, Josiah Henson, Louis Hughes, Elizabeth Keckley, the Reverend J. W. Loguen, Reuben Maddison, Solomon Northup, J. W. C. Pennington, John Thompson, and L. Tilmon, to mention a few of the more famous; but the Abolitionists did not engender the passion for freedom in their hearts and, as they told it, in the hearts of the overwhelming majority of the slaves. If anything, the Abolitionists were engendered by their passion. And Carter Woodson's *Negro Orators and Their Orations* adds the testimony of a host of black orators before slavery died that freedom for the slave was the major theme for their oratory.

In this connection, note the incisive but obvious meaning of "O, Freedom!" Note that it does not say, "Before I'd be a slave anymore," or "Before I'd accept being a slave very long." It says "Before I'd BE a slave" in the first place. The last line, "And go home to my Lord and be free," is palpably a tag line for the white people. The real meaning is in the second and third lines. The poet slave is clearly saying that in his heart and mind—the only place where it ever counts with people—he was never a slave, and he will die before he ever is one. And this is what free men all over the earth have been saying since the dawn of time.

If Booker T. Washington, by virtue of his so-called desire to accommodate to prevailing white mores to give his black brothers a chance, is thought to fall outside these radical precincts, let the thinker be quickly disabused. Booker T. Washington was born a slave. In *Up from Slavery* (1901), his standard autobiography, he writes that his mother prayed fervently that Lincoln and his armies would win the Civil War and she and her children be free. He adds,

> As the great day [end of the War] drew nearer, there was more singing in the slave quarters than usual. It was bolder, had more ring, and lasted later into the night. Most of the verses of the plantation songs had some reference to freedom. True, they had sung those same verses before, but they had been careful to explain that the "freedom" in these songs referred to the next world. Now they gradually threw off the mask, and were not

afraid to let it be known that the "freedom" in their songs meant freedom
of the body in this world.

An interesting phase of the slave's freedom passion is the desire for freedom of religion. The slave looked forward to the day when he would not
have to "steal away" and "go way down yonder" to hold secret religious
meetings, as Charles H. Wesley explains in his essay, "The Negro Has Always Wanted the Four Freedoms" (1944).

Long before the Civil War, the slave looked forward to freedom of every kind. The free-at-last songs were numerous in the emancipation year,
but they were not new. *The Negro in Virginia* demonstrates this fact. It
also indicates how remarkable was the number of escapees and the quality
of the escapes in spite of patrols, punishments for the captured fugitive and
his helpers, swamp life, snakes, wild animals, "nigger dogs," and barking
house dogs. All this is realistic testimony to the passion for freedom in the
folk community of the Afro-American spiritual.

Some of the free-at-last songs are quite homely, and they prove false the
notion that the spiritual has no humor. Listen to these lines,

> Mammy don't you cook no mo'
> You's free! You's free! . . .
>
> Rooster, don't you crow no mo' . . .
>
> Ol' pig, don't you grunt no mo' . . .
>
> Ol' cow, don't you give no mo' milk . . .
>
> Ain't got to slave no mo'.

And to these,

> Ain't no mo' blowin' dat fo' day horn,
> Will sing, chillun, will sing.
> Ain't no mo' crackin' dat whip over John
> Will sing, chillun.
>
> Tain't no mo' sellin' today
> Tain't no mo' hirin' today
> Tain't no mo' pulling off shirts today
> It's stomp down freedom today.
> Stomp it down!

And to this one from the book of a Southern lady who was proud of the
good relationship between masters and slaves. She describes a "black
crowd" in the track of Sherman's army singing now in unison, now in
parts:

> I free, I free!
> I free as a frog
> I free till I fool
> Glory Alleluia!

❪ The Slave Sang of This Earth

Few will deny that the white spiritual was primarily and almost exclusively otherworldly. Its creators were people who looked beyond the troubles and disappointments, even the partial success (such as being white), of this life and yearned for the perfections of heaven. True and complete salvation was in their every thought. Because their religion was a compartment in their lives, a kind of Sunday exultation, instead of the whole thing, they could afford this kind of preoccupation. Because they were lacking in a long and deep religious tradition as well as a song tradition, they had had little practice matching artistic symbols with the affairs of everyday life. They stuck to raw, simple, desperate expressions of hope for themselves as individuals in the great beyond.

With the Negro creator almost everything was the opposite. His traditions in song and wholehearted religion were deep enough, his everyday life was hard and brutal and to him unjust enough, his use of mask and symbol was skillful enough, his faith in earthly future was intense enough that he could sing of his earthly life and do it artistically. In any case he sang of this earth, as many thoughtful students and observers have testified.

Ernest Borneman, for example, declares that the Southern Negro was by nature a realist, and that his music "even in its most sugary phases, never ceased to retain a close touch with reality." In *Composer and Nation* Sidney Finkelstein nails down the same point. Realism, or the immediate truth of life, he says, is vividly apparent in the American Negro spiritual. Julia Peterkin goes even further. She declares that each spiritual is re-created by singers to express the immediate emotion, the starkest kind of realism. And she adds that these Negro songs go far deeper than they appear to do on the surface.

Pursuing the literary expression demanded by his miserable lot, the black slave, as Gerald W. Haslam (in 1968) clearly sees, utilized and perfected such African modes as mythic histories, slave tales and chants, animal stories, religious shouts and songs, clandestine protest rhymes, and uniquely interpreted songs and verses from his Afro-American setting. Forty years before Haslam, Alberta Williams saw the same breadth in the spiritual. She says it encompasses every phase of the slave's life—history, news, the rhythm of his work, humor, religious fervor. By singing the same song in different ways the black worker reveals varying facts of his life. Weatherford calls the slave's songs folk music true to the life of the whole people. It is a record of traditions, beliefs, customs, and longings "such as no individual literature could possibly possess." Fredrika Bremer notes that improvisations in the songs followed the patterns of daily life; also that songs were made on the road, during journeyings, upon rivers, and at cornhuskings.

In a perceptive article on "The Psychology of Negro Spirituals," Albert

Sidney Beckham shows how the spiritual recalls the panorama of slave life. It tells of life in the fields, he says, in the shops, at home, in religious meeting. It includes songs inspired by faith. Its vivid emotions and escape mechanisms, its real spirit and sincerity make its appeal well-nigh universal. From the most banal incidents of everyday life it ranges to a philosophical humility and to other commentaries upon the economic and social life.

What S. I. Hayakawa has said about the blues approach in his unusual essay, "Popular Songs vs. the Facts of Life," he could easily have said about spirituals. After deploring the false idealization and the frustration and demoralization bestowed upon people by popular songs, he praises the blues for giving people "real equipment for life." Blues, he says, face up to life's problems and take a tough attitude toward them. Popular songs interfere with emotional maturity. The life problems of the spiritual are far deeper and more challenging than those associated with the blues. All through the spirituals the singer lays them out clearly and unblushingly. Then he offers his solutions to them. While requiring much strength of character, the solutions are well within human capacities and are dead on the bull's-eye of the problems concerned. Take, for example, spirituals like "Study War No More" and "Keep A-Inchin' Along Like a Po' Inch Worm."

Dr. Hermine Barz's review leads her to the conclusion that the spirituals were not religious songs in the narrow, special, or "simple worship" sense. They covered, she says, the whole range of group experience, except sex. It is only a minor correction to have to state that even sex is included in some spirituals directly and by implication. Dr. Barz is confirmed by E. B. Reuter despite his well-known bias against Negroes. Professor Reuter says that the songs grow out of daily plantation life, work, and play; that they vary with local conditions; and that they express the hopes, joys, and fears of a primitive group in an alien environment. He is aware that they are all not strictly religious; he calls the majority of them "semi-religious." And he adds the reason for their broad scope: Song was almost the only means these people had for expressing their emotions.

William Faux, the English farmer-visitor of 1823, adds "plaintive love songs" to the list. He is seconded by W. H. Thomas who adds economics to love. From economics it is a simple step to a number of writers who mention the interrelationship of spirituals and work songs during slavery times. Jeannette Murphy recalls that the Negro sang religious music at work. This is undoubtedly true. It is a fact which prevents the logical separation of work songs and spirituals. This fact was especially true of rowers, as Faux, Fanny Kemble, and the *Nation* reviewer of *Slave Songs in the United States* (1867) all emphasized. The reviewer set down as unforgettable his hearing "O Deat' He Is a Little Man" by a crew rowing the ferry between St. Helena and Beaufort. The fugle man of the crew was particularly effective with his "O Lord, remember me; *do*, Lord, remember me!"

But spirituals as work songs did not stop with the oarsmen. As *The*

Negro in Virginia shows, they were used by railroad builders (singing mournfully of being beaten, whipped, or sold away); by spinners (singing, "Keep yo' eye on de sun, See how she run, Don't let her catch you with your work undone, I'm a trouble, I'm a trouble, Trouble don' las' alway"); by potato hoers; by celebrants of all kinds, especially those thinking of marriages and Christmas.

Should anyone try to draw a line between these and purely religious spirituals, he will get himself into all kinds of trouble. Any such line would eliminate such remarkable samples as "Hammering," "Michael, Row the Boat Ashore," "Heave Away," and "Many Thousand Gone."

While Joseph Hutchinson Smith credits the claim that the imagery and sentiments of the Afro-American spiritual grow from American conditions, Frederick J. Work (in 1907) goes further: "Since they tell faithfully the Negro's inmost life, both intellectually and spiritually, they are the only true source of our history. If any man would read the Negro's life, let him study his songs."

Sterling Brown and Anne Kenny have noted the range of poetic ideas in the titles alone. This range is equally suggestive of a wide horizon of subject matter. The fact that there is a religious catchphrase in most songs (such as the name of the deity or some other Biblical character, or reference to a Biblical event or to heaven) is not the significant thing at this point. The main thing is the pithy element of life suggested by the poetic grist of the title. For example, in "We Are Climbing Jacob's Ladder," the story of Jacob is just a point of departure. The really important expression the singer is pouring out is his determination to rise from his low estate and to progress up the material and spiritual ladder, "round by round." Jacob's experience has been chosen because it is the most available, the most dramatic, the most impressive and acceptable simile. And please note, his poetic point relates to his life on earth. In the mythical heaven, one is already as high as one can go.

Deep readers of the Afro-American spiritual have reported another noteworthy characteristic: these songs are narratives of personal experiences. Though lacking affection for Negro songs as a whole, Edmund S. Lorenz, in *Church Music: What a Minister Should Know about It*, confesses that the spirituals are frequently narratives of personal experience and, therefore, really "sacred ballads." Joseph Hutchinson Smith, though disrespectful to his "old darky woman" singer says that "Um! Most done toilin' here" was created in this personal way. Lucy McKim Garrison quotes a respectable house servant, who had lost all but one of her twenty-two children, concerning the "Poor Rosy" song in *Slave Songs of the United States* (1867), "can't be sung widout a full heart and a troubled sperrit!" clearly implying the sympathetic way in which it was created. A gem of an explanation of the creative process from an old Kentucky female creator is supplied by Jeannette Murphy: "Us ole heads use to make 'em up on de spurn of de moment, arter we wrassle wid de sperrit and come thoo."

It is doubtful that the Afro-American spiritual, with all its powerful ingredients, would ever have become nationally and world famous had not the original traveling singers been predominantly former slaves. Both the Fisk singers who started singing and traveling in the fall of 1871 and the Hampton singers who set forth in the spring of 1873 were people who sang the agonies and aspirations of the life from which they had been recently released. Arna Bontemps's *Chariot in the Sky* (Philadelphia, 1951), a fictionized story of the Fisk group and particularly of one member, is accurate and poignant in this respect.

These young men and women selected for their program the songs they had sung, and their fellow slaves had sung, when they lived within the cauldron of slavery itself. Through interviews they have revealed their own experiences, their sense from the beginning of having been utterly unfit for slavery (they did not have the essential slavish mind or character); their resistance and the resistance of those about them; their being sold, some more than once or twice or three times; their running away to swamps and being pursued by men and bloodhounds; their involvement in all the great ordeal and ingenious cruelty of American slavery; and their singing through it all. These men and women are the nearest thing in the record to the prototypes of actual creators of the Afro-American spiritual.

So deeply scarred had they been that, although they sang the spirituals every day while eating, dressing, carrying out their chores, and walking to and fro, individually and in groups, when the Fisk singers first began traveling, no Negro songs were on their program. The white director wanted them, but the Negro singers, all people of outstanding talent and sensitivity, hesitated to spread their deepest reactions to most terrifying experience on the record. Only when it seemed that the tour might fail from lack of audience interest did they permit one or two songs each time to be programmed. From this point the success of their tours for many years to come, as amateurs and as professionals, was assured.

The big point here is that the songs were of this earth, of the most harrowing and irresistible experience a human being can undergo. If they had been singing white men's songs served up in rehash; if they had been "happy slaves" singing like automatons the glories of the plantation and the "big house," the sweetness of "ol massa," "ol mistus," and lovely, kind overseers, they could never have convinced all those thousands of audiences in the Northern and Western United States and in many foreign countries. Because they had gone through these gradations of hell, far worse than anything Dante imagined, because they had resisted and been broken in pieces everywhere except in heart and mind, they could create and sing the mighty songs that had been written in their blood. Every audience who heard them was struck dumb for having caught a tiny glimpse into real life at its most terrible, but exalted by human endurance, human determination to resist or at least to hold fast, and human faith in a better world on earth, sponsored by a religion that all the time worked quietly in them, and from time to time fired them up with song.

Before Professor Reuter mentioned the fact referred to above—that the songs vary with local conditions—Professor Kelly Miller had written (in 1906) of their adaptation to local environment. He had described the songs as music autochthonous to the American continent, racy to the soil, baptized with the blood and watered with the tears of the slave. He downgraded the African influence and insisted that scene, circumstance, and aspiration in the spiritual were applicable to the slave's abiding place, not to a land of sojourn.

Booker T. Washington directs us to another undoubted source of spiritual ideas: slave discussion and the slave "grape-vine telegraph." Not all the supervision and snooping of overseers, drivers, and their henchmen, even when the snooper was black and a racial traitor, prevented lively discussion of important questions among slaves. Often these discussions led to secret meetings of carefully chosen groups in secret places. The fact that these meetings were sometimes discovered and dispersed by prevailing authority, and the participants severely punished, did not stop these gatherings.

The "grape-vine telegraph" was a true phenomenon. Of this phenomenon William Loren Katz has offered John Adams as his witness: In 1775 Adams wrote, "The Negroes have a wonderful art of communicating intelligence among themselves; it will run several hundred miles in a week or a fortnight."

How a group without newspapers or any mass media, and mostly without the ability to read or write, kept informed on all kinds of things—news of the day, inventions and discoveries, the approach of underground agents, the details about David Walker and Nat Turner, the ebb and flow of wars, the success or failure of runaways to reach their destinations—can hardly be explained. The incontrovertible fact is that all this happened by a regular system, as well-informed historians of the private life of the slaves have repeatedly testified. From this kind of communication, and the resultant close interrelationship, the songs acquired impetus, ideas for poetic development, and power for dissemination.

One of the strong, earthly drives of the Afro-American spiritual was the great concern of the slave with personal character. As Dr. Barz said, he was aware of his pain and hunger and of what his reaction to them meant. Jim Morse concludes that his concern with heroes overcoming great obstacles was his means of expressing resentment without incurring punishment. Clearly, it was also a sign of ingrained respect for the character of heroes and a silent indication that they were striving to exhibit such character.

The grandson of a firebrand Baptist preacher, the late Louis E. Lomax, author of *The Negro Revolt* (New York, 1962) and a television discussant, declares that the Afro-American spiritual is a product of the black masses. Tracing the songs from African tribal psychology through folkways revolving around Christian and burial societies, Lomax establishes these important character traits: "plaintive reaffirmation of the dignity of the individual soul couched in a rousing denunciation of this world's ways." Pharaoh, he says, would have emerged looking suspiciously like a Southern white man.

An interesting report on what was called extensive research is given by Clarence Cameron White in his background study of the spiritual "Nobody Knows the Trouble I've Seen," published in *The Musical Observer* for June 1924. Far from being a naïve peddler of stories, Clarence White was a concert violinist, a composer of Negro music, a historian, and a respected critic and teacher. His research reveals that "Nobody Knows the Trouble I've Seen" sprang from the heart of a Negro slave whose trials were almost more than he could bear. After wife and children had been sold away, he withdrew to his cabin and poured out his sorrow in this song. The mere creation or singing of such a song, from the standpoint of personal character, is a great victory over adversity.

The progress of the black man in America since Emancipation was foretold by his great ardor for self-improvement and education. If you read the autobiographies of the runaway slaves (like those listed above) you will find that the thing which drove them to risk their lives, repeatedly, to be free, even more than cruel and unjust treatment, was the prospect of living forever in mental and spiritual darkness. We have already shown how the "Jacob's Ladder" song (and there was a whole series on the theme) bespoke the determination for self-improvement more than any other thing. The dozens of songs on the subject of reading and writing (e.g. "My Lord's Writing All the Time," "My Mother Got a Letter," "O Lord, Write my Name," "Gwine to Write Massa Jesus," "De Book of Revelation God to Us Revealed," to recall but a handful of a large group) are proof of this preoccupation. One of the most incisive was printed in the *Southern Workman* for March 1907. It begins undisguisedly, "I know I would like to read . . . like to read."

One function of the Afro-American spiritual we have slanted against several times already was the morale-building function. "Walk Together, Childun, Don't You Get Weary" is one of a large series. Even when the song did not spell out this function, its purpose was implicit. As late as 1964, Joseph R. Washington, Jr., tells in *Black Religion*, how black students in jail in the 1960s still sang repeatedly "Lord, I Want to Be a Christian" as a morale builder.

Related in character and purpose are the consolation hymns for those sold away. Jacob Stroyer, another literary runaway slave, who published

My Life in the South in 1879, and a new and enlarged edition in 1889, tells how slaves composed and sang together such songs, with fiddle or banjo accompaniment, and even to original dance. One was,

> When we all meet in heaven,
> There is no parting there;
> When we all meet in heaven,
> There is parting no more.

Certainly it is clear that the words of such songs were not nearly so important to the singer as the heartlessness and poignancy of the events which inspired them. Recognition of a similar reaction to such experience is recorded in Edith Talbot's "True Religion in Negro Hymns" (1922),

> *Solo:* Mother, is massa gwine to sell us tomorrow?
> *Answer:* Yes, yes, yes! . . .
>
> Gwine to sell us down in Georgia?

One of the religious factors in this spiritual is a certain sense of destiny. Gilbert Chase describes the background from African cultism (where religion and magic meet), that the individual believed he had a fighting chance to alter his destiny if he could get the intercession of a kind deity. Chase does not stop to record the dozens of spirituals developing this sense with only the change that the American God is substituted as the source of power.

Joseph R. Washington insists that many spirituals fall outside the Christian faith. While he does not document his case, he assuredly raises an interesting and believable point. If the slave was blending African and American elements and adopting the Christian religion, not in imitation of his masters (he never admired hypocrites), but because it promised hope on earth as well as beyond, it is logical to read extra-Christian meanings into them.

Though not fooled by the Christian mask worn by the whites around him, the slave songwriter did express gratitude for true benevolence. The Reverend Samuel Davies, writing in 1757, tells of having baptized 150 Negro adults (slaves) and having sat down "at the Table of the Lord" with 50 of them. Without attempting to trace a cause and effect, one can logically state that lines like "I'm gonna sit at de welcome table" probably arose from some such experience. The pattern of the songs shows that the creator relied on uplifting personal experiences rather than on abstract principles of benevolence. In this regard, with respect to his descendants in the here and now, little has changed. It is pretty definite, as Joseph Washington states, that many of the songwriters thought of Bishop Francis Asbury as Moses, though many others reserved this spot for Harriet Tubman. Asbury, says Washington, lost his health working in behalf of Negro slaves, and they were grateful.

On the other hand the songwriters do not refrain from sharp reaction to bad treatment, even on the part of their owners or others in high place, in spite of the fact that for any Negro to speak disrespectfully of whites was often prohibited by law. Cresswell (1774), Faux (1823), and the reviewer in the *Nation* (1867) have told how the early Negro songs related to usage received from master, appropriately for good or bad. Stroyer describes the gathering of slaves to view the remains of a not-too-kind master. The slaves shed false tears, saying, "Never mind, missis, massa gone to heaven." Their real meaning, adds Stroyer, was, "Thank God, massa gone to hell." Whatever their irony, it did them no good. Mistress proved a great deal worse than master.

According to Joseph Washington, however, the phony white religionist received the full brunt of their contempt. He calls the Negro spiritual a criticism of missionaries, revivalists, evangelists, and the whole Protestant coalition bent on casting out the devil in the Negro, but who became for the Negro the devil himself. In his famous book, *The Confessions of Nat Turner* (New York, 1967), William Styron shows how the white preacher delegated to the slaves was a close ally of the power structure, a paid prostitute, harping only on the parts of the Bible that required obedience of servants, ignoring all the rest of its admonitions for charity, love, and constructive cooperation with one's brother in creation. He also reflects the contempt of Nat and other slaves for the whole despicable conspiracy. His dramatization is truthful and effective for the general idea, but he has probably understated the cause.

When the slave singer reached the point of defiance, he was fully defiant. George Washington Cable comments in passing that the Creole slave songs originated in a masculine mind. They were quite strong when they lamented the fate of a famous Negro insurrectionist in "The Dirge of St. Malo." They were stronger still when they rose from the throats of former Creole slaves, now runaways.

The crowning proof of defiance in the spiritual and the crowning evidence that the slave created and sang songs of this earth is in the authenticated stories on Harriet Tubman. They are too numerous to detail at this point. Before summarizing their chief features, however, it is important to recall Jim Morse's note that the constant reference in the songs to chariots, trains, ships, rivers, the sea, the promised land are a trend for escaping slavery, which is right at the fore of the slave mind.

Of the many fine studies of Harriet Tubman, for a summary picture with regard to the issues being discussed here, Earl Conrad's " 'General' Tubman, Composer of Spirituals" is hard to surpass. This article by a sharp-eyed journalist appeared in the *Etude* for May 1942, along with pictures of General Harriet at ages forty-five and ninety-two.

Harriet acquired her general's stars from John Brown. Five feet tall, carrying to her grave bruises and ailments caused by her slave experiences, she ran away repeatedly from slave territory and carried between two and three hundred slaves with her. About to depart for free country, she would sing her farewells to her fellow slaves:

> I'm sorry I'm going to leave you,
> Farewell, oh farewell;
> But I'll meet you in the morning,
> Farewell, oh farewell.

One of the reasons it is impossible to believe Professor Guy Johnson and his coterie when they say that freedom in the Negro spiritual meant freedom from sin is seen in Harriet's next stanza,

> I'll meet you in the morning,
> I'm bound for the promised land,
> On the other side of Jordan,
> Bound for the promised land.

For her pithy song Harriet appropriated a Methodist air, but the words were her own. And they were loaded with earthy meaning. Of her hundreds of liberated passengers (slaves she guided to freedom), she had this to say, and it was truth: "I never ran my train off the track and I never lost a passenger."

With other songs she soothed those she was about to free,

> Hail, oh hail, you happy spirits,
> Death no more shall make you fear,
> Grief and sorrow, pain nor anguish,
> Shall no more distress you there.

The verses (the stanza quoted is one of the many) had a Methodist ring, but they were pure Tubman.

"Old Chariot" was one of the names they gave her. As a get-ready song, she used these lines,

> When the old chariot comes,
> I'm going to leave you,
> I'm bound for the promised land,
> I'm going to leave you.

In spite of redoubled patrols, in spite of increasing rewards which began at $1,000 and finally reached as high as $40,000 (at least a $.5 million in today's currency), General Harriet kept returning to slave territory, kept bringing out slaves like some omniscient, unselfish, incomparably fearless and brave Pied Piper, kept marching them along to the tune of "Old Chariot," "Go Down, Moses," "Steal Away," "The Gospel Train is Coming," "There's No Rain to Wet You," and "Didn't My Lord Deliver Daniel?" to freedom, to complete freedom on this earth, in Canada, if necessary.

It is noteworthy that she had a sublime faith and hope in the American way of life. When during the Civil War, she was leading three hundred Negro troops on a raid up the Combahee River in South Carolina, at the behest of Colonel James Montgomery, she believed firmly that her country would do right by its freedmen. It is a pity that the land of the free and the home of the brave let her down. Nevertheless, she sang her own patriotic song to her troops:

> Of all the whole creation in the East or in the West
> The glorious Yankee nation is the greatest and the best
> Come along! Ca! Don't be alarmed;
> Uncle Sam is rich enough to give you all a farm.

In the farriery of the black spiritual, then, the forge used a double material. First, there was the African tradition, extraordinary, as we have seen, in song and poetry. The power, ingenuity, depth, and variety of this tradition asserted itself characteristically in the American product. The hammer was the natural gift and urge of the transplanted folk to sing their reaction to a new life and intertwine their everyday pain, joy, and hope, and their far-flung aspirations.

Second was the institution of American slavery. If John Wesley's phrase may be repeated, it was "the vilest that ever saw the sun." On the other hand, it gave the slave numerous opportunities for poetic arousal. In a sense, however, the cruelty, malice, and bitterness of American slavery; its frenzied effort to shut out all hope of freedom from the black man in a land of the free; its vast and vain expenditure of energy to block every channel by which chattels could become men and spiritual personalities, all these helped to make the black spiritual more colorful and intense. The African slave was determined to have the shoes, the harp, and the wings that would fulfill his yearnings. When the two irresistible forces clashed, out of the hearts and mouths of the irrepressible slave bards burst forth these songs.

And for generations the hammers, and the songs, "kept-a-ringing!"

PART II / *The Slave Sings Free*

*— And before I'd be a slave,
I'd be buried in my grave—*

CHAPTER FOURTEEN

Basic Characteristics of a Folk Song

⟨ Nature of the Folk Community out of Which a Folk Song Grows

EVERY folk song, verse, and melody, is the product of a folk community. The community supplies its themes and its subject matter. Its unique language has been previously grown in the community's own soil and under the community's atmosphere and weather conditions. Within the community, and nowhere else, are its conventions, its social, moral, theological, and legal principles, its open and hidden prides and prejudices. Many of these run counter to established law and custom in the large society. From its community a body of folk song derives its natural history, its anthropology, its mythology, its subtle implications. As Nettl has said, folk music, both old and contemporary, is representative of the people's ancient traditions as well as an indicator of their current tastes. So far as its whole body of songs and other expressions is concerned, the folk community is a law unto itself.

What is a folk community anyway? The tendency of writers is to leave the term purposely loose. To get at the inner meanings of folk things, we must tighten up the term.

We begin with a people of common backgrounds—social, economic, ethnic, sectional, urban, rural, mountainous, occupational. The backgrounds must have developed over a period of generations, so that they are well set in the minds of the group. The educational system of the group has instilled in the people a sense of its unique character as a group.

To common backgrounds are added common goals, interests, and values. These provide a magnetic field in which every member of the folk group has been caught. Perhaps most vivid of all are the common pressures.

The folk group is ubiquitously aware of these pressures. More than any other one thing, the pressures mold the folk community into a unity, allowing room for insistent individual differences.

From backgrounds and common goals and awareness of common pressures evolves a common psychology. Again, there is room for demanding variety in interpretation. But the common psychology determines the folk mind of a given subject. Variant verses in folk songs illustrate some deviation, but the fact that a song develops a theme in accordance with a straightforward plan of thinking is proof of the predominance of a common psychology in the folk community.

When the folk become a nation, the general principles broaden and intensify. All national music, say Downes and Siegmeister, is an amalgam of racial strains and historical processes consequent upon wars, migrations, trade, and other forms of interpenetration. The richer and more characteristic the folk strains of a people, the more vivid and colorful the music is likely to be.

As said before, the folk community makes its own rules. Robin Hood, for example, was an outlaw to the general community. His nobility of purpose made no difference; he was an outlaw, capable of being destroyed on sight by the law-abiding citizenry. But to the folk community who made the songs, he was a splendid hero. Its values placed the elements of character in which the folk delighted above the legal condemnations.

The "Frankie and Johnny" song wastes no time in stating the primary value in life: It is love. To these people, living in insecurity, love was the ultimate desideratum, the only real security. Frankie and Johnny not only had love, they practiced it; they were lovers and they loved. Besides the practical life, they had sworn vows of love. To the singing folk, nothing in life could have been better, greater. Thus, when Johnny broke his vows and practiced elsewhere, he had to die. Poetically and logically, Frankie had to be the one to kill him. That the killing was a capital crime in the eyes of the great society outside (which encompassed the folk community) was a secondary issue. The matter was solved when Frankie, convicted and standing on the scaffold, looked up to heaven and said, "Good Lord, I am coming to Thee."

These examples point to the key characteristics in the expressive phase of the folk community. There must be a capacity within the community for reaction to things; there must be a need for expression; there must be a common language—whether in words, instruments, dances, art pieces, or some other device—overt and covert, and there must be a fully developed craft and art of expression.

Actually, folk expression is an intragroup thing. Those of us who study folklore have merely developed a capacity for reading people's private mail. Occasionally, a folk group may have some reason to communicate with the outside world and something to say outside. Most of the superior pieces of folk expression, however, are within the group. If, therefore, we truly wish to know what is being said and done, we must get inside the group's mind and read from there. It is only a pale, secondary thrill to interpret from the outside or to make up our own minds from a distance about the meaning of folk art.

Proof of the intragroup expression is found in innumerable folk songs going back to Homer, and perhaps farther. In the Scottish ballad, "The Bonny Earl of Murray," the call in the opening verse is,

> Ye Highlands and ye Lowlands,
> O where hae ye been?

In "Bonny Barbara Ellen" the red rosebud and the sweet brier over the joint graves of Barbara Ellen and her fateful swain are twined in a true-lover's knot "For all true lovers to admire."

The American folk singer is very explicit about the fellow members of his folk community, whom he naturally expects to become involved in his song. Look at the following list of lines and songs.

Line	*Folk Song*
"Sons of pleasure, listen to me"	"James Bird"
"Young people, who delight in sin"	"Wicked Polly"
"Come ye sons of Columbia, your attention I do crave"	"Fuller and Warren"
"Come all of you young people who lives near and far"	"Poor Goins"
"Come all young men, please lend attention"	"(A) Silver Dagger"
"Ye doctors all of every rank With their long bills that break a bank,"	"Calomel"
"Come all you rounders for I want you to hear"	"Casey Jones"
"Come you tender Christians, wherever you may be,"	"Charles Guiteau or James A. Garfield"
"Come all ye tender Christians and hearken unto me,"	"The Death of Bendall"
"Come all my friends and listen to me, While I relate a sad and mournful history"	"Young McFee"
"Come you bold undaunted men, you outlaws of the day"	"Jack Donahoo"
"Come all you Texas Rangers wherever you may be"	"The Texas Rangers"
"Come along, boys, and listen to my tale"	"The Old Chisholm Trail"
"Come all you pretty girls and listen to my noise, I'll tell you not to *marry* the Cheyenne boys,"	"Cheyenne Boys"
"Now, all you poor sinners, I hope you will stay,"	"Starving to Death on Government Claim"

"Now don't get discouraged, you
    poor hungry men."
"Come all you jolly fellows and   "The Buffalo Skinners"
    listen to my song,"
"My friends if you'll listen to a   "The Dreamy Black Hills"
    horrible tale"

The folk song wears group clothes when it needs to, and personal clothes when they are more appropriate. When calling for rain or warding away pestilence, it is a group song. When dealing with loneliness and aloneness, with love, especially betrayal by a lover or the pain and ecstasy of returned and of unrequited love, it is supremely personal. It is stern about duty, friendship, marriage, pride. It recognizes generational gaps (youth and old age), fading youth, bravery, double-dealing. It delineates sharp experiences of occupations—fishermen, agricultural workers, coachmen, soldiers, ferrymen, boatmen and seamstresses—to mention a very few. It reacts to unemployment and poverty; to the helplessness of the rich and powerful; to the beautiful and the strange; to the foreboding and the tragic; to the ever-fabulous manifestations of nature. In singing of nature it does not merely lay appreciative hands upon flowers, trees, birds, and animals; it is finely observant of the special features of rosemary, violet, and rose; of maple and birch; of the woods themselves; of nightingale and swallow; of the horse, the pig, the heifer, and of monsters of land and sea, even the hated shark. It revels in mountains, clouds, stars, and darkness.

([Necessity and Use of Mask and Symbol

When any person outside the folk group attempts to interpret the folk song, he should keep in mind the natural qualities we have just reviewed. If all he wants is to turn the song to his own ends, he is free to do so; but he should not call this operation significant interpretation.

Perhaps the most usual misinterpretation is to read a folk song "literally," that is, without regard to the peculiar language of the folk community. Consider the language of a close family when members are communicating with each other. It is full of oral shorthand, symbol, meaningful but peculiar accent, irony, and significant silences. These elements are not embellishments; they are the natural routine of close communication. The same sort of thing is true of the communication of a folk community.

But with the folk community the complexity of the language is accentuated even more. Since the folk community has many people to communicate with, it insists upon a more lasting method. It resorts to art. In its art, as Nketia points out, it uses "mask, irony, human values, dimension." Russell Ames also stresses the persistent use of irony, especially in Negro folk song. The interpreter who does not take all these elements into account, and the specific reasons for them, is not doing his job of clear and perceptive interpretation.

⟪ Quality and Purpose of the Song

The quality of a folk song obviously depends upon the depth of involvement of the folk group and the success of the artistic devices employed. Songs that tell stories must maintain a high degree of narrative skill. The Scottish ballad "Sir Patrick Spens" is a good example. Poignancy is often used to introduce emotional depth. In "The Dying Cowboy," for example, the lead character begs not to be buried "on the lone prairie" amid mournfully howling coyotes, weeping cold winds, and waving grass—in a place where no sunbeam ever rests. And yet his buriers ignore his plea,

> "In my dreams I say"—but his speech failed there;
> And they gave no heed to his dying prayer;
> In a narrow grave six feet by three,
> They buried him on the lone prairie.

The stanza lays bare a world of feeling not only from within the cowboy's community, but for anyone who can feel at all.

The quality of the song is sometimes judged by this universal appeal. This is hardly fair. The song should be judged by its quality in relationship to its community. Hardly any railroad man feels relaxed in the presence of "Casey Jones."

The purposes of the folk song have already been indicated. It is created to highlight matters of deep concern to its community. The fact that, by probing the human depths of the community as a group and as individuals, it often reaches out to capture the people at large is only coincidental. Under Joseph Conrad's rule, if art can compel men to "pause for a moment at the surrounding vision of form and color, of sunshine and shadow," it can reveal "all the truth of life." Whenever one group, through the magic of art, finds solution or release in one of the many complexities of life, it opens the door for every human being to feel a little bit more secure.

The folk song always deals with the heart of life. As Rabindranath Tagore says, it speaks of intense yearning of the heart for the divine in man. It is often the people's only form of worship.

⟪ Character of the Actual Creators of the Song

For many years an argument waxed in folklore circles concerning the question of group composition of folk songs. Does the folk group create its songs as a group or is the chore turned over to talented individual members? Very few folklorists any more give credit to the folk group for the actual creation. The songs too often show signs of imagination, organization, and style which is far above the capacity of a large committee. Occasionally, they rise to heights of the very best poetry. The best folk songs are tightly unified. For these and other reasons a talented individual, respectfully anonymous, is suspected.

Acceptance of this talented individual does not rule out partial participation by the group in the creative process. Often the individual misjudges the capacity or current tastes or plain stubbornness of the group. When he creates the song and gives it to the group, the group generally accepts, but reserves its veto power. It may strike off portions that, in the singing or in the present mood, do not fit. It may even add a phrase or a line. Over the period and range of transmission of the song it may add stanzas, and has often done so.

These developments take nothing from the original creator. He is spokesman for the group. In every way he is in the blood, heart, guts, and brain of the group. He is likely to know them better than they know themselves. He knows what they need to sing, what they want to sing, what will solve their emotional complications, what will lift their spirits. As a true poet he has mastered the literary phase at least as far as he needs to. As a true poet he has the art of striking deep into the consciousness of his people and putting their ineluctable cry into thoughts and words and pauses that reveal the depths. As a true poet he knows the rhythm and the harmony of his community and sings in accordance.

But he is more than spokesman. He is creator because he is an individual with philosophy and style. His peculiar characteristics will be reflected in his song. In a body of songs from a given folk group will be a variety of philosophies and styles expressing a single community attitude. This variety reflects the molding of individual creators. It is not just a variety of moods of the community. And the community is aware of this double variety, both in its thoughts and moods and in different ways of expressing them. It is proud of its arsenal of different creators.

⟨ Specific Elements of Literature in the Song

The folk community reflects the musical and literary conventions of the total people. They are very rarely revolutionaries. Full of invention and device within the conventional pattern, they follow the regular methods of expression. This they do partly because of a need for explicitness and for being fully understood.

Thus, within the folk song are the literary vogues of a given period. Though these are given all kinds of original touches, pursuant to the unique genius of the folk community and its individual creators, they are repeated again and again.

The original touches are often quite remarkable. They often go beyond invention in a new mode. They are also full of basic soil and elements. This latter fact is proved by the fact that so much of great literature and great art music stems from folk expression. Even a "realistic" dramatist like Ibsen trained himself in the legends of his people before turning to such masterful and surgical analyses of his everyday neighbors as one finds in *Ghosts*, *A Doll's House*, *Hedda Gabler*, *The League of Youth*, and *An Enemy of the People*.

⟪ Relationship to Dance and Instrument

In most primitive societies the arts are all one. This principle is especially true of the musical arts—singing, instrumentalizing, dancing. Even the traveling poets sang the legends and epics of the people to musical accompaniment and often with dances in background or foreground. The earliest dramas, based on folk pieces, are intermixtures of beautiful singing, beautiful playing of instruments, and beautiful dancing. This was the practice not only in the West—ancient Greece, for example—but also in the East.

The folk song may not seem always to show its relationship to the instrument and the dance, but the relationship is always there. In Africa, it was always overt. In other countries the song may have somehow escaped its inveterate partners, but it never escaped their influence.

Every folk song is written to dance music and is sung against a background of musical instruments. This background accounts for its setting and its rhythm. It also reflects the inherent determination of the folk community to have a full artistic, as well as philosophical, experience.

❖❖

CHAPTER FIFTEEN

The Afro-American Spiritual as Folk Song

. .

To WHAT extent is the Afro-American spiritual a folk song? Is it a folk song at all? The best way to answer these questions is to apply the criteria of Chapter 14: Was there a valid folk community to produce the songs? Did these songs have the qualities and purposes of folk songs? What was the character of the creators, and was this a folk character? What were the basic literary elements, and can these be identified as folk elements?

There was indeed a valid folk community. The chief determinants of this community were two: The African tradition shared by all those who inspired, composed, and sang the songs; and the American experience of slavery. With the magnetic field created by both these factors vigorously at work, a community of several million people from Virginia and Kentucky to Texas was primed to express itself in song.

The basic African element has already been described in Part One of this book. Also, it has been shown by competent evidence that this element was not eroded by American slavery. On the contrary, the evidence points to the conclusion that the ruggedness of American slavery developed the African element in new and unexpected ways. The songs, African in root and branch, were charged with new life and new color by the challenges and chemistry of an utterly brutal slave experience. The fact that they were African is attested by President Senghor of Senegal, by Nicholas George Julius Ballanta Taylor, and by other Africans. These incontestable witnesses have affirmed that the identical melodies and the sentiments of many songs have been heard for centuries and can still be heard in the outlying districts of Africa.

How old is this folk community? Alan Lomax estimates "at least 2,000 years," but other estimates say 5,000 years or more. Without question it is the oldest musical folk community on earth. Ballanta Taylor speaks of its slowness to change over the long, long years. He tells also how its music was painstakingly developed over centuries and how it became inextricably intertwined in the lives of all the people. Evidence gained from a recent tour of nine African countries and from Afro-American communities in North and South America and the West Indies clearly proves that, despite changes, the folk community that produced the Afro-American spiritual is still very much alive.

Far from having been wiped out by violence, this folk community was toughened by it. According to Reginald Nettel, the best of the black captives were chosen by traders; the remainder under their control were slaughtered without compunction. H. C. Brearley, writing in W. T. Couch's *Culture in the South*, says that only a third of the Negroes secured in Africa eventually reached the Southern fields. Among many of those finally settled on plantations, the cruelty and brutality of slavery aroused the determination to survive and even to overcome the monster against whom they were pitted. Of course there was a determination by slaveholders to suppress the African inheritance. This campaign was met by an equally determined resistance. More times than not, the resistance triumphed. What was called shiftlessness and perversity was obviously a subtle form of warfare and survival tactics.

What is the geographical range of the community? On the eastern side, stress has been given to West Africa, but Elizabeth Donnan (in her *Documents Illustrative of the History of the Slave Trade to America*) and others tend to say the whole of Africa. Considering the relics of African music in both Americas and in the islands, and considering the kinship of the songs in these areas, one would have to say that the western range was also many thousands of square miles.

The Afro-American spiritual, then, is just one expression of one segment of a very large folk community. The segment which produced the spiritual requires more elaborate definition and description, which are forthcoming. As this elaboration proceeds, however, the overall community, its ancientness, its gradual progress and maturity, its capacity to expand and absorb, and its general toughness and resiliency, should not be forgotten.

⟨ *The Afro-American Blend in the Spiritual Folk Community*

No one can understand any folk song without understanding the peculiar nature and experiences of the general and specific folk communities out of which the song is born. This does not mean that one cannot sing and attribute to it whatever meaning he cares to. But the richness of meanings inherent in folk tradition is available only to those who know the engendering community, its human essence, its standards of value, its impressive experiences, its reaction to impressive experience, its goals and failures, its hopes and defeats, its need for singing, the secrets underlying its song, what it is willing to suffer, what it is willing to fight and die for, its peculiar religion, its sense of community and isolation.

We therefore must turn to the blend of African and American elements that characterized the spiritual folk community. From our definitions of song and folklore in Part One let it be remembered that a folk community dictates and sings the entire range of its deep concern. Often its songs are ritualized, depending on the depth and formality of the concern. Often they are spontaneous, depending on the slant and excitement of given experiences. They are never the borrowed concerns of other people; they are always uniquely the original expression of the community at hand, bathed in its tradition, formed in images respectable to the community at the moment, swept along by its contemporary enthusiasms and its desires for making a special point at a particular time. And because of the need for protecting the community's and each individual's precious thoughts and feelings, they are usually shaped through mask and irony.

Because the number and range of the spirituals are great, it is necessary to display the folk community that spawned them in considerable detail. Before taking up the most significant phase of the community, a few general points must be emphasized.

First is the interlocking relationship between black and white communities. Although the slaveholders were a decided minority (only 7 percent of the Alabama population in 1860 owned slaves), they set the tone for the black relationships. The law and the poorer whites were subservient to them. The mythology which they had to invent and which, in spite of the facts, they firmly believed, controlled everything. They handed it down, or tried to hand it down, to their children. In Bishop Gregoire's book is reference to white children serving an apprenticeship in inhumanity by tormenting black children.

The mythology was partly due to economics and partly to the fact that the slave owner could not control his slaves without it. If he had dealt kindly with his slave, the whole story might have changed. But how does one deal kindly with millions of people who do not want under any circumstances to be slaves? He was probably as generous as he could be, until he found his generosity and his investment confronting each other.

Parts of the mythology were rooted in sheer ignorance. The slave owner's paid historians had told him that blacks were always slaves, and had so been since time began. Bishop Gregoire addressed himself to this point by showing how often blacks had been free and independent, and how often whites had been slaves. The slave owner had also been told that Africa was a land of pagans, heathens, and barbarians. The fact that he was paying his "scholars" to tell him these things is momentarily beside the point. He needed to believe them, and he made the necessary arrangements. How surprised he would have been had he been able to afford a serious look at African history!

Out of the above myths arose the myth that slaves were eternally docile, stupidly happy, and of low intelligence. Herskovits, Borneman, and Elkins have amassed the evidence to destroy this myth, but their late arrival and the fact that they would not have been believed anyway contributed little to the realistic circumstances. Even Elkins has to some extent sided with the happy-slave theory of the Southern dreamer-historian, Ulrich B. Phillips. This he has done in spite of enormous instances of slave revolts, of slave runaways, and of the fears of Southern whites.

The happy-slave theory is the basis for much misinterpretation of the spiritual and its folk community. Along with a capacity for being happy in spite of the brutal treatment they received, the slaves, say these theorists, swallowed in a gulp the white man's version of Christianity. One of these theorists, James Battle Avirett, says that at no time in history was a peasantry so happy as the Negro slaves of America. The slave, he goes on, loyal to his master, closed the fetters upon his own limbs. Avirett's ignorance and stupidity were so useful, however, that he had slaves singing such plantation songs as "Way Down on de Swannee River," "Massa's in de Cole, Cole Groun'," and "Carry Me Back to Old Berginny." The last of this group was written by a black minstrel composer years after slavery had disappeared.

Another happy-slave theorist, Elmer T. Clark, emphasizes the Christian angle. He proclaims it doubtful that any people ever lived so free from want and on a higher moral plane than did people of the old South, black and white. It is a fact beyond dispute, he declares, that slavery took the Negro from the rankest paganism to a Christian civilization. If a Christian civilization meant the use of Christianity to support and expand the most inhuman slave practices in history, then he was right.

Another, and most disturbing, portion of the myth was the belief that the African was ambivalent to family relations. For centuries, the family, alive and dead, had been one of the African's most fundamental faiths. But it was necessary, for the maintenance of internal slave trading, for the slaveholder to believe in this ambivalence. Thus he believed.

Against the background of such mythology the Afro-American folk community developed. It was not a happy community, as mountains of evidence show. In some small respects it accepted Christianity, but not as the white man taught it. It judged the slave owner and his myths by the eternal principles of human right and human justice. For these and other reasons that we are about to unfold, it was a community in perpetual and unyielding conflict.

YOUTH AND RESILIENCY

Frank Tannenbaum is one of many historians who have called attention to the youth of the Negroes put on the slave ships for delivery in the New World. He says the age range was between 16 and 30 years. Slaves under

25 were believed less likely to die of grief. These facts are highly significant to anyone truthfully examining the psychology of the people on the Middle Passage and of those who survived to enter slavery.

The census figures, however, are even more revealing. In 1850, for example, 45 percent of the slaves in the Southern United States were under 15 years of age; 56 percent were under 20; and almost 74 percent were under 30. Slavery was no game for the middle-aged or the elderly. It is, therefore, all the more remarkable that people still interpret the songs of this slave community as though the singers were primarily old folk.

Also in 1850, the median age for Negroes in the United States bond and free, was 17.3, two full years under the figure for whites. The same youth and physical strength that went into the cultivation of the fields and enriched the planter were present in the general energy and mobility of the slaves. Charles Ball, a slave for forty years, said that the work of the slave required mainly superior agility and wakefulness. The same resiliency which enabled a single slave to maintain himself for an extraordinary time under the dehumanizing pressures of slavery and to master a variety of routines, skills, and crafts, produced the vast problems of control. The increase in the patrolling system during the 1850s and 1860s was a vain answer to the slave's youthful and vigorous activity. The determination to run away from slavery, the attempted escapes, and the actual escapes, in the face of a series of almost impossible hurdles, is further witness of this youth and resiliency. The control problem would have been infinitely simplified had the average slave been a few years older and a bit more relaxed.

If we could not prove youth and resiliency from the behavior and testimony of planters and reliable observers, we have much other incontrovertible evidence. For example, a planter dies suddenly and his slaves are put up for auction. The auction catalogue gives names, ages, accustomed employment, and other data concerning each slave. By far the great majority are between 20 and 28 years old. Very rarely did a slave live beyond age 55. The whole number of slaves in a typical probate sale in 1837 was 130. Only three, or about 2 percent, were over 40. Thirty-five females in the group were 16 to 33. Thirteen children were under 13 years of age. One should remember that age 30 under the conditions of American slavery would be roughly equivalent to age 60 or 70 among people today.

More important, though, is to recognize the fact that the folk community of the American slave is predominantly that of tough, resilient, overworked young people, generally in their late teens and twenties. The plantation tradition stereotype of the typical slave is a white-thatched, bald-on-top old man, or a correspondingly elderly old woman, who had grinningly given up on life and thought only of pleasing "ol massa" and "ol mistus" as he stepped gingerly toward the grave. Perhaps this stereotype could have produced the kind of songs the analyst with the plantation tradition mind had conjured up. It is inconceivable that the actual slave could have. He was vigorous, imbued with African pride, utterly uncompromising with the idea of his being a slave for life, young, and determined to improve his lot on this earth before he died.

As early as 1833, John Rankin wrote that the African was not created for slavery. They are, he testified, rational creatures, human, possessing all the original properties of human nature. Men with such properties desire to obtain knowledge, wealth, reputation, liberty, and the vast variety of objects necessary for complete happiness.

One of the ironies of slavery was that the needless brutality and stringency challenged the African to put forth his best efforts in resistance. At this point one does not have to enter the debate of whether the great majority of the slaves accepted things regardless of their personal opinions. The evidence clearly shows that tens of thousands of slaves were mentally and physically rebellious. This activity undoubtedly affected the "peaceful" slave, broke the calm and aroused the fears of the ruling class and of all other whites. The resultant tension was one of the important conditions in the air affecting the creation of the songs.

The youth and resiliency of the African, galvanized into fullest action by the challenges of slavery, were not isolated elements of character. They were part of a combination of personality traits. Thomas Jefferson declared the slave as brave and more adventurous than the white man; he required less sleep and was more transient in grief. Too often the African was known by those characteristics—idleness, deceitfulness, troublemaking —which were part of his campaign to show his disapproval of slavery and to undermine it. Many Southern whites have written of the so-called good slave, the one who did not fight and who was lovable, loyal, brave, and sweet. When unchallenged and undriven by the forcing elements of slavery, the everyday African naturally exuded a spirit of youthful love of life and a recurring desire to live the good life. To fail to consider this sense of youth when interpreting the songs is to engage in perverse distortion.

In her memorable book, *The Homes of the New World*, Fredrika Bremer recommends a journey to the South for three reasons: "to eat bananas, to see the negroes, and hear their songs." Dwelling on the second, she heightens the effects of vitality and resiliency,

> But the negroes are preferable to every thing else. They are the life and the good humor of the South. The more I see of this people, their manners, their disposition, way of talking, of acting, of moving, the more am I convinced that they are a distinct stock in the great human family, and are intended to present a distinct form of the old type man, and this physiognomy is the result of temperament.

Just after slavery was over, observers meeting blacks at close range for the first time echoed their resilient sentiments. One of them, Elizabeth

Kilham, offers an almost statistical reply to a statement that blacks are idle, vicious, weak in body, and with brains half-organized. After close examination, her conclusion is that in these blacks are the qualities of greatness. "They have," she continued, "soul, affection, devotion, music, beyond any other people, and no lack of wit."

SENSITIVITY TO SURROUNDINGS

Only a person who can believe that the African was utterly without feelings can accept the fantasies of some historians about the master-slave relationship or about the slave's personal psychology. Not only would he have to believe that the slave was a literal chattel, incapable of blood reaction to physical and psychological stimuli. He would have to ignore the evidence of thousands of years of keen sensitivity in the African background.

The purpose of the present examination of sensitivity is not to inveigh against slave owners or the slave system. Our concern is entirely with the folk community of the spiritual. Sensitivity to surroundings on the part of that community is a fundamental question in the making of these songs.

Let each reader put himself in the slave's place to whatever extent he can. If you are like most of your colleagues in slavery, you are not only distressed by but indignant over your slavery. On your arrival in the colonies you are sometimes exposed naked, without distinction as to sexes, to brutal examination by your purchasers. You are driven against your will to work from dark to dark. You are often forced to work without any clothes (if Sir Harry Johnston is to be believed). Your food and lodging are subminimal. You hear cloth and shoes referred to as Negro cloth or Negro shoes because of their sleaziness. Your stated name is rarely used; you are generally called upon in burlesque terms or in curse words. You see your closest relatives and friends sold in an instant and forever. You can be sold without being made aware of the fact until your new master comes to pick you up. You are compelled to watch the murderous beatings of your fellow slaves. One of your number was whipped because he cried when he saw his fellow slave and friend beaten to death.

This is just an introduction, but let it serve as a test. You would have to shut your eyes to the legal aspects of your situation, for how could you ever reconcile yourself to the fact that some man or woman owned you, held papers showing that you belonged to him for life and were forced to obey him in every respect, at the expense of being beaten or sold. You are held to strictest account, but no promise ever made to you is binding, legally or otherwise. The fact that you could never understand how such a life was your life would be the beginning of your perpetual sensitivity. In this regard you would be in almost exactly the same situation as those African slaves.

In a recent, highly informative article, "The System of Psychological Control," Gladys M. Fry has demonstrated two other practices of the slave owner that most certainly heightened the slave's sensitivity. One of these was the slave owner's deliberate manipulation of supernatural beliefs for the purpose of control and coercion. The other was the wide use of informers, usually house slaves variously induced to spy and tell. As a result insecurity reigned in all slave gatherings.

As long as there were slaves imported directly from Africa and as long as such slaves had any influence, which was during all of the slavery period, there was strong sensitivity about the comparison between African and American slavery. Nearly all of the slaves brought from Africa came from the middle and upper classes and not from slave groups. But all Africans were aware of the nature of African slavery. As early as 1795, Mungo Park had described African slavery. He had told that slaves outnumbered freemen in a ratio of about three to one, that they were treated with kindness or severity depending on the character of masters, but that custom prevented brutality to slaves. The authority of the master extended only to reasonable correction; a master could not sell a slave without a public trial.

If this kind of slavery had existed in America, there would certainly have been a different type of slave community folk song.

The sensitivity of the slave to raw, deliberate brutality was undoubtedly a factor in preparing his song. The most striking example of such brutality was the floggings by the master or one of his agents, which the slaves, more often than not, were required to observe. Thirty-nine lashes was supposed to be a normal punishment, but on numerous occasions floggings went far beyond that number, sometimes reaching a thousand lashes or more. Following these whippings, which had to be ordered and administered by men of pathological mentalities, other brutalities were piled on. The lacerated body of the whipped man was bathed in salt and red pepper. It was forbidden to apply healing salves of any kind.

Jacob Stroyer describes a situation in which a slave received three hundred lashes from an overseer for disobedience. The overseer called this a "light flogging" and promised more the next time. Assuming the observing slaves to be human beings, what would be the expected reaction among them of watching one human being vigorously applying a heavy strap to the bare body of a fellow human being (who happened to be the same color as the observers) three hundred times!

Interviewed about his life as a slave, Charlie Moses of Brookhaven, Mississippi, summed things up in a great flood of sensitive remembrances:

> Slavery days was bitter an' I can't forgit the sufferin'. Oh, God! I hates 'em, hates 'em. God Almighty never meant for human beings to be animals. Us Niggers has a soul an' a heart an' a min'. We ain't like a dog or a horse.

If one ignores the testimony of observers, Northern and Southern, and sticks to evidence taken from runaway advertisements in Southern newspapers, he can accumulate an amazing haul. Scars from whippings about neck, cheeks, lips, chin, back, arms, thighs, hips could begin the story. When one realizes that the average lash was seven to eight feet long and made of cowhide (or something similarly strong and cutting to human flesh) and that a routine whipping might be seventy to one hundred lashes, one gets a clearer picture. A child of nine or ten might have her flesh cut into strings or her lips glued to her teeth, and often did.

Besides floggings, which (as shown) might be concluded with red pepper or salt rubbed into the wounds, there were tortures of various kinds. Compared to the planters and their employees, ancient and medieval torturers and inquisitors were pikers. Tortures relate to punishments, since they were often the reward and reminder for runaways, but they often also had an identity and a motivation all their own. Note a few of these,

A yellow boy named Jim with a large lock chain around his neck.

A Negress Carolina with a collar which had one prong turned down.

A Negro boy committed to jail wearing a large neck iron, a huge pair of horns, and a large bar of iron on his left leg.

A mulatto with a pair of handcuffs and a pair of drawing chains.

A man named John with a clog of iron on his right foot weighing four or five pounds.

A woman with the letter M burned into her left side.

A man named Henry, his left eye out, some scars from a dirk on and under his left arm, and many whip scars.

A man with shots in his left arm and side.

A girl named Mary with an eye scar, many teeth missing, and the letter A branded on her cheek and forehead.

A man named Jim with a piece cut from each ear and other scars.

A man named Fountain with holes in his ears, a forehead scar, bullet marks in the hind parts of his legs, many whip marks on the back.

Runaway Bill with a dogbite on his leg, scar over his eye, burn on his buttock from a piece of hot iron in the shape of a T.

A man with the tip of his nose bit off.

(In spite, perhaps because, of their hopples and disabilities, all the above were runaways, as reported by the newspapers.)

Iron collars, chains, fetters, handcuffs on slaves were common. No one, except the slaves, paid much attention when a master or his overseer flogged a slave until he was exhausted, rested awhile, and resumed flogging. It was equally uneventful, except to fellow slaves, when a master flogged a slave to death, often for trivial or capricious reasons, cut a slave's throat from ear to ear, tortured him periodically while drinking with friends, or placed the head of a runaway on a pole, starved a proud slave to death, cleft the skull of a slave with an axe, or maimed a female slave who suddenly decided to resist unwanted sexual advances. One planter who owned three hundred slaves generally had one slave trained and assigned exclusively to tracking down runaways. When asked why he had fired his physician for slaves, he replied that it was cheaper to lose a few Negroes every year than to pay a physician. This man was a presidential elector in 1836.

To realize that you have no status in the law and that your master will not be held accountable even for maiming you would arouse sensitivity even in a community lacking in sensitive traditions. In 1851 a Virginia judge ruled that a master could not be indicted for beating his own slave even if the whipping and punishment were "malicious, cruel, and excessive." In a similar case, a South Carolina judge declared that "the criminal offense of assault and battery can not, at common law, be committed upon the person of a slave." Omit for the moment the legal manifestations; concentrate on the feelings aroused in the breast of the slave as he daily contemplates his position.

Frederic Bancroft points to accusations that Negroes were indifferent to family separations through sales. He also records the great amount of refutation available. It should be remembered that these slaves were Africans with an ineradicable sense of family identification. Not even death could break their families; the dead members of the family enhanced rather than forfeited their status. Thus the wrenchings of separation through sales of brothers and sisters, fathers and mothers, husbands and wives, sons and daughters were far keener among these people than among the great majority of folk. This keenness of feeling about family separation is reproduced in hundreds of songs.

Not all the sensitivity was of a bitter kind. Ruby Elzy, born in Pontotoc, Mississippi, who sang Serena in the first *Porgy and Bess*, reports that millions of slave owners had affection, respect, and regard for their slaves, and vice versa. And Clarence Cameron White says that songs created in Maryland and Virginia were lighter and more joyful because slaves changed masters less frequently. There was undoubtedly some truth in both of these observations and in the direction toward which they point. The African was as sensitive to good treatment as he was to bad.

A very large body of testimony supports the view that the African was ingeniously sensitive to pleasant surroundings. Much of this testimony comes from foreign travelers and Northerners, but by far the greatest part of it comes from Southerners. As early as 1793, William Bartram, an Anglo-Irishman, writing of his travels in Georgia in the 1770s, declares, "at the same time, contented and joyful, the sooty sons of Afric forgetting their bondage, in chorus sung the virtues and beneficence of their master in songs of their own composition." In 1838, Caroline Gilman, in her *Recollections of a Southern Matron*, reiterates the theme.

Writing for the *Continental Monthly* in 1863, H. G. Spaulding describes the strong feeling of former slaves for home. In such a home, marriage relations were observed, family ties were knitted together, there was stimulating rivalry among cultivators in the field, and houses were erected by black carpenters. The music was plentiful, and most of it was spirituals.

In 1913, Elizabeth W. Allston Pringle wrote *A Woman Rice Planter*, which she followed in 1922 with *Chronicles of Chicora Wood*. Both of these books contain many proud stories and pictures of slavery worthy of great praise. One of the pictures is of a slave woman "who promised not to war any more." Mrs. Pringle says such things as "Negroes are by nature aristocrats, and have the keenest appreciation and perception of what constitutes a gentleman."

Archibald Rutledge, a patriotic South Carolinian, has written many books containing such sentiments, since 1918. One of his poem titles in *Deep River* (1960) is "Aristocrats of Africa"; and he specifies Ephraim, Amos, Pino, Abel, London, Linus, Lewis, Gabe, Sambo, Rollins, and Gideon. Another poem is called "Black Angel," and it describes "Black Sue Alston" who taught him well. In *God's Children* (1947) he corrects the notion that Negroes are lazy, superstitious, and laissez-faire toward life; he pays tribute to the intelligent Negro. In *It Will Be Daybreak Soon* (1938), he writes of the black man's psychic power, faith, spiritual sagacity, delicate perceptions, and compassion.

Similar thoughts, with accompanying spirituals, emanate from the Gullah sketches of Marcellus S. Whaley, in *The Old Types Pass* (1925) and from Orland Kay Armstrong's *Old Massa's People* (1931), where the old slaves tell their story. One of these old slaves was cook and body servant for Robert E. Lee during the Civil War. Henry William Ravenel's "Recollections of Southern Plantation Life," published in the *Yale Review* for 1936, gives good and bad sides to the picture. He speaks of the Negro's pride and of his refusal to retaliate against bad masters. "Could any other race have passed through it (the temptation of revenge) with clean hands?" But he also declares that the improvidence of the Negro is proverbial.

One of the most outspoken books in this group is Caroline Couper Lovell's *The Golden Isles of Georgia* (1932). Based primarily on the life of Captain Charles Spalding Wylly of Darien, Georgia, it has Negro atmosphere throughout. Loyalty of Negroes to masters, says Mrs. Lovell, is repeatedly proved. Negroes demonstrated fully their intelligence, honesty, and industry. Morris, a trusted slave, had the sense and judgment "of the white race, rather than the black."

Thus, the sensitivity of the African slave is proved to be a balanced sensitivity, appropriate response to the bitterness and the good treatment of whites. The sense of balance in the African community, even under the pressures of slavery, is a cornerstone of the spiritual.

The slave was also aware that slavery cut through racial patterns and was often more economic than racial. In Carl Sandburg's *Abraham Lincoln: The Prairie Years* is reference to the fact that forty-five hundred free Negroes owned slaves as early as 1830; and that a Negro Baptist minister in St. Louis in 1836 owned twenty slaves. The spirituals generally reflect the principles of evil rather than the race or class of the evildoer.

Wherever he could, the African slave violated the laws that deprived him of an education. He was most sensitive to the policies of the slave-holding class that deprived him of the cherished privilege of self-improvement. This sensitivity is exemplified in many songs.

Throughout the slave land, the African was aware of the fight being waged outside to see that he got his freedom. In the eyes of one slave, described by Kate E. R. Pickard, only his free papers made him a man. This awareness was the basis for his personal struggle to be free, often by risking his life and health again and again. His songs reveal that freedom to him was more than a thing he personally desired. It was a dream to be fulfilled throughout the life of man, wherever man lived. It was a song itself. It is remarkable that in the "land of the free and the home of the brave" no literature treats the concepts of freedom with such great respect, endearment, and dedication as the poems created by American slaves.

All these sensitivities the slave sang. As W. L. Hubbard points out, because his song was his sole means of expressing his emotions and feelings, from these songs came the truest judgment of his character and disposition. He sang in the fields, in his cabins, in his secret meetings, in quietude to himself. He did not merely sing his sorrows and his joys. He sang his suppressed hopes and his broken, bleeding heart. He sang his rash resolutions. As his African ancestors had been doing for centuries, he lived to the hilt the cruel life handed him and sang the totality of that life.

RECOGNITION OF RELIGIOUS HYPOCRISY

Although many people, even outstanding scholars, still spread the stories about the African slave's intensive religious background, and the development of spirituals through that background, a careful examination of the facts to their roots will not support these stories. It is absolutely clear that the great majority of slaves never had any conventional religious experience whatsoever. Numerous evangelists and campaigners for the religious instruction of the slaves have proved this point. One of the first was the Reverend Samuel Davies in his *Letters . . . Shewing the State of Religion (Particularly Among the Negroes) in Virginia*, published in London in 1757. He declared flatly that thousands of Negroes in Virginia continue as unconverted as they were in Africa. One hundred and one years later, a report from the *North Carolina Presbyterian* to the *Evangelist*, the national organ of the Presbyterians in America, is called "Instruction of the Colored Population." There is a statement of gratification that the late session of the Orange Presbytery had witnessed interest in regard to the instruction of slaves. But most of the report deals with the "sinful neglect of their spiritual interests" and with the problems involved in bringing whites and blacks together into the church and with preparing the "milk of the Gospel" rather than the "strong meats" for the blacks. Assessing the obvious formidability of these problems one could see that the chances for progress were quite slim. And this was only five years from the end of the slavery period in the United States.

Similar evaluations apply to the Methodists and Baptists, in spite of the great talk about camp meetings. As any minister can tell you, religious involvement is not a question of a few isolated meetings. It is a matter of strong policy by some governing body, of well-conceived plans for carrying out the policy, and of unrelenting hard work in executing the plans. None of these things ever happened on any considerable scale.

As a matter of fact, throughout the slavery period, most Southern whites thought of African slaves as pagans and infidels, incapable of being converted or at least extremely difficult to convert to any American religion. The slaves themselves were told that the Bible cursed them as forlorn descendants of the wrong son of Abraham. Bishop Hopkins' (of the Episcopal Church) letter on this point was "ripped up" by many biblical scholars. A law of Maryland, passed in 1717, prevented Negroes from testifying in court against Christians. Far fewer than 10 percent of the slaves were listed on the books of all the evangelical religions as members or as "having been converted." Even these figures were extremely generous and hopeful.

Sir Harry Johnston compares the attitude toward slavery and religion between North and South America. In 1789 the Spaniards in the South passed an ordinance requiring all slaveholders to instruct their slaves in the principles of Roman Catholicism. Slaves also were required to be baptized during their first year of residence in these Spanish domains. Each slave, under this broad religious ordinance, had a separate bed. Not more than two slaves occupied a single bedroom. An infirmary was required for sick slaves. Debilitated slaves had to be taken care of; they could not be "given liberty" to avoid liability. Masters were instructed to prevent unlawful intercourse and to encourage matrimony. The master could give as punishment a maximum of twenty-five lashes; anyone else beating a slave could be punished. All dead and runaway slaves had to be reported within three days. If such a program had been established and enforced in the United States, the whole picture of slavery and the attitude of the slave toward religion would have been radically different.

All this happened over more than three centuries to a people who belonged to a tradition that was totally religious, and to a people who for thousands of years had faithfully demonstrated their religious susceptibility. Since they were in the market for new concepts, a religion containing the doctrines and precepts of the Christian religion should certainly have appealed to them. Why did it fail to do so?

The answers are extremely simple and well documented. First, the everyday slave never got acquainted with the Christian religion. Standing between him and a knowledge of Christianity were two impenetrable forces: the domineering master and the might of the state. For various reasons the master generally wanted no part of a religious doctrine, and especially the Christian doctrine, to be taught to his slaves en masse. According to Charles Sydnor, writing on *Slavery in Mississippi*, the religious Negro was thought by some planters to be the worst on the plantation. The master was afraid of the power of the very cloak in which he pretended to wrap himself. And the state, dictated to by many slaveholders, was afraid of any congregation of slaves for any purpose. One state declared that five black males in one place constituted a dangerous element and had to be dispersed.

Whereas Timothy Flint records that in Louisiana masters allowed slaves entire liberty to attend public worship, Fredrika Bremer declared flatly that in most places no religious instruction was allowed. Miss Bremer visited a number of the slave states. She does mention the Methodist missionaries who went about preaching the gospel to slaves.

In his doctoral thesis on "The Religious Development of the Negro in Virginia," Joseph Earnest expresses the summary reaction that Virginia merely apologized for the way the slave was treated. There was much display of good intentions but little proof of determination to give the slave or other blacks religious instruction, let alone religious freedom. He offers much supporting evidence. The free Negroes of Richmond, for example, were denied a petition to have their own church, after proving themselves deprived and excluded from other places of public devotion. According to Sir Harry Johnston any meetings of slaves "under pretence of divine worship" might be dispersed and the slaves could receive twenty-five lashes on the bare back without trial. After Nat Turner, the Virginia legislature passed a hard bill prohibiting any Negro ordained, licensed, or otherwise from holding religious or other assemblies at any time. To hold or to attend such a meeting called for thirty-nine lashes.

Innumerable witnesses support Earnest's views, not just for Virginia but for the whole South. Stanley Elkins quotes several of them, including Morgan Godwyn and Marcus W. Jernegan. Elizabeth, a colored minister of the gospel, born in slavery, wrote that where she lived in Maryland there was, for slaves, no preaching and no religious instruction. If a slave wanted to pray, he had to do so in secret behind the haystacks. This fact is illustrated by many spirituals where religion must be practiced in the wilderness or in some other hideaway place.

When the slaves tell their story in the *Slave Narratives*, they reiterate these deprivations of religious instruction. For a few, a master made them go to church, or they could go if they got permission, or they were never forced. For the great majority it was no church allowed, the slaves did not need religion, their owners never made arrangements, the slaves were not allowed freedom of worship. Sir Harry Johnston gives one reason why many slaves did not go to church: Their Sunday holidays were entirely a gift of the master. In South Carolina and Georgia, he says, slaves seldom got their Sunday day of rest except in the slackest winter months. In Phyl Garland's *The Sound of Soul* is a reference to the fact that in the late years of slavery religious meetings were encouraged as a preventive to insurrection. The overwhelming evidence of slave owner practices clearly destroys this opinion.

Linda Brent tells how a slave chapel in her community was spitefully demolished. In 1821, a slave church was closed when it was discovered that reading was being taught. In the records of R. Q. Mallard of New Orleans, a slavery enthusiast, is evidence that as late as 1834 there were only five churches in the slaveholding states built expressly for the use of Negroes. Not a twentieth part of the Negroes attended divine worship on Sundays, there were no Bibles for them, and the blacks depended for their religion mainly on their own color.

One of the chief spurs to the sense of religious hypocrisy among the slaves was the behavior of the men of the cloth. Linda Brent reports that a pastor who has a child by a white woman not his wife was dismissed from his charge; if he has one by a black woman, he is not touched. When a pastor told the slaves that God saw their disobedience of their earthly master and, as their heavenly master, he felt offended, the slaves went home highly amused. They were, no doubt, equally amused when they heard or read that the First General Assembly of the Presbyterian Church in the Confederate States of America refused to condemn slavery as a sin but assumed "the souls of our slaves" as a solemn trust. On the same subject, Nancy Williams, a former slave quoted in *The Negro in Virginia* and quoted again in Julius Lester's *To Be a Slave*, declares,

> That ol' white preachin' wasn't nothin.' . . . Ol' white preacher used to talk with their tongues without saying nothin', but Jesus told us slaves to talk with our hearts.

In the spirituals is much upholding of this view. The slave adopted the symbols of the Christian religion but not the hypocritical practices. He recalled that Christianity had introduced the slave traffic; that, as Linda Brent said, there was a great difference between religion and Christianity; that, as Matlock proves, Christianity in the South was founded in regions where the people were too poor to keep slaves. He was no fool. In many areas he accepted Christianity but only on his terms; he did not accept the white man's broken and bespattered Christianity.

When the master, sometimes under the influence of the mistress, broke down and permitted a few of his slaves to attend church or brought church to them, he carefully censored the doctrine. About all of the Bible most slaves heard, if they heard any of it at all, was Saint Paul's edicts for servants to obey their masters in the Lord. The canned St. Paul service was a staple on hundreds of plantations; and even this was delivered under the watchful eyes of the master's guards. For most masters the rest of the Bible was not good enough or was too good for the slaves.

It is true that many slaves, by learning to read and other devices, learned about the Bible, Old Testament and New. And having learned, they taught their fellows. But the Bible acquired in this fashion was less religious doctrine and more the kind of pithy story the African had been used to for centuries. Many slaves, for example, immediately identified themselves with the Hebrew children. One effect of this method of disseminating the Bible was a questioning of why something so holy and wise, containing so many keys to the good life, was kept from the slave.

This kind of questioning leads into a tremendously significant feature of the mind of the slave community: its sense of religious hypocrisy. If the master had been thinking clearly, he would have reviewed the facts thusly: These people are intelligent enough to master intricate crafts and skills; they do most of the work of running this plantation, which is my source of income and social status; how can they be fooled by our proclaiming Christian principles and living the opposite?

The *Cavalcade of the American Negro* tells us that some masters suffered qualms of conscience trying to reconcile human bondage with Christian ideals. Apparently very few did. In any case, most felt it necessary to avow Christian principles while furthering their inhuman and supremely economic, slavery-propelled enterprises.

Whatever their religious stance and false logic, the slave was not fooled. From thousands of slave testimonies are overt statements and implications, expressing and decrying religious hypocrisy. Many slaves are reported to have agreed with Charles Ball's grandfather. Although he prayed every night, he never went to church (even when permitted) because he held religion in the United States to be false. It was no religion at all, he said. It was the invention of priests and crafty men who hoped to profit by the ignorance and credulity of the multitude. Because of the slave's great respect for religion and its totality in life, it would have been better, if the purpose was to brainwash him, for the master and the other whites to have announced in advance the doctrines which accorded with their practices, and then to have proceeded to go on and live by those announcements.

The slave was also fully aware that this breakdown in religion, as it affected him, permeated the whole life of the governing class. The following statement was written by Thomas Ashe, an Englishman who toured America in 1806; it might well have been written by a slave with the perceptions of a Frederick Douglass, for it expresses the general opinions of most slaves.

> For the southern States, nature has done much, but man little. Society is here in a shameful degeneracy . . . political licentiousness, . . . doctrines here found by experience, to make men turbulent citizens, abandoned Christians, inconstant husbands, unnatural fathers, and treacherous friends.

The incompatibility of the concept and the operation of slavery with any kind of Christian philosophy was doubtless recognized by almost every slave, certainly by many thousands. Most of them believed as John Woolman believed, that slavery was impossible on principle and inconsistent with Christianity. In his incisive paper on "Slavery and Conversion in the American Colonies" (published in the *American Historical Review* for 1916), Marcus W. Jernagen states explicitly that a slavery antagonistic to the conversion of the Negroes won out in the long run. He adds that slavery also prevented important religious advances among the whites.

In the mind of the slave the sense of religious hypocrisy, a part of the air which one breathed, was deepened by the fact that the institutional religions, instead of trying to lead their parishioners away from the inhumanity of slavery, supported slavery at nearly every turn. The Savannah River Baptist Association, for example, voted that the separation of married slaves through one of them being sold away was civilly equivalent to death and "that in the sight of God it would be so viewed." George Whitefield, the great Methodist evangelist and emissary of the Wesleys, urged the Georgia Trustees in 1751 to allow the introduction of slavery. In America, the Church of England never interfered with slavery. And Jernagen reports that a Presbyterian church was presented a slave as an endowment.

All this happened in spite of the fact that many church leaders and ministers were clear and straight in their judgments on slavery. As everyone knows, John Wesley was a determined opponent. In his *Thoughts on Slavery* (1774) he wrote,

> I strike at the root of this complicated villainy. I absolutely deny all slaveholding to be consistent with any degree of natural justice. . . . Liberty is the right of every human creature as soon as he breathes the vital air, and no human law can deprive him of that right.

Writing in his *Diary* two years later, Asbury complained of masters forbidding their slaves religious instruction. Two years after that he wrote: "O Lord, banish the INFERNAL SPIRIT OF SLAVERY [the emphasis is Asbury's] from thy dear Zion."

Under these influences slaveholding was outlawed by Methodist rules in 1784. But the founders of Methodism were completely ignored by their American constituents in later years. Not only did the Georgia Conference in 1838 declare slavery *"not a moral evil,"* but the Maine Conference in 1839 refused to condemn slavery. Meanwhile, the South Carolina legislature passed a law authorizing any person to disperse any Negroes found at Methodist meetings.

In South Carolina and Georgia slaves were sold for church and mission benefits. In certain areas slave houses were searched for Bibles, hymnbooks, and other books. If any were found, a slave was whipped until he told how he came by them. The slave of a Mr. Emerson of Portsmouth, Virginia, was caught praying in the back part of his master's garden; for this offense he received thirty-nine lashes. In spite of the alleged predilection of slaves for religion, on most plantations during most of the slavery period, slaves were not allowed to attend church on Sunday, their only possible day off.

Often the wielders of whips and branding tongs upon slaves were staunch members of the church, even ministers. *American Slavery As It Is* (which used mainly sworn testimony and newspaper clippings) reported the case of a Presbyterian minister who had moved from North Carolina to Georgia. He owned an unusually intelligent slave. He began by whipping this slave unmercifully. Next, he nearly drowned him as a punishment. He then put him in an ingenious type of stocks (made by manipulating the corner of a worm fence). There his slave with the uncommon mind died. Apparently unconcerned, the minister went on with his preaching.

A Kentucky Methodist preacher is reported as having taken, among other produce, five slaves to New Orleans and having sold them there. Coming up to Natchez, he purchased seven more slaves and sold them also. His gospel preaching, meanwhile, was uninterrupted. When fellow passengers aboard a river boat who had seen him in the "slave shambles" of Natchez and New Orleans learned that he was a minister, they had much sport at the expense of "the fine old preacher who dealt in slaves."

One Charleston lady, a staunch Presbyterian church member, flogged at least one slave every day. She kept "pancake sticks" (cowhides in small paddles) in four different apartments of her house and used them for small offenses, or for no fault at all. After a revival meeting in 1825 she opened her house to social prayer meetings. The room assigned to these meetings had been regularly used for two things: (1) her only devotions three times a day, and (2) the thrashing of her slaves who often lost large pieces of flesh. She thought it entirely proper to send her "unruly" slaves to prison, to be worked on the treadmill or to be more thoroughly flogged than she she was capable of doing. When these beaten slaves returned, they were kept out of the house until they were rid of the unendurable smell arising from their wounds.

This kind of practical evidence of the everyday workings of religion was far more impressive upon the slave's attitude toward religion than the propaganda culled from the Bible about servants obeying their masters in the Lord, the slave catechisms (one of which was reprinted in *Frederick Douglass' Paper* in 1854 from the *Southern Episcopalian* of Charleston, South Carolina, stressing God's gift of master and mistress and the slave's need to obey his masters, do his work, and avoid wickedness and laziness), and the windy theology of camp meetings.

Although the slave maintained a definite religious faith, based on his broad background and his selective borrowings from American religions, he was not "taken in" by American protestations, unsupported and flatly denied by practice. The religious supports of the spiritual are thus unique.

They, however, definitely decry American hypocrisies in religion. And they are rooted in the comprehensive concept of religion practiced for centuries by the African.

RECOGNITION OF LEGAL HYPOCRISY

Surrounded by religious hypocrisy, the African slave was even more bothered and worried by legal hypocrisy. Regardless of what whites thought (and think), the African was a proud man. He had every reason to be. His tradition had led him to believe in the importance of human identity. The accident of slavery, which he generally accepted as temporary, had no effect upon this belief. On top of this, he was a producer, the major producer of his community. Why should he not think highly of himself?

And yet, in the eyes of the white man's law, he was nothing. He had no rights whatsoever. He had no status in court, except to testify against another slave. One legal opinion held that a slave's word was assessed at the same value as "the cry of an animal." Someone else determined what kind of labor he should perform, what kind of treatment he should receive, what kind and how much food, clothing, and other necessaries he should have. Howell Henry reports that there were laws against his becoming a skilled craftsman, even when he had the ability.

Aside from being a nonentity in the general law, he was subject to the strictures of his local despot, the slaveholder, who made and executed his own law. In *DeBow's Review* for 1856, one commentator writes,

> It is true he is amenable to public opinion and any flagrant outrage is visited by the laws; but there are a thousand incidents of plantation life concealed from public view which the law cannot reach.

This legal nonentity was incapable of owning anything—the state of North Carolina once passed a law specifically preventing him from owning any animal. He was incapable of any contract, even matrimony—all slave marriages were fictional and at the convenience of the existing master. He found himself the occasion of laws which said that his being baptized had no effect upon his bondage. At any moment he was subject to being sold, mortgaged, leased, even against his master's wishes if the legal necessity demanded. As already pointed out, and as further attested by Richard Hildreth, he was surrounded by spies and informers, in defiance of any true legal process. A Florida law prevented him from hiring his own time under any circumstances. A law passed in Tennessee in 1839 was called "an act to prohibit the practice of permitting slaves to act as if they were free."

However injured, except by another slave, he had no redress. Though constantly accused, he was without legal or quasi-legal defense. Howell Henry, a Southerner, admits that accusations of low intelligence, deformed character, and bad behavior against Negroes were often no more than a defense of the slave system; and further, that precautions against these items offered opportunities for delinquency among whites.

The great contribution of the slave system to destroying the manhood of Southern whites is often an occasion for sadness on the part of visitors. Fredrika Bremer declares that the curse of slavery has warped the sense of truth and degraded the moral nature of the whites. The South is far behind the North in moral and intellectual culture because of slavery. The fetters of the slave bind, more or less, all and everyone.

She even states that slavery degrades the white man more than it does the black. It works, she goes on, against his judgment and the education of his children. Men otherwise amiable and attractive are unjust and severe to slaves. There are very few good and tender masters. Passion and insanity in the treatment of slaves is common.

The tribunals of Carolina and the better class of the community, she asserts, have fresh in memory the deeds of cruelty done upon house slaves, which rival the worst abominations of heathen times. Some of the blackest deeds are done by women in the higher class of Charleston society. Public tribunals take cognizance only of cruelties too horrible and public to pass over.

As a slave you were fully cognizant of the fact that if you were beaten to death by your master or his overseer, or if you were mistaken for another slave and met death in the street from a vicious white attacker you had never seen before, the chances of anyone's being punished for your death were nil. Not until 1821, in South Carolina, was murder of a slave made punishable by death; even then, if the deed was committed in sudden heat and passion, the penalty was $500 fine and six months in jail. You were sometimes deliberately worked to death in the pestilential rice swamps on the theory that it was more economical to get all the work you had in you in a few years than to have you hang on to an invalid and mildly expensive old age.

Your whole legal system inhered in one man—your master. It was he who dominated the legislatures and got all the laws passed. It was his overseer who held court every morning on the plantation, often assessing punishment on the basis of personal feelings. It was his wife who on one occasion, as reported by John Rankin, pulled from the socket the eyeball of a black cook.

The legal prerogatives of your master are almost beyond bounds. As you have seen, he does not hesitate to stab, shoot, hang, or burn the best beloved of his servants if his control is endangered. In one instance in Livingston County, Kentucky, as you have probably heard, a master called his slaves together. He produced his bound slave George. With a broad axe he chopped him up, throwing piece after piece into the fire. Meanwhile he lectured his slaves, threatening like punishment to all who disobeyed, ran away, or even talked of the present incident.

As you well know, if a slave dies while being "corrected," his death is no felony. The law says that it cannot be presumed that malice would induce a man to destroy his own estate. As you also know, maiming was a part of the law. In North Carolina (in 1741) false testimony of a slave could result in his having both ears nailed to a pillory, and then cut off; followed by thirty-nine lashes. You have seen your fellow slaves whipped to death by master and overseer and, if not to death, whipped unmercifully by patrollers. You have seen circumstances such as that related by Uncle Israel, Dorothy Scarborough's friend in Louisiana, when "ol' marse" would grease his slaves down with tallow and whip them until the blood ran down; then he would spread tallow over them and hold a candle to it and burn them.

Perhaps you have not read the record, but you are well aware of the general circumstances of other slave punishments. After many years of study, Sir Harry Johnston records, for example, that in Virginia there were sixty-eight capital crimes for slaves, and only one for whites; in Mississippi thirty-eight capital crimes for slaves, which if committed by whites called for fine or punishment; in Alabama, for slaves death for almost every offense, and no offense for which death was prescribed for whites. As late as 1856, the Maryland Constitution required that a black man convicted of murder would first have his hand cut off, then he would be hanged, then beheaded, then quartered, and finally have his head and quarters nailed up in a public place. You know of "nigger dogs" (a cross between a Spanish bloodhound and a mongrel) and their being trained to hate all black people; and how, if they catch up to a runaway, they are allowed to bite and tear him to satisfy their rage. You know, also, that in spite of these dogs and all other terrors, you and large numbers of your community continued to run away, to freedom!

It is true that occasionally a white man, even a master, was tried for murdering a slave. In the term of 1821, the Honorable J. G. Clarke of the Mississippi Supreme Court handed down a decision against Isaac Jones, accused of slave murder, containing these high-sounding sentences:

> Has the slave no rights, because he is deprived of his freedom? He is still a human being, and possesses all those rights, of which he is not deprived by the positive provisions of the law . . . but no law gives master power over the life of a slave. The slave is a *reasonable creature*, i.e., a human being. They cannot be murdered with impunity.

Justice Clarke then overruled the motion to arrest judgment and sentenced Isaac Jones to hang on July 27, 1821. But there is no record that Isaac Jones was ever hanged.

In a notable case reported by Helen T. Catterall, taken from the statutes of the state of Georgia for June 1857, a runaway girl, 13 years old, was given between four hundred and a thousand licks by an overseer using a three-ply leather strap. At times, he turned her on all fours, at times head down, at times head up. He kept whipping her after white froth appeared on her lips (says he thought she was "possoming"). Indicted for murder, he was convicted of involuntary manslaughter and recommended to the mercy of the court.

You are now musing over your legal predicament as a slave. You remember that slavery is hereditary and perpetual. You recall the laws that deny you the benefits of any kind of education, even learning to read and write. If you do not recall the reasons why, you may profit from a reminder by J. Lumpkin, quoting from a Georgia statute of 1853:

> The *Status* of the African in Georgia, whether bond or free, is such that he has no civil, social or political rights or capacity, whatever, except such as are bestowed on him by Statute. . . . A white man is liable to a fine of five hundred dollars and imprisonment . . . for teaching a *free* negro to read and write; and if one *free* negro teach another, he is punishable by fine and whipping, or fine or whipping, . . . these severe restrictions . . . have my hearty and cordial approval. . . . Everything must be interdicted which is calculated to render the slave discontented.

It is obvious that Mr. Lumpkin does not credit the black man with feelings or human desires.

If the slave had shown no feelings about all these things, the multiplication in the slave states of laws demanding his respect for whiteness would hardly have taken place. By law, the slave had no right of self-defense against any white person; by law in Virginia, in 1748, a slave received thirty lashes for merely lifting his hand against a white person; by law in Texas, a slave or a free person of color was punished with stripes for abusive language to whites.

All this happened in a country where the slave heard people perpetually proclaim the land to be the "land of the free." Assume the densest ignorance on the part of the slave (and rule out the possibility of explaining his management of the plantation and the high performance of thousands of runaways), and you would have some sense inside him of the legal hypocrisy under which he lived. Assume the African as he was, and you had a welter of such feelings. Assume men and women with the character requirements for making the spirituals, and you get the deep sense of legal hypocrisy plus the philosophic and artistic skill to put things in perspective.

From the tens of thousands of variant records there is little doubt that the slave, generally speaking, was a free man at heart. He felt that he was entitled to freedom of movement. Freedom was meaningful to him. He observed it in the possession of people around whom he esteemed no better than, and often not as good as, himself. Not least, he was impressed by the fact that he was living in a free country, a country founded on the idea of freedom, a country in which the word *freedom* was the greatest in the vocabulary. He alone was denied it at every turn. Even a famous Episcopal bishop from Vermont, writing about slavery, said that the Declaration of Independence was no part of the then American system.

For him alone, according to a Southern Carolina statute quoted by Catterall, the word *Negro* had a fixed meaning—*slave*. Even the national capital, according to Bancroft, was the seat and center of slave marketry.

The idea of freedom was antagonistic to the color of the skin. Manumission was severely restricted in most states. In Mississippi, in 1842, any free Negro entering the state could be sold out of hand. Henry states that a free Negro with good evidence had trouble withstanding a challenge to his freedom in court. On the authority of Francis Butler Simkins, free Negroes kidnapped for the slave trade were as numerous as slaves who escaped bondage by flight, meaning that the number was up in the hundreds of thousands. In spite of all this, Miss Bremer says that the slave population increased daily in numbers and intelligence through the influence of free blacks and mulattoes.

The movement of all blacks was severely restricted. Passes were required everywhere; impromptu regulations of the patrollers endangered any black man in the street. With the smallest provocation the policeman and the justice of the peace could arrest and jail any black man for drunkenness. A Kentucky law of 1838 prohibited Negroes from traveling. A Maryland law of 1841–42 made it a felony for free Negroes to receive even slightly suspicious papers in the mail. A Charleston, South Carolina, ordinance of 1813 prohibited Negroes from swearing, smoking, or walking with a cane in the streets; or from dancing or parading without permission of the city's wardens. In 1848 an ordinance passed in Charleston prevented any blacks from going into a park without the master's or the employer's permission.

Is there any wonder that freedom was the outstanding theme of the spirituals?

In line with the religious fears described above, any kind of congregation of slaves produced panic in the heart of the white brother. In 1802, the Corporation of the District of Columbia acted to restrain night meetings of slaves, free Negroes, and mulattoes. A penalty of forty stripes was placed upon the violator. An Alabama law of 1832 specified that slaves could attend religious services conducted by whites, but could not preach to other slaves unless licensed by some neighboring religious society and before five respectable slaveholders.

In spite of all these restrictions, and perhaps because the restriction had irresistibly aroused their sense of freedom, the slaves often broke loose. In defiance of specific laws, they learned to read and write, they worked at forbidden employment, and they married and had families. In spite of articles keeping attendance at funerals down to fifteen or twenty persons, three to four hundred Negroes would use the funeral to congregate. And the secret meeting of large groups of slaves, cradle and inspiration for many a spiritual, was a commonplace.

SKILLS AND TALENTS

It is not remarkable that many of the spirituals are directly or indirectly concerned with skills and talents. For the African slave a large and important part of living was fulfilling the gifts with which he was endowed. Since slavery seemed inevitable, at least for the foreseeable future, many slaves were determined to make the most of it. A major reason for running away was the utter lack of opportunity to discover and develop natural endowments.

In his descriptions of his travels in the interior districts of Africa, Mungo Park (in the late eighteenth century) had often referred to the unusual gifts of the Africans. He spoke of their practicing their own arts of making gunpowder. He said that most African blacksmiths were acquainted with a method of smelting gold. Naturally, he had many comments on their love and perpetual practice of music and their taste for poetry.

Even before Mungo Park was in Africa, Nicholas Cresswell toured the South. In his journal, covering the years 1774 to 1777, he mentions the unique agricultural gifts, in growing tobacco, wheat, and Indian corn, of the Negroes in Nanjemoy, Maryland.

In his *History of Louisiana*, Charles Gayarré refers to the military talents of the blacks. In the Battle of New Orleans, he recalled, there were black troops on both sides. After the battle there were negotiations to return slaves who had run away from the British.

The classified advertising sections of Southern papers rarely failed to include reference to black skilled workers. The *Alabama State Sentinel* (of Selma) of January 9, 1855, carried a request for Negro men to work with the Selma and Woodville Railroad for the balance of the year: liberal wages and monthly payments are promised. It is well known that slave laborers built track all over the South; in Georgia alone they built more than a thousand miles of railroad. On the other hand, the *American Beacon and Norfolk and Portsmouth* (Virginia) *Daily Advertiser* of January 3, 1825, offers four excellent Negro bakers and a house carpenter for hire for the balance of the year.

In advertising for the return of their runaways, slave owners have laid bare a great array of talents. A long article in the *Journal of Negro History* entitled "Eighteenth-Century Slaves as Advertised by Their Masters" spends all its time building up this picture. Slaves were described as "exceedingly artful," capable of speaking properly and well and of "telling a plausible tale." Many, it was admitted, could read and write; some could preach and print; some could cobble and drive carriages; some could shave and dress hair. Two or three were tailors and sawyers by trade.

A great many played instruments, fiddles and fifes especially. The languages they could speak covered a wide range: Dutch, French, Swedish, to mention a few. It was clearly indicated that they could sustain themselves in the make-believe role of free men because they were competently self-educated and excellent actors.

Aside from singing talents of slaves, which were proverbial, there is often mention of their instrumental talents. In Frederick Law Olmsted's *A Journey in the Seaboard Slave States* is the announcement that there were Negro bands, often of great excellence, in all Southern cities. One group of runaway slaves was good enough to band together as "scientific musicians" in 1847 and to play its way out of Louisville to Cincinnati and Canada.

In the competent histories of slavery and the Negro is a much fuller story of the slave artisan, skilled worker, and craftsman. In the West Indies, nine-tenths of the mechanics were black slaves. In the United States well-skilled slaves worked on the plantation and in the urban centers. John Hope Franklin places more than one-tenth of the slaves in 1850 in urban communities. Describing town slaves in Mississippi, Sydnor says that they were found in foundries; tin, copper, sheet iron, and brass works; saddle and harness manufactories; cotton gins and cotton mills; brick, lumber, shingle, boot, and shoe factories; on railroads and in river transportation.

In South Carolina the slave boys worked as apprentice cabinetmakers along with white boys. They ranged from part-time specialists on the small plantations to managerial functions on the large plantations. The slave was the backbone of agriculture and industry in the South.

By combining the lists of Professors Franklin and Stampp, one gets the following catalogue of positions involving some medium or great skill in which slaves were regularly engaged: blacksmiths, brickmakers, business directors, butlers, cabinetmakers, carpenters, chair spinners, chambermaids, children's nurses, coachmen, cooks, coopers, draymen, engineers, footmen, gardeners, hostlers, housemaids, hucksters, inventors, labor foremen, landscapers, laundresses, lumberers, mechanics, millers, mine operators, painters, personal (body) servants, plasterers, production managers, seamstresses, shoemakers and bootmakers, stevedores, stone masons, tailors, turpentine producers, weavers, and wheelwrights. Besides these occupations, slaves worked in bakehouses, on cotton presses, in ditching, on docks, in hotels, on iron furnaces, with livestock, in mills, on railroads, in saltworks and shipyards, on steamships, and in tanneries, tobacco factories, and warehouses.

To the above list C. L. R. James adds dyers, tanners, and makers of things on the plantation from nails to plowshares. In Frederick Douglass one reads of cart menders and grinders along with many other craftsmen. From other sources one can add woodcutters, quarry workers, deckhands and firemen on river boats, construction and maintenance workers, and canal, navigation, and bridge workers.

Professor Franklin says that the number of slave carpenters in Charleston in 1848 was greater than the number of carpenters who were free Negroes or whites. In the field of invention, he mentions Henry Blair of Maryland, who was given patents on corn harvesters in 1835 and 1836.

Lewis C. Gray has testified that under the severe conditions of rice and indigo cultivation, black labor was superior to white. Quoting Parkinson, he called them "the best servants in America." They had clearly demonstrated their ability to operate factory machines. On the plantations their advice was often requested by their masters.

The slave was deeply desirous of being trained for a skill. He considered his talents a precious thing. And the spirituals of his community reflect in significant and beautiful ways this special standard of value.

OCCUPATIONAL SINGING

In line with a keen sense of being possessed of skills and talents and of developing them, the African slave produced much music through them. Gilbert Chase, the music historian, puts strong emphasis upon the Afro-American's desire to sing while working; he says the religious motivation has been overstressed. In some occupations the ability to sing, and to sing in a certain way, was a badge of membership. Almost none of the boatmen or railroad workers was without an appropriate song. Josiah H. Combs speaks of occupational songs of the Negroes which were adapted by Highlanders.

If one were choosing the outstanding occupation for singing spirituals and other songs it would have to be that associated with the boats, the ships, the rivers, and the sea. In *The Myth of the Negro Past* (and in other works), Melville J. Herskovits has pointed out the African identification with water and the ways in which that identification has passed over to the Afro-American. The evidence from the spirituals offers impressive support. Here is a small roll call of researchers in the field:

Mary Dixon Arrowood and Thomas Hoffman Hamilton
> Spirituals sung by boatmen: "Bredren, Don' Git Weary," "Roll, Jordan," and "De Ship Is in de Harbor"

Thomas Ashe
> Reference to boathands singing "The Beauteous Month of May" in paddle cadence

William E. Barton
> Constant recurrence of "Old Ship of Zion" hymns on his extensive tour in search of spirituals in the late 1890s

John Mason Brown (who wrote "Songs of the Slave" in 1868)
> Also reference to many ship hymns and to songs that came from Negro crews, especially firemen, on steamboats in the West and South for years

W. (William) Faux
> Songs of galley slaves, regulated by the motion of the oars

Frances Anne (Fanny) Kemble
> Chants of steersmen, in time with the stroke

"Letter from St. Helena's Island" (by C. F.)
> Songs of her rowers when she first came in from Beaufort, their own songs, "peculiarly wild and seldom," sung with singular swaying body motion which made the songs more effective

Caroline Couper Lovell
   Singing of the Negroes rowing up and down the Altamaha
Sir Charles Lyell
   Black oarsmen making moods echo to their song; improvised verses; an
   occasional Methodist hymn; one of them took the lead, improvised verse
   complimenting the master's family and a celebrated black beauty of the
   neighborhood, the other five joined the chorus (According to Jay B. Hub-
   bell, who presented Lyell's descriptions in a separate article, their songs
   reflect the high efficiency standards of the boatmen.)
James Miller McKim
   Many boat songs
William Wyndham Malet
   Boatmen's epic song with women's voices mingling
Frederick Law Olmsted
   Boathand singing in Louisiana
Elizabeth W. Allston Pringle
   Nothing like rhythm and swing of Negro boat songs from six splendid
   oarsmen
Reviewer in the *Nation* (1867)
   "Then there is the quaint 'O Deat' he is a 'Little Man,' which we remember
   ourselves to have heard sung by a crew rowing across the ferry between
   St. Helena and Beaufort. The fugle man on that occasion—a fellow of inky
   blackness, with the sweat of a summer's day streaming from every pore, and
   his eyes squinted under the sun's glare—can never be forgotten as he poured
   forth energetically, 'O Lord, remember me; *do,* Lord, remember me!' "
Mary Wheeler
   The spirituals in her "Folk Songs of the River Packet Era" from her *Steamboatin' Days*

Great as they were, the singing boatmen were only part of the story.
There were army slants on songs from singing soldiers. There were spirituals from cornshuckers and cotton field hands, delivered in their peculiar
ways. There were family songs. There were harvest songs from farm
workers. There were songs by humorists, lovers, and outlaws, potato
workers, railroad workers, rice workers, sawmill workers, sugar field
workers, and tobacco workers, waiters, and wheat grinders. *The Negro in
Virginia* tells of slaves singing while hoeing potatoes; E. F. Murphy describes songs arising from rice swamps and sugar bottoms; Natalie Burlin
tells of illiterate and ignorant black laborers sorting tobacco leaves in a big
tobacco factory—crude and primitive in looks and speech but their collected voices never sweeter or more appealing; Lemmerman reports tobacco group singing where three or four songs were in the air simultaneously; and James McKim recalls workers grinding at the mill in time to
hand music.

In spite of the richness of his occupational singing, the slave never forgot
that he was a member of a community and that in the community was his

real strength and protection. The most typical community song was probably the shout song, which Abigail M. H. Christensen traces from Africa. In the shout spiritual, which was really a dance, the group clapped hands, urged one another on by name and invited nonparticipants to join in.

The Afro-American community song had considerable range. Not only did it take care of funerals and of slaves who had served terms in jail (note the "Paul and Silas" series), but it was also the backbone of the Christmas celebration. It had in its repertory marrying songs. It even had songs to commiserate with the fellow who got a hundred lashes and a short peck of corn. C. Alphonso Smith writes that the Negro hymn, which can last all night in a well-knit community, is the best example of a communal composition in the United States.

In a sense, community singing was occupational. In living through a thing like slavery, the task of keeping up the morale and the fighting spirit of the group is a regular job for each member. He must devote his imagination and time and energy to it. In many spirituals this job is reflected. Without the need for invigorating the community, there would probably never have been a spiritual.

EDUCATION

For thousands of slaves the desire for education was the strongest of desires. In many slave narratives and commentaries the point is made that facing the future without education was the most unbearable part of slavery. It motivated innumerable escapes and attempts to escape.

It is true that reading and writing were not generally a part of the educational system in Africa. This fact did not mean that there was no education. The African child was very carefully educated in the most exacting ways. Vocational training was pursued with systems of apprenticeship and other methods of inducting the young into gainful employments. Mungo Park, among many others, has told how deeply the Negro loved instruction. When education is defined as enlightened training for a place in society and for the individual's personal development, it was a thing highly respected in Africa. It must be remembered, also, that the slave came from the middle and upper classes of African society. And the Afro-American continued and intensified the respect for education.

The Afro-American's great desire to read and write was two things at least: It was recognition of what he would need to compete in the new world to which he had been brought and it was in line with his determination to develop his skills and talents. In the mid-eighteenth century the Reverend Samuel Davies wrote of the eagerness of the Negroes he had met to learn to read.

Several perceptive writers have drawn clear inferences about the educational outlook of slaves from an analysis of their lives. In John Rankin's work one reads that the African, by weathering slavery, has exhibited strong mental capacity. Russell Ames tells us that, if unlettered working people produce art of high quality, hard experience has hammered realism, wisdom, and ironic humor into their heads.

People with such skills as those we have just described had the implicit intelligence that warranted education. The power structure of the plantation South was determined, out of pure fear, to limit or prevent this deserved education. "Knowledge and slavery are incompatible," wrote a citizen in Woodville, Mississippi, in 1832. In the methods they used to deprive the slave, as Hildreth has shown, they set up a strong barrier against education for all whites.

The Maryland code in 1683 stated that "the inhabitants shall have all their rights and liberties according to the great charter of England"; and, further, "all Christian inhabitants (slaves excepted) to have and enjoy all such rights, liberties, immunities, privileges and free customs," et cetera! The fact that slaves were highly sensitive to this exception among Christian inhabitants all over slave country, and highly resentful too, has been often ignored even by Negro historians.

Shortly after the Nat Turner uprising a delegate arose in the Virginia legislature and frankly admitted,

> We have as far as possible closed every avenue by which light may enter slaves' minds. If we could extinguish the capacity to see the light our work would be completed; they would then be on a level with the beasts of the field.

Out of one side of their mouths the slave owning powers said that such education would be useless, since the barbaric slave was utterly incapable of absorbing it. Out of the opposite side they worked hard to prevent education for fear it would lead to dissatisfaction, insurrection, rebellion, and "manifest injury of the citizens" (as an act to prevent the teaching of slaves, passed in North Carolina in 1830, put it). In late years of slavery, the fear that slaves would read abolitionist literature was given as a reason for preventing education. Punishments for teaching slaves to read ranged from fines for whites to death for Negroes in Alabama and Louisiana. As early as 1804 in Virginia it was no longer lawful for overseers of the poor to require master or mistress to teach black or mulatto orphans reading, writing, and arithmetic. Also in 1838 educated free Negroes were prohibited by law from returning to Virginia.

In spite of these restrictions John Hope Franklin reports that many slaves got educated. He quoted one observer who said that one of every fifty slaves in the Southwest could read and write, and another observer who estimated that five thousand of Georgia's four hundred thousand slaves were literate.

On the word of Francis Butler Simkins, in *A History of the South*, slaves overrode prohibitive laws and learned to read and write. Sydnor says that even in Mississippi many slaves learned to read. One Mississippian advertised in a weekly paper (in 1818) a school for blacks. He was told he could be fined $30 or be imprisoned for thirty days and given thirty-nine lashes. In Mississippi and elsewhere slaves were teaching themselves and receiving pointers from their fellows. Linda Brent tells of a black man, age 53, who all his life had wanted to read more than anything else. He begged her to teach him. She taught him. Allen W. Read concludes that during the colonial period the success of the black man in learning English was equal to that of any other immigrant body. And as C. L. R. James has reminded us, the Bible was the most readily available book. "It was," as he says, "a course in the alphabet, a first reader, and a series of lessons in the history of mankind." It is most ironic that the people who prided themselves so greatly on being a Christian nation and section should exert such brutal force to prevent their charges from learning to read the Bible.

Concerning the slave's ability to learn when given the opportunity, many writers have commented. Most say his learning power was considerable. Certainly one reason for this progress was an almost overwhelming motivation. Timothy Flint said that slaves were quick of apprehension and that they learned to read faster than whites. It would be difficult, though, he said, to teach them arithmetic.

Frederick Douglass and other ex-slaves who gained education, chiefly through self-teaching, have testified as to the desire of slaves to command the benefits and broad outlook which education conferred. They have also spoken of help they received from whites. It is notable that the laws often paid respect to such whites and, at the same time, threatened them with penalties. In Douglass's case, a kind mistress (Mrs. Auld) had taught him, out of sheer humanity, to read and write. When her husband convinced her that slavery and education were incompatible with each other, she tried to undo her teaching. She snatched away from him a newspaper or book he was quietly reading and scolded him for his persistence. But like many slaves with quick minds, Douglass had gone too far to turn back. As he puts it,

> In teaching me the alphabet, in the days of her simplicity and kindness, my mistress had given me the "inch," and now, no ordinary precaution could prevent me from taking the "ell."

Douglass persisted most stubbornly, carrying a copy of Webster's spelling book in his pocket, having his white playmates "review" him in vocabulary, and otherwise enlarging his educational horizons. In these respects and in defiance of the stereotype, the comprehensive evidence shows him to be a sample of many thousands who learned by various means to read. Thousands more yearned for the opportunity.

The impact of education upon assembled Negroes was anticipated partly because of actual cases in which educated Negroes proved hard to handle or ran away, and partly because of assorted fears. Howell M. Henry in *The Police Control of the Slave in South Carolina* devotes a whole chapter to "Negro Gatherings for Religious and Social Purposes" and another to "Slave Insurrections." Under the latter he describes an act of 1800 which made all assemblages of slaves and free Negroes for mental instruction unlawful, even with whites present, if held behind closed doors. No meetings could be held between sunset and sunrise. This law interfered with Methodist meetings, especially class meetings. It was strengthened several times, particularly in 1837, obviously in response to growing anticipations. Hurd also lists an Alabama law of 1832 that prohibited the attempt to teach any slave or free person of color to spell, read, or write.

The most chilling fears about the slave's education arose from slave uprisings the leaders of which were often literate and sometimes well educated. Following the Nat Turner insurrection in 1831 and the dissemination of the information that Nat was an enormous reader who knew the Bible almost by heart, the state legislatures of the South were busy passing laws to forestall any semblance of slave education. The blood of each one of the sixty to eighty whites slaughtered by Nat's hand was assigned to the set of circumstances under which Nat had learned to read. Throughout the South slaves suspected of education were detected, tortured, and killed for no other reason than their dangerous literacy. Negro meetings were further restricted, even funerals, after it was learned that Nat had used funerals to reach three to four hundred slaves at a time; attendance at funerals was kept down to fifteen or twenty. Following the abortive Vesey revolt, free Negroes (Vesey was free) were denied the right to hold meetings.

On a smaller scale Jacob Stroyer testifies that his owners were shocked when they learned that he could read. After he had run away to freedom, he wrote a book and announced that the proceeds from sales would be used to further his education. Tom Fletcher relates that his grandmother's greatest ambition was to learn to read the Bible. Following the practice of many house servants, he was taught by white children.

The slave preacher has been often described as a man with an unusual storehouse of information, general and special, whether he could read or not. The very famous John Jasper, a black preacher of the late nineteenth century, tells how as a slave he "thusted for de bread uv learnin'." Although books were sealed to him, he longed to break the seal. A fellow slave finally taught him from the *New York Spelling Book*. He also learned to read the Bible. Several writers have said that the slave preacher was one of the first slaves to learn to read; one writer voices a strong suspicion that most spirituals were written by slave preachers.

Allison Davis wrote that the ancestors of the Afro-American left him this heritage, "the determination to survive and to wrest a home and education for their children from a hostile environment." And in his highly significant book, *The Education of the Negro Prior to 1861*, Carter G. Woodson has two compelling chapters, "Learning in Spite of Opposition" and "Education as a Right of Man." Both are directly in line with the predominant spirit of the slave folk community.

When the slave was unable to get formal education (and sometimes when he was able), he often cultivated memory as a substitute. Besides learning to read, Fletcher's grandmother would often select a chapter of the Bible and memorize it. Bernard Robb, in *Welcum Hinges*, writes of a former slave named Uncle Woodson who could not read, but who knew by heart large portions of the Bible and of the Episcopal service.

The slave preacher was famous for his memory, especially of great and dramatic portions of the Bible. Ball, Earnest, Sydnor, and others have cited innumerable cases. By embellishing these, he could maintain complete control of his service and congregation. No doubt many of the makers of spirituals were poets who remembered striking passages from the Bible and from other literature and used them effectively.

As Frederick Douglass proved, and delineates in his autobiography, learning to read and write and otherwise educating oneself were among the slave's sharpest weapons in his fight against slavery. Of course it was dangerous to be caught with a book. By using care and taking advantage of every opportunity, the slave could master reading. There was usually some friendly white person, or at times another slave or free Negro, who was willing to teach him how to write. Once he had captured writing and reading he was already on his way out of the most abject slavery. At the very least, he could write passes for himself and read signs on his route to freedom. Remember, though, that the everyday slave was not really an illiterate. His expression in conversation, story-telling, proverb, song, and other folklore were a strong form of literacy. Not only did he communicate; he left a sharp impression, often an impression of wisdom. The songs he created went far beyond the one language he was taught to use; they spoke, and still speak, in a universal tongue both in melody and in thought. Formal education the slave saw not as a means of getting started but as a weapon for intensifying and coordinating his natural gifts.

The attitude of the folk community toward the enlarging power of education is clearly reflected in numerous spirituals. Spirituals about books, letters, reading and writing, about souls shining in a new environment where opportunities for personal expansion are great, were enthusiastically composed and sung. From thinly veiled songs like "I Know I Would Like to Read," in Fenner's Hampton series, to broad symbolisms like "This Little Light of Mine," "Oh My Little Soul Goin' Shine Like a Stahr," and "I Have a Right to the Tree of Life" state an educational desire and determination which only the totally blind can miss. If the writing in early stages must be done by others ("De Angel in Heben Gwin to Write Muh

Name"), eventually, when the slavery chain is broken, it will be done by the man himself. "My soul is a witness," just as was Methusaleh, who lived "nine hundred and sixty-nine," about whom "you read in the Bible and you understand"; just as was Samson, the strongest man, who pulled down a building; just as was Daniel who lay down and slept with lions all about.

The number of songs about reading and writing is proof of the front position these cherished skills occupied in the slave's mind. There was a good reason why. Slavery was proof of the distorted world. That world needed to be changed, had to be changed. The mythology of the Christian religion was a mythology of change, radical change. But the real change had to be a change in human beings. And where best to begin than with oneself?

THE FUGITIVE AND INSURRECTIONARY SPIRIT

After the reader's review of the sensitivity of the keen sense of distortion the slave felt in the world around him, his fugitive and insurrectionary spirit should come as no surprise. Remember his African pride. Remember the African habit of solving unbearable assaults upon human pride by physical means. Most of all, remember that his cup was filling up at least a little each day; and when it ran over, an explosion was to be expected.

A number of writers, former slaves and more or less objective observers, have declared that the desire to be free was present and driving in the breast of almost every slave. Uncle Tom, for instance, in both novel and play, was certainly no symbol of rashness as a slave. He was as agreeable a slave as you could find, deferring always to his masters no matter how personally distasteful his life was. And yet, in conversation with his most charming, kind, and loving master, he said that he would rather be a poor freeman than a rich slave: freedom was the thing he yearned for most.

In spite of the Uncle Toms, let us concede that there were many slaves who found slavery agreeable. They liked, let us say, the notion of belonging to a powerful family; of being assured of board, lodging, and the minimum necessities of life; of having whatever small status their occupations brought them. They looked down upon poor whites because they were rootless and insecure. They developed genuine friendships with their masters and mistresses and with other whites around them.

Making this concession merely sharpens the image of freedom in the hearts of the great majority of slaves. It cannot be forgotten that the overwhelming majority of these people never thought of themselves as fit for slavery. If they tolerated their condition, they did so under a quiet but definite personal protest: "Better to bear the ills we have, than to fly to others that we know not of."

Already, in tracing other characteristics of the folk community that created the Afro-American spiritual, we have seen the runaway and insurrectionary spirit. Such a spirit was omnipresent and almost inescapable in the mind of the slave, whether he acted upon it or not. The slave was merely recognizing a fact of life. He was in a perpetual state of war. (Equiano had called American slavery a war between slave and master years before.) Hildreth has put it quite clearly. Every plantation in the slave states was the seat of a little camp. The war was not limited to a single neighborhood as with an invading army; it was diffused over the whole country. In 1840 Hildreth predicted the eventual outcome: "If the system of slavery in the United States be not first extinguished by some peacable means, it will sooner or later, come to a forcible termination."

Although the slave was at heart peace loving, he recognized the existing warfare in his songs. A few songs, like "Ain't Gonna Study War No More," are peace seeking. A far greater number cast the slave in the role of a soldier, fighting a perennial and bitter fight. Using a thin religious coating, he was reflecting the battlefield of his everyday life.

Describing his battlefield, one may begin with the home of the master. The sleeping quarters of the slaveholder were more often not protected by knives and pistols. One slaveholder said that if the slaves were not made sure that immediate death would be their portion for the slightest insurrection, they would reenact "the St. Domingo tragedy."

In the dining room, the master and his family were far from safe. Florida, in 1843, passed a law prohibiting the sale of poisonous drugs to Negroes. Henry reports that following several executions of slaves for poisoning their masters, South Carolina passed a law offering four pounds to any slave or free Negro who gave information on any such poisoning that led to a conviction (false information made the witness liable to punishment for the crime being tried). Even so, "it was difficult to get one slave to inform against another." Occasionally they did as in the Camden insurrection of 1816 and the famous Vesey plotting of 1822. Peter Prideau, who "preached" on the Vesey plotters, was voted by the legislature the cost of his freedom and $50 a year; his stipend was raised to $100 when his master refused to free him; it was raised to $200 in 1857.

If the bedroom and dining room were dangerous, so was the whole plantation. The patrol emerged in the late seventeenth century not only to forestall runaways but also to protect the lives of whites and prevent insurrection, called by Henry "the greatest possible danger to be feared from the African population." In 1816, following two attempted insurrections, the patrol law in South Carolina was tightened. By 1819 all white males over 18 were made liable for patrol duty, although there many abuses of the law followed.

Hurd and Catterall join Henry in reflecting through legal citations the great fear of insurrection in all the slave states over a period of two centuries. The story they tell by direct statement and implication, of insurrections full-blown, of insurrections attempted, of insurrections imagined in every shadow, on every breath of air, is even more awesome than the actual list of hundreds of slave outbursts described in Herbert Aptheker's *Negro Slave Revolts in the United States, 1526–1860*. The terror under which Southern whites perpetually lived, not able to trust their most "trusted" chattels, on farm or in a big house, day or night, in field or city, alone or in groups, is a large sheaf of pitiable pages in American history. The laws restrained sympathetic whites as much as slaves and free Negroes, although whites were authorized smaller punishments than the other two groups. Just to be on the safe side a Georgia law in 1792 decreed that "no congregation or company of negroes shall under pretence of religious worship assemble themselves contrary to the act for regulating patrol."

Slaves were punished for being near arms or ammunition; for being disorderly—a Virginia statute of 1705 provides that a disorderly slave may be dismembered on order of the court; for "tumultuous meetings"; for drinking, carousing, or gaming; for offering anything of value for sale; for "insolence" (which might be a look, a pointed finger, or slowness of move); for using abusive language to whites; for failing or refusing to show leave papers to patrollers. Even whites were in violation if they purchased corn, rice, peas, bacon, flour, tobacco, indigo, cotton, ham, chicken, turkeys, or a host of other items from slaves. Punishment could be as much as thirty-nine lashes unless the offender were a white woman.

Seditious and incendiary publications could not be circulated (sometimes under penalty of death); Negroes could be jailed for asking for or receiving such papers at the post office for any reason. Slaves could not travel on the road without permission. To kill a slave resisting coercion was no felony in Virginia from 1669 on. As the nineteenth century grew older, it became harder and harder to free slaves; free Negroes were absolutely prohibited from entering or settling in many states.

One of the reasons for laws against incendiary publications was the publication and circulation in 1829 and thereafter of David Walker's *Appeal to the Colored Citizens of the World*. Although not calling for outright rebellion, it predicted the overthrow of the slave power and the downfall of slaveholding Christians. It declared the condition of the Israelites in Egypt better than that of blacks in America; it said Roman slavery was far worse than ours. Curiously enough, it made its thrust on a religious basis; it quoted the Bible voluminously and skillfully, and insisted that God did not support American slavery. Somehow it gained circulation all over the South, among slaves, free Negroes, and whites. Southern papers denounced it in editorials. Elaborate searches were conducted to root it out. Riding in pursuit of Walker's appeal, the Southern plantation owner almost completely overlooked a far more dangerous incendiary item, the revolutionary songs of his slaves, which also used the Bible with great skill.

In "Day by Day Resistance to Slavery," Raymond A. and Alice H. Bauer point up a movement that is described in numerous documents of slave life.

The chief methods the Bauers trace are the labor slowdowns, the organized strikes in protest against severities, the fires started by slaves, the feigned clumsiness, the costly malingering, the pretense of pregnancy, the feigned disabilities while on the auction block, the actual mutilations, the suicides, and the killing of children by mothers to prevent the imposition of slavery. It is easily seen how the everyday war was being fought from the slave's side. Knowing his value and his closeness to the master's property, knowing that the large numbers could not always be successfully watched, the slave fought with weapons at hand. Needless to say, he inflicted heavy financial losses.

Sydnor says that slaveholders feared the existence of free Negroes in the neighborhood as a source of discontent among slaves. No doubt they were right. Since the color black meant slave, a white man could be miserably disconcerted by the appearance of a black man who was not a slave. By the same appearance a slave could be brought to do some hard thinking.

Randall Ware, a blacksmith and a leading character in Margaret Walker's *Jubilee*, was based on a real free Negro who eventually became rich and a large property owner in the South. Articles like James B. Browning's "The Free Negro in Ante-Bellum North Carolina" demonstrate that there was sufficient quantity and quality among free Negroes in the South to inspire and arouse a good many slaves.

Act after act, sometimes on quite trivial subjects, would have in its preamble the phrase, "for the better preventing of insurrections by Negroes." And an 1846 law in Tennessee reached the nadir, or the zenith as you like, when it was called "an act to prohibit the practice of permitting slaves to act as if they were free." It was followed eleven years later, in Tennessee, by an act "providing voluntary enslavement of free Negroes."

None of these flailings by terror-stricken whites, nor the tortures, nor the burnings and hangings—sometimes on the basis of insurrections read about hundreds of miles away—nor the cajoleries, nor the distracted experiments in attempting to induce fear among slaves caused the insurrections to stop. They continued right down to 1864, the last year of the Civil War. Rather than prove that the slave folk community was barbaric, they proved that sizable portions of the community had refused to cooperate with slavery even at the risk of their lives. The "valiant-hearted men," the singers "with swords in their hands," and those who swore in song that "I will die in the fiel'" are a part of the evidence that the spiritual fully echoed this militant noncooperation in the face of increasing pressures from the well-armed enemy.

Miles Mark Fisher in his well-written book, *Negro Slave Songs in the United States,* insists that the predominant characteristic of the folk community was the desire to return to Africa. It would be most interesting if this characteristic could be proved. In view of the great opportunities the slave had to be freed if he agreed to go to Africa and the limited acceptance of these opportunities over a century and a half, an impartial observer can hardly credit this suggestion as a decisive element of the folk community.

The case against colonization is solidly stated by Peter Williams, pastor of St. Phillips Episcopal Church (reprinted by Carter G. Woodson in *Negro Orators and Their Orations*). The Reverend Williams says, "We are NATIVES of this country, we ask only to be treated as well as FOREIGNERS." He invites the influential members of the African Colonization Society to see that Negroes receive justice here rather than be sent to Africa. At the end he declares quite emphatically, "Very few free people of colour *wish* to go to that *land*." Fredrika Bremer reports that free Negroes in Cincinnati preached and shouted against African colonization. The evidence shows that the African slave was of the same mind as his free brother even should he have to forgo the implied emancipation.

The sentiment of both slave and free Negroes concerning the American land was best expressed years later (1891) in a poem in the *Atlantic Monthly*,

> De white man done drive off de Injun,
> done mos' drive off de fox,
> but Brer Rabbit, he say he gwine stay.

But running away to free land in America and running away in general were decisive elements in the folk community as increasing pressure from the law and overwhelming direct evidence clearly prove. The first fugitive slave laws in Virginia appear in 1642–43, twelve years after the first laws providing for the return by force of runaway indentured servants; thereafter, throughout the South, similar laws fell like heavy rain. There were penalties for enticing slaves away and for advising slaves to abscond (a white man got six years in the penitentiary). New powers were given to patrols for arresting and punishing Negroes.

Running away was not merely the folk community's declaration of independence; it was also the community's protest against brutality, inhumanity, and plain meanness. Although several historians give a reasonably full picture of the runaway slave, the evidence offered by Stampp in *The Peculiar Institution* seems more revelatory of the mind of the folk community in which the spiritual developed. Thus, our authority for most of the following data on fugitive slaves is Stampp.

Early in his account Stampp quoted Olmsted to the effect that few planters, large or small, were not plagued by runaways. Remedies and prevention techniques were never successful. While usually under 30 and male, they were often over 60 and female. Some "ran" only once; others repeatedly. More ran in summer than winter, to avoid bitter cold and frostbite. To leave Stampp a moment, we may note that Henry quotes a phrase from Pollard's *Black Diamonds* as suggestive of the general spirit of the slave of every class, "Lord, foot help body."

Stampp's facts mow down innumerable stereotypes about black slaves:

Stereotype	Fact
1. Mulattoes, more agressive through white blood, were the chief escapees.	1. The runaway was not predominantly mulatto, but predominantly black. But light-colored slaves forged free papers and went off to jobs in fisheries, on wharves and river boats.
2. Field slaves ran; house slaves stayed put because they were well fed, well clothed, and treated like members of the family.	2. All classes ran; domestics, field hands, skilled artisans, house and domestic slaves—all!
3. Humble, meek, good-humored, inoffensive, cheerful slaves never or rarely ran—the industrious ones did not.	3. Typical on this point is the testimony of a Louisiana master who lost three at one time: number one was very industrious, always answered with a smile; number two addressed whites humbly and respectfully; number three was well-disposed and industrious, very timid, and spoke humbly, hat in hand, to whites.
4. Runaways sneaked out alone, keeping their guilty secret from their closest associates.	4. Runaways might be single or in groups of two, three, or a dozen; in a few instances, more than fifty; one Maryland case on record, eighty in a group.
5. Kind masters were not afflicted by runaways.	5. Masters were often amazed at the runaway's reaction to kind treatment; they called this reaction ingratitude and depravity. One said, "Poor ignorant devils, for what do they run away? They are well clothed, work easy and have all kinds of plantation produce."
6. Other slaves never helped runaways.	6. Other slaves often gave aid to fugitives. The literate wrote passes; when detected, they, too, would go. Slaves took food to runaways; would accept beatings rather than reveal hiding places.

According to W. E. B. Du Bois, there were four main geographical paths for runaways: (1) the swamps along the coast from Norfolk to North Florida; (2) the Appalachian range, the safest path north; (3) through Tennessee and Kentucky and the heart of the Cumberland Mountains, using limestone caverns; and (4) the valley of the Mississippi.

Runaways had no single pattern of behavior. Some would live in forest or swamp, squatting huts and camps, storing food, utensils, and blankets. The prospect of certain failure did not deter them; the floggings, maimings, brandings of the unsuccessful or the recovered did not discourage them. Most fled to the North (following the North Star). Some fled to the British in the Revolutionary War and the War of 1812; and to the Spanish before the Louisiana and Florida purchases. Some joined up with Indians and Mexicans. Some stole boats and went to the Bahamas. Although often helped by whites, the runaway usually trusted only fellow slaves. They usually fought desperately to prevent recapture.

One of these pitched battles was reported in the *Wytheville* (Virginia) *Gazette* and reprinted in the *San Francisco Herald* in 1851. Four fugitive slaves armed with knives, spears, and weapons made of broken English scythes, were overtaken by five or six whites. One of the whites had his head split open and died within eight hours. Another had his left wrist and hand almost severed. Another was stabbed. Another had his skull cloven from temple to temple but could possibly recover. Another was severely injured by rocks. Of the fugitives two were captured and two escaped.

The incident just related followed a pattern: A gang of runaways with weapons would normally kill whites and die themselves rather than accept capture. They would commandeer food and supplies from their plantations and have no compunction about stealing since they had given more than their share to the wealth of the plantation. In 1802 a South Carolina judge called slaves "in general a headstrong, stubborn race of people." Another white man spoke before the Louisiana Supreme Court: The desire for freedom "exists in the bosom of *every* slave—whether the recent captive, or him to whom bondage has become a habit."

The idea of running away was in the mind and secret conversation of the slave perpetually. One slave woman in Mississippi merely disappeared when it seemed that she would no longer be able to fight off her overseer's demand for sex. In talking to her brother, Linda Brent suggested that he earn money and some day *buy* his freedom. He quickly assured her that he did not intend to buy his freedom.

Reliable figures on the number of runaways are hard to come by, for obvious reasons. Franklin estimates between 1810 and 1850 a loss of a hundred thousand slaves valued at more than $30,000,000. During debate on the Fugitive Slave Bill of 1850, Southern congressmen, led by Senator Butler of South Carolina, loudly protested that they had lost thousands of slaves and millions of dollars in property. Roy F. Nichols reports that the number of free Negroes grew by way of escapes from 59,557 in 1790 to 488,070 in 1860, or 11 percent of the Negro population in the United States. On this basis about six thousand slaves a year ran away. If it were possible to accumulate all the evidence from all sources, it is highly likely that the actual number of runaways was several times this figure. When the process became fully developed, the slaves ran away in droves.

In many books are stories of the fugitive slave. In spite of all these books, Fredrika Bremer could not understand why the histories of fugitive slaves do not become subjects of romances and novels in American literature. Even so, the well-organized Underground Railroad and its associated activities are described by William Still, William H. Siebert, and Henrietta Buckmaster. Four mighty examples of successful fugitives are displayed in miniature in *Four Took Freedom,* by Philip Sterling and Rayford Logan. These four are Harriet Tubman, Frederick Douglass, Robert Smalls, and Blanche K. Bruce.

Some very interesting individual stories have been published in numerous places. Benjamin Drew, in *The Refugee* (1856), offers narratives of fugitive slaves in Canada, related by themselves. In the *Atlantic Monthly* for February and March 1866, is William Parker's "The Freedman's Story" which gives many insights into American slavery and repeats John Wesley's designation of it as "the sum of all villainies." Parker tells that he first heard of runaways safe in Canada when he was 10 or 11 years old. Tired of working without pay, he needed no further excuse for leaving. He ran for the woods after wrestling with his master over a stick, taking his brother with him. Following these movements, he and his brother went back to the slave quarters to make up bundles and say farewells to friends. Then off to Baltimore.

In his *History of Louisiana* Gayarré tells how, in 1808, Negro slaves ran to Texas in large numbers, believing the foreign flag would improve their conditions. And *The Negro in Virginia* calls the number of escapees remarkable in view of constantly increasing patrols, increased punishments for fugitives and their helpers, swamp life, snakes, wild animals, "nigger dogs," and barking house dogs.

Larry Gara, in *The Liberty Line,* has attempted to show that the Underground Railroad was not as powerful an operation as its describers have said it was. But even reducing it by a great amount, no one can deny that it was massive, with massive results. Nor can anyone deny that the fugitive mind was perpetually at work and, as a result, the highways and byways leading North were filled with hopeful slaves. The *Boston Daily Globe* reports that on one occasion a fugitive slave was captured on the Capitol steps in Washington.

Perhaps the most interesting and revealing source of the fugitive is the advertisements in the newspapers announcing his departure and the rewards for his return. It is not merely that the master and his script writer are disclosed in their subtle glory. After one has read several thousands of these ads, the relationships between masters and their reluctant slaves are generously spelled out.

Quite often the advertisement would say that the runaway could read and write and had written his own pass as a feature in his escape. Sometimes he would be acknowledged as a fine craftsman. David, wanted by a Nashville, Tennessee, subscriber was admitted to be blacksmith, shoemaker, tool handler, and farmer. Occasionally, he would be called a pleasant, obedient fellow, and the reader would have to wonder how he ever got such strange ideas as those which made him a fugitive.

Almost invariably the advertisement would speak of scars. It is hard to tell if the master was proud of his workmanship or, if in trying to assemble the materials for a good identification, he was also trying to hide or play down the fact that this was not the first time a particular slave had run away. Whatever the reason, these evidences of mayhem abounded—teeth missing, scars on lips, eyelids, forehead, ankles, or back. Just on the basis of the scars there is small wonder that the fugitive spirit remained high in the slave community.

Perhaps most fugtives were peaceful men and women, concentrating only on their freedom; but some decidedly were not. Stroyer says that the runaway would not hesitate to fight, with knives, stolen guns and powder, and other weapons; he knew of cases when runaways killed the bloodhounds that pursued them. And Parker, a principal actor in the Christiana riot (which cost the United States $50,000) tells of the singing of his group. One song sounds very much like several spirituals,

> Leader, what do you say
> About the judgment day?
> I will die on the field of battle,
> Die on the field of battle,
> With glory in my soul.

If so many people had not effected a release from slavery by putting forth a strong effort, this toleration of slavery might have rested more quietly in the upper hearts of the great majority of the slave community. But the fact that these people tried to break free, often again and again, and the fact that thousands of them, some from every community, did break free, stirred the minds of millions to estimate their own chances. For this reason, perhaps more than for any other, the fugitive mind was a large phase of the folk community mind of the Afro-American slave. Overtly and covertly, he carried the fugitive idea as far as he possibly could in his spirituals.

The fugitive mind motivated the Afro-American in a variety of ways. It made him a keen student and practitioner of mask and irony in his everyday dealings with the white man—a mask and irony which the large body of literature shows the white man, even down to the second, third, and fourth generations, did not understand. It steeled him to absorb mistreatment and brutality and his own temptation to break out on the basis of everyday unbearable situations. It developed in him an ingenuity, a great courage, and the rashness he had to have either to run away or to keep thinking that some day he was going to.

The reaction of the whites to the runaway problem intensified the community's fugitive spirit. Although considerable effort was made to paint this reaction as primarily economic—the loss of valuable property—it was not primarily economic. It was primarily psychological. The runaway was striking at the morale of the slave community, including the owners and their white cohorts. The reaction to this attack on morale was read by the slaves as an admission of the guilt of slaveholders and the whole slavery system. If the runaway was caught, brought back, and punished; especially, if he was sold—the greatest fear of the runaway—the slave group did not suffer a feeling of deterrence. Its determination to be a successful fugitive was merely intensified. The failure of so-called deterrent methods used by the slaveholder, and the lawmakers who did his bidding, never seems to have been understood by these people. They therefore cooperated in increasing the number of self-freed slaves, and this cooperation was not lost on the members of the slave community.

From the fugitive to the insurrectionary mind is sometimes a very small step. The extent of the acceptance of slavery by the slave on the one hand and of his physical resistance to masters and slave policemen on the other has never been satisfactorily evaluated. There was certainly some acceptance; there was a great deal of physical resistance.

Henrietta Buckmaster's opening statement is quite appropriate:

> If "the negro on the whole yielded to the slave status with little show of resistance" as an eminent historian has said, how does one account for the fact that he employed sabotage, engaged in strikes, committed suicide, and mutilated himself; ran away, turned guerrilla, struck at his master through arson and murder? And more than anything kept the South in a real or imagined ferment? Why did armed men patrol the roads at night, or a Georgia woman write that she dared not trust her life with a single person on her plantation and never went to bed without an ax near her pillow? Why did state legislatures pass continuously repressive laws, taking away from the slave, one by one, the few privileges he had been allowed, until in 1860, when a flame of revolts broke out, he would hardly be classed as a human being with human rights?

Before going further with the insurrectionary spirit, one must point out that the lack of physical resistance was no proof of the acceptance of slavery by the slave. The runaway showed more intelligence and more courage than the physical resister. He also struck more deeply at the heart of slavery. He was better at agitating the slaveholder and the white population. As Du Bois said, his was the really effective revolt. In addition to the runaway, a great many slaves who despised slavery suffered in silence and were fuses waiting to be ignited or engagers in underground activities which were never discovered. Many of these activities are detailed in the very large number of slave narratives.

Listings of slave revolts have been often made. Perhaps the most complete listing is Herbert Aptheker's *Negro Slave Revolts in the United States, 1526–1860*. Some interesting smaller listings are Joseph C. Carroll's *Slave Insurrections in the United States, 1800–1865*, Wendell P. Dabney's "Slave Risings and Race Riots," Harvey Wish's "American Slave Insurrections Before 1861," and John Dixon Long's "Negro Insurrections" in his *Pictures of Slavery in Church and State*. Wish enumerates 55 slave mutinies between 1699 and 1845; he says his list is far from exhaustive. The Gabriel Prosser uprising in 1800, he says, was inspired by the San Domingo rebellion and the Israelites of the Bible. June P. Guild says that the Preamble to the Virginia Constitution of 1776 accused George III of prompting Negroes to rise in arms.

Gayarré gives several pages to a slave insurrection of January 1811 in the Parish of St. John the Baptist, thirty-six miles above New Orleans. He tells how the slaves set fire to houses on four or five plantations and compelled other slaves to join. It goes without saying that such insurrections were ruthlessly put down, and that the whites took an inordinate amount of revenge. In this case the militia had to be called. Sixty-six slaves were left dead on the field; many others were hanged on the spot. Sixteen were sent back to the city for trial. Corpses were found daily. Heads were placed on poles.

Revolts among slaves in other countries were not unknown to American slaves. The uprisings in Haiti were a shock to whites and blacks alike in the American South. Throughout the West Indies, as we know from Sir Alan Burns, slaves were repeatedly in revolt. Burns records uprisings in Suriname, French and Spanish Hispaniola, Spanish Puerto Rico, French Montserrat, and in the English colonies of Antigua, Barbados, Bermuda, British Guiana, Dominica, Grenada, Jamaica, St. Kitts, Tobago, and Trinidad. Nowhere was the African slave a docile creature. Word of these foreign uprisings often reached the ears of black slaves in North America.

Once freedom was in the air, the insurrectionary spirit naturally increased. Remember Charlotte Forten's conversation with the retiring young black man in South Carolina in 1861. He had, of course, been freed by the Union Army. When she asked him what he would do if they tried to put him back into slavery, he responded very quietly, "I'd fight 'em, miss."

In the *Richmond Enquirer* for October 18, 1831, is an account which bears the headline, "Atrocious Murder." It gives the details of how John Henry Lewis was murdered in his bed by his slaves, who then robbed the house and destroyed it by fire. Five of them were caught and confessed. One of them, Kit, had been taken up a week or more before for "uttering expressions indicating his hellish purposes against the whites." Condemned to be hanged, he was freed when his sentence was commuted by the governor and his council. The writer of the story interpolates that if Kit had been hanged, John Henry Lewis would still be alive and well.

The big uprisings of Gabriel and Denmark Vesey and Nat Turner shook the whole Southland with fear. Many Southerners did not understand how things like this could happen. They were well aware, however, that if they could happen at one place, they could happen anywhere in the South. Thus, the effect was the same as though they had happened in each white person's immediate neighborhood. As to Vesey's conspiracy, aside from blaming slaveholders who allowed slaves to learn to read and write, one Southern observer called it "religious fanaticism." The fact that the leaders of slave uprisings were often churchmen was another factor operating against allowing the slaves too much religious experience.

To read the Southern papers for the summer and fall of 1831, from the time when Nat Turner's murderous assaults were first reported, is to receive a lesson in the ways the Southerners had of terrifying themselves. The long weeks when Nat could not be found were a period of fearful excitement all over the South. Not just that he had to be caught and hanged, but who knew when he would explode from some nearby swamp and strike again? According to the Southern newspapers, Nat was seen everywhere, in mountain and valley; he was suspected of having gone to Ohio with free Negroes; he was reported drowned; he was sought through the flimsy leads of a coat and hymnbook.

At last, "Gen. Nat Turner" was apprehended. Confirmation had come from Governor John Floyd of Virginia. He was now ready to be placed in his proper light and not painted in beautiful colors as the *Albany Fabulist* had done with Gabriel. This "murderous bandit" had been taken; soon he would receive his just deserts.

In an issue of the *Norfolk Herald* for November 1831, there is a story with the heading, "The Last of Nat." The writer of the story had with his own eyes seen the culprit expiate his crimes on Friday, November 26, at twelve o'clock. He reported that the hurried executioner showed no emotion. He sold Nat's body for dissection and spent the money on ginger cakes.

As the slave community watched all this boiling terror and efforts to conceal it, as they saw innocent blacks suffer and die for the actions of a man hundreds of miles away, as they noticed the evolving character of whites under pressure of a physical challenge, they read the realities. They could see that they were not dealing with valiant, noble, and indomitable hearts. They did not put away their own suppressed insurrectionary desires.

Almost as bad as insurrection itself was the dread of insurrection. In a way the dread was worse, for it was ever-present. One of Fanny Kemble's earliest notations is about the patrols everywhere, the tolling of bells, the beating of drums, like old fortified towns where the tocsin sounded as if invasion were momentarily expected; the persistent dread of domestic insurrection; the curfew, recalling early feudal times. Fanny adds, "Still I should prefer going to sleep without the apprehension of my servants' cutting my throat in bed, even to having a guard provided to prevent their doing so."

After the devastating Nat Turner experience, a writer calling himself Appomatiox declared that insurrections such as Gabriel's and Nat's showed the need for chasing out all free Negroes. He recognized the problems. The Northern states would not accept Virginia's forty to fifty thousand Negroes; large Negro tribes in Canada and Haiti would be undesirable neighbors; the expense of the removal would be almost prohibitive.

Appomatiox was not alone in these solutions for terror. A writer in the *Petersburg* (Virginia) *Intelligencer* reported that sentiment was gaining ground in Virginia that the whole African race ought to be removed. "Many people," he insisted, "feel unwilling to die and leave their property exposed to all the ills, which, from the existence of slavery in our State, they have themselves so long felt." He said that some were moving, and there were others to follow.

One very serious student of the problem wrote a *Letter to a Member of the General Assembly of Virginia, on the Subject of the Late Conspiracy of the Slaves* (Baltimore, Bonsal & Niles, 1801). Praising by implication the organization of Gabriel's conspiracy, he declared that no man denies the magnitude of the danger arising from domestic slavery. He blamed in part the slaves who could read and write and who thus became centers of instruction. In part, also, he attributed slave insurrections—which he seemed to think inevitable—to the fact that love of freedom was an inborn sentiment, flourishing at any good opportunity. More rigorous laws and enforcement, he said flatly, would be "vain and nugatory." Not only would the blacks increase in population more rapidly than the whites; they also had links with fanatical and religious whites. The only hope, he concluded, was to free all the slaves and transport them. He suggested the West Indies or a purchase from the Spanish government or the Indian country of Georgia. At the end of his little book he set out an elaborate system of arrangements and taxation to support his transportation suggestion.

The creators of the songs held all these things in mind. Many songs directly reflect the fighting spirit of the slaves. But, generally speaking, the creators looked beyond the gory details and, like true artists and philosophers, concentrated on the universal principles involved.

RELIGIOUS ATTITUDE

There is a decided difference between the slave's awareness of religious hypocrisy in his atmosphere and his own religious views. The former is more negative, the latter more positive. The former is something the slave could hardly help developing; the latter is something he developed deliberately and consistently in spite of the bitterness and brutality of his surroundings. The former is somewhat simple; the latter, very complex indeed. Reginald Nettel says the extent of religious influence on Negro song has been exaggerated. Perhaps he should have said that the extent of a certain notion of religious influence has been exaggerated. In any case, without a clear understanding of his religious attitude, one can never understand the complex religious aspects of the spiritual.

To begin with, the Afro-American retained much of the African's tendency to consider religion as a totality, a unifying element in his life. This fact, alone, would prevent his swallowing whole the religious views of his masters, even if the masters had consistently imparted them to him. It is also an insuperable barrier to his wooden imitation of the white camp meeting song. The slave could plainly see that what he called his religion was just a compartment of the white man's life. Most often, it was a very small compartment. He obviously went to church, supported churches financially, and mouthed the religious doctrines with his fingers crossed. It was clear that he never intended to carry them out. His true religion, the guiding force in his life, the set of principles he lived by, was a combination of economic and sociological factors. The slave could see this every day; and the slave knew him better than he knew himself.

But the slave was part of a tradition in which religious theory and practice dominated the lives of people. In his heart he was confused and outraged by people who would profess to follow a true and deep religious philosopher like Jesus Christ and who would, simultaneously, indulge in such practices as were necessary to maintain the kind of slavery he experienced. He could never understand people who went out of their way to call themselves Christians and fearers of a benevolent and just God, and who at the same time held their brothers in bondage, fomented brutalities, and subordinated everything to money-making.

At this point it needs to be remembered that the slave learned about Christianity and the white man's God, not through, but in spite of the white man. He learned about them as he learned about most other things, through his grapevine—a few slaves listening or observing, a few slaves reading, and the information bursting through the veins and arteries of the slave community like the rush of blood.

If he had been taught Christianity by devout masters, his religious attitude would have been somewhat different. Henry William Ravenel, the planter and botanist, born and reared in the South, emphasizes the fact that there was not much exertion to give slaves religious instruction at all. What they got was really a little ridiculous. Read, for example, Andrew Flinn Dickson's *Plantation Sermons*, a two-volume publication for the use of white mistresses to give religious instruction to their slaves on Sunday afternoons. One does not need to be able to penetrate the mind of the slave very deeply to know how they reacted to that kind of talk, especially in the face of the realities.

The Reverend Charles Colcock Jones of Savannah, Georgia, in his *Religious Instruction of the Negroes* (1832), pleads for the effective teaching of slaves. His sermon was twice delivered to associations of Southern planters. In the sermon he admits to his audiences that Negroes lie, steal, blaspheme, are slothful, envious, malicious, inventors of evil things, deceivers, covenant breakers, implacable, grossly immoral, greatly wanting in natural affection, improvident, without understanding, and drink freely when liquor is available. But these are no reasons why masters should disobey the express commands of God to teach them the religious ways. They can teach them themselves or employ others to do it.

He offers a plan for planters to form a voluntary association to take instruction into their own hands, during weekdays and on the Sabbath. Ignorant and wicked as their slaves are, they all, he said, need religious instruction. The results would be better relationships between master and slave, decrease in Negro crime, saving the souls of the slaves, and relieving ourselves of great responsibility. "Are not," he begs, "their souls more precious than their bodies?" How inconsiderate it is to send the gospel to foreign lands, public prisons, and destitute settlements in our own country, and deny it to the poor Negroes.

It is quite likely that his pleadings, however well calculated they were to gain and hold the attention of his audience, fell on very deaf ears. It is probably just as well. Knowing the masters as they did, the slaves would probably not have put very much trust in their religious messages. The whole project was doomed from the start.

What was the real attitude of the slaves toward Christianity? Dorothy L. Conley and Alain Locke believe that the spirituals themselves prove a profound acceptance of Christianity on the part of the slaves. Mrs. Conley says that there would have been no Negro spirituals had the slave not accepted Christianity. This statement failed to consider the natural tendency of the African to sing wherever he was and his further tendency to utilize whatever was in the air around him.

Professor Locke goes further than Mrs. Conley. He says that a "naïve and spirit-saving acceptance of Christianity is the hallmark of the true spiritual"; and, further, that the spirituals "although the most original and universally effective expressions of elemental Christian faith and feeling, are merely the artistic by-products of an emotional interpretation of Christianity that in time may be regarded as a greater gift." But Professor Locke's opinion, in this instance, seems to be based upon personal philosophic insight rather than upon inductive evidence.

Writing in 1862, W. W. Malet says that he is certain that the four million Negroes "are all professing Christians, and all have spiritual as well as temporal provision." Such an opinion can hardly be taken seriously. In

1905, Frederick Morgan Davenport, then professor of sociology at Hamilton College, said that the most prominent activity of the Negro race was religion and that practically every Negro was a member of some church. So palpably and widely inaccurate a statement would also have to be disregarded. A. M. Chirgwin's declaration that Christianity saved the slaves from demoralization and decay can be held in abeyance.

A scientific approach to our question can be found in an article by Professor John B. Cade, who wrote "Out of the Mouths of Ex-Slaves" for the *Journal of Negro History* in 1935. Professor Cade's sampling was from Louisiana. He says that of the 150 ex-slaves interviewed, only 10 had been Christians. He notes that they generally recalled that, in their experience, religious services had been forbidden. Slaves prayed face down to prevent the sound carrying. When slaves wanted to sing or pray, they had to steal into the woods. If heard singing and praying, they were whipped all the way home.

In the secret (contraband) prayer meetings everyone was his own preacher, and all sang and prayed. Pots were placed over the door to keep down the sound. The speaker talked into or over a vessel of water to drown the sound. Hands were placed over the mouths of any who became animated.

From much other evidence it is clear that things were not as bad all over as they were in Professor Cade's Louisiana. In William Faux's visit to a slave church in Denver, Delaware, on May 11, 1820, the services were lively, merry, and instructive. Perhaps the conditions farther north were generally better than they were in the deep South. But Professor Cade's evidence and a great deal of similar evidence destroy the myth that the slaves went regularly to camp meetings or to church, that they heard the gospel preached in some full way, that in the normal course of things they listened to Christian preaching and accepted Christianity in large numbers.

It has already been shown that the Presbyterians admitted their incompetency in the proselyting of slaves. The Methodists seemed far ahead of other denominations, and they made only a slight inroad. John Wesley was distressed by the neglect of the conversion of slaves by Americans. It is reported that Methodist slaves in church were strong supporters of Denmark Vesey. According to William Loren Katz, Vesey read to his partners of the delivery of the children of Israel from Egyptian bondage and urged them, likewise, to free themselves by force. He says that the slaves were driven away from their church, and the church shut up.

One Negro preacher, known to an Englishman before the Civil War, had a memorable sermon on the peculiar Methodists. They were peculiar because they had love feasts, because of the way they took "de Supper of de Lord" on their knees, and because of the manners of both preachers and people. The Methodist preacher "speaks right out to de people. Dey raises der voices to de third heavens, until it reverberates and strikes de people dumb." Others may get to heaven, but the Methodists, said this black preacher, get there by the right road; "de Methodists, de peculiar people, haul de oder congregations right up to heaven. Bredren, I have done."

Although there is little evidence that slaves were more than casual attenders at camp meetings (and in comparatively small numbers), John Dixon Long says that camp meetings were an unmixed delight to those slaves who did attend. They provided the slaves with a season of rest. They provided a holiday without drunkenness or profanity. Best of all, they gave the slaves a chance to see their relatives from neighboring plantations and to sing and jump to their heart's content.

C. V. Bruner's doctoral thesis on the religious instruction of the slaves attempts to divide the course of this movement into periods. In the period before 1740, says Bruner, the Negro clung tenaciously to primitive beliefs. Much manumission resulted from the belief that one Christian might not hold another in bondage.

The period 1740–90 was called the "great awakening." Attracted by intense emotionalism, the black man was welcomed by Presbyterian, Baptist, and Methodist. The period 1790–1830 was characterized by a general retardation of missionary work, by increases in the effects of the anti-slavery movement, and by greater activity on the part of the Negro churches, the A.M.E.s and the A.M.E.Z.s.

In the period 1830–45, again there was retardation, partly because of the impact of Nat Turner. Schisms between the Methodists and Baptists, breaking into Northern and Southern groups, did not help the work among slaves. Bruner says that the period between 1845 and 1860 showed a remarkable religious development among the Negroes. Planters became convinced that religious instruction increased the slave's value; they also, he says, wanted to promote the happiness and welfare of the Negro.

In summary, he cites the remarkable result that, by 1860 one-fourth of the slaves over 18 were members of the church, as compared with one-third of the whites of the same age. When one recalls that 55 percent of the slaves were under 19, this figure is not very impressive. It becomes less and less impressive as one muses on the slave's opportunities for maintaining and fulfilling his membership; and less impressive still as one rereads Bruner's book and notes that he is straining to make the planter look good. His statements about planters wanting to promote the happiness and welfare of the Negroes, for example, are without serious documentation.

In both his religious faith and his songs, the slave used the Bible, but he made his own unique interpretations. He was unimpressed by the biblical quotations of his masters and his master's prostitute preachers, which advocated slave obedience. He measured his adoptive (American) religion almost entirely by the yardsticks of freedom and humanity it espoused and by the failure of its white adherents to obey its edicts of equality before God and charity with respect to fellowmen. He enjoyed the emotional and imaginative experience of his adoptive religion more than he did its neglected and abstruse dogmas. A most interesting and painfully objective analysis of the religious environment of the spiritual is found in Theo Lehmann's *Negro Spirituals: Geschichte und Theologie* (1965), not yet (like some of Lehmann's other works in folklore) translated from German to English.

Since slaves in various states were differently treated, both in general and in specific matters affecting religious development, the slave's religion was a great and complex hodgepodge of things. William Francis Allen, Charles Pickard Ware, and Lucy McKim Garrison in their epoch-making *Slave Songs of the United States* (1867) have documented this complexity in their songs from different states and sections, such as Northern Seaboard slave states (Delaware, Maryland, Virginia, and North Carolina); Southeastern slave states (South Carolina, Georgia, and the Sea Islands); and inland slave states (Tennessee, Arkansas, and the Mississippi River). Other spiritual analysts have carried these distinctions farther by such exclusive treatment as *Thirty-Six South Carolina Spirituals*, *In Old Alabama*, *Negro Songs From Georgia*, and *Cabin and Plantation Songs*, originating mainly through students at Hampton Institute. The songs in Dorothy Scarborough's *On the Trail of Negro Folk-Songs* came mainly from Texas and Louisiana. Often because of these different locales the same basic song will have curious variants in phraseology, spelling, accent, imagery, and social emphasis.

In the life of the Negro slave, especially, religion had a strong role to play in conflict resolution. In this regard, as Melford E. Spiro has said,

> religious behavior is appropriate to, rather than disruptive of, the behavioral environment . . . and a religious world view is consistent with, rather than a distortion of, "reality" . . . religion serves as a highly efficient culturally constituted defense mechanism.

The slave's life was so full of conflicts of great size that without religion, or something like it, he could not have mentally and emotionally survived. Tough as he was, rooted as deeply as he was in strong backgrounds, he needed a perpetual supply of spiritual nourishment.

Some have raised the question of the great discrepancy between the slave's concern with religion and his questionable morals. The main advertiser of his questionable morals was his master and other whites who defended slavery. It was to their advantage to make him appear immoral, as justification of their holding him in bondage because he was incapable of caring for himself. Without doubt they contributed to his apparent immorality. Their laws prevented him from legal marriage; from their concupiscence no slave girl or woman was out of danger; and yet they complained that he was sexually loose. From his labor they amassed material fortunes; and yet they often accused him of stealing. Keeping him under strict controls, they invited him to make distortions that would give him some leeway; when he made them, they accused him of lying.

Of the so-called stealing, Charles Ball, slave for forty years, said,

> I was never acquainted with a slave who believed that he violated any rule of morality by appropriating to himself anything that belonged to his master, if it was necessary to his comfort. The master might call it theft and brand it with the name of crime; but the slave reasoned differently when he took a portion of his master's goods to satisfy his hunger, keep himself warm, or to gratify his passion for luxurious enjoyment.

From his observations in four decades as a slave Ball also found strong religious views among slaves concerning the brutality and unfairness of masters. He said that slaves firmly believed their tormentors would be tormented in the hereafter. They could not see how a just God could admit masters and mistresses to the joys of heaven. They believed that overseers would get all their lashes back. These ideas of revolution in the conditions of whites and blacks are a cornerstone, Ball reiterates, of the black's religion.

Both the slaves and many whites opposed the notion that the Bible or Christianity upheld slavery, as many books and articles attempted to prove. This is one reason they could not accept the particular Christianity handed them by the Southern white man. They could never have believed in a Christianity that countenanced bondage. Dozens of spirituals can be called in witness. Their views were expressed by John Rankin, who proved that the Bible prevented slavery. Even at best their Christianity, as Albert H. Stoddard has shown, was modified by their African past.

But their religious experience was genuine and full. They often got good preaching from their own slave preachers, even when their meetings were forbidden or secret. They reveled in the powerful prayers delivered by their fellow members. They thoroughly enjoyed conversion. Read, for example, *God Struck Me Dead*, religious conversion experiences and autobiographies of Negro ex-slaves published by the Social Science Institute of Fisk University.

From the earliest times they craved their own meetings and churches. When there was slavery in Massachusetts, Cotton Mather helped a group of Negroes, at their request, to organize a Society of Negroes. The Society, whose rules have been published, met every Sunday evening, prayed together by tunes, recited a Psalm between two prayers, and listened to a sermon. They also studied one of three catechisms Cotton Mather recommended: The New-English Catechism, the Assemblies Catechism, or the Catechism of the Negro Christianized.

The founding of the Silver Bluff Church was a venture of slaves and sympathetic whites. The earliest Negro Baptist church, it was established on an estate in Georgia between 1773 and 1775. When the British took Savannah, the church had thirty members. Two of its pastors were banished for fear they should stir the slaves in the direction of freedom. The British commander, the Earl of Dunmore, promised the slaves and the white indentured bondmen their freedom if they helped the British. The Reverend George Liele of Silver Bluff went from plantation to plantation telling his fellow slaves of the blessings of salvation he had experienced.

In *The Negro's God As Reflected in His Literature*, Benjamin Mays concludes that the ideas of God in the spirituals adhere to "the traditional, compensatory pattern" and follow the ideas found in the Bible. This conclusion can be honored only if one admits that the Bible presents a variety of presentations of God, and that the spiritual does also. Reading hundreds of spirituals with direct or implied concepts of God, one cannot always see the identicalness.

In Hugh Proctor's *Between Black and White* is a chapter on "The Theology of the Songs of the Southern Slave." He breaks down the divine concept into the three parts of the Trinity. The songs, he says, reveal God in the consciousness of men as a power (king of kings) and as a Father capable of helping even the lowest. They reveal Christ in terms of his divinity and kingliness, his humanness, his existence as friend, and his worthiness to be believed. They exercise belief in the Holy Spirit through Peter filled with the Holy Ghost, through the Holy Ghost as "the heavenly breeze," and through the fact that no one can be a Christian without the witness of the spirit in his breast.

Beyond this, Proctor says, the songs show a belief in angels and a belief in the Christian life. This latter included strict morality plus highly wrought emotion, personal honor, and integrity even above personal freedom (Christian slave women, for example, who accepted beatings rather than submit to lust for exemption from drudgery, and for ease, luxury, and gold), and a life of activity, robust piety, and growth. The climax of the Christian life was holiness. The songs, he avers, are not materialistic and exhibit no spirit of revenge. They are otherworldly, emphasizing heaven for the righteous and hell for the wicked, and the glories of the happy land.

Proctor's readings are certainly thorough and consistent. They seem, however, to be based on just a handful of songs. They also are superficial, since they take the poems as direct statements, just as though they were prose, and they ignore the realities of life in the community which produced the songs.

Perhaps the closest interpretations based on the facts and the poetry are those of Denis Preston and Albert McCarthy in "Poetry of Afro-American Folk Song" and those of Joseph R. Washington, Jr., in *Black Religion*.

Preston and McCarthy open by quoting Alakija, "The African just danced his way into Christianity." That this is more than a figure of speech will be shown in a few pages.

Preston and McCarthy also emphasize the heterogeneous emotions in slave poetry which slavery had inverted and repressed. This is an incisive, truthful emphasis. Likewise is their emphasis upon the tension and upon the fact that in the songs is little resignation to earthly lot—more of sweeping eagerness and ring of triumph for a world emotionally the slave poet's. Their only weakness, a slight one, is their use of "sometimes" when referring to the songs as a reflection on the slave's social condition. How could it ever be otherwise?

Joseph R. Washington, Jr., states flatly, "From the earliest days, the Negro was much more concerned with the freedom of this world than with the religion of the next." He says the slave was resourceful enough to perceive that the religion of the whites, sanctioned by masters and overseers as means for harnessing his energy for production, was his best route to freedom. He also states flatly that the Negro spirituals lie outside the Christian faith.

Such a statement may be somewhat strong. In one sense, though, it is not an overstatement. A great many spirituals were undoubtedly written by Christian believers. Washington, however, is doing a service by smashing the notion that the spirituals were nothing more than the slave poet's becoming converted to Christianity and setting about spouting Christian doctrine. This kind of oversimplification has interfered for years in the full and proper appreciation of these very great folk songs. If they were nothing more than Christian slave philosophy, they would be lacking in the basic qualities of great folk poetry.

Washington further states that the spirituals were a criticism of missionaries, revivalists, evangelists, and the whole Protestant coalition bent on casting out the devil in the Negro, but who became for the Negro the devil himself. Although this may be a slight exaggeration, it is not far from the display of the awareness and condemnation of religious hypocrisy which has already been presented. Christian doctrine cannot mean very much when it comes from people who supported, or who did not fight, the slavery system as it existed and goes to people who were and who felt themselves heavily victimized by that system.

Taken all together, the slave's religious beliefs were certainly not simplistic. Seeing what he saw daily; hearing from his own sources the chief tenets of the Christian religion; liking what he heard, especially the part about the preciousness of each individual soul and the freedom of people from tyranny; the slave certainly had an inclination toward Christianity. The camp meeting strengthened the inclination of the relative handful who got the chance to express their emotional feelings and to throw off the mental burdens they had carried around a long time.

But seeing very little devout application of Christian doctrine, the slave did not rush into this religion. An African, he still wanted a religion which could unify and organize his life. He saw no need for religion as a sideline or as a small compartment to which one turned on Sundays or on prayer meeting nights. He did not seem to be very much impressed by preaching which reiterated the necessity of his obeying his master in the Lord.

Most of the religious meetings that were meaningful to him were secret meetings, proscribed by the establishment. In these he could let himself go, he could commune with his true friends, those to whom he was bound in danger as well as in faith, and he could sing, clap his hands, and shout. Here, also, he heard about Biblical heroes and events from the preachers and others among his fellow slaves who could read or who came by the news in various ways.

As to his religious beliefs, they were his own, and probably a unique set for each person. On evidence from the songs and elsewhere, there was a unifying framework. First of all, the slave undoubtedly dismissed conventional Christianity as the work of faint-hearted believers, hypocrites, and people who thought they were fooling the Lord. They never forgot, also, that Christianity built and reinforced the slave trade; that Christian preachers and communicants in America justified slavery with incessant and interminable arguments, dragging in the Bible to "prove" their points. They probably blamed Northern Christians, too, for not making the Southerners put a stop to this outrage.

But the singing slave did not eliminate all Christianity. He might be said to have built his own Christianity. It was based mainly on his concept of Christ as a god of compassion and suffering, a promulgator of freedom and peace and opportunity, a son of an omnipotent Father. Christ and his Father had proved themselves. They had brought justice out of many impossible situations and could and would bring it boldly out of slavery, when the time came. They were already bringing it out, to some extent, since they were guiding so many black people (runaways) to the realms of freedom. Denmark Vesey, it can be recalled, appealed to hundreds of slaves by showing that the Bible instructed them to fight for their own freedom.

Grouped around Christ were selected heroes from the Bible. All these people demonstrated the truth and workability of Christ's principles. If Christ and his Father could work through them, they could also work through slaves. Thus religion was a matter of tying yourself in with this system, giving it your body and soul, keeping your eyes open for opportunities, anticipating good things both on this earth and in the land beyond the grave, sticking out the evils of slavery, and joining in with all the other good people.

Marion Starkey says that the spirituals evolved in the African church. Whether this was true or not, they certainly resulted from the kind of religious faith just described, plus an awareness of the solid principles in all the other factors of the slave's life.

SUMMARY OF FOLK COMMUNITY

The folk community that produced the spiritual was thus African at its base and maintained its African attitudes and psychology in many ways. But it was greatly transformed by the American slave experience. In fact, its experiences in slavery and its feelings about that experience are the greatest single factors in molding it into a special community, a branch of the basic African community.

Within this special community a number of characteristics are outstanding. First was physical and mental youth and resiliency. Second was a certain sensitivity to surroundings. Third was recognition of the religious and legal hypocrisy of its slave position. Fourth was awareness of its skills and talents and a determination to exploit them in every possible way. Fifth, growing out of fourth, was its tendency and ability to bring songs out of particular occupations. Sixth was its exalted attitude toward education, its desire for education, and its determination to get a competitive education. Seventh was its fugitive and insurrectionary spirit. And eighth was its real religious attitude.

Without knowing the community in terms of its characteristics, one cannot begin to know the meaning and essences of its artistic expression. To read a few dozen or a few hundred spirituals and to try to interpret them in the broad senses of their apparent meanings is wasteful and misleading. Unfortunately, most interpretation of spirituals has been in these categories.

Even without interpreting the spirituals, to know this community in its humanness, its courage, its resourcefulness, its ideality is to be truly uplifted. To go from there to the deepest interiors of its songs is almost to be carried away.

H. L. Mencken once said that a folk group does not write songs; it only chooses which songs survive. This slave community, as a community, most likely did not write or compose these spirituals. But they supplied the poetic and philosophic stuff.

⟨ Necessity and Use of Mask and Symbol

It has already been shown that mask and symbol are indispensable to folk song. The job here is to show in what peculiar ways they were indispensable to the Afro-American spiritual.

Generally speaking, the mask was for protection against whites; the secrecy was for binding the slaves together through messages of assurance. There is first the normal practice of the African in his everyday dealings.

Ian Cameron, writing on "Negro Songs" in the *Musical Times* of London in 1922, has understood this practice. In part he says, "No self-respecting negro of the old type will ever be 'sassy' to a white 'gen'lman,' but he will by sly innuendo of saying and song express his opinions, his wishes, and his sarcasm."

Rising from individual to group expression, the use of mask and symbol becomes an even greater necessity just to get the idea across. If one is speaking for a group that has a single intention, but many individualistic ways of making its intention known, one is almost compelled to choose a mask of some sort or resort to symbolic phrases.

One of the most perceptive analysts of Negro folk song, Russell Ames, has said that it is not, as generally thought, simple, emotional, nonsensical, artless, and crude in form. At its best, Ames says, it is sophisticated and ironic in meaning, classical and subtle in the use of forms. B. A. Botkin joins in the opinion that the spirituals (and the blues) possess irony. Oscar Brand declares that many people have found disguised longing in such songs as "Let My People Go" and "The Walls Came A-tumbling Down." Sidney Finkelstein underscores the idea by showing how the slave in the spiritual drew upon biblical images to mask his yearning for freedom and his defiance of tyranny.

In tracing double meaning in the songs, Gerald W. Haslam relies to some extent upon Sterling Brown. On his own, also, he asks several pointed questions aimed at illustrating double meaning in black folk expression: Who was Brer Rabbit? Who the dull-witted Bear? How many hymns about going to Canaan and setting people free were actually concerned with the plight of Old Testament Jews? Perry Bradford quotes Grandma Betsy Bradford, a former slave, to the effect that "Steal Away to Jesus" always meant to go up north to the promised land.

For close examination of mask and symbol take a simple spiritual like "Lord, I Want to Be a Christian." The words go,

> Lord, I want to be a Christian
> In my heart, in-a my heart,
> Lord, I want to be a Christian
> In-a my heart.

The group's intention is often misunderstood. It is not saying that each member of the group is a Christian, or that any member is a Christian. It is saying that there seems to be some advantage in being and behaving like a Christian. This advantage depends upon whether or not the individual is a true believer—"In-a my heart"—not a surface operator, and intends to carry out in every respect the obligations and responsibilities of the Christian.

That is the surface meaning of the words. What has probably happened is that the group, as individuals, have seen a lot of people who profess Christianity and did not behave as Christians are supposed to behave. As though it has held a discussion of the matter, it has concluded that it wants to make known its disgust with phony, insincere Christians. It is tired, for example, of Christians who practice selfishness and brutality. It is tired of so-called Christians who go to church on Sunday morning and come home and beat their slaves on Sunday afternoon. So, using the mask of a song which seems to be praying for the Christian experience, it makes a commentary on the need for true religion, and the honest practice of the fine set of doctrines encompassed in Christianity. If this were not its intention, why does it phrase its poetic idea as it does, "I *want* to be a Christian" . . . in-a my *heart*"?

As great poets, the makers of the spiritual had stronger reasons even than these for using mask and symbol. They knew, by instinct, if you will, that mask and symbol are a part of the means of hurling the poetic point into the heart of the listener with devastating effect. Direct language tends to stumble over local and insignificant concerns. They also knew that the real purpose of artistic inspiration is not expression but impact.

Take as a sample one of the most powerful and justly popular of the spirituals from the first collection published in America. It is called "Lay This Body Down." It opens with this stanza,

> O graveyard, O graveyard,
> I'm walkin' troo de graveyard;
> Lay dis body down.

The first effect of the poet is to bring the listener into a spooky atmosphere. As an example of a funeral song, a relic of Africa, the spiritual quite naturally offers a graveyard scene. But before the first stanza is over the mask begins to show. Notice that the emphasis is not upon a corpse, but upon the singer. He is the one who is walking through the graveyard. Of his own free will he is about to lay down his body. If the listener has any curiosity at all in his soul, he wants to know why. The poet goes on,

> I know moonlight, I know starlight,
> I'm walkin' troo de starlight;
> Lay dis body down.

Being quiet and unencumbered, graveyards are naturally places where moonlight and starlight are full and free. The singer not only walks through the graveyard; he walks through the moonlight and starlight. Quite obviously he intends to make a theatrical performance of his putting himself away. Later in the poem, he says,

> I lay in de grave an' stretch out my arms; . . .
>
> I go to de judgment in de evenin' of de day . . .
>
> And my soul an' your soul will meet in de day
> When we lay dis body down.

It is now clear what mask the poet is wearing and for what purpose. Under the guise of a funeral poem he is stating an unabashed confidence in the ability of life to conquer death. Bather in moonlight and starlight, he revels in the graveyard, defying death, making engagements in the face of death. In the process he has invigorated his listener and written a beautiful poem. Could he have done all this and left the same memorable impression had he engaged in direct talk?

And so, in common with folk songs of all ages, the Afro-American spiritual employed a mask and symbol. Its creatures carried these two to a very high pitch. Using them as they did, they were able to write songs that dealt with every phase of the slave's life and to do so without fear of being punished. They were even able to depict the slaveholder as tyrant and hypocrite and to further the flight of the fugitive.

⟪ *The Qualities and Purposes of the Spiritual*

The Afro-American spiritual has certain qualities and purposes as a folk song. As a general rule, it is personal for each member. The use of the personal pronouns *I* and *we* is deliberate. Such a quality is a style of presentation rather than an overemphasis on ego. It is probably intended, however, as an ego builder. It is also probably intended to place the singer in the midst of major actions and feelings. A community of millions of people, each one recognized as important, produces a powerful folk effect.

The religious quality in the poems is often there for reasons other than the expression of Christian doctrine. Nettie Fitzgerald McAdams says that religion is the great theme in these songs both in its consolation for this life and in its hope for the life to come. Death is merely the necessary means of transition to that other glorious life. But Mrs. McAdams seems unaware of the fact that the principle of religion being followed is African. The songs merely recall the totality of religion as a unifying and organizing force. The slave was fully aware that he needed such a force. The master class attempted to supply it, but the slave had mental reservations against the master class. He needed a totality principle from a source he respected and believed in.

Another reason for the religious quality was a time-honored one: the acquisition of depth and dignity. Religious poems have always dealt with the most important topic of man's existence, with the nature of the world, with the world's creations and their operation and control, with the essences of being, with the relationship between man and whatever God or gods he accepted. To give the spiritual religious tone and religious subject matter was to force upward the slave's meditations as he sang. It was like a liberal education.

Within expression the folk community wanted to communicate. Their targets were their own members, men of goodwill and believers in justice, and powers (the divinity of the powers was often symbolic) who could move the apparently immovable oppressors. If his songs are proof, the slave singer never believed that the master class was in an impregnable position, or that he was doomed to be a slave for life on this earth. He constantly expressed confidence that thick walls would "come a-tumb-a-lin' down." He had seen them come down. All around him he had seen powerful emperors cut down, their empires reduced to rubble, their possessions (even their slaves) scattered to the four winds. If justice and deliverance could come to Daniel, why not to every man? Why not to me?

Since there was every kind of human being among the slaves and innumerable situations and experiences among the folk community, it turned out that there was every kind of spiritual. Distinctions between spirituals, work songs, blues songs, animal songs, and the like, are likely to be more artificial than real. In the first large collection of slave songs, *Slave Songs of the United States* (1867), there is every kind of folk song imaginable and the family relationship among them all is quite clear. Examination of this and later collections will underscore this variety even among songs that the more simpleminded insist are spirituals and nothing more.

"Songs of the Coffle Gang," "Slavery Chain," "Paul and Silas Bound in Jail," for example, are prison songs if ever there were prison songs. "Hammer Ring" and a hundred others are work songs. Animal songs abound in expression about sheep, birds, cows, bees, etc. "Michael, Row the Boat Ashore" is one of a dozen that come near being sea chanteys. And where are there better blues songs than "Nobody Knows the Trouble I See," "I'm Er Pore Little Orphan Chile in de World," "Sometimes I Feel Like a Motherless Child," and "I Wish I Had Died in Egypt Land."

Dena Epstein demonstrates that in the middle of the eighteenth century slave songs ranged from obscene and warlike to plaintive and melancholy. In *From Jehovah to Jazz*, Helen Kaufmann differentiates "settin' spirituals" from "runnin' spirituals" (i.e. shouts). Newman I. White, in *American Negro Folk Songs* (1928), has made a number of categories and subcategories, but nearly all of his differing types can be found among so-called orthodox spirituals: "Upstart Crows," "Social Songs," "Songs About Animals," "Gang Laborers," "Rural Labor," "General and Miscellaneous Labor," "Songs about Women," "Recent Events," "Race Consciousness," and "The Seamier Side."

Mrs. Epstein has also noted that some owners, suspicious of all forms of musical expression by slaves (as early as 1842), prevented their chattels from singing at all. Others prohibited melancholy tunes or words and allowed only cheerful music and senseless words. These curious masters thought thereby to prevent the slave from dwelling on the nature of peculiar hardships. It is difficult to conceive of such blindness and insensitivity by the rulers of the realm.

Probably to try to dispel the notion that the spirituals were trifling, Frederick Douglass in his earliest autobiography had characterized spirituals in this fashion,

> I have sometimes thought, that the mere hearing of these songs would do more to impress truly spiritual-minded men and women with the soul crushing and death-dealing character of slavery, than the reading of whole volumes of its mere physical cruelties. They speak to the heart and to the soul of the thoughtful.

Later, he adds,

> They were ones, loud, long and deep, breathing the prayer and complaint of souls boiling over with the bitterest anguish. Every tone was a testimony against slavery, and a prayer to God for deliverance from chains.

In the spiritual section of *The Negro in Music and Art* (1966), Lindsay Patterson, the editor, has perpetuated the debate over the question of the predominance of misery and sorrow in the songs. He reprints first the memorable essay of W. E. B. Du Bois, "Of the Sorrow Songs" (from *The Souls of Black Folk*, 1903). Du Bois (in this one of the greatest efforts by a master of belles-lettres in America) rightfully stresses the sheer beauty of the spirituals, the ancient origins, and the message. He brings out the hope which shines through the sorrow. The slaves, he says, in an exquisite manner, were "singing to the sunshine."

The negative side of the debate is in Zora Neale Hurston's "Spirituals and Neo-Spirituals" in 1933. Miss Hurston says, "The idea that the whole body of spirituals are 'sorrow songs' is ridiculous. They cover a wide range of subjects from a peeve at gossip to Death and Judgment." In this view Miss Hurston is right, although she did not give Du Bois full credit. But she veers away from precision when she says, "The nearest thing to a description one can reach is that they are Negro religious songs, sung by a group, and a group bent on expression of feelings and not on sound effects." Obviously the songs are not always religious in the American sense. And sound effects, in both music and words, are one of the strong points of their art.

Let it be underscored, then, that the Afro-American spiritual has great variety of purpose, beginning with pure expression and communication, and fanning out over a wide field. It cried for a union of the folk against a common enemy and for the common goal of freedom of the body and of the human spirit. It provided for every type of individual and group method of singing. The great span shown by its arrangers (note the spiritual section, pp. 454–82 in Charles Haywood's *Bibliography of North American Folklore and Folksong*) is not an accomplishment in arrangement but a development of the natural elements in the song.

The spiritual, as we have seen and shall see again more specifically, was preeminent in message bearing, in setting the record straight, in appeals to the highest courts of human values, in advocacy and declaration of change, and in the African-inspired tradition of poetry as magic. Russell Ames and others have recorded how Harriet Tubman used "Go Down, Moses" to call up her candidates for transportation to free land; she also used "Wade in the Water" to warn her friends how to throw bloodhounds off the scent. Nat Turner used "Steal Away" to call his conspirators together. "The Chariot's A-Comin' " was a clear reference, via "singing telegraph," to the overhanging shadow in the neighborhood of a conductor for the Underground Railroad. "Good News, Member" reported by the same great telegraph that a runaway slave had reached freedom. "Foller de Drinkin' Gou'd" (the drinking gourd was the Big Dipper in the sky) was a musical and poetic map of one line in the network of the Underground Railroad.

About 1839, as recorded by Dena Epstein (from the *Liberty Bell*, a magazine), Charity Bower, an ex-slave born in Pembroke, North Carolina, about 1774, was interviewed by Lydia M. Child concerning the meanings of spirituals. Among other evidence she insisted that praying or singing immediately following the Nat Turner "rising" was a dangerous occupation carried out by slaves. For so doing, the slaves might be killed by "low whites" before the masters or mistresses could get to them. She remembered several prohibited spirituals, but especially this one,

> A few more beatings of the wind and rain,
> Ere the winter will be over—
> Glory, Hallelujah!
> Some friends has gone before me,—
> I must try to go and meet them—
> Glory, Hallelujah!
> A few more risings and settings of the sun,
> Ere the winter will be over—
> Glory, Hallelujah!
> There's a better day a coming—
> There's a better day a coming—
> Oh, Glory Hallelujah!

If the helpless slave, immured in slavery, was merely singing about heavenly rescue in such songs, why was he prohibited even by a master who was slow on the uptake?

A few years ago the late T. K. Whipple in a memorable essay, "Men, Machinery, and Magic," helps to explain why poetry has lost its popularity. He reiterates the experience of many literary critics of the past by establishing poetry as magic, words capable of performing powerful things. Not being magic any longer, poetry has lost out to engineering, which is magic and therefore the most modern of poetry.

The folk community of the spiritual believed in poetry as a maker and a reflector of change so powerful as to constitute magic. "Ain't I Glad I've Got out the Wilderness," for example, is more than Biblical and personal rescue; it is part of a magical process. This process is described at length in later chapters.

Coleman and Bregman in *Songs of American Folks* make an interesting observation on the purposes of these songs. They say that no matter how colloquially phrased or "comically" twisted, these songs are fundamentally serious moral tales: the songs "have one overwhelming advantage, however, over other serious, moral tales; they are never dull!" Downes and Siegmeister, on the other hand, note that they are not all serious and exalted. Many, they say, are "exuberantly gay." They set down as the most remarkable characteristics of the songs their truthfulness, spontaneity, and uninhibited rectitude.

The word of a trained psychologist may be valuable. Albert Sidney Beckham wrote on "The Psychology of Negro Spirituals." He notes that many have thought the spirituals were never intended to appeal to the intelligence, that they were merely stimulants of emotional fervor. This point Beckham is willing to concede. He accepts the fact that the spirituals were generally created in an emotional atmosphere and in the poetry and life of an oppressed people. But an appeal to intelligence is often found, he declares, for example, in the warnings against hurtful gossip. Discontent and hope are the most common of emotional appeals. The spiritual, however, goes farther and wages a fight for freedom.

In selecting experiences upon which songs could be built, the slave poet concentrated on those which had parallels in the slave's own life, or those from which parallels could easily be made. The experiences of Moses and Daniel are obvious enough, but those of the New Testament are equally appropriate. "Po' ol' Lazarus, po' as I, / W'en he died, he had a home on high" is more than a promise of reward after death. The singer achieved status immediately upon recognizing his worth in the category with Lazarus; the home on high was merely a final acknowledgment of his status. Note the present tense in the chorus line, "I got a home in dat rock, don' you see?" He does not have to wait for the home in the rock; he has that now. Likewise, "Rich Man Dives" is already demoted. The home in hell awaiting him is the final judgment, but having no home in the rock, he is already doomed, like other rich men floating around.

As folk songs, the spirituals were created to seem simple, but actually to be profound. This was to induce meditation and new discovery as the singer sang the song over and over again. If they had been as simple as they seem, or as many interpreters try to make them, they would not have encouraged resinging even with the beautiful music. But because they perpetually repaid new singing and new thinking about the meaning, they became popular with a great many slaves over a vast territory.

In line with the African imagination, the Afro-American spiritual was picturesque and concrete on top. The walker in the graveyard bathed in moonlight and starlight; the gory details of the "great gittin'-up mornin' ";

the mountain tops and the revealing wilderness; a soul anchored in the Lord—thousands of elaborate and exciting pictures to catch the fancy of the singer. But the pictures and the concrete items merely opened the subject. Underneath there is always the magnetic point. "Babylon's fallin' . . . to rise no more." Yes, but what does it all mean? Why did it fall? What does Babylon's fall mean to me?

Emotionally the range of the songs is almost as great as it can be: from very lively to very slow; from very happy to very sad; from songs of assurance and confidence to songs of great mystery and not knowing what to do. The folk mood had to be reached as it turned on a wide axis. The varying tempos of the folk had to be accommodated. The need for excitement and the need for something to sing when one felt like being quiet still deserved equal attention.

Some have insisted that the spirituals are otherworldly. G. R. Wilson in "The Religion of the American Negro Slave: His Attitude toward Life and Death" did a B.D. dissertation at the University of Chicago to try to prove this point. Some have said they are entirely worldly: Rosey Pool of England and Holland and Janheinz Jahn of Germany, to mention only two. Some have made them out to be purely traditional; others, to be purely contemporary.

All these are right, up to a point. The Afro-American spiritual was worldly, otherworldly, traditional, and contemporary. It was a true folk song in that it blended the experiences and poetic imaginations of one folk group and created songs for the universal human heart. The fact that it has been sung and cherished around the world, and is still being sung after hundreds of years, is testimony of the extent to which it has dug deep into the universal human heart.

To summarize, the purposes of the Afro-American spiritual can be simply stated:

1. To give the community a true, valid, and useful song
2. To keep the community invigorated
3. To inspire the uninspired individual
4. To enable the group to face its problems
5. To comment on the slave situation
6. To stir each member to personal solutions and to a sense of belonging in the midst of a confusing and terrifying world
7. To provide a code language for emergency use

(*The Character of the Spiritual's Creators*

As is usual in the folk tradition, the community provides the stuff of the songs and the dominant themes; some genius in the community creates the songs themselves. In Africa, this genius was carefully designated and trained over a period of years. In America he was probably well known to his local group, but his name has since become shrouded in mystery. His character can be fairly well established from internal evidence and the results of the searchings and insights of scholars.

Bruno Nettl has written, "As in Africa, the Negroes of the United States have developed song makers who composed or improvised songs, or who created material out of songs already in existence, and who became masters recognized by the community."

Characterizing the individual creator of the spiritual more specifically, however, G. Malcolm Laws (in *Native American Balladry*) has declared (speaking just of the narrative spirituals),

> The Negro singer is dramatist first, moralist second, if at all, in contrast to the white singer, who often lets his moralizing interfere with an otherwise vivid story. The Negro uses words well, if not always in an orthodox manner. And he is so keenly aware of the truth and realism of the story he tells that he holds his hearers by his own sincerity. Limited as they are in range and incident, these narrative folksongs of the Negro are moving and intense, and they have added immeasurably to the richness of American balladry.

By instinct, says Louis Achille, the anonymous composer has placed himself in the universal conscience as the soloist before the choir. The individual has only distinguished himself from the mass in order to express the common emotions or the simple unmistakable solidarity which imposes the commonality upon the skin. For an instant, and without investigating a personal success in originality, he takes in charge experience vibrant to the group and frames in doing so a message to the whole of humanity.

Oscar Seagle, a white Southern singer, says that the leader improvised the verses and allowed the melody to follow the word line. There followed repetitions, additions, deletions.

In the estimation of H. L. Mencken probably one poet wrote "Swing Low," "Deep River," and "Roll, Jordan, Roll." "He was one of the greatest poets we have ever produced, and he came so near being our greatest musician that I hesitate to look for a match for him."

For opening the game of reconstructing the identity of these masterful songsmiths, a most appropriate poem is available. Consider, therefore, the first three stanzas of James Weldon Johnson's "O Black and Unknown Bards":

> O black and unknown bards of long ago,
> How came your lips to touch the sacred fire?
> How, in your darkness, did you come to know
> The power and beauty of the minstrel's lyre?
> Who first from midst his bonds lifted his eyes?
> Who first from out the still watch, lone and long,
> Feeling the ancient faith of prophets rise
> Within his dark-kept soul, burst into song?

Heart of what slave poured out such melody
As "Steal away to Jesus"? On its strains
His spirit must have nightly floated free,
Though still above his hands he felt his chains.
Who heard great "Jordan roll"? Whose starward eye
Saw chariot "swing low"? And who was he
That breathed that comforting, melodic sigh,
"Nobody knows de trouble I see"?

What merely living clod, what captive thing,
Could up toward God through all its darkness grope?
And find within its deadened heart to sing
These songs of sorrow, love and faith, and hope?
How did it catch that subtle undertone,
That note in music heard not with the ears,
How sound the elusive reed so seldom blown,
Which stirs the soul or melts the heart to tears?

An opening element of character is immediately apparent. As one writer has said, whoever wrote these songs was gifted with a free spirit and was unfit to be a slave. Applying this rule, since the stuff of the songs was prepared by the slave community, none of them deserved to be slaves. It is certain that in many congregations where these songs were sung, and doubtless where they were created, free and slave Negroes sang together. It is not inconceivable that some of them were written by free Negroes, identifying with their slave brothers. Denmark Vesey was free.

Olmsted remarks that the creators showed a readiness in the art of music, the power of memory, and a gift for improving ideas given to them. Clark says that they were probably sensitive human beings rather than great thinkers. Hall is struck by their lovableness, and many writers have mentioned their lack of vindictiveness. The latter comment is a tribute to the sense of art in the creators; very few poets have succeeded in turning out great songs if their minds were split between the work of creation and getting even with somebody. Barry is impressed by the creators' individuality.

The comment on individuality raises the usual argument about how much of the individual and how much of the communal is in these songs. Ballanta Taylor, who was born in Africa, but who spent much time in the United States, says that everything in America is individual, and everything in Africa is communal. Landeck attributes the verses of the songs to the individuals and the choruses to groups; she adds that adaptation was continuous. Jeannette Murphy quotes one former slave as saying that the songs were made up by the "old heads" in the group "on the spurn of the moment." William L. Dawson and Esther MacTaggart credit the group. Dawson specifically eliminates any individual composer or poet; Mac-

Taggart, who says she saw a spiritual born (in 1940), shows how the group put the song together.

H. L. Mencken insists that there is no such thing as a song bursting full-grown out of folk. Folk songs, he underlines, are written by individuals. "Ah," he says, "that we could discover the authors of some of them!"

Undoubtedly Robert T. Kerlin agrees with Mencken. He dedicates his whole book, *Negro Poets and Their Poems,* to the spiritual writers.

Actually, as has been said, the songs were written by both the group and the individual, at times with greater emphasis on the group, at times with greater emphasis on the individual. By and large, because of the artistic skills demonstrated, one would have to give predominance in most instances to the individuals.

The most likely individual for a great number of songs was the Negro preacher. In *God's Trombones,* a series of sermons and prayers presumably delivered by one or more Negro preachers, James Weldon Johnson has shown the strong parallels between the sermon and the spiritual—the narrative technique, the picturesqueness and the concreteness, the emphasis on personal characteristics, the familiarity with the deity, and all the rest. The preacher also had the knowledge, the memory, the imagination, the skill with phrases, and the requisite poetic soul. He possessed the leadership to impress his songs upon the congregation and get them well started on their way. Russell Ames adds one other powerful characteristic of the black preacher: the quality of living drama.

Haskell says the songs could have been created by preacher or member. There is no reason to believe that many of them were not written by members. The important thing is not the position but the basic character of the creator. Whether preacher or member, while he was delivering the song, he was in a leadership role.

A great many writers have given pictures and examples of creators at work. Abigail Christensen indicates that the shout spiritual was probably led by the best singers, who opened the religious dance built around the song. This dance could accelerate until singers and dancers were "clean beat out."

In *Lincoln and the Music of the Civil War,* Kenneth Bernard tells of Lincoln's experiences with spiritual singers. On more than one occasion the President found himself singing with the group. The leader in the group was Aunt Mary Dines, formerly a White House employee, a singer and a writer. When the group sang "Nobody Knows the Trouble I've Seen" and "Every Time I Feel the Spirit," the President found himself wiping tears from his face. When they sang "I Thank God I'm Free at Last," the President bowed his head. Aunt Mary Dines was undoubtedly a spiritual creator.

Joseph Hutchinson Smith tells of an old Negro woman who just wanted a new song. As a result she created "Um! Most Done Toilin' Here." At a re-

ligious meeting in the Georgia woods, T. G. Steward saw and heard a tall
black woman sing this song which she seemed to have created,

> Dark clouds a-risin'!
> Thunder-bolts a-bustin'!
> Master Jesus comes a-ridin' by
> With a rainbow on his shoulder.

The searchers after and the recorders of spirituals have found many
creators who must have belonged to a tradition hundreds of years old.
William E. Barton describes Sister Bemaugh. In Marion Kerby's records
are Parson Jacobs of the Sycamo Baptist Church in the Mississippi Delta;
Old Aunt Becky of Greenville, Mississippi; Aunt Etta from the Measury
Estate in Cleveland Park, Thomasville, Georgia; and Uncle Eph who lived
twenty miles from Tuskegee Institute, Alabama, and who was well known
by Booker T. Washington.

Lucile Price Turner met, in Arkansas, a creator named Tom. Tom was
a treasury of anecdote, legend, and folklore. He sang and prayed at work.
In his great repertoire was an original verson of "All God's Chillun Has
Shoes." In his church Tom did the singing, the praying, the testifying, the
speaking in tongues, and the "dancing in the Spirit." He also created songs,
one of which went,

> O Lord, search my heart; O Lord, search my heart;
> For you know when I'm right, when I'm wrong.
> Please, Jesus . . . Holy Spirit, . . .
> I'm so glad, . . .

Beyond any doubt the most brilliant description of spiritual creators is
found in James Weldon Johnson's essay which became a part of the Preface to *The Book of Negro Spirituals*. This great personality in the spiritual tradition addresses himself first to the question of whether the spirituals "were the spontaneous outburst and expression of the group or
chiefly the work of individual talented makers." His answer is that some
of them may be the spontaneous creation of the group, but that he believes
that the far greater part is the work of talented individuals. He speaks of
modifications that still continue, of variations in melody, of interchange
and substitution of lines.

Then he turns to the "barding" which he associates with the production
of many spirituals. The bard, he said, had to have a gift for melody, a
talent for poetry, a strong voice, and a good memory. He had to know
how to compose an appealing tune, how to fashion graphic lines, how to
pitch the tune and lead it clearly. He also had to remember all the lines.

Turning to his childhood (he was born in 1871), he recalls two striking
personalities: "Ma" White, a great leader of singing, and "Singing" Johnson, a maker of songs. "Ma" White was a laundress and a busy woman,
but she was always at church ready to lead the singing when the choir and

the organ did not edge her out. Her shrill, plaintive voice quavered above all the others. "One of her duties was to 'sing-down' a long-winded or uninteresting speaker at love feasts or experience meetings, and even to cut short a prayer of undue length by raising a song." She knew sources of spirituals, but probably never composed any.

As to "Singing" Johnson, singing was his only business. He went from church to church, often singing and teaching new songs. He received a collection, food, and lodging. In his leisure time he originated new words and new melodies, and new lines for old songs. He was admittedly not as striking a figure as some of the great Negro preachers, but on special occasions he was only slightly less important. He could improvise lines on the moment. He was a great judge of the appropriate song to sing "and with a delicate sense of when to come to the preacher's support after a climax in the sermon had been reached by breaking in with a line or two of a song that expressed a certain sentiment, often just a single line."

Always singing with his eyes, or eye, closed, "Singing" Johnson marked the tempo by swinging his head and body. "When he warmed to his work it was easy to see that he was transported and utterly oblivious to his surroundings."

James Weldon Johnson insists that "Singing" Johnson was one of a line of great bards of an earlier day, bards who composed the spirituals. Their stories and songs were influenced and modified by the group in action. He also cites parallels with African bards.

Since the spirituals obviously reflect the deepest thoughts, reactions, philosophies, dreams, and hopes of the community, the community cannot be ruled out as a co-composer. But the actual work of formulating the song had to be the work of experts in music and poetry and in what would capture and overwhelm the human heart.

❨ Basic Elements as Literature

A discussion of the precise literary elements of the spiritual will appear somewhat later in this book. At this stage the role of the spiritual as folk song is being developed. Since nearly all folk songs are literature to some extent, it is necessary to examine these basic literary elements.

The folk community and its poet in residence followed certain patterns. These can be roughly divided into *mechanical* and *nonmechanical*. In the mechanical pattern is generally a basic declaration of some truth or reaction to some truth. For example,

> There is a Balm in Gilead,
> To make the wounded whole . . .
> To heal the sin-sick soul

or "I'm so glad trouble don't last alway." This declaration is iterated and reiterated—the spiritual often opens with the refrain—probably to make sure it sinks in as well as for mnemonic reasons. After the refrain, the song turns to stanza, and from that point refrain and new stanzas alternate.

Also in the mechanical phase there is sharp phrasing. The one-syllable word and the clear, tough, vigorous Anglo-Saxon word predominate. There is original use of single words, idioms, phrases, clauses; of resolutions; and of unanswerable questions, like "Were You There When They Crucified My Lord?" or "Death (sometimes spelled "Det'"), Ain't You Got No Shame?"

The repetition so flagrant in the spiritual has already been partially explained. It is there both to make the song easy to carry and to harp on words and ideas of key significance to the groups. Sometimes the repeated phrases are code words with hidden instructions in them. Lomax says that the brevity and speed of patterns of repetition restrict the song to "those bits of information which culture members agree are paramount in importance."

Personal pronouns are greatly favored. Most spirituals declare or presuppose *you* or *I*. Side by side with the personal pronouns are the family and community terms (beloved of the African mind): *father, brother, sister, mother, member, seeker, sinner*, etc. There is emphatic use of vocatives, as in "Walk Togedder, Children, Don't You Get Weary."

The spirituals interchange phrases, verses, stanzas without compunction or confusion. Words of the same song may be hard to distinguish because of variations in dialect and because of the idiosyncrasies of arrangers.

Also mechanical is the beat and the rhyme. Most spirituals follow simple beats, iambic tetrameter alternating with iambic trimeter, but, over the range, dozens of beats are used. The rhyme scheme is often *abcb*. But again, looking widely one can find many rhyme schemes. Whatever beat and rhyme schemes are used, they are likely to be easy for the multitude to sing and to develop into rhythmic and harmonic patterns. Often there is no rhyme. But there is always rhythm. There is always a sequence of words to catch the beat.

In the nonmechanical phase perhaps the outstanding element is simplicity with a core of subtlety. Even Theo Lehmann in Germany has learned the old saying that the white man talks with the back of his head (shows you his whole mind); the Negro talks with the front of his head (shows you only the surface of his thought). Lehmann also seems convinced that when the song speaks of being saved from sins, it means being saved from slavery at the same time. He refers to the fact that "Oh Mary, Don't You Weep" expresses both joy about salvation through Christ and a reminder that the listener should not be sad when the singer leaves to escape.

This subtlety within simplicity is not confined to double meanings like those above. When, for instance, "the wall comes tumbling down" at

Slave procession in Benin, Africa.

Slaves working cotton gin, 1793.

Torture device used on slaves who tried to run away.

A slave being whipped.

A slave mother has killed her children rather than let them be returned to slavery.

Iron collar used for torture and punishment of slaves.

A free Negro is kidnapped and made a slave.

Slaves dancing in Congo Square, New Orleans.

A slave learning to read.

A slave woman
committing suicide
by leaping from a
building.

A slave running from
bloodhounds.

White minstrels imitating slave
humor and songs.

Slaves fighting off pursuers.

Fighting off slave-catchers,
pre-Civil War era.

A group of runaway slaves fighting pursuers.

Former slaves who fled Florida and rose high in the Seminole Indian nation.

Ann Wood leads a group of slaves to freedom in 1855.

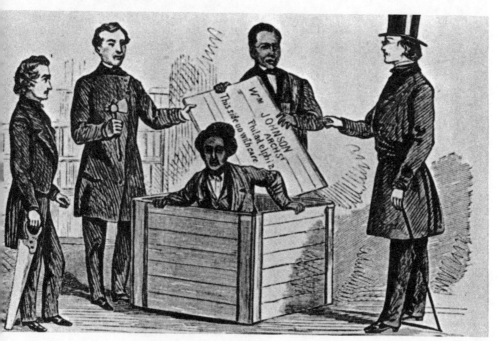

Slave Henry "Box" Brown emerges from the box in which he escaped from slavery.

Learning to read together: a slave and his master's children. FROM THE NEGRO COLLECTION OF THE MOORLAND ROOM, HOWARD UNIVERSITY LIBRARY

Harriet Tubman: born a slave, she freed herself and hundreds of
other slaves; she used many spirituals as code messages in the process.
THE ASSOCIATED PUBLISHERS, INC.

Jericho, you have the following clear meanings: (1) the Biblical story as a basis; (2) the destructive power of the slave against those who have imprisoned him, similar to the power of Joshua and his marchers; and (3) the universal principle that, if it is aggressive and persistent, right will triumph over wrong because that is the kind of world we live in.

The next, very important, nonmechanical element is immediacy. In the usual religious hymns and white spirituals Biblical events happen at a distance or through simile or other figure of speech. In the Afro-American spiritual, as Ames put it, "Biblical history is taking place right before your eyes or even . . . you are included in the action." Thus, you are there when Christ is born ("Go Tell It on the Mountain") or when he is crucified. Daniel, Noah, Moses, Paul, and Jesus himself are at arm's length or easily reached.

A third nonmechanical device is the critical attitude or approach. Mrs. Epstein said that on Sundays, even as early as 1774–77, slaves played on the gourd (a kind of a guitar) and, through droll music, "relate the usage they have received from their Masters or Mistresses in a very satirical stile and manner." In later chapters this critical approach will be fully documented.

There is use of command and urgent request; the purposeful selection of topics, especially of personalities for topics; there is mask and irony, as has already been shown. There is, finally, among this selected list of nonmechanical elements the use of the listener as a creative device. In "We Are Climbing Jacob's Ladder" is a stanza that asks the sinner, "Do you love my Jesus?" The next stanza inquires, "If you love him, why not serve him?" This method is obviously more than call and response. It presumes that the listener is a part of the song. What he thinks and feels, how he reacts to the whole big event, are part of the song. This utter involvement is invigorating to singer and listener. It helps to account for the spiritual's perennial popularity.

So much, then, is the folk community. We now turn to the major topics and to the songs themselves. Whatever they are, they can be interpreted only in terms of this particular folk community. Whatever they are, they are as unique as fingerprints, as indeed are all folk songs vis-à-vis their folk communities.

As folk literature the spiritual puts its strength in the first line. First lines are the summation of the community's and the poet's philosophical discovery. First lines are the creative explosion of wisdom, sentiment, and beauty on which the originality and appeal of the song rest. First lines get the song off the ground and into the air where its full development takes place.

Look at some of the first lines in the *Slave Songs of the United States*, the first thoroughgoing spiritual collection. "I hold my brudder wid a tremblin' han'." Note the tension, the suggestion of mystery. "What make ole Satan da follow me so?" The pithy question that seems to be at the root of all the singer's problems. Whom is he thinking of as Satan? Why, in fact, is he being pursued? What is the effect on his life and being of his being perpetually followed around, as though by furies?

Occasionally, the first line carries a blend of apparent opposites: "Walk in, kind Savior, No man can hinder me!" Occasionally, it is a sudden and deeply thoughtful picture: "Oh Deat' he is a little man, . . ." Every now and then, it is a peremptory order: "Hunt till you find him, Hallelujah, . . ." "Michael row de boat ashore, Hallelujah!" "Sail, O believer, sail, . . ." "Turn, sinner, turn today, . . ."

Considering that first lines are often repeated and that second and third and later stanzas are often interchanged with other songs, the first line is the real indicator of the original spiritual.

Though not as sharp and powerful, on the whole, as the first lines, the refrains and choruses are next in order of importance in the construction of the spiritual. "Blow your trumpet, Gabriel" is not a first line, but it gives the song a great boost. "Lay dis body down" is a refrain line. It is not as beautiful, nor as poetic, as "I walk in de moonlight, I walk in de starlight"; but it provides a central station from which the remarkable poetics of the poem radiate. "Religion so sweet," also a refrain line, by repetition at regular intervals induces a feeling of incomparable satisfaction in the singer's mind.

Most poems are a careful organization of a vivid first line, a middle refrain line, and a chorus. The repetitions are mainly singing devices, memory aids, and means of enlisting and holding the support of the group. These methods appear in many folk songs, but in the spiritual they are generally meshed with originality and taste.

The themes of the spiritual are both pointed and comprehensive. If one remembers that the mask of Christianity and religion is a mask, not of itself a theme-maker, and goes on from there to concentrate on the real themes, he will see how pointed and comprehensive. Even if one conceded that the songs were all-Christian—an overwhelming concession in the face of the facts—this concession would not at all affect the nature of the case.

Take a well-known spiritual like "Study War No More." The idea comes from Isaiah 2:4 (and Micah 4:3), "and they shall beat their swords into plowshares, and their spears into pruning-hooks: nation shall not lift up sword against nation, neither shall they learn war any more."

Let it first be noted that, even if slaves had gone to church regularly and had been given Christian instruction consistently, Isaiah is not an area of the Bible that was taught to them. The topic of the song thus came from some enterprising slave who found out about Isaiah and his theory of war and peace on his own.

Notice two other things: the association of the sword and the shield and the shift from "learn war" to "study war." The Bible associates shields with spears, for that association is normal; it never mentions shields and swords together. Probably for poetic reasons the makers of this song rejected the spear and shield association and joined sword and shield. Not only did they have smoother sounds, but a broader symbolism.

"Study war" was a great improvement over "learn war" for the purpose of singing. You needed the extra syllable. You also needed a stronger, more persistent term than "learn war."

In its apparently original form this spiritual had three stanzas; it is very rarely adapted. The three stanzas represent three steps: (1) "lay down my sword and shield"; (2) "put on my long white robe"; (3) "talk with the Prince of Peace." All of this takes place "down by the riverside." What more logical a place!

What is the real theme of the song? Does the *I* refer to everyone? Is this a suggestion of what everyone must do? Of course. It is an unequivocal peace poem. But its theme is inherent in the word "study." Wars take place, says the poet, because people's minds are not turned from them and from all things that produce them. To dispense with the weapons of war is not enough. One must find a way to transform the minds of men so they will not stray into pathways of thought that result in war. Our whole educational system must be changed. We must learn to "study" the ways of peace; that is what the singer's talk with the "Prince of Peace" will be about.

No matter that the basic idea comes from the Bible—it could have come from the newspapers or from some other source which told of the misery and uselessness of war. The theme of the poem is not a mere complaint against war. It is an advocacy of educating the people to peace. One does not have to dig for the theme. It is right there in front of the eyes of anyone who reads the poem patiently, thoughtfully, and without preconceived ideas.

So it is with the themes of most of these poems. Why a slave who was conducting a war against slavery should be so strong for peace is a separate matter. The answer is not too far away. There are many spirituals in praise of war, poems in praise of valiant soldiers, poems advocating that the slave die on the field of battle. Aside from the fact that there were many points of view among a large group of people like the slaves, the war poems and the peace poems are not necessarily in contradiction even were the maker of all the poems a single man. In the everyday struggle, he had to fight. The oppressive enemy gave him no alternative. In the calm of his thinking he was well aware that peace was the only condition to generate and cherish the greatest accomplishments of the human soul and the human body. Loud as this song is, it probably grows out of the maker's moments of calm.

Figure of speech is a staple of folk songs. It is an outstanding quality and accomplishment of the Afro-American spiritual. The similes, the metaphors, the personifications, and other figures are generally bold and exciting. Similes like "O the religion that my Lord gave me,/ Shines like a mornin' star"; metaphors like "My mother's broke the ice and gone"; and personifications galore. "Death ain't nothin' but a robber, don't you see" is one of the most powerful because the robbery is spelled out,

> Death came to my house, he didn't stay long,
> I looked in the bed an' my mother was gone, . . .
>
> I looked in the bed an' my father was gone, . . .
>
> I looked in the bed an' my brother was gone,
> Death ain't nothin' but a robber, don't you see.

The figures with rocks are usually quite striking. If one deliberates, a home in a rock is far more picturesque and incisive than it seems at first blush. But examine the "rock" figures from Revelation. All John, the writer, gives is a picture of kings, mighty men, free men and bondmen hiding themselves in the dens and in the rocks of the mountains, and saying to the mountains and rocks, "Fall on us, and hide us from the face of him that sitteth on the throne, and from the wrath of the Lamb."

In some songs, however, you get the exact reverse:

> O rocks, don't fall on me,
> O rocks, don't fall on me,
> O rocks, don't fall on me,
> Rocks and mountains, don't fall on me.

In other songs, you get a very plaintive situation. After these men have cried out to the rocks, the rocks answer,

> Went to the rocks for to hide my face,
> Rocks cried out, "No hiding place,"
> There's no hiding place down here.

Or the rocks say,

> I'm burnin', too,
> I want to get to heaven just as much as you.

Not only is there a drama based on John's more simple situation. There is the expression of the eternal law of justice. If you do wrong, regardless of your status in life, you pay. Standing up for stern morality, the rocks made clear that they were not made to shield the wrongdoer from his just punishment. Even the rocks are an agency of the moral law.

This example leads to the last of the basic elements of the Afro-American spiritual as folk literature: the element of inherent philosophy. Each individual song expresses a philosophical idea, as has been shown for several. When one examines the general philosophical expression of the thousands of poems, one is deeply impressed.

One notices that the philosophy or philosophies are well in line with the characteristics of the folk community. They are a full appreciation of the slave's personal, legal, religious, educational, and general social positions, as he saw them. They voice his aspirations on the basis of his relative positions. Protected by its mask and symbol, the community does not hesitate to be quite frank and free about all this.

The fundamental elements of the community's philosophy will be given and documented in later pages. It is sufficient here to declare that the Afro-American spiritual is a folk song, philosophically speaking. As sung around the world, the philosophies of the songs have inspirited the people.

Like the literature of all great bodies of folk song, the Afro-American spirituals can be primarily interpreted only in terms of their original folk community. Whatever they are, they are as unique as fingerprints. All true folk songs vis-à-vis their folk communities are like ours.

❰ Relationship to Dance and Instrument

Anyone who has studied African folk expression even casually is aware of the almost unbreakable union of instrument and dance and song. For centuries the drum was the key. The drummer was (and is still in many parts of Africa) a master not only of his instrument but of the feelings of the people. He knew enough about the community to put their essential feelings into his drumming. And when they recognized their feelings through the drumbeats he could, through his drum, guide them to higher and higher rungs of feeling.

He did this partly through his control of the dance. In and out of ritual, the community danced when the drums played. Ritual dancing was formalized, but there was plenty of room for individual expression. Dancers like the Sierra Leone Dance Troupe still demonstrate both forms.

Usually after the drums and the dance were well established, the singing would begin. The songs grew out of the setting and atmosphere established by the dance, but they had a certain independence. Taken all together, they had a very wide range of forms and subjects. They saluted the great and honorable; they praised and condemned; they commented on the problems of the people; they spoke of the honored dead as though they were still alive; they engaged in sexual declarations, though not for the sake of mere sex; they stirred the community to dream and aspiration.

In Afro-America, after a while the drum was missing. But there were substitutes in other instruments, especially one unfailing instrument, the human hands. In Africa, handclapping by the dancers often went along with the drums. As we have told already, this writer saw a folk festival in Africa in which handclapping accompanied the instruments, and when the instruments suddenly stopped, the handclapping took over as full accompaniment and guide to the dancing and the singing.

Since it is extremely likely that most spirituals were composed in secret meetings, the handclapping took the place of the drum and shouting and other highly rhythmic body movement were substituted for the dance. The rhythm of many spirituals clearly indicates this process. As an example, take "In Dat Great Gittin' Up Mornin'." It could hardly be delivered without handclapping and body movement. And, as in Africa, the tempo accelerates as the song proceeds.

Reference in many songs to certain instruments presupposes the sound of the instruments in the consciousness of the singer. Take the trumpet, for example, especially Gabriel's trumpet. Note the dramatic roles given to bells.

In his mental appreciation of the harp the slave found a most unusual thrill. It is highly unlikely that very many slaves either saw or heard a harp in their whole lives. But the very word harp seemed to set them to dancing. The fact that David, a most prepossessing fellow with the slaves, played on his harp and danced to his harp, probably had something to do with it. The fact that angels had harps and used them extensively was another probable strong motivation.

In the great song that describes the shouting all over God's Heaven, the "I got a harp" section seems to be the most rapturous. Shoes, wings, crown, yes—but to have a harp, to play it, to dance to it, is really and truly heaven. The fact that the commercial harp is a big, unwieldy instrument that you have to sit down to play and that you can hardly swing in a dance never worries them. Tribes of East Africa had light maneuverable harps.

Another instrument which finds great play in the spiritual is the hammer. True, it is primarily a carpenter's tool, but it rings. Its ring betokens death, and such a relationship fascinates the slave. They were not afraid of death, but they engaged in many poetic commentaries about it.

Louis Achille has put the whole matter felicitously. Behind the instrumental music, he says, lived and prospered a singing Negro music, in solo and in choir. That the spiritual is an African song associated with dances and instruments helps to account for its remarkable gift of rhythm. The fact that, in the heart of the African, music is ever-present gave these rhythms depth and unerringness. Whoever sings spirituals today without a sense of varying dance rhythms is probably not getting as much from them as he might.

CHAPTER SIXTEEN

The Search for Meanings in the Spiritual

. .

To GET inside the Afro-American spiritual one must search for themes and meanings in accord with the desire and need for expression of the folk community just described. One must read the songs as comprehensive folk poetry, not primarily as isolated outbursts. One must examine with care a sufficient number of poems from a sufficiently wide distribution so as to be reasonably sure of the groove cut by them.

G. Malcolm Laws has declared that one-twelfth of the native ballads current in America owe their existence and perpetration to the Negro. That is not to say that the Negro spiritual represents one in twelve of all American folk songs. Certainly Laws intends to include more than spirituals in the Negro portion; and folk songs, generally, include more than ballads. On the other hand, Laws, like other good evaluators, may have underestimated the total number of spirituals which developed during the 340 years of African slavery in America.

Whatever the percentage of the Afro-American spiritual in the total mass of American folk song, it represents a very large proportion. From all evidence it is the largest single type with uniform characteristics. The Americanized Scottish ballad, the patriotic song, the white spiritual, the sea and river songs, the comic and nonsense song, the nursery and children's song, the play-party song, the courtship song, the dance song, the historical song, the crime song, the jailbird song, the railroad ballad, the hobo and bum song, the drinking song, the street song, the mountain song, the mining song, the temperance song, the cowboy and cattle song, the lumberman's song, and the songs of countries from which Americans come, or of states which they call home—any one group is small by comparison with the American slave song. Several of the large groups listed would have to be massed together to equal the black spirituals in number.

This fact is not surprising. A group with rich folk backgrounds, in America since the early seventeenth century, expanding from about seven hundred thousand in the first census of 1790 to about four million in 1860, working and singing continuously, under conditions as described in Chapter 15 above, would be expected to produce a very large number of songs. If lost songs could have been saved, the established number might be several tens of thousands instead of, as at present, something less than ten thousand. It is fortunate that a strong preservation movement was started about a hundred years ago.

Although some writers have attempted to date particular poems, the evidence of time and chronology is quite skimpy. Even if all the poems could be accurately dated, the range of style and patterns is so great as to make a chronological treatment self-defeating. The idea here, therefore, is to trace patterns of development in the whole spread.

It does seem possible to reproduce the patterns in terms of developing steps. Although there are many themes and accents, the major patterns are few. It is possible to show how they develop and how they relate to one another.

Assuming that these patterns grow from certain propaganda aims in the songs, one can state these aims and show how the poets fulfill them. But one can go further than that. Even though the poets had points to make, they also reacted to their experiences in writing the poems. Tracing the outcomes of their poetic experience is one of the most profitable ways to read, study, and enjoy the songs.

For the benefit of those who desire a more strictly literary presentation, there will be a definition and an examination of the literary elements. This will include forms, genres, and styles.

At the end of Part Two will be a discussion of the relevancy of the poetry of the spiritual to the present day. In the broad sense, the folk community which produced the spirituals still exists; in more narrow senses, it has undergone a number of changes, and some very great changes. The fact that the spiritual is still alive and working in the broad community is one proof of its relevancy.

The spiritual has been adopted by a very large group of people who are neither African nor Afro-American. Some sections of Part Three will describe this adoption, both historically and in the present. But the comment on relevancy will bear, to a limited degree, in the direction of this large group of non-Africans.

The songs displayed here have come from a great variety of places. The words of many have been recorded by the author from listening to hundreds of choirs and other singing organizations. Many others have been reported by the dozens of searchers who have been combing the folk community for at least half a dozen generations. Unless designated otherwise, they are all folk songs, created by the people without specific authors. The spelling changes reflect the varied ways different groups of singers express themselves. These range from rare provincialisms to standard English. Even here the unique manifestations of poetry and philosophy are present.

✿◇

CHAPTER SEVENTEEN

Radical Change in the Existing Order of Things

. .
.

◖ Sense of Change: Evolutionary and Revolutionary

THE fundamental theme, though perhaps not the greatest, that pervades the spiritual is the need for a change in the existing order. No one can deny that this theme is equally fundamental in Biblical Christianity. A close reader of the spiritual is compelled to conclude that this fact provides the prime reason for the slave poet's selecting the Bible for his main source when a harvest of sources (his work, his fellow slaves, the people he worked for, the phenomena of nature, his legends handed down from African ancestors, and many others) were available.

If this declaration of key theme seems to deny the religious motivation of the songs, let us quickly explain. No doubt, as we have demonstrated, the spiritual is often a religious song; it is just not a simple religious song and nothing else. What we are examining here is why it is a religious song. As shown above, in Chapter 15, religion was adopted by the greatest leaders of the slave revolts, undoubtedly because it was the most radical method by which their personal feelings, their criticism of slavery, and their need for a frame of secrecy could be expressed. So the slave folk poet and all his band chose religion as the chief field of their expression. This choice did not mean that they thought any less of their religion or, on the other hand, that they were necessarily predominantly religious. Religion does not automatically inspire literature in its practitioners. But if a slave, even a religious slave, seeks an outlet for expression, he wants and needs a system capable of direct language and undercurrent symbolism at the same time.

Nothing fits this need better than the Christian religion. It has a firm base in traditionalism. But it strikes out in two other directions, a much better and radically different life on earth and a supremely better and revolutionary life in a world beyond the grave. Since poets are helpless without symbolism and since slave poets find symbolism indispensable (as self-protection and as prevention of the destruction of their creative product, if for no other reasons), the Christian religion was made to order for the slave poet we are studying. He seized upon it and put it to as good use as poets anywhere have done.

In his expression of radical change he relies first upon the evolutionary process. Things will happen, he declares, in a certain way as to make things different. Not for a moment does it occur to him that anyone will doubt that things need changing, from top to bottom; a world with the bitter, degrading injustice of slavery in it obviously could not be a good or a tolerable world. This poet is sure that the folk band who will join in his choruses fully agree in the need for radical change. His song naturally assumes that this view is the consensus everywhere.

His own troubles are the symptoms of the most immediate level of change.

> All my troubles will soon be over with,
> Soon be over with, soon be over with,
> All my troubles will soon be over with,
> All over this world.

In only two ways can this prophecy come true. He will die and go to a better world for him, or the current world will be transformed to eliminate his troubles. Since he says nothing about dying in this particular song, suppose we assume the latter way. To change his troubles means a very big change either in the slave system or in his removal from it. This sense of change recurs hundreds of times in these songs.

If the die-hard believer in death has his own solution upheld, that fact does not change in the slightest the slave poet's concept that a fundamental overhaul of things is desirable and required.

In a similar song, the poet takes himself, as individual, out of the picture. He talks about trouble in general. Obviously, he means to suggest a system of troubles that need eradicating. And he predicts with great joy—note the "Hallelujah"—that the eradication is sure to come.

> I'm so glad Trouble don't last always; . . .
> Hallelujah, I'm so glad trouble don't last always.

Naturally, the poet uses death as a symbol of change. This does not necessarily mean physical death as an infinite number of poets before and since these have shown. Whether or not it means physical death (and new life beyond the grave), the point about need for evolutionary change is sharp and deeply embedded.

> Death's gwineter lay its cold icy hands on me.
> I'm ready fo' to cross ol' Jordan's stream.

He would certainly not be ready to accept this deepest of changes if his current situation were profitable.

Evolutionary change is often credited as God's work:

> Oh, yes, bow yo' knees upon de groun' . . .
> An' ask yo' Lord to turn your roun',

or

> Oh, can't you rise an' tell what de Lord has done for you?
> Yes he's taken my feet out of de miry clay
> An' he's a placed 'em on de right side of my Father.

And note that all this took place before the robber death intervened.

Occasionally the radical change is perpetrated by the individual himself, and once in a while he will specifically ask that others keep hands off.

> Do don't touch-a my garment . . .
> Good Lord,* I'm gwine home
> (Also do don't touch-a my slippers)
> Touch me not little Mary,
> Good Lord,* I'm gwine home.

The most striking declarations of change, however, are revolutionary, not evolutionary. The slave poet saw too many things wrong with the existing order to hope that a few alterations here and there would satisfy. He was too impatient, generally speaking, to accept the slow process of gradual development and improvement by enlightened forces. Directly or indirectly, therefore, there had to be revolution. Once more using the Bible, he projected both bloodless and bloody revolution. In hundreds of songs, it should be noted, his root thinking is more important than his surface words. Considering that the songs came from individual creators all over the South, representing folk opinion everywhere, the consistency and persistency of these views is inescapable.

Let us begin with songs in which revolution is implied rather than planned and developed. These songs stress situations that cannot take place unless the old (current) order is abolished and a new order is established. Since we are dealing with the poet's mind and his intentions, whether the new order is in heaven (the next life) or on earth (this life, South or North) is irrelevant. From a study of the social history, however, there is little doubt that the slave singers were talking about this world, not some other (see Chapters 13 and 15).

---

* The injunction not to touch is not directed against the Lord; "Good Lord" here is merely a holy byword.

Since John the Apostle wrote the Book of Revelation, projecting and predicting a complete new order, he is a favorite point of departure,

> Tell all the world, John, Tell all the world, John.
> Tell all the world, John, I know the other world is not like this.

As in all folk literature, repetition here is not only for mnemonic convenience but for deep and varied emphasis.

Switching from John to Mary (who ran to the supposedly occupied tomb of Jesus on Easter morning and found it empty), the poet reaches very nearly the same position,

> Run, Mary, run, (repeated twice)
> I know de udder worl' is not like dis.
> [Changes probably due to local transcription]
> Fire in de Eas', an' fire in de Wes',
> I know de udder worl' is not like dis.
> Boun' to burn de wilderness,
> I know de udder worl' is not like dis.

In the New Testament of the Bible are several references to great healing operations conducted when a deformed or paralytic individual waded in a stream after the water had been "troubled" by an angel of the Lord. This sort of belief is age-old and worldwide, being very much alive in India (and other places) today. The theory of the spiritual poet is that, if one person can be transformed by such a process, why cannot the same thing work for a whole crowd or nation of people. This theory is very little different, in the poetic sense, from a doctrine of implied revolution; only the method needs working out. If God is going to supply the method, you do not have to worry about that part anyway; thus,

> Wade in de water, children (repeated twice)
> God's a-gwineter trouble de water.

So far, the revolutionary principle has inhered in God or other outside forces. The spiritual poet often initiates the revolution in himself. The *I* of the spiritual, however, is not a single person. It is every person who sings, everyone who has been oppressed and, therefore, every slave anywhere.

The slave poet sometimes finds himself utterly disgusted. His patience gives out. In his heart he can no longer bring himself to work and pray and wait. The patchwork here and there suggests nothing so much as futility. And so he sings,

> If I had my way,
> O Lordy, Lordy,
> If I had my way;
> If I had my way,
> I would tear this building down.

In other songs the poet says,

> I'm a-goin' to lay down this world,
> Goin' to shoulder up my cross,

or

> Yes, one o' dese mornin's 'bout twelve o'clock,
> Dis ol' worl' am gwineter reel and rock.

Either way, the revolutionary spirit is satisfied especially if you read the first one (as from the evidence you have every right to do) to mean that he is going to accept all the hazards and run away to freedom.

In the civil rights legislative discussion of the 1960s there was much talk of the revolutionary effect which would derive from digging up and throwing away the deep-seated tradition of separate eating facilities for white and black races. Orators and pseudo-sociologists equated the tradition with deep ramifications of an orderly society; they likewise equated the destruction of the tradition with social disorder, mongrelization, white genocide, and other dire outcomes.

Although the slave was probably not interested in intermarriage as such, he was certainly an integrationist, largely on the grounds that anything less was degrading and insulting. To be denied the ordinary treatment of a human being was unbearable to him. He was not in position to say so flatly, but he did not hesitate to say so poetically,

> I'm goin' to eat at the welcome table,
> O yes I'm goin' to eat at the welcome table some of
> these days hallelujah!

Not only was he going to have the right to eat at a table where good food was served (note the impossible food of the slave). He was also going to live in a world where he would be welcomed to a good table. Later in the song he was going to be equally welcome to "drink at the crystal fountain." From the viewpoint of the late 1700s and early 1800s, the probable time of the creation of most of these songs, such practices would involve the mightiest of revolutions.

Nothing could be more revolutionary than the slave running away to freedom, inducing others to run away, or advocating running away. First, the slave was a chattel and his departure was a violation of the laws of property. Second, the slave system was considered by the South an economic and political necessity; any loss of slaves undermined the system, any advocacy of running away was economic and political revolution. Third, the religious leaders of the South, relying upon the Biblical passages which they said supported slavery, demonstrated that inducing a slave to leave his bondage was morally wrong and religiously sinful.

Even so, the slave advocated running away in his songs. Set aside for now the "Go Down, Moses" series. It is beyond question that the chief desire of the slave (see Chapter 15) was for physical freedom here and now. He had many friends in the North and the example of many runaway slaves to encourage him in his desire.

One of the creative singers wishes to remind the crowd that freedom is not an impossible way out of their troubles. He comes by a suitable rhythm and stretches it into song,

> Steal away,
> Steal away,
> Steal away.

And then the danger of his position confronts him. He cannot openly advocate escape and insurrection; it would do no good. He knows that his yearning is already shared by the crowd around him and that they all understand what he is trying to say. He searches for a medium with appeal and force. Knowing the religious bent of his companions, he settles on "To Jesus!"

Now, he is in the clear. From now on, he can say whatever he pleases. The oppressor, always close by, is satisfied that this is a purely religious enterprise; his suspicion, aroused by the first "Steal away" is fully allayed. But the slave poet goes on,

> Steal away, steal away home,
> I ain't got long to stay here!

The trusting oppressor never knew (or believed) until too late that the slave had probably already made contact with a representative of the Underground Railroad or some other slave stealing organization. But the surrounding slaves knew well the implications of the first verse,

> My Lord calls me, He calls me by the thunder;
> The trumpet sounds within-a my soul,
> I ain't got long to stay here,

To support this interpretation is the testimony of one of many hundreds of testifying slaves, Frederick Douglass, who ran away successfully and became a great man in a free society. Of the spirituals he writes,

> They were tones, loud, long and deep, breathing the prayer and complaint of souls boiling over with the bitterest anguish. Every tone was a testimony against slavery, and a prayer to God for deliverance from chains (*My Bondage and My Freedom*, p. 99).

The revolutionary song at its best is a powerful production. As nearly always, the slave chooses a revolutionary chapter from the Bible. Note that nearly all of the Biblical personages the slave poet deals with were involved in upheaval and revolution (Moses, Daniel, David, the Hebrew children, Samson, Elijah, Gideon, Jesus, Paul). This fact alone should warn the reader what the songs import if the reader were genuinely interested in reading the literature, rather than in singing or in being lulled to quasi-religious sleep.

One of these big productions is called "Joshua Fit de Battle ob Jericho." Historically, Joshua, Moses' successor, is in the final stages of a major conquest by a group of recently freed slaves over a well-equipped and superior army of Philistines. The walls of Jericho are symbolic of a long-standing tradition which kept the ex-slaves out of Canaan, their promised land. If the above characteristics and their revolutionary implications had not been inherent in the subject matter, the slave poet would certainly have passed over Joshua and his prize battle as a dramatic theme.

The basic ingredients established, the poet gives Joshua's pedigree,

> You may talk about yo' king ob Gideon,
> You may talk about yo' man ob Saul,
> Dere's none like good ole Joshua,
> At de battle ob Jericho.

Step by step the poet follows Joshua. (1) "Up to de walls of Jericho, He marched with spear in han'," (2) " 'Go blow dem ram horns,' Joshua cried, 'Kase de battle am in my hand.' " (3) After the horns and trumpets blow, "Joshua commanded de chillen to shout, An' de walls come tumblin' down."

Only the most naïve reader misses the point that what Joshua did can be done again and again, wherever wrong and evil are to be overthrown, wherever promised good and right are to be established. Once the walls are down, the ex-slaves walk into the capital of Canaan, free men in a free land. Getting into the singing heart and mind of the slave poet (especially when the song is sung with the proper vigor and gusto), you can appreciate the thrill of a group of singing slaves, with a certain expectation in their hearts, following their leader through:

> Dat mornin', Joshua fit de battle ob Jericho,
> An' de walls come tumblin' down.

⟨ *Deliverance Through Power and Association with Power*

It perhaps needs to be repeated that religion was an essential quality and ingredient of the spiritual. The chief injunction remains the avoidance of overemphasis upon conventional religion or upon religion as something relaxing and taken for granted. The slave relied upon religion, not primarily because he felt himself "converted," but because he recognized the power inherent in religious things.

What he needed most was power and a feeling of closeness with power. It is probably strange that one must say that he cared little for subtle power or mystical power (usually religion's greatest selling point). The slave had

to have physical, realistic, and even material power. Those who say he
was singing quietly religious songs associate his creative mind with ultimate, distant power; they seem to think he conceded immediate power
because he was a helpless slave.

This view is unsupported by the songs. Of course he believed in ultimate
power; but he believed in immediate power too, lots of it, close at hand.
His relationship with the Deity presupposed anthropomorphic as well as
omnipresent beings, capable of miraculous performance and always on
call. His reading of the Bible had conditioned him to miracles and mighty
feats of power. In his predicament, only this kind of deity was worth trusting. He trusted, but he demanded every resource of his contract.

The slave's association with power naturally meant a radical change in
the existing order, heralded by his songs. This change was reflected in his
everyday life, in the prospect of doom for his enemies (just as it was with
"the chosen people" of the Bible), and in the assurance of the best possible
life beyond the grave. Since he was in bondage, the key concept of the
change he sang about was deliverance.

Hardly a song is without some evidence of this sense of powerful deliverance and of the slave's reliance upon it. In refrain or verses the recurrence of the symbols of power, Jesus, the Lord, God, the angels, and various inanimate things, is so great that a comprehensive list of examples
would be little less than a dozen volumes of poems and poetic phrases.
Some effort is made here, however, to give examples that are representative of this widespread display.

One example purports to be representative of one other phase of the
subject, the rank of the symbols. For instance, if one makes a close examination of 260 spirituals, carefully selected for their representativeness, one
will find about fifty developmental references (not simple mentions) of
Jesus, the Lord, and God. Of these fifty, a little over half talk of Jesus, a
little more than one-third of the Lord, and less than one-tenth of God.
Rarely does the spiritual poet mix up the three except in bywords like "O
my good Lord" or "Yes, my Lord" mingled with a reference to Jesus or
God.

On the basis of this examination one might, very cautiously, say that the
spiritual poet thought of God as the ultimate and final source of power,
more or less removed like an unbelievably massive and inexhaustible dy-
namo; of the Lord as a more available series of power stations; and of
Jesus as readily available, always at hand. Angels are the messengers of
any one of the three.

The functions of Jesus as a deliverer are far-reaching. He is, first of all,
an indomitable ruling king who does not hesitate a second in favoring his
subjects, "Ride on King Jesus! No man can hinder him," or "Ride on King
Jesus, I want to go to heav'n in the mornin'." He rides "on a milk-white
horse" and performs all manner of useful and difficult services,

> When I was blind and could not see,
> King Jesus brought that light to me.

Since he favors his people on earth, he will certainly extend his benevolence to the extracurricular world:

> When every star refuses to shine, . . .
> I know King Jesus will be mine.

Occasionally, the poet bursts into a paean of praise for his gracious King. Although he works with and for men, he is clearly above them and capable of cutting down wrongs and building up rights.

> He is King of Kings, He is Lord of Lords,
> Jesus Christ the first and last, no man works like him.
>
> He built his throne up in the air, . . .
> And called his saints from everywhere, . . .
>
> He pitched his tents on Canaan's ground
> And broke the Roman kingdom down.

But Jesus, in the poet's eyes, can also be powerful as a Lamb (often a dying Lamb), who rescued man from sin by pulling the destructive sting from death. "I'm purchased by the dyin' Lamb" constantly recurs. He is a tender, sympathetic Lamb as the song "Sittin' Down beside O' the Lamb" proves. But these inherent qualities detract nothing from his delivering power.

> In the river of Jordan John* baptized,
> How I long to be baptized,
> In the river of Jordan John baptized unto the dying Lamb. . . .
>
> We baptize all that come by faith unto the dying Lamb. . . .
>
> Here's another one come to be baptized unto the dying Lamb.

It is always touching when the poet, after recognizing the power and the deliverance conferred on him by his closest friend (Jesus), unabashedly gives his heart,

> O Lamb, beautiful Lamb; I'm going to serve God til I die. . . .
>
> Never felt such love before, I'm going to serve God til I die. . . .
>
> Looked at my hands, and they looked new, . . .
> Looked at my feet, and they did too.
> I'm going to serve God til I die.

In "Jesus Will Come Bye-an'-bye" the slave poet learns a great fact about power. If you are deserving and if you move persistently in the right direction, power will meet you halfway,

---

* John the Baptist, differentiated from John the Apostle.

> Keep a-inchin' along,
> Keep a-inchin' along,
> Jesus will come bye-an'-bye.

One reason the poet leans so heavily on the power of Jesus is that he has conquered even a meaner world than the slave confronts, the world of death. Many songs speak of the crucifixion; many more of the resurrection,

> Go and tell ev'rybody
> Yes, Jesus is risen from the dead.

If a power can overcome death, the poet reasons, he can certainly handle slavery, all personal troubles, and all sinful weaknesses of all the people. But Jesus did not stop with mere overcoming. He maintains a dynamic victorious attitude afterwards, one that is more appealing to an imaginative slave.

> Jesus rides in the middle of de air, . . .
> He's callin' sinners from ev'rywhere.

"Jesus rides" is not a rare, but a favorite phrase. It carries the implication that if you are pinned down (as the slave was at the time), you can still hope for deliverance from a benevolent king who moves about.

The delivering Jesus of the afterlife is impressive, but he is the more conventional symbol. "I'm goin' up to see my Jesus, O some sweet day after 'while" is pretty much what you would expect from a slave songwriter. The following lines, however, are somewhat off the beaten track,

> You needn't min' my dyin' (repeated twice)
> Jesus goin' to make up my dyin' bed. . . .
>
> I'll be sleepin' in Jesus, . . .
>
> I'll be restin' easy.

And a very generous thought,

> When I get to heav'n I want you to be there too,
> When I cry "holy" I want you to say so too.

He obviously infers that Jesus will make up more than one dying bed and will try to keep friends together. Another mildly unconventional touch delineating deliverance in the afterlife is in a military vein,

> We'll shout o'er all our sorrows, An' sing forever more,
> With Christ an' all his army, On dat celestial shore.

Without a doubt, however, the really powerful Jesus of the spiritual works on earth, in this life, in the here and now, today and tomorrow. At his very best the spiritual poet sings,

> Nobody knows de trouble I see,
> Nobody knows like [or but] Jesus
> Nobody knows de trouble I see,
> Glory, Hallelujah!

A sad song is turned into exultation by sudden appreciation of Jesus' delivering power.

Again and again, in wonderful strokes of his brush, the amazing poet
echoes poignant variations on this idea,

> I'm troubled, I'm troubled, I'm troubled in mind,
> If Jesus don't help me I sho'ly will die. . . .

> When you see me on my knees—
> Come here, Jesus, if you please. . . .

> When you hear me calling, Jesus,
> Hear me, Jesus, if you please.

The pathos of the last two songs is matched only by their gentle courtesy.

Sometimes, Jesus is not expected to do a major act of salvation. Sometimes, a bit of psychoanalytic listening or talking will do.

> O a little talk with Jesus makes it right, all right, . . .
> Troubles of ev'ry kind, Thank God I'll always find
> That a little talk with Jesus makes it right.

It is therefore not surprising that the poet declares, "You may have all
this world, Give me Jesus." Or that he is grateful for that happy day
"when Jesus wash'd my sins away." Or that he appreciates more deeply a
King who preached to the poor,

> Did you ever see such love before, . . .
> King Jesus preaching to the poor,
> I do love the Lord.

If the reader is beginning to wonder how these private services relate
to radical change, let us remind him that the slave felt that he had to be
sustained from day to day before he could accomplish his transformation.
American slavery with its isolation, its backbreaking toil under hot sun or
in inclement weather, its lack of family life, its poor food and housing, its
persistent threat of being sold "down the river," and its other disabilities
was very hard to take. Even the first acts of the slave stealers were related
to upholding the prospective escapee until he could be delivered. These
concepts of Jesus were, in this regard, effective and necessary.

But Jesus contributed a greater concept than any of these to the slave
mind through the spiritual—the feeling that he was already free at heart
and already a denizen of democracy.

> When Jesus shook the manna tree, . . .
> He shook it for you and He shook it for me, . . .

> Hallelujah to the lamb! . . . Jesus died for ev'ry man.

And the more expressive lines, because of their Biblical implications,

> Jesus Christ, He died for me, Way down in Egypt land:
> Jesus Christ, He set me free, Way down in Egypt land.

The fact that Jesus was not around when Moses and the Hebrew children were freed from Egyptian bondage is irrelevant. The poet is not a theologian or historian, as so many people have apparently given him credit for being. He is concerned with his private desires, and the greatest of these is freedom. The quickest route to freedom is through the transforming power of Jesus.

The Lord in the spiritual is somewhat more comprehensive than Jesus and definitely farther away. But he is power beyond all the needs of the slave. The Lord readily cuts through laws, conventions, power structures, and all other sociopolitical forms to make things right for those he favors, for those who return his trust. Thus, the slave creator appeals directly to the Lord when the need is great. The implied answers to his appeals often connote radical departures from natural as well as social law. Note these two,

> My Lord's done just what He said,
> Healed the sick and raised the dead. . . .

> Didn't my Lord deliver Daniel, deliver Daniel, deliver Daniel,
> Didn't my Lord deliver Daniel, An' why not every man.

The song containing the second quotation also refers to Jonah's delivery from the belly of the whale and the saving of "de Hebrew chillun" from the fiery furnace. The rescues of Daniel, Jonah, and the trio Shadrach, Meshach, and Abednego were not ordinary acts of deliverance. They involved suspension or repeal of the laws of nature, the nature of hungry lions to eat available flesh, the nature of whales to retain their food, the nature of fire to burn human flesh. In the slave's mind, his situation within the rigid and crushing system of slavery, which seemed to all others immovable and unchangeable, was in the category of hopelessness with Daniel, Jonah, and the three fire-eaters. But the Lord had proved He was equal to the occasion; and the slave had proved he was deserving. Thus the miraculous deliverance was inevitable.

To the slave, Pharaoh was earthly power to the highest degree. He was in the class with the slave master. The Israelites were in a hopeless position against such power. So is the slave in a hopeless position. Both hopeless, except for one thing—the existence of the Lord and His determination to side with the helpless good against the powerful bad. Not just his determination; also, his command of power, supreme power, unlimited power. He had such power that he could pronounce,

> Your enemies you see today,
> You never shall see more.

All the helpless good had to do was to call upon him. For Pharaoh read the combined power of the slave owners of America, their errand-running, subservient politicians, their military might,

> When the children were in bondage,
> They cried unto the Lord,
> To turn back Pharaoh's army,
> He turned back Pharaoh's army.
>
> When Pharaoh crossed the water,
> The waters came together,
> And drowned ole Pharaoh's army,
> Hallelu!

Using the same logic and magnificent poetic faith, the spiritual poet told of other great deliverances which he intended to be relative to his own. Through the creative strength of his idea and his simple, but overwhelming, directness, he carved out marvelously touching lines:

> O, de blin' man stood on de road an' cried.
> O, de blin' man stood on de road an' cried.
> Cryin' O, my Lord, save-a me,
> De blin' man stood on de road an' cried.

The poet's blind man, like the poet, and like the reader if he is sensitive, is fully aware of the bigness of the job he is asking the Lord to do. The job involves preeminent social and psychological, as well as medical, skills. But the poet is never doubtful of the Lord's ability to perform it.

The poet often projects himself into this complex field of sociopsychological welfare. Listen to this,

> Lord help the po' and the needy,
> In this lan' . . .
> In this great getting up morning we shall face another sun,
> Lord help the po' and the needy,
> In this lan', In this lan'. . . .
>
> Lord help the widows and the orphans, In this lan' . . .
>
> Lord help the motherless children, In this lan' . . .
>
> Lord help the hypocrite members, In this lan' . . .
>
> Lord help the long-tongue liars, In this lan' . . .

Note several things: The poet does not join the poor and the needy; he separates them. He does not request help for just the worthy; he includes the unworthy and the obnoxious. And most radical of all, he indicates that this kind of help points toward a time when all the conditions that cry for help will be removed.

Although the slave poet's personal appeals to the Lord imply more limited changes, they are radical enough. First, they are far more numerous than all other appeals combined; when their total weight is added up, they cover a broad range of changes and of implicit modifications in the social structures. For example, "O Lord I'm hungry, I want to be fed" and "O Lord I'm naked, I want to be clothed" would assault the economic structure by adding greatly to the slave owner's food and clothing bills. Second, if the prayers are answered, the slave himself would be so basically transformed that he might be much less useful, and more uneconomic, as a slave. Third, the slave would acquire elements of character and personality that would make slavery even less palatable than it was, if that were possible, and would increase the slave's desire to escape. Study the implications in the following,

> Do Lord, do Lord, Do remember me, . . .
> When I'm in trouble, Do remember me, . . .

It seems that the Lord with his gigantic whip would be standing above the overseer who overshadowed the slave.

> Oh, Lord, Oh, my Lord! Oh my good Lord!
> Keep me f'om sinkin' down,

obviously meaning, don't let me give in to threats, overwork, and oppression; stiffen my resistance.

> It's me, it's me, O Lord,
> Standing in the need of pray'r
> [Not my brother, my sister, my mother, my elder].

In spite of the deep sense of community in the spiritual as a whole (see Chapter 19) songs like this reinforce the sense of individual identity. Again and again the spiritual poet stresses the need for strength of individual character (see also Chapter 19, "Development Through Character and Right Living") as opposed to group unity. Such individual spiritual strength, derived from the Lord, would not be conducive to good slave psychology and was a commodity the slave owner, dealer, and overseer greatly deplored and feared, even fought against. Not Emerson himself ever preached a sharper sermon on self-reliance.

We have several times referred to peaks in spiritual poetry, and shall again. One of these peaks is the poet's immersing himself within the boundless power of the Lord and emerging into everyday life clothed in and invigorated by that power, like some Achilles dipped completely (not held by a heel) into the Styx.

At first, he gradually launches in, almost like a toe trying the water, "Lord, I want to be a Christian/ In my heart, in-a my heart." Being a Christian means being more loving, more holy, less like Judas, more like Jesus, all in his heart.

Next, he loses any modesty and dives in, partly because, like the Biblical people, he has found the Lord wholly reliable,

O, ain't I glad I've got out the wilderness, . . .
Leaning on the Lord.

At length, he reaches complete understanding. Adapting one of his inscrutably glorious figures of speech from the world of work, he declares,

In de Lord, in de Lord,
My soul's been anchored in de Lord. . . .

Befo' I'd stay in hell one day,
My soul's been anchored in de Lord.
I'd sing an' pray myself away,
My soul's been anchored in de Lord.

I'm gwineter pray an' never stop, . . .
Until I reach de mountaintop,
My soul's been anchored in de Lord,
O Lord, my soul's been anchored in de Lord.

See my father in the gospel
Come wagging* up the hill so slow,
He's crying new as he cried before
My soul's been anchored in the Lord.

To go from the Lord to God is to go from the top to the topmost top. The slave's god is the God of Moses and Daniel and other such Old Testament heroes; His prime function is in His role as the Deliverer. In being the Deliverer, He is at times not gentle,

My God is mighty man of war, man of war,
  (repeated twice)
Sinner, please don't let this harvest pass,
And die and lose your soul at last.

The emphasis is strong that all of God's might and martial strength cannot deliver a man who refuses the opportunity to believe and the action necessary to meet deliverance partway. As we have seen, He can trouble the water and turn it into a gigantic hospital and great society. Although standing in proper "fear" and respect, who would not love such a God and strive to be in his presence.

O mother, don't you weep when I'm gone.
For I'm going to Heav'n above,
Going to the God I love.

Like Christians from everywhere, the spiritual poet and his band, from "dat great gittin' up mornin' " on, will "live wid God forever."

That God is his friend and protector no one can ever doubt. In these

---

* Means "toiling, moving slowly," a truly wonderful usage.

phrases he must have included overseers and other brutalizers in his warning,

> I'm gonna tell God how you treat me (repeated twice)
> ... some of these days.

In spite of the poet's gratitude for all other manifestations and associations with God, nothing surpasses his pride over the fact that this friend of his is the greatest power in reality or imagination.

> God is a God! God don't never change!
> God is a God! An' He always will be God!
> He made the sun to shine by day, He made the
>   sun to show the way,
> He made the stars to show their light, He made
>   the moon to shine by night, sayin'
> God is a God, God don't never change! ...
>
> The earth his footstool an' heav'n his throne,
>   The whole creation all his own,
> His love an' power will prevail, His promise
>   will never fail, sayin'
> God is a God! An' always will be God!

With such a friend and deliverer, the slave poet has every right to warn enemies, detractors, and oppressors that their day of control and dominance will be short. God would certainly carry out his just requirements. "My God ain't no lyin' man," the poet sang.

The angels are important only because they carry out the edicts of Jesus, the Lord, and God. From time to time, however, they can be quite colorful. At one place the poet demands that you "Listen to the angels shoutin'." One thing they shout gives them parallelism with the slaves: "I hear them shoutin' 'I've been redeemed.'" And much is said of the angel chorus "that hailed our Savior's birth."

But mostly the angels (and archangels) are engaged, under orders, in the work of deliverance, with notable efficiency. One of them is celebrated in spirituals because he rolled the stone away at some time between Good Friday evening and Easter sunrise. (Rarely, though, does the angel of the spiritual work alone.) Others are busy with difficult chores,

> Way over yonder in the harvest fields,
> The angels shoving at the chariot wheels.

The slave poet does not hesitate to ask for the services of the angels as if they were a regular transportation company,

> O bretheren, my way, my way's cloudy, my way,
> Go sen'-a dem angels down.

Or from a very famous song,

I look'd over Jordan, an' what did I see
Comin' for to carry me home,
A band of angels comin' after me,
Comin' for to carry me home.

An extremely interesting responsibility for angels is to make certain that all the good folk get their rewards. There is little doubt that in the following song the poet is projecting one or both sides of a double meaning—reward in the afterlife and assurance that he will be in the next batch from his plantation to be carried up to freedom on the Underground Railroad.

O, write my name, (repeated twice)
De Angels in de heav'n gwineter write my name....

Write my name in de Book of life,
Yes, write my name in de drippin' blood,
De Angels in de heav'n gwineter write my name.

Death and Judgment Day are likewise methods of defeating the system of slavery. It cannot be repeated too often, however, that very likely death means merely deliverance into a system of freedom, that is, a free land, and Judgment Day merely that great day (like V.E. or V.J. Day) when the liberation is accomplished.

Considering the background and psychology of the slave and the nature of folk expression, as clarified in Chapter 15 above, only a weak or perverse imagination could overlook the implications in such a song as the following, and there are hundreds like it. "The heavy load" is certainly slavery, not life; the "robe" is the opportunity to live freely; the "gate of hell" is the tribulations of the slave that defeat his true expression; Jesus, as usual, is the deliverer. Why go all the way to heaven when you can begin your deliverance on earth?

O Bye and bye, bye and bye,
I'm goin' to lay down my heavy load....

I know my robe's goin' to fit me well, ...
I tried it on at the gate of hell....

O Christians, can't you rise and tell
That Jesus hath done all things well,
I'm goin' to lay down my heavy load.

The same pattern of interpretation will fit "Somebody's Buried in the Graveyard," "O My Little Soul," "Deep River," "Mos' Don Toilin' Here," "My Ship Is on de Ocean," "O Wasn't Dat a Wide River," "Po' Mourner's Got a Home at Las'," "Roll, Jordan, Roll," "Walk in Jerusalem Jus' Like John," and hundreds of other so-called death spirituals. Likewise, "You May Bury Me in de Eas'," "When the Roll Is Called up Yonder," "See the Signs of Judgment," the fabulous "In Dat Great Gittin' Up Mornin'," and perhaps a hundred other judgment day spirituals.

Deliverance is often expressed in the spiritual in impersonal ways and things. Note the following, each of which is a mere sample of a very large group,

Balm: "There is a Balm in Gilead, To make the wounded whole,
                There is a Balm in Gilead, To heal the sin-sick soul."
Chariot: "Roll de Ol' Chariot Along"
                ("Ef de devil's in the way Jus' roll right over")
City: "You'd Better Run, Run, Run-a-run . . . to the City of Refuge"
                "I'm Seeking for a City, Hallelujah"
Rock: "Got a Home in That Rock"
                "O Hide Me over in the Rock of Ages"
                ("O Rock of Ages cleft for me")
Ship: "I'm Gwine Cling to de Ship o' Zion"
                ("Try my bes' for to serve my Lord")
Train: "Same Train"
                "De gospel train's a-comin', I hear it jus' at han',
                I hear de car wheels movin'
                An' rumblin' thru de lan' . . .
                Git on board, little chillen,
                Dere's room for many a mo'.

There is thus little doubt that the spiritual poet thought always of his deliverance or that he could approach the subject from a thousand directions. He realized that only the greatest power could deliver him; he discovered and sang of the power and of its multifarious manifestations. In spite of his confidence in ultimate victory, he devoted many songs and parts of songs to the terrible hazards of the course. But when he rose to the heights in "Nobody Knows de Trouble I See," "My Soul's Been Anchored in the Lord," or "God Is a God, God Don't Never Change," he was at his very best. This best was as good as a folk song ever gets to be.

([Goals and Coming Great Events

Though ranking high as a folk song, the spiritual is open to serious criticism as poetic form. The slave creator used the standard measures of his day, used a limited vocabulary, and oversimplified his rhythms (see Chapter 21). He tended to preoccupy himself with just a few themes, although he found in these few considerable imaginative variation. Like Perry Mason, he and his people rarely lost a case. He was unabashedly superior, hobnobbing with only the supreme members of the universal society, past, present, and future.

On the other hand, he was nearly always exciting. His sense of dramatic action was extremely high. He knew how to choose the right simple words to fit the sharpest occasions. He knew how to probe the human heart and reveal with curiosity and wonder what he found. He commanded a rich, tragic vein and a delicate comic touch. But one his greatest gifts was in his ability to eliminate the trivial and to point his flaming arrows toward the stars.

Much of the radical change he managed to infer from his intense interest in goals and coming great events has already been reviewed in the earlier sections of this chapter. Our concern now is not so much with the details as with the devices and the creative outlook. For example, what are some things that will happen when the miracle of social and economic transformation is accomplished?

A first simple answer is found in this representative song,

> Bye an' bye, bye an' bye, good Lord! . . .
> Ev'ry day'll be Sunday bye an' bye.

There was more to it, however, than holiness and quiet and passivity. Before setting down some of the internal details, we should note that most of this category of the spiritual's planning went far beyond the slave and embraced the hopes of every decent, upright man. Action was the order of the day.

> Great day! Great day, the righteous marching,
> Great day! God's going to build up Zion's walls.

The action was sometimes in the field of preparation. The slave was not just waiting to have greatness thrust upon him. He was willing to put forth effort to deserve. Whatever the final rewards, he wanted to earn them. He sang,

> I want to be ready,
> I want to be ready,
> I want to be ready,
> To walk in Jerusalem just like John.

Through his own merits he wanted to be worthy of his great goal. He wanted to fulfill his opportunities.

In spite of the peacefulness of "Deep River" and "Study War No More," many songs are calls to arms, probably more on the order of the Johnsonian "war on poverty" than of literal and bloody battles.

> Going to take my breast-plate, sword, and shield, . . .
> And march out boldly in the field.

The modus operandi of reaching the goals and preparing for the great events to come is varied, but there are consistent notes whenever the subject is discussed. First of all, you had to live rightly for "you shall reap what you sow . . . On the mountain, in the valley." Second, nothing was going to be easy,

> I ain't got time for to stop an' talk,
> The road is rough an' it's hard to walk.

Whether or not this view is remarkable coming from a slave whose daily

life was gruesomely hard depends on your viewpoint. If he's inventing a
new order, you might suppose that he would give himself an easier time;
you might be surprised that he insisted that the gospel war required him to
say,

> An' I will die in de fiel' . . .
> I'm on my journey home,

or that he kept saying he was "ready to die." In fact, you were enjoined to
stay ready all the time. On the other hand, since his salvation was assured
through the power all around him, perhaps his self-respect required that he
do his share (see Chapters 19 and 20). Or you could surmise that this religion, his personal philosophy, or both, demanded hard work for the glorious reward to come.

> Wet or dry I 'n-tend to try . . .
> To serve the Lord until I die.
> My Lord says he's comin' bye and bye.

As previously suggested, there are two usual ways to reach your goal, or
great event, and you will have them both. One is your own death or deliverance in some other fashion; the other is the Day of Judgment. Both are
solid opposites to and corrosive criticisms of the miserable life the slave
now leads. Both lead to suitable lives for people like the singers, for the
singers keep saying things like,

> I'm on my journey home . . .
>
> My Jesus will meet me in-a that mornin' . . .
>
> De streets up dere am paved wid gol' . . .
>
> I'm gonna feast on milk an' honey . . .
>
> See de heabenly lan'
> It am brighter dan-a dat glitterin' sun.

Furthermore, it is generally higher in geographical altitude and in social
level than anything on earth. The fact that most of these items are part of
a general Christian belief is quite beside the point; the slave singer took
what he chose and adapted or invented according to his own designs. Some
of his death songs, in fact, have elements that are quite un-Christian in
sentiment,

> After death got to fill an empty grave,
>   (repeat twice)
> An' I wouldn't mind dyin' if dyin' was all.

Judgment Day has already been mentioned twice. It was a grand opportunity for dramatic maneuver by the slave whose sense of drama was near
the realm of genius. Beside the slave, the Calvinist was a piker on the subject. On a grand stage all people who have ever lived are assembled. You

can see "coffins bustin'," dragons being "loosened," "dry bones a-creep-in'," "elements a-meltin'," and perhaps a great performer like Belafonte leading the mighty glee club in "Fare You Well, Fare You Well."

Not only are all people and nations assembled; they are judged.

> Got to go to judgment, stand your trial,
> Can't stay away.

No one is allowed to pray any more or do good deeds that might improve his record. Sinners cry out "Down I'm rollin', Down I'm Rollin'," and they say "Amen" to their own damnation. Hell, uncapped and burning, waits to receive its mighty share. Thunder and lightning are magnificent and every-where intermingled with blood and fire.

But on the other hand, "glory" (heaven) is ready to receive the good people:

> Oh yes, I'm gwine up, . . .
> Gwine up to see de hevvenly land.

Earthly class distinctions have been wiped out. The misrepresentations and subterfuges of the slave civilization are now laid bare; it is inevitable that mistreaters of the slave have used up all their superiority (like Dives) and the righteous slaves (like Lazarus) are headed home for glory, to join the blessed and the "snow-white angels." Everything is now for keeps; the ups and downs of history are at an end. "Fare you well," repeated over one hundred times during the song, clearly means that the good slave and all other good people are waving goodbye to the bad people of whatever rank and station.

Considering the fierceness and gusto of these Judgment Day songs, no doubt the slave poet got great satisfaction in evening things out for good. To look forward to this lasting settlement of the world's people on a fair basis probably enabled him to endure the unbearable, but temporary, rigors of slavery, in which his personality was as severely damaged as his body.

Perhaps he was overly cruel and presumptuous. Perhaps he was too sure of his being hand in glove with God.

> Although you see me coming long so
> To the promised land I'm bound to go. . . .
>
> Sometimes I'm up, sometimes I'm down,
> But still my soul is heavenly bound.

Without question he was a Utopian socialist, constructing a new and proper and harmonious society and showing precisely how it would come into being. But he never told it all down here.

> When I get to heav'n I will sing and tell,
> When I get to heav'n I will sing and tell,
> When I get to heav'n I will sing and tell
> How I did shun both death and hell.

CHAPTER EIGHTEEN

❀◇

The Agencies and Models of Transformation

. .

N ow that we know the chief aims, purposes, and goals of the spiritual as literature, we can turn to the next interesting phase: the methods and devices by which these were accomplished. Naturally there is some overlapping. You cannot illustrate the goals without bringing in some of the devices. The important thing here, however, is not what was used, but why and how certain things were used. The whys and hows penetrate the poetic instincts, powers, and skills of these unique creators of folk literature.

Many people, for instance, rest their case for the purely religious origins of the spiritual upon the fact that the black poet used the Bible and borrowed from the camp meeting forms. The first no one can deny. Even if the second were true, did not Shakespeare use Holinshed, Plutarch, Cinthio, and old plays? The questions are, what did he do with what he borrowed and how do his borrowings differ from the originals? The answers to those questions are the beginnings of the explanation of Shakespeare's genius as a poet.

So with the spiritual creator. He used the Bible, the world of nature, things around him, occupations, even other songs. But his poetic approach was different, often unique. He borrowed only the things that fit his poetic philosophy. He used his material only in certain ways. These original processes are now the subject of our investigations.

Let us turn first to the camp meeting songs. I offer a representative comparison:

Camp Meeting (same as old Methodist Hymn)	Afro-American Spiritual
"And then away to Jesus On wings of love I'll fly."	"Dey'll take wings and fly away, For to hear de trumpet soun' In dat mornin'."

The camp meeting poet (author of the so-called white spiritual) was interested in the abstract values of religion, the simplest possible exposition of the relationship between the Deity and man, and what happens as a result. The spiritual poet is always more spirited, more vigorous, more dramatic, more colorful, more sensual. His purpose was to stir and galvanize his hearer, not merely to inform him or to join in the repetition of old important truths.

⟨ Objects as Devices

The spiritual poet employed hundreds of simple objects as devices. Rarely were the objects unobtrusive. They assured the quality of things with hidden meanings suddenly revealed.

The hammer and nails reminded the singer of Christ on the cross or of the simple, but glorious, act of building, a form of constructive behavior that appealed mightily to the slave. The ladder was that of a new Jacob. Climbing was terribly important to the slave; he felt he had been kept down for too long. He specialized in gates (especially pearly gates) which opened to some new life; fountains with peculiar powers of refreshment and new strength; nets, which meant fish, food, and profitable occupation; rods which symbolized magical deeds; and keys which opened doors that other people considered unopenable, like the door of the grave or the door to freedom. The sword and shield were connotative of wars which sometimes had to be fought, as in the Bible.

Examples are legion, but perhaps a few will get the point across.

Hammer and nail:	"Dey nail'd His han' an' dey nail'd His feet, De hammer was heard on Jerusalem Street." "King Jesus built me a house above, An' He built it tout* a hammer or a nail."
Ladder:	"We are climbing Jacob's ladder, . . . Ev'ry round goes higher 'n' higher."
Gates:	"I haven't been to Heaven, but I've a-been told, Not made with hands; O, the gates are pearl and the streets are gold, Not made with hands, O brethren."
Fountain:	"Been drinking from the fountain, (repeated twice) His name's so sweet." "I'm goin' to drink at the crystal fountain, . . . some of these days."
Net:	"Peter, (Peter) . . . on de Sea o' Galilee (repeated) Take yo' (take yo') (repeated) Take yo' net an' foller me."

* tout = without.

Rod: "Jordan's river is a river to cross,
         I know de udder worl' is not like dis,
         Stretch yo' rod an' come across."

Key: "Too late, too late, sinnah . . .
         Massa Jesus lock de do',
         Carry de key an' gone home."

Broom: "Mas' Jedus gib me a little broom
         For sweep my heart clean!
         I sweep it clean by de grace o' God—
         O trial's in my way!"

Needle: "See how de worl' come ag'in' me,
         Small as a needle."

Window: "O look through de diamon' window, Lord!
         I ain't got de army bymbye!
         I look through de diamon' window—new moon a-comin'."

The use of wearing apparel (robes, slippers, crowns) and musical instruments (harps, bells, ram horns, trumpets, drums), usually suggested creative talents; they are, therefore, interpreted later (see Chapter 19). Likewise, houses and building pointed toward elements of character (see Chapter 19).

The employment of a pen, sometimes a golden pen, to keep the record of each individual clear and straight, is a sign of eternal justice (see Chapter 20). But the golden altar, on which John saw the holy number sitting, is a sacred sign that you are one of the chosen people and an indication of the slave's leaning toward predestination. The Christian banner certifies a motto that is new as well as old with "repentance and salvation . . . graven dere in gold."

The streets, lanes, and roads are usually status symbols. If you end up living in or walking the right streets, your fortune is truly made.

Road: "Marching up the heavenly road, . . .
         I'm bound to fight until I die."

Street: "O, the gates are pearl and the streets are gold, . . .
         Gwineter walk dem golden streets."

Lane: "Jesus calls you, down de lane, . . .
         In de heab'n, down de lane, . . .
         Walk, Mary, down de lane."
         "King Jesus built me a house above,
         An' He built it on Jerusalem lane."
         "I want my Elder to go with me,
         (repeated twice)
         To walk down Jerusalem lane."

But remember our previous reference to the hammering on the cross that was heard on Jerusalem street and an earlier reference to the fact that "the road is rough an' it's hard to walk." References of this latter type are rare; those of the former type are predominant.

By far the most striking and numerous of the objects employed as poetic devices by the spiritual poet came from the realm of transportation. In his imagination, the slave was constantly on the move, partly because of his desire for a new life and partly because of his fascination with fast-moving vehicles.

If you begin with his borrowing from the Bible, you will concentrate on arks and chariots, the latter far in the lead. The ark is, of course, associated with Noah and with the marvelous drama of the choosing of pairs of birds and animals from over all creation. These associations are variously adapted,

> O, in-a dat ark de little dove moaned,
> An' a Hallelujah to dat Lam'
> Christ Jesus standin' as de corner stone,
> An' a Hallelujah to dat Lam'.

The best ark song and one of the greatest of all the songs is "The Old Ark's A-Movering." Notice that the Afro-American spiritual poet says "a-movering," not "moving" or "a-moving" as the white spiritual or camp meeting poet would certainly have done in a like circumstance. As a word, disregarding its suggestion of appropriate action in sound, *a-movering* is in a class all alone. And when it becomes triplets and has colorful vignettes attached, it becomes a poetic expression of considerable size.

> Th' old ark she reeled, the old ark she rocked,
> [Sometimes "Co-lock she rock"]
> Old ark she landed on the mountain top.
> O, the old ark's a-movering, a-movering, a-movering,
> The old ark's a-movering, and I'm going home.
>
> See that sister dressed so fine?
> She ain't got Jesus in-a her mind.
>
> See that brother dressed so fine?
> Death's goin' a come for to carry him away.
>
> See that sister coming so slow?
> She wants to go to Heav'n fore the Heaven doors close.
>
> Th' ain't but the one thing grieves my mind;
> Sister's gone to Heav'n and left-a me behind.

Led by "Swing Low, Sweet Chariot," a spiritual classic, the songs about chariots cover a wide range and much depth. Of course, the slave could be referring to the Underground Railroad which had taken to glory (free land) many of his friends and fellow workers. Assume he is not. This is one of a family of songs in which a great golden vehicle, powered and directed by God, manned by angels, comes down from heaven through the skies to pick up and elevate a particular individual. It far outdistances a rich friend sending his limousine to take you to his home for dinner. Close your eyes and try to imagine a more picturesque scene.

Some of the chariot songs are even more picturesque,

O my good Lord,—Show me the way, (repeated twice)
Enter the chariot, travel along.

Way up on de mountain, Lord! Mountain top, Lord.
I heard God talkin' Lord!
Chillun, de chariot stop Lord!

Sometimes the chariot was most remarkable in appearance and composition: "I'm gonna ride een duh glycerin' cha'ayut." The weight of the chariot is often phenomenal:

> The good ol' chariot passing by,
> She jarred the earth an' shook the sky.

The idea of "rocking," very close in meaning to the rock operations of the seventh decade of the twentieth century, is quite common in the spiritual. It seems to apply primarily to chariots, but it also refers to other things. One spiritual is called "Rock Chariot." Its orders are,

> Rock, chariot, I told you to rock!
> Judgment goin' to find me!

"Rock Mount Sinai," "Rockin' Jerusalem," and "Mah Lawd Gawd Rockin' in de Weary Lan' " are three other famous rock spirituals. And in "Mary Had de Leetle Baby" is not only the talk about rocking, but the rocking itself,

> Mary had de leetle baby
> Born in Bethlehem
> Ev'ry time de baby cry
> She rock in a weary lan'
> Ain't dat a rockin' all night
> Ain't dat a rockin' all night
> Ain't dat a rockin' all night
> All night long

Twelve milk-white horses are usually the agency of God's power. The poet dramatically reproduces the whole operation,

> Milk white horses over in Jordan, . . .
> 'Hitch 'em to de chariot, (repeated four times) . . .
> How I long to see dat day.

Sometimes, you do not ride along (as on the Underground Railroad you often did not); you belong to a righteous group that has earned salvation. Then, one dawn you ride,

> Gwineter ride up in de chariot, Soon-a in de mornin' . . .
> An' I hope I'll jine de ban'.

At last, the appeal goes out to all who earnestly desire the chariot ride,

> O mourner, O mourner, you must believe, . . .
> And the grace of God you will receive,
> Going home in the chariot in the morning.

In the more secular world the poet of the spiritual read the symbolism in ships and trains. A very beautiful and poignant, though lesser known spiritual, is entitled "My Ship Is on de Ocean." Here, the poet uses a magical ship to separate himself from worldly things and unite himself to the goodly and the permanent. The poignancy arises primarily from his deep care for the sinful friend from whom he is compelled to part.

> My ship is on de ocean, (repeated twice)
> Po' sinner, fare-you-well.
>
> I'm goin' away to see de good ol' Daniel,
> I'm goin' away to see my Lord, . . .
> I'm goin' away to see de weepin' Mary . . .
> Oh, my ship is on de ocean,
> Po' sinner, fare-you-well.

Songs about trains are a minor miracle. The railroad train did not come into America until the late 1820s; it did not reach the slave country to any great extent until the 1830s and 1840s. Even then, the opportunities of the slave to examine trains closely were limited. Yet, before 1860, many spiritual poems exploited the train, its seductive sounds, speed and power, its recurring schedules, its ability to carry large numbers of passengers at cheap rates, its implicit democracy.

We have already referred to "Same Train" and its sharp implications. In many similar songs, the poet of the spiritual, finding an especially productive device to ride, urged his listeners to use the train,

> Got my letter, Got my letter, Got my letter.
> Goin' to hail the train. . . .
>
> Got my letter, goin' to ride the train.

Train talk appears in spirituals even when there is no regular train on the track. "O gambler, you can't get on a-this train" is in anticipation of a glory-bound train that has not yet arrived. The same is true of "O sister, have you got your ticket signed?"

The right train has a way of bringing together people of a kind, of inspiring strenuous efforts, and of encouraging punctuality.

> I'll meet you at the station when the train comes along.
> I may be blind an' cannot see, . . .
> I may be lame an' cannot walk,
> But I'll meet you at the station when the train comes along.

The outstanding "train" spiritual is "Git on Board, Little Chillen," sometimes called "The Gospel Train." It is a clear command for the Underground Railroad or for the slave to attach himself to some trainlike method of swift advancement or departure. It refers to "car wheels movin', An' rumblin' thro' de lan'," to the cheapness of the fare and the availability of the train for all, and to the fact that there is plenty of room. It seems to be saying, "If you don't get down to the station and board this train, you have only yourself to blame."

The uniqueness of this particular train and the poignancy of missing it are strongly stressed,

> No signal for another train
> To follow on the line,
> O, sinner, you're forever lost,
> If once you're left behind.

James Baldwin's title *Tell Me How Long the Train's Been Gone* is based on a spiritual which deplores the awful fix in which missers of this wonderful train find themselves. The title of the spiritual is "How Long de Train Bin Gone," or something quite similar, depending on the locale where the song is sung. Like Baldwin's book it hints that fundamental changes in our way of life are terribly long overdue,

> Train been gone a long time . . .
> Oh yes Lawd.

In somewhat of a surprise, the mill as a place of normal evolution is used by the spiritual poet. No matter what kind of a front people put up, no matter how they may try to evade, they cannot escape "Jordan's Mills,"

> Jordan's mills a-grinding
> Jordan's a-hay, . . .

The sturdiness and incorruptibility of the mills are certified by the facts that they are "built without nail or hammer" and run "without wind or water."

The success of Joshua's people in bringing down walls of tyranny and injustice by simply walking around them causes a group of songs to be composed on the subject of going around the wall. One of these is called "That Suits Me." To go around the wall is a sure way of straightening things out, especially inveterate wrongs,

> Come on mama le's go roun' the wall,
> Come on mama le's go roun' the wall,
> Come on mama le's go roun' the wall,
> Don' wanna stumble an' don' wanna fall—
> An' that suits me.

⁅ Occupations

Like certain objects, certain occupations stood out in the spiritual poet's mind. These are generally related to acts or products which the poet considered essential to his goals or glorifying.

The bell ringer is found in many interesting songs. The ringing of bells alerts the listener to poetic possibilities of every sort and to thoughtful contemplation of both tradition and potentiality for the future.

> Oh, Peter, go ring dem bells, (repeated twice)
> I heard f'om heav'n today.

After this introduction the bells stir in the poet-listener wonder about where his mother and sister Mary are gone. The answer to the wonder is implicit,

> I thank God an' I thank you too
> I heard f'om heav'n today.

Few spirituals are more genial and delightful than "Mary an' Martha Jes' Gone 'Long,"

> Mary an' Martha jes gone 'long, (repeated twice)
> To ring dem charmin'* bells,
> O, Yes sister
> Free grace an' dyin' love, (repeated twice)
> To ring dem charmin' bells. . . .
>
> O, 'way over Jordan, Lord, (repeated twice)
> To ring dem charmin' bells.

How many bell ringers are so wonderfully embellished!

The boatman is still famous today in a spiritual-derived song, "Michael Row the Boat Ashore," made famous by the marvelous readings of Harry Belafonte and others. He is not a regular among the occupational personalities of the spiritual, but he does appear occasionally, as in this fragment from "No Hiding Place,"

> Boatman, boatman, row one side,
> Can't get to heav'n 'gainst wind and tide,
> There's no hiding place down here.

The carpenter was a builder; also, Jesus Christ was a carpenter. Each self-respecting slave thought of himself as to some extent a carpenter because building was a way to rise.

> I'm workin' on the buildin' for my Lord, . . .
> If I was a gambler I tell you what I would do,
> I'd throw away my gamblin' dice an' work on the buildin' too.

It took engineers to run trains and the Christian's engineer was the Bible, which guided and let out the power of the gospel train.

> The Bible is our engineer
> That's what Satan's a-grumbling about;

* Charming means chiming, but what a beautiful touch!

> It points the way to heav'n so clear,
> That's what Satan's a-grumbling about.

The farmer and the husbandman, who sowed, reaped, nurtured, and gathered into barns, were substantially the same in the spiritual. His origin is Biblical, and he is, among other things, an agency of freedom.

> I am the true vine, (repeated twice)
> My Father is the husbandman.
> I know my Lord has set me free,
> My Father is the husbandman,
> I'm in Him and He's in me.

Through Peter, a spiritual favorite, the fisherman gained quite a vogue.

> Fisherman Peter—out on the sea—
> Stop your fishin', Peter, Come and follow me.

That the gambler is one of the easiest sinners to identify is attested by his numerous appearances in spiritual songs. His prevalence in the slave community is harder to attest. Perhaps the slave observed the white gambler from afar and was impressed by his dazzling color and by the rapidity of his rise and fall. Perhaps he considered himself the greatest of "longshots" in life. Whatever the case, he loved to sing about gamblers, especially dice shooters, as a brilliant model of evil.

> O, gambler, git up off o' yo' knees,
>   (repeated twice)
> End o' dat mornin', Good Lord, (repeated once)
> End o' dat mornin' when de Lord said to hurry.
>
> O, gambler, you can't ride on his train.

As we have seen, hammers and hammering were a favorite subject. Thus, also, the hammerer by implication. As at Christ's cross, the hammerer was ominous, but in a poetically fascinating manner.

> The hammers keep ringing on somebody's coffin,
>   (repeated twice)
> Makes me know my time ain't long.

In the above song, the hammering is linked with the crunch of hearse wheels. Note the indirect artistry of,

> The hearse wheels rolling somebody to the graveyard, . . .
> Makes me know my time ain't long.

As Noah made the ark famous and Peter the fisherman's net, so David glorified the harp. As harpist, David rivaled the angels and the greatest of all trumpeters (greater than Louis Amstrong), Gabriel. When David the harpist appeared and when the slave aspired to become a harpist, the slave poet was at his zenith.

> Little David, play on your harp, Hallelu! hallelu!
> Little David, play on your harp, Hallelu!

The horseman also was glorified. As with medieval romance, the horseman on his mount was pure glory and a performer of mighty services. When the horseman was King Jesus, no evil could withstand him and no deed exceeded his ability.

> King Jesus rides on a milk-white horse,
> No man can hinder him.
> The river of Jordan he did cross,
> No man can hinder him.

Since the burdens of slavery and the winning of freedom were best represented by rugged mountains, the mountain climber is a perfect model. The slave liked to think of himself not merely as enduring but as advancing.

> Lord, I'm climbin' high mountains,
> Trying to get home.

The preacher was held in high esteem. As we have shown, the preacher occupied a strategic position because the slave accepted his leadership and the white man considered him useful; he could lull the slave with escapist theories about another world. Not until many slave revolts were led by preachers did the white man awaken. The slave, however, revered the act of preaching and the preacher himself and expected much of him.

> Purtiest preachin' ever I heard, Way ovah on de hill, . . .
> Preachin' wid a sword in ma han', Lord (repeated)
> Preachin' wid a sword in ma han'.

and

> O preacher, can't yo' hold out yo' light, (repeated twice)
> Let yo' light shine aroun' de world.

No occupational personality, however, exceeded the shepherd in the slave's respect. The slave poet seemed overwhelmingly impressed by the shepherd roles of David and Jesus: kindness, care, bravery, protectiveness, rugged endurance, fearlessness of wolves, all intermixed with a well-rounded personality and a sense of function of major importance in the world.

Nothing broke the heart of the slave poet more completely than thoughts of a shepherd falling down on his job.

> Shepherd, Shepherd, where'd you lose your sheep?
>   (repeated twice)
> O the sheep all gone astray—The sheep all gone astray. . . .

and

> Hear the lambs a-cryin' . . .
> O Shepherd, feed my sheep. . . .
>
> My saviour spoke these words so sweet,
> Sayin' "Peter, if you love me, feed my sheep."

The bravery, power, and victorious feeling of the shepherd, even as a boy, are summed up in David,

> Little David was a shepherd boy,
> He killed Goliath and shouted for joy.

There is even more pathos in the victory song of the shepherd who left the ninety-nine sheep, searched for the one lost sheep, and found him,

> Done foun' my los' sheep, (repeated twice)
> Hallelujah, I done foun' my los' sheep. . . .
>
> Sinner man trablin' on trembling groun',
> Po' los' sheep ain't nebber been foun'
> Sinner, why don't yo' stop and pray,
> Den you'd hear de Shepherd say,
> Done foun' my los' sheep.

Near the top of the hierarchy was the trumpeter, and Gabriel was the greatest ever known. No one ignored his performance, no one wherever he was, whatever he was doing.

> Where shall I be when de firs' trumpet soun'
> Where shall I be when it soun' so loud,
> When it soun' so loud till it wake up de dead,
> Where shall I be when it soun'? . . .
>
> Gwine to try on ma robe when de first trumpet soun'.

All this was going to happen "In Dat Great Gittin' Up Mornin'."

> De Lord spoke to Gabriel, Fare you well, Fare you well,
> Go look behin' de altar, Fare you well, Fare you well,
> Take down de silvah trumpet, . . .
> Blow yo' trumpet, Gabriel . . .
> Den you'll see po' sinners risin', . . .
> Den you'll see de worl' on fiah.

And so on and on. But if you think Gabriel was the only trumpeter, you are mistaken,

> I'll take my gospel trumpet, and I'll begin to blow,
> And if my Savior helps me, I'll blow wherever I go.

One can see, therefore, that occupations were not merely incidental to the slave poet and his songs. The slave poet was sensitive to the depth and function of the individual occupations. More important, he knew how to use this sensitivity and knowledge to fashion songs that told his peculiar story and underlined his unique philosophy.

❨ *Biblical Characters, Places, and Fulfillments*

To say that the slave poet borrowed from or utilized the Bible is to say very little about his literary propensities or values. His special attitude toward the Bible, his selectivity with respect to its contents, and his special way of turning Biblical materials to imaginative purposes make him quite distinctive. In some respects his use of the Bible is a religious manifestation; in others, it is without overt or even apparent religious significance. The slave poet was not an evangelist; he was simply a literary man commanding a vast mine of ore.

Occasionally he would group a number of Biblical characters together. On "The Gospel Train," for example,

> There's Moses, Noah and Abraham,
> And all the prophets, too,
> Our friends in Christ are all on board,
> O, what a heavenly crew.

With such a crowd and in delightful surroundings he and other stout mortals were going to have good times to end all good times,

> We'll shout o'er all our sorrows,
> And sing forever more,
> With Christ and all his army,
> On that celestial shore.

Obviously, the intent here is not so much to glory in the world beyond as to demonstrate his worthiness to associate in the best of high company.

In introducing his Biblical characters, the slave poet strikes some very odd angles. Wisdom and strength growing out of foolish appearances are exemplified in the song "They Called Old Noah a Foolish Man." In "Wrestle On, Jacob," Jacob shows character in wrestling, but also "Jacob hang from a tremblin' limb." The mold of Moses is generally heroic, but not always. As "an infant cast away," Moses overcame great handicaps; but in "Wheel in a Wheel," you see another Moses,

> I wonder weh is Moses he mus' be dead,—
> De chillun ob de Israelites cryin' fo' bread

> I wonder weh wuz Moses when de Church burn down—
> . . . Standin' obuh yonder wid his head hung down.

Samson is glorified, not primarily as a Biblical character, but as a man who uprooted evil. Obviously he is needed now, as the insistent tone of "Sampson Tore the Building Down" clearly suggests. Compassion goes out to Job as to all men and women who are in the class of sufferers with the slave. In "Job, Job" and in "Job, All Your Children Are Gone" is the expression of common ground. Sometimes all David's other exploits are forgotten in recalling his majesty, as in "King David." And sometimes Daniel's great exploits are subordinated to two significant facts: in "Two White Horses," "Daniel was a man, Daniel was a man," and "De good Lawd proved to be Daniel's frien'."

The story of Adam and Eve in Eden was fascinating to Carl Sandburg as to many others. One of its best versions is in the spiritual "Dese Bones Gwine to Rise Again." Not only is it a beautiful example of narrative skill; it is told in such a homely way that it makes the Eden scene thoroughly believable. We, therefore, give it here.

The refrain, given at the end of the first stanza, follows every stanza. The rhythm line "Dese bones gwine to rise again" follows every verse. It is as though the Eden story were the kind of experience man is fated to repeat over and over, as long as he lasts.

> Lord, he thought he'd make a man,
> Dese bones gwine to rise again;
> Made him out of mud and a little bit of sand,
> Dese bones gwine to rise again.
>
> Refrain: I know it, 'deed I know it,
>   Dese bones gwine to rise again.
>
> "Adam, Adam, where art thou?"
> "Here, Marse Lord, I'se comin' down."
>
> Thought he'd make a woman too;
> Didn't know 'xactly what to do.
>
> Took a rib from Adam's side;
> Made Miss Eve for to be his bride.
>
> Put 'em in a garden rich an' fair;
> Tole 'em to eat what they found dere.
>
> To one tall tree dey mus' not go;
> Dere mus' de fruit forever grow.
>
> Ol' Miss Eve come a-walkin' roun';
> Spied dat tree all loaded down.
>
> Sarpent he came roun' de trunk.
> At Miss Eve his eye he wunk.
>
> Firs' she took a little pull;
> Den she filled her apron full.

Adam he come prowlin' roun';
Spied dem peelin's on the groun'.

Den he took a little slice;
Smack his lips an' said 'twas nice.

Lord, he spoke with a mighty voice.
Shook de heavens to de joists.

"Adam! Adam! Where are thou?"
"Yes, Marse Lord, I'se a-comin' now."

"You et my apples, I believe?"
"Not me, Lord, but I 'spec 'twas Eve."

Lord den rose up in his wrath;
Tole 'em beat it down de path.

"Out of my garden you mus' git,
"For you an' me has got to quit."
Dese bones gwine to rise again.

I know it, 'deed I know it,
Dese bones gwine to rise again.

It is highly significant that with all the Biblical characters, incidents, parables, sermons, and historical features to choose from, the slave, in thousands of songs, selected relatively a few and turned these to only a few
ends. The secret of his genius was in the skill of his adaptations, not in the
volume of his selections. He could take the same character or incident and
give it many dazzling facets. He was more interested in genial touches than
in serious sermonizing. His sense of the grotesque or humorous and his
comparisons of some Bible personality with ridiculous or hidden aspects of
his own world were often the key to his final treatment.

We will have to assume that the reader is generally knowledgable of the
main backgrounds in the Biblical references we are about to explore. Even
the slave poet "picked up" his knowledge rather than read the book or
mulled over its theological connotations. We will refer to these Bible references roughly in chronological order for the several categories, and we
will mention only those used in the spirituals a representative number of
times. We will give the name of the character or other item and the most
significant connotation found in the spirituals.

Before beginning these chartings, it should be said that the Biblical item
is selected most often for reasons already examined—symbolization of the
deliverer or overcoming the oppressors; inspiration from notable accomplishments under almost impossible circumstances (the slave considered
himself a potential accomplisher in a universe where he had little or no real
hope but great expectation); and exemplification of the workings of faith
and power.

Chart of Use of Biblical Items in the Spiritual

Item	Connotation

BOOKS

Item	Connotation
St. Luke (Gospel, Chap. 21)	Prediction of the judgment time is close by
Revelation (of St. John)	The book of the seven seals to be unfolded on that mighty day

PLACES

Item	Connotation
Jordan (a popular name in the spiritual)	The river as dividing line between time and eternity or between slave land and free land; a river chilly and cold that cannot stand still
Egypt (a very popular name in the spiritual)	Always the land of slaves from which free men emerge; the land leading to the wilderness ("I Wish I Had Died in Egypt Land"); the country symbolized the drive for freedom ("way over in Egypt's Land, you shall gain the day . . . you shall gain the victory"); the land of miraculous deliverance ("As I went down into Egypt, I camped upon the groun',/At the soundin' of the trumpet, The Holy Ghost came down")
Red Sea	God's sink of judgment upon pursuers of the chosen people (obviously intending a parallel between the Israelites fleeing Pharaoh's army and escaping slaves; note "Tryin' to Cross the Red Sea")
Canaan	Free, promised land
Jericho	Site of any famous battle where the forces of good overwhelm the Philistines (bad people) of the earth
Galilee	Home country of Jesus Christ and his friends (slaves in the front ranks, "Going to hang my harp on the willow tree,/It'll sound way over in Galilee");/also meeting place of the faithful ("Mother told me to meet her in Galilee")
Roman Kingdom	Symbol of entrenched evil and imperialism which are sure to fall from the battering of the forces of Jesus; if in all its greatness it could fall, then other oppressors, however well entrenched, can fall and will in due time

PEOPLE: OLD TESTAMENT

Adam and Eve	Inhabitants of Eden paradise; the first makers of terrible mistakes
Methusaleh	As the oldest man that ever lived on earth (969 years of time) and went to heaven, the best available witness of my Lord
Noah	Commander of the ark (by virtue of his goodness and manhood) and of the ancestors of every living animal; promoter of the dove of peace and the rainbow, but symbol of the fire next time
Abraham	Father Abraham, to be revered and imitated for his close speaking relationship with God
Isaac	A ransom
Joseph	A man betrayed by his own brothers
Jacob	Symbol of those who rise step by step as by a ladder ("Jacob's ladder deep an' long")
Moses (one of the most popular of the spiritual figures)	Symbol of deliverance of a whole people, of true leadership, and of the opportunity for each person to be free
Pharaoh	Symbol of oppression overcome and destroyed ("Didn't old Pharaoh get los' In de Red Sea") ("O Mary, don't you weep, don't you mourn,/Pharaoh's army got drownded,/O Mary don't you weep")
Pharaoh's Daughter	A good woman arising from bad stock; preserver of Moses
Joshua	Miracle worker, in sacking heavily fortified Jericho and in gaining God's confidence so as to stop the sun from setting; also a man who finished his job ("Joshua was de son of Nun/He never would quit till his work was done")
Gideon	Evidence of how a small band can work together to overcome outnumbering forces
Samson	Witness in pure strength, but easily fooled
Delilah	The duper of the world's strongest human ("She shaved off his head just as clean as your hand,/And his strength became as any other man's")
Samuel (Hannah's child)	Secret sharer with the Lord
David	All-around hero; shepherd, fighter, musician, and ancestor of Christ
Ezekiel	Interpreter of life through wheels and dry bones

Daniel (another extremely popular spiritual figure)	Defier of kings and their lions; proof that all men can resist slavery and be delivered; interpreter of life's dreams and puzzles
The Hebrew children: Shadrach, Meshach, and Abednego	Defiers of kings and their furnaces; proof that God will send an angel to prevent even a hair of any good man being singed in the flames; further proof that God will deliver every man who believes in Him
Nebuchadnezzar	Evidence of the transitoriness of glory and power if one does not maintain a standard of goodness (his fall symbolized by "the han' writin' on de wall")
Jonah	Proof that disobedience is big trouble (you can be swallowed by a whale); but proof also that God's servants, when repentant, can be delivered ("He delivered Daniel f'om de lion's den,/Jonah f'om de belly of de whale")

PEOPLE: NEW TESTAMENT
(Jesus omitted because treated earlier)

Mary, mother of Christ	Symbol of the motherhood most glorious, but with considerable suffering and some puzzlement about what to name her one and only child
John the Baptist	A great preparer of the faith (by baptizing Christ); a mighty preacher; a believer in immersion (" 'Twas at the river of Jordan,/Baptism was begun,/John baptized the multitude,/But he sprinkled nary one")
Apostle Peter (another great favorite of spiritual poets)	Model fisherman, preacher, ringer of bells; receiver of message from Jesus to shepherd the lambs (look after all the faithful)
Apostle John	Prophet who foresaw the world beyond our world, and who lives in our memory as messenger of hidden truth
Apostle Thomas	Doubter, who will eventually be stronger in the faith because of strong conviction
Nicodemus	Seeker after mysterious knowledge ("How can a man be born when he is old?")
Mary and Martha, of Bethany (sisters of Lazarus)	Deep sympathizers and friends of Christ in his sorrows, who will some day be joyous

Mary Magdalene	Reclaimed from sin and devils; anointer of Christ's feet; weeper* who will some day weep no more
Lazarus	Friend of Christ (whom Christ wept about and rescued from death) who had security in heaven, though poor, because he had built spiritual credit while on earth
Dives	Rich man on earth who ended up in hell because he had built no spiritual security
Pilate	A ruler with no character who failed the challenge to stand up for good against evil
Paul	A gifted pray-er
Prodigal Son	A symbol of improvident loneliness

EVENTS

Birth of Christ	"Glory! Glory! Glory to that new-born King! Wasn't that a mighty day, . . . When Jesus Christ was born"
	"That's what made the glory manger"
	"Mary had a baby, Yes, Lord! Mary had a baby, Yes, my Lord"
Crucifixion of Christ	"They crucified my Lord, an' He never said a mumbalin' word, (repeat) not a word, not a word, . . .
	The blood came twinklin'** down, and He never said a mumbalin' word, . . .
	He bow'd His head an' died, an' He never said a mumbalin' word, . . . Not a word, not a word, not a word"
	"Ev'rytime I think about Jesus, (repeated twice)/Sho'ly He died on Calvary"
	"Were you there when they crucified my Lord? . . . Were you there when the sun refused to shine? . . . Oh,—sometimes it causes me to tremble, tremble, tremble"

Resurrection of Christ

"Dust and Ashes"

"He rose, he rose, he rose from the
dead, . . . /An' de Lord will bear
my spirit home"

"In-a this-a band we have sweet music,
(repeated twice)/Jesus is risen
from the dead.
Go tell Mary and Martha, (repeated
twice)
'Yes, Jesus is risen from the dead'."

" 'Twas on one Sunday morning,
Sunday morning, Sunday
morning—
'Twas on one Sunday morning, Just
'bout the break of day
An Angel came down from
Heaven, . . .
And rolled the stone away
John and Peter came a-running, . . .
And found an empty tomb.
Mary and Martha came a-weeping,
And lo! their Lord had gone."

A remarkable variation is a song in
which the slave imitates his Jesus in
death and resurrection:
"I'm so glad, (repeated twice)
I've been in the grave an' rose again,
I'll tell you how I love the Lord . . .
With a hung down head an' achin'
heart"

---

* "Weeping Mary" refers variously to the mother of Christ, Mary of Bethany, and
Mary Magdalene
** In some spirituals the blood "came tricklin' down."

A close comparison with the real people and happenings of the Bible will
reveal the slave poet's broad or delicate emphases and variations, his outright departures, and something very important, the Biblical items, events,
and people he does not emphasize. Note, for example, that Paul's reputation
rests on this ability to pray rather than on his great apostleship; Joseph's
great rulership is ignored; and Ruth, Esther, Solomon, Isaiah, Jeremiah, and
Amos do not appear in the current list (although it is hard to say flatly that
they are never mentioned in the songs). It is reasonably sure that there is no
considerable body of talk about them in spiritual literature.

Thus, the Bible of the spiritual writer is not everybody's Bible and is not
the Bible of the theologian or of any doctrinaire Biblical philosopher. It is
a thin Bible with some names and events recurring quite often, others mentioned but rarely, and still others of alleged importance never mentioned. It

is a source book, not a textbook or a book of rules. Compared to the secular worlds, of nature, social living, individual psychology and human ethics and justice taken all together, it may not be the spiritual's largest source. But it was his greatest source. It usually led outward into themes most dear to the slave's heart. As an example, take the spiritual called "Holy Bible":

> Holy Bible, Holy Bible,
> Holy Bible, book divine, book divine—
> Before I'd be a slave, I'd be buried in my grave,
> And go home to my Father and be saved.

❪ The Magical World of Nature

The numerous references so far to objects of nature have certainly impressed the reader with the slave poet's sensitivity to his natural world. This sensitivity is, first of all, a wide-eyed wonder and appreciation. It expands to love. It even becomes kinship, for often the spiritual poet compares his fate with that of some other natural being. His references to nature are not casual; they are full of wonder, awe, and delight. It might be remembered, also, that some African religions had invested natural objects—sun, moon, sea, rocks—with deistic qualities.

As in previous cases, the number of such references is so great that only a representative selection can be used here. This selection is divided as follows: heavenly bodies and forces, waters, other airy elements, other earthly elements, flora, and fauna.

Of the heavenly bodies the sun, of course, takes preeminence. The sun's power is reflected in "The Sun Mows Down." Worship of this power is seen in these lines,

> I got my religion from out the sun—
> I clapped my hands and began to run.

These lines may sound like the pure sun worshipping of the East, but there is no evidence in support. There is much evidence of God's control of the sun such as the sun's refusing to shine at the crucifixion and the declaration,

> He made the sun to shine by day,
> He made the sun to show the way.

Among these thoughtful slaves the need for light, especially spiritual light, was paramount. Since the sun brought physical light, it might also be an agency of spiritual light.

> Sun don't set in de mornin', Lord, . . .
> Light shine round de world.

Turning one's face to the sun is a sign of looking upward in one's own life and of being ready to receive the bounty.

> When I fall on my knees, Wid my face to de risin' sun;
> Oh, Lord, have mercy on me.

But the sun we shall face from Judgment Day on will be different,

> In that great getting up morning
> We shall face another sun.

The sun was also a measurer and a regulator. It measured brightness, for heaven would be "brighter dan-a dat glitterin' sun." It measured individual progress,

> Watch the Sun, how steady she runs,
> Don't let her catch you with your work undone.

As everyone knows, when Joshua was at the Battle of Jericho,

> Joshua prayed for to stop the sun,
> The Sun did stop till the battle was won.

Unlike her popularity with romantic poets, the moon occupied a lesser poetic position in the spiritual than the sun. Like the sun, however, it was God's creature, "He made the moon to shine by night." Very often it was used to reflect phenomenal changes; for instance, after "the moon run down in a purple stream," "King Jesus shall-a be mine." At the Great Judgment, also, you would "See de moon a-bleedin'."

Shining was the star's chief business; there is hardly any reference to astronomy or astrology—"He made the stars to show their light." One star was greatly meaningful: "Dere's a star in de Eas' on Christmas morn." The injunction went out to you and shepherds alike,

> Foller, foller, rise up Shepherd an' foller, foller,
> Foller de star of Bethlehem, Rise up Shepherd an' follow.

The star also provided a model of radiancy toward which the earthly individual could aspire.

> Goin' to rise and shine,
> Shine like the morning star.

or

> Great big stars—'way up yonder, (repeated)
> All aroun' the heav'n goin' to shine, shine . . .
> O my little soul's goin' to shine, shine.

And when things happened to stars, the whole universe was in trouble. On that fearful day every star would disappear; with your own eyes you would "See de stars a-fallin'."

The wind was another good indicator:

> De win' blows eas' and de win' blows wes',
> It blows like de judgment day.

If you could control it, you would prevent the fulfillment of things:

> Hol' de win'! Hol' de win'!
> Hol' de win', don't let it blow.

Often the wind grows ominous:

> Wind blows hard, wind blows cold,
> What you goin' to do when your lamp burns down?
> Lord have mercy on my soul.

And when the wind blows hard and snow clouds come, you have winter. Of this season the slave poet sings, "O de winter, de winter, de winter'll soon be ober, children."

Turning to the permanent waters, you do not hear as much of the ocean as you do of the sea, but when the ocean does come into play, it is supreme. Once your "ship is on de ocean," the only word is "fare-you-well," and that is finality.

The sea is rarely uproarious; "the sea of glass" is a favorite phrase. Perhaps the fact that Christ (through faith) walked on the waves encourages the poet to declare and to repeat, "I'm going to stand on a sea of glass."

For the Baptist-minded the sea was a generous baptismal font and with obviously strong magic in its waves.

> Hallelujah! an' a hallelujah!—Hallelujah, Lord!
> I been down into the sea.
> O, I've been to de sea an' I've done been tried, . . .
> O, I've been to de sea an' I've been baptize',
> Been down into the sea.

But there are rivers galore, the most talked about being Jordan's chilly stream (see above in this chapter). It is a deep river, as the song of that name will attest. It is also a wide river.

> O, wasn't dat a wide river, . . . Wide-river!
> Dere's one mo' river to cross.

Whether it was the Jordan River or one closer by, alongside the Underground Railroad, when God troubled the water everything changed— "God's A-Gwineter Trouble de Water." It was certainly Jordan where the ritual of baptism began, but any river provided the basis for transportation by the Baptists (the Methodists went by land),

> But when they get to heaven,
> They'll shake each other's han'.

Along with rivers were fountains with powers both of refreshment and healing. "I've Just Come from the Fountain" is, therefore, a highly significant song.

Airy elements are often brought into spiritual poetry and nearly always under some special touch. In the following lines is a suggestion that the seeker was out early trying to make contact:

> Head got wet wid de midnight dew,
> What yo' gwine to do when yo' lamp burn down.
> Mornin' star was a witness too.

Clouds also are often present, realistically and figuratively. "O bretheren, my way, my way's cloudy." The clouds come, but the promise is that they will not always remain.

> Ol' trouble it come like a gloomy cloud
> I know de udder worl' is not like dis
> Gadder thick an' thunder loud.

The rainbow is a great favorite. Not only borrowing from Noah's experience, the poet gets a great personal thrill from the contemplation of the idea and the word. In a spiritual called "Comin' een de World Bum-bye," he sings,

> Comin' een de rainbow, . . .
> Comin' een de cloud, . . .
> Comin' een de breezes, . . .
> Comin' through de darkness, . . .
> Comin' een de rainbow.

And following the clouds come rain, often with thunder and lightning, again both actually and figuratively, a threat that one would like to stop but that one is powerless against.

> Thund'ring and lightning and it looks like rain,
> Hol' the win', don't let it blow.

One day, says the poet, it will be even worse, "O on you heaven will rain fire."

The poet deals in thunders and lightnings of great variety. He may begin with flashes of lightning and rolls of thunder. He may move to forked lightnings and muttering thunder. His Judgment Day special is still forked lightning, but Gabriel's trumpet will be "loud as seven peals of thunder."

The same idea shows up again in "Tall Angel at the Bar." The term "sleeping nation" seems to refer to America's dangerous unawareness of the terrible risk she runs in perpetuating slavery. A tremendous shock is needed to awaken her.

> Blow it loud as thunduh,
> Tall angel at the bar,

> Seven claps o' thunduh,
> Tall angel at the bar.
> Wake de sleepin' nation, . . .
> All de sleepin' nation.

And the spiritual's lightning does more than fork. It also jumps.

> O see dat forked lightnin'
> A-jump from cloud to cloud.

Thunder and lightning are sometimes messages, like Morse code.

> My Lord calls me, He calls me by the thunder; . . .
> My Lord calls me, He calls me by the lightning,
> The trumpet sounds within-a my soul.

In "Loose Horse in the Valley" the Lord also talks through the thunder.

The more earthly items are equally picturesque. Feet in miry clay are the Deity's opportunity to show his redemptive power. Although it is God's footstool, one day this old earth will reel, rock, and crack open.

For the time being it is a place of highways, roads, and lanes. The gospel highway predominates. One of the lanes is Mary's walking place and yours also if you accept Jesus' invitation. Along one of the roads the blind man stood, crying to the Lord, begging not just to be made to see but to be fully saved and given the expressive powers of life.

Roads lead to cities, and three are famous in the spirituals. The first is the city of Jerusalem, which, beginning with an association with Jesus, becomes any city where the slave reaches fulfillment, obviously one in a free land. He is perfectly willing to work and suffer to get to this city.

> I'm seeking for a city, hallelujah! . . .
>
> Lord, I don't feel no ways tiahed,
> Children, O glory hallelujah!

The second city is the one John saw, sometimes intermixed with the first city, but usually identified by the elaborate description, or some part of it, to be found in the Book of Revelation. For instance, there are twelve gates leading into it, from all directions; and the city lies "foursquare," as long as it is broad. The singer announces, "I am seeking for a city, hallelujah," or he expansively observes,

> O, what a beautiful city, O what a beautiful city,
> O, what a beautiful city, Twelve gates to the city, hallelu!

A third is the city of refuge, famous in the Bible and in the hearts of the slaves.

> You'd better run, run, run-a-run, (repeated)
> You'd better run to the city of refuge,
> You'd better run, run, run.

The slave loved to think and sing about rocks. Somehow, he felt his life to be on shifting sand. Although he saw no immediate end of slavery, only an ultimate end to all oppression, he did not believe that he himself would be forever enslaved, even in this life. He therefore thought in terms of rocks to take the place of the quagmire of slavery.

One interesting Biblical adaptation on this theme was Daniel's interpretation of the stone cut out of the mountain. Daniel interprets the dream of Nebuchadnezzar (Daniel 2:31–45), a part of which concerned "a stone (which) was cut out without hands," which smote an image upon his feet of iron and clay and broke them in pieces. Daniel read in this vision the ascendancy of the kingdom of Nebuchadnezzar and his heirs, but it was ultimately destroyed by a kingdom of the God of heaven.

The spiritual poet was fascinated by the vision and its interpretation.

> Daniel saw de stone, Rollin', rollin'
> Daniel saw de stone,
> Cut out de mountain widout hands.

He was always fascinated when things built on false power, however seemingly indestructible, were overcome by things built on true power, however seemingly weak. Such parables gave him hope.

The Rock of Ages naturally drew him. It was, paradoxically, associated with Christ's bosom; it was cleft for him personally. Like Lazarus, he had a home in this rock for he was living truly.

> I got a home in-a dat Rock, Don't you see?
> Between de earth an' sky,
> Thought I heard my Savior cry,
> You got a home in dat rock, Don't you see?

But even the rocks could be insecure in that last day.

> O, rocks, don't fall on me, (repeated twice)
> Rocks and mountains don't fall on me. . . .
>
> O, in-a dat great great judgment day, . . .
> De sinners will run to de rocks an' say—
> Rocks an' mountains don't fall on me.

No natural element inspired the slave poet, however, more than the mountain, and especially the mountain top. The mountain was something he needed, rising high above all troublesome land. Although at judgment it also would flee away, it was the solidest thing he had on earth. His mountains began with Zion's hill where he went up to sing. They rose quite high. "Go tell it on the mountain," he sang,

> Over the hills and everywhere, . . .
> That Jesus Christ is born.

Only on a mountain top could a slave, or anyone else, reach his zenith. Here only on earth he came on equal terms with God.

> Way up on de mountain, Lord!
> Mountain top, Lord!
> I heard God talkin', Lord!

It was the goal of his endless climb.

> I 'ntend to shout an' never stop, . . .
> Until I reach the mountain top.

It was his challenge to refuse an existence bound to the flat earth.

> Lord, I'm climbin' high mountains,
> Tryin' to get home.

In so many words he was saying that he belonged in the high places, not in the low, despicable areas. Hardly anywhere in literature is a slave's ambition more firmly or more sweepingly displayed than in those constantly recurring mountain songs.

The opposite of the mountain, the valley is mentioned rarely compared to the mountain. It is usually referred to as a place of prayer. All are invited to go down to the valley to pray—brothers, sisters, children, preachers, everybody—"let's go down," says the poet.

> I went down in the valley to pray,
> Studying about that good old way.
> O who shall wear the starry crown,
> Good Lord, show me the way;

or,

> Brother [Sister, Mourner], didn't your conscience come and tell you,
>   (repeated twice)
> To go down 'n the valley an' pray.
> No I ain't a-shame' (repeated twice) to honor my Lord,
> No I ain't a-shame' to go down 'n the valley an' pray;

or,

> Where've you been, poor sinner? Where've you been so long?
> Been low down in the valley for to pray, And I ain't got weary yet.
> [Sometimes last line reads: "And I ain't done prayin' yet."];

or,

> If you wanter catch dat heab'nly breeze, Oh, yes, Oh, yes.
> Go down in de valley on yo' knees an' pray.

But the valley has other uses. One is to inspire self-reliance.

> I must walk my lonesome valley, I got to walk it for myself,
> Nobody else can walk it for me, I got to walk it for myself.

Another is to bolster the courage of all who must face death and to reduce fear and anxiety.

> We shall walk through the valley and the shadow of death, . . .
> If Jesus Himself shall be our leader,
> We shall walk through the valley in peace.

The things that grew on earth were full of meaning to the slave. Since the slave was an agricultural being, one wonders why there is not more interest in flora by the spiritual poets. Curiously, most of the references stem from the Bible, such as,

> Sinner please don't let this harves' pass,
> An' die an' lose yo' soul at las';

or such as the tree to which Christ was nailed,

> O, see dat cruel tree, see dat cruel tree, Lord!
> Sinner, O see dat cruel tree,
> Where Christ has died for you an' me, for you an' me, Lord!

Once in a while he would mention another tree, a secular one, "You can weep like a willow," he'd say. Or he would plan "to hang my harp on the willow tree" and he would double back with an exclamation,

> O the willow!
> And the children!
> Couldn't sing!

Besides trees, the spirituals claimed many a flower. Love of flowers is one of the things that attract the singer to heaven, or to the upward life.

> Roses bloom in the heaven I know, . . .
> Lilies bloom in the heaven I know, . . .
> I can't stay behind.

Fauna are more persistent than flora in these songs. Sheep lead, partly because of the poet's great respect for the business of shepherding. The poet identified himself with sheep.

> My Lord had a hundred sheep,
> One o' dem did go a-stray
> That jes lef' Him ninety-nine,
> Go to wilderness, seek an' fin',
> Ef you fin' him, bring him back,
> Cross de shoulders, Cross yo' back;
> Tell de neighbors all aroun'
> Dat los' sheep has done been foun'.

In another striking parallel with humans, the wisdom of elderly sheep is praised over the inexperience of young lambs.

> Oh, de ol' sheep done know de road,
>   (repeated twice)
> De young lam's mus' fin' de way.

Young sheep are the greatest of favorites in spirituals. With them the poet is particularly tender. "Don't you hear them little lambs crying?" he plaintively asks. Then he turns the question around,

> Listen to the lambs; Listen to the lambs;
> Listen to the lambs cryin', I want to go to Heaven when I die.

God's bleeding Lamb (Christ) is one of the reasons people strive for heaven.

> Want to go to heab'n, when I die, When I die, when I die,
> Want to go to heab'n, when I die, To see God's bleedin' Lam'.

But the poet does not overlook the comparison between the sheep and his enemy,

> False pretender wears sheep clothin' on his back,
> In his heart he's like a raving wolf.

Lions in the Afro-American spiritual are treated with respect. Often they are associated with Daniel, but sometimes the emphasis is upon the mighty beast himself and the supreme challenge he offers, as in "Go, Chain the Lion Down." The call to courage is even greater in a grueling song, mentioned by Frederick Douglass as one of the things which motivated him to claim his freedom, "Run to Jesus, Shun the Danger." One of the dangers is depicted in these lines,

> Oh, I thought I heard them say,
> There were lions in the way.

Horses are generally associated with chariots or as being the mount of a king like Jesus. If they are described at all, they are usually white or milk-white. In one spiritual about a horse is a reminder of Arthurian legend. Only the righteous can ride this horse.

> Loose horse in the valley
> Aye
> Who goin' t' ride 'im
> Aye
> Nothin' but the righteous
> Aye, Lord
> Time's a drawin' nigh.

The dove is the main bird in the spiritual, largely because of his mourning propensity, the ease of his flight, and his role in Noah's ark. "Mourn like a dove" comes through on several occasions. On one of these you are asked, "Don't you hear them turtle dove a-mourning?" Mourning is a spe-

cial gift and a kind of paradoxical pleasure of the poet (see Chapter 15).
Since no one was traditionally better at mourning than a dove, the dove becomes a model.

As to his flying ease, the poet adapts an early piece,

> Sing a ho that I had the wings of a dove,
>   (repeated twice)
> I'd fly away and be at rest.

It was Noah's dove, however, one of only two left in the world at the
time, who won the spiritual poet's prime attention. First, Noah sends him
out,

> Noah sent out a mourning dove, . . .
> Which brought back a token of heavenly love.

At last, the dove returns. Apparently, Noah is slow in readmitting him. The
slave poet seems disturbed that, like many people, Noah seems not eager to
bring in as quickly as possible tokens of love and peace. He therefore urges
Noah to hurry,

> Open the window, Noah! (repeated twice)
> Open the window, let the dove come in.

> The little dove flew in the window and mourned, . . .
> The little dove brought back the olive leaf.
> Open the window, let the dove come in.

Along with its doves, the spiritual has its eagles as in "Sometimes I feel
like a eagle in de air" and a whole song called "Eagle's Wings."

Cows and bees seem not to be mentioned directly, but indirectly they are
a necessity. The spiritual heaven would starve except for milk and honey.

In the spiritual, therefore, everywhere nature works to fulfill the good
man and divine purposes. Like man, nature is colorful, restless. Through
nature man learns remarkable truths, religious and secular. Most of all, man
learns through nature to stand as tall and climb as high as he can, to endure
and conquer and, through faith, not ever to fear.

⟪ Personality Change

Never did the slave excuse himself from the transformation process.
Again and again he offered himself as a sacrifice on the altar of his ideals.
He was realistically aware of his shortcomings and of his crying need for
personal rerouting. Remember how he sang,

> It's me, it's me, it's me, O Lord,
> Standin' in the need of prayer.

If on the last day he had to be judged on the wholesomeness of his personality, he was willing to begin at once to make the necessary changes. He did not intend to be found wanting. He did not intend to use his powerful friends and associates for matters he knew himself to be personally responsible for: such as the purity and rightness of his own heart, such as his own courage and fortitude, such as his personal toughness and faith. When he sang of the demands of Judgment Day, he did so mainly to prepare himself against those demands. He knew that changes of such great magnitude did not come all at once. He knew it would take time for him to change himself under the hardest discipline.

> Oh you got tuh walk-a that lonesome valley,
> You got tuh go tha by yo'sef,
> No one heah to go tha with you,
> You got to go tha by yo'sef.
>
> Jurdun's stream is cold and chilly,
> You got tuh wade it faw yo'sef,
> No one heah tuh wade it faw you,
> You got to wade it by yo'sef.
>
> When my dear Lawd was hangin' bleedin'
> He had tuh hang tha by His-sef,
> No one tha could hang tha faw Him,
> He had tuh hang tha by His-sef.
>
> When you reach the rivah Jurdun,
> You got tuh cross it by yo'sef,
> No one heah may cross it with you,
> You got tuh cross it by yo'sef.
>
> When you face that Judgmunt mawnin',
> You got tuh face it by yo'sef,
> No one heah tuh face it faw you,
> You got tuh face it by yo'sef.
>
> You got tuh stan' yo' trial in Judgmunt,
> You got tuh stan' it by yo'sef,
> No one heah tuh stan' it faw you,
> You got tuh stan' it by yo'sef.

Once you had done all you could for yourself and had set your heart unswervingly and unflinchingly in the right direction, then you could apply to the powers for help. Then you could "Let Your Heart Catch on Fire" through the Holy Ghost or some other moving supreme force. When the whole change was well under way, you might say irreversibly, then you could look at your hands, and your hands would look new; you could look at your feet, and they would look new, also. And, because you had undergone the personality change necessary for your transformation, the powers would recognize the fact and would change your name. And you would say, "Thank God the angels done changed my name."

❀◇

CHAPTER NINETEEN

The Methods of Transformation

. .
.

IF THE poet, on behalf of his ambitious fellow slaves, was to turn himself into a new being, he was going to be methodical about it. He did
not believe in putting all the work on the Lord or his son Jesus. The
Deity is mentioned numerous times in the spiritual, but one person is
mentioned many more times, *I*.

The spiritual *I* is very much like the Whitman *I*. The poet is not brag-
ging or complaining as a matter of course. He believes in self-reliance and
self-responsibility. He is willing to earn his reward, to accept his unique
fate, to develop his special talents. In his estimation the greatest thing that
can happen to him on heaven or earth is fulfillment. Fulfillment will change
him from a small spirit to a great one, and from a weakly to a strongly considered man. Only rarely does he have small faith in himself, but he wants
the whole world to share his sense of growth. When he proclaims,

> It's me, it's me, it's me, O Lord,
> Standing in the need of prayer,

he does not mean he is helpless or that he intends to do everything alone.
He means that, by calling upon his own energies to the limit, he cannot be
everything he wants to be. When to his forces is added outside power,
especially divine power, then he can properly grow.

❲ Sense of Family and Community

Much as he relied upon an enlightened egotism and upon the divine
power, the slave poet (and the host of slaves for whom he was spokesman)
did not overlook the strength in community. He also did not depart from
the African reverence for family. He took a comprehensive view of nearly
everything. Examining life and the human condition broadly, he saw com-

munity power as a vast resource. The community he defined as a group of individuals, each struggling for fulfillment as hard as he could. Being a member of the community did not restrict your individual expression (as Emerson, Thoreau, and others seemed to think); it reinforced you. The community role did not substitute for the individual role, nor did it encroach upon the individual role. Yes, you had to walk the lonesome valley for yourself, but from another standpoint, when you combined with your "band" or with your relatives and friends, you could get more and different things done. You could also have experiences that gave you a different slant and insight from those of the individual alone.

The simplest form of community recognition is for the singing folk poet to call upon various immediate associates for recognition and reassurance. It is a kind of adult ring game. In "Casey Jones" the call was "O come all you rounders"; "The Jam on Gerry's Rock" is clearly directed to fellow lumbermen, at least in the first instance.

The spiritual poet constantly cries out "O brethren!" or just "Brothers"; "O children!" or "Tell it children" usually meaning fellow sufferers and believers, children of the Deity; "O sisters," and "O preachers." You often hear (or read) "Seekers" (fellow searchers after truth) and at times "Sinners" or "Mourners" or "Neighbors." You also often find in the songs references to the "great 'sociation" and the "union." Like the members of any well-organized group, the singers recognized their leaders: "I'm gwine down to Jordan, wid de elders in de lead."

It is significant that the great majority of songs which do not begin with some first person pronoun (*I, my,* or *me*), are addressed to some *you,* either as command or entreaty. A good many are prayers aimed directly at the Deity and a few are directed to significant people or things, such as "O Mary, Don't You Weep," or "O, Gambler, Git Off o' Yo Knees," or "Swing Low, Sweet Chariot." By far the greatest number are "I-songs" and "you-songs." The poet had a keen feeling of being surrounded by an attentive audience which was ready to share his sentiments.

Sharing sentiments and more than sentiments is indeed one of the hallmarks of the family and community spiritual.

> I want my sister to go with me
> To feast on the heavenly manna

is typical, as is "You're my brother so give me your han'," and

> My lovin' brother, . . . My lovin' sister,
> When the world's on fi-yah
> Don't you want Christ's bosom
> To be your pillow?

and

> Ain't you glad, ain't you glad
> You got good religion?

and "When I get to heav'n I want you to be there, too."

The family and family relationship are never forgotten in the spiritual. Slightly less recurrent are members of his community outside the family. His community includes his preacher, neighbor, fellow church member, and all mourners (sinners who are trying to be saved). In Africa, the "extended family" had included all close friends. Community never includes any master, overseer, auctioneer, or any member of the family of any of these. Jesus was the slave's only recognized master. If the slave loved slavery, as some say, he had thousands of opportunities to take his earthly masters and mistresses and their families on his chariot rides and in through heaven's pearly gates. He never did so. Actually, he secretly includes them among the hypocrites and among the condemned rich, like Dives. Only white songwriters praise masters in the slave's behalf.

After the community is recognized as people with mutual aims and interests and a desire to share good things among one another, the next step is to keep the group together. Many songs have this as a primary purpose.

> Walk together, children, Don't you get weary, . . .
> Talk together, children, Don't you get weary, . . .
> Sing together, children, Don't you get weary.

and

> Members, don't git weary,
> For de work's most done.

Standing the storms of life as a group is much easier than standing them individual by individual. The slave poet and all his singers knew that the breaking down of the group morale of the slaves was considered to be a necessity of the governing classes. If the master and the overseer could handle them one by one, they could inflict upon them all any kind of discipline. But if they held together as a group, their resistance would be hard to overcome. Thus they sang,

> We'll stand the storm,
> It won't be long,
> We'll anchor by and by.

As we have explained, the slaves often thought of themselves as engaged in a war. It was not a religious war. Religious symbolism was adopted to enable them to sing openly and loud. In this war they were besieged by owners and their cohorts. To defend themselves properly, they needed the disciplines of the group. Under such circumstances they sang songs like "Come, All of God's Children,"

> Come, all of God's children,
> In the field . . .
> In the field of battle
> Glory in-a my soul.
>
> The preachers want warriors, . . .
>
> Oh, we'll shout when we get in the field.

Many songs were pure morale builders and nothing else. As with all large groups, some slaves were strong, others much weaker. The songwriter appealed to the strength of the tough slave to help pull the weak ones through. And so he had them all sing "Let Us Cheer the Weary Traveler" and "Don't Get Weary." In the latter song is the suggestion that the struggle will not be endless,

> My brethren, don't get weary,
> Angels brought de tidings down;
> Don't get weary,
> I'm hunting for a home.

"Don't You Let Nobody Turn You 'Round" is a group song warning against compromises with the establishment. Under the circumstances of slave life, it could not be otherwise. The song could certainly not be encouraging the slave to continue cooperating with his oppressor. Fitting into the pattern of the other builders of group morale, it merely says that if we all hang together, we will find a satisfactory way out of our misery. It ends with the injunction, "keep straight in the narrow way." The narrow way refers to the tightrope the slave had to walk when he was planning something better.

The temptation just to give up was always great. The enemy seemed overpowering and circumambient. What could the poor slave do but give up? Inherent in the songs urging him not to give up were silent reminders that many slaves had got free and got clear out of slavery. Thus, the message of such songs as "Hold Out to the End" and "Keep Your Hand on the Plow, Hold On" was quite clear to the members of the community, no matter how much it sounded like a religious or an otherworldly song to others.

Very often the songs which mentioned or implied heaven were created to encourage the group to look upward, to reach for high goals. Remember that the slave never thought of himself as slavish in heart or mind. While he was struggling in slavery, he could not let his spirits droop. He had to think of the time when things would be better for him.

> Keep prayin',
> I do believe
> We're a long time waggin' o' de crossin'.
> Keep prayin',
> I do believe
> We'll git home bimeby.

Every once in a while a note of impatience entered:

> I'm bred and born a Methodist,
> When shall I get there?
> I carry the witness in my breast,
> When shall I get there?

At other times, he was in no doubt at all about the certainty of his destination. "I'm Seekin' for a City," he would sing. And within the song would be reminders of his group affiliation: "Oh, bredren, trabbel wid me, Hallelujah" and "Hallelujah, will you go along wid me?" Whether or not an escape from slavery was in the plan, there was certainly a reaching for the stars.

Sometimes the group song was pure celebration. "What a happy New Year" one song declares.

The camp meeting gave the slave a special opportunity to sing his original songs. Although few slaves had the privilege to attend, many imagined it a fine opportunity. At the camp meeting, not only did people have an ecstatically good time as individuals and as a group, but they felt responsible for one another. A sinner or a mourner was a fellow sufferer who had somehow not seen the light and, as a result, was risking a dire future. Saving him was an act of benevolence, but also one of great joy. Shouting and singing were the accompaniment to this salvation and to the constant reiteration of one's own salvation. It was the zenith of excitement and pleasure.

Thus, the slave poet could think of heaven as being little more than a series of gigantic camp meetings where the community as a whole gained joy and benefit. The "Walk Together, Children" song usually ended, "There's a great camp meeting in the Promised Land." And there were other powerful camp meeting songs, like this one,

> Get you ready, there's a meeting here tonight,
> Come along—there's a meeting here tonight,
> I know you by your daily walk, there's a meeting here tonight . . .
>
> Camp meeting in the wilderness, I know it's among the Methodes'
>   [or, "Don't you let that sinner have no res' "]
> There's a meeting here tonight.

The song encouraged mourning, praying, and flying, all pleasurable activities. It commended handclapping. You can imagine the gusto with which a camp meeting song like this was sung.

Often, songs in this sense-of-community series carried a direct or implied warning. If you did something wrong or failed to do something right, you ran an eternal risk. The poet, on behalf of the community, tried to see that you avoid this great danger.

> Watch out, my sister, how you walk on the cross, . . .
> Yo' foot might slip an' you soul get lost;

or

> Brother, [Sister, Sinner] you shall reap jus what you sow
> On the mountain, in the valley;

or

> An' a brothers an' sisters one an' all, . . .
> You'd better be ready when de roll is call,
> An' a Hallelujah to dat Lam';

or "O, keep yo' lamp trim'd an' a-burnin' for de work's mos' don."

Going beyond mere warning are the expressions of need for community reform:

> All I do, de church keep a-grumblin',
> All I do, Lord, all I do.

And when the need becomes critical, a higher authority steps in:

> We got deacons in de church,
> Dey ain't straight,
> Who's goin' to straighten them?
> God's goin' to straighten them,
> He says he's goin' to straighten them,
> God's goin' to straighten all de people in His church.

There is much talk of the community banding together for the crucial trip to heaven. Once again, it should be recalled that this trip to heaven may sometimes mean a trip to free land. There is much evidence that slave runaways and even slave revolts resulted from banded action of slaves rather than independent action.

But whether the deliverance was earthly or heavenly matters little to the poet. The language and the poetic fervor were the same. The important element was the deliverance itself, and the fact that it was right and just, and the implied fact that the thing from which they were being delivered was wrong and sinful.

The band was often called together in the first instance to celebrate a religious event. One was the Resurrection of Christ, important to the slave because it was a deliverance from one of the strongest institutions known, the institution of death.

> In-a this band we have sweet music, (repeated twice)
> Jesus is risen from the dead.

The band held together in honoring the faith it shared:

> Christians, hold up your heads! (repeated twice)
> Got religion all around the world. . . .
>
> Neighbor, you bear your load! . . .
> O, then I'll shout a "Glory!" . . .
> Got religion all around the world.

Notice that in this song the band is a universal group of Christians, not a group of slaves yearning for religion as escape. As the band was not re-

stricted by space, it was not restricted by time. Any believing group belonged to the band or host, from immemorial history, so long as they honored the delivering faith.

> See dat host all dressed in white,
> God's a-gwineter trouble de water;
> De leader looks like de Israelite, . . .
>
> See dat ban' all dressed in red, . . .
> Looks like de ban' dat Moses led, . . .
> Wade in de water, children,
> God's a-gwineter trouble de water.

The band could be,

> Old Zion's children marchin' along, marchin' along,
>   marchin' along,
> Old Zion's children marchin' along, Talking about the
>   welcome day.

Or it could be a group walking "through the valley and the shadow of
death" with Jesus himself, who had tied back the jaws of death, as the
leader.

It mattered not how large the band grew: it would never be cramped for
room. "Don't stay away!" sang the slave poets, "my Lord says there's room
enough." At another time they gave assurance,

> There's plenty good room. There's plenty good room,
> Way in the Kingdom . . .
> [or, "In my father's kingdom"].

The ultimate destination of the band was in heaven or in someplace quite
similar. There, after you had been cleared through the general roll call,
you would be united to the Deity and the angels and reunited to your
sanctified (or free) friends and relatives.

> I'll be there in the mornin'
> When the gen'l roll is called,
> Yes, I'll be there.

"An' I hope I'll jine de ban'," is a common phrase in spirituals. Joining
the band means reunion with mother, brother, sister, and friends; it means
walking and talking with Jesus and a "chatter wid de angels." The spiritual
poet constantly requests other members,

> If you get there before I do, . . .
> Tell all my friends I'm coming too.

The association ("I'm Gwine To Jine de Great 'Sociation") and the
union ("Who'll Jine de Union?") were just other names for the band.
When they all worked together, they created group benefits as well as

individual benefits. One of the results of joining "de great 'Sociation" is seen in this prediction, "Den my little soul's gwine to shine."

([Creative Expression and Education

The poet perpetually makes known his passion for creative expression and education. It is not his passion only; it is one shared by slaves in general. Often what is taken for simple religious participation is a determination to be a whole person, without regard for any religious activity. The slave life and the realization of being a slave inhibited the natural creative yearnings of the slave. He tried to get his creative expression back by making songs and singing them. The obvious inference is that he would have used any channel, religious or secular, to fulfill this essential part of his life.

In Africa the slave's ancestors had been artistically inclined, almost universally. The homes of the African tribes were a vast art gallery, indoors and out. The great number of relics, art pieces, and artifacts that have been acquired by Americans and the French particularly, as well as by other nations, are a small index of this universal feeling. The number which still remain in Africa today are still another index. Nothing happened on the way over or in the unartistic realms of slave territory to eradicate this feeling; it was merely inhibited. The slave song and other folk expression released it.

Just as important in the literature of the spiritual as the slave's desire for creative expression was the poet's interpretation of the desire, sometimes delicate, sometimes robust, sometimes in between. If you are not careful, you may confuse this intention with more practical purposes, such as thinking of prayer as a mere religious routine or as the purely mechanical thing it often is with uninspired church members. If you read hundreds of spirituals from their roots up, you can easily see when the poet is resorting to pure or preponderant creative activity. The test is whether the action and the spirit that moves it are primarily aesthetic rather than functional. The tag ends (dragging in some conventional religious phrase) are not the determinants. From the purely religious standpoint one big thing that seemed to motivate the writer of spirituals was his apparent belief that, since God was primarily a creator and he was made in God's image, then he was primarily a creator on his level.

Before receiving examples of creative expression in these poems, the reader should reflect upon the talents of the slaves, beyond ordinary artistic desire or motivation. The common view is that the slave population consisted of hundreds of thousands of unskilled laborers. If this had been true, Southern agriculture would have had to rely upon a great army of white craftsmen and would have had to pay them handsomely, thus putting a great dent into plantation economics.

To the contrary, the slave was the talented worker and he did not have to be paid (except when he was farmed out to factories or the like, and even then he was engaged in skilled or semiskilled crafts). His room and board were a negligible item, as we pointed out in Chapter 15. Frederick Douglass reports that on his plantation the slaves bossed, directed, charted everything—horseshoeing, cart mending, plow repairing, coopering, grinding, weaving, "all completely done by slaves." The scope and proficiency of the slave's talents were a fruitful ground for the cultivation of his creative expression.

The slave was proud of his skills. He wanted them developed and used for the people as a whole. So he sang, "I Want to Live So God Can Use Me."

If one has talent, one needs education. We have already seen how highly the slave esteemed education, reading, writing, and all the rest. His songs show that education and the tools of education are constantly on his mind.

> There is a school on earth begun
> Supported by the Holy One.
>
> I had a little book, an' I read it through,
> I got my Jesus as well as you;
>
> I know I would like to read, like to read,
> Like to read a sweet story of old;
>
> I got a letter dis mornin'
> . . . Aye, Lawd
>
> My Lord's writing all the time.

The slave respected the ability to write as though it were a magical creative exercise.

> O, write my name, O write my name, O write my name,
> De Angels in heab'n gwineter write my name.

The logical starting point for the slave poet's demonstration of creative expression is his talk about musical instruments. In "Michael Row the Boat Ashore," Michael's boat was "a musical boat." Since the slave poet always used good models (Jesus taught him how to love; angels taught him how to sing and shout), we are not surprised at this song,

> Little David, play on your harp,
> Hallelu!

or

> Little David, pluck upon your harp,
> Halleloo.

But he is not slow in learning this wonderful instrument; he has one ready at hand, and somehow he has mastered the skill.

> I've a harp up in the Kingdom,
> Ain't that good news!

and

> I've got a harp, you've got a harp,
> All of God's chillun got a harp;
> When I get to Heaven, goin' to play on my harp,
> Goin' to play all over God's Heav'n.

And he has an added touch in store:

> Going to hang my harp on the willow tree,
> It'll sound way over in Galilee.

Gabriel's trumpet is, of course, a mighty instrument since, in the spiritual as in the concert hall or on television, the test of an instrument is the far-reaching effect it produces. The effect seems mild enough in this song,

> Blow, Gabriel, blow, Blow, Gabriel, blow,
> Tell all the joyful news.

But later, the effect grows most terrifically,

> Where shall I be when de firs' trumpet soun' . . .
> When it soun' so loud till it wake up the dead.

And finally, on Judgment Day, it goes out of this world when Gabriel's silver trumpet grows "loud as seven peals of thunder," wakes "all the living nations," and, ready or not, draws them to the judgment seat.

As he learned from David how to play the harp, so he learned from Gabriel how to handle the trumpet.

> I'll take my gospel trumpet, And I'll begin to blow,
> And if my Savior helps me, I'll blow wherever I go.

Often, the creative effect of the trumpet was a reverberation: "The trumpet sounds with in-a my soul."

Like the silver trumpet, the ram horns were a powerful instrument. At Jericho,

> Den de lam' ram sheep horns begin to blow
> Trumpets begin to soun',
> Joshua commanded de chillen to shout,
> And de walls come tumblin' down.

Bells and the ringing of bells are considered a most delicate and effective creative achievement. To begin once more at the very top of the profession in this category, the poet says, "I hear archangels a-ringin' dem bells." He then asks Mary and Martha to do the same. We have already referred to another song in which we are told:

> Mary an' Martha jes' gone 'long, (repeated twice)
> To ring dem charmin' [chiming] bells.

Likewise, Peter is invited,

> Oh, Peter, go ring dem bells, (repeated twice)
> I heard f'om heav'n today.

When the sound of ringing bells gets into the heart, it can and should touch the individual deeply.

> Live-a humble, humble, humble, Lord;
> Humble yo'self, de bell don ring.
> [sometimes "rung"]

And in more than one spiritual bells and drums are linked: "De Bell don ring, de Drum done beat."

Some garments express the creative urge as much as musical instruments. They transform the slave from the ordinary worker and being some people (including masters, overseers, auctioneers, and some twentieth-century folk) consider him into the personage of extraordinary capacity he considers himself. All he needs is the chance. He has talents, abilities, programs in his repertory, all manufactured, ready to wear. Either freedom or the land beyond the grave can give him his chance, preferably the former.

> I got a robe, you've got a robe,
> All God's chillun got a robe;
> When I get to Heav'n, goin' to put on my robe,
> Goin' to shout all over God's Heav'n.
> Heav'n, Heav'n,
> Ev'rybody talking 'bout heav'n ain't going there,
> Heav'n, Heav'n,
> Goin' to shout all over God's Heav'n.

What was true of his robe was true of his shoes and crown. Immediately upon his arrival in Heav'n—wherever that was—he would don his robe.

> I'm a-going to put on my long white robe
> Down by the riverside, down by the riverside, down by
>   the riverside;

and his slippers,

> Oh, dem golden slippers, oh, dem golden slippers,
> Golden slippers I'm bound to wear
> 'Cause dey look so neat,
> Oh, dem golden slippers, oh, dem golden slippers,
> Golden slippers I'm bound to wear
> To walk de golden streets.

He warns others not to interfere in this gloriously expressive act,

> Do don't touch-a my garment, . . .
> Do don't touch-a my slippers.

They are indeed quite special in appearance, and they have special uses,

> What kind o' shoes are those you wear, . . .
> That you can walk up in the air?

Only those of us who, in moments of what we consider supreme accomplishment, never "walk on air," will not understand.

The crown, though apparently an unnecessary elegance, was a device that could inspire creativity just by the owner's putting it on.

> I got a crown,
> You've got a crown,

and

> Ef yo' mother want to go,
> She shall wear a starry crown.

But even the starry crown was not indispensable. As with every great creator, the creator's joy in accomplishment takes precedence over the thing accomplished, however perfect.

> Walk into heaven, and take my seat,
> And cast my crown at Jesus' feet,
> Lord, I want to cross over into campground.

Singing, talking, shouting, praying, preaching, mourning, writing, telling, flying ("All God's Chillun Got Wings"), running, serving Jesus, even dying ("I Want to Die Easy when I Die") were all creative enterprises.

Running and flying were particularly indicative. If a man believes himself creative and knows that he has been held down, he wants to make up for lost time. Running and flying, moreover, are very great challenges. The slave felt that in his life the greatest possible challenge was appropriate. These two activities also represent the acme of invigoration and, never forget that the slave was resilient.

The running songs pointed in a variety of directions. Two fairly unorthodox samples from the group are "I'm Runnin' On" and "Yo' Better Run, Run, Run." In the former the singer runs to leave the world behind, to cross "the separatin' line," to be free and glad. He promises that he will never turn back. In the latter the runner has a definite incentive,

> Yo' better run, run, run, and run in time—
> Keep yo' hand upon de throttle
> And yo' eyes upon de prize.

As to flying, the singer constantly calls for strong wings,

> Oh! give me the wings,
> O, good Lord, give me the wings, . . .
> My good Lord, give me the wings for to move along.

He is well aware that the great promoter of flying has in stock the kind of wings he wants.

> Lawd I wish I had an Eagle's wings . . .
> I would fly all de way to Paradise, . . .
> O Lawd, fly all, O Lawd, fly all, fly all de way to Paradise.

His flying will not stop when he gets *to* Paradise. He says quite frankly that he's "goin' to fly all over God's heav'n." In song he also lays out his method of flying,

> Jes' wait till I get up on the mountain top,
> Goin' to make my wings go flip'ty flop.

But not even flying brought him more peculiar satisfaction and fulfillment than singing. "When I get to Heav'n, goin' to sing a new song," he says. He is full of new creative ideas.

When he got thoroughly disgusted with the way things were—and he often did—his singing was martial,

> Singin' wid a sword in ma han', Lord, . . .
> Shoutin' wid a sword in ma han'.

Singing was one of his great loves, "Oh, I'm a gwinter sing, gwinter sing, gwinter sing all along de way." Shouting was not far behind singing,

> We'll shout o'er all our sorrows,
> An' sing forever more.

And in another place he says,

> I long to shout,
> I love to sing—.

And in still another,

> I know you shoutin' happy so sit down! . . .
> Sit down an' rest a little while.

Many examples of creative praying and preaching have already been given. The reader of the spirituals should be reminded, however, that when the spiritual poet referred to these two, he normally did not mean routine church services. "I'm going to sing/pray/shout when the spirit says," is far from what goes on in regular churches, except perhaps in something like a Quaker meeting.

The poet learned from masters, as usual.

> Purtiest preachin' ever I heard,
> Way over on de hill,
> De Angels preach an' I preach'd too.

In the song the same went for praying and mourning. And never forget that they were going to use a golden pen and write the name "in de drippin' blood." Morever, Daniel's interpreting was most impressive,

> Dere's a han' writin' on de wall, (repeated twice)
> Oh, won't you come an' read it, See what it say,
> Dere's a han' writin' on de wall.

Telling was equally efficacious as singing and writing. "I'm going to tell God how you treat me," "Go tell it on the mountain," and

> If you cannot sing like Angels,
> If you cannot pray like Paul,
> You can tell the love of Jesus,
> You can say he died for all.

That form of creativity in which the inspired individual cannot refrain from "letting out" is often represented in the spiritual. Note this song,

> Stan' still, Jordan, (repeated twice)
> Lord, I can't stan' still. . . .
>
> When I get up to glory, (repeated twice)
> Lord, I can't stan' still.

We have already mentioned the slave's determination to borrow a creative function of stars, and just shine. This form of creative expression is the spiritual at its best. In some of the other forms there is the possibility of confusion with practical or routine things, or with religious purposes. In this one, such a possibility disappears.

> Hold out yo' light, you heav'n boun' soldier,
>   (repeated twice)
> Let yo' light shine aroun' the world.

One reason for shining is that you worship a Deity who created light and who deals in it. But light as described in Genesis is sheer creative expression. God is not creating it, in the original instance, for any stated reason. Simply "God said, Let there be light, and there was light." The spiritual poet feels exactly the same way.

> O 'rise! shine! for thy light is a-comin'
>   (repeated twice)
> My Lord says he's comin' bye 'n' bye.

The very best example of shining in this sense is "This Little Light of Mine." The idea, of course, comes from John, "Let your light so shine before men that they may see your good works and glorify your father who is in heaven." But the poet develops his own special slant, with little or no theology in it.

The poet is fully aware that his is a modest talent; nevertheless, he is going to put it forth with all the power he can. Though it is just a *little* light, any bit of light can penetrate a mighty lot of darkness. He is proud to be a light and to know that he has the gift of shining. No matter how much energy and trouble it takes, he is determined to be a beacon. He will never let his light go out, die down, or be hidden.

> This little light of mine, I'm goin' t' let it shine,
> This little light of mine, I'm goin' t' let it shine,
> This little light of mine, I'm goin' t' let it shine,
> Let it shine, let it shine, let it shine.

> All through the night, I'm goin' to let it shine, . . .

> Everywhere I go, I'm goin' to let it shine, . . .
> Let it shine, let it shine, let it shine.

If he had no other creative concept, this one alone would admit him to the ranks of respected poets.

⟨ Development Through Character and Right Living

Because of the constant reference to the Deity and his guidance, the reader of the spiritual may sometimes overlook the explicit principles of character and right living which the poet required of his people. The Deity was all around, yes; the poet called on him for help, yes ("Come here, Lord!"); but to bring about the hoped for transformation, the individual had much to be and do on his own.

To begin with, he had to be a man of character. When the poet sang,

> Lord, I want to be a Christian
> In-a my heart, in-a my heart,

he was not making a routine statement. He was joining this religion not for show, but because he expected it to help make a man of him. He said "in-a my heart" to differentiate himself from Christians in name only.

In the same song he said he wanted to be "more loving" and "more holy." These were not easy goals for people in his position. He chose them deliberately when he did not have to.

Next, he said he did not want to be like Judas. Overseers and other managers of the slave felt it necessary to play slaves off against one another; they offered premiums to members of the group who would tattle and betray. Regardless of the material benefits he could gain from betraying and, regardless of the lack of material benefit in being "more loving" and "more holy," the slave firmly chose the latter.

> Lord, I want to be like Jesus
> In-a my heart,

was more than a prayer; it was a declaration that, from this point, he was going to follow the man-god he admired. We have already seen the traits of Jesus' character the slave stressed: his royal manner, his performance of useful and difficult services, his desire that every man be free (for this he died), his concern for the poor and the troubled, and his determination to save mankind from error. If Jesus had had no religion or church, the slave would have wanted to follow this example of character. He said so in his songs many times.

In a song related to the one above, "Lord Make Me More Holy," the poet spells out this declaration of character further.

> Lord, make me more faithful, . . .
>
> Lord, make me more humble, . . .
>
> Lord, make me more righteous.

As we have seen, he admired the Biblical heroes largely because they represented solid traits of character. Noah for his goodness, manhood, and concern for peace. Jacob because he showed how a man could rise step by step. Moses for his leadership and preoccupation with freedom. Samson for his strength, but not for his folly. Daniel for his courage and wisdom. Shadrach, Meshach, Abednego for courage that defied flames and a king's anger. Lazarus because he built a home in the rock.

This rising step by step appealed to the slave. Again and again he showed that he expected to accomplish his transformation the hard way, slowly, unyieldingly, never giving up, grinding through solid rock.

> Keep a-inching along, Keep a-inching along,
> Jesus will come by-and-by.
> Keep a-inching along, like a poor inch-worm.
> Jesus will come by-and-by.
>
> It was inch by inch that I sought the Lord, . . .
> And inch by inch that He saved my soul, . . .
> We'll inch and inch and inch along, . . .
> And inch and inch till we get home.

In the long run, he was sure that the way of firm character was the best way for him.

> I would not be a sinner [gambler, liar],
> I tell you the reason why,
> 'Fraid my Lord might call me,
> An' I wouldn't be ready to die.

He wanted to be ready for the most rigid inspection at any time. "Hol' de light," he sang, "de Angels lookin' at me." "Oh, get right, And stay right," he sang, "be ready when yo' Jesus come."

Having sound character resulted in right living, the slave poet believed.

> My soul is a witness for my Lord,
> My soul is witness for my Lord.

Then, he went down the list of witnesses, beginning with Methusaleh, who after living "969 years" assuredly went to Heaven. The song ends, "Who will be a witness for my Lord?" Who else is willing to live the good life for the incomparable rewards?

Repeatedly, the slave declares that he has tried hard to live right. He has chosen and remained in "dat ol'-time religion," because "it's good enough for me." He has followed his own advice.

> Don't you let nobody turn you roun', turn you roun',
>   turn you roun',
> Don't you let nobody turn you roun',
> Keep the straight an' the narrow way.

He has worked "on the buildin' for my Lord." He is proud that he can truthfully report,

> Good Lord, I done done, (repeated twice)
> I done done what you told [or "ask"] me to do.
>
> You told me to pray [mourn, shout] and I done that too, . . .
> I prayed and prayed till I come through,
> I done done what you told me to do.

The Lord is his guide, but the man feels that he has done the work. If religion is the fortune the slave thought it to be ("Religion Is a Fortune I Really Do Believe"), he had been the big investor and had supplied the substantial part of the capital; or so he announced through his songs.

The values which promoted right living and which were sharpened by right living and good character are often referred to in the songs, at least by implication. He felt himself "sanctified" after hard struggle. He felt he was living "humble" although this feeling carried no implication of inferiority. Jesus had been humble, but he had not been or felt himself "inferior." A song called "The Gift of God" seems to sum up the case:

> When I was seeking Jesus,
> And thought he couldn't be found,
> The grace of God came in my soul,
> And turned me all around.

Maintaining this life of grace automatically resulted in a great reward; "O the gift of God is eternal life," and not maintaining it equally automatically meant an opposite payment, "And the wages of sin is death."

In reading the songs, however, one gets the feeling that the reward was a thing apart and distant. The important thing here and now is to live right.

Although he knew that many of his temptations to do wrong were the result of distortions in the ways of slavery, he was not going to use these as an excuse. It was worth more to him to build himself up strong than to blame others or the system.

> I feel all right, no condemnation,
> Feel all right, no condemnation,
> Well, I feel all right, no condemnation,
> No condemnation in mah soul.
>
> I been bawn of God, no condemnation.

And so he held himself and all his band to strict account. "Plumb the Line," he demanded, taking a figure from one of the occupations in which he was skilled. "Norah," Joshua, Daniel, Shadrach, Moses, "all God's children got to plumb the line."

> Gambler, you got to plumb the line, . . .
> Can't get to heaven thout you plumb the line.

This particular song ends in a prayer,

> Lord, help me plumb the line
> Lord, help me plumb the line
> Lord, help me plumb the line
> I can't get to Heaven without I plumb the line.

Another song, stressing character and taken from his homely, everyday activity, was "Draw Lebel." Drawing level had to do with rice measures.

> Draw lebel, de ainjul am a-comin' down,
> Comin' down, comin' down, . . .
> Down tuh duh groun'.
> Draw, membuhs, draw,
> Draw roun' duh haltuh,
> Draw, membuhs, draw,
> Draw tell de break ob day.

The deacon, the "preachuh," his sister are all told to "draw lebel."

The weak members are especially warned, for they are in greatest danger. One way of weakness is being just plain foolish. For such "The Ten Virgins" is sung. The lesson of the five foolish virgins who took no oil with them is hammered home. It is hammered home in the climbing line, "Depart, I never knew you, said the bridegroom, then."

Being weak, avoiding the necessary personal discipline, never overcoming the temptation to do wrong are eventually paid off in the coin of damnation.

> Oh, there's Bill Thomas, I know him well,
> He's got to work to keep from hell;
> He's got to pray by night and day,
> If he wants to go by the narrow way.
>
> There's Chloe Williams, she makes me mad,
> For you see I know she's going on bad;
> She told me a lie this afternoon,
> And the devil will get her very soon.

But the complexity and unpredictability of the Afro-American spiritual is shown by the fact that sometimes there is salvation without goodness. In "Round About the Mountain" are these lines,

> The Lord loves the sinner,
> The Lord loves the sinner,
> The Lord loves the sinner,
> And he'll (she'll) rise in His arms.

Aside from good character and right behavior, good living in the spiritual consists of fulfilling one's opportunities. "Sinner, please don't let this harvest pass" was a serious matter, as much for the lack of fulfillment as for the certain damnation at the end. "Rise up Shepherd and Foller" called for sacrificing your regular job to cash in on the big opportunity. "Let Us Cheer the Weary Traveler" was twofold suggestion: The traveler along the heavenly way was fulfilling himself; whoever cheered him along was doing likewise.

On this theme of fulfillment the slave poet reaches a pinnacle in "Somebody's Knocking at Your Door," in philosophy as well as style. Once again, the source is Biblical ("Behold I stand at the door and knock; if any man hear my voice, and open the door, I will come into him, and will sup with him, and he with me.") But the poet gives a new direction to his source.

He sets up a dramatic sequence. A sinner is at home. Someone knocks. The sinner inside is no fool, he knows he can rush right to the door. But the miraculous beauty and fulfilling strangeness of the knock overwhelm him and freeze him where he is. He senses that if he opens he will have unspeakable joy. But he will also have to make deep sacrifices and accept grueling responsibilities. Thus, he hesitates between two unendurable extremes.

The poet tries to awaken him,

> Knocks like Jesus, Somebody's knocking at your door, . . .
> O—o—o sinner, why don't you answer?
> Somebody's knocking at your door.

Taking advantage of the suspense in the sinner's delay and of the growing revelation the song brings to listeners, the poet goes on,

> Can't you hear Him, . . .
>
> Answer Jesus, . . .
>
> Jesus calls you, . . .
>
> Can't you trust Him?

Whatever the lyric quality, the main thrust of the song is to remind every unfulfilled person that he must answer the knock of opportunity. Even partial fulfillment is not enough. The knock continues. And the query as to why you do not answer fully continues, too. Since all of us are at least partially guilty of unfulfillment, the song bites deep into the universal heart, slave or free.

⟨ *Appreciation of Things Going Wrong and of Riddles in the World*

The Afro-American spiritual was not a song of unmitigated joy, despite its recurrent optimism. Even the expectation of victory presupposed a long, hard struggle. On the other hand, the title "The Sorrow Songs" given the spirituals by W. E. B. Du Bois in his magnificent essay in *The Souls of Black Folk*, does not fit the whole case either. In fact, there is not a great deal of pure sorrowing. Even the mourning is creative and sometimes joyful.

Close examination proves that the spiritual cannot be encompassed by simple phrases, as so many people have tried to do in writing about, thinking about, or dismissing the songs. These songs are a complex lot. Even individual songs or a group of songs on a single theme are full of complexity. These poets and the folk around them are torn between agonies and anticipated joys, between assurances and doubts, between realities and fantasies, between surface meanings and undercurrent connotations, between serious philosophy and playful humor, between acknowledgment of ignorance and hunger for incisive truth.

They did not delude themselves either about their everyday predicament or about religion. If religion was mild escape for them, it was also a serious method for building character and facing problems, as we have just seen. In those songs, in which they were undoubtedly promoting free land to the runaway, they knew the risks they were taking. They were ready to die rather than remain enslaved, but they had no intention of throwing their lives uselessly away if they could avoid it. They spent little time looking on the surface of things; they probed deeply for hidden meanings, for booby traps, for unknown springs beneath the rocks. They gazed in the skies for an outline of a proper home for their aspirations.

These are some of the reasons why they chose the Christian faith and developed it in their terms. To put the case more succinctly, the Christian faith offered meaningful rewards for struggle and upright living by people who had to begin at the bottom. Its gods made friends with the poor and offered the highest boons, e.g. everlasting life, to any man who could muster the faith and carry out the works. That was all the slave wanted, a chance to live by merit on the highest level. He had felt all along the injustice of having been treacherously seized and brutalized and then of being denied things like freedom and the exercise of his talents. He would never have joined a religion which did not have provisions for his deliverance, spiritually and otherwise.

His songs are full of the evidence of these attitudes and beliefs. His songs show, further, that he believed the world and time, unlike the slavery institution and the greedy owners and unprincipled politicians who upheld it, to be essentially just. Thus, he could line up on the side of justice and await certain ultimate verdicts.

Once again, however, the Afro-American spiritual becomes complicated. Although the prevailing view is essentially optimistic, the spiritual is honeycombed with realistic doubts and fears. Sometimes, the poet is not sure he has what it takes; or that religion is strong enough to override evil (did they not even crucify Christ, the Son of God?); or that justice is not man's greatest illusion; or that death can be ringed and tied for long; or that every lost sheep will eventually be found; or that some terrible riddles simply have no answers; or that the whole business of living, dying, and living again is not some murky joke.

Right alongside the indomitable "Go Down, Moses," with its fierce command, "Tell old Pharaoh 'Let my people go!' " is this song,

> O, I can't stay away, (repeated twice)
> I wish I had died in the Egypt land.

The song makes apologies for the expression of defeat, but it advertises defeatism nevertheless.

From Egypt of the period centuries before Christ to the trouble of their own day is just a small jump:

> One day, Lord, one day, Lord,
> Walkin' long, Lord, Wid hung down head, Lord!
> Chillun,—an achin' heart, Lord!

Or note this apparent sample of persecution complex:

> Down on me—Down on me—
> Looks like ev'rybody in the whole round world's down on me;

or this need for secret consultation with a great power,

> I'm ladened with trouble, an' burden'd wid grief;
> To Jesus in secret, I'll go for relief;

or this deeply plaintive cry for help,

> Oh Lord, Oh, my Lord!
> Oh my good Lord!
> Keep me from sinking down;

or "Lord, have mercy. Save me now."

The next song carries a distant hope, though no assurance, of help from Jesus. Even with that hope, the feeling expressed is one of almost overwhelming despair.

> I'm troubled, I'm troubled, I'm troubled in mind,
> If Jesus don't help me I sho'ly will die;

or, "O wretched man that I am . . . I'm bowed down with a burden of woe"; or, "Poor me, poor me, Trouble will bury me down." And these lines are very nearly as disheartening,

> Ol' trouble it come like a gloomy cloud, . . .
> Gadder thick an' thunder loud.

Occasionally, the poet will sum it all up,

> I'm a-rollin', I'm a-rollin',
> I'm a-rollin' through an unfriendly worl',
> I'm a-rollin', I'm a-rollin', through an unfriendly worl'.

Sometimes it hardly helps to know that you are caught in an unfriendly world. Things are just as bad. Your situation and your blues have not improved. You still are forced to run for your life.

> Ef ennybody ax yo' what's de matter wid me
> Jis tell him I say I'm runnin' fo' my life . . .
> . . . mo'nin' fo' my life . . .
> . . . prayin' fo' muh life.

Sometimes crying is the only thing that will help. And so there is a spiritual, "Can' Help from Cryin' Sometime," and another spiritual, "Wring My Hands and Cry," which goes something like this,

> Sometimes I feel like
> A moanin' dove
> Sometimes I feel like
> A moanin' dove
> Wring my han's an'
> Cry, cry, cry,
> Wring my han's an'
> Cry, cry.

Other stanzas in the spiritual tell of feeling "like I gotta no home," "like I'm troubled all day long," "like I gotta no frien's."

If there is so much trouble, someone is to blame. Another spiritual tells who, "Fault een Me." The singer links himself with Jonah,

> Oh duh fault een me, eh Lawd,
> Oh duh fault een me, eh Lawd,
> Jonah cry out, Eh Lawd,
> Duh fault een me.

But the singer is not the only one having trouble. "Somebody Got Lost in de Storm." And who was the somebody? "Po' sinner got lost in de storm."

If there is any consolation, trouble has always been a condition of living. The spiritual "Troubles Was Hard" says so. Trouble was hard for Adam and Eve, for David, for members struggling to get to heaven.

> 'Cause dey troubles was hahd,
> Yas dey troubles was hahd, Lawd, Lawd;
> Oh dey troubles was hahd,
> Yes indeed, dey troubles was hahd.

Naturally, the people themselves were to blame. They were the ones who had made God angry.

> God got angry on his throne,
> He called the angels and they began to mourn;
> They dropped their wings and veiled their face,
> And cried, have mercy on the human race.

In times like these, the good man can ease his way with prayer. But there comes a time when things are too heavy even for prayer.

> How can I pray . . .
> when my heart is burdened down
> Oh Debble's in de way . . .
> When my heart is burdened down.

Now all of life is dark. Pain, trouble, the hopelessness are in complete command. Apparently nowhere is there even a thin shaft of light. But once again the slave poet reverses his field. He finds a realistic answer. He sings,

> I'm so glad trouble don't last always
> I'm so glad trouble don't last alwaaays,
> I'm so glad trouble don't last always
> O my Lord, O my Lord, what shall I do?
>
> Christ tol' the blin' man,
> To go to the pool an' bathe;
>
> Christ tol' Nicodemus,
> He mus' be born again; . . .
>
> O my Lord, O my Lord, what shall I do?

Added to the general toughness of life is the inexcusable carelessness and irresponsibility of people. "De people keep a-comin' and de train done gone," says one song. In a number of songs you will find these same lines,

> Watch out my sister (or "Mind out brother")
> How you walk on the cross,
> Yo' foot might slip an' yo' soul get lost!

And the poet gives indication often that this very mishap has overtaken a large number who thought they had been saved. He returns to the theme in far more famous lines, "Ev'rybody talkin' 'bout heav'n ain't goin' there."

Sometimes the carelessness is sheer perversity,

> And I couldn't hear nobody pray, O Lord!
> Couldn't hear nobody pray,
> O, way down yonder by myself,
> And I couldn't hear nobody pray.

The song obviously refers to more than prayer as a fulfilling exercise; it clearly suggests that people just will not do right when they have the opportunity. Halfway house is not much better.

> Some seek God's face, but don't seek right,
> Pray a little by day and none at night.

This line of thinking leads the poet to the conclusion that the world is just too full of sinners, gamblers, liars, and hypocrites. Please note that no one is born bad. In the lexicon of the spiritual the very word *sinner* means a person of potential goodness who, for some peculiar reason, keeps making mistakes. He is always a candidate for salvation. Every one of the saved begins as a sinner and continues to sin, at least slightly, on occasion. But the good ones continue to wash themselves in the blood of the Lamb and continue to come out clean.

The confirmed sinner is he who allows himself to get dirty and to remain so. After a while he simply does not take the trouble to wash; it is too much trouble even to think about it. In the eyes of the spiritual poet this is the man who is on his way to hell.

In numerous songs the implication seems to be that at one time the number of sinners was few, like a sky with hardly a cloud in it. But recently the sky has filled with clouds. The number of sinners has become so great that the sky is dark and gloomy, and the poet is distressed because it seems that little can be done to clear the sky again.

> O the downward road is crowded, crowded, crowded,
> O the downward road is crowded
> With unbelievin' souls.

Besides sinners and gamblers galore, there are hypocrites and backbiters,

> You say the Lord has set you free, . . .
> Why don't you let yo' neighbor be. . . .
>
> Jes' let me tell you what a hypocrite'll do
> He'll talk about me an' he'll talk about you!

Not that any of these people are going to get away with anything! They will surely pay a heavy price, the worst possible price, eternal damnation. But the poet is heavily distressed by all this waste. On this "great gittin' up mornin'," they will rise through the fire and cry out for cold water. And this is only the beginning. Here on earth their plight is bad enough,

> Yo' low-down ways, yo' low-down ways,
> God's goin' to get you 'bout yo' low-down ways.

Claims to goodness will avail little,

> You may be a good Baptis'
> An' a good Methodes' as well,
> But if you ain't the pure in heart,
> Yo' soul is boun' for hell.

Reference to Methodist and Baptist identification leads to the topic of the trouble with the church in general.

> All I do, de church keep a-grumblin',
> All I do, Lord, all I do.

The poet is genuinely worried about his church. As we have seen, he values his community interest and benefit extremely highly. He also builds a little suspense, "There's somethin' on my mind that's worryin' me," (repeated twice). His first expressed worry is a limited one,

> Fathers drinkin' with their sons,
> That's what's worryin' me.

Finally, he gets to his main worry,

> The church is out of union,
> That's what's worryin' me.

If the flock are disjointed, the sheep are sure to get lost.

> Shepherd, Shepherd, where'd you lose your sheep?
> (repeated twice)
> O, the sheep all gone astray, the sheep all gone astray.

The result for many slaves was a recurring feeling of sheer loneliness. With a little thought, imagination, and reconstruction of the crime, the reader can join this penetrating sense of loneliness that must have swept many individuals on the plantation. They are proud, sensitive people dumped by circumstances and greed into a cruel world they never made. Around them were whites practicing bitter domination and cruelty, expressing hidden fears, or pretending benevolence, and fellow slaves knuckling under ignominiously or craftily biding their time. The sensitive slave finds himself unsympathetic with all these points of view and often there is no one who can share his spoken complaints or silently share his miserable contemplations. The only breast on which he could lay his head for comfort is the rocky ground. Even the hope of escape or rescue is momentarily blacked out. At times like this, even his beliefs, so powerful most of the time, fail him. Immersed in such hopelessness but still possessed by his poetic heart, no wonder he was able to create so poignant a classic as this song,

> Sometimes I feel like a motherless child,
> Sometimes I feel like a motherless child,

Sometimes I feel like a motherless child,
A long ways from home; a long ways from home.
True believer, a long ways from home, a long ways from home.

Sometimes I feel like I'm almost gone,
Sometimes I feel like I'm almost gone,
Sometimes I feel like I'm almost gone,
A long ways from home; a long ways from home.

Meanwhile, Satan is very busy:

Ol Satan's jes' like a snake in de grass, . . .
He's watchin' for to bite you as-a you pass.

And death is running wild:

The hammers keep ringing on somebody's coffin— . . .
The hearse wheels rolling somebody to the graveyard—.

Death is not merely unrestrained. He is a nonrespector of persons. He is an unbridled criminal.

Death ain't nothin' but a robber, don't you see? . . .

Death came to my house, he didn't stay long,
I looked in the bed an' my mother was gone, . . .

I looked in the bed an' my father was gone, . . .

I looked in the bed an' my sister was gone, . . .

I looked in the bed an' my brother was gone,
Death ain't nothin' but a robber, don't you see?

If all these troubles and evil circumstances had befallen only bad people, the poet could possibly understand. If they had happened just to people, like himself, who, while struggling upwards, had not fully proved themselves, he might still understand. But the world is so constructed that they happen to the nicest, the most generous, the most sacrificial, the best man who ever lived—Jesus Christ. How can anyone understand that? or the awfulness of life in such a world?

Wasn't that an awful shame,
He hung three hours in mortal pain!

and

Those cruel people! Hammering! (repeated three times)
They nailed him to the tree . . .
You hear the hammers ringing;

and

He had to wear a thorny crown, (repeated four times) . . .

Dey licked him wid violence, (repeated four times) . . .

An' den dey nailed him to de tree;

and

> Dey whipped Him up an dey whipp'd Him down,
> What yo' gwine to do when yo' lamp burn down?
> Dey whipp'd dat man all ovah town,
> What yo' gwine to do when yo' lamp burn down?

On top of everything, in spite of all his struggles, self-denials, and sacrifices, sometimes heaven seems terribly far away,

> Heaven's so high, I am so low,
> Don't know if I'll ever get to heaven or no,

and

> O, de river of Jordan is so wide,
> One mo' river to cross,
> I don't know how to get on de other side:
> One mo' river to cross.

The number who will be successful is so small a percentage of the people on earth; can he dare to hope that he will be one of these rare souls?

> The Heav'n'ly land so bright an' fair,
> There are very few seem going there.

The riddles are very much in the vein of the things going wrong. Under normal conditions there are no riddles. You live in a difficult, or at least a dubious world. You know how to improve your condition. You know the sources of power. You simply ally yourself with them and make yourself work hard to insure your proper reward. That is all there is to it. You cannot possibly go wrong if you follow the right instructions.

In spite of this apparently simple process and the overwhelming evidences that it works, the slave poet found many riddles. A few of them are listed here:

Where shall I be when de firs' trumpet soun'?
Where shall I be when it soun' so loud,
When it soun' so loud till it wake up de dead;
Where shall I be when it soun'?

O, po' sinner, O now is yo' time, O po' sinner,
What yo' gwine to do when yo' lamp burn down?

O, nobody knows a who I am, a who I am, till the judgment morning.

I'm so glad trouble don't last always, . . .
O my Lord, O my Lord, what shall I do?

Where shall I go? Where shall I go?
Where shall I go for to ease my "troubled in mind"?

Oh! sinner Oh! sinner man Oh! sinner
Oh! which way are you going?

There's a heavenly home up yonder, . . .
Oh! When shall I get there?

Done took my Lord away, away, away;
Done took my Lord away!
Can't ye tell me where ter find him?

O how long, watch-a-man? How long?

They led my Lord away, away, away,
They led my Lord away,
O tell me where to find Him.

Were you there when they crucified my Lord?

Before this time another year, I may be gone.
Out in some lonely graveyard, O Lord, how long? . . .
By the grace of God I'll follow on, O Lord, how long?

O wretched man that I am, (repeated twice)
O who shall deliver po' me?
I'm bowed down with a burden of woe, (repeated twice)
O who shall deliver po' me?

❲ Prevailing Attitudes

Although the items we call "basic attitudes" or "prevailing attitudes" have been referred to in their original contexts, to get a complete picture one should see these items in the total context of the philosophy of these folk poems taken somewhat as a whole. They are the permeating influences of transformation as the spiritual poet envisages the process. Explicitly, one or more of them appears in almost every poem. They carry the emphasis, the drive, the magnetic pull of the relationship between the life the slave lives and that which he hopes for and expects.

JESUS

The first of these is the love and power of Jesus, and the slave's friendship and alliance with him. Although the Jesus of the spiritual is derived from the Son of God, the Christ who lived, died, and was resurrected, and from the living Saviour and Comforter, all of the Bible, he is far more than a staid, religious figure in the songs. He resembles the Jesus of basic Christian doctrine, but, all told, is not the same personality. He lacks the aloofness and untouchability of a god. The slave is on familiar terms with him. Moreover, Jesus is available for services of every kind, on earth and in heaven, in life and death. The fact that he arouses the spirit of freedom in the slave and encourages him to yearn and strive for it is highly significant. Equally significant is the fact that, without religious implications, Jesus helps to inspire manhood, creativity, and self-reliance in the slave. Jesus, as he sang it, was his door,

> Oh, I am the Door, I am the Door, children,
> I am the Door,
> Oh! who will enter in?

As the closest link to the Lord and God, Jesus is the slave's channel to omnipotent power, and the slave leans heavily on this power. Besides sheer power, Jesus embodies the dignity and majesty of a king and this king is the slave's friend. The result is a delicacy and a sense of the magnificent that give the songs a very special flavor.

The details which identify the various aspects of this attitude are often quite interesting. In the matter of the origin of Jesus, for instance, the fact that he chose to be humbly born made a solid impression on the slave singers. It drew him closer to them, of course, but it also made them oversympathize.

> Po' li'l Jesus, Hail Lawd,
> Child o' Mary, Hail Lawd,
> Bawn in a stable, Hail Lawd,
> Ain't dat a pity an' a shame.

They were proud that he had chosen to be a rock. Without his "rockness" they would have been at an awful disadvantage.

> We are building on a Rock,
> On high, on high, . . .
> Christ Jesus is the Rock.

How he could "fix" things in his own life was also a delight to them. Life must have been as complicated in Jesus' time as it was now, but "Jesus Got His Business Fix." From the time his work was "just begun" through the stages when he preached in Galilee, preached "to the po'," and "turned the dead alive," he knew how to keep things in order. He also knew the trick of ascending to heaven.

If Jesus could do it for himself, he could do it for them or help them learn to do it. And so another of their songs says "Fix me, Jesus."

> Fix me right,
> Fix me so I can stand, . . .
> Dig my grave with a silver space. . . .
> And let me down with a golden chain.

The slave singer did not hesitate to make very unusual demands of his friend Jesus.

> Meet me, Jesus, meet me,
> Meet me in de middle of de aiah,
> So's if my wings should fail me,
> Meet me wid another paiah.

There was never any doubt about their friendship to him, and what was the great deal more important, his friendship to them.

> When my face become a lookin' glass, . . .
> When my room become a public hall,
> King Jesus is my ondly friend.

Wonderful to be friends with a king and to have a king for a friend! According to the next spiritual, the friendship was very deep.

> Gwine to roll in my Jesus' arms,
> Gwine to roll on my Jesus' breast.

When the slave needed a bondsman, he was going to "Wan' King Jedus Stan' My Bon'."

But the most wonderful and attractive things about Jesus were that he could bounce back and he could take it. "Look-a How They Done Muh Lawd," the slave would sing. "He went right down to hell." And in the next breath, they "killed poor Jesus, . . . and laid him in a tomb," but "he arose."

> My Jesus rise.
> I feel him rise.
> Ain't yo seen 'im w'en ee rise
> An' gone to Heaben on a Sunday mornin'?

Knowing how to take it was the greatest character attribute a slave in America could possess. Even if you steeled yourself against the hard work, the bad food, the beatings, the separations from loved ones, things you had grown to expect, you were still not proof against the horrible surprises. You still could not handle the unexpected anger or whim of a cruel overseer or of a towering master; so you had to learn to take whatever came. And sometimes you had mighty trouble learning.

But Jesus knew how to take it, all the miseries of life, all the anguish which death could lay upon him.

> Oh, dey whupped him up de hill, up de hill, up de hill,
> Oh, dey whupped him up de hill an' he never said
>   a mumbalin' word,
> Oh, dey whupped him up de hill an' he never said
>   a mumbalin' word,
> He jes' hung down his head an' he cried.
>
> Oh, dey crowned him wid a thorny crown, . . .
>
> Well, dey nailed him to de cross, . . .

Well, dey pierced him in de side, . . .

Den he hung down his head, an' he died.

In another famous version of this great song, the singer asks, "Were you there when they crucified my Lord?" The emphasis is on two words, *you* and *my*. If you were there, what were you doing? How in the world could you have let it happen? "Were you there when the blood came a-twinkling down?" Surely, you could not have stood there watching and done nothing. To think of your unspeakable neglect,

> Ooooo-oooh, sometimes it causes me to tremble, tremble, tremble,
> Were you there when they crucified my Lord?

The setting, the phrasing, the powerful momentum of this poem surely make it one of the great poems of all time. Every great wrong, it says, is committed under the eyes of frightened or uncaring people. For the wrongs of humankind, the finger points at us all. We are all guilty. We are guilty not so much because of what we do, as what we allow to happen. And without a doubt, the slave singer was including the slavery of human flesh in the bill of indictment.

On the making of this song, J. N. McKim said of the creator, they "work it in—work it in, . . . till they get it right."

Other versions of this song have been recorded with other themes predominant. In some the *you* is changed to *I*. The singer admits that he was there.

> I uz dere win he walk'd in Galilee, Galilee, . . .
> Oh sometimes my trubbles make me trimble, trimble,
> I uz dere win he walk'd in Galilee, Galilee.

> I uz dere win dey nailed 'im to der cross, to der cross, . . .
> Oh-o! how hit makes me sadder, sadder, win I think how
>   dey nailed 'im to der cross.

> I uz dere win dey took 'im down, took 'im,
> I uz dere when dey took 'im down,
> Oh-o! how it makes miah spirit trimble, trimble, win
>   r'calls how dey took him down.

SATAN

The Satan of the spirituals is the same as the devil and old Nick. In a hundred uses of the three, old Nick will appear once, the devil about nine times, and Satan all the rest. Satan is a real person, invisible and untouchable, but real. First, he is a liar, a conjurer, a trickster, and a snake in the grass. As liar, he will tell the slave, "de God I seek I never find." He will tell him to stop praying because it does no good.

As conjurer, he must be handled with great care. If you don't watch

out, he'll "conjure you," "cut you in two," or "cut you through." As a
trickster, he is trying to "git his grip on me." As a trickster he also swept
Eve and Adam to destruction. As a snake in the grass, "ef you don' mind
he'll git you at las'."

Renouncing methods of remote control, Satan establishes direct contact,

> What make Ole Satan follow me so?
> Satan hain't nottin' at all for to do wid me.

> Stand back, Satan, let me come by.

> Old Satan told me to my face, . . .

> I an' Satan had a race, Hallelu, hallelu
> (Satan mount de iron gray. Ride half way to Pilot-Bar.)

> O Satan told me not to pray,
> He want my soul at Judgment Day.

> Wrestle with Satan and wrestle with sin,
> Stepped over hell and come back again.

> Go 'way, Satan, I don't mind you, . . .

> The Devil he thought he had me fast, . . .
> But I thought I'd break his chains at last.

Never giving up, Satan stays "bery busy." "He roll stones in my way."
It is Jesus who rolls the stones away. But,

> O brethren, brethren, you'd better be engaged, . . .
> For the devil is out on a big rampage.

For all his activity and determination to contest for souls, Satan is constantly a loser, and most often a poor loser.

> What make ole Satan hate me so?
> Because he got me once and he let me go.

> The Devil's [Satan's] mad and I am glad,
> He lost this soul, he thought he had.

> And I won't stop praying,
> That's what Satan's a-grumbling about.

> Old Satan tremble when he sees
> The weakest saints upon their knees.

> Fier, my Savior, fier,
> Satan's camp a-fire;
> Fier, believer, fier,
> Satan's camp a-fire.

> If you want to see de debbil [or "Old Satan"] run
> Just pull de trigger o' de gospel gun.

> And then I seen Old Satan,
> And they bound him with a chain,
> And they put him in the fi-ar,
> And I seen the smoke arising,
> They bound him in the fi-ar,
> Where he wanted to take my soul,
> Old Satan gnashed his teeth and howled,
> And missed po' sinner man's soul.

In spite of some discomfitures, Satan still has a chance to win; you must, therefore, be constantly on guard against him.

> Brothers, will you pray for me,
> And help me to drive old Satan away?
>
> An' ef you don' mind he'll git you at las'.

Sometimes it takes angels to ward him off,

> Dem-a snow white angels I shall see,
> See de heabenly lan'
> Den de debbil am-a gwine to let-a me be,
> See de heabenly lan'.

Thus, the Satan of the spiritual is no mere evil spirit. He is a hard-working and clever adversary. Only the true believer at his best, with the ready help of Jesus, is proof against him.

DEATH AND LIFE

Death is another basic attitude. Hardly anywhere in the spiritual can we find the blatant horror of death. The bleeding Christ on the cross and the bleeding moon on Judgment Day are real, but more like sacrifices on altars. Yes, Death is a robber and a sneak. But there is something gentle and thoughtful about him, too, like John Oakhurst, the bad man in "The Outcasts of Poker Flat." "Death's goin' to lay his cold, icy hands on me." After all, Death is only doing what he has to. He realizes that if he let you know far in advance, you would only build a grand case of nerves. In the spiritual, Death hardly ever pounces and drags you away, screaming.

The fact that death is associated with rewards and deliverances softens his image considerably. The fact that Death is an undercurrent symbol for the road to freedom on earth makes him, many times, a positively welcome figure. "Come lovely and soothing Death," says Whitman, as well might the slave when death means freedom. The river of Death is "chilly and cold," but it chills only the body; the soul revels in it.

The land beyond death, Canaan or camp ground, is nearly always a symbol for free land. As the one thing nearly every slave yearned for above all else, it was home. Remember that even Uncle Tom, with all his patience, told his kindest Master that above all else, even above St. Clare's kindness and Eva's angelic worship of him, he wanted his freedom, with all its hazards and drawbacks.

It should be reiterated that no one can begin to read spirituals for true meaning unless he accepts the slave's desire for freedom as his prime cause. It should be reiterated that the slave could discuss this prime cause only through symbols. Thus, Death and Canaan are most often symbols of release from slavery without meaning release from life.

Where Death does mean release from life, the African concepts are likely to be present or pronounced. Philip Quaque of Cape Coast, Africa, points up the depth of ancestor worship and the belief that the living and the dead are linked in permanent association. The living, he continues, must pay constant attention to the dead since the spirits of departed ancestors guide and influence the fortunes of the clan on earth.

In the dozens of songs which speak of reunion with mothers, fathers, sisters, brothers, and other beloved dead, these African beliefs are assuredly being perpetuated. "Goin' to see my mother some o' these mornings" is both hope of salvation and recognition of a blessed and permanently favorable influence. "Hope I'll jine de band," the usual refrain for the above first line, is a statement of the union of the good in heaven and on earth. The faith of the little girl in Wordsworth's "We Are Seven" is multiplied a thousand, perhaps even a million, times.

The case cannot rest, however, completely there. Many slaves had close relatives who had escaped to freedom or whose purchase had been consummated. They often thought and spoke of joining their relatives in a free land. Harriet Tubman, remember, came back and freed her relatives. A number of successful runaways at least tried to do the same, and the number of successes was surprising. Some of these songs must have referred to this phase of "the band." In this case death would symbolize the bridge between the hopeless and the hopeful life.

The particular poems dealing with Death are quite expressive. The thought of Death inspires the spiritual creator quite deeply. Reasons for this are easy to find: the fact that his African ancestors were on friendly terms with Death, the notion that Death and life are partners and not enemies, the feeling that Death offers angles of which life is incapable.

Most of the time, death is anthropomorphic.

> Oh Deat' he is a little man,
> And he goes from do' to do',
> He kill some souls and he wounded some,
> And he lef' some souls to pray.
>
> Death he ain't nothin' but a robber, don't you see?
> Death came to my house, he didn't stay long,
> I looked in de bed an' my mother [father, sister,
>   brother] was gone,
> Death he ain' nothin' but a robber, don't you see?

Death's gonna lay his cold, icy hands on me.

One dese fine mawnin's at break of day, . . .
King Death gwine fin' me hyeah at my play.

He is a creeper: "Soon one mawnin' Death come creepin' in yo' room." He
is a knocker: "Soon one mawnin' Death come knockin' at yo' do'." He
is a caller: "Hush! Hush! There's some one callin' mah name."
He works in the dark and springs suddenly upon you:

> But death had fixed his shackles
> About his soul so tight
> Just befo' he got his bus'ness fixed,
> The train rolled in that night.

He is a shaker,

> Let me tell you, my brother, 'bout the natchel fact,
> Death going to shake this body of mine.

He can be very cruel with sinners,

> Just spare the man, don't cut him down, . . .
> While he crumbling to the ground.
> Oh! Death! Oh! Death! a sinner crying oh—! Death!
> How can I go with you?
> I'm just a flower in bloom . . .
> Why will you cut me down so soon?

(It is interesting to note that there is no religious reference in the whole
of the above song.)

> Death went out to the sinner's house,
>   come and go with me.
> Sinner cried out, I ain't ready to go,
>   I ain't got no trav'lin' shoes.

But in the spirituals as a whole, more often than cruel he is easy,

> O de sperrit say I want yuh fo' to
> Go down, death, easy,
> I want yuh go down, death, easy,
> I want yuh go down, death, easy,
> An' bring my servant home.

> I want yuh creep to de bedside, easy, . . .

> Cut loose de heaht-strings, easy,

> Step to de graveyahd, easy,

> Pass ovuh Hell-flame, easy,
> An' bring my servant home.

Oh, when I die, when I die,
I'm gwine to rock from side to side when I die.
I'm gwine to set in de armbow chair,
I'm gwine to rock from side to side,
Yes, rock from side to side 'til I die,
'Til I die, 'til I die.

I'd like to die as-a Jesus die,
An' he die wid a freely good will.

But sometimes the mortal questions him accusingly,

Det' ain't yuh got no shame, ...
Tek my chile en gone, gone, ...
Tek my ma en gone, gone, ...
Tek my pa en gone, gone, ...
Det' ain't you got no shame?

Whether he intends it or not, Death causes wake songs and hanging crepe. A famous wake song is "Sim-me [See me here], yuh muh leaduh,/ All roun' duh body, sim-me yuh." And as the hammer rings, "de crepe keep a-hangin' on somebody's doorbell." And yet he is not to be feared. "I am not afraid to die," the singer openly says. Every once in a while, the singer is defiant of him.

If the member has the least twinge of fear, let him go and get Jesus.

We shall walk through the valley and the shadow of death,
We shall walk through the valley in peace,
If Jesus himself shall be our leader,
We shall walk through the valley in peace.

Wan' King Jedus stan' my bon', ...
Way een duh middle-night,
W'en det' come creepin' een duh room,
Wan' King Jedus stan' my bon'.

The difference in the attitude toward Death of sinner and Christian is told in a beautiful song called "Rule Death in His Arms," probably reported to the public first by William E. Barton. The refrain goes like this,

O didn't Jesus rule Death in His arms,
Yes, rule Death in His arms,
On the other side of Jordan,
Ah! rule Death in His arms.

In the first stanza you hear God commanding Michael to stretch a dividing line between the sheep on his right and the goats on his left. In the second stanza the scene changes to earth. You are present in the bedroom of the sinner,

See the sinnah lyin' on his deathbed,
An' a Death come a-steppin' in;

You heah the sinnah say to Death,
"Let me pray God for my sin!"
An' you heah Death say to the sinnah,
"You been heah long enough to pray
God for your sin."

. . . "God Almighty has sent me heah for you,
An' I can't let you stay."

In the meantime Gabriel blows the silver trumpet, calling the living to
judgment and the dead to come forth from their graves.

See the Christian lyin' on his deathbed,
An' a Death come a-steppin' in;
You heah dat Christian say to Death,
"O Death, you are welcome."

LOVE AND HATE

The words *love* and *hate* are very rarely mentioned in the spirituals; the
word *hate* hardly at all. The fact that the spiritual has no word for hate
seems to suggest that hate is a useless commodity in the slave's marketplace.
Time and energy devoted to hate, the slave seems to be saying, might well
be used for some constructive purpose, like helping to make freedom a real
thing in the world.

Although the word *love* is not often used, the spirituals are full of the
demonstration of love. When the word is used, it is usually in a religious
context. "I'm goin' to see my lovin' father when I git home," for example.
Or "Love an' Serve the Lord," "Love Come Trickling Down," "Love
Come Twinkling Down," "Love King Jesus."

Once in a while religion goes out of it. Take, for example, the spiritual
"When You Feel Like Moanin',"

When you feel like moanin', it ain't nothin' but love. . . .
When you love everybody, taint nothin' but love.

Considering the enormous number of instances when love is depicted,
the slave had a powerful need and yearning for true love.

HEAVEN AND HELL

A full discussion of the spiritual's treatment of heaven will be found
in the next chapter. Because they are part of the slave's overall attitude,
his attitudes toward heaven and hell are briefly summarized here.

Whatever religion the slave had, he firmly believed in the reality of
heaven and hell. Very often the word *heaven* has been misinterpreted to
refer exclusively to the place of reward beyond the grave. Occasionally, it

signifies free land, or the place at the top of an upward climb; and at times it does mean the place of reward beyond the grave. Hell always means the place of punishment beyond the grave. There is no suggestion that it had any symbolic meaning whatsoever. When the spiritual poet says that on Judgment morning, "Hell shall be uncapped an' burnin'," he means just that. His friends and relatives, for the most part, will be in heaven.

This attitude toward heaven and hell is perfectly in accord with the slave's realistic existence. When one lives under a canopy of injustice, he needs to keep in the front of his mind both a place of justice on earth and one beyond the grave. He needs a hell to assign just locations to people who simply will not live right and who withstand all warnings.

We have already seen many examples of the latter; there were many others. In the next chapter we will see that his own brother and the "white man" are not exempt from hell if they transgress the law of justice and right, and will not be called to repentance.

But the slave's views about heaven are considerably more fluid. First, it was a beautiful place. The slave singer loved beauty in almost any form. One reason it was beautiful was the natural reason, and another reason was that it contained no liars, gamblers, sickness, backsliders, backbiters.

Second, the place had plenty of room. "Room enough in de Hebben" appears a hundred times in the songs and in a variety of forms. Third, he had relatives there; his mother first. Considering the precariousness of the family relation in slavery and the African love of family life, this was a power recommendation.

Next, since he was striving to live right, heaven was his natural home. He told his friends, in his songs, that they could not claim heaven if they did not strive to live right.

> If yer wanter go ter heben when you die,
> Stop yer long tongue from tellin' a lie.

And so to heaven the slave had to go, both to the heaven on earth and to the equally certain one in the skies. "I'm gwine up to heab'n anyhow," he sang, "Yes, I want God's heab'n to be mine."

One of the best proofs that the slave poet was not predominantly other-worldly is found in several poems which sculpture his attitude toward heaven. Great as the thrill of heaven is, it exacts a certain terrible price. That the slave had hopes for his life on earth and did not want to exchange it, even for heaven, is seen, for example, in this spiritual,

> One moment in glory
> To satisfy my min'
> A-settin' down wid Jesus
> Eatin' honey an' drinkin' wine!
> [Sometimes it is "Feastin' on milk an' honey an' wine!"]

Marchin' roun de throne
Wid Peter, James, an' John—

But yo' body
Got to lie
In de groun'.

WAR AND PEACE

We have already shown the nature of the everyday war in which the slave was engaged, and in which he felt himself to be engaged. The fact that there was available a symbolism of the Christian fighting a war therefore appealed to him very much. He merely adapted the terms of this Christian war to his everyday war. In his songs the whole thing had very little to do with life after death.

At heart, however, he was peaceful, and a lover of peace. The war was not of his own choosing. He was fighting it because he had been projected into it. It had to be won before he could settle down to the fruitful ways of peace.

The songs of war and peace ranged all the way from the character of his God as a God of war to his own character as a soldier. A rousing demonstration of the former is found in "My God He Is a Man—a Man of War, An' de Lawd God Is His name." Confidence in his own soldierly arms is expressed in the song "End This War":

We will end this war, brethren,
Down by the river,
End this war,
Down by the riverside.

The implication of putting a quietus (or of at least *wanting* to put a quietus) on the whole slavery institution is almost too strong to be avoided.

Although a God of war, God was also a creator. The songs stress his role as maker of the sun, moon, "stahrs," birds of the air, earth aroun', beast of the field, serpents of the groun'. The clear implication is that once his war is over, through victory over slavery, he can be a creator, too.

Songs emphasizing the warlike character and glory of his heroes are quite numerous. The generalship of Moses and David was a favorite subject. At Jericho Joshua appeared with spear in hand.

"Soldier for Jesus," "You Got tuh Join That Christian Army," "Stay in the Field," "Keep on the Firing Line," and "Die in de Fiel'" are samples of a very large body of songs that depict him as a necessary warrior. As we have seen, he even sings, moans, and prays "wid a sword in ma han'." Since he did not fear death, and since slavery was utterly dishonorable, he was fully prepared to "die in de fiel'." So he sang on numerous occasions.

On perhaps even more occasions he proved himself a lover of peace and of the ways of peace. He was in his strongest element when he sang that he was going to lay down his sword and shield and "ain't gonna study war no more." As the supreme symbol of peace the turtle dove stirred his deepest admiration. One of his most enthusiastic songs is "Norah Hice [Hoist] duh Winduh,"

> Chorus: Oh Norah, hice duh winduh, Norah,
> Hice duh winduh, Norah,
> Hice duh winduh,
> Hice duh winduh, let duh dub come een.
>
> Oh turkle dub 'e flewd away, . . .
> Rain keep rainin' all aroun', . . .
> Oh turkle dub come flop dis way, . . .
> All yuh dry bones you're alibe, . . .

VIOLENCE AND NONVIOLENCE

As with his views on war and peace, the slave in his songs was essentially nonviolent, but did not rule out violence as an essential in getting things straight. Violence was, ruefully, the only answer to the persistent harms and brutalities of wicked men. It, therefore, had to be used, but only so long as necessary.

When it was necessary he made no apologies. Not only did he sing, shout, mourn, pray, and preach "wid a sword in ma han'." He called on the Lord to help him,

> In mah han', Lawd
> Help me sing it.

One reason he was sure that sometimes violence was needed was that in his estimation the Deity at times had to resort to it. Of course, Jesus Christ was well acquainted with it; he had received it,

> Dey licked him wid violence
> Violence.

But, although the Prince of Peace, Jesus Christ himself had to use it,

> My Jesus Chris', a-walkin' down de hebbenly road,
> Den-a
> An' out o' His mouth come a two-edged sword,
> Den-a.

God had no hesitancy in destroying the wicked. "Babylon's falling, to rise no mo'," at God's behest because in its wickedness it could not be saved. God had already wiped out the whole earth once; when the time came, he would do it again. "My Lord, My Lord, My Lord says he's gwineter rain down fire."

PATIENCE

Knowing he was on the right side, realizing God to be a god of justice, the slave in his songs was reasonably patient. On several occasions he said that "religion gib me patience."

His patience he expressed in a variety of ways. Having gained a deep assurance, he sang: "Po' mourner's got a home at las'." Calmly he could wait for the day when "God's A-Gwineter Trouble de Water." All doubt had been removed from his mind, because already "My Ship Is on the Ocean." Not far off, he sang, was the great day,

> Great day! Great day, de righteous marchin',
> Great day! God's gwineter build up Zion's walls.
>
> Dis is de day of jubilee, . . .
> De Lord has set his people free, . . .
> God's gwineter build up Zion's walls.

And if all else failed, "Gabriel's trumpet going to blow, By and by, by and by."

Never does the spiritual concede that slavery is permanent. In many songs the individual is on his way to freedom soon. In others, the whole slavery institution is doomed in the not-too-distant future. Such is the prospect in this song which carries an underlay of recommended patience,

> O the winter, the winter, the winter soon be over, chillen,
> The winter, the winter, the winter soon be over, chillen,
> The winter, the winter, the winter soon be over, chillen,
> And we'll all arise and go.

TRANSITORINESS

Like all great poets he believes in the transitoriness of things—of life and fortune, especially. Since he was a slave and a true poet, he naturally believes in the transitoriness of slavery and of his low social position that cheats him of his rightful creative expression. Had he been legally free, the evidence suggests that he would still yearn for a higher and higher life as time went on. Since he was free in spirit, the evidence is valid without additional supposition. The slave poet was aware that, in some sense and to some degree, every man is a slave.

Backed by great power, he is on his way up. As a romantic poet, he is filled with assurance. As a realistic poet in the same skin, he knows and he sings that nothing is sure. We can only yearn and strive and sing and hope as hard as we can. And because we are valiant-hearted, we will never give in!

❖◇❂◇

CHAPTER TWENTY

Outcome of the Poetic Experience

. .
.

A FTER all his thinking and planning and the dark night of the soul and flight, what is the poet left with? What proof is there that he has had a poetic experience? How does his experience differ from those of other poets? What indelible truth has been written on his heart?

⟨ A Sense of Well-Being

That the slave poet sustained a sense of well-being is quite remarkable, all things considered. His everyday life did not encourage him to such a sense. If he had been slavish or without sensibility, he might have ignored his everyday life and buried himself in religious faith that was actually escapist and narcotic. But we have seen much evidence that he was not escapist; that often with, or despite, his religious faith he was left bewildered and forlorn. We have seen that he adopted Christianity more because his peculiar brand of Christianity fit his concepts, goals, and purposes than the other way around.

Exactly from whence, then, did the slave poet's sense of well-being stem? The answer is found in two things: his tough character and his belief that he was on the right road for overcoming his disabilities.

Although lacking conventional education, the slave was well aware of what was going on around him. So Southern a book as *Gone with the Wind* refers to "that black grapevine telegraph system," as do many more authoritative works. Siebert and Still, in their books on the Underground Railroad, clinch the belief that the majority of slaves were constantly collecting information, seeking outlets, and plotting and planning. The slaves knew how their masters suffered economically and mentally. They were well aware of the political battle over slavery and its extension, and of the strenuous activities of antislavery and abolition groups. So many thousands could not have escaped in spite of national and state fugitive slave laws and heavy patrols around the plantations, if the slaves had not kept their information and contacts up to date.

Thus, the sensitive slave had every reason to believe in the eventual collapse of the slavery system. Whenever a single slave successfully freed himself, the slave system had already collapsed for him. There was hardly a slave who did not believe that this boon could fall to him in the early or the distant future. Many firmly believed that it would fall to them soon. This is one reason they worked for and prayed and helped their escaping fellows.

The important thing, though, is that they were men and women of such character that they were determined to fight for their freedom and for other right principles, regardless of the possible outcome. In this fight they were bolstered by their Christian faith. It is clear that the determination to fight normally preceded the Christian faith. Once the faith was adopted, however, its symbols reflected the determination. It provided an outlet for expression and reassurance which the slave needed.

And so it is that the songs often express the poet's sense of well-being because he knows he is part of a movement that cannot fail. He and others are bound to benefit, at once internally, and eventually externally. All they must do is to stand up like men and to keep connection with their source of power. In this knowledge they can sing,

> O religion is a fortune, I really do believe;
> O religion is a fortune, I really do believe,

and "I'm so glad I got my religion in time."

Whatever they call this total faith, they are going to sustain it. Here, it is called the ship of Zion. Here, grit and endurance count even more than faith.

> I'm gwine cling to de ship o' Zion,
> Try my bes' for to serve my Lord;
> I'm gwine to cling to de ship o' Zion,
> Hal-le-lu-jah.

But faith is a power also, and an evidence of character. Only the strong in heart know really how to believe. Only they can exult in faith.

> O the religion that my Lord gave me,
>   Shines like a mornin' star, (repeated)
> O Brother, [Mourner, Sister], you'd better
>   believe, believe, (repeated)
> To shine like a mornin' star.

Along with faith go loving and being loved.

> O make-a-me ho- holy, I do love, I do love,
> O make-a-me ho- holy, I do love the Lord. . . .
>
> Down on my knees when the light passed by, . . .
> I thought my soul would rise and fly.

Having such firm foundations, this is no casual romance.

> O Lamb, beautiful Lamb, I'm going to serve
> God till I die, (repeated) . . .
>
> Never felt such love before, . . .
> Made me run from door to door, . . .
>
> Looked at my hands, and they looked new, . . .
> Looked at my feet, and they did, too,
> I'm going to serve God till I die.

In exchange for such worship, the Power does his part.

> My Lord's done just what He said, (repeated twice)
> My Lord's done just what He said,
> Healed the sick and raised the dead,
> All my sins been taken away, taken away.

The washing away of his sins is more than a stage in his ultimate deliverance; it is a form of reassurance, it reinforces his determination. In his kind of world such periodic reinforcement is an absolute necessity.

As usual, all of this feeling becomes at length a community concern.

> Hallelujah! Hallelujah!
> I do belong to that ban', hallelu!

and

> Hail! Hail! I belong to the bloodwashed army, . . .
> My name's written on high.

According to our poet, it is not enough to be strongly determined and on the right road. One must also gain regular improvement in one's lot. There must be visible and recognizable signs of progress as one goes along. Since these signs appear, the slave poet maintains his sense of well-being.

A particular storm has been ridden out, and it carries the symbolism of all trouble.

> Hallelu–, Hallelu–,
> O yes, the storm is passin' over,
> Hallelu.

A period of meditation with the Leader is remedy for various trials, troubles, and temptations, from time to time.

> O a little talk with Jesus makes it right, all right,
> Little talk with Jesus makes it right, all right,
> Troubles of ev'ry kind, Thank God, I'll always find
> That a little talk with Jesus makes it right.

Occasionally, the troubles will be very great, in fact so great as to approximate a minor death. This also can be overcome, following the model of the Leader:

> I'm so glad, I'm so glad,
> I'm so glad I've been in the grave an' rose again.

Sometimes, the feeling of victory over life's problems is so complete that it seems like a message from above. The illusion is great, but it is not necessarily mystical. This overwhelming feeling is often experienced by nonreligious people who describe the reaction in different ways.

> I heard f'om heav'n today,
> I heard f'om heav'n today,
> I thank God an' I thank you, too [or,
>   "It's good news and I thank God, too"],
> I heard f'om heav'n today.

The sense of well-being in the spiritual will sometimes rise to a general happiness. It will appear in exclamations for verses in some songs, such as,

> O, I'm happy!

> Left my burden!
> At the river!
> In the valley!

> Going to Heaven!

> Now I'm getting happy!

Sometimes it becomes an all-encompassing shout,

> O Lord! Shout for joy!
> O Lord! Shout for joy.
> Early in the morning—
> Shout for joy!

Some writers, including the memorable James Weldon Johnson, have ruled out humor in the spiritual. On the evidence of verses from spirituals already given, this seems a mistaken view. Note the jokes about Baptists and Methodists and the double-talk in "Mary Has a Baby, Yes, Lord!" which begins perfectly seriously and continues so down to "Name him King Jesus" and suddenly turns off to,

> Yes, Lord!
> De people keep-a comin' an' de train done gone.

One of the most humorous verses appears in several spirituals and at odd times,

> Old Satan is mad an' I'm so glad, . . .
> He missed de soul he thought he had,
> Oh, sen'-a dem angels down.

How can anyone dramatize this line in his mind without a chuckle? You can see Satan, sometimes with a considerable expenditure of energy, corrupting souls, bagging them up and taking them off to hell. As he crosses a certain point, one soul is released, or releases himself, from the bag and gets away to freedom. Satan does not even know he is gone. Not until he gets inside hell at the counting station is he aware of the one that got away. Undoubtedly, the poet meant this episode to be taken humorously, whether we follow him or not.

But there is better evidence of the happiness that inspires laughter. It is in several songs, but especially in one called "Come Here, Lord!" It goes,

> Come here, Lord! Come here, Lord! Come here, Lord!
> Sinner cryin' come here, Lord.
> O little did I think He was so nigh,
> Sinner cryin' come here, Lord.
> He spoke an' He made me laugh an' cry,
> Sinner cryin' come here, Lord.

Obviously, the whole song is gay and vital.

The supreme test of the sense of well-being is the time of confrontation with death or achievement of free land. One song envisions a soul's new arrival to heaven on earth or in the skies. He is greeted,

> Sit down, servant, sit down! (repeated twice)
> Sit down an' rest a little while
> Know you mighty tired so sit down, . . .
> Know you shoutin' happy so sit down,
> Know you shoutin' happy so sit down! Sit down!

If he was "shoutin' happy" when he got inside, he must have approached and entered under suspicious conditions.

A famous song already referred to declares, "I want to die easy, when I die, when I die." Another song on the same topic carries the details much further,

> You needn't min' my dyin', (repeated twice)
> Jesus goin' to make up my dyin' bed.
>
> In my dyin' room I know, somebody's goin' to cry,
> All I ask you to do for me, jes close my dyin' eyes.
> I'll be sleepin' in Jesus, . . .
>
> In my dyin' room I know, somebody's goin' to mourn,
> All I ask you to do for me, jes give that bell a tone. . . .
>
> I'll be talkin with the angels, . . .
> Jesus goin' to make up my dyin' bed.

⟮ Fortitude

By definition, fortitude means endurance in the face of misfortune, pain, and calamity; constant and firm courage. Many of the songs specialize in these and similar characteristics.

We have already mentioned, in part, a keynote declaration of the spiritual:

> We want no cowards in our band,
> We call for valiant-hearted men,
> You shall gain the victory, you shall gain the day.

In another song using the first two lines of the above triplet, the opening chorus goes,

> Great day! Great day, the righteous marching
> Great day. God's going to build up Zion's wall.

The spiritual poet was proud of the brave members of his band.

For fortitude, as for other great characteristics, the poet pointed to Biblical models. Since these have been discussed several times in various connotations, we will review here only those connotations which bear precisely upon fortitude, Moses from the Old Testament and Jesus from the New.

In the song, "Tryin' to Cross the Red Sea," sometimes called, "Didn't Ol' Pharaoh Get Lost," the poet draws heavily upon the grit and lasting quality of Moses as one of the main elements in Pharaoh's defeat,

> Didn't ol' Pharaoh get lost, get lost, get lost,
> Didn't ol' Pharaoh get lost, yes, tryin' to cross the
> 　　Red Sea.
> Creep along Moses, Moses creep along, Creep along Moses,
> 　　I thank God.

Anything involving the overthrow of Pharaoh and the victory of Moses was a favorite theme, since it was taken to refer to the wholesale freeing of slaves. The fact that it was done in part by tough stick-to-itiveness on Moses' part made it all the more to be recommended.

In the spiritual Jesus was rarely praised for his meekness and mildness; he was often praised for his resistance to unbearable circumstances and for his resiliency after being downed. The slave's confidence in him was largely the result of his possession of such qualities as these, and not a wooden following of doctrines, as it is with so many millions of Christians.

> And if you meet with crosses
> And trials on the way,
> Just keep your trust in Jesus,
> And don't forget to pray.

Naturally, the most impressive thing about Jesus, even more impressive than his resurrection, was his behavior on Good Friday or Calvary's hill. It is as though the slave poet were saying, "When all your friends, apostles, admiring multitudes, and even your Father God have forsaken you, then your real true character comes out." Had Jesus died in some other way than the one he did, he would certainly have had many fewer followers among the slaves. He died not like a god but like a great man, this they could understand; in this they reveled. Under the lash and other heavy punishments they themselves had "taken it" up to and over the point of death and without cracking. Those who watched these executions never cracked either. And so, all praise to Jesus!

> They led Him to Pilate's bar,
> Not a word, not a word, not a word, not a word. . . .
>
> They all cried, "Crucify Him,"
> Not a word, not a word, not a word, not a word. . . .
>
> They nailed Him to the tree,
> Not a word, not a word, not a word, not a word. . . .
>
> But he never said a mumblin' word,
> Not a word, not a word, not a word, not a word. . . .
>
> Wasn't that a pity and a shame.

If you prefer another version,

> They crucified my Lord, . . .
> They pierced Him in the side, . . .
> The blood came twinklin' down, . . .
> He bowed his head an' died, an' He never
>   said a mumblin' word;
> Not a word, not a word, not a word.

Of course, these versions are somewhat un-Biblical: the various gospels report seven famous last "words," each of which was a sentence containing several words. But in the mind of the slave poet, these few scraps of words were insignificant. The important thing was that Jesus (note that Christ is rarely mentioned) took death, the greatest punishment of all, like a good, strong man, the best and strongest of all. For perpetual reminder, this fact was worth more than one great song.

The other side of the spiritual's crucifixion cycle is a challenge to the listener. Granted Jesus was behaving like a great man; you have announced your undying fealty to him and to what he stands for. The people and the apostles deserted; Judas betrayed; Peter denied; what were you doing all this time? What do you do each time from now on when Jesus is betrayed and deserted? Do you have the fearlessness and stamina to speak out for him against the raging mobs, against the engines of death?

Were you there when they crucified my Lord? (were you there?)
Were you there when they crucified my Lord?
Oh! . . . Sometimes it caused me to tremble, tremble, tremble,
Were you there when they crucified my Lord? . . .

Were you there when the sun refused to shine?

The trembling is hardly a sign of fear; it is a recognition of the magnitude of the challenge.

A similar challenge to fortitude is found in the late verses of "We Are Climbin' Jacob's Ladder." To live the principles of Jesus in the face of a perpetually corrupt, mean, and harassing world is one of the greatest displays a man can make of his inner strength, in the eyes of the spiritual poet. Only a committed soul and a genuine fighter can manage it. Thus,

Sinner, do you love my Jesus?
Sinner, do you love my Jesus?
Sinner, do you love my Jesus?
Soldier of the cross.

If you love Him, why not serve Him?
If you love Him, why not serve Him?
If you love Him, why not serve Him?
Soldier of the cross.

One of the by-products of fortitude is the ability to make strong vows and to strive to keep them. The spiritual poet vowed to complete his difficult journey regardless of any obstacle thrown in his path.

Anyhow, anyhow, anyhow, my Lord!
Anyhow, yes, anyhow;
I'm gwine up to heab'n anyhow.

To accomplish this purpose meant hurdling some very difficult troubles.

If yo' brudder [sister, preacher, deacon] talk about you,
An' scandalize yo' name,
Down at de cross you mus' bow,
I'm gwine up to heav'n anyhow.

Assuming the end of the journey to be heaven beyond the grave or heaven in free land, the faith and endurance required were precisely the same. The main thing was that you meant to see things through and not use short cuts. You had already convinced yourself of the superiority of the rugged road you had chosen over roads less rugged and momentarily more pleasing. Now, you were at pains to honor your conviction to the last mile.

Until I reach-a ma home, Until I reach-a ma home,
I nevah inten' to give de journey ovah,
Until I reach ma home.
True believer.

The best of the "vow songs" is one in which the Lord is the recipient of the declaration but the vow puts the weight on the individual. In the main chorus there is no assurance of reward; the vow-maker is going to honor his vow just the same.

> Done made my vow to the Lord and I never will turn back,
> I will go, I shall go, to see what the end will be.
> Done opened my mouth to the Lord and I never will turn back
> I will go, I shall go, to see what the end will be.

Living up to one's vows involves a great variety of sufferings, narrow escapes, failures, reversals, and hard trials which one must bear without losing faith and from which one must rebound. The poet proclaims,

> I'm a going to do all I can for my Lord, . . .
> I can't do no more.

He seems to take for granted that his best will always be good enough. In other poems, he ignores the steps along the way and concentrates on the goal, as in,

> I tell you what I mean to do; . . .
> I mean to get to heav'n, too.

He never ignores the depth and complexity of the obstacles and energetic evil forces in his path; "O, this is a sin-trying world," he declares and repeats. We have already seen that it is an unfriendly world. The burdens he must bear are excessively heavy; the mountains he must climb are high ("Tryin' to Get Home"). In his "Exclamations for Verses" is one shout he will do periodically, "Hard trials!" The trouble is so great that he predicts that it "will bury me down," but he quickly adds,

> Sometimes I think I'm ready to drop, . . .
> But thank my Lord, I do not stop.

He admits that he has "been long time a-talking 'bout my trials here below," but he is just as ready with, "Don't ever feel discouraged," "Neighbor, you bear your load!," and that well-known trouble-shooter,

> O stand the storm, it won't be long,
> We'll anchor bye and bye.

In the preceding chapter, when we were demonstrating the spiritual's concern with "things going wrong," we cited a song which began "Sometimes I feel like/A moanin' dove" and which ended "Wring my han's an'/Cry, cry." While the earlier stanzas of this song are full of trouble and woe, the last stanza exposes the way the slave singer shakes off his discouragement and picks himself up from the ground.

> Sometimes I feel like
> A eagle in the air

> Sometimes I feel like
> A eagle in the air
> Spread my wings an'
> Fly, fly, fly;
> Spread my wings an'
> Fly, fly.

Another famous song shows how the slave rises from the ashes of oppression to the heights of glory. In this one he takes the symbol of his oppression with him, on his back.

> I been 'buked and I been scorned, [or " 'bused"]
> I'm gwine ter lay down dis world,
> An' shoulder up my cross,
> An' take it home ter Jesus,
> Ain't dat good news.

As has been shown, the call to fortitude may be on a group basis, "Walk together, children, Don't you get weary," or it may be strictly individualistic,

> I must walk my lonesome valley,
> I got to walk it for myself, . . .
> I must go and stand my trial, . . .
> Nobody else can stand it for me,
> I got to stand it for myself.

A strict constructionist will quickly say that this song is inspired by the Twenty-third Psalm ("Yea, though I walk through the valley of the shadow of death, I will fear no evil, for thou art with me") and that, therefore, the song refers to physical death. He will probably be right about the inspiration, but wrong about the conclusion. There are many experiences in life which happen in what may connotatively be called "the shadow of death" besides death itself. The poet has chosen to emphasize the unique demands upon the individual rather than some other phase of his "source." His song logically applies to any topic in a very large subject.

The poet likes to remind himself and each individual that, when he bravely faces tribulation, he is in excellent company.

> Jesus walked his lonesome valley,
> He had to walk it for himself,
> Nobody else could walk it for him,
> He had to walk it for himself.

Now and then the poet backslides. The load gets too heavy and he seems to beg that the tension be loosened. He sings as though in parody,

> Swing low, sweet chariot into de Eas' . . .
> Let God's children have some peace, . . .
>
> Swing low, sweet chariot into de Wes' . . .
> Let God's children have some res', . . .

Swing low, sweet chariot into de Norf, . . .
Give me de gol' widout de dross, . . .

Swing low, sweet chariot into de Sout', . . .
Let God's children sing and shout.

He does not, however, remain very long in this humorously down position. Before very long he is back to a characteristic position of fearlessness,

Walk, Mary, down de lane. . . .
I'm 'fraid nobody, down de lane,
'Fraid nobody, down de lane,
'Fraid nobody, down de lane,
'Fraid nobody,—down de lane.

Several writers have accused the spiritual of often being an expression of
self-pity. John A. Lomax, B. A. Botkin, and Albert Sidney Beckham have
done so and have offered in evidence some of the songs referred to here and
in the section on "Appreciation of Things Going Wrong" in Chapter 19.
Botkin says that self-pity is a trait of the Negro, "bred in him by centuries
of oppression." According to Beckham, although there is no self-pity in
songs like "O Freedom," there is in songs like "Sometimes I Feel Like a
Motherless Child" and in "Poor Me, Poor Me, when I Get Home." In such
songs, says Beckham, there is no palliative and no finding of a way out.
He also cites songs which show pity for the world.

The issue is on drawing the line between self-pity and fortitude. It is not
self-pity to recognize that life is tough and that one has come, momentarily,
to the end of one's resources. Some of the world's greatest poetry is in this
category—for instance, the soliloquies of Hamlet. It is a sign of the most
admirable realism and analytical power when one faces up to hard truth in
his life. American slavery was the hardest of hard truths. Only the very
strongest of men were able to even contemplate it. When the slave said,
"There it is and there am I within it, and the chances of my maintaining
any identity at all are practically nil," he was showing great intelligence
and strength of character.

If that is self-pity, then a few songs do fall in the category. But only a
few. The slave poet nearly always went farther than that. After his analysis of the bitter truth, there followed a plan for improving his state. Either
he aimed for outright freedom or for strength and device to withstand his
predicament. By no stretch of the imagination could this kind of attitude
be called self-pity. And Botkin is wrong. There is no "trait" or tradition of
self-pity in the literature of the Afro-American. Even in the blues is an
undercurrent of excitement and enjoyment.

In the tradition of literature written by slaves, for slaves, no more remarkable a body of songs can be found than these which emphasize the
kind of fortitude generally reserved to the free. If evidence were needed,
this body of songs proves that the slaves who created them were not slavish.

They were what they said they wanted, "valiant-hearted men." They predicted that this condition would gain them the day, and their predictions came true. By maintaining this kind of heart during their own struggle and by so inspiring others to help them, they earned the victory of the physical freedom which they ultimately received.

❲ Commitment to Freedom and Democracy

Closely related to their songs of fortitude are the songs demonstrating their commitment to freedom and democracy. All along we have been seeing various phases of their concepts of freedom. The songs we are about to display and interpret go much farther than concept. In Joseph Conrad's words, these are "the thing itself."

Far from the slave's religion being a calming influence, it was, as we have seen in Chapter 15, one of the greatest stimulators of the slave's love for and determination to have his freedom. And thus, the commitment to freedom in spirituals begins, as one might say, with songs about Old Testament heroes and devils. The greatest hero is Moses; the greatest devil is Pharaoh. Nearly every song about Moses is intended to chide Americans, South and North, about permitting slavery and to issue a solemn warning that slavery will not be indefinitely tolerated. If this is not true, then the Southern states whose legislatures passed laws making it a crime for white or black to sing were bitterly deceived. And the many slaves freed by Harriet Tubman, partly through the use of this song, are hard to explain. Denmark Vesey, leader of the abortive Charleston revolt in 1822, also used the song.

Usually the song of freedom is a coin with two sides: the condemnation of the slaveholder and the insistence upon immediate freedom for the slave. One of the (anonymous) clergymen who strongly objected to the defense of slavery by Bishop Hopkins (in an article entitled "Bishop Hopkins' Letter on Slavery Ripped Up and His Misuse of the Sacred Scriptures Exposed") declared that whoever pleaded for heathen slavery deserved in justice, under the terms of Matthew 7:2, to be himself a slave. (Matthew 7:2 says that "with what judgment ye judge, ye shall be judged.") The spirituals do not go quite so far as this, but they do proclaim both sides of the coin. The Pharaohs are emphatically denounced, again and again. The claim for immediate freedom is put forth hundreds of times.

"Go Down, Moses" is direct statement all the way. It does not employ the undercurrent symbolism of "Steal Away to Jesus" and other such poems. Only a very obtuse listener can miss its point. It says flatly that Moses freed these Egyptian slaves boldly and justly because slavery is wrong. It clearly projects the principles of this experience to all the world: Wherever men are held in bondage, they must and shall be freed.

The "Let my people go!" refrain is thunderous. It does not argue economic, sociological, historical, and racial points. It does not concern itself with what the Pharaohs of the world shall do for substitute labor. It is one of the great freedom declarations of literature and history, as final and absolute as *The Trojan Women* is against war.

As a poem, it wastes no words and moves relentlessly toward its goal of filling every listener with a pervasive contempt for oppression and a resounding enthusiasm for freedom, wherever either one is found. It sets the penalty for violation as though it were a judge wearing a black cap. It makes arrangement for the immediate reimbursement to the slave for his unrewarded toil. When it is spoken or sung in anything close to the way it was conceived and composed, it leaves an indelible impression. The listener cannot be casual about slavery or freedom ever again.

The song is organized so that in each stanza the leader intones the first line, the chorus pronounces the second line, the leader returns with the third line, the chorus with the fourth, and both deliver the refrain. Although many songs, even famous ones, are adapted by arrangers, "Go Down, Moses" is about the same in nearly every book of spirituals.

> When Israel was in Egypt's land,
> Let my people go!
> Oppressed so hard they could not stand,
> Let my people go!

Refrain:
> Go down, Moses, 'Way down in Egypt's Land,
> Tell old [or "ole"] Pharaoh, Let my people go!

> "Thus saith [spoke] the Lord," bold Moses said,
> Let my people go!
> "If not I'll smite your first-born dead,"
> Let my people go!

> No more in bondage shall they toil,
> Let my people go!
> Let them come out with Egypt's spoil,
> Let my people go!

Refrain:
> Go down, Moses, 'Way down in Egypt's land,
> Tell old Pharaoh, Let my people go!

"Go Down, Moses" is only one of many freedom songs on this theme, but unquestionably the best. A song with at least a dozen stanzas in some versions is "Didn't Old Pharaoh Get Los'?" In one version, the story is told by stanzas, like this,

Stanza 1: Isaac's ransom; Moses' rescue by Pharaoh's daughter

Stanza 2: Joseph's rise; Samuel's predictions

Stanza 3: The Lord's first orders to Moses to go to Pharaoh

Stanza 4: Den Moses an' Aaron, To Pharaoh did go,
"Thus says de God of Israel, Let my people go."
Refrain: (same after each stanza)
Didn't old Pharaoh get los' get los', get los'
Didn't old Pharaoh get los' In de Red Sea.

Stanza 5: Pharaoh resists; Moses warns that the Lord hears his people pray

Stanza 6: The Israelites cry for bread; the downflow of manna

Stanza 7: Moses exhorts his people to stand fast

Stanza 8: Moses predicts the dispersal of the enemy

Stanza 9: Down came raging Pharaoh,
Dat you may plainly see,
Old Pharaoh an' his host
Got los' in de Red Sea.

Stanza 10: Smiting the rock, Moses gets water for his people

Stanza 11: An' de Lord spoke to Moses, From Sinai's smoking top,
Sayin', "Moses lead de people, Till I shall bid you stop."
Didn't old Pharaoh get los'.

In another version of "Go Down, Moses," which extends for twenty-five stanzas, Egypt is called "the proud oppressive land." When the Israelites finally get to the free side of the water, "They sang a song of triumph o'er." The cloud "cleaves" the way; "a fire by night, a shade by day." The children of Israel are promised that they will not be lost in the wilderness because they will have a lighted candle at their breast. The fall of the walls of Jericho and the possession of "fair Canaan's land" are predicted. At length, there are these lines,

O, let us all from bondage flee, . . .

And let us all in Christ be free, . . .

We need not always weep and moan, . . .

And wear these slavery chains forlorn, . . .

This world's a wilderness of woe, . . .

O, let us all to Canaan go, . . .

In "March On," two things are stressed, the victory and the resultant freedom. The fact that "you shall gain the victory!" and "you shall gain the day!" are repeated like a chant throughout this song which deals with adventures " 'way over in Egypt's land" clearly portends the slave's expectations in his own land.

"He's Jus' the Same Today" combines Moses with another great freedom fighter, Daniel. The first stanza repeats one of the Moses episodes with a different and very important emphasis.

> When Moses an' his soldiers f'om Egypt's lan' did flee,
> His enemies were in behin' him, An' in front of him de sea,
> God raised de waters like a wall, An' opened up de way,
> An' de God dat lived in Moses' time is jus' the same today.

Once more in the spiritual is incontrovertible evidence that human slavery is doomed because God will not stand for it. The same God who delivered Moses and the enslaved Israelites, who ran from their masters to set up a free society, says the poet, will deliver slaves for the same purpose in the nineteenth century.

The slave admired Daniel because he would not submit to the tyrant no matter how much power the tyrant had. In the slave's eyes, he and Daniel were in the same boat; the slave would not submit in his heart to the institution of slavery, although he momentarily worked as a slave. In encouraging slaves everywhere to resist in the name of a God who supported resisters to tyranny, the second stanza of "He's Jus' the Same Today" is quite as insurrectionary as the first.

> When Daniel faithful to his God, would not bow down to men,
> An' by God's enemy he was hurled into de lion's den,
> God locked de lion's jaw we read, An' robbed him of his prey,
> An' de God dat lived in Daniel's time is jus' de same today.

The best song of freedom is, however, "Didn't My Lord Deliver Daniel?" It is as bold and explicit as "Go Down, Moses." It makes no reservations or allowances. The white people who heard it sung and permitted it, must have been trusting souls indeed!

> Didn't my Lord deliver Daniel, deliver
>   Daniel, deliver Daniel,
> Didn't my Lord deliver Daniel,
>   An' why not-a every man!
>
> He delivered Daniel f'om de lion's den,
>   Jonah f'om de belly of de whale,
> De Hebrew chillun f'om de fiery furnace,
>   An' why not every man!

Obviously, these were all impossible deliverances. Only the Lord God could make them. Only an impossible deliverance could get the slave his freedom. But if the Lord God had done it several times already, why will he not continue? The clear implication is that he will. For those who hang on to the discredited notion that these songs deal with deliverance beyond the grave, how irrational is it that all the slave's models deal with people delivered from impossible situations here on earth, in the interest of further earthly living!

As we have shown in Chapter 19, the great champion of freedom was Jesus. Many times it is the Lord who sets the slave free ("I know my Lord has set me free, . . ./I'm in Him and He's in me"), but most often it is his son Jesus: "King Jesus died for ev'ry man," and

> Oh, shout-a my sister for you are free, . . .
> For Christ has bought yo' liberty,

and

> Came down here and talked to me,
> Went away and left me free.

The slave poet was fully aware that freedom in a democratic society imposed obligations.

> You say the Lord has set you free, . . .
> Why don't you let yo' neighbor be!

The terms *Jubilee, Canaan,* and *camp ground* are flat symbols for free land.* Many times in the spiritual one sees lines like,

> This is the day of jubilee, . . .
> The Lord has set his people free.

and

> Set my foot on de Gospel ship, an' de ship begin
>   to sail,
> It landed me over on Canaan's shore, An' I'll never
>   come back no mo'.

Canaan was the free land of the chosen people who were, in many respects, a model for the slave; the parallelism is unarguable.

"Deep River," one of the most beautiful of spirituals, is also one of the most deadly to the institution of slavery. It talks about the promised land (Canaan) with very little disguise. The singer says again and again, "Lord, I want to cross over into camp-ground." Once more, the listener who thinks he means a land beyond the grave is either obtuse or not privy to the yearnings of the slave's heart. Into this song the slave poet poured his whole soul of desire for freedom, earthly freedom. As such, the song has irony and comes out more beautiful still than if it is interpreted as after death. Better still, let it mean both free land and heaven after death. The slave singer aimed at both.

In many of the songs so far has been an assurance of freedom that need only be noted here. When the poet, on behalf of his fellows, says,

> One o' dese mornin's—it won't be long,
> You'll look fo' me, an' I'll be gone,

or when he sings—

> Git yo' bundle reddy I know it's time,

* For connotations of heaven in this connection, see Chapter 20, "Heav'm," below.

he doubtlessly means the words literally, although he "covers up" with talk about Judgment Day, as almost anyone would do in his shoes.

As reported by Thomas Wentworth Higginson, a white colonel of the Federal Army and a famous literary man, at the outbreak of the rebellion, black men were jailed in Georgetown, South Carolina, for singing "We'll Soon Be Free." A portion of this spiritual goes,

> We'll soon be free, . . .
> When de Lord will call us home.
> My brudder, how long, . . .
> 'Fore we done sufferin' here?
> It won't be long
> 'Fore de Lord will call us home.
> We'll walk de miry road, . . .
> Where pleasure never dies. . . .
> We'll soon be free . . .
> When Jesus sets me free.
> We'll fight for liberty . . .
> When de Lord will call us home.

As a black drummer boy told Colonel Higginson, "*de Lord* mean for say *de Yankees.*"

When real solid freedom finally came, the songs showed little change. One of the first "solid freedom" songs was "Many Tousand [thousands] Go,"

> No more peck of corn for me, no more, no more;
> No more peck of corn for me, Many tousand go.
>
> No more driver's lash for me, . . .
> No more pint o' salt for me, . . .
> No more hundred lash for me, . . .
> No more mistress' call for me.

Another is the famous "Free at Last." The song carries the same code of religious terms as many of the previous songs, even after the need for secrecy has been removed. This fact does not mean that the spiritual writer was not religious at all, it means that he was not just religious.

> Free at last, free at last, I thank God I'm free at last;
> Free at last, free at last, I thank God I'm free at last.
> 'Way down yonder in the graveyard walk, . . .
> Me and my Jesus goin' to meet and talk, . . .
>
> On-a my knees when the light pass'd by, I thank
>   God I'm free at last,
> Thought my soul would rise and fly, I thank God
>   I'm free at last.

Still another is "Done Wid Driber's Dribin',"

> Done wid driber's dribin',
> Done wid massa's hollerin', . . .
> Done wid missus' scoldin', . . .
> Roll, Jordan, roll.

To return to the slave's commitment to freedom, one finds an idea that is often found in freedom songs wherever they are composed and sung; namely, that the tree of liberty must be watered by the blood of patriots. Or, to state it more simply, freedom cannot be handed to an individual, the individual must fight for it.

Joshua at Jericho is a good example: "Dere's none like good ole Joshua." Usually, the emphasis is on his bringing down the walls with a shout from his army ("de chillun"). But when one considers what Joshua was really fighting for and the penchant of the spiritual poet to glorify only those who did things of significance to him and his code of values, one can read the deepest reason for the creation of the song.

Going back to the period just before Joshua, one poet has written of the children of Israel,

> Yes, the children they did right, . . .
> When they went and had that fight.

Not just the children of Israel, but every group and individual wishing to live the good life must fight, some of these poets say. The forces of evil are deeply entrenched and belligerent; you cannot win without fighting.

> Marching up the heavenly road, (repeated)
> I'm bound to fight until I die, . . .
> My sister, have you got your sword and shield, . . .
> I got 'em fo' I left the field,
> Marching up the heavenly road.

Another song of the field shows the unyielding determination of a patriot and attempts to spread the contagion.

> Oh, what-a you say, seekers, (repeated twice)
> About dat Gospel war.
> An' what-a you say, brothers,
> Oh, what-a you say, brothers (repeated)
> About dat Gospel war.
> An' I will die in de fiel', will die in de fiel', will die in de fiel'
> I'm on my journey home.
> Sing it ovah—I will die in de fiel'.

The same spirit seems implicit in "Singin' Wid a Sword in Ma Han'," in which the creator and the fighter are joined, François Villon-style,

> Singin' [Shoutin'] wid a sword in ma han', Lord,
> Singin' wid a sword in ma han',

In ma han' Lord,
Singin' wid a sword in ma han'.

It is hard to see what quiet, peaceful interpretation the white listeners gave to this song, or to "Our bondage'll have an end, by and by, by and by."

That the spirit of the Underground Railroad providing transportation to freedom and the runaway slave pervaded and doubtless dictated some songs is unquestionable. A song like "Don't Be A-Stoppin' an' A-Lookin' " is almost certainly an invitation for travel to free land.

Oh! de song of salvation is a mighty sweet song,
Den don't be a-stoppin' an' a-lookin'.

"Git on Board, Little Chillen" is a clear invitation to ride the train. It reiterates that plenty of room is available; that the train can be heard close by; that it is "rumblin' through de lan' "; that

De fare is cheap, an' all can go, De rich an' poor are dere,
No second class aboard dis train, No differunce in de fare.

Perhaps the gospel train did refer to a train running from earth to heaven. It shows, however, a remarkable likeness to the Underground Railroad, which was running trains and transporting thousands from stations all over slavery land to free land. Had I been a slave with my knowledge of both trains and my right to choose, I think I would have unhesitatingly chosen the latter, with all its perils. Hundreds of slaves did so choose.

In "Same Train," the poet refers to a train, now "ablowin' at de station," which carried his mother, sister, and implicitly others to some desirable destination. You can easily deduce heaven as the destination. But Harriet Tubman was one of several who, after freeing herself, came back to free her relatives and friends among many others. "Be back tomorrer" has a far more pleasant ring if it refers to an earthly train with a free destination. One can always use the heavenly train later.

The same principle works for the ship. Just after "Didn't my Lord deliver, Daniel, An' why not-a every man" in one version are the lines,

I set my foot on de Gospel ship, an' de ship begin to sail,
It landed me over on Canaan's shore,
An' I'll never come back no mo'.

In the interpretive literature of the spiritual there are numerous references to the organs of freedom. Botkin asserts that trains are familiar in both the spiritual and the blues; the train is most frequently encountered as a symbol of freedom and vicarious expression. In a critique of Finkelstein is reference to the spiritual's drawing upon Biblical images in its yearning for freedom and in its defense against tyranny. He underscores the fact that these spirituals were employed as signals on the Underground Railroad. Haslam contrasts the oblique reference to freedom in "Go Down, Moses" with the open references in "No More Auction Block for Me." Long before emancipation, say Downes and Siegmeister, the slave sang of freedom. At first freedom was symbolized in such religious songs as "The Great Jubilee," "Dat Great Day of Mornin'," and "Kingdom Come." They also quote Frederick Douglass to the effect that a keen observer would have detected the freedom note in the repeated references in the songs to "O Canaan, sweet Canaan."

Freedom and democracy, fought and died for, confer certain rights in the spiritual. Eating at the welcome table, drinking at the crystal fountain, attending "the big baptizin' " were all proper rights of the sanctified.

But there were rights beyond these about which the slave poet sang. They are described in a number of songs, but one brilliant song, which reads like the Declaration of Independence, is a sufficient illustration. It is called "You Got a Right." Like the Declaration of Independence, it is rooted in divine justice. It sings,

> You got a right, I got a right,
> We all got a right, to de tree of life.

> De very time I thought I was los',
> De dungeon shuck an' de chain fell off.

> You may hinder me here, But you cannot dere,
> 'Cause God in de heav'n gwineter answer prayer.

> O bretheren,
> O sisteren, You got a right, I got a right,
> We all got a right to de tree of life.

In the exercise of such rights, the man invested with freedom is invincible.

> O no man can hinder me!
> O no man, no man, no man can hinder me!

❰ Awareness of a Just Universe

In spite of his slave condition, the brutalities of slavery, his recurring sense of personal insecurity, and the hazards of running to the freedom he felt he deserved, the slave poet proclaimed a just universe. The way he put it, justice did not emanate exclusively from the Deity. Under the eye of the Deity much of the injustice continued, although the slave poet did not blame the Deity for it. He did see the Deity as promulgating and administering just acts and just situations. The essential justice, however, was in the nature of things. People and things just naturally received the rewards and punishments they were due according to their character and behavior. Botkin quotes Alain Locke to the effect that the slave got his democratic sentiments not from the Bill of Rights, but from the moral justice of the Hebrew prophets. There is, however, another possibility. In Africa, strict justice was almost a religion. Africans had a law of reparation. Under this law, if a man steals, he or his family must give equal in value to the robbed person or his relatives. A murderer must give his own children to carry out the function of a murdered person. The underlying principle is a life for a life rather than a death for a death.

The rewards we have discussed in various connections. On the gospel train there was no second class because obviously all the sanctified are equal. When Heaven's pearly gates open, there will also be only first-class accommodations—welcome table, milk and honey, apartments on the golden streets. All of this arrangement follows the eternal principle which pervades life.

> You shall reap jes' what you sow, Brother
> [Sister, Sinner],
> You shall reap jes' what you sow,
> On the mountain, in the valley,
> You shall reap jes' what you sow.

He recognizes that it applies to him as much as to anyone else. "I'm gwine to jedgement bye an' bye."

Since his appeal is more to sinners than to the sanctified, the slave poet seems to spend more time on the punishments than on the rewards. In either case and in both cases he is advertising the natural justice in things.

> Too late, too late, sinnah,
> Hm—too late, too late, sinnah,
> Carry de key an' gone home.
> Massa Jesus' lock de do',
> O Lord! too late; . . .
>
> Too late, too late, false pretender,
> Hm—too late; too late, too late, backslider,
> Carry de key an' gone home.

Perhaps the workings of justice are just as strong on the other side when the key is in the hands of the man who says he is good.

> I got a key to thuh Kingdom
> I got a key, Oh, yes, I have-a now.
> I got a key to thuh Kingdom
> An' the worl' can't do me no harm.

Often, the message is a good deal more dramatic.

> Oh, de sinner man he gambled an' fell, (repeat)
> Oh, de sinner man gambled, he gambled and fell;
> He wanted to go to hebben, but he had to go to hell,
> Dere's no hidin' place down dere.

When he boarded his ship on the ocean, en route to his earned reward, he says to the sinner who did no such earning, "Po' sinner, fare-you-well." He tells the gambler to "git up off o' yo' knees" because he is not now going to be admitted to the train, having wasted all his chances for a proper ticket. He deplored the fact that

> the downward road is crowded, crowded, crowded,
> with unbelievin' souls,

and he adds a special touch on the subject of your expecting to cash in benefits when you have made no deposits,

> Some people say they believe in Him,
> An' then won't do what he says,
> You can't ride the empty air
> An' get to heaven that day.

He reiterated his warning about dice shooters:

> Done told you once, done told you twice,
> There're sinners in hell for shooting dice.

Even his own brother is not exempt from the workings of the immutable laws.

> Yonder comes my brother
> Whom I loved so well,
> But by his disobedience
> Has made his home in hell.

On a comprehensive basis the punishment can be pretty strong.

> My Lord, (My Lord) My Lord, (My Lord,)
> My Lord says he's gwineter rain down fire;

Sometimes the spiritual poet will place conditions and reservations upon the behavior of people in the hope that the message will get through and the individual will save himself in time.

> You mus' hab dat true religion, You mus' hab yo' soul converted,
> You mus' hab dat true religion, You can't cross dere.

As above with his brother, his sister is warned,

> O sister, have you got your ticket signed,
>   (repeated twice)
> In-a that morning, O my Lord, . . .
> In-a that morning when the Lord says "Hurry!"

He is liberal with unsolicited advice to sinner, gambler, and dancer. If I were you, he says, I'd throw away sinful ways, gambling dice, and dancing shoes, and work on the building for the Lord. He reminds Baptists and Methodists that mere church membership is not going to get them through;

they must be pure in heart if they expect to avoid hell. Under the regulations, unfortunately, only a few can enter the slave poet's bright and fair heavenly home. But the situation is open for repair.

> If you wanter catch dat heab'nly breeze, Oh yes, Oh, yes,
> Go down in de valley on yo' knees an' pray.

Better still, become fully sanctified.

> Jordan's stream is chilly and wide,
> None can cross but the sanctified.

If you decline,

> You can weep like a willow
> You can mourn like a dove,
> But you can't get to heaven
> Without Christian love.

The most courageous and downright warning went to members of the master race:

> You may be a white man, White as the drifting snow,
> If your soul ain't been converted, To Hell you're sure to go,

or

> Oh, you may be a white man
> White as de dribberlin' snow
> Ef yo' soul ain't ankeld [anchored] in Jesus
> To hell you sho'ly go.

When it comes to Judgment Day, all warnings and merciful allowances are off. Eternal justice is in control and there are no exceptions. The poet makes early announcement that all may have full notice.

> See the signs of judgment, (repeated twice)
> The Time is drawing nigh.

He begs that the people begin their monitoring early.

> You'd better min' how you talk [sing, shout],
> You'd better min' what you're talkin' about,
> For you got to give an account in Judgment,
> You'd better min'.

The justice bar is a fine dramatic setting for the spiritual poet. Like any trial scene it is theatrical and full of suspense. The fact that the poet is naturally sensitive to the injustices in the world enhances the anticipatory effect. Those who have been trading in injustice and benefiting from it, keeping the worthy people low, will finally get what is coming to them. The worthy people, after years, generations, centuries of inappropriate misfortune, will finally rise to their rich estates. Best of all, the settlement at this bar is permanent. Things can never slip back. Eternal justice will see to that.

> O mourner: (repeated twice)
> Look at the people at the bar of God.

If the slave owner, his lawmakers, his judges and juries, and all his other hosts who had been making and enforcing "black laws," with reckless disregard for the human being underneath, had listened carefully to the black singing, they might have heard,

> Just as you live, just so you die,
> And after death, Judgment will find you so.

Some will, of course, try to evade, but this is what will happen to them,

> In dat Resurrection Day sinner can't find no hidin' place,
> Go to de mountain, de mountain move,
> Run to de hill, de hill run, too.
> Sinner man tremblin' on trembling groun',
> Po' los' sheep ain't nebber been foun'.

The remedy for all this condign justice must be taken well in advance of the Day.

> Sinner, why don't yo' stop and pray,
> Den you'd hear de Shepherd say,
> Done foun' my los' sheep, Done foun' my los' sheep,
> Done foun' my los' sheep.

The instability of the wrongdoer's position on the Day of Final Justice is brought home by contrast with the most acceptedly stable things on earth —rocks, hills, and mountains.

> O rocks, don't fall on me, (repeated twice)
> Rocks and mountains, don't fall on me.
>
> Look over yonder on Jer-ri-cho's wall, . . .
> And see those sinners tremble and fall, . . .
>
> In-a that great, great Judgment Day, . . .
> The sinners will run to the rocks and say:
> "Rocks and mountains, don't fall on me."

It is contrasted also with the rightdoer's position at the same time:

> The trump shall sound, and the dead shall rise, . . .
> And go to mansions in-a the skies.

When called upon, the rocks and mountains will give no comforting answers.

> There's no hiding place down here, (repeat)
> Went to the rocks to hide my face,
> Rocks cried out, "No hiding place,"
> There's no hiding place down here.

Or worse,

> O de rock cried, "I'm burnin' too," (repeat)
> Oh de rock cried out, "I'm burnin' too,
> I want to go to hebben as well as you,"
> Dere's no hidin' place down dere.

We have several times seen "Dat Great Gittin' Up Mornin' " in its full, glowing color; it is not necessary to rerun that dazzling scene at this point. Let the reader merely be reminded that everything in the scene, the thunderous trumpet, the creeping dry bones, the loosened dragon, the burning world, the bleeding moon, the falling stars, the glorified Christians, and the one hundred and fifteen "Fare you wells," are all necessary and are dictated by the demands of justice to reward and punish, to show that at the last justice will not be mocked.

All this relates to the end result. Or the beginning, if one is viewing the scene from the standpoint of eternal life. It is important to know that the force which rises to so mighty a climax has been working a bit at a time all along.

> We got deacons [preachers, members] in de church,
>   Dey ain't straight,
> Who's goin' to straighten them?
> God's goin' to straighten them,
> He says He's goin' to straighten them,
> God's goin' to straighten all de people in His church.

Day by day, God is an engine of justice.

> My Lord's goin' move this wicked race
>   —this wicked race, this wicked race,
> My Lord's goin' move this wicked race, Lord, Lord
> He's goin' raise up a nation that shall obey.

Not only day by day but generation by generation God will administer justice. He will sometimes select a man he can trust to be his surrogate:

> God called old Moses on the mountain top, on the
>   mountain top, on the mountain top,
> God called old Moses on the mountain top, Lord, Lord,
> An' he stamped His law on Moses' heart.

Also, it was only through the inexorable demands of justice that God sent Moses to,

> Tell old Pharaoh
> "Let my people go!"

His justice worked throughout the Bible,

> Tell ol' Nebucaneezah dat he's weighed in de
>   balance an' foun' wantin',
> Dere's a han' writin' on de wall.

Even in the case of God's own son, justice was an irresistible force against strong earthly powers.

> De soljahs der a-plenty, standin' by de do'
> But dey could not hinder, De stone done roll away....
>
> Ol' Pilate an' his wise men, didn't know what to say,
> De miracle was on dem, De stone done roll away.

No finer case of universal justice has been recorded than the story of Dives, the typical rich man, and Lazarus, the typical poor one, as related in numerous Afro-American spirituals. We have room for only one version:

> Poor old Lazarus, poor as I, Don't you see? Don't you see?
> Poor old Lazarus, poor as I, Don't you see? Don't you see?
> Poor old Lazarus, poor as I, When he died had a home on high.
> He had a home in-a that Rock, Don't you see?
>
> Rich man, Dives, lived so well, Don't you see? Don't you see?
> Rich man, Dives, lived so well, Don't you see? Don't you see?
> Rich man, Dives, lived so well, When he died found home in hell,
> Had no home in that Rock, Don't you see?

And so it happens that in the Afro-American spiritual, universal justice straightens all, clarifies all, judges all, at long last. It may allow distortions and deviations for seeming ages, but in the end it serves all men fairly according to their adherence to principle and right. It is no judge one can corrupt or bribe. It cares not at all for social or economic or political position, for class or rank, for bond or free. Eventually, it will give you what, in the rock, you have earned. Nothing less. Nothing more.

Don't you see!

⟨ Determination to Struggle, Resist, and Hold Fast

Many people honestly do not believe that the spirituals use mask and symbolism. If they could accept symbolism, they would never accept a symbolism of resistance and struggle. Too many histories written by proponents of the plantation tradition have brainwashed them. Although they accept a handful of troublemakers, they believe in the docility of the slaves. They believe that slaves and their masters were sweet and loving partners.

The evidence offered in earlier portions of this book, taken from unimpeachable authorities, destroys these views. The great majority of slaves wanted to be free. If their masters had been utter darlings to them, they would still have wanted to be free. Besides their wanting to be free, their masters were the exact opposite of utter darlings. Thousands planned escapes from slavery, and a large percentage of these planners were successful. Where the slave could not escape, or until he could escape, he tolerated slavery and cooperated with it only to survive as long as he could. A few recklessly threw themselves into the mouth of the dragon and were burned in his flames. But most of them had resistance in their hearts; and they had resistance in their songs, most of the time carefully masked. Where it was not resistance, it was the determination to hold fast until help came.

The writings of Frederick Douglass and Booker T. Washington, summarized in Part Three of this book, clearly demonstrate the resistance and the spirit of freedom. Hundreds of other former slaves said the same things they said, felt the same way they felt. So far, under other headings, we have offered dozens of songs which express resistance and struggle; the point needs to be emphasized as an important outcome of the poetic experience of these slaves.

After hundreds of years of such mask and symbolism, the Southern white man had finally penetrated to the core. Ignoring the symbolism of "de Lord" and "Jesus," he at last realized that this spiritual, as hundreds of others before it, was blatantly opposing slavery and proclaiming freedom. Had the slaveholders throughout the South done similarly, and jailed every slave who sang of freedom and resistance, the plantation territory would have been covered with jails.

Since so many songs of this nature have already been given, only a few remarkable samples are necessary. Often songs about building upon rock are for the purpose of demonstrating the determination of the slave to hold fast in his personal antislavery feeling until he can manage a personal escape. Look at this one called "Bound to Go,"

> I build my house upon de rock, O yes, Lord!
> No wind, no storm can blow 'em down, O yes, Lord!
> March on, member, Bound to go;
> Been to de ferry, Bound to go;
> Left St. Helena, Bound to go;
> Brudder, fare you well.

The same general message is carried by "I've got a home in-a that Rock, Don't you see?"

We have already shown how the spiritual stressed the soldier theme. The mask of the Christian soldier was an excellent one for the kind of realistic war in which the slave realized he was engaged. As a soldier he could not only fight his necessary way, at least in his heart and in his songs; he could also develop his manhood. As a soldier he could build up his determination to resist. And so he sang,

> O stay in the field, childeren-ah
> Stay in the field, childeren-ah,
> Stay in the field,
> Until the war is ended.
>
> I've got my breastplate, sword, and shield,
> And I'll go marching thro' the field,
> Till the war is ended.

And again he sang,

> Oh, my feet are shod with the gospel grace,
> And upon my breast a shield;
> And with my sword I intend to fight
> Until I win the field.

In "No Man Can Hinder Me," the slave poet once again uses the mask of Christianity to hide his personal determination to struggle. But the obvious buildup of the poem, its iteration and reiteration of a point which is not religious, its bringing in of "Saviour" and "Jesus" as sidelines, just as "We'll Soon Be Free" does, all prove the true meaning of the spiritual.

> Walk in, kind Savior,
> No man can hinder me!
> Walk in, sweet Jesus,
> No man can hinder me.
>
> See what wonder Jesus done,
> O no man can hinder me!
> See what wonder Jesus done,
> O no man can hinder me!
>
> O no man, no man, no man can hinder me!
> O no man, no man, no man can hinder me!

The singer, the member, the seeker is fixed in his plan. He will not allow himself to be frightened out of it.

> I shall not, I shall not be moved,
> I shall not, I shall not be moved,
> Like a tree that's planted by the waters,
> I shall not be moved.

If he does decide to move, then it will be irresistibly toward a new and free goal.

> I'm on my way and I won't turn back, . . .
> I'm on my way, Great God, I'm on my way.
>
> I'm on my way to the heavenly land, . . .
> I'm on my way, God knows, I'm on my way.

⟨ Heav'm

The word *heaven* is spelled many ways by the various arrangers of the spirituals (heavem, heaven, heav'n, Heav'n, heab'n, hebben, hebb'n—to mention a few). When it is sung by a good chorus with good conductors, its sound depends to some extent upon its position in the series of words or sounds. When John W. Work, one of the outstanding arrangers and anthologists of spirituals, wrote instructions for singing "Heav'n, Heav'n" in the famous song, "Goin' to Shout All over God's Heav'n" (also known as "All God's Chillun Got Wings"), he said, "Let the last syllable of heav'n be a hum." This direction makes the words come out "Heav'm," and "Heav'm" is a topmost subject of the spiritual.

We will not belabor further the point that, since freedom is the slave's preoccupying thought, when he sang "when I get to heav'm," he undoubtedly meant "when I get free." It is the belief of the present writer that most of the time he does mean "when I get free," but perhaps not every single time. Sometimes, he undoubtedly means the universe beyond the grave. It is possible that, at times, he means the free land first and the universe beyond the grave later. The songs were composed and popularized by many creators; they are entitled to a variety of views.

The solution to this problem interferes but little with the display of the evidence about heav'm, culled from hundreds of songs. No one concept so inspires him. No one concept better demonstrates the complete transformation he envisions, from the small organism he starts with to the gigantic thing he sees as the never-ending development if he is given the chance or under the omnipotent power it has been his good fortune to link up with.

If the reader thinks his heav'm is a theological or otherworldly thing, the evidence ought to disabuse him. The heav'm of the Afro-American spiritual speaks more to the slave's appreciation and criticism of the things and values of his earthly life than it does to anything else. When he mentions a heavenly thing or value, he more than likely has an earthly thing or value in mind—like Homer who had two names for certain characters, one for earth and one for the heavens—and the reader should take pains to search his meanings. The spiritual poet was no visionary or speculator in the usual senses.

Because the subject requires a separate book for full development, the present appreciation is highly selective. Some four or five hundred key spirituals have been thoroughly investigated for the purpose. The references about heav'm have been organized into family categories rather than into individual ideas. The categories are presented in descending order of number of usable references. This means that the first category has the largest number of references and the number declines with each category. The last six or seven categories have only one or two references each.

THE NATURAL GOAL, END, AND REWARD
OF THE SANCTIFIED

If you are one of the sanctified, says the spiritual poet, to heav'm by one way or another you are headed. The nature of being saved has a built-in magnetism which propels you to heav'm. Everything else is incidental.

Sometimes, the song stresses the fact of going, including the being on the

way. Sometimes, it shows the irresistibility of the driving impulse. Again, it
may concentrate on the desire, but that is no different from the going itself.
If you are determined to go and have been permitted into the magnetic
stream, forget everything else, you are going! Saying you want to, longing
and yearning for the day are mere fillips. Again and again, the song describes the method—ship, chariot, or someone coming to get you who can
take you right in.

If heav'm is free land, one can understand the emphasis on the irresistibility through the slave's need to be saved. If he was going to attempt this
variety of salvation, he would certainly want to feel that his chances of
failure were minimal. There is plenty of evidence that he yearned for the
day of freedom, no matter what the method. He would want to feel that he
was "on the way" and "bound to go" and that nothing could stop him. His
enthusiasm would be without bounds, as it was in these songs.

If heav'm is the land of reward for the sanctified beyond the grave, then
the irresistibility is appropriate, but in a different sense. Frankly, the slave's
preoccupation with the things of the earth is so great that it does not seem
likely that he would have so deep a concern for a land beyond the grave so
early in his career. If, in spite of appearances, he had such a concern, he had
given up hope of earthly betterment and was putting all his hopes and plans
into his postearthly career. If this is indeed the case, he would want nothing
to interfere with that sole remaining hope, however far away its time of
materialization.

It is easy to see that the songs are more insistent if the immediate hope
and enthusiasm are greater. It is also quite clear that the slave was like most
of the rest of us, we have our heav'ms within reach and those far away.
Very few of us surrender all the immediate ones and resign ourselves totally
to those far away. If we do, we rarely write songs of vigorous enthusiasm
about the process. Especially, if we are like the people and singers whose
concerns have been described in the preceding pages.

In certain essential respects, you could have either polar interpretation
and still have the same songs. The poet is having a wonderful time talking
about rewards and goals. Incidentally, he is talking about the good life
(that people of soul and energy and spirit have discussed in literature from
time immemorial) and why it is a fine thing to lead. To have strong goals
is a sign of character; to work unremittingly for them is an even better sign.
To expect the rewards of good living is natural and inspirational; it makes
you keep up your standards and steels you against discouragement and defeat. In the case of the spiritual poet, it developed his fine, aesthetic sense as
we shall see in the next section of this chapter.

So, heav'm is a place to which the sanctified are on the way. "Thank
God, I'm on My Way to Heav'n," they sing in one song. "Let us cheer the
weary traveler, Along the heavenly way," they sing in another. "Gwinter
Sing All along de Way," they sing in still another. While singing, they raise
high a golden banner upon which is written: "Repentance and Salvation."

They are going, going, going, and nothing can stop them.

> For I'm goin' to Heav'n above,
> Goin' to the God I love.

So mother, do not weep; just get ready to go, too, when your turn comes.

I am "goin' meet King Jesus in the air," says still another. "Goin' to take my wings an' cleave the air" is a common declaration, although never is it told when and where "my wings" are to be issued, tested, and certified. "Oh, yes, I'm gwine up, gwine up, gwine up all de way, Lord, Gwine up, gwine up to see de heavenly land," and presumably to visit there a while. "Gwine reach heab'n by an' by" is another statement delivered with certainty. "Anyhow, anyhow, anyhow, my Lord! Anyhow, yes, anyhow; I'm gwine up to heab'n anyhow."

All these declarations presuppose the proper credentials, knowledge of the route, and no hitches caused either by the individual's relaxation of his good life or by some authority's disagreeable manner or error. Some of the declarations, however, are stronger still; some people are bound to go. "But still my soul is heavenly bound," says one. "My soul is boun' for that bright land," says another. "I will go, I shall go," says one. Nothing can stop me, indicates another, because "de Angels in de heab'n gwineter write my name . . . in de Book of life . . . wid-a golden pen, . . . in de drippin' blood." "You shall have a new hiding place that day," is the firm assurance granted by still another.

Sometimes, although the arrival is sure, the method is of some concern. "Got my letter, goin' to ride the train," is all the message that is necessary in the heart of one poet. For another poet, to be on a ship that is definitely going is the right way, "My ship is on the ocean, We'll anchor bye and bye." For another whose ship is on the ocean, there is no thought of the sureness of the voyage and the landing; he has time to think of whom he wishes to see after arriving; he chooses "good ol' Daniel" and "weepin' Mary." For a more particular passenger, "gwineter ride up in de chariot, Soon-a in de mornin' " is adequate.

One singer ignores the method but says he sees the angels beckoning and adds,

> I tell you what I mean to do; . . .
> I mean to go to heav'n, too.

Another wants to be escorted,

> My way-my way's cloudy, my way,
> Go sen'-a dem angels down.

Another will be satisfied with no less than Jesus himself,

> How can I die when I'm in de Lord?
> Massa Jesus is comin' bye and bye.

Another suggests that you "hang on behin' the old chariot that's headed for heav'n." This one adds that

> Ef yo' mother want to go,
> She shall wear a starry crown.
> An' she must hang on behin'.

One other is telling sinners, liars, gamblers, and backsliders that they cannot cross "de ribbuh ob Jordan" and implies that he himself can. Still one other gives assurance that "dere's one mo' river to cross," but this one ("Jordan, Lord") is very wide indeed.

Many make the declaration that they want to go without saying precisely that they are going. Such a declaration is tantamount to already being in the magnetic stream.

> Say, don't you want to go to heav'n,
> How I long to see dat day.

The writer of a very famous song put it this way, "I want to go to Heaven when I die." A colleague wants to go after he dies "to hear old Jordan roll." Another writer repeats the wish, includes a desire to see mother, father, sister, and Jesus, and ends with,

> Good Lord, when I die,
> Good Lord, when I die.

Perhaps, there is no doubt that these two refer to the afterlife for sure.

The sister in "The Old Ark's A-Movering" wants "to go to Heav'n 'fore the Heaven doors close," a reasonable wish. Another maker of good wishes intones,

> I know I have another building,
> I know it's not made with hands, O brethren,
> I want to go to Heaven, and I want to go right,
> Not made with hands;
> O, I want to go to Heaven all robed in white,
> Not made with hands, O brethren.

This one also has,

> A holy band of angels coming after me,
> Not made with hands, O yes.

"This holy band" might just be Quakers in the Underground Railroad. Still another, besides being dressed in white, wanted "to be in Heaven when the roll is called." Already he can hear

> Heav'n bells a-ringing,
> The saints all a-singing.

In one version of still another very famous song, "Lis'en to de Lam's" are these lines,

Come on sister wid yo' ups an' downs,
Wan'-ta go to heaben, when I die.
De angel's waitin' for to give you a crown,
Wan'-ta go heaben when I die.

Another declarer wants

to go to heab'n, when I die, . . .
To see God's bleedin' Lam'.

Another sweet singer makes clear his preference after what seems to have been a long period of meditation and soul-searching.

Yes, I want God's heav'n to be mine,
To be mine, to be mine;
Yes, I want God's heab'n to be mine,
Save me, Lord, save me.

Once in Heav'm, he is there for good:

When I get to heav'n, gonna sing and shout,
Nobody there for to turn me out.

THE PLACE FOR THE FULL EXPRESSION OF THE PEOPLE

The songs which dilate upon the place Heav'm itself are also quite numerous and expansive. They seem to spend most of their time and energy on the layout and the fittings. When they are closely examined, this illusion disappears. The layout and the fittings are just setting for something else. These songs demonstrate over and over again that heav'm is a place for the full expression of the people.

We have already shown (in the section, "Creative Expression and Education," in Chapter 19) the main reasons why this need for expression is so important. A few further clarifications might possibly help. Although the slave owners had "free" labor, they were not skillful in applying it to the best advantage. They had little knowledge of and less faith in the special talents of slaves. As in the armed forces in the old days, a great waste of energy resulted from failure to discover and to channel these special talents. A battery of efficiency experts at work could have greatly improved the social, economic, and public relations aspects of this vast institution.

If slave owners or managers learned, more or less accidentally, that a slave had some gift or occupational aptitude which could be especially useful or profitable, they might or might not take advantage of it. For example, they might assign such a slave to a craft activity or farm him out to a nearby factory and take all or most of his pay. House slaves were often chosen for special aptitudes, but often again because of pure whim or favoritism. Female house slaves were often selected because of apparent sexual qualifications and brought into an area of convenience.

The governing principle of owners and their lieutenants was doing with their property as they pleased. An owner or overseer could beat a slave literally to death, as Legree did Uncle Tom, or shoot him or cut off fingers, ears, toes, or other portions of the body, or rape his female slaves, or sell any slave out of hand in any show of anger or pique, and he was well within his rights. No law or law enforcement reached out fingers for him.

Such a system riled the slaves for many human reasons. In spite of their alleged savagery, many of these slaves had come from cultured backgrounds and were sensitive, intelligent, talented people. Whatever their backgrounds, they deeply deplored the lack of humanity and reason in the way they were treated. They deplored most deeply the fact that slavery gave them little chance to be the kind of people they wanted to be, occupationally, morally, or culturally.

Their deepest curse was in being unfulfilled. This truth emerged from the records of hundreds of slaves who, after being freed, took up gainful activity. The slave was not naturally or generally indolent and shiftless, as many Southerners complained. His industry brought great wealth to his owners in spite of the poor management of plantations. Where he was not industrious, he was often protesting against brutal or inconsiderate treatment or he was not being employed in work suitable to his talents.

Thus, the heav'm of the spiritual served a prime purpose of fulfilling the unfulfilled. Its finest, most obvious characteristic, on the basis of the evidence of the songs, was that it was substantially different from most things on the slave's earth. Look at the chart on page 349.

The fact that some of these details correspond to some in the hymns and songs of the whites is not germane. The backgrounds, except in a few details, are entirely different. To make true parallels, one would have to search the backgrounds of the white revivalist groups and show how their songs developed from their backgrounds. This writer has done sufficient searching to support his conviction of fundamental difference. The presentation of parallelism and constrast on these points does not seem to be a logical part of the present book.

Let us turn to the evidence from the songs. Often, robes, crowns, wings, shoes, are intermixed; always the emphasis is on fulfillment of unfulfilled talents, never on mere acquisition or possession of beautiful or desirable things.

> I've got a robe [crown, shoes, wings, harp, song],
>   you've got a robe,
> All of God's children got a robe,
> When I get to Heaven, goin' to put on my robe,
> Goin' to shout all over God's Heav'n.
> Heav'n, Heav'n,
> Everybody talking 'bout heav'n ain't going there,
> Heav'n, Heav'n,
> Goin' to shout all over God's Heav'n.

Item	Earth	Heav'm
Clothes	Skimpy much-worn rags	Well-fitting long white robe
Headgear	None or greasy hand-me-downs	Starry crown
Shoulder gear	None or insignificant	Wings
Foot gear	None or much-worn shoes	Fine shoes, golden slippers
Living quarters	Broken-down shacks, crowded quarters, earth-floors, leaky roofs	Mansions; plenty good room
Musical instruments	Mostly none; occasional guitar; human voice; hands for clapping	Harp, bells, trumpet; angel choir; own unrestrained voice
Drinking water	Muddy stream, old wells; old buckets	Crystal fountains
Food	Chiefly cornmeal with salt	Milk and honey; best corn and wine; gospel feasts
Punishment	Beatings with lash (often a hundred lashes at a time); mayhem; branding; murder	None
Transportation	None except with masters, slave drivers, temporary managers, patrollers, or auctioneers	Golden chariots
Meetings	Church meetings and camp meetings under supervision	Great jubilee type camp meetings, fully free, fully expressive
Family and friends	Often kept apart even when on same plantation; often divided when one or more sold down the river	Always together, including best friend, King Jesus
Entrances and exits	Barbed wire fences guarded by pattyrollers (patrollers)	Pearly gates
Streets	Miry and dusty pathways and roads	Golden streets

Note several things. Robe, crown, shoes, harp, and song are talents already in his possession but obviously not used. How else does he have them before he gets to heav'm? When he gets to heav'm, he is going to put on these talents, that is, begin using them. "*Shout* [italics mine] all over God's Heav'n" obviously means to employ these talents to the fullest degree, in the most expressive and stimulatingly effective ways. What is true of him is true of "*All* [italics mine] of God's children." This clearly means that the whole slave community is a group of talented individuals who are not being called on to use their talents. The fact that some people who talk about heav'm are not going there suggests unsanctified members of either the white or the black community. Following the undercurrent symbolism and sniping of many songs, the sentence probably is a back-handed slap at the white community. The slave knows that many of these people have put him down as without a soul and not booked for heaven. In a manner similar to the Lazarus-Dives story, the slave slyly turns the tables, without calling names.

It is clear that in all of this, heav'm could refer to free land. He has the talent; when he gets to free land and thus captures the opportunity to use his talent, he will use it as widely and deeply ("shout all over") as he can. Some who think they will be freed are not going to be, but he is! Considering the realism of his talents and his desires to use them, and the fact that passing through death may bring profound changes, the "free land" interpretation is more logical for this song than the "afterlife" interpretation.

Let us go back for some details. In several songs there is assurance that "the robe's goin' to fit me well" because "I tried it on at the gates of hell," or some variation of this idea. In one song the wearer will don the robe "down by the riverside," which seems to be before he gets to heav'm. But since it is his robe ("my long white robe") in advance, the time he puts it on makes little difference. One song peers into the whole experience of what will happen after the fulfillment starts, "Oh, Yes! Oh Yes! Wait 'til I Git on My Robe."

The crown is often starry, but not always; since King Jesus is one's friend, it is suitable, almost necessary, conferring the proper dignity and status even in this classless society. Sometimes, there is question as to who shall be entitled to wear it ("O who shall wear the starry crown"), but most of the time the people with credentials are well defined.

As to wings, one version of the "All God's Chillun" song says, "Fly all over God's Heab'n" instead of "Shout." Another song says that the flying will have an additional function to self-expression, "Going to fly about Heav'n and tell the news."

The shoes, says one poet, are made for walking in the air. Sometimes, they are golden slippers, which will "outshine the glittering sun." They must be golden to be suitable for wearing on the golden streets. They will confer upon the wearer a new position:

> Golden slippers, I'm bound to wear, . . .
> I'm goin' to jine the heavenly choir
> Yes, yes, yes, my Lord,
> I'm a soldier of the cross.

Like the wings, they will also be a news-bearing agency, although the news of the flyer above is likely to be somewhat fresher.

> When I get to heab'n gwine put on my shoes, . . .
> I'll walk all over heav'n an' spread de news.

But note that the wearer of the shoes wants to be of creative service.

The bell players have been mentioned in reference to a beautiful song called "Mary an' Martha Jes' Gone 'Long." Their purpose is "to ring dem charmin' [chimin'] bells." They will be joined in the bell-ringing process by at least the preacher, elder, mother, father. The bell ringing will take place "O, 'way over Jordan, Lord," which puts the location well within the heavenly boundaries. Along with the bells, the ringers will cry, "Free grace an' dyin' love"; they cannot help making an altogether impressive, touching, and charming impression.

When cultivated, the human voice is a great instrument. Singing frees the inner soul, communicates miraculously, and develops creative and artistic form. All three the spiritual poet and his company believed in and practiced. If they have nothing else, all God's children have a song. When slave masters and managers permitted singing, they thought it would work in their favor. It turned out that singing was the most easily available and most successful key to cabals, runaways, and revolts. Eventually, singing was allowed only under heavy supervision, some songs were interdicted, and in certain places group singing was interdicted.

In the spiritual's heav'm, singing is unrestricted and a natural delight. The spiritual itself had taught the slave to believe in singing to the utmost. One of his heavenly ultimates was being admitted to the choir up there.

> Sheet of blood all mingled wid fire, mingled wid fire,
>   mingled wid fire;
> Sheet of blood all mingled wid fire,
> To see God's bleedin' Lam'.
> An' you jine dat heab'n-ly choir, heab'n-ly choir,
>   heab'n-ly choir,
> An' you jine dat heab'n-ly choir,
> To see God's bleedin' Lam'.

He would also sing and shout at the great camp meetings in the skies. Singing was one thing he had learned well on earth ("Sing together children, Don't you get weary") and he would be perfection in heav'm. At times, he would stop singing to march a little and when he marched, "O yes, march wid de talles' angel."

The slave poet found the contemplation of the whole vast array of fulfillments an utter delight.

> I've a crown [harp, robe, slippers] up in the Kingdom,
> Ain't that good news! . . .

> I'm a-goin' to lay down this world, Goin' to shoulder
>   up my cross,
> Goin' to take it home to Jesus, Ain't that good news!

Note that he didn't expect to get to heav'm cheaply; he was willing to shoulder up his personal cross (as Jesus did) before he began stretching himself in his unlimited talents and enjoying unspeakable delights.

One need not apologize for wanting to express one's talents to the full. The gems of purest rays deep in the ocean and the desert flowers blushing unseen are typical of nature's greatest tragedies. "Beauty is its own excuse for being," said Emerson of a woods flower which represented all nature. In the same vein, you can sum up the slave poet's yearning to be himself, complete and outgoing at last; he was a proud child of nature. Comparing himself to another one of nature's proud children, he sang,

> Great big stars—'way up yonder,
> Great big stars—'way up yonder,
> Great big stars—'way up yonder,
> O my little soul's goin' to shine, shine, . . .
> All aroun' the heav'n goin' to shine, shine,
> All aroun' the heav'n goin' to shine, shine.

UP WHERE JESUS LIVES

The best way to introduce oneself to the significance of heav'm as Jesus' permanent home and yours by virtue of his friendship and invitation is to jot down a few of the actual references to the phenomenal facts and to observe the references minutely. To this purpose here are some samples:

"Some sweet day after 'while, I'm goin' to see my Jesus."

"Hallelujah! Troubles over. In the kingdom! With my Jesus!"

"O Mary, O Martha, Sit at my Jesus' feet."

"I'm going back with Jesus when He comes, when he comes."

"Keep a-inching along, like a poor inch-worm, Jesus will come by-and-by."

"Dis sinner gwine to heaben, . . .
Howdy, Mas' Jesus; how's yo Pa?
Howdy, Mas' Jesus; how's yo Pa? . . .
Makin' a curt-sey-a to de Lamb."

"Massa Jesus is comin' bye and bye."

"When I get up in Heaven, And-a my work is done,
Going to sit down by Sister Mary, And chatter with the darling Son."

"I'll go to heav'n an' take my seat, An' cast my crown at Jesus' feet."

"I'm a-goin to talk with the Prince of Peace, Down by the riverside."

"[Of King Jesus] He built his throne up in the air, No man works like him,
And called his saints from ev'rywhere."

"I'm just a-goin' 'way over Jordan, I'm just a-goin' over there,
I'm goin' home to see my Jesus, I'm just a-goin' over there."

"King Jesus built me a house above, . . .
  He built it 'tout [without] a hammer or a nail."

"My Jesus will meet me in-a that mornin'."

"Oh, when I come to die, Give me Jesus."

"When ev-ah-ry star refuses to shine,
  Rocks and mountains don't fall on me.
  I know dat King Jesus will-a be mine."

"I want to see my Jesus when I die,
  Shout salvation as I fly."

"Meet my Massa Jesus, soon-a in de mornin', . . .
  Walk and talk wid Jesus, soon-a in de mornin'."

"Want to go to heav'n when I die, When I die, When I die,
  Want to go to heav'n when I die, To see God's bleedin' Lam'."

Several things are immediately clear. As we pointed out in Chapter 17, the spiritual elects Jesus as the slave's closest, most reliable friend. The other deities are powerful and concerned; Jesus is powerful, sympathetic, experienced in the ways of man, an intercessor and arranger, and the hope of the people. Since he is a king and lives like one, he commands all necessary facilities and services on a permanent basis. He is just and will see that justice rules in all final decisions. Though majestic, he is easy to know. Note that some songwriters are willing to have him as master, although the master part may be derived from the Bible and not from the system of slavery.

Perhaps the closeness of the relationship in the slave's mind is cemented through Jesus' having taken heavy punishment unjustly, as the slave feels he had often done. God and the Lord never were chastised with thorns, never hung on a cross, never were cursed and chided, never had sharp weapons dug into their sides. Jesus and the slaves did. This gives them one big thing in common. If you are going to heav'm anyhow, is it not natural that you would first seek out the personality in power with the most sympathetic heart?

In some ways, note, Jesus is coming in person to gather up his friends and take them to heaven; in some, he will send for his friends; in some, the whole issue will await the Judgment morning; in others, as soon as you die, you go to Jesus' apartment: he is ready and waiting to meet you there, wherever and whenever that may be.

Arrangements for your accommodations seem, mostly, to be taken for granted; one poet has a seat, however, and another has a house built without benefit of hammer and nail. But, without question, the accommodations will be perfect and everlasting. There will never be any trouble about them, such as holes in the golden streets, moldy corn with the wine, low pressure on the crystal fountain, poor service at the gospel feast, broken strings on the harps, smudges on the white robes, malfunctioning of the wings, tarnish on the crowns. The flat promise is—"Trouble over." Apparently, there will be work to do ("When I get up in Heaven, And-a my work is done"), but it will be quite fulfilling work and not the kind that wears you out. This is a rewarding eternity you are about to spend.

Some poets stress "seeing" Jesus, although there is little doubt that "seeing" covers all phases of the life together. Some envision the closest possible eternal relationship ("King Jesus will-a be mine"). Some will be satisfied with nothing less than walking and talking with him ("chatter with the darling Son" is a darling line!). Notice that all references carry the warmest affection without loss of high respect and dignity.

Some critics will offer a series of poems like this as incontrovertible evidence that the spiritual is purely religious and nothing else. Such a conclusion is unwarranted. Religious these verses are in some degree, no doubt, but not exclusively so. The closeness of the relationship is counter to pure religious practice. Where else are there deities (outside of classic and Norse mythology) who are on such friendly terms with their worshippers? Could even the elders and officers of the churches be depended upon to make living arrangements, to build homes, to await guests and chatter with them at their convenience, to pick up countless numbers of friends, charter many chariots, and carry all these people home! The deities and nobility of churches generally consider such activity far beneath their responsibility and dignity. It is they who are to be served, not their flock.

No, the most significant thing about heav'm as the home of Jesus and his sanctified, as the spiritual tells the story, is the fact that the slave needed friends or a friend. Jesus is elected as their friend because he had, in their conception, all the essential qualifications. If you have a friend with large, permanent estates, and you are poor and maltreated, you expect eventually to go to your friend's place, and, if he welcomes you, to stay there.

Remember also that, on top of everything else, Jesus was the agency of freedom and liberty, as we have proved many times. Perhaps Jesus' home and the earnestness of his invitation were a part of the process of freedom. Certainly, the heav'm where Jesus lives is the freest land of all.

THE PLACE OF THE UNION OF FRIENDS
AND RELATIVES

If Jesus was the best friend and they were going to be united with him in heav'm, it follows that all other good friends and relatives would have to be there, too.

Once again the feeling is realistically understandable. Close family ties and close friendships have been, for centuries, the support of nations, societies, and smaller societal organizations. The commerce of slavery ignored these powerful ties. Even a very small child might be sold away from his mother after his mother and father had been sold to different owners. The rights of husbands, wives, sisters, brothers, and close friends to live together, to help each other build useful lives, were trampled almost daily. Few slaves knew where their relatives were or if they were still alive. When a slave sang that he wished to see his mother in heav'm, he often meant that he just wanted to see her again, and heav'm was the likeliest place he could think of.

Once more the religious element is not the governing factor. If the slave had had a decent family organization, he would probably not have confined his songs of union and reunion to a heavenly scene. This kind of song is an argument for the "free land" interpretation. Many slaves, freed by their own endeavors or through some effective slave stealing process, began working at once to free their relatives. They often succeeded.

The reunion songs are quite simple in form. The poet merely expresses a desire, usually an intense desire, to see his friends and relatives in heav'm. He knows the conditions for going to heav'm; he naturally assumes that his friends and relatives, and he, have lived and will continue to live in such a way as to earn heav'm. He does not seem to be expecting special favors. Remember the song in which the singer openly admitted that by disobedience his own brother had made his home in hell.

The reunion was expected to be pleasant, fulfilling for all concerned, and of course permanent. Often Jesus is brought into the picture with the singer and his relatives and friends. Apparently, they will all be intermingled in heaven's activities. The fact that this process will involve probably millions and billions of people, an unbelievable number of arrangements, and countless amounts of equipment and facilities, never seems to cross the singer's mind. Things like this just naturally happen in heav'm. Heav'm is that kind of place. The details will take care of themselves. Don't worry about them.

It is interesting to observe the degree of popularity of friends and relatives. In twenty songs which have reference to a friend (sometimes an ancient from the Bible) or relative, selected at random, the score turns out so:

Friend or Relative	Number of Mentions
Mother	9
Sister	5
Brother	4
Father	2
Sister Mary (from the Bible)	2
Grandmother	1
All fellow Baptists	1
All friends	1
Daniel (from the Bible)	1
Elder (in the church)	1
Leader (in the church)	1
Seeker	1

George Leonard White, founder and first director of the Fisk
Jubilee Singers. FISK UNIVERSITY LIBRARY

Poster advertising a concert of the Fisk Jubilee Singers in New
York, January 14, 1873. FISK UNIVERSITY LIBRARY AND HOWARD
COOPER, PHOTOGRAPHER

THE
JUBILEE
SINGERS

OF

Fisk University, Nashville, Tenn.,

WILL SING AT

STEINWAY HALL

TUESDAY EVENING, JANUARY 14th, 1873;

THE ORIGINAL COMPANY

HAS BEEN

ENLARGED and IMPROVED

BY

IMPORTANT ACCESSIONS
MANY NEW AND TOUCHING SONGS

Have also been added to those formerly sung. The Concert will SURPASS, both in

VARIETY AND POWER

Those which were received with such

UNIVERSAL FAVOR AND ENTHUSIASM

A YEAR AGO.

THESE STUDENTS ARE ENDEAVORING TO INCREASE THE

TWENTY THOUSAND DOLLARS

OF LAST YEAR, TO

SEVENTY THOUSAND,

THIS SUM WILL PAY FOR THE

NEW SITE OF TWENTY-FIVE ACRES,

AND COMPLETE

JUBILEE HALL.

TICKETS,..............50 CENTS RESERVED SEATS,..............75 CENTS

SALE OF TICKETS WILL BEGIN THURSDAY, JAN. 10th, at Steinway Hall; the Methodist Book Concern,
No. 805 Broadway; and at the Rooms of the American Missionary Association, 59 Reade St.

DOORS OPEN AT 7.   CONCERT WILL BEGIN AT 8 O'CLOCK.

Metropolitan Print, Herald Building, cor. Broadway & Ann Street, N. Y.

The first troupe of Fisk Jubilee Singers to tour Europe. FISK UNIVERSITY LIBRARY

Saturday Afternoon, 2 1-2 o'clock.

Programme.

PART I.

1. JOHN SAW.

   John saw de holy number
   Setten on de golden altar.
   Worthy, worthy, is de Lamb
   Setten on the golden altar.

2. SWEET TURTLE DOVE.

   Sweet Turtle Dove, she sing a so sweet;
   Muddy de water so deep;
   An we had a little meeting in de mornin,
   A for to hear Gabriel's trumpet sound.

3. KEEP ME FROM SINKING DOWN.

4. GIDEON'S BAND ON MILK WHITE HORSES.

5. OLD FOLKS AT HOME.

6. JUMP FOR JOY.

PART II.

1. OH, DE OLE ARK A MOVERIN ALONG.

   Jes wait a little while, I'm gwine to tell you 'bout de ole Ark,
   De ole ark, a moverin, a moverin along,
   De Lord tole Noah for to build him an ole ark,
   De ole ark moverin, a moverin along.

2. MY LORD, WHAT A MORNIN.

3. MOST DONE TRAVELLING.

4. MY OLD KENTUCKY HOME.

5. HONOR DE LAMB.

6. DUST, DUST AN ASHES, (The Slaves' Easter Hymn)

Thursday Evening.

Programme.

PART I.

1. HEAR DE ANGELS SINGING.

   Oh sing all de way,
   Sing all de way,
   Sing all de way, my Lord,
   Hear de Angels singing.

2. MY BRETHEREN DON'T GET WEARY.

   My bretheren don't get weary;
   Angels brought de tidings down.
   Don't get weary, I'm hunting for a home.

3. OH, SWING LOW, SWEET CHARIOT.

4. ZION, WEEP A-LOW.

   Oh, look up yonder, Lord, a what I see,
   Den a hallelujah to de lamb,
   Dere's a long' tall angel a coming arter me,
   Den a hallelujah to de laub.

5. OLD BLACK JOE,—Bass Solo and Chorus.

    I'm coming, I'm coming, for my head is bending low;
   I hear their gentle voices calling old black Joe.

6. MY LORD DELIVERED DANIEL.

PART II.

1. BRIGHT SPARKLES IN DE CHURCHYARD.

2. I WANT TO GO TO HEAVEN IN DUE TIME.

   I want to go to Heaven in due time of day,
   Before de heaven gates shut against me.

3. GO DOWN, MOSES.

   Go down, Moses,
   Way down in Egypt's land,
   Tell ole Pharaoh
   Let my people go.

4. OLD FOLKS AT HOME.

5. AH, DEM A UNION BRETHEREN.

   All you brothers gwine ter help me ter sing,
   Start yourself right in a dis ring.
   If my memory sarves me right,
   We're gwine to hab a big shout ter night.

6. OH DE WINTER 'LL SOON BE OVER.

An early troupe of the Cotton Blossom Singers of Piney Woods,
Mississippi, and the bus-hotel in which they toured. PINEY WOODS
SCHOOL

Girls of the Cotton Blossom Singers in their cotton dresses. PINEY
WOODS SCHOOL

St. George's Church

STUYVESANT SQUARE   NEW YORK CITY

16TH STREET, EAST OF THIRD AVENUE

ELMORE M. McKEE, *Rector*

17th Annual Service of Negro Spirituals

Sunday, May 12th, 1940, at 4 P. M.

Soloists—Harry T. Burleigh, Orville E. Race,
Carol Brice, Mildred Cunningham

Choir of 60 Adults and Junior Choir

Organist and Choirmaster, George W. Kemmer

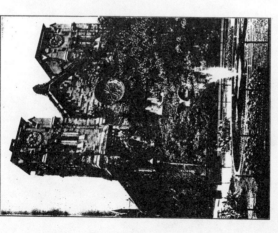

The Order of the Music

✠

PRELUDE   Largo, from "The New World Symphony"   *Dvorak*

PROCESSIONAL HYMN   495   O brothers, lift your voices   *"Waters"*

SPIRITUALS   Great Day! de Righteous Marchin'   *har. and arr. by Alston W. Burleigh*

Great day de righteous marchin'
God's a-gon-a build up Zion's walls.
Chariot rode on de mountain top,
My Lord spoke an' de chariot stop.

Marchin' on! an' you shall gain the day
Way over in de Egyp' lan',
Heard good news from de Promis'd Lan',
God's a-gon-a build up Zion's walls.

We are climbin' Jacob's ladder   *har. and arr. by Burleigh*

mixed voices and Junior Choir

We are climbin' Jacob's ladder,
Soldier of the cross.
Every roun' goes higher'n higher,
Soldier of the cross.

Sinner do you love my Jesus?
Soldier of the cross.
If you love Him, why not serve Him?
Soldier of the cross.

SENTENCES

PRAYERS

SPIRITUALS   Steal Away   *har. and arr. by Kemmer*

mixed voices and Junior Choir

Steal away, steal away, steal away to Jesus.
Steal away, steal away home, I ain't got
long to stay here.
My Lord He calls me, He calls me by the thunder;
The trumpet sounds within-a my soul;

I ain't got long to stay here.
Green trees are bending, Poor sinner stands
a-trembling;
The trumpet sounds within-a my soul;
I ain't got long to stay here.

The following have been harmonized and arranged by Harry T. Burleigh

Sometimes I feel like a Motherless Child

women's voices

Sometimes I feel like a Motherless Chile,
A long ways from home—
Sometimes I feel like I'm almos' gone
A long ways from home.

Didn't my Lord deliver Daniel?

mixed voices

Didn't my Lord deliver Daniel,
An' why not every man?
He deliver'd Daniel from de lion's den,
Jonah from de belly of de whale,
An' de Hebrew chillun from de fiery furnace,
An' why not-a every man?
Didn't my Lord deliver Daniel,
An' why not-a every man?

De win' blow Eas' an' de win' blow Wes',
It blows like de judgment day.
An' ev'ry poor soul that never pray
I'll be glad to pray that day
I set my foot on de Gospel Ship,
An' de ship it begin to sail.
It landed me over on Canaan's shores,
An' I'll never come back any more.

Swing Low, Sweet Chariot

women's voices and Junior Choir

Swing low, sweet chariot,
Coming for to carry me home.
Swing low, sweet chariot,
Coming for to carry me home.

I look'd over Jordan, what did I see,
Coming for to carry me home?
A band of angels coming after me,
Coming for to carry me home.

Dig my Grave

mixed voices

Dig my grave long and narrow!
Make my coffin long and strong!
Bright angels to my feet,
Bright angels to my head,

Bright angels to carry me when I'm dead.
Oh, my little soul gwine shine,
Oh, my little soul gwine shine like a star,
Good Lord, I'm bound to Heav'n at last.

Partial program of a service at St. George's Church, New York. Burleigh was chief soloist at St. George's from 1894 to 1949. Specializing in spirituals, he sang every other conceivable type of vocal music. He sang "The Palms" on 54 consecutive Palm Sundays. ST. GEORGE'S CHURCH, NEW YORK

Harry Thacker Burleigh, composer and arranger: Antonín Dvořák used his arrangements of spirituals as the chief source for his American pieces. ST. GEORGE'S CHURCH, NEW YORK

Program of a concert given by The Hampton Institute Choir in New York in 1931. NEW YORK PUBLIC LIBRARY

Conductor William Levi Dawson and the Tuskegee Choir, which sang spirituals on the premiere program of Radio City Music Hall, New York, December 27, 1932. TUSKEGEE INSTITUTE

Denmark, with groups from Denmark and Norway.

Jester Hairston teaching spirituals around the world. JESTER HAIRSTON

Yugoslavia.

Nigeria.

Ghana.

The Jamaican Folksingers, directed by Olive Lewin. OLIVE LEWIN

Louis T. Achille directing a section of the Park Glee Club of Lyons, France. FRANCE-REPORTAGE

HOME

In spite of the fact that you were going to be King Jesus' guest and were going to have friends and relatives strung around your neck like beads, a thing of vital importance was that heav'm was going to be your home, your home for good and all. As a slave, you never had a real home. Oh yes, you might stay under one roof or in one slave shack for years, but this was no home. You never yearned to come back to it. You might be well enough satisfied with it, and one day you would be sold away from it in the twinkling of an eye to a place (still not a home) you hated or simply could not live in because of insects, vermin, crowded conditions, or unruly and unhygienic companions. To be sold, you did not have to offend anybody; you might be a part of a good business deal, or your previous owner needed the money, or he died and his estate had to be settled, or someone saw you and made an offer he could not resist, or his womenfolk needed new wardrobes, or he "fancied" one day that he saw you looking sullen or unhappy, or for any number of other reasonable or unreasonable reasons.

Thus, as with friends and relatives, the slave needed a home. His poetry invented one—heav'm. Although the poet used afterlife terminology, he was not necessarily talking about a home after death. The emphasis is on the idea of home and the idea of the slave at last having and reaching his home.

Here are a few illustrations:

"Lord, I'm bearin' heavy burdens, . . . climbin' high mountains,
 Tryin' to get home."

"Soon-a will be done with the trouble of this world,
 Going home to live with God, . . .
 When I get to heav'n I will sing and tell,
 How I did shun both death and hell."

"Going home in the chariot in the morning."

"Sometimes I feel like a motherless child, . . .
 Sometimes I feel like I'm almost gone, . . .
 A long ways [or "Far, far away"] from home."

"Swing low, sweet chariot, Coming for to carry me home." [Sometimes a question, "home?" This song very likely referred to free land.]

"Some of these days, it won't be long,
 Goin' home to sing my song."

"I've got a home in-a that Rock, Don't you see?"

"Between de earth an' sky, Thought I heard my Savior cry,
 You got a home in dat Rock, Don't you see?"

"No harm, no harm,
 Poor mourner's got a home at last."

"An' I will die in de fiel', ...
I'm on my journey home."

"Ride on Moses, I know de Lord would pass dat way,
I want to go home in de mawnin'."

"We'll camp a little while in the wilderness, few days, few days, ...
An' den we'll all go home."

"Until I reach-a ma home, ...
I nevah inten' to give de journey ovah,
Until I reach ma home."

"O, de ol' ark's a-moverin', ... an I'm goin' home."

"Do don't touch-a my garment, Good Lord.
I'm gwine home."

THE PLACE FOR THE GOOD AFTER JUDGMENT

If heav'm encompasses a life after death, then you can go there two
ways: whenever you die and on Judgment Day. The latter is considered
by some to be unquestionably at the end of life; again, not necessarily.
The surface language of the songs certainly projects it into the far future.

But consider one thing. The slave was deeply impressed by the distortions of life, especially as they affected him. He had heard the Biblical
stories which showed how, miraculously or otherwise, monumental distortions and injustices were set to right without waiting for the Judgment
Day described in the Bible (e.g., Noah's experience with the Deluge). It is
true that this latter occasion offered grand opportunities to his redoubtable
imagination. But his sense of the need for correction was so strong that he
was ready to accept as Judgment Day any comprehensive day of reckoning, or to have both that and the regular Judgment Day. If it were the latter, then the heav'm that followed was clearly a place after death; if the
former, then the eventuality could be a revolution followed by a period
and place of heavenly justice somewhere on earth.

As we have seen in similar cases, various songs are written in such a
way as to allow for the one, the other, or both. "Where shall I be when
de firs' trumpet soun'?" he asks. Then he answers, "Gwine to try on ma
robe, When it soun' so loud."

"My Lord, what a mornin' " is sometimes delivered "My Lord, what a
mournin'." In either case, it is the beginning of a great day of justice, accompanied by falling stars, moaning sinners, thundering trumpets, nations
awaking underground, and, of course, shouting Christians gliding toward
heav'm.

"O Rocks, Don't Fall on Me" produces a similar setting: You see the
dead rising and going to their mansions "in-a de skies." Likewise, in "You
May Bury Me in de Eas' " [or "Wes' "], the good soul will hear the trumpet wherever he is.

> Good ole Christians in dat day,
> Dey'll take wings an' fly away.

You do not have to be told that their destination is heav'm.

In "In Dat Great Gittin' Up Mornin'" there is one additional, very delicate, touch. Gabriel's instructions from the Lord as to the loudness of the trumpet call are twofold. The second time he blew normally, "Loud as seven peals of thunder." The first time, however, the Lord said,

> Blow it right calm an' easy,
> Do not alarm my people.

As we have several times shown, this song insures no mercy for sinners, who must say "Amen" to their damnation, but for true Christians, the blessings of Heav'm.

> Dere dey live wid God forever, . . .
> On de right hand side of my Savior,
> Fare you well, Fare you well.

THE PLACE OF SALVATION (FREE LAND)

Some of the songs are bolder in their connotations of heav'm as a free country on earth than others, which disguise the connotation carefully, or place the door on hinges which swing either way. There can be little doubt about "Holy Bible,"

> Before I'd be a slave, I'd be buried in my grave,
> And go home to my Father and be saved
> [or "to my Lord and be free"].

There is good disguise, but reasonable strength in the lines,

> This world's a wilderness of woe,
> So let us all to glory go.

The poet must have read "free land" under his breath for "glory," but he did not come right out and say so. The same sort of thing is true of "My way's cloudy, Go sen'-a dem angels down," especially if you spent some time reading the runaway advertisements in the contemporary papers or the records of the Underground Railroad.

"By an' By," the spiritual says, "I'm gwinter lay down my heavy load." When speaking of the fit of the robe, it says,

> I know my robe's gwinter fit me well, . . .
> I tried it on at de gates of hell.

Why the gates of hell? Did the saved person have to circle hell to get to heaven? A much simpler explanation is that the robe means free opportunity and the trying on was done before he left the slave world.

The gospel ship that landed the good slave "over on Canaan's shore" in the memorable "Didn't My Lord Deliver Daniel?" must have had an earthly engine and must have been engaged in an earthly enterprise. The import of the song is too bold and direct for anything less.

"I Thank God I'm Free at Las' " is impeccable "free land" propaganda. Even so, it speaks of the soul rising and flying and of meeting Jesus "in de middle of de air." It is evidence, not very rare either, that the freedom songs, even when overt, were intermixed with earthly purposes and heavenly trappings.

THE NEW JERUSALEM

Heav'm and the New Jerusalem described in the Apostle John's Book of Revelation (the last book of the Bible) are often intertwined in the spiritual. John's name, language, and symbols were a delight to the spiritual poet. One of the most characteristic spirituals is "I Want to Be Ready,"

> I want to be ready, I want to be ready,
> I want to be ready to walk in Jerusalem
> Just like John.
>
> O John, O John, what do you say? . . .
> That I'll be there at the coming day.
> John said the city was just four square, . . .
> And he declared he'd meet me there,
> Walk in Jerusalem just like John.

"Sittin' Down Beside the Lamb" begins with the shouted "New Jerusalem!" two times. "Rockin' Jerusalem" uses the same rousing device, although not at the beginning. It also says,

> I hear archangels a-rockin' Jerusalem,
> I hear archangels a-ringin' dem bells.

"King Jesus Built Me a House Above" promises that the new dwelling is on Jerusalem lane. "John Saw the Holy Number" tells the family story of "the golden altar" and the shout "Worthy, worthy is the Lamb."

"THERE"

Often, heav'm is just "there" or "over there" without specifying place or direction. The use of "there" is somewhat like a password known well and only to those in on the secret. It is not an uncommon poetic device.

> I'll be there in the mornin' . . .
> When the general roll is called, yes, I'll be there,

or "When the roll is called up yonder, I'll be there."

In "Death's Goin' to Lay His Hand on Me" the poet says to some unspecified *you,*

> If you get *there* [italics mine] before I do, . . .
> Tell all my friends I'm a-comin' too.

"I'm Just A-Goin' over There" gives a direction, but goes beyond the indicated point into some wonderful unknown.

> I'm just a-goin' 'way over Jordan,
> I'm just a-goin' over there.

SOMETHING TO FIGHT FOR

In one group of spirituals, heav'm is something really important to fight for.

> Marching up the heavenly road, . . .
> I'm bound to fight until I die.

After asking his sister if she has her sword and shield, the poet continues,

> O fare you well friends, fare you well foes,
> Marching up the heavenly road,
> I leave you all my eyes to close,
> Marching up the heavenly road.

As we know, the poet is sometimes a heaven-bound soldier, holding out his light. The tendency is to put the emphasis on the beautiful lines expressing the radiance—"Let yo' light shine a-roun' de world." One should not forget, however, that, in the first instance, the poet is presenting a soldier, a fighting man, and that in the second instance, this soldier is fighting his way up to heaven. Beautiful as it is, the light holding seems incidental to the poem's chief thrust. The same kind of thing is true in "We Are Climbin' Jacob's Ladder." The climbing part and its implicit advancement are most attractive. But the climbing to heav'm is being done by "soldiers of de cross." It is a fighting operation, not a sports activity.

THE PLACE OF GENUINE AND PERMANENT REST

Considering the grueling, hard work the slave was compelled to do, dawn to dark, day after day, it is not surprising that an important attribute of heav'm is just plain rest. For some people who do little work or normal work (say forty hours a week), heav'm is also a place of rest. Besides one or two days at Christmas, the slave had no vacations, paid or otherwise. Rest was something he cherished.

> Wish I's in heaven settin' down, settin' down, (repeated)
> O, Mary, O Martha, Wish I's in heaven settin' down.

> Wouldn't get tired no mo', . . .
> Wouldn't have nothin' to do.

Again, he thinks first of rest after the earthly grind is over:

> You may bury me in the East, you may bury me in the West.
> But in that morning my soul will be at rest.

In a somewhat more famous song, he declares,

> O, by an' by, by an' by.
> I'm gwinter lay down my heavy load.

Here, his rest is automatic.

Paradoxically, he also thinks of heav'm as a place of great activity.

> I got a mother in heaven, . . .
> Lord, I can't stand still.

> When I get up in glory, . . .
> Lord, I can't stand still.

GOD'S CAPITAL, THE PLACE OF HIS THRONE

Among many other wonderful things heav'm is the seat of the kingdom of God; in it are the throne of God and all the appropriate elements which surround the throne. "The earth is his footstool an' heav'n his throne," sings the Afro-American poet, as many other religious poets have sung. Added significance is given to the throne by some other lines in the same poem:

> God is a God! God don't never change!
> God is a God! An' He always will be God! . . .

> The whole creation all His own,
> His love and power will prevail,
> His promises will never fail.

THE PLACE OF ENDLESS SUNDAYS (SABBATHS)

Related to the rest theme is the spiritual's periodic reminder that heav'm is endless Sundays. The slave did not always have a rest day on Sunday, although in most places he did. But besides rest, Sunday or the Sabbath means worship on the authority of Holy Bible. In heav'm will be perpetual worship, for there will be much to glorify.

In "Religion Is a Fortune I Really Do Believe" are the lines,

> Gwineter walk-a wid de Angels, I really do believe,
>   (repeated)
> Gwineter see my Massa Jesus, I really do believe,
> Where Sabbaths have no end.

One song, however, is devoted entirely to the theme of endless Sundays. It is called "Ev'ry Day'll Be Sunday,"

> Bye an' bye, bye an' bye, good Lord!
> Bye an' bye, Ev'ry day'll be Sunday bye an' bye. . . .

> One o' these mornin's bright an' fair, . . .
> Goin' to take my wings an' cleave the air, . . .

> One day, one day as I's walkin' along,
> I thought I heard the angels song,
> Ev'ry day'll be Sunday bye and bye.

THE UNCROWDED PLACE, THE PLACE FOR THE RESOLVING OF DIFFERENCES, THE PLACE OF THE LORD'S VIEWING STATION, THE PLACE OF COMPLETE PEACE

These last four attributes of heav'm, although separate ideas, can readily be grouped together, since they seem to be only rarely mentioned.

In spite of the millions of worthy dead, heav'm will never be crowded. The song pays tribute to the spaciousness of heav'm and to the efficiency of the Deity's arrangements. It seems to imply that, unlike the situation in many of earth's establishments, no one need ever stop trying to get there for fear the place will fill up or grow crowded. Apparently, everyone who will be there has already been counted and accommodated in advance.

> O brothers [sisters, mourners], Don't stay away,
> (repeated three times)
> For my Lord says there's room enough,
> Room enough in the heav'n for us all,
> My Lord says there's room enough,
> So don't stay away.

Although taking in many kinds of folk, heav'm is a place for the resolving of differences. On earth, Methodists and Baptists often engage in bitter rivalry. Their interpretations of the methods for reaching heav'm are in conflict. Heav'm will admit the members of both groups and will find a way to smooth out their conflicts.

> The Baptist they go by water,
> The Methodes' go by lan',
> But when they get to heaven,
> They'll shake each other's han'.

To make certain that all his laws are being obeyed by the vast congregations of the earth's peoples and to keep being sure that justice and goodness prevail, the Lord must have a good viewing station. That station is situated in heav'm.

He's got His eyes on you, He's got His eyes on you—
My Lord's sittin' in the Kingdom, He's got His eyes on you.

At the very end, heav'm is a place of complete peace. The spiritual poet often calls Jesus the Prince of Peace. Peace among nations is a function of religion, in his eyes. On earth, peace is difficult to obtain. It seems, sometimes, that wars, conflicts, large or small, and the attendant hatred and bitterness are everywhere among nations and smaller groups of peoples. Should they seem to stop in some places, they invariably continue or break out in other places. Wouldn't it be wonderful if there were a place where everybody and everything is truly and fully at peace?

Such a place is available, declares the poet of the spirituals. It bears the cherished name of heav'm. You go there if you will. Do you not want to go there,

> To that gospel feast,
> That promised land, that land, where *all*
> [italics mine] is peace?
> Walk into heaven—

❀◇

CHAPTER TWENTY-ONE

Literary Characteristics in the Body of Spirituals

· ·
·

AS LITERATURE, the spirituals lack many of the qualities which academicians require. They were not written down, book fashion. They were not in fashionable or, even, grammatically correct English. Most times they rhyme; often they do not; sometimes their rhyming is clumsy or banal. Many times their language is not literary at all. Like most folk songs, theirs is the language of the people. The hope of their creators was communication, not inclusion in an anthology.

Even so, they possess a number of authentic literary qualities. They have poetic exaltation and often a care for language in the best poetic senses. They have definite themes and theme development. Borrowing from the Bible and from other sources, they show a creditable, and sometimes a remarkable, adaptive skill and result. They have a sense of purpose and style. They use sound and repetition with telling effects. As Mrs. McAdams says, they have an intimate, confidential tone accounted for by a naturally sociable spirit, which led the singers to work, play, and worship in company. And as Irving Schlein says, an innate beauty always comes through in these songs.

In the fundamental skills of writing, exposition, description, narration, and argumentation, the spiritual ranges from passable to outstanding. A song like "All God's Chillun Got Wings" clearly explains the slave's awareness of his skills and talents and his determination to use them when he gets the chance. It does so, both by direct statement and by implication. Hardly anyone listening to this song could fail to get the point and to be impressed by it.

Many good descriptions are found in these songs. A handy one is "I Couldn't Hear Nobody Pray." The details are striking, the atmosphere is skillfully painted, the effect is well contrived. An even better one is "De

Blin' Man Stood on de Road and Cried." Besides skillful manipulation of detail, the song introduces and develops genuine pathos.

The number of good narratives is very great indeed. Of narrative spirituals, Botkin says that instead of merely dialect versions of evangelical Protestant hymns, they demonstrate a native balladry that converts Biblical symbols of freedom and old Bible stories into folk poetry of a high order. The songs about David present the character of this young king through pointed selection of his major characteristics. It also sharply employs incident. In the various song stories of Noah and his ark, emphasis is on incident, but character is well developed also.

The many songs about the birth of Christ tell the story in a variety of interesting ways. From the Mary's baby theme, to the manger scene, to the adoration of shepherds and wise men, each story is told with dignity and with pride, and sometimes with great gusto. The story in the song it introduces, "Go Tell It on the Mountain," is a clarion call.

One of the very best and most fully developed narratives is "Joshua Fit de Battle ob Jericho." The marshaling of detail in this story is not short of being masterful. If the song is sung as it is written, the climactic tumbling down of the walls is a great triumph each time. The character and skill of Joshua as a great commander are unquestionably displayed.

Examining the spiritual's narratives critically, however, Nettie Fitzgerald McAdams finds confusion and fragmentariness and abrupt beginnings. Many spirituals, she says, are like the Scottish ballad "Edward," consisting entirely of unintroduced dialogue, e.g. "What kind of shoes you going to wear?" She rightfully states that the prevailing stanzaic form is the couplet, usually iambic tetrameter. Perhaps her critique would have been more definitive had she written later than 1923 (up to 1923 only a few hundred songs had been published).

In "No Hidin' Place" are reports of several good arguments. Perhaps the most interesting is about the gambler. For some reason gamblers constantly recur in the spirituals. They may have been secretly admired by the creators of the song, but they are always losers. In "No Hidin' Place" the sinner man gambled and fell; he wanted to go to heaven, but he went to hell. The fact that the sinner man wanted to go to heaven is the key to the argumentative note in the song.

One phase of the literary career of the songs is letter writing. "My Lord's A-Writin' All de Time" includes even a listing of the contents of the Lord's letters, all you do, all you say. "De Angels in Heab'n Gwineter Write My Name," "Dere's a Han' Writin' on de Wall," and "Got My Letter" are titles of a few of the other spirituals which carry on the letter writing excitement. In "Got My Letter" acquisition of the letter gives the receiver immediate authority to "hail the train."

Prayer is another literary form in which the spiritual specializes. "It's Me, O Lord," is one of the best prayers because it places responsibility directly on the singer, nobody else. If he is standing in the need of prayer, he is ready to shoulder his responsibility.

Other striking prayers, which qualify as literature, are "Ev'ry Time I Feel de Spirit," "Keep Me f'om Sinkin' Down," "Oh, My Good Lord, Show Me de Way," and "Come Here Lord!" In this last one, the singer commands the Lord in the name of sinners. One of the stanzas of "Come Here Lord!" carries a touching warning,

> Some seek God's face, but don't seek right,
> Pray a little by day and none at night.

Many spirituals could qualify as sermons. Two of these are "Gimme Dat Ol' Time Religion" and "Humble Yo'Self, de Bell Done Ring [or "Rung"]." In the former the singer builds his sermonic point like a regular preacher. In the latter the notion of humility is probably not the same as being submissive to the white folks. Unless this song departs from the patterns set in hundreds of others, it is stating a universal principle. Humility is a sane way to live. It is the opposite of dangerous pride. Embrace humility.

In his *Art of the American Folk Preacher*, Bruce A. Rosenberg says, "One is inclined to approach the origin of the changed sermon by the circuitous route of the spiritual for several reasons." One is the use of vivid repetition in both spiritual and sermon. Another is the large number of sermonic lines which come from spirituals. Still another is the recurrence of spiritual rhythms and the informal, concrete, personal relation with God, as in one sermon, "Jesus Said to Me Last Night." Rosenberg, in summary, says that the chanted sermon is the ideal conflation of prose sermon and spiritual.

Some of these poems engage in a practice that might be called philosophizing. They present one small bit of philosophy to enlighten and encourage the member who needs it. "Die in de Fiel' " is such a poem. In so many words it encourages the member to stick by his principles even though at great expense to himself. In "Didn't My Lord Deliver Daniel?" the "And why not every man?" is such a bit of philosophy. Such bits appear like nuggets in a great many songs.

Moving from elemental literary forms to more complex and conventional ones, the reader might examine the epic sense in the spirituals. Dorothy Scarborough has written of the epic proclivities of the slave poet, "Who else is capable of such epic largeness of gesture, such eloquent roll of eye, such expressive hesitation in speech?" By bringing together all the songs on Moses and all the references to Moses, one would have the materials for a pretty good epic. In the view of the spiritual poets, Moses did not stop by freeing the Hebrew people from the Israelites. He is the symbolic leader of all oppressed people who are bound to overthrow their oppressors. The steps Moses took in accomplishing this Gargantuan task could easily be sections of an epic poem. The fact that he was victorious offers hope for the people.

The Afro-American slave was fully aware of the depth and breadth of his predicament. Even the most hopeful did not anticipate an early deliverance. They knew of the efforts being made to abolish slavery, but they respected even more the strength of the South in maintaining the institution. They understood the policies of the fight. Knowing and appreciating all this, they lavished great attention upon Moses. He was no legendary figure, he had actually lived. Through him a very bitter slavery had been overthrown. If it could happen once, it could happen again.

Some of the Moses songs run for twenty-five stanzas. This length and mass of detail put a great strain upon the memory of the lead singer. But for Moses every detail was important. In "Go Down, Moses," the most popular of the Moses songs, and the most deadly, there is a line, "Let them come out with Egypt's spoil." The feeling that compensation should accompany manumission was very strong among the slaves. In the years immediately following the Civil War there was much grumbling among the former slaves about the absence of the promised forty acres and a mule per man.

The Moses epic definitely gave a solid place to Pharaoh. Symbol of the oppressor, he was looked upon with fascination. The fact that he struggled hard to uphold his tyranny and finally was destroyed abjectly, completely, is an inevitable part of the story. It was not revenge that motivated the singer slaves; it was all-pervasive justice. If the foundations of the world did not rest in the concrete of justice, then all life was meaningless. Thus, "Didn't Old Pharaoh Get Los'" was a very popular song.

One of the very important portions, perhaps the climax, of the Moses epic was its application to the Afro-American slave. A spiritual sometimes bearing the title, "He's Jus' de Same Today," is one of several bringing the Moses story into contemporary focus. One reason that the slave could believe in God was that the word *God* meant for him eternal principles of right. He knew that he was being done wrong. He did not believe that the wrong being done to him was going to last. He did not know how the change would take place, but this Moses system was one way it could take place. If this God up there plowed through the darkness of the Israelites and used a Moses to bring freedom to a large group of people, He was worth believing in, hence the power of the spiritual line, "The God that lived in Moses' time, Is jus' the same today."

There is one other great epic idea in the spirituals and it, too, is built on the theme of eternal justice. This is the epic of Judgment Day. Their great excitement about Judgment Day was a combination of their deep concern with eternal justice and their love of highly dramatic, colorful situations. "My Lord, What a Mornin'," "My Lord Says He's Gwineter

Rain Down Fire," and "In Dat Great Gittin' Up Mornin' " are three of a very large group of songs which enlarge upon the earth's final judgment.

The gorgeous display of detail, the fierce piling of action on action, the combining of the Book of Revelation in some of these Judgment Day poems suggests that they were written by slaves who could read and who had pored over various sections of the Bible. The fact that "In Dat Great Gittin' Up Mornin' " carried the refrain, "Fare you well, fare you well," suggests that the slave singer is in the clear; it is other people who have problems. The fact that it is the last time around for all of earth's inhabitants, including those who have been corralled from their graves, puts a cap on the whole proceeding.

But the slave singer is probably not concentrating upon getting even with those who have mistreated him, although these people most assuredly come in for their just deserts. He is more interested in sorting out his world and its values. The writers of the songs probably believed in a real Judgment Day at some time in the future. But the songs are more of an exercise in imagination. Since Judgment Day is not yet here, let us presuppose it and see what happens. It gives all the singers a chance to examine the world from a very high and revealing vantage point. It is, therefore, epic in scope as well as in significance.

The individual poems of the Judgment Day series are, as has been said, highly dramatic. Although not many spirituals are outright dramas, a great many are set in the midst of dramatic situations. Adam and Eve in Eden, Joshua at Jericho, Daniel in the lion's den, Ezekiel and his wheel, Noah and his ark, and hundreds of other dramas are depicted or assumed.

The spiritual picks up drama from the everyday life of the slave. In the words of Dorothy Scarborough, "The Negro is a born dramatist." "Done Made My Vow to the Lord" is a good example, whichever way you decide to read it. Suppose it is a poem that has nothing to do with religious conversion, as some intelligent readers will have it. Suppose it is an announcement that the slave has decided to free himself by whatever means. Think of the agony he has gone through in overcoming his fears, in deciding to cut himself away from his friends and surroundings, in planning his escape, every move of which is packed with danger. Suppose it is a poem of religious conversion; the man (or woman) has struggled with himself, has resolved to cast off his sinful ways, which must have been sweet and comfortable to him. In either case he faces a perilous future, as the song clearly indicates. The experience of seeing what the end will be demands every ounce of his strength and watchfulness.

The same sort of thing is true of "Steal Away." Whether or not this song was written as part of the fugitive apparatus, as is most likely, it was certainly used by Harriet Tubman and others in the fugitive apparatus. It was certainly used to call slaves to secret meetings. Thus the very singing of the song introduces a note of mystery, a note of danger. The fact that, in the verse lines, the Lord calls by thunder and lightning intensifies this note.

A prelude to expressionistic drama is found in "Who'll Be a Witness for My Lord?" After establishing "my soul" as a witness, the song goes back into the past and brings in great personalities. As each personality comes forward, his whole career is presented through the calling of his name. Each is a witness on a different score: Methusaleh for his ability to live almost a thousand years; Samson for his strength; Daniel for his ability to lie down and sleep in the presence of hungry lions.

Lyric poetry abounds among the spirituals. Recall the lyric quaintness of "Sometimes I Feel Like a Motherless Child." The real poignancy in the poem comes in recalling that the African slave was utterly devoted to home and family, and here he has lost both. Although many of the spirituals were written to keep up the spirit and the morale of the group, it is equally poetic to have a poem that admits that all such efforts have failed, that the slave feels utterly lost and alone, "almost gone."

One of the most remarkable lyrics among spirituals is a "Negro Hymn of the Judgment Day,"

> Done yo' see de chariot ridin' on de clouds?
> De wheels in de fire how dey roll, how dey roll!
> O dat mornin' you'll hyar a mighty roarin',
> Dat'll be de earth a-burnin',
> When de Heabens fly away.
>
> Done yo' hyar de trumpets blowin' fo' de dade?
> Done yo' hyar de bones how dey shake, how dey shake!
> O dat mornin' you'll hyar a mighty roarin',
> Dat'll be de earth a-burnin',
> When de Heabens fly away.
>
> Done yo' see de graves dey open an' de dade arisin'?
> An' de bones in de fyar how dey burn, how dey burn!
> O dat mornin' . . .
>
> Done yo' see de eyes throo de lids how dey stare?
> An' de living worms how dey gnaws, how dey gnaws!
> O dat mornin' . . .
>
> Done yo' see de king a-comin' on de clouds?
> See de nail prints in his han's how dey shine, how dey shine!
> O dat mornin' . . .
>
> Done yo' see His robes a-flowin' on de light?
> An' he hade an' he hair white as snow, white as snow!
> O dat mornin' you'll hyar a mighty roarin',
> Dat'll be de earth a-burnin',
> When de Heabens fly away.

Two other strong lyrics are found in "Christmas Carols from Georgia," unearthed by Emma M. Backus for the *Journal of American Folk-Lore,*

> De leetle cradle rocks to-night in glory,
> In glory, in glory, . . .
> De Christ-chile born.
> Peace on earth, Mary rock de cradle . . .
> De Christ-chile born in glory,
> In glory, in glory,
> De Christ-chile born in glory.
>
> De Christ-chile am passin'
> Sing softly,
> De Christ-chile am passin',
> Sing low.
> Don' yo' hear he foot on de treetop,
> Sof' like de south win' blow?
> Glory hallelu!
> Glory, glory, glory
> Glory hallelu.

Other lyric samples illustrate the following styles:

Love Song: "I Never Felt Such Love in My Soul Befo' "
"When You Feel Like Moanin' "

Epigram: "Ev'rybody Talking 'bout Heav'n Ain't Going There"

Celebrational Poem: Birth of Christ, "Go Tell It on the Mountain"
"A Happy New Year"

Elegy: "Were You There?"
"They Crucified My Lord"

Satire: "Satan's a Liar an' a Conjurer, Too"

It is clear, then, that these unlettered men had mastered much of the poetic art. Most important of all, their poetry stuck in people's hearts.

❂◇

CHAPTER TWENTY-TWO

The Poetry of the Spiritual and Its Relevancy for Now

· ·
·

WHAT relevancy does the poetry of the spiritual have for to-day? This is not a new subject. It has been broached many times in the hundred years since the songs began to be pub-lished. Although usually broached by literary people, it is a question raised by historians, educators, theologians, sociologists, and psychologists.

As early as 1899, the Hampton Negro Conference, held at Hampton In-stitute, Virginia, discussed the relevancy of Afro-American music in its section on "Music, Literature, and the Drama." Along with an attack on and defense of ragtime, there was unanimity that the Afro-American needed "the beautiful plantation melodies" as a part of his progressive de-velopment. One speaker especially urged that all concerned should "hunt them out and preserve them with care." The conference was told by Dr. H. B. Frissell, then of Hampton,

> There is a great future for the race that produced the plantation melodies. What can any people want better than a songlore that has had power to move the hearts of men and women all over the world? Walter Damrosch, who is himself a great master of music, and knows the elements that make it divine, has distinguished these melodies by his commendation.

Seven years later, Kelly Miller, an Afro-American sociologist and po-lemicist, addressed himself to the relevancy of the songs in an article en-titled "The Artistic Gifts of the Negro." After insisting that they were American and not African, he turned to the disposition of the "more sensitive Negro" to affect to feel ashamed of these melodies. This affecta-tion he called a fear to acknowledge a noble influence because it proceeded from a lowly place. "All great people," he added, "glorify their history, and look back upon their early attainment with spiritualized vision. . . . A people who are afraid of their own shadow must forever abide in the shade."

He then declared that the spirituals were the Negro's chief contribution to purifying influences that soften and solace the human spirit. He said that they possessed the quality of endurance. He strongly urged that the rising Afro-American carry them along on his upward climb as an indispensable item of baggage.

More than half a century later, Francis L. Broderick and August Meier in their *Negro Protest Thought in the Twentieth Century* (1965) offered a comparison of the spiritual's approach to problems with those approaches of later periods.

One of the most intensive treatments of the question appeared in several places in Buell G. Gallagher's doctoral thesis (published by the Columbia University Press in 1938), *American Caste and the Negro College.* Apparently not having read many spirituals or overly impressed by Du Bois's title, Gallagher insists on referring to spirituals as "sorrow songs." This feeling narrows his focus, but does not prevent his raising effective questions.

In his first reference to the songs he recalls that the singing of the slaves was more than whistling to keep up courage when passing the graveyard. "This is a definite psychohygienic technique for keeping a modicum of equanimity and sanity in the face of crushing circumstance." This attitude poured out of undefeated hopes and deep yearnings of spirit into songs "which have been unequaled in American musical development for sheer poignancy and emotional meaning." Here Gallagher makes the usual mistake of attributing to the slave in his songs a look to the hereafter for compensation and solace.

A little later in his book, though, Gallagher gets down to real cases. He asserts that the Negro artist can get wide acclaim from the white caste by interpreting what whites think are "Negroid" materials. Admitting the Negro is making a cultural contribution, Gallagher asks if at the same time his net effect is but a buttressing of the barriers of social distance.

The Negro artist, he continues, sometimes wonders if contributing to the cultural advance is worth the price of caste which he pays. "Are the spirituals worth the sorrow and suffering out of which they were born? And if they are, why should the artist have to pay, rather than the patron?"

White audiences need to know, Gallagher points out, that not only does the Negro sing spirituals well when well trained but that a professor of political science can shed light on world developments regardless of his skin color. In this pronouncement Gallagher strikes at the tendency of whites to have all things "Negroid" apply only to a Negro world. It is good to denounce this tendency. If these songs are valuable at all, they are valuable because their readings of life are universal. Truth, justice, and creative expression are not confined to any race, no matter where the original philosophy about them comes from. As the spiritual poet most generously proved, freedom is indivisible.

In his article "Tradition Challenges the Negro" (1946), B. A. Botkin declares that the will to survive and the will to be free are the heritage of all oppressed people. They take on a special significance and poignancy in the Negro who cries, "Before I'd be a slave, I'd be buried in my grave." Using these truths as a jumping-off point, Botkin shows how the Negro's stubborn and rebellious will to freedom is expressed in his folk songs and folk sayings. He clearly suggests that these characteristics are germane to the time and people for whom he is writing.

He makes one other important suggestion. Only by constantly reexamining and reasserting this tradition, he affirms, can the Negro destroy the myth of Negro inferiority and acquiescence, and challenge the underlying assumption of the uniformity of American life. To one who knows the thousands of spirituals, it was a most appropriate suggestion. Nothing is more characteristic of these songs than the idea that the battle of freedom and integrity and soul must be conducted relentlessly, every moment, until it is firmly won.

In 1951, writing on "Implications of Negro Folk Song," Russell Ames declares, "One cannot recognize American Negroes as great thoughtful artists in jazz and folksong and then continue to tolerate racism." Equal in significance to this truth is his next statement of truth which is, that to say that Negroes are "different" with some inborn superiority in singing and dancing is a form of discrimination. He notes, finally, that hidden protests and disguised meanings were growing less common in Negro life of the early 1950s although oppression was being intensified.

In a very recent article (1969) on "Two Traditions in Afro-American Literature," Gerald W. Haslam quotes Ralph Ellison on the contribution of black folk stuff. Ellison says that it has much to tell of the faith, humor, and adaptability to reality necessary to live in a world which has taken on much of the insecurity and blues-like absurdity known to those who brought it into being. Haslam makes the appropriate current applications.

A negative view of the relevancy of the spirituals is given by Sir Harry Johnston in his *The Negro in the New World* (1910). In Sir Harry's view these were nonsense songs. They might be excusable "in poor, despairing ignorant slaves," but they were "unworthy of a growing-up race of hopeful men and women."

Many members of the present Afro-American community have dismissed the spiritual as a religious cry of slavish people. They feel that the present community needs neither religion nor slavishness. Quite obviously, they have read the songs on the surface. They associate them with some of the people who still sing them, people of a fundamentalist religious cast. They also are not well acquainted with the slaves who produced them, men and women of considerable self-respect and courage.

Many of the people who still sing the spirituals in churches and in other congregations think and feel likewise. For them the songs are precious because of a surface sentimentality, or because they are associated with ancients in their families, or because they are beautiful and touching. Quite often these "lovers" of the spiritual are not well acquainted with the deep underlying meanings of individual songs, and certainly not with the powerful meanings of a number of songs on the same subject, taken together. Through its beguiling ways, the spiritual has discouraged intensive study.

Although it is rare for a folk song, written under a precise set of conditions, to continue to be meaningful to people hundreds of years later, who live under quite different conditions, parallels can be drawn. Many Afro-Americans consider themselves to be still enslaved, by discriminatory customs and practices, by the nonenforcement of laws for equal treatment, by the perpetuation of black ghettos, by the cynical refusal of a rich nation to provide jobs, decent housing, fair education, and equal opportunity to people solely because of black skin. Hardly any Afro-American is satisfied with these conditions. Some are not very vocal, and are willing to work cooperatively with the establishment to try to correct matters. An increasing number are full of disgust and are determined that things shall change immediately.

In these respects the breakdown is similar to that among the slaves. Hardly any slave was satisfied with the system. Many grudgingly cooperated. A very large number determined on change and worked out their own methods of change—flight to the swamp or free land, sabotage, physical resistance, or the destruction of some individual who was a symbol of oppression.

According to the songs, the first topic for discussion in evaluating the validity of the philosophy of the spirituals in the world of today, is the concept of freedom. If you ask today's Afro-Americans to define the freedom they want and must have, you will get a great variety of answers, almost as many as there are people. Most of these answers would have several things in common, but the trend of the times is to be individualistic. Each man includes in his definition of freedom what he personally desires or thinks he needs. Often his desires and estimates of need are not carefully thought out, even from the standpoint of his own best interests. A part of freedom is having the right to make and to advocate mistakes, however costly to the individual and his society.

In the songs of the slave freedom had no such broad individualism. It was more a community than a personal matter. It meant simply not being owned or controlled by someone else or by laws which attempted to make him the property of someone else. It meant the right and the privilege to develop his own talents, to choose and work in his own occupation, to have his own religion, to select his own stars and to aim his life toward them. Perhaps the lessons that he cruelly learned from slavery taught him to subordinate minor details to major considerations.

No doubt the primary reason for limited progress in today's thrust for freedom on the part of the Afro-American is the fact that he has not learned this lesson. He lacks essential unity because each little group insists that its way is the only true way. Even the so-called radical thinkers and activists are widely divided—Carmichael versus Cleaver versus Baldwin versus Rap Brown versus the leaders of the Black Panthers versus the leaders of the Black Muslims. The so-called liberals are even more widely divided. The remaining so-called leaders are still more widely divided. The people who would like to follow a winner turn this way and that and know in advance that the road to progress is blocked. Very few of the self-appointed leaders realize that unity is more important than any individual scheme. This inexorable fact they could learn from the spirituals. If the slaves or their song-makers had been divided on details, their progress to freedom would have been ever so slow, or even nonexistent. They might never, by their heroic moves, have inspired an Abolition movement and a war to set them free, as they did.

No more passionate songs have ever been written to proclaim the concept of freedom. Perhaps the American slave knew more about freedom than anyone who has ever lived. Whether or not this is true, his songs declare freedom as well as or better than it has ever been declared: "No more peck o' corn for me, No more, no more," "And why not every man?" "Tell ol' Pharaoh Let my people go," "If I had my way, . . . I'd tear this building down," "Before I'd be a slave I'd be buried in my grave," "Done 'wid driber's dribin'," "No second class aboard dis train"—for the concept of freedom, where can you find their superiors! Who speaks today for freedom in such glowing terms? Who understands so well the soul of freedom? Who better ties together the dream and the reality!

Next to the concept of freedom in this evaluation is the concept of eternal justice. The concept of justice on a universal plane is somewhat different from the concept at any one point in history and quite different from the application of justice. The slave knew that to keep hammering at the universal theme was the only hope of society. Since local manifestations are always watered down, if there is slippage in the general concept, all hope is lost.

In today's fight the Afro-American very often sacrifices universal justice for local expediencies. Outside Afro-America the attacks on those principles of the Constitution which represent eternal justice are quite ruthless. Since the most earnest and realistic campaigns for uplifting the Afro-American are rooted in the universal principles of the Constitution, any cooperation given to these ruthless forces (which represent greed and the tyranny of the few over the many) is a form of tortuous suicide. The slave's faith in the ultimate triumph of elemental justice was one of his main supports from day to day and as he looked to the future. A little more of that kind of faith would not hurt the present Afro-American.

If Christianity as the slave understood it had not been infused with such a concept of justice, all indications are that the slave would have rejected it outright. What he took mainly from Christianity anyway was its symbolism—a just God, just principles, a son of God who lived and died to see to it that justice would come to all people, including the poor and the untouchable and those who made mistakes and those who had little to offer besides their mere small selves.

By devoting himself to universal principles of justice, the slave automatically renounced such doctrines as racial separatism. Justice is not inherently a matter of race; if race enters the picture, that is a question of application. The slave realized that to some extent each man was a slave. He realized that to a very large extent his masters and other oppressors were more severely enchained than he was. His reference to such characters as Satan and rich man Dives were undoubtedly references to such people. But he did not withhold from them the benefits of eternal justice if they would merely observe the rules. Whoever observed the rules could cash in on the benefits. Whoever did not observe the rules, white men, rich men, even members of his own very precious family, was doomed.

What would the songs, through their basic philosophy, have to say about present-day suggestions for overthrowing the capitalistic system and substituting a socialistic or a communistic system? There is no doubt that the slave was predominantly revolutionary where slavery was concerned. He wanted it destroyed root and branch. But he looked to the world outside slavery as a heaven on earth, a place where he could fulfill himself. With all its faults this world offered him opportunities. Many slaves were able to keep in touch with successful fugitives. They were aware that these ex-slaves were living good lives and growing economically and spiritually. Whether he would have wanted to see this world of opportunity destroyed because of its economic malorganization is doubtful.

Yet if these people, tutored by their slave experiences, were alive today and could see the severe limitation placed upon opportunity exclusively because of race, they might be persuaded to vote for a complete revolution. Once again, the thing that mattered was elemental justice. If elemental justice turned out to be unavailable under the present system, then they would be for a new system. In this, it would be less their personal desires and more their belief in the ultimate triumph of elemental, universal, eternal justice, regardless of the wishes and machinations of little, selfish men.

In his songs the slave came out for full employment. "All God's Chillun Got Wings," he said. This undoubtedly meant that if everybody had wings, he was entitled to fly, or as the song put it, to "shout all over God's heaven."

When he was forced to work, and when he was given something to do that challenged his capabilities, the slave did not seem to be unhappy with the working phase of his life. He was definitely unhappy with the forcing part. But appropriate work was a means of self-fulfillment. He was lazy and shiftless only when he did not have appropriate work, or when it was necessary to protest the whole operation of slavery.

To get appropriate work and to fulfill himself through it were two of the main reasons for his running away. "I don't care where you bury my body, . . . My little soul's gonna shine"; the meaning is quite clear. In whatever geographical area he finds true opportunity, he will grow. This he guarantees.

He showed contempt for those who, having a true function, did not carry it out. Look, for example, at "Shepherd, Shepherd." Being a shepherd was a useful and significant occupation. It offered a career with poetry and soul. Not to perform in such a career was inexcusable.

Shepherd, Shepherd, where'd you lose your sheep? . . .

O the sheep all gone astray—The sheep all gone astray.

Without any question the slave would have been horribly distressed if, as a "free" man, he had to live in a world where unemployment is a regular thing and is caused by capitalistic manipulation or the refusal of employers to train and hire qualified people on the basis of race. He would probably have written some very strong songs on these matters.

Education, if one reads the songs carefully, was one of the great desires and yearnings of the slave. It should be recalled that he was never really uneducated. The people who advertised him as a savage or as one step from a savage were doing so to justify their holding him in bondage. In addition, they were contradicting themselves. If he was so uneducated and so uneducable, how could he have carried the South's business and economy on his broad black back for so many years?

As a matter of fact he knew a great many things to begin with; and he learned things rather quickly, often intricate things. He could be depended upon to carry out his intricate learnings and duties. Most slaves were men and women of character, in the midst of their occupations and society. What more can education do for a man than train him to be a useful citizen?

But the slave was not satisfied with this kind of education. He wanted an education that would be competitive in American society. He desired to learn to read, write, and figure, and to do all the other things that would enable him to grow with the society.

It is only a guess, but today's educational struggles might confuse him a great deal. He might understand that to continue to be competitive in a rapidly changing society, education would have to undergo rapid changes. He probably would not understand the things some people, black and white, are doing, under the guise of making education more fit, to water education down and to make it less useful in our newest world.

He would probably be ashamed of the fact that some of the most famous leaders in Afro-America are decidedly uneducated men and women by almost any standard. If he accepted this condition as a temporary thing, something that one had to put up with to get through a period of change, he would want to hurry back as soon as possible to a world in which educated people did the leading and the planning and in which, as far as possible, educated people did the following, too. In his day the standards for an educated man were quite clear. After the necessary changes, he would want clear standards again. In the mere name of change he would not want to be misled by thoughtless loudmouths and energetic fools.

As has been shown already, the use of the personal pronoun *I* in a large number of spirituals is an artistic device. It is not merely to put the singer into the center of important actions; it is to give him a sense of personal responsibility.

The aspiring slave believed very strongly in personal responsibility. He believed in a community of personally responsible individuals. Christian conversion was meaningful to him on the basis that the individual was deliberately weighing all the consequences and taking up his life and devoting it to a great cause. After he made this decision, he did not step aside and let the cause rule him. He followed his progress every step of the way. He worried about what happened to him; and if the spirituals, as some say, are not Christian but merely wearing a Christian mask, then the point is doubled and redoubled.

The slave's great emphasis upon personal responsibility meant that any campaign for changing the world had to start with him as an individual. Thus, personal transformation is ever-present in these songs. "Marching up the heavenly road, *I'm* bound to fight until I die," he sings. "Death's goin' to lay his cold icy hands on *me*," he sings.

The pronoun *you* carries the same force as that *I*. "Don't you let nobody turn you roun'," the poet sings. You are responsible just as I am. In you, personally, is the germ of transformation, just as it is in me.

In today's world the notion of personal responsibility and the sense of need for personal transformation seem somewhat dim. The idea seems to be that the group is the ethical center, and that what is good for the group is good for each person in it. When a person joins the group, he joins without consulting his own heart or his own interests. He allows the leaders of the group to make up his mind for him.

If the groups now fighting for freedom and justice for the Afro-American in America were composed of dedicated individuals, each with a dedication of his own and each a member of the group because of personal conviction, the fight would be a great deal more vigorous. Nothing is more apparent to a cunning enemy than the lack or thinness of conviction on the part of the individual member of a group. When the enemy determines this lack of thinness, all he needs to do is to buy or cajole or frighten the leaders, and the group is dead.

The integrity of the individual is the foundation for the individual's role in society. In the spiritual, membership in the "band" is based on each person's individual offering. As the spiritual says,

> The more come in with free good will,
> Make the band seem sweeter still.

Perhaps on this point the spiritual poets and today's practitioners are sometimes close together. In the business of helping the less fortunate, the group is generally composed of individuals who each have a great and peculiar desire to be of service.

The reliance upon society to motivate the individual, an idea dear to the heart of the spiritual poet, is, however, probably not strong today. The poet said,

> O walk together children—Don't you get weary, . . .

> O talk together children—Don't you get weary,
> There's a great camp meeting in the Promised Land.

Suppose one looks at this from the standpoint of the present-day relationship between the black masses and the more or less educated black middle class. The latter does not take its strength from the former. It hardly knows the black masses except at secondhand. When it essays to help the masses, it does so on its own inspiration or at the command of its leaders. The promise of the poet that a walking and a talking together will result in a "great camp meeting" is not pursued. If anything is needed among Afro-Americans today, it is a knowledge of the masses by the middle class, and a determination of the middle class to give the masses the assistance and uplift and inspiration they need, the need determined by experience. It is the linking of middle class to masses for one grand, continuous assault.

The question of goals was very important to the poets of the spiritual. The word *heaven* usually referred to ultimate goals; on the basis of all intelligent indications, it very rarely meant the place of rewards after death. It must be remembered that the slaves were predominantly young people, mostly under twenty years of age. If they had the motivation to write the kind of songs they wrote, they must have been deeply concerned about their futures.

Some of them decided quite early that they were not going to put up with slavery and began planning escape. Others were available for an opportunity to escape should one arise. Perhaps the great majority were just hopeful that somehow soon slavery would be abolished, or at least they would be let out of it. Very, very few complacently anticipated a full life of slavery without the possibility of freedom.

It should be remembered also that the white preachers and other religious spokesmen gave them very little hope for much change in heaven. Many of these spokesmen described heaven as built pretty much along the

lines of earth, the whites in command and the blacks existing at their suf-
ferance. Even so, it was better than hell, where raging punishments took
place. The quickest route to hell was through disobedience of the people
God had placed over you. Thus, this tepid heaven was far better than hell,
and it was the best that destiny offered the black man.

The fact that this doctrine was preached on many plantations, inside and
outside of religious services, helps to defeat the interpretation that heaven
in the songs refers to a place of rewards after death. But this is a minor argument. The major argument is that the spiritual community was primarily
concerned with life on this earth, and they made their songs in accordance
with this concern.

On this basis their immediate goal was freedom, and their ultimate goal
was a world where all men were free. This world included their ambitions
in the field of skills and talents and in the field of education. It rested upon
universal justice. It was a heaven on earth.

The Afro-American community is older now, but most of its worthwhile goals are the goals of its young people. Like their slave ancestors they
want a world where people are really free, free to develop themselves, free
to live where things are best, free to get the education they need and want,
free of the domination of capitalist bosses, free of war, free to the individual
soul. They are willing to work for this kind of world. Although undercut
and misled by their leaders, they have demonstrated their chosen goals and
their determination to accomplish them. Also, like their slave ancestors,
they will settle for nothing less.

The methods of change described in the songs are a good point to use for
comparison with the present day. As revolutionaries, the spiritual folk
community was always concerned with overturning the world they lived in
and molding a new world. As shown already, they often began with themselves and their own society. They worked to keep the group together
under pressure; they worked to keep it in good spirits. They sought help
from sources more powerful than they. They tried to correct and win over
the stragglers and the derelicts. They studied and followed good examples
from the past. They kept up-to-date on the world around them, both the
world of nature and the world of industrialism (for example, trains, ships,
mills), and worked to make themselves comfortable in that world. They
were very studious in trying to avoid mistakes, especially those which injured or destroyed the personality. They spent much time building an interest in things human and things spiritual.

Their counterparts today are probably not so energetic, on the whole, as
they were. Today's young people have many things done for them, and
they get in the habit of expecting things to be done for them. The young
slaves had practically nothing done for them, and they got in the habit of
doing for themselves.

But today's young people are a deeply concerned lot. In spite of their seeming selfishness, it seems clear that they care a great deal for improving the condition of the world. They band together in improvement groups. They make sacrifices. They stick their necks out. They are not easily frightened. Perhaps not many of them risk their lives, or would risk their lives, as thousands of young slaves did, for personal freedom. But a great many of them suffer greatly for their beliefs and actions in working for what they have decided is the world's improvement.

Perhaps the greatest drawback to the present young Afro-American is the sluggishness of his elders. Generation gaps are inevitable from natural causes, but the generation gap of today is unnecessarily wide and injurious. Too few of the elders behave as though they believed in change. They often resist changes on the part of their young people merely because the new things are different from the old. They do not take the time or the trouble to examine the real value of the new things in light of the needs and creative drives of the new generation.

The educational system is a case in point. Of course there are fundamentals in education—the ability to read well, to write and speak adequately, to be proficient in basic mathematics and science, to understand society and one's place in it, to understand the arts and their indispensability to the inner growth of man—which can hardly be bypassed for this generation or for any other. Beyond these fundamentals, however, today's world and the evolving world offer many alternatives, any intelligent combination of which constitutes a good education.

The spirituals demonstrate that the slave showed considerable flexibility in meeting problems of change. If today's elders would follow their example, the educators would not be shocked at the demands of young people for a "relevant" education. Even the fundamentals listed above can be taught in a number of ways. As to this part of the superstructure which is placed atop the fundamentals, what is wrong with working out a separate program for each student? Given a certain amount of balance and coordination, each program can be unique and quite effective.

The spiritual's way of putting responsibility on each individual presupposes a unique life for each person, and therefore unique preparation for that life. Some of the suggestions of today's young people are quite wild and would have to be rejected. The main thing today's young people seem to want, however, is a recognition of change. In spite of their persistent use of the word *nonnegotiable*, they are on most occasions quite reasonable.

The final question for the estimation of the validity of the spiritual's meanings in today's world is a very big one: Where does the power lie? In spite of the great emphasis on realism in the spiritual, in spite of the fact that the slave persistently sang of this world, the creator of the songs and the community he wrote for did not believe that the power lay in things material.

The slaves and today's people are quite alike in one particular: Both move from a world where opportunity and genuine living have been denied to a world where they must be granted. When making such a transition, it is easy to put the emphasis upon the immediate things—food, shelter, jobs, necessary training, and other necessary materialisms. In the early stages of the tradition the emphasis belongs on such things. Some of today's leaders, however, seem to be suggesting that material benefits are the whole story; that if the Afro-American gets them and gets future chances at his share of the material wealth of the nation, the whole problem will be solved.

It is at this point that the spiritual begins to earn its name. It may or may not have been a religious song; it was unquestionably a spiritual song. It subordinated material to spiritual values. This does not mean that it eliminated material values. It fought very hard for the material foundations, but for the spiritual, material things were only foundations. Real living was spiritual.

In so many words and in many songs, the singer stated unequivocally that the human being would be unfulfilled or stunted if he did not have a spiritual life. He believed in soul, not just for personal enjoyment, but for personal expansion. In his eyes the individual could live a life of limited spirituality if he chose; but if he did, he was cheating himself out of real living. He was also cheating himself out of real power.

The God, the Lord, the Jesus Christ of the spirituals were symbols who provided basic material necessities, yes; but, most of all, they provided an unlimited horizon and an unlimited area for growth. When these slaves took their lives in their hands and ran away; when they talked about the need for education and a chance to develop their talents; when they did so much as think about freedom and justice, they were planning the biggest possible life. The life of the spirit. The life of the soul.

With them, therefore, the power lay with things spiritual. With many people today it lies with the merely material. Thus the slave who sang the spirituals was a bigger man than most of the members of the folk community of his descendants. He demanded and expected more from life. He was willing to risk more to achieve his demands. He believed more in the masses and in the right of each member of the masses to have, not only material needs, but spiritual expansion.

His whole spiritual platform was expressed in a single stanza of one of his songs:

> You got a right,
> I got a right,
> We all got a right to the tree of life.

And the tree of life was more than a natural tree. It was a symbol of unlimited horizons for men on earth.

PART III / *The Flame*

He's got the whole world in his hands
He's got the big round world in his hands
He's got the wide world in his hands
He's got the whole world in his hands

He's got the wind and the rain in his hands
He's got the moon and the stars in his hands
He's got the wind and the rain in his hands
He's got the whole world in his hands

He's got the gambling man right in his hands
He's got the lying man right in his hands
He's got the crap-shooting man in his hands
He's got the whole world in his hands

He's got the little bitsa baby in his hands
He's got the little bitsa baby in his hands
He's got the little bitsa baby in his hands
He's got the whole world in his hands

He's got you and me brother in his hands
He's got you and me sister in his hands
He's got you and me brother in his hands
He's got the whole world in his hands

Oh he's got everybody in his hands
He's got everybody in his hands
He's got everybody here right in his hands
He's got the whole world in his hands

✿◊

CHAPTER TWENTY-THREE

Some Preliminary Considerations

. .
.

THE forge of the spirituals and the creativity and meanings of the songs are no less wonderful than the way the songs have been received. They have always spoken directly and immediately to the heart of the listener. When they are read or thought about, they have spoken also to the intellect. Written as communication between slaves under great pressure, they have become messages of great incisiveness and power to innumerable groups and individuals.

They have worked like a flame. First, they burn in the heart. Because of their homely and beautiful truths, they bring warmth. Because of their simple and beautiful language, they bring color. They bring incandescent light into the darkness of anxiety and despair. Because of their insights, like a flame they prepare the raw flesh of life for absorption and digestion. Finally, like a flame, they leap from heart to heart and often consume a whole congregation of people with inspiring fire.

We therefore turn to the nature of the spiritual as flame, in the way it has grown and caused reactions over the world and down through the years. Before doing so, it may be worthwhile to recall that Samuel Baud-Bovey has said that folk music cannot survive the changes of the social conditions from which it was born. We shall see that with the Afro-American spiritual, in the sense of the pure and original song created by slaves, this statement is true; in the sense of the same song inspiring adaptations to fit peculiar feelings and uses, it is not. More appropriate, perhaps, is Albert Sidney Beckham's declaration that the vivid emotions and escape mechanisms, the real spirit and sincerity of this spiritual, make its appeal well-nigh universal.

One might recall also other writers who have accounted in various ways for the universal appeal of the Afro-American spiritual. Botkin has said,

"Because poetry, like religion, in the words of Santayana, gives him another world to live in, the hard-pressed Negro takes naturally to song as prayer and to prayer as song. . . . the longing for freedom motivates the spirituals and accounts for their universal appeal." As to popularity, Botkin declares that the final decisions on folk songs are made by the masses. In *They All Played Ragtime*, Rudi Blesh and Harriet Janis have the Negro masses taking the spirituals back from the trained singers like Paul Robeson and Marian Anderson. According to Downes and Siegmeister, the Negro in his songs freed the white man's art from a long period of regimentation and domination by a foreign tradition.

As we approach the evolution of the influence of the spiritual, it is interesting to note that in some respects it is not unique. From a story in the *San Francisco Chronicle* for January 27, 1970, on the death of Max Myerson at age eighty-seven, one learns that as a young man in Russia he and his group in the leather factory sang songs against the czar. This was before the Russian Revolution. Not being free to speak, they sang: "The more we sing, the more we fight for freedom." Myerson always maintained that working and singing went together. When he came to America, he joined certain workers in singing against the sweatshop; "Though the bosses didn't like it, we sang . . . to educate the workers."

The Afro-American spiritual was a folk song produced and sung by a fraction of the several million slaves who inhabited the South in the seventeenth, eighteenth, and nineteenth centuries. Although it was sung with regularity and a wild beauty, it was generally ignored by the whites who heard it. When, in the last quarter of the nineteenth century, it became known to large numbers of people, it achieved a tremendous popularity. It was adopted not only by members of the Afro-American community who were no longer slaves, but by American whites, North and South, and by millions of others.

This broad popularity and this worldwide adoption of a folk song produced by a relatively small group of people can be fully described only by the word *phenomenon*. But its influence did not stop with popularity. It became useful and instructive to many people in many different fields. Its usefulness ranged from entertainment to revelations in anthropology, politics, history, religion, music, and a number of other fields.

Its influence has not diminished to the present. To trace the phenomenon of its influence is almost to tell a separate story from the origin and meanings of the songs. But origin and meaning help to make the influence understandable.

❀◇

CHAPTER TWENTY-FOUR

Earliest Evidences of the Spiritual

. .
.

A NUMBER of music historians and other writers have contributed to the history of the spiritual as a living thing. In the following historical note, there will be a summary of the evidence as given by several of the more important of these writers. Since Dena J. Epstein has told a continuous story in "Slave Music in the United States Before 1860: A Survey of Sources," she will be saved for separate testimony at the end.

The first thing is to turn to a definition in Gilbert Chase's *America's Music*. Chase declares flatly that the Negro spiritual is not an unvarying, musicopoetic entity. Any printed version, he says, is arbitrary and artificially static. The Negro spiritual is a composite and infinitely varied creation, existing only when sung.

Although substantially true, the statement is not as remarkable as it sounds. In the first place, it is true of every folk song, it is a description of what is meant by the oral tradition. When people create songs and pass them along orally, on the basis of memory, this sort of thing is what you have. To collect the songs, either by having them taken down by musicians who hear them or by tape recorders or any other method is to perpetuate variety. Whatever group the collector hears gives its version; the collector can get another version by going to another group in the same folk tradition. He will get substantially the same song, but there will always be some change. Thus are the vagaries of the popular memory and of the popular emphases and values.

In the second place, there is a substantial lowest common denominator upon which many original singers and collectors agree. This is, and must be, the basic song. Most times, in most songs, the changes are very minor. They are signs of the continuous creative urge of the folk writer and composer. They add vitality and luster to the songs. To put a song in a book and nail it down is to have a dead song or a stone song. To have it "fooled with" by more or less inspired creators and adapters is to have it stay alive.

Actually, this liveliness affects very little the study of the songs. The melodies are very little changed; the sentiments and meanings remain about the same. If one singer says, "The blood came a-trickling down" and another, "The blood come a-twinkling down," there is a thrill in the poetic difference, but not a very great change in the meaning. The interpretation is adjusted to these colorful, but small, differences. The remarkable thing is the amazing poetic quality in each of the differing versions.

The ignoring of the songs by Southerners for so many years is a far more serious matter. According to Miles Mark Fisher's very scholarly *Negro Slave Songs in the United States*, the spirituals are traceable to the early eighteenth century and might possibly have existed in the seventeenth century. Neither of these dates is an unreasonable surmise. The conditions which made the spiritual possible were already in place by the late seventeenth century at least.

It was not that the South made no pretense at caring about music. There were many advertisements relating to music, musical performances, and musical instruments in the Southern newspapers. It was just that the Southerner felt it bad policy to give slaves credit for any type of cultural achievement. Once the spiritual was "discovered" by Northerners and Europeans, a good many Southerners joined in with reports of spirituals they had heard. This took place, of course, well after the time when slavery was abolished.

One of the Northern discoverers, Thomas Wentworth Higginson, writing in the late 1860s, said that he personally had heard these songs for years. He had heard them in South Carolina long before the Civil War. Lydia Parrish cites what she calls "unmistakable evidence" that the spirituals antedated the American Revolution. They were already in the Bahamas at the time of the Revolution and had been unquestionably imported from the Southern United States. John Work's researches place the songs in full-blown existence before 1800.

Although "Roll, Jordan, Roll" appeared in sheet music in 1862, the group which collected and produced *Slave Songs of the United States* in 1867—William Francis Allen, Charles Pickard Ware, and Lucy McKim Garrison —were the real saviours of the spiritual. As Dena Epstein has shown in an article devoted to Mrs. Garrison, she was the musician of the group. As early as 1860 she had received from an uncle in Georgetown, Delaware, a copy of a spiritual much admired by the Negroes there. Her mother's family had been associated with the Underground Railroad in Pennsylvania. She went to the South Carolina Sea Islands shortly after they became Union territory in November of 1861.

The publication of the book of songs and of Higginson's article in the middle of 1867 brought forth the spiritual for the world to see. But real public interest in the songs did not arise until the tours of the Fisk Jubilee Singers in the Middle West and the Northeast in the later 1860s.

Dena Epstein's article on "Slave Music in the United States Before 1860" paints in early origins of the spiritual in Afro-Portuguese music of the fifteenth century. She cites lamentation singing by African Negroes captured by the Portuguese in 1444 and brought to Portugal, as described by Gomes Eannes de Azurara in *Cronica Do Descobrimento E Conquista De Guiné* (translated by Sir Arthur Helps in *The Spanish Conquest in America, and Its Relation to the History of Slavery and to the Government of the Colonies*). There is also other evidence of the display of the African propensity for dancing, singing, instrumentalizing, and poetizing, all four inseparably joined. Mrs. Epstein quotes Donnan concerning the songs by Africans on the Middle Passage, melancholy lamentations of exile from the native country. Tracey adds that a Franciscan monk, André Fernandes, gave out the texts of two African songs in 1562.

Mrs. Epstein also sums up an interview with Charity Bower, an ex-slave, born in Pembroke, North Carolina, about 1774. From her childhood she remembered songs both religious and secular. She also remembered quite vividly the fact that just after the Nat Turner rising, slaves found praying or singing were killed by "low whites" before masters or mistresses could get to them.

In 1773, Mrs. Epstein states, some slave songs were reported as being obscene and warlike; others as being plaintive, expressive of the misery of the slaves. In 1778 Dr. Rush said that slave songs were not marks of happiness but "symptoms of *Melancholy Madness*, and therefore . . . certain proofs of their misery." Between 1774 and 1777, slaves are reported as playing on a gourd (a kind of guitar) and through droll music relating "the usage they have received from their Masters or Mistresses in a very satirical stile and manner."

After 1800, religious songs are described by George Tucker in *Letters from Virginia* (1816); Levi Coffin, who tells of spirituals in North Carolina; Peter Neilson (1830), who tells of spirituals emphasizing the downfall of Satan; Caroline Howard Gilman (1834); Charles Colcock Jones (1842); and Ella Storrs Christian (in the 1840s).

❊◇❊◈◇❊◇

CHAPTER TWENTY-FIVE

Development of the Spiritual
as a World Phenomenon

· ·
·

⟪ Development Through Touring Choral Groups

THE BOOK of *Slave Songs* and the article by Higginson in the *Atlantic Monthly* in the middle of 1867 aroused a few hundred music lovers, scholars, and general readers. For the great majority of Americans, even cultured Americans, the Afro-American spiritual was still an unknown quantity. It was not to remain so for very long.

In the ten years following the Civil War a number of church organizations decided to dedicate themselves to the education of the new freedmen. One of these was the American Missionary Association, established by the then Congregational Church. One of its first acts was the founding of Fisk University. Voted into being in 1865, Fisk opened its doors to students, "irrespective of race," in January 1866. Like most such colleges and universities it became immediately engaged in a death struggle for funds.

Although many of its teachers worked for little or nothing, Fisk University was on the verge of bankruptcy and closing by 1870. George L. White, a music teacher, suggested a student concert tour to raise funds and to publicize the school. By his mere suggestion he set Fisk trustees, students, and teachers into an uproar. Most of the opinion was decidedly negative. George White, nevertheless, went on with his preparations. Not ever receiving permission from the trustees, he nevertheless decided to move in the summer of 1871.

On October 6, 1871, George White and his nine black singers, all ex-slaves but one (Miss Minnie Tate), left Nashville by train and traveled up to Cincinnati. At this point they were not called the Fisk Jubilee Singers or Jubilee Singers at all. According to the basic picture, the original group was, seated, left to right: Miss Minnie Tate (contralto), Mr. Greene Evans (bass), Miss Jennie Jackson (soprano), Miss Ella Sheppard (soprano and pianist), Mr. Benjamin Holmes (tenor), Miss Eliza Walker (contralto); standing, left to right: Mr. Isaac P. Dickerson (bass), Miss Maggie Porter (soprano), Mr. Thomas Rutling (tenor). In the following years, the personnel of the singers changed from time to time, and the number rose to eleven at one time. But the original group was nine, five women and four men.

Their original programs did not contain spirituals, although Fisk students sang them in chapel. Only after apparent failure faced the enterprise were two spirituals inserted into the program. When these were enthusiastically received, more and more were introduced. Even as late as November 29, 1871, the program in Mansfield, Ohio, had sacred anthems, an Irish ballad, sentimental songs, temperance songs, patriotic songs, and only two spirituals.

The early weeks of the first tour were very, very hard for the members of the tour. It was difficult even to get the opportunity to sing, and even more difficult to find places to sleep and eat. Occasionally the group lived in the train station. The early concerts were without fee; a collection for the singers was taken at the close. The first appearances were at the Vine Street Congregational Church in Cincinnati, in Columbia, and in Chillicothe, Ohio. The Chillicothe concert, on October 12, 1871, was a benefit for the sufferers of the Great Fire, which had practically burned down Chicago on October 8 and 9.

The group then moved back to Cincinnati; then to Springfield and sang for the Presbyterian Synod (where it picked up $105); on to Yellow Springs and Xenia, where it sang in a Negro Baptist church, the chapel at Wilberforce University, and the Xenia City Hall; and to Charleston, London, Columbus, Worthington, Delaware, Wellington, Cleveland, and Oberlin, all in Ohio. It was in Columbus, while harassed by debts and frost, that George White named the company "The Jubilee Singers" (October 29–30, 1871).

After concerts in several other Ohio cities, the new Jubilee Singers moved through Meadville, Pennsylvania, into New York state. At Jamestown, in upper northwest New York, it announced a concert for the Sabbath day and gave the concert in spite of objections.

On December 5, the Jubilee Singers reached New York City. They gave a concert in Town Hall and finally, on December 18, they sang in the famous Plymouth Church (Congregational) of Henry Ward Beecher in Brooklyn. Not only was the contribution generous and the applause enthusiastic, but this appearance put the Jubilee Singers solidly on the national map. They returned to Plymouth Church several times during their winter tour of New York, New Jersey, and New England. In New York alone, they sang for six weeks.

Concerts now came easily and the money rolled in. At Allyn Hall in

Connecticut, they earned $600. In New Haven they even forced postponement of a lecture by their great Brooklyn benefactor, Henry Ward Beecher. This event somewhat compensated for the papers' calling them "Beecher's Minstrels."

During the week of March 15, 1872, with concerts at Milford, Middletown, Bridgeport, New London, and Norwich, all in Connecticut, they were paid $3,900. In spite of these great successes, when they returned to Jersey City on February 29, they were denied accommodations at the American Hotel.

A few days later they sang at the Y.M.C.A. in Washington, D.C., and were welcomed by the students of Howard University. They were also greeted by President Grant. After this interlude they returned for demand concerts in Connecticut, New York, Massachusetts, and Rhode Island. At Tremont Temple in Boston they received their highest income for a single concert, $1,235. Along the way they were selling many copies of the jubilee songs. They even traveled to upper New England and visited and performed in Maine and New Hampshire, including Dartmouth College.

By the end of April their original mission was completed. They had earned the $20,000 they had set as their goal, clear and above expenses. Leaving New York City on May 2, they headed for Nashville. Along the route they stopped for a last concert in Louisville, Kentucky.

The *Illustrated Christian Weekly* (New York) on Saturday, May 4, 1872, said that they were "likely to sing themselves into history." It noted that many other such bands were probably available, but these had no George L. White. Without tricks or trappings, with utmost sincerity, it said, these singers delivered with native simplicity the "quaint, grotesque, yearning melodies of the old slave-life, and carried them home to the hearts of the people."

In June of 1872, the triumphant singers returned north by invitation to sing at the World's Peace Jubilee in Boston Coliseum. After their performance the great hall rang with cheers, "The Jubilees! The Jubilees forever!"

The Fisk Jubilee Singers had several rivals from the start. In March of 1872, their management was warned that the Hutchinson Family had sung "Room Enough" and "Turn Back Pharaoh's Army" from versions copyrighted by W. A. Pond & Company under the title *Camp Songs of the Florida Freedom*. Fisk had sung both these songs in their own versions. Also George L. White went to more than one New York town in October of 1872 to hear the Canaan Jubilee Singers. He reported to his home people that they did not have very good voices. But when he heard them, they had already earned $43,000.

On April 8, 1873, the Fisk Jubilee Singers reached the continent of Europe, landing at Liverpool. Their first appearance was private. To Willis's Rooms in London, on May 6, the Earl of Shaftesbury invited a large and very distinguished company. From such London journals as the *Times*, the *Daily News*, the *Standard*, the *Daily Telegraph*, the *Guardian*, the *Globe*, the *Graphic*, and *Punch*, these unique singers received a most elaborate press.

The next day they sang before Queen Victoria. The songs the Queen commanded were "Steal Away to Jesus," "Go Down, Moses," and the Lord's Prayer (a chant). After reporting that the Duke and Duchess of Argyll, the Duke and Duchess of Northumberland, and Dean Stanley were also listeners, the *Daily Telegraph* said that "Her Majesty expressed gratification with what she heard."

The *Standard* was unequivocal about the private concert: "It is the best entertainment of the kind that has ever been brought out in London." It stressed the fact that the interest, amusement, and delight of the audience never flagged. It mentioned how terrible it was to think that people like these had been bought and sold. It was shocked that only one pure-blooded African (Miss Jennie Jackson) was in the singing party. Miss Minnie Tate, it said, seemed to hail from the South of France. Misses Lewis and Gordon could pass in any drawing-room as "fair English belles" with but a strain of foreign blood. Later in a long review the *Standard* said:

> There is something inexpressibly touching in their wonderful, sweet, round bell voices, in the way in which they sing, so artless in its art, yet so consummate in its expression, and in the mingling of the pathetic with the unconscious comic in the rude hymns, shot here and there with a genuine golden thread of poetry.

The *Daily Telegraph* was almost as strong. Not one listener, it insisted, "is likely soon to forget." It referred to "frequently moistened" eyes among the audience and to the prospect of "unqualified admiration" as the singers journeyed through the country. To the *Daily News* there was striking contrast in people "unmistakably slave-derived" singing like the best English chorus singers in clear, rich, highly cultivated voices. The fervor, wild melody, and quaint expressions were unlike anything heard before. The *Daily News* reviewer hoped that these "genuine minstrels" would receive every encouragement, as they deserved.

They were entertained and praised by Prime Minister and Mrs. Gladstone. They were exalted for being minstrels with dignity, without "bones," a banjo, or a tambourine, who could keep an audience perpetually entertained. *Punch* said that they caused the hearts of thorough black and English white to vibrate in unison. They won over the Quakers who were supposed to object to singing as part of public worship; the *Christian World* reported that the Quakers were intensely excited. Nobility and commoner mingled at their concerts and vied with one another in making compliments.

In his prepared statement about them, the Earl of Shaftesbury said,

Now, these excellent young people have almost all passed through the ordeal of slavery. Most of them have been sold not once or twice, but thrice, and even oftener. Some of them, too, have been in the dismal swamp, pursued by their masters and by the savage bloodhound, but by God's mercy they escaped, and they come here to show to you what the negro race are capable of if you will give them those benefits and opportunities which you have yourselves enjoyed.

Their first public concert was at the St. James's Theatre on the evening of June 6. After three months in London they invaded and conquered the the rest of the British Isles. Beginning in January 1874, they had concerts (occasionally more than one per place) in the following cities: Dunfermline, Scotland; Manchester, Liverpool, Rochdale, Stockport, Macclesfield, Wakefield, Sheffield, Derby, Wolverhampton, Coventry, Norwich, Ipswich, Cambridge, Nottingham, Leicester, Birmingham, Newport, Swansea, Cardiff, Bristol, Bath, Tunbridge Wells, Brighton, Southampton, and Birmingham again. On April 10, 1874, they sang in the Temperance Hall of Leicester. One concert in Scotland brought in $1700.

In Europe, says W. L. Hubbard, those who did not understand the language were moved to tears by the charm of the music. In Holland they sang in cathedrals because other halls were too small. They won the acclaim of the *Musik-Zeitung* (Berlin), one of the most critical journals of its time, because of their shading, accuracy of declamatic, high artistic talent, finely trained taste, and extraordinary diligence. Franz Abt, the German composer and conductor, said that they could not equal these "freed slaves" in generations if they trained their own peasantry.

After touring Europe several times, the original troupe disbanded in Hamburg in 1878. Another troupe, with several of the original singers, and permission from the university, toured and sang until 1885. Wherever they went, they were happily received. They gave the Afro-American spiritual a lofty fame and respect, from which it has never declined.

These recent ex-slaves with their remarkable songs and voices had received adulation and friendship from the President of the United States, the Queen of England, the King of Prussia (Frederick the Great) and his family, the King of Holland, the Czarevitz and Czarevna of Russia, and a number of other national rulers. Again and again they had delighted and deeply touched hundreds of thousands of people in audiences. Honoring them, dozens of the most famous names of the world had given parties and receptions, as, for example, the breakfast party of the great British statesman, W. E. Gladstone. One of their number (Mabel Lewis) had modeled herself on Jennie Lind and her travels carried her to a meeting with the great singer. One troupe had sung "Praise God from Whom All Blessings Flow" in the room of Martin Luther in the old monastery at Wittenberg. A much later troupe had been praised by the great French composer Ravel.

Their singing had not just established high standards of poetry and art. It had paid for big college buildings and for college operations. It had justified in many hearts and minds the elimination of slavery in the United States and Great Britain and all its territories. It had set up a new movement for the freedom and rehabilitation of Africa. Like the songs they sang, they started a conflagration for freedom which spread around the world.

Returning home in 1875, the original Jubilee Singers attended the commencement at which Jubilee Hall, the first building they had "sung up," was dedicated. Three of the singers remained permanently in Europe as expatriates.

In 1890 the F. J. Loudin Company of the Jubilee Singers sang to an invited group in the Taj Mahal, as reported by the *Gazette* (Delhi). In 1904 the summer's tour of the Fisk Jubilee Singers included Missouri, Kentucky, Mississippi, Alabama, and Georgia, not to mention Fisk Day at the St. Louis World's Fair. In 1925 a letter to the editor of *The New York Times* urged people to attend the coming Town Hall concert; the writer said she had gone from London to Paris to hear them the previous spring. Not only would Americans enjoy them, she said, but New York City must not be behind Europe in appreciation. Dozens of Fisk tours in the United States and other countries have happened since.

As early as 1872, in the midst of the first national tour, books about the singers began to appear. The Reverend Gustavus D. Pike of the American Missionary Association was the original author. H. L. Mencken reported that, in spite of the Reverend Pike's crudeness, his books in various editions had sold 180,000 copies by 1893.

His first book was called simply *Jubilee Songs* and sold for 25¢. In 1873 he brought out *The Jubilee Singers, and Their Campaign for Twenty Thousand Dollars*. Besides a story of the first national tour, it contained sixty-one spirituals. In 1875, he told the first adventures of the singers in England in *The Singing Campaign for Ten Thousand Pounds*. It contained seventy-one spirituals. By the 1880s the Reverend J. B. T. Marsh was writing the stories. The 1886 version was copyrighted in the Australasian colonies, including New Zealand and Tasmania, and contained 127 spirituals.

Nor were the stories and song scripts confined to publishers in the United States and England. *Die Geschichte der Jubiläums-Sänger* appeared in Berlin, under the imprint of Rudolf Mosse, in 1877; *De Geschiedenis van de Jubilee-Zangers Met Hunne Liederen* was brought out in Amsterdam by Het Evangelisch Verbond also in 1877. These were two of a considerable number of foreign publications of the Pike-Marsh series. The Fiskiana Collection has several copies of the German edition, bound in velvet and stamped in gold.

In later years, Frederick J. Work of one generation and John Wesley Work of the next picked up and creditably performed the jobs of directing singers at Fisk, collecting, arranging, and publishing spirituals. John W.

Work's *American Negro Songs* (1940) is an extremely useful volume of song words, melodies, and notes. In 1951, Arna Bontemps published *Chariot in the Sky*, a fictionized story of the Jubilee Singers, especially one from Charleston, South Carolina.

The same sort of thing happened at Hampton Institute in Virginia. On February 2, 1872, the *Southern Workman*, published at Hampton, referred to the warming and quickening religious influence of the Fisk Jubilee Singers in New York, Brooklyn, and vicinity. In February of 1873, a group of sixteen Hampton students were organized as singers, to travel and sing spirituals and help raise $75,000 needed for a chapel, dining room, girls' dormitory, all under the same roof. Their collection of songs was quite large and had grown from the old associations and vivid recollections of the singers. Three of their songs were, "I'm Weary; Good-night, Good-night," "Hammering," and "Then My Little Soul Goin' to Shine, Shine."

They first appeared in Washington, D.C. After being entertained at Howard University, they were interviewed by President Grant, who in his turn made them a speech. Their program included "The Milk-White Horses," "In Search of Liberty," "Ef You Want to See Jesus, Go in de Wilderness," and "The Soldier's Farewell." They used no instrument. They were greeted with many rounds of applause.

After two more concerts in Washington, the Hampton Singers moved to Philadelphia. The *Philadelphia Bulletin* of February 22, 1873, was full of praise. Among other things, it said,

> The weird, the wild, the grotesque, the pathetic, the religious, and the comic elements in the African nature seem to be all represented in the songs they sing. No language can portray the effect of such songs as "Dust and Ashes," "Swing Low, Sweet Chariot." If Meyerbeer ever heard these songs, he could have introduced them into his operas with a stranger and more striking effect than any chorus in his *Africaine* can produce.

During three concerts in New York, the Hampton Singers received high praise. The *New York Weekly Review* (a journal devoted to literature and music) devoted several columns to them, over two numbers. In sum it said, "It has remained for the obscure and uncultured Negro race in this country to prove that there is an original style of music peculiar to America."

The Hampton Singers continued through Connecticut, New Jersey, and Massachusetts. Before very long, they had earned enough money to build Virginia Hall. Thomas Fenner, their music teacher, and others agreed that they had built the reputation of the school by singing and good deportment.

In the winter of 1874 the Hampton Singers were again on tour, this time in New York, Pennsylvania, and New Jersey. As with the Fisk group, they inspired books, the first of which was *Hampton and Its Students* by Mrs. M. F. Armstrong and Helen W. Ludlow, containing a complement of slave songs by T. P. Fenner.

Letters from the Singers appeared periodically in the *Southern Work-man*. One, dated June 8, 1874, from London, Ontario, spoke of their being refused accommodations at St. Catherine's, seven miles from Niagara; also of their being refused at two first-class hotels in Toronto and having to go to a low-class, filthy hotel.

But another described a visit to Cambridge, Massachusetts, to the home of Professor Henry Wadsworth Longfellow (where the group sang two songs) and to the grave of Senator Charles Sumner. The singer had words of gratitude for Sumner's courage and persistence in the Negro cause. He wrote, "Our hearts thrilled with enthusiasm while we stood silently around the grave of this noble defender of justice—this Union Star of America." Sumner's last words, "Don't let the Civil Rights Bill fail," were remembered. At his grave the Hampton Singers sang "O Dust and Ashes" and "My Lord, What a Morning."

The *Southern Workman* of March 3, 1875, reported that the Hampton Singers were now commencing a campaign to raise $25,000 for a boys' dormitory. They expected to do so in New York state, California, Utah, Colorado, etcetera.

All but one of the Hampton Singers were of Southern birth, Carrie Thomas was from Philadelphia. Sopranos included Alice Ferribee and Rachel Elliott of Portsmouth, Virginia; Lucy Leary and Mary Norwood of Wilmington, North Carolina (Lucy Leary's father had fallen at Harper's Ferry in John Brown's raid). Altos were Maria Mallette, cousin of Lucy Leary and also from Wilmington, and Sallie Davis, of Norfolk, Virginia. Tenors were Joseph Mebane, of North Carolina; Hutchins Inge and Whit Williams, of Danville, Virginia; James C. Dungey, of King William County, Virginia; W. G. Catus, of Winston, North Carolina, and J. B. Towe of Blackwater, Virginia (shout leader and improvisator, "Dat Great Gittin' Up Mornin'" was his specialty). Basses were James H. Bailey, of Danville, Robert H. Hamilton (set free by the Union Army), James M. Waddy, of Richmond, Virginia, and John Holt, of New Bern, North Carolina.

Unlike the Fisk group, which gradually gave up their education, the Hampton students took books with them and later passed examinations. They kept their own accounts and wrote journals. They sang at Buxton, Canada, founded in 1849 as a homestead for slaves purchased in Louisiana by the Reverend William King, and set free by him. They also sang freedom songs at Plymouth Rock. When waitresses refused to serve them at Troy, New York, lady guests volunteered as substitutes.

The paths of the Hampton and Fisk singers crossed at Steinway Hall, Brooklyn, on March 27, 1873.

In February of 1874 the Hampton programs included the following spirituals: "Ef You Want to See Jesus, Go in de Wilderness," "Oh, de Ol' Sheep Dun Know de Road," "My Lord, What a Morning," "Jerusalem Morning," "The Great Camp Meeting," "Plenty a Room," "Peter, Go Ring

Dem Bells," "My Bretherin, Don't Get Weary," "Keep Me From Sinking Down," "I Hope My Mother Will Be There," "Gideon's Band," or, "Milk-White Horses," "Danville Chariot," "Humble Yerself, de Bell Dun Rung," "Ain't That Hard," "Bright Sparkles in de Churchyard," and "Zion Weep A-Low." Each program also included some Stephen Foster song or other general favorite, such as "Old Folks at Home," and "Massa's in de Cold, Cold Ground."

Admission prices to the concerts were 35¢ and 50¢. In some places a ticket admitting three persons was $1. A children's ticket was 25¢.

Also, as at Fisk, the spirit of the spirituals was maintained over many years with the entire student body singing together several times a week. Numerous Hampton visitors reported the effects of hearing these students in newspapers, national magazines, and books on various subjects. One of them, writing for the New York Sun of September 8, 1903, said that the Hampton students provided the best choral music in America; they had volume, flexibility, noble harmony, and perfect balance of male and female voices. He said that they were vastly better than touring groups, more massive, less conscious, less professional. Their singing, born of genuine musical emotion, thrilled the hearer, and brought tears. Their voices rolled up in perfect diapason, with perfect moderation.

Also like the Fisk groups, the Hampton singers continued to travel every year. In succession they were directed by two of the leading composer-conductors of spiritual history—R. Nathaniel Dett and Clarence Cameron White.

Although Hampton's singers lacked the international reputation of those from Fisk, they did have several memorable international tours. One of these was in the spring of 1930. Dr. Dett took twenty-seven women and twenty-five men singers on a European tour, covering England, Holland, Belgium, France, Germany, Switzerland, and Austria.

In London, they sang on Tower Hill (Tower of London), at Westminster Abbey, and for Prime Minister Ramsay MacDonald. The Prime Minister requested (and got) "Were You There When They Crucified My Lord?" He commented that this spiritual had the title of Mark Symon's modern conception of Christ crucified which was then a part of a Royal Academy exhibition. The group sang several other spirituals at the request of Mr. MacDonald's daughter, Ishbel.

From faraway South Africa, the Sunday Times (Johannesburg) of June 4, 1930, had a comment to make on the Hampton Singers' appearance at Westminster Abbey. It was made under the title, "London's Negro 'Fluff.'" It began, "One gets rather nauseated with the manner in which London loses its heart to anything black." For evidence was listed the "lying, sentimental Uncle Tom's Cabin by black theatrical companies, Paul Robeson, and now Dett with a band of blacks at Westminster Abbey." The writer then quoted from a news story, "It will be a unique occasion in the history of the Abbey when the soft negro voices float through the nave in the plaintive protest of the spirituals." The South African writer then ended, "Protest . . . against what?"

Later in the 1930s the Hampton Choir appeared on network radio. It inaugurated a series of half-hour programs over NBC, Red Network, in 1935. Clarence Cameron White, director of the choir, was informed that fifty million listeners heard the choir do its spirituals on the Byrd broadcast, Sunday night, November 18, 1932.

Looking back over the music world before and after the first appearance of the Fisk and Hampton singers, some striking results are evident. The first of these has to do with the minstrel tradition in America. The white man with the cork face, the black distortion in character, and the phony black songs had made a powerful impression upon the stages and horizons of both America and England. Not many of his very large audience believed that he was not depicting a true and honest Negro. Because he was a generally efficient and skilled entertainer, he cut a deep groove of credibility. The black man in America has spent more than a hundred years, already, overcoming the terribly false impression he left, and he has not yet completely succeeded.

When George L. White unveiled his honest black singers to the world, almost everybody, even the good-hearted church whites, thought of them as minstrels. When the *Cincinnati Commercial* of Monday, October 9, 1871, reviewed one of their earliest programs, the review headline read: "Negro Minstrelsy in Church—Novel Religious Exercises." Note that it was the religious exercises which had changed, and not the minstrel tradition.

As the reviewer got down to cases, he called the Fisk singers something of a sensation "in a band of genuine negro minstrels." The minstrels, he continued, were of both sexes, of ages from ten to twenty-five, and of several shades, from quadroon to pure black. The standard of value was clearly that of the regular minstrel who was always a white man painted jet black.

One of the reviewer's fellows, he said, left at once with the remark, "No bones, no end man, no middle man." If the disgusted devotee of burnt cork had remained, he went on, he would have heard "some very fine music—at times funny, but deep and rich."

When the *Cincinnati Daily Gazette*, the *Commercial*'s chief rival, published its review, it called attention to the *Commercial*'s previous announcement: "A band of negro minstrels will sing in the Vine Street Congregational Church this morning. They are genuine negroes, and call themselves Colored Christian Singers." It was also delighted to add that this kind of reporting was characteristic of the anti-Christian paper and of the man who conducted it. In the same issue with its review the *Commercial*, underscoring the variety that was asserting itself in religious exercises in the city, referred to a man who called himself a missionary and who was going to lecture, in a Chinese costume, at the Christian Church on Sixth Street.

When the Fisk Jubilee Singers sang for Henry Ward Beecher and his elegant parishioners in Plymouth Church, Brooklyn, New York, just after Christmas in 1871, the minstrel atmosphere pervaded the reviews. The nicest approach was that of the *New York Tribune*, Greeley's liberal paper. The *Tribune* said that long enough had there been coarse caricatures in corked faces; it also said that the Fisk singers were a relief from the labored fun and dubious sentiment of professional Negro minstrels.

The *World* and the *Herald* were far more brusque. The *World* complained that only four of the nineteen selections on the program were camp meeting songs [this was a misstatement of fact], and that poor work was made of the other fifteen selections. Calling the singers an "amateur troupe of negro minstrels," the *World* reviewer commented also on the fact that Brother Beecher's church had no aversion whatever to laughter, stamping, clapping, and other theatrical modes and forms. "They sometimes touch up in this way the brother himself."

The *World* ended on this note:

> Probably the management know their own interest best; but it seems better that the troupe should sing camp-meeting and nigger melodies proper than venture on opera. Your colored individual is not good at Ernani but when it comes to something about the golden streets or "de heaven gate" is all at home. It was noticeable in the singers that they had the air of well-trained monkeys when put upon scientific, but as the programme touched a wild darky air, [they] limbered out instantly and sung with mellowness and life.

But the *New York Herald* put a cap on the climax. Its headline read, "Beecher's Negro Minstrels." Its subtitle went like this, "The Great Plymouth Preacher as an 'End Man'—a Full Troupe of Real Live Darkies in the Tabernacle of the Lord—Rollicking Choruses, but no Sand Shaking or Jig Dancing."

The review opened by noting that this was Beecher's first time as a manager of Negro minstrels, or as "end man." Ladies in the audience were dressed as if at a matinee at Hooley's or listening to a tambourine solo at Bryant's Minstrels. As the curtain rose, nine black darkies were seen sitting close to each other in parallel line and sitting in awkward fashion. The biggest girl, Miss Jennie Jackson, was dressed in a cheerful blending of colors which lent "irridescent (*sic*) charm to her features, which were as black as stovepipe." Despite her hideous brown dress, Miss Maggie Porter had a really exquisite voice, "fresh as a lark and tuneful as the harps of Zion. . . . If some of our crack minstrels desire to hear singing that will take them down a peg, let them go and hear Miss Maggie Porter."

Much of the rest of the review was the report of a dialogue conducted by such listeners as "BLONDE GIRL WITH THE DIMPLE," "BRUNETTE WITH WICKED EYES," and "NUISANCE OF A BIG BROTHER." The dialogue included such comments as these:

Do you like to hear colored people sing when they are so badly dressed?

I suppose the reason Beecher is so successful is because he allows everybody to make a joke of religion; and men and women are like monkeys—all they want is a leader, and they are willing to walk in the broad way of destruction. Now this is a precious humbug, to see all of these people come here and patronize these poor niggers, who ought to be home in their beds. People of a superior race—or who fancy they belong to a superior race—like to patronize those whom they fancy to be of an inferior or docile race.

The review ended with a warning to Hooley's (minstrel theater) that Beecher was an established rival; and that Beecher's congregation was now supplied with "all the necessary attractions and amusements that can make life endurable and cheerful."

The Fisk Jubilee Singers did not escape overt references to their being minstrels, even in England. A reviewer in the *Daily Mail* (Birmingham) for Friday, April 10, 1874, said, "Their melodies are exceedingly primitive and often characterized by the merry 'nigger' refrains of ordinary Christy minstrels." A Liverpool reviewer commented that even when the singers were performing a very pathetic and solemn piece, "our association of the negro minstrelsy with what is grotesque and comical often made the audience laugh when such a display was not in keeping with the spirit of the song."

In spite of reviews like those in the *World* and the *Herald*, literally hundreds of other reviewers, in America and in Europe, took pains to make the comparison between the Fisk and the Hampton singers on one hand and the minstrel singers on the other, to the very great discredit of the minstrel singers. After a few years it became apparent that these singers of spirituals were well on the way toward removing the stigma which the minstrel tradition had levied upon all black people. Utter sincerity, beautiful songs, and singing skill on the part of real black people were driving the phonies and their baleful influences from the field.

Most of the reviewers stressed basic characteristics of the music and the singing. Some mentioned the plantation accent of the songs; one English reviewer said that they sang "with all the unction and vigor of the frequenters of American revival meetings"; others noted the fact that there was an intermixture of the serious and the humorous. Many referred to the genuineness, the earnestness, and the fervency both of songs and singing. One Englishman said that the earnestness and expressiveness were sometimes so remarkable as to produce a great effect on the audience. An American said, it was "genuine soul music of the slave cabin, before the Lord led his children 'out of the land of Egypt, out of the house of bondage.'" One, from Portland, Maine, said that all songs received the heartiest applause except that grotesque song, "Didn't the Lord Deliver Daniel." To one, the opening song, "Children, You'll Be Called to Die in the Field of Battle," was a deeply pathetic incentive to Christian exertion. To him, also, the masterpiece of the evening was "Go Down, Moses," both because of its sad, earnest, and pathetic beginning and its great swell to rapturous grandeur after the deliverance of the Israelites. He found "Mourn, Jerusalem Women" the only crude and incoherent song. Another remarked the voices of rare sweetness with a sympathetic tone peculiar to the singers' race. Still another declared the unaffected simple fervor remarkable and touching. A Boston reviewer, as well as one in Edinburgh, called the style of the program original and effective. The *Courant* (Edinburgh, Scotland) praised the singers for general intelligence and refinement in their singing, and for "a strong expression of triumph" and enthusiasm in songs relating to freedom.

The *Express and Eastern Counties Weekly News* (Cambridge, England) said that, despite a few persons whose expectations were not realized, the vast majority of the listeners considered the singing "an event by itself in a lifetime. . . . It will be like a sunbeam in his life for many a day." The reviewer spoke of the spell the singers threw upon the audience. "I am persuaded," he said, "that its secret lies among the deep springs of the heart of man, which are too seldom touched."

From William C. Chambers, of the *Chambers's Journal of Popular Literature, Science, and Art*, of Edinburgh, Scotland, came some very interesting reactions. He said that the singing of the slaves could be compared to the notes of a bird in captivity—to be admired, but pitied. He said, further, that the slaves had sought solace in the outpouring of their song. If the Negro was not intellectually brilliant, he was entirely vivacious.

A good many of the reviewers had things to say about the singing troupes themselves. One from Cincinnati said that the singers compared favorably with the best class of colored citizens in his city. Another reviewer said that, sitting on the stage, their countenances were sad as if they hardly realized they were no longer bondmen. Mr. Chambers had a somewhat long description of the twenty-four singers he had met. Except for a few mulattoes, he said, they were all of the pure Negro type. They had not been badly affected by great success. None of them used tobacco or alcohol. Considering their temptations and the deprivations of their early lives, there was not a little to admire in their conduct and accomplishments, their energy and modesty.

As many reviewers had done, Chambers also commented on the way they had been treated. He recalled the caste prejudices with which they had been visited. Railroad employees had treated them with indignity; in certain places, they had had to wait on themselves and blacken their own boots; they had been refused accommodations by one steamship line after another.

Reports on the results of the singing were revelatory. In Boston one apparent result was the advertisement of the Chelsea Choral Society in the newspapers for tenor and bass singers to complete its "Jubilee Chorus." Farther south, the McAdoo Jubilee Singers were organized; they were soon singing in Great Britain, South Africa, and Australia. Fisk was advertising to the world its training of teachers and of missionaries to Africa. The Hampton group, seeking endowment funds for the school, was praised for being a "brave little band of singers" doing what the world had been waiting for Negroes to do—help themselves. Robert R. Moton, Booker T. Washington's successor, said that Hampton, Fisk, and Tuskegee had nurtured Negro folk music and were encouraging the Negro in the appreciation of his own traditions.

In quite a few respects these singers were called unique or unusual. A Cincinnati reviewer said that they were the first Negro troupe to sing in Cincinnati's Mozart Hall. The same reviewer declared that by any standards Minnie Tate was unusual. Chambers said that the enterprise of the Fisk Jubilee Singers had no parallel and that the unselfish and noble endeavors of these humble melodists stood out as something to applaud and to redeem human nature. Of the Hampton Singers, the *New York Weekly Review* said, "At last the American school of music has been discovered." Also of Hampton, the *Haverhill* (Connecticut) *Bulletin* remarked, "One of the finest concerts to which it was ever our good fortune to listen."

Summing up the case for the Fisk Jubilee Singers and for black singers in general, W. L. Hubbard, editor of the *History of American Music*, resorts to high superlatives. The career of the Jubilee Singers, he declares, is unique in the music annals of the world. "That these uncultured singers could bring all Europe to their feet by the inherent beauty of their song and by their characteristic rendition of the same, demands for the negro a distinct place in the musical world."

The nature and reaction of audiences were of very great significance. On innumerable occasions, applause was said to be enthusiastic or rapturous. The fact that so many influential people were listeners and that audiences were most deeply affected had much to do with the establishment of the spiritual as a worldwide phenomenon. One New York reviewer said that in his audience he saw gray-haired men weep like children. The high appreciation of kings, queens, emperors, princes and princesses, dukes and duchesses, earls, prime ministers, presidents, governors, and others of like rank caused many middle-class folk and lower-class people to search out these singers, partly for curiosity. When the Right Honorable William E. Gladstone, for example, said, "Isn't it wonderful? I never heard anything like it," he undoubtedly contributed to future audiences. It was worth noting that one-third of the audience to an early Cincinnati concert was colored. George White said that although the audiences in the South were chiefly colored, a good many whites attended, including former slaveholders.

To sum it all up, the 1870s were a period of musical revolution in a large segment of the Western world. That revolution was caused by the dissemination and absorption of the Afro-American spiritual.

While student singers from Fisk and Hampton were popularizing the spirituals and winning attention for their schools as educational institutions, students at Howard University in December of 1909 were rebelling against being asked to sing spirituals. Early indications of the rebellion were seen in an editorial in the student newspaper, *Howard University Journal*, for December 17, 1909, signed by B. H. Locke, a sophomore. After reviewing the visit by Coleridge-Taylor to Howard a few years before, he descended to the fact that as a rule slave folk songs were crudely sung. Since they are painful reminiscences of the sad days of slavery, we can well afford to forget them, he went on. He noted that Andrew Carnegie on a visit more recent than Coleridge-Taylor's was more moved by an anthem sung in Latin by Howard students than by anything else. Howard, he was forced to conclude, was sufficiently northern to take on northern ideals of culture. Since our sister institutions had succeeded so well with these songs, "wouldn't it be a wise plan to have one negro college paying especial attention to the study of the great masters?"

Two days later, a very big storm broke. A front page story in the *Washington Post* for Sunday, December 19, was headed "Balk at Folk-Songs: Howard University Students Threaten to Revolt." The *Post* described an uprising which had gained strength over the alleged forced singing of "religious rags" or plantation melodies. President Thirkield (a white man) was accused of having general students, teachers, the choir, and the glee club do these songs to amuse his visiting friends. A *Post* story the next day said that in a meeting a large percentage of the students had repledged support to the President, but there were pockets of strong and bitter resistance.

The event was taken up by the *Sun* (New York) in an editorial on December 21 entitled "A Just Rebellion." The editorial was emphatic that the rebellion had proper cause since the songs were not composed by the ancestors of the black students but by "maudlin Northern whites" to touch the sympathies of Northern audiences. The Negro, the editor informed his readers, has no folk songs. And so these "trivial melodies" which did not speak for them should not be "imposed upon them by pedagogues."

This editorial was answered three days later in a letter to the *Sun* by Professor Kelly Miller of the Howard faculty. Mentioning the ingeniousness of the *Sun*'s theory on the origin of the plantation melodies, Professor Miller declared that there was no spirit of rebellion at the university, only one of good will. He was sure that the students would continue, as they had in the past, to follow their own preference and taste in any matter relating to plantation melodies.

As the university developed, the singing of spirituals assumed respectability and power. Under the conductorship of Warner Lawson, trained at Fisk and an arranger of spirituals, the Howard Choir won a considerable reputation in the spiritual field. Besides making tours, it cut albums of spirituals. On June 17, 1960, it left New York for a Latin American Tour, planned by the National Theatre and Academy and sponsored by the State Department's People-to-People Program. Before returning eighty days later, it had given 91 performances in fifteen countries plus Jamaica, Trinidad, and Martinique. It had covered 27,000 miles and had sung before 222,000 people, not counting hundreds of thousands on six televised concerts. It received excellent reviews in such cities as Mexico City, Quito, Caracas, La Paz, Bogota, Lima, and Santiago. In Santiago it gave four live concerts, one before 7,000 listeners at Vina del Mar's Casino Municipal. *El Universal* of Mexico City called the tour one of the greatest musical events of the last decade.

And so did the Howard University Choir inspire hundreds of thousands of music-lovers south of the border to new admiration and respect for spirituals and other songs.

We have already mentioned one book which stemmed from the Hampton expedition. Another was prepared by the first director of the Hampton Singers, Thomas P. Fenner, who published *Cabin and Plantation Songs* in 1878. To some extent this book was based upon the fifty cabin and plantation songs published in Armstrong and Ludlow, *Hampton and Its Students* in 1874. After several revisions, a new series was instituted in 1909, *Religious Folk Songs of the Negro as Sung on the Plantations*. When Dett became director, he published *Religious Folk-Songs of the Negro as Sung at Hampton Institute* (1927). Later, in 1936, Dett developed his own series, *The Dett Collection of Negro Spirituals*, in four groups. Dett's published spirituals, however, extended far beyond this series.

Besides Fenner and Dett, Hampton had another bright star in the spiritual firmament—Natalie Curtis Burlin. Before coming to Hampton, she had distinguished herself in the field of Indian folklore. At Hampton she not only collected and published spirituals; she also wrote incessantly and extremely well about the meanings of the songs and their backgrounds. Her study of backgrounds included African songs, as is proved by her *Songs and Tales of the Dark Continent* (1920).

Another student choir which has given the Afro-American spiritual popularity and distinction for a number of years is the one at Tuskegee Institute in Alabama. Although favored by good and sometimes great singers, its rise to fame was occasioned by the greatness of its founder and director for twenty-five years, William L. Dawson.

If you talk with Dawson, the first thing he will tell you is that the songs in question are not spirituals; they need another name for they carry, not narrowly religious overtones, but the universal implications of human life. He should know. His directorial genius propelled his choir into a very strong national spotlight. And his *Negro Folk Symphony*, based primarily on themes in the spiritual, was given its world premiere on November 14, 1934, by the Philadelphia Symphony Orchestra, at the Academy of Music with Leopold Stokowski conducting.

In 1931 the Tuskegee Choir was born just after Dawson was made head of the new School of Music at Tuskegee. A year later, Roxy (S. L. Rothafel) was traveling over the country searching for attractions with which to open his Radio City Music Hall. After he heard the Tuskegee Choir, he signed them up for this memorable occasion.

Seven thousand people heard and saw the first program at Radio City on December 27, 1932. Along with the Tuskegee Choir of 110 voices were Titta Ruffo, Coe Glade, Ray Bolger, Weber and Fields, DeWolf Hopper, Martha Graham and group, Patricia Bowman, the Berry Brothers, and a ballet corps of eighty dancers. The original program lasted for four weeks.

Following this star performance, Dawson took his Tuskegee Choir to the birthday party of President-elect Franklin D. Roosevelt, at the invitation of his mother, Mrs. Sara Delano Roosevelt; to a concert in Carnegie Hall, New York City; and to the White House at the invitation of President Herbert Hoover.

In 1933, the chancel windows of the Tuskegee Chapel, in commemoration of the spirituals, were completed, each eighteen feet high. The panels reproduced words from eleven spirituals: "We Are Climbin' Jacob's Ladder," "Roll, Jordan, Roll," "Joshua Fit de Battle of Jericho," "Oh, Sing All the Way, oh Lord," "Shout All Over God's Heaven," "Rise Up Shepherds and Follow," "Steal Away," "My Lord, What a Mournin'," "Go Down, Moses," "Deep River," and "Swing Low, Sweet Chariot." Through an unspeakable misfortune a few years ago, fire destroyed the chapel and its historic windows. The windows, their colors, and their songs have, however, been restored.

Although the tour of the British Isles, Continental Europe, and the Soviet Union, announced by Roxy as manager, did not materialize, the Tuskegee Choir was in demand throughout the United States for years. In 1936, Stirling Bowen of the *Wall Street Journal* called it "The World's Finest." It was especially popular in the South and with predominantly white audiences. During the 1937–38 season it did a series of half-hour broadcasts each Sunday afternoon over the National Broadcasting Company network. In 1945 it did a series for the Columbia Broadcasting System. In 1946 it did a special for the American Broadcasting System. It also did recordings for the Westminster Record Company.

Under the direction of C. Edouard Wright, the Tuskegee Choir of today is still a choir of distinction. Although built along classical lines, it has no hesitancy in incorporating effective modern elements of Afro-American music.

To understand the peculiar use and power of spiritual singing at the Piney Woods Country Life School in Piney Woods, Mississippi, one must know something of the origin and development of the school. The school is set in a particularly slow-moving section of the state, twenty-one miles south of Jackson. It was founded in 1909 by Dr. Laurence C. Jones, and he has been its only president. Coming from Iowa and eschewing other opportunities for personal success, President Jones decided six decades ago to dedicate his life to the education of his people in a section where education was really meaningful. His main principle of education is to develop both the brain and the hand. Every student must learn one or more useful manual trades while pushing forward his intellectual development. No student is allowed to pay his way out of the manual requirements. No student is ever turned away for lack of funds; often students present themselves with no money at all and no other material resources; they are fully received into the school.

The singing started almost at once within the school. President Jones and his faculty felt that this music was a means of providing the students with artistic expansion and giving them pride both in their personal accomplishments and in their honorable heritage. He feels that only Negroes can give the true interpretation to the songs, because only they have in their blood the feeling for the origins, trials, and tribulations out of which the songs grew.

In about a dozen years, the spiritual singing burst out of the school and into the world beyond. Piney Woods organized the Cotton Blossom Singers. The first group was composed of five singers—three women and two men—and a director, who traveled in an old-fashioned touring car. They toured the Middle West and brought back donations from churches, civic groups, and individuals. Avoiding the problem of hotels, which had plagued the Fisk and Hampton Singers, they slept in their car. The Cotton Blossom Singers of this time did not charge an admission fee; they depended entirely on free-will offerings. Even so, at Marshalltown, Iowa, for example, where Dr. Jones had grown up, the Rotary Club sponsored a concert and cleared $1,000 for the school.

When asked why the Cotton Blossom Singers were organized, Dr. Jones answers that raising money was important but not the main reason. The main reason was to create friends. Another reason was to advertise the school.

After this, the Cotton Blossom Singers grew to an organization with many forms and functions. Groups of five, six, or seven singers, traveling with a director and sometimes with the president, toured the entire country. They sang spirituals (and sometimes other songs) in lowly churches, in small and large auditoriums, in the open air, and for private gatherings. They sang for mayors and governors, for President Franklin D. Roosevelt at Warm Springs, for the Wrigley family in Southern California. They sang again and again at folk festivals in Washington, D.C., St. Louis, Missouri, and elsewhere.

Sometimes the group was only boys, sometimes only girls, sometimes mixed. Several groups were composed exclusively of blind students. Sometimes a girls' group would wear only cotton dresses.

The big touring car was replaced by what Dr. Jones called "house cars." In inventing this model, with all the comforts of home, Dr. Jones antedated the modern trailer and should probably have applied for a patent. Many people, after a concert, would come up to congratulate the singers and to make a thorough inspection of the singers' combination traveling and living quarters.

The Cotton Blossom Singers gave a beginning to some very unusual performers. George Hall left their ranks to sing with the Eva Jessye Choir and DePaur, and later to perform on Broadway. Henry L. Spencer and Thomas J. Pruitt became nationally known. A recent graduate, Angela Bethea, whom this writer has heard, has a most promising voice.

Spirituals are still sung each Sunday night by assembled students and teachers at Piney Woods. In addition to all other effects they bring a unity to the school. They are sung with warmth and excitement, a sense of proud black heritage, and a deep touch of originality.

Since the original successes of Fisk and Hampton, dozens of predominantly Negro colleges and academies and at least some predominantly white ones have had spiritual choirs or choirs which on occasion sang spirituals. In 1937, for example, a Wellesley Verse Speaking Choir did a number called "The Black Man," composed of "God's A-Gwine ter Move All de Troubles Away" and "Ride On, Jesus." Many of these groups have toured, keeping the sound of the songs ever fresh and various in the ears of American audiences. A number of colleges have used the spirituals for student congregational singing. In most instances the testimony has been that they produced a spirited and unifying effect.

The Penn Normal, Industrial, and Agricultural School at St. Helena Island, Beaufort County, South Carolina, has had an unusual history in the spirituals. Set in the geographical area from which the first published book of spirituals came, it draws upon a continuity of Negro settlers of more than ten generations. In 1928, it was reported that Penn School pupils sang spirituals every Wednesday at noon. In the praise houses of the neighborhood spirituals were sung three times weekly. Frances R. Grant wrote an article for the *Outlook* entitled "Negro Patriotism and Negro Music." In this article she essayed to show how the old spirituals at Penn School, Hampton, and Tuskegee promoted Americanization.

In the 1920s the Penn School had one other stroke of good fortune. It turned out to be the place where Nicholas George Julius Ballanta Taylor, born in Freetown, Sierra Leone, worked. In understanding and arranging spirituals he was an accredited genius. At Penn School he recorded and transcribed spirituals and sent them to New York to be published. His *Saint Helena Island Spirituals* is one of the finest collections.

At Bennett College in Greensboro, North Carolina, Mary Allen Grissom directed a choir and published a volume of forty-five spirituals, *The Negro Sings a New Heaven* (1930). For selection and arrangements of songs, this volume is outstanding.

Calhoun School in Alabama was another notable center for the singing and dispensing of spirituals. At the very beginning of the twentieth century, Emily Hallowell directed music there. She published several volumes of Calhoun plantation songs.

The Utica Jubilee Singers of Utica, Mississippi, were another well-known school group. They were encouraged and assisted by J. Rosamund Johnson. The Morehouse College singers went to the White House in 1933 at the invitation of Mrs. Roosevelt.

In the midst of the successes of Fisk and Hampton, professional non-student groups arose, singing the songs and making a great deal of money. Such groups still abound, sometimes lasting only a few years each, in all parts of the United States. A few of the professionals have won distinction both as accomplished musicians and for the quality and imagination of their interpretations.

The Dixie Spiritual Singers, sponsored by a Richmond, Virginia, radio station, were popular in the early 1930s. Their director was Frederic C. Cheatham. Illustrating their interpretations, he published *Twelve Negro Spirituals* in 1932.

Three professional groups specializing in spirituals blossomed in the 1930s—the Golden Gate Quartette, the Southernaires, and the Wings Over Jordan Choir. Each of them did land office businesses in public concerts, radio, and records. Each of them published books of spirituals reflecting its unique methods of singing. The arranger for the Golden Gate Quartette was Frederick Conrad.

The Southernaires specialized as an NBC radio quartet. They sang regular spirituals, but they also adapted spirituals to special religious purposes. "Prayer of Love," for example, was based on "Swing Low, Sweet Chariot." They sang each Sunday morning and achieved an enormous following.

Worth Kramer was arranger and Glenn T. Settle the originator and leader of Wings Over Jordan. In eleven years they sang in forty-seven states in spite of "White Only" signs. Besides traveling, they sang regularly for the CBS network. Critics called their style "spontaneous, highly emotional, expressive." Esther Overstreet, soprano soloist, cited instances in which they actually overcame prejudices in people. They helped a Baptist church in Shreveport, Louisiana, pay a $1,200 mortgage by singing a benefit spiritual concert. They also transformed a Birmingham businessman from a Negro hater to a donator of three music scholarships for worthy Negro students. In *Thunder an' Lightnin' Britches*, Leroy C. Townsend says that Wings Over Jordan had forty million listeners, of every race, creed, color, and sect, every Sunday morning.

The great success of student and professional groups in popularizing spirituals aroused a number of amateurs to form groups and to try their hands at singing spirituals in public. This in turn created a demand for spirituals arranged for choirs and soloists. The demand was filled by a very large number of choral volumes of spirituals. Two such volumes, as samples, were Hollis Dann's *Fifty-Eight Spirituals for Choral Use* (1924) and Charles L. Cooke's *Robbins Choral Collection*, Negro spirituals for mixed voices (1942).

Many commentators complain about the adulteration or watering down or desecration of spirituals by singing groups. This kind of complaint flies in the face of what is known about the nature of folk song. Every folk song is created at the behest of a given folk community and is kept alive by the community and by people joining with the community. As it passes from one branch of the community to another—for example, as a spiritual passes from Virginia to Mississippi or Texas—it undergoes change dictated by the new branch. It does not become a new song, but the variation gives it a different flavor. This theory of variation is related to H. R. Rookmaaker's view that the most remarkable thing about the Afro-American spiritual is not melodies or words, but method of delivery.

In the unusual circumstances of a folk song lasting for generations and passing into communities far different from those of its origin, the variations sometimes become more marked. But every folk branch, or ally of a folk branch, has the right and the creative privilege to adjust the song to the peculiar conditions of its locale. This is part of the folk process and is a highly desirable thing rather than a bad thing. As Jean Wagner has said, "Whatever the reader or listener gets is part of the song."

The preserving of songs by putting words and music into print or by making records of them is also highly desirable. But one should remember that what is preserved is a particular version from a particular place at a particular time in the song's development, not all the versions, not the whole song in its many ramifications. There are no facilities for preserving the whole song. Even if there were, to insist upon these as the final body of the song would be to kill and bury the song. The folk process is just the reverse of this kind of murder. The song is kept alive by having new people it has inspired present it in their own creative ways.

Thus, there is no such thing as adulterating a spiritual. There is no superstandard to begin with; there are only people creating and singing what is in their hearts, what is on their minds as they survey the living scenes through the eyes and other senses of their art. This incontrovertible fact takes nothing from individual spirituals. The fact that they passed from subgroup to subgroup is a testimony of the unity of slave thinking, feeling, artistic purpose, and method. As new groups interpret them in new ways, they insure that the spiritual will stay alive. If people were forced to sing the songs the way some arbitrary authority decides or not sing them at all, the spiritual would quickly die. And would be better dead.

([*Development Through Churches and Other Community Congregations*

The perpetuation of the spiritual through the Afro-American community during the past hundred years has been a many-sided operation. First, the Afro-American community never stopped singing spirituals as the result of emancipation or manumission, either during the slavery period or since. On a wide scale there has been one continuous flow of spirituals. Second, following the Civil War the singing of the songs took on an extraordinary variety of uses and purposes as the result of changes in the life of the community. Third, non-Afro-American communities adopted the spirituals and have been singing them in their communities or in mixed communities for almost the entire century.

The number of books of spirituals planned, printed, and sold since the 1870s is a good indicator. To the 180 thousand plus copies of Fisk collections sold in the last two decades of the nineteenth century were added many thousands of lesser-known collections. The spurt of popularity reached by the spirituals about 1917 was followed by a steady and rising period of favor in the 1920s, the 1930s, and the 1940s. Hundreds of thousands of spiritual collections were sold. And, since it is a fairly well-known fact that American Negroes were slow about buying books, the great majority of these sales were made to whites.

But this evidence is not to suggest that the Afro-American community was not using the spirituals during these times. They had no need to buy songs which were part of their family, parental, grandparental, and general community inheritance. Until the present generation, singing of spirituals by individuals to themselves and around the home fireside was not an uncommon thing. Books of spirituals for use at home were edited and published by many arrangers, as, for example, Dick and Beth Best, Virginia Thomas, and Florence Hudson Botsford.

In hundreds of Afro-American churches today, what Dorothy Scarborough said in 1925 is still true: "You can break loose with an old spiritual in a meeting and move the church." In Mays and Nicholson, *The Negro's Church* (1933), are several references to the use of spirituals in Negro churches. To write their book, Mays and Nicholson investigated 609 urban churches and 185 rural churches. They reported the spiritual as prominent in Negro services, along with regular hymns. Eighty-five per cent of the 609 urban churches had choirs which often led the congregation in the singing of hymns and spirituals.

In 1945 Drake and Cayton, in their *Black Metropolis* (a study of Negro life in a Northern city), declared that spirituals were seldom used for congregational singing in Bronzeville churches, gospel hymns and traditional Protestant hymns being preferred.

Later in their book they state that the prevailing attitude of Bronzeville's lower-class church people can be summed up by the old Negro spiritual,

"Gimme That Old-Time Religion." The apparent contradiction is understandable because of great variance in the practices of many churches.
There is hardly a church, middle or lower class in the Bronzevilles of the
cities, even today, where spirituals are not sometimes sung. But, except in
a few churches, the spiritual has been replaced as a regular diet. The most
recent editions of hymnals of various Protestant churches include some
spirituals.

A great many white churches have used and still use Afro-American
spirituals, both in their choirs and in congregational singing. When asked
why, they reply that people like them or that spirituals are one of the store-
houses of good and inspiring music. Most of the time, their method of
singing them is quite different from the method in the Afro-American
churches. Quite often they will employ a competent black director to lead
them in the singing of these songs, but the result is only a little bit different.
If a folk song is adopted by any group, however, its being sung is the main
thing. The white church singer invests his imagination and his heart and
produces a result which is satisfactory to him, and often to his audience.
The spiritual stays alive and continues to function along one or more of its
many electrical lines. Only the narrow-minded will complain.

The singing of spirituals over the years has not been unanimously done
or advocated by members of the Afro-American community. As early as
1873 it was frowned on by Bishop Henry McNeal Turner (1833–1915) of
the African Methodist Episcopal Church. Bishop Turner was the compiler
of the *Hymn Book* for the church, commissioned in 1868. His *Hymn Book*
was called a collection of hymns, sacred songs, and chants. In the "Compiler's Remarks," Bishop Turner very frankly said that under the head of
"Revivals," he was using a large number of old "Zion songs." He added:

> This may elicit the disapproval of some of our poetic neologists. But they
> must remember we have a wide spread custom of singing on revival occa-
> sions, especially, what is commonly called SPIRITUAL SONGS, most of which
> are devoid of both sense and reason; and some are absolutely false and vul-
> gar. To remedy this evil, and to obviate the necessity of recurring to these
> wild melodies, even to accommodate the most illiterate, these time honored
> and precious old songs, which have been sung since the time "whereof the
> memory of man runneth not to the contrary," have been as it were resur-
> rected and regiven to the church.

There are in print and in circulation a great many books of spirituals and
spiritual sheet music designed for church use. One of these, Virginia C.
Thomas's *Old Time Spirituals*, has original settings for Hammond or pipe
organ registrations. Others have made efforts to select and present texts and
music which are generally favored by church congregations.

Besides regular church services, spirituals are widely used, and have been
for at least a century, in prayer meetings and young people's meetings, and
for revivals. Madam A. E. Duncan of Americus, Georgia, published a

Handy Songster for Revivals, Churches and Sunday Schools. Under the auspices of the National Sunday School and Baptist Young People's Union Congress of America, E. M. Barnes published *Seven Songs*, containing spirituals. Away back in 1883 Marshall W. Taylor published *A Collection of Revival Hymns and Plantation Melodies*, with music by Josephine Robinson. The use of spirituals for revivals is certainly not unusual. For many years the power of the spiritual in bringing hardened sinners to the mourner's bench and thence to the conversion table, has been fully acknowledged.

Some churches have been especially acclaimed for their spiritual singing. Collectors from the early days of William E. Barton, and down through the periods of John A. Lomax, Dorothy Scarborough, R. Emmet Kennedy, Marion Kerby, and Alan Lomax have mentioned churches in the South that gave forth with the pure spiritual. Phillips Barry in "Negro Folk-Songs from Maine" spoke of songs emanating from Negro prayer meetings in Brownsville, Maine. From such churches songs have been culled and recorded particularly by members of folklore societies. One of the remarkable reports of such a song was made by Martha Emmons for the Texas Folklore Society. The song was "Walk around My Bedside." It was printed in Dobie and Boatright's *Straight Texas* (1937).

Down through the years spirituals have been published at the request and for the special use of schools and colleges. Among these are Dick and Beth Best, *Song Fest*, containing seventeen spirituals. This book was especially used by college outing clubs of the Northeast, members of an intercollegiate association.

One interesting community use of spirituals was the Negro spiritual contest, held several times in Columbus, Georgia. Groups of not more than fifty boys and girls from each playground constituted the participants in the contest. Each group prepared four spirituals, and the winner received a prize. The choruses were named for such famous Afro-Americans as Booker T. Washington, Paul Laurence Dunbar, and Phillis Wheatley. While the judges were voting on the winner, a band of community singers sang for the large audience "Little David" and "Swing Low."

❨ Development Through Musical Artists

A great host of musical artists, concert singers, instrumentalists, composers, collectors, arrangers, conductors, and others, and scholars have devoted much rare talent to turning the spiritual into a phenomenon on a national and international basis. There is not time to discuss them all. There is time, there must be time, to give a few brief notes on the contributions to the development of the spiritual by the most important.

To open the discussion, one can do no better than introduce Mrs. E. Azalia Hackley (1867–1922). She gave up a career as a concert singer to devote herself to providing opportunities for promising Negro artists. Several of the members of the following list owed their best opportunities to her. It is to the credit of the Detroit Public Library that its Negro collection is called the E. Azalia Hackley Collection.

WILLIAM F. ALLEN (1830–89)

The primary editor of *Slave Songs of the United States* was a classical scholar born in Northboro, Massachusetts, son of a Unitarian clergyman. He graduated from Harvard College in 1851 and did postgraduate studies in Göttingen and Berlin in 1854. After seven years as associate principal of the English and Classical School of West Newton, Massachusetts, he was employed by the Freedmen's Aid Commission to teach new freedmen. He went to St. Helena Island, South Carolina, in November, 1863. For several months in 1865 he was assistant superintendent of schools of Charleston, South Carolina. For a year, 1866–67, he was professor of ancient languages at Antioch College. In 1867 he assumed the chair of ancient languages and history at the University of Wisconsin, which he held until he died.

Besides nine hundred articles and reviews on classical, historical, political, and other subjects, he produced several books for students of Latin, including an edition of Tacitus and *A Short History of the Roman People* (1890).

Slave Songs of the United States contains an elaborate introduction (thirty-eight pages) written almost entirely by William Francis Allen. The introduction tells how the songs were acquired and prepared, and gives essential background for understanding them. He says, for example, that these particular slaves never sang secular songs, and that the hymns presented illustrated "the feelings, opinions and habits of the slaves." To get religion with them was to "fin' dat ting." One female slave told the collectors, "Couldn't fin' dat leetle ting—hunt for 'em—huntin' for 'em all de time—las' found' 'em." Allen tells about the shout, about songs for rowing, about how the songs were made, about the absence of part singing, and about the peculiarity of the slaves' dialects. *Huddy*, for instance, means "how-do?" *Titty* means "mother" or "oldest sister." *Enty* is a corruption of "ain't he" or "Is that so?" *Day-clean* is used for "daybreak." *Strain* is a favorite word with a variety of meanings, as in "Dat tune so strainful." Language at praise meeting was colorful. "Arter we done chaw all de hard bones and swallow all de bitter pills," was part of a benediction; a prayer asked "dat all de white bredren an' sister what jine praise wid we to-night might be bound up in de belly-band ob faith." And here is a description of love,

> Arter you lub, you lub, you know, boss. You can't broke lub. Man can't broke lub. Lub stan'—'e ain't gwine broke. Man hab to be berry smart for broke lub. Lub is a ting stan' jus' like tar; arter he stick, he stick, he ain't gwine move. He can't move less dan you burn him. Hab to kill all two arter he lub 'fo' you broke lub.

Allen was fully aware that the editors had merely broken the surface of a very large field. He predicted great wealth for future collectors.

GEORGE LEONARD WHITE (1838–95)

The man who assembled the Fisk Jubilee Singers, who outfaced the varied and killing problems associated with the national and international tours, who had the psychology and the gift for keeping the group together and its delicate individuals satisfied, who had the imagination, the drive, and the savoir faire for the infinity of steps in the years of struggle and success, was born in Cadiz, New York. His father was a blacksmith who played in a band and accounted for his early love of music. His formal education ended when he was 14, in high school. At 20, nevertheless, he taught school in Ohio and taught Negroes to sing in Sunday school. He served in the Civil War, as an enlisted man in the Seventy-third Ohio; he was at Chancellorsville and Gettysburg. After the war, he joined the Freedmen's Bureau under Clinton B. Fisk (for whom Fisk University is named). He was appointed instructor of vocal music at Fisk University in 1867. His singing troupes raised $90,000 for Fisk in less than six years.

Untrained as a choirmaster, he learned the art and used it with great distinction. He made contacts and arrangements. He kept many of the financial books for the travelers, indicating in the columns what places and people could be trusted, who and what were difficult and impossible. He settled morale problems, disputes among the singers, homesickness, financial matters, fears, and excitements. At home with managers and businessmen on both sides of the Atlantic, he was also the gracious mingler with nobility and royalty. He was endlessly resourceful and indefatigable; the whole company, all the various companies, relied on him for every kind of need.

It is safe to say that without George L. White there would have been no Fisk Jubilee Singers and no phenomenal successes for the spiritual throughout America and abroad. Without these successes, it is quite possible that the spiritual, after a few years, would have relapsed into a state of mildly academic curiosity.

ROLAND HAYES (1887–)

The first Afro-American to win immortal respect for the spirituals through solo concert singing was Roland Hayes. More than one "critic" of the spirituals has said that they were created for group singing and are not supposed to be sung by individuals. This, of course, is nonsense. Even when they were created, the first presentation of many of the songs was made by an individual to the group. Collectors have acquired many songs from individuals. For most of the songs, except those with built-in choral requirements, the individual is just as capable of communicating their true and deepest meanings as a quartet or a chorus.

Back in 1923 Samuel Chotzinoff reported that the first American concert singer to include spirituals in programs was Alma Gluck. Roland Hayes was the first black singer to win recognition as an artist from American audiences and American critics. As Sterling Brown wrote, when Roland Hayes sings, the world, however briefly, forgets both its tyranny and its submissiveness. As Heywood Broun wrote, when he sang of Jesus, you knew that this was what religion ought to be.

He was born in Curryville, Georgia, on June 3, 1887. He is still alive, living in Brookline, Massachusetts, and engaged in musical enterprises. He was the child of slaves. Educated in part at Fisk University and in part through sheer application to the business of working wherever he could, saving his money, and gradually acquiring the best voice teachers in America and abroad, he promoted himself on tours through the United States, 1916–20.

He went to Europe in April of 1920 and sang his first London recital on May 31, 1920. He did command performances before King George V of England in April 1921 and before Queen Mother Maria Christina of Spain, April 1925. He was awarded the Spingarn Medal in 1925.

The *Literary Digest* of January 5, 1924, reported that he sang Negro spirituals as did many white musicians, but that he wanted to be a universal artist, not just a singer of spirituals. He became one. In *My Songs* (1948) he told the story both of the songs and of his dealings with them. Of "Good News" he said, "Liberty, freedom, were realities of their earth, not far removed from celestial promises found in their Bible, their religion."

Of Roland Hayes and his spirituals, Henrietta Straus wrote in the *Nation*, "And the 'spirituals,' like no other songs in form and content, will shine as pure gold, bearing a strange kinship to old masters like Bach, as tho they were merely repeating a familiar message in new words." She reiterated, however, that the spirituals—in which Hayes was supreme—were only a part of his art. He had been able generally to transmute art "from an expression of formal beauty into spiritual utterance."

Olin Downes noted (in 1923) that Hayes was the first black singer ever to appear with the Boston Symphony Orchestra. It had been many seasons since any singer had received so enthusiastic a reception. "Go Down, Moses," Downes said, was sung in the tone and manner of one who prophesies. Downes summed up Hayes as a thoughtful and sensitive interpreter who deserved the many encores he received following his last programmed spirituals.

In Deems Taylor, however, one finds perhaps the most significant commentary on Hayes and his powerful songs:

> The people who filled Carnegie Hall to the brim last night, and crowded in packed rows upon the platform itself, were there for one reason and one only: because when art leaves the lowlands of mere polished excellence and rises towards the peaks of greatness, it appeals to something universal, some-

Roland Hayes, internationally famous tenor and popularizer of spirituals. ROLAND HAYES

Marian Anderson singing before 75,000 people at the Lincoln Memorial, Easter Sunday, 1939. SCURLOCK'S, WASHINGTON, D.C.

Paul Robeson, one of the greatest of spiritual singers in America and on the international scene. Audiences in Communist countries relished his spiriuals for their humanistic value. THE ASSOCIATED PUBLISHERS, INC.

Sir Jacob Epstein's bronze of Paul Robeson. THE CARL VAN VECHTEN ESTATE AND THE RESEARCH LIBRARY OF THE PERFORMING ARTS OF THE NEW YORK PUBLIC LIBRARY

William Levi Dawson, arranger, composer, and conductor. WILLIAM
L. DAWSON

Hall Johnson, one of the most highly respected arrangers of spirituals and a most successful organizer and conductor of spiritual choirs.
MRS. ALICE J. FOSTER AND MRS. SUSAN E. JORDAN, PASADENA, CALIFORNIA

William Grant Still, famous Afro-American composer, at work on a symphonic score. WILLIAM GRANT STILL

James Weldon Johnson, poet, historian, and pioneer interpreter of
spirituals. MRS. JAMES WELDON JOHNSON

The Reverend Howard Thurman, interpreter of spirituals in books and lectures. HOWARD THURMAN

Imamu Amiri Baraka (LeRoi
Jones), critic and interpreter of
Afro-American folk music.
IMAMU AMIRI BARAKA

John Littleton, European-
American singer and recording
artist, at Turin, Italy, April,
1969. JOHN LITTLETON

Dr. Crista Dixon, whose scholarly *Wesen und Wandel* presents a thorough examination of the theological background of the spirituals.

The Reverend Peter Smith of Sheffield, England, who uses folk songs in a new way to attract youth. ROGER HURRELL

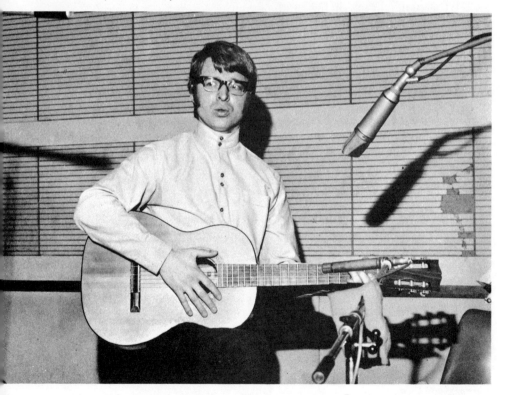

thing beyond the emotions and far beyond the intellect, something that you may be pleased to call the soul. And somewhere concealed, oddly enough, nearly everybody has one. It does not matter, particularly, whether Roland Hayes is black or white or green. What does matter is that he is an artist, and a great one.

MARIAN ANDERSON (1902–)

For a number of reasons Marian Anderson, the internationally famous contralto, has been a powerful force in popularizing the spirituals and in maintaining the respect and dignity of the songs. As a child of six she sang in the junior choir of the Union Baptist Church in Philadelphia where she was born. From age 13, her singing duties had aroused in her a deep sense of responsibility. She was educated in the public schools of Philadelphia. It soon became apparent that she had the remarkable voice, the ability to respond to training, the understanding of the spirituals, and the easy ability to place a spell upon her listeners when she sang spirituals.

"My religion," she says in her autobiography, "is something I cherish. . . . I carry my troubles, and I don't sit back waiting for them to be cleared up." Her stout declaration is similar to that of the courageous slaves, whose songs she reproduces.

She always included spirituals in her programs. She sang them in dialect as they were born, holding this to be an essential part of their character. Before going to the Soviet Union, she was warned against singing religious songs. She nevertheless sang the spirituals there, and her Russian audiences were greatly enthusiastic, demanding encores. Reporters at the Salzburg (Austria) Mozarteum say that the audience, on her first appearance there, was paralyzed by her rendition of "The Crucifixion." She has refused to "jazz" the spirituals; she sings them as she sang Handel, Brahms, Schubert, Verdi, and Finnish songs, according to her estimate of their merits.

In her famous appearance before seventy-five thousand at the Lincoln Memorial in Washington, D.C. on Easter Sunday (April 9), 1939, she sang three spirituals: "Gospel Train," "Trampin'," and "My Soul Is Anchored in the Lord."

The scope of her dissemination of spirituals is seen in the breadth of her concert tours. By 1950 she had sung in 285 cities, 780 auditoriums, before 3.75 million listeners in America alone. She had also sung over most of Europe, and in Africa, Mexico, South America, the West Indies, Hawaii, Asia, Australia, and New Zealand.

The appreciation of her art has been seen in numerous ways. In 1938 she won the Spingarn Medal and a degree of doctor of music from Howard University. She has received honorary degrees from a great number of educational institutions within and outside the United States.

One reason for her great success in singing spirituals to the world was her tremendous investment of thought and feeling. "The Crucifixion" she describes as one of the most deeply emotional songs she knows; she feels that it captures all the terror and tragedy of that awful moment in the world's history. For her, "Trampin' " represents an army of people bowed down, whose only solace is in marching along the road to heaven. In her visit to the Holy Land, she found the Jordan River not nearly so wide, and the walls of Jericho not nearly so high as they are in the songs. "Deep River" and "Heaven, Heaven" are full of excitement for her. The images in the spirituals as a whole she imagines as vaulting as the Negro's aspirations. For her people the making of song was an act of liberation, a desire to escape from confining restrictions and burdens.

The greatest of spirituals for her is "He Has the Whole World in His Hands." Everything and everybody is here—the wind and the rain, the lying man, the gambling man, the little bits-a-baby, you and me, brother and sister, specifically "everybody here." Besides everybody there are cry, appeal, meaning for her, more, much more, than any number on a concert program.

In the spirituals the singer, oppressed and persecuted, dreamed of a City called Heaven, a new home of peace and love. In the spirituals the singer captured the essence of reality and went far beyond it to express the deepest necessities of the human predicament. Thus, Marian Anderson, ardent philosopher, dwells at the heart of Marian Anderson, singer.

PAUL ROBESON (1898–)

One of the most accomplished of the spiritual singers, in his heyday, was Paul Robeson, who was born in Princeton, New Jersey. His father had traveled the Underground Railroad from slavery to freedom. Paul had honored his father by earning a bachelor's degree from Rutgers University —earning Phi Beta Kappa, four letters in athletics, and the position of end on Walter Camp's All-America team—and an LL.B. from Columbia University. He gave his first concert as a basso interpreter of spirituals in 1925. Carl Van Vechten reviewed this concert for *Theatre Magazine*. He said that Paul Robeson and Lawrence Brown (Robeson's accompanist and an arranger of spirituals) had revealed the wealth of melody and emotion of the Negro folk song.

For five years as a singer, Paul Robeson sang only Negro folk songs. His brother, the Reverend Benjamin C. Robeson, said that in his singing of these songs Paul was the personification of his father with his own personality added; he visions himself as breaking down centuries-old barriers. During one of the controversies over Robeson's difficulties in getting permission to travel outside the United States because of his left-wing views, J. Dover Wilson, the famous English literary critic and teacher wrote to the *Times* (London), "Let him loose upon us! . . . We want his breath for spirituals and other songs." He indicated that in England Robeson would not have time to waste on politics. Edward F. Murphy, calling Robeson and Hayes artists supreme, said that they kept raising the spiritual to new heights of fervor and appeal.

Robeson has sung spirituals to appreciative audiences all over the world. In East and West Germany, Russia, England, Hungary, France and elsewhere, he has been almost worshiped. His physical appearance, voice range and control, and tremendous emotional color and variety are only a few of the reasons why he is spiritual singer par excellence.

HARRY THACKER BURLEIGH (1866–1949)

Harry T. Burleigh is credited with having done more than anyone else in preparing the spirituals for use by concert singers, both individuals and groups. In his article on "Negro Music" for the *International Cyclopedia of Music and Musicians*, R. Nathaniel Dett said that Burleigh was preeminent in advancing the art of serious Negro music. His "Swing Low," says Dett, was related to Old China and Amerind and his "Go Down, Moses" to the music of the Magyars of Hungary. Not only were his arrangements used by Roland Hayes, Paul Robeson, Marian Anderson, and other Afro-American singers, they were used by many white singers. Oscar Seagle, a white baritone, was the first artist to include an entire group of Burleigh spirituals in a vocal recital of significance. Seagle complained, however, that some white singers dropped Burleigh's music when they learned that the composer was black.

Burleigh's preparation for music preceded his birth; it reverts to his grandfather, Hamilton Waters, escaped slave from Somerset County, Maryland. Waters, though blind from slavery's cruelties, was on his way to Canada when Harry's mother, Elizabeth, was born in the family wagon. The Waterses never reached Canada; they settled in Erie, Pennsylvania. In spite of his blindness, Hamilton Waters found work as lamplighter and town crier. As Harry led his grandfather around by hand, the latter sang plantation songs to him and told him plantation stories. At school Harry was discovered to have a good voice. He sang in choirs on Sundays and in synagogues on Saturdays. He eventually got a scholarship to the National Conservatory in New York City. During his first summer in New York, he worked at Saratoga in a hotel where Victor Herbert led the orchestra. He and Herbert became intimate friends.

The high point of his second year at the Conservatory was the arrival of the new director, Antonín Dvořák. Harry studied with him and received much time outside of class. With an engraver's precision he copied the master's manuscripts. He also copied scores for an opera house in exchange for tickets.

Harry played and sang, over and over, spirituals for Dvořák, spirituals he had learned from his grandfather. Dvořák was deeply impressed. He said the theme of "Go Down, Moses" was as great as a Beethoven theme. According to Harry Burleigh, Dvořák, in composing the *New World Symphony*, the *String Quartet*, and the *Quintet*, saturated himself with the spirit of the spirituals and then invented his own themes.

In 1903 Harry Burleigh began singing at St. George's Protestant Church in a service of spirituals by a choir of eighty voices. He used his own arrangements, plus those of Hall Johnson and other arrangers. He sang the spiritual "Calvary" at the funeral of J. P. Morgan, a senior warden at St. George's. St. George's honored him on the occasions of his twenty-fifth, thirtieth, and fiftieth anniversaries with the church. He sang "The Psalms" on fifty-two consecutive Palm Sundays.

His first compositions were not spirituals. From 1898 he wrote such famous songs as "Jean," "Little Mother of Mine" (frequently sung by John McCormack), and "Just You." He also did minstrel melodies, Scottish-type songs, Swedish-type songs, and traditional Surrey. He transcribed his first spirituals in 1901. He wrote for solo voices, quartets, and choruses. His "Deep River" in 1917 is considered a signal achievement and a model. In all he did 250 songs, including 100 spirituals. He was a charter member of ASCAP and an editor at Ricordi and Company, music publishers. One of the finest sketches of his life was done for the *Hymn* (a church music publication) by Charlotte Wallace Murray, herself a former concert singer.

ANTONÍN DVOŘÁK (1841–1904)

After Dvořák's arrival in the United States in the fall of 1892, he was written up in many American newspapers and magazines. In many interviews he stressed the importance of Negro music in America, challenging American composers to use the wealth of material in this treasury of folk music. He reiterated that the Negro spirituals and their derivations were a genuine folk music upon which a national music could be developed. He said specifically, "In the Negro melodies of America I discover all that is needed for a great and noble school of music."

In spite of statements by music critics that *From the New World* used Czech themes, Dvořák's biographer, Paul Stefan-Gruenfeldt says, "At all events, this music (Negro and Amerind) it was that inspired Dvořák to write his *American Symphony* and to compose several chamber-music works while in this country." He says further that although *From the New World* contains no "original American melodies," it is composed out of a spiritual affinity with American folk music (he quotes Dvořák and members of his family in support of this view). He adds that in the symphony are echoes of "Swing Low," "Somebody's Knockin'," "Seeking for a City," "Roll, Jordan, Roll," "Didn't My Lord Deliver Daniel," and others of the same kind.

Dvořák himself said, "Everyone who has a nose must smell America in the symphony." He says he would never have written it had he not seen America. But he adds, "I wrote my own themes, embodying in them the qualities of Negro or Indian music and, using these themes as subject, I developed them with all the resources of modern rhythm, harmonisation, counterpoint, and ochestral coloring."

Tim Dennison, Sr., says that the "Largo" of the symphony was a Negro lullaby, "Mammy's Chile," and that it had been sung by Afro-American mothers to their children long before Dvořák came to America.

William Arms Fisher seems to have summed up the case. First he quotes W. A. F. (himself), a pupil of Dvořák, to the effect that the composer did not incorporate Negro themes but invented his own "after the negro manner." W. A. F. continues, "He was ever seeking fresh musical material and in the Negro spiritual he rejoiced to find something that from the old-world point of view was unhackneyed and moreover indigenous. He saturated himself in it and then simply and naturally gave rich expression to his 'discovery.'" Then, Fisher writes,

> The *Largo*, with its haunting English horn solo, is the outpouring of Dvořák's own home-longing, with something of the loneliness of far-off prairie horizons, the faint memory of the red-man's bygone days, and a sense of tragedy of the black-man as it sings in his "spirituals." Deeper still it is a moving expression of that nostalgia of the soul all human beings feel. That the lyric opening of the *Largo* should spontaneously suggest the words "Goin' home, goin' home" is natural enough, and that the lines that follow the melody should take the form of a negro spiritual accords with the genius of the symphony.

In 1947, the Knoxville (Tenn.) Symphony Orchestra, conducted by Lamar Stringfield, introduced its rendition of *New World Symphony* with an offstage choir singing "Swing Low, Sweet Chariot."

FREDERICK DELIUS (1862–1934)

Frederick Delius called his *Appalachia* "Variations on an Old Slave Song with Final Chorus." The title derives from the Appalachian Mountains. The theme is an old Negro melody.

To get his mind off his desire for a musical career, Delius's father, who wanted his son in business, sent Frederick to Florida to manage the family orange grove. In Florida the songs of the plantation workers sank firmly into his memory. In later years he spoke with great admiration of the musical instincts of these Negroes. He remembered that all took keen delight in singing; he remembered one who could whistle passages in thirds. Although unacquainted with any music except their traditional songs, they could improvise, he said, inner parts when sung in chorus with extraordinary taste and skill. Their harmony was not that of the hymn book, with which such

Negro melodies as have been published are always associated; it was something far richer and stranger. It aroused Delius's enthusiasm. It baffled the efforts of music theorists to analyze or explain it.

Delius hired one of the Negroes to sit in front of his cottage, strum a guitar, and sing the old slave tunes. Although *Appalachia* is broadened to include the whole of North America and psychologically to express universal human feeling, the Negro singer and the musical traditions of his race are intended to play a large part in the final version of the composition.

SAMUEL COLERIDGE-TAYLOR (1875–1912)

Although born in England, of African and British parentage, Samuel Coleridge-Taylor had a great deal to do toward building the prestige of the Afro-American spiritual. As a very young man he was deeply affected and inspired by the Frederick J. Loudin troupe of the Fisk Jubilee Singers. Always proud of his African blood, he had used "Nobody Knows the Trouble I See" in his *Song of Hiawatha* (1899). Late in his life, he wrote hot letters to the newspapers, complaining about uncomplimentary remarks concerning the Negro people. He called Du Bois's *The Souls of Black Folk* the greatest book he had ever read.

His first visit to America in 1904 was mainly at the instance of the Samuel Coleridge-Taylor Choral Society of Washington, D.C. During his stay in America he conducted his *Hiawatha* and his *Songs of Slavery*, also based on the works of Henry Wadsworth Longfellow. In Chicago he appeared as pianoforte soloist in "Three Negro Melodies Symphonically Arranged from Set of Twenty-Four," a new work he was then engaged in composing. Harry T. Burleigh assisted in this concert.

Upon returning to London, he included five of his "Characteristic Negro Melodies" in a recital at Public Hall. He collaborated with Paul Laurence Dunbar in an orchestral piece. He soon developed the idea of producing compositions which would do for Negro music what Brahms had done for the Hungarian, Dvořák for the Bohemian, and Grieg for the Norwegian.

As the result of an invitation from the Oliver Ditson Company of Boston, he published in 1905 *Twenty-Four Negro Melodies Transcribed for the Piano*. Of the melodies in this volume, four were from southeast Africa, two from South Africa, one each from West Africa and the West Indies, and all the rest from the Afro-American spirituals. In distinguishing African from American music, he said the African was more martial and free, the American more personal and tender. Later in his career he returned to the spirituals in his *Symphonic Variations on an African Air*. To open a concert for the Philharmonic Society in 1906, he played "I'm Troubled in Mind." On the basis of hearing his wife play "Keep Me from Sinking Down," he considered using this melody for a composition he was then working on; he later rejected it for the melody of another spiritual, "Many Thousand Gone"; the composition was *Violin Concerto*.

The publication of *Twenty-Four Negro Melodies* was an event in its day and is still a milepost in the evolution of the Afro-American spiritual. W. L. Hubbard calls the compositions gems of their class. Besides Coleridge-Taylor's foreword, providing the Negro a "musical personality," it contains a memorable introductory essay by Booker T. Washington. The main contents of the essay will be given shortly under the heading of Booker T. Washington. Concerning Coleridge-Taylor specifically, Booker T. Washington had this to say,

> It is, I repeat, a cause for special gratitude that the foremost musician of his race, a man in the zenith of his powers, should seek to chronicle, and thus perpetuate, the old melodies that are so rapidly passing away.
> Mr. Coleridge-Taylor is himself an inspiration to the Negro, since he himself, the child of an African father, is an embodiment of what are the possibilities of the Negro under favorable environment. In his preface to the *Cabin and Plantation Songs*, as sung by Hampton students, Mr. Thomas P. Fenner said, . . . "The freedmen have an unfortunate inclination to despise this music [Negro music] as a vestige of slavery; . . . It may be that this people which has developed such a wonderful musical sense in its degradation will, in its maturity, produce a composer who would bring the music of the future out of this music of the past." May we not look to Samuel Coleridge-Taylor for a fulfillment of this prophecy?

R. NATHANIEL DETT (1882–1943)

Dett was born in Canada of parents who were educated and musically inclined. Very early in life he learned to play by ear and to earn through his genius free tuition in music. He also listened to his grandmother's perpetual rendition of primitive Negro songs, which to him sounded strange, weird, unnatural, but fascinating. He was educated primarily at Oberlin College. At Harvard, in 1920, he won the Bowdoin Prize for an essay on "Emancipation of Negro Music." As a young man he was grateful to Henry Edward Krehbiel who, through his *Afro-American Folksongs* (1914), drew the attention of the literary world to the artistic possibilities of Negro music. Another strong influence on his life was Madame E. Azalia Hackley, who had sent Carl Diton, the pianist-composer, and Clarence Cameron White, the violinist-composer, to Europe for extended study. Through Madame Hackley's influence he went to Hampton Institute in 1913 as director of music. Here, he led the Hampton choirs until his resignation in 1931.

His contribution to the evolution of the spiritual did not stop with his being an outstanding music teacher and choirmaster. He was also an arranger and composer. He arranged and recast many spirituals in his *Religious Folk-Songs of the Negro* and in *The Dett Collection of Negro Spirituals*. A part of his inspiration came from attending meetings of ex-slaves in the backwoods. He saw how their faces showed a self-abnegation, evidencing their being transported to another world. Besides spirituals, he composed other works on Negro themes, such as the motet, *The Chariot Jubilee* (1919), and the oratorio, *The Ordering of Moses* (1937).

Dett was a firm believer in the religious significance and power of the spirituals. Not only was he sure that religion was the primary motivation of the slaves who created the songs; he believed they were right. The term *spiritual* he derived from the fact that the creators and singers were moved by "the Spirit." He felt the spiritual "become very sincerely the voice of a divine power, as wonderful as that which wakens the magnolias into their gorgeous bloom, hurls a Niagara over a thundering precipice, wakens the trill of the morning bird or paints the glories of a sunset sky."

WILLIAM LEVI DAWSON (1899–)

In 1956 the American Embassy in Madrid, Spain, issued a report signed by Antonio Gonzáles de la Peña, concerning the activities of William L. Dawson in Spain. The excerpts from that report are as follows:

> The aims of these concerts are multiple; on the one hand they attempt to establish a true knowledge of the beauty of American music—in this case the Negro spirituals in Spain—and to make known in the United States the compositions of some of the Spanish musical geniuses. . . . On the other hand they try to let both the American and the Spanish public know that there exists both in Spain and in the United States excellent music of the people written by great and good composers representing the temperament and the true soul of their people; a music which sings to God or to their earthly loves, with real inspiration and beauty, without commercialism or vulgarity. This may be accomplished by having these songs, directed by a native composer or director, and taught to the singers by him. . . .

> From his first efforts, when he was rehearsing with the members of the Orféon Donostiarra in San Sebastián, until his last performances at El Ferrol and at the Cathedral of Santiago, with the choral group of the Empresa Bazán, he has left an unforgettable memory with the members of the choruses and with his audiences.

This kind of superlative has been used to evaluate the work of William L. Dawson during most of his life. Since the time he sold his bicycle for $6 to go to Tuskegee and arrived on campus with $1.50 in his pocket, he had insisted upon the highest standards of performance for himself and those he directed.

About the interpretation and direction of Negro folk songs, Dawson has some very definite ideas. A part of his philosophy is expressed in the lines, "Every melody has a personality. . . . Every time you sing you hear something you never heard before. . . . Everything going on today, the creator of Negro song has already said it."

He took over the Tuskegee choir in 1931, and began teaching them Negro folk songs (he never uses the word spirituals because, in his estimation, it is too limited for the songs). He says these folk songs will last for a thousand years and will be the one thing American blacks will be remembered by.

During his twenty-four years at Tuskegee, he and his choirs won many prizes for excellence and superiority. After the premiere performance of his *Negro Folk Symphony* (composed 1931) by Leopold Stokowski and the Philadelphia Symphony in 1934, he was in demand as a composer. He had also written interpretively of the songs.

His *Negro Folk Symphony* had three movements, of which the third was designated "O Le' Me Shine, Shine like a Morning Star."

After leaving Tuskegee, he was for a year conductor of the Fisk University choir. Since then, he has been regularly engaged as guest conductor and lecturer in this country and abroad. No one has made a stronger contribution to the presentation and understanding of the Afro-American folk song.

HALL JOHNSON (1888–1970)

Hall Johnson is important in the history of the spiritual because of his remarkable success in directing choirs, arranging songs, and teaching to others the arts of directing and arranging and the genuine flavors of Negro music. His sisters—Mrs. Alice J. Foster and Mrs. Susan E. Jordan of Pasadena, California—remember the instruction he received from their father, the Reverend William Decker Johnson, an A.M.E. minister, both in religious training and in solfeggio. From an older sister he learned to play the piano.

He was born in Athens, Georgia, in the midst of a snow blizzard. Most impressive of his childhood memories was the rich and habitual singing of the former slaves in revivals and in other congregations. He received his basic education from Knox Institute, Allen University, Atlanta University, and the Hahn School of Music. He was graduated from the University of Pennsylvania in 1910, largely on the strength of a prize-winning composition.

Later he attended the Institute of Musical Art in New York. He studied theory, violin, piano, and his specialty, composition. Of all his teachers, Percy W. Goetschius was his favorite. Having gained musical maturity, he took intensive graduate courses in German and French at the University of Southern California.

Early in his career he played the violin in the personal orchestra of Mr. and Mrs. Vernon Castle. He was also violinist in the original orchestra of the production of *Shuffle Along* (1921).

Among his earliest compositions was an operetta entitled *Coophered*. In 1946 he produced at the New York City Center a Negro Easter cantata, *Son of Man*, which he had composed and directed. In this producing company were soloists and a choir of 300 voices. If his compositions had been confined to the arranging of spirituals, however, his reputation would have been exceedingly high. Besides being sensitive and touching music, his arrangements delineated the basic Negro idioms and the unique racial flavors. No wonder his spirituals were selected for programs by soloists and singing groups, white as well as black, all over the world.

In September, 1925, he organized the first Hall Johnson Negro Choir. The key to his success was his determination to make all his trainees into serious musicians. He was director of the choir that sang the twenty-three spirituals in *The Green Pastures,* which opened on Broadway on February 26, 1930. After this very great triumph he directed many singing groups called the Hall Johnson Choir. He also led the Festival Negro Chorus of Los Angeles. Arvey and Still credit him with the development of choral singing through the full elaboration of unusual Negro voices.

His choirs performed in movies, concerts, general theater, radio, television, as well as on Broadway, and also made recordings. Among the movies he helped to celebrate were *Swanee River, The Green Pastures, Way Down South,* and *Cabin in the Sky.* He composed the music for *Run Little Chillun* (1933) on Broadway. Besides editing *The Green Pastures Spirituals,* he arranged and edited *Thirty Negro Spirituals* (1949). The latter work was republished in Zurich, Switzerland, in 1965.

With his choir, and singing spirituals, Hall Johnson toured France, Germany, and Austria on good-will missions for the United States government. In 1951 his choir sang at the International Festival of Fine Arts in Berlin.

He was awarded a doctor of music degree in 1934 by the Philadelphia Music Academy. In 1962 Mayor Robert F. Wagner presented him with a citation from the City of New York for thirty-five years of cultural contribution to the world. New York honored him again on March 12, 1970, when Mayor John V. Lindsay followed with the George Frederic Handel award for his unusual achievements and contributions.

Less than three weeks before he died, a large group of his followers gave "A Musical Tribute to Hall Johnson" at the Salem Methodist Church in New York City. Tributes were delivered by Marion Cumbo, Camilla Williams, Marian Anderson, and Marguerite Avery, a member of the first Hall Johnson Choir. In most of the music sung—adult songs, children's songs, choral selections, and a cantata—Hall Johnson's name appeared as composer.

J. ROSAMUND JOHNSON (1873–1954)

The brother of James Weldon Johnson, J. Rosamund Johnson prepared the music for *The Book of American Negro Spirituals* (1925) and *The Second Book of American Negro Spirituals* (1926). These collections of spirituals served for many years as the standard collections. In 1940 when the two were brought together as *The Books of American Negro Spirituals* the new collection lost none of the prestige of the early two.

J. Rosamund Johnson was educated at the New England Conservatory of Music and in Europe, where he studied piano, organ, and voice. From 1896 to 1908 he was supervisor of music in the public schools of Jacksonville, Florida.

Besides arranging and adapting—his *Sixteen Negro Spirituals* (1939) were dedicated to the Southernaires—J. Rosamund Johnson has been an ardent student of Afro-American song. His *Rolling Along in Song* (1937) was a chronological survey of American Negro music. With eighty-seven arrangements and notes he presented ring shouts, regular spirituals, jubilees, plantation ballads, minstrel songs, jailhouse songs, work songs, ragtime, street cries, and blues.

CLARENCE CAMERON WHITE (1880–1960)

Clarence Cameron White was a concert violinist, a director of choirs and music schools, an arranger and composer, and a regular contributor to magazines. In all these spheres his primary passion was Afro-American music.

Born in Clarksville, Tennessee, he was educated in the public schools of Washington, D.C., and at Howard University. He then took a degree in violin from the Oberlin Conservatory. He was a pupil of the distinguished Russian violinist, M. Zacharewitsch.

As early as 1918 he published *Bandanna Sketches,* four Negro spirituals for violin and piano. The first was a chant, "Nobody Knows de Trouble I've Seen"; the second a lament, "I'm Troubled in Mind"; the third was a slave song, "Many Thousand Gone"; and the fourth, a Negro dance, "Sometimes I Feel Like a Motherless Child." In 1921 he published *Cabin Memories,* using "Nobody Knows de Trouble I've Seen" and three new spirituals. His "Nobody Knows de Trouble I've Seen" was programmed for concerts by Fritz Kreisler and recorded by Kreisler under the Victor label. In 1927 White did *Compositions: Opus 18, From the Cotton Fields,* containing three spirituals and two original songs, and *Concert Paraphrases of Traditional Negro Melodies,* containing three spirituals and "Water Boy," which he offered as a camp song. In 1927 he brought out a long expected volume, *Forty Negro Spirituals.*

For his *Ouanga,* an opera about Dessalines in Haiti, written in collaboration with John F. Matheus (who did the book), White received the David Bispham Medal. He also directed music at West Virginia State College, 1924–32, and at Hampton, 1932–37.

Among his many articles are three of more than average historical value, "Negro Music: A Contribution to the National Music of America," which appeared in the *Musical Observer,* from November 1919 to March 1920;

"The Story of the Negro Spiritual 'Nobody Knows the Trouble I've Seen,' " which was published in the *Musical Observer* for June 1924; and "The Music of the American Negro," which came out in the *Southwestern Christian Advocate* for August 1924.

FREDERICK J. WORK (1880–1942), JOHN WESLEY WORK II (1871–1925), AND JOHN W. WORK III (1901–)

These three musicians were members of the team who carried on the very great tradition in spirituals at Fisk University. All were educated at Fisk. All were engaged in searching through the South for new spirituals, and recording them. John Wesley Work III was professor of music theory at Fisk until his retirement.

In 1907 Frederick J. Work brought out *Folk Songs of the American Negro*. In the preface to this volume are two significant statements. The first, "Even the Negro himself, whose music this is, has little by little overcome his resentment against it, notwithstanding that this resentment sprang from the idea that these songs were very closely connected with slavery and all that slavery meant." The statement describes an important historical development. It is understandable that in the closing years of the nineteenth century, as the American Negro was struggling to establish himself with respect and dignity in the full society, he would be suspicious of anything which reminded him and others of his recent status as a slave. Not having studied thoroughly enough the backgrounds of the songs to know that, although created by slaves, they were the opposite of slavish, he naturally acquired the resentment. His resentment was not helped by white musicians who tried to make the songs a part of the "happy darky" tradition of the Old South. His resentment was overcome when he began to understand the truth of his own music.

The second statement is also quite perceptive, "Since they [the spirituals] tell faithfully the Negro's inmost life, both intellectually and spiritually, they are the only true source of our history. If any man would read the Negro's life, let him study his songs." The preface also makes clear that the swaying of the body during the singing of spirituals was in dead earnest, not fun. It does not refer to the perpetuation of the African dance tradition.

Other significant volumes by members of the Work team are John Wesley Work, *Folk Song of the American Negro;* and three by John W. Work, *American Negro Songs, Ten Spirituals*, and *Jubilee*, which also contains ten spirituals, though not the same ten as the 1952 volume.

WILLIAM GRANT STILL (1895–)

William Grant Still and Nathaniel Dett were named by Philip Gordon as two of fifty good, productive American composers in 1947, recognized skilled creative craftsmen. Still was also mentioned proudly by Howard Hanson, in 1951, as among the young composers whose works had first performances at Eastman (Rochester). Without a doubt, whenever original composers in the spiritual or the Afro-American field are reviewed, Still will be in the list. More than that, he is an original composer in any field. Cowell says that in his compositions Still uses Negro themes and feelings as a base, but always works out something new. On his part, Still declares that American Negro music possesses exoticism in itself without straining for strangeness.

Still has proved that the Negro spiritual, when harmonized according to inherent racial qualities, shows little Caucasian influence and does not sound like an Anglo-Saxon hymn. He published *Twelve Negro Spirituals* in 1937. Along with the music were "Literary Treatments," in which he depicted Negro life at the time the spirituals were inspired. In 1956 he published *Three Rhythmic Spirituals* for voice and keyboard instruments. And in 1961 he brought out *The Devotion of a People*, containing thirteen spirituals.

From the spiritual and beyond the spiritual he has created a great deal of inspiring music. Perhaps he is best known for his *Afro-American Symphony* (1931). His *Symphony in G Minor* (1937) he has called *Song of a New Race*. His *Works for Band* (1945) includes "From the Delta," part work song, part spiritual, part dance. His *Four Indigenous Portraits* for string quartet and flute has a section called "North American Negro," an original theme in the style of a spiritual. In the rest of the piece he traces relationships between the North American Negro and the South American Negro and both North American and South American Indians.

MAHALIA JACKSON (1911–1972)

Although world-famous as a gospel singer, Mahalia Jackson has contributed a great deal to the popularity and general appreciation of the Afro-American spiritual. She was born in New Orleans—her grandparents were slaves—and educated in the New Orleans public schools. She was brought up in churches where the people sang a great many spirituals, such as "Let's Go Down to the River Jordan." Her first choir solo was "Hand Me Down a Silver Trumpet, Gabriel."

Shortly after she began to sing in public, she specialized in such spirituals as "Standing in the Need of Prayer" and "Sometimes I Feel Like a Motherless Child." She also enjoyed singing an old spiritual she remembered from childhood,

> One of these mornings I'm going to lay down my cross
>   and get my crown
> As soon as my feet strike Zion, I'm going to lay down
>   my heavy burden

> I'm gonna put on my robes in glory and move on up a
> little higher

The title of her autobiography is *Movin' On Up*.

Others of her favorite spirituals, which she has helped to maintain in the public heart, are "Joshua Fit the Battle of Jericho" and "Didn't It Rain?" Again and again she has aroused her audiences with this one,

> I've been 'buked and I've been scorned.
> I'm gonna tell my Lord
> When I get home,
> Just how *long* you've been treating me wrong.

As reported by Milton Okun, Miss Jackson's all-time favorite is "Balm in Gilead."

Like most successful singers of spirituals, Miss Jackson is deeply sincere about them and deeply committed to the message she believes they carry. "When I cry when I'm singing," she has written, "I'm not sad like some people think. I look back where I came from and I rejoice." It is interesting to remember that through the spiritual the slave often projected into the future, where he believed his community would "shine."

The remarkable appeal of Mahalia Jackson as a spiritual singer is exemplified in a sketch written by Rudi Blesh and found in *O Susanna* (1960). This time the place was the Newport, Rhode Island, ball park; the time was just after midnight on Saturday, July 7, 1958. Despite the heavy rain thousands of people, wet to the skin, sat, waiting. Blesh picks up the story,

> Mahalia Jackson came out on the stage. Gently, as though speaking to children, she spoke. "I don't know," she said, "if you want to hear me and you want to stay in the rain, I'm just getting warmed-up." Immediately then, over the deafening cheers, she soared into *Didn't It Rain*. Our time had never heard it sung like that, even by Mahalia. The rain slackened. The rain stopped. Then—all over God's heaven—the stars came out.

Summing up Mahalia Jackson, Blesh has written,

> There must have been many great singers of her sort back long ago in Sojourner Truth's day, when her people were in slavery. But no one within our memory has rocked the old songs—so miraculously and sweetly distilled from the bitterness of servitude—as she rocks them, her great figure swaying and the great husky voice rolling out in torrents of sound. Fine art, folk art—all the terms become meaningless, even impertinent, when Mahalia sings.

HARRY BELAFONTE (1927–)

For originality and popularity in the singing of spirituals, in concerts, on records, and on television, Harry Belafonte is outstanding. Since Belafonte produces his own records, his basic originality is untouched. His book,

Songs Belafonte Sings (1962) includes six spirituals. His personal choice, according to Milton Okun, is "I've Been 'Buked and I've Been Scorned."

Belafonte shows the spiritual as a member of the family of African and Afro-American songs. He styles each song in accordance with his unique imagination and study of backgrounds. Each song is then delivered with a special emphasis. In solo work or in leading a chorus he is equally exciting and effective.

Spirituals to which he has brought unusual popularity are "Buked and Scorned," "Michael, Row the Boat Ashore," "My Lord, What a Mornin'," "March Down to Jordan," "In That New Jerusalem," "Take My Mother Home," "Noah," "In That Great Gettin' Up Mornin'," "Go Down, Moses," "Sometimes I Feel Like a Motherless Child," and "When the Saints Go Marching In." Oscar Brand has written that Belafonte makes "Let My People Go" sound like exciting entertainment rather than propaganda.

JESTER HAIRSTON (1901–)

Jester Hairston has had a remarkable career in organizing and directing spiritual choirs. His background for this activity has also been remarkable. Born in Homestead, Pennsylvania, he learned his music at Tufts University and the Juilliard School. In 1929 he decided to go into show business. His first show was with Chic Sales, *Hello Paris*, in 1930. Even before *The Green Pastures*, Hairston was a member of the Hall Johnson Choir. He sang in *The Green Pastures* and helped Hall Johnson organize his other choirs.

Since leaving Hall Johnson, his choral work has been extensive. He was choral director of a WPA chorus; he has often been a motion picture choral director; he organized the Festival Negro Chorus of Los Angeles; and he was choral director on a Harry Belafonte tour, 1960–62.

His choir work in the motion pictures has been highly praised. He has conducted professional choirs in *Carmen Jones*, *Land of the Pharaohs*, *Portrait of Jenny*, *Foxes of Harrow*, and *Friendly Persuasion*. In addition, he has acted in a number of films, on radio, and in television. He has published two books of spirituals and has arranged fifty spirituals for individual presentation through sheet music.

In 1949, at the College of the Pacific (now the University of the Pacific) in California, he began teaching young people how to sing spirituals. In the past twenty years he has trained hundreds of spiritual choirs all over the United States and in foreign countries. In 1969 alone, with his trained spiritual choirs, he produced sixty concerts. His festivals, on more than one occasion, have involved more than two thousand voices.

At the instance of the State Department he began training spiritual choirs abroad in 1961. In 1961, he worked in Germany, Austria, and Norway; in 1963, he trained choirs in Germany, Yugoslavia, Denmark, Norway, Sweden, and Finland. In 1965 and 1966, he taught spirituals in Mali, Ivory Coast, Nigeria, the Cameroons, and Ghana; and in 1968, in Ghana, Senegal, and Ivory Coast. He gives slave history when he teaches the songs. He is credited with having altered lives and attitudes and with having been a "bridge of communication" in both white and black communities.

Jester Hairston did the choral music for the motion picture, *Lilies of the Field*. His arrangement of "Amen" was the one used by Sidney Poitier in winning the Academy Award for best actor. It is very likely that Jester Hairston has been the cause of more people singing spirituals in more places than any other single individual.

LEONTYNE PRICE (1927–)

For the past half century most of the outstanding Afro-American concert artists have been judged in the first instance by their ability to sing spirituals. When Roland Hayes mastered European song and delivered it as well as any concert singer, he was still told by some music critics to stick to his spirituals, or at least to concentrate on them.

It is a refreshing fact that just the reverse is true of Leontyne Price. Although she is a superlative singer of spirituals, her reputation has been built upon her general concert work and her greatness in opera. When she sings spirituals now, the critic tends to judge this performance by the standard she has already maintained.

The headline on one critique read, "Soprano Gives Flawless Recital." After praising Miss Price for her supreme mastery of difficult and rewarding music, the critic then wrote, "Her last group was devoted to Negro spirituals to which she brought the same sense of excitement which had characterized her entire concert."

Another critic followed the same pattern with equally great praise, "The program closed with a group of Negro spirituals. Miss Price sang them without condescension. Her voice glowed with beauty, and the beloved old hymns had never sounded with more sublime and heartfelt reverence."

Like the majority of the truly great Afro-American singers, Miss Price served her apprenticeship in church choirs. She followed her mother who gloriously sang hymns and spirituals in the choir of the St. Paul's Methodist Church in Laurel, Mississippi. She did a great deal of home singing. At Central State College, as she told one interviewer, she sang in choir, glee club, and shower. She also said that she never went on stage without saying a prayer. This practice would be a tribute to her art as well as to her religious faith. One of the things that has kept the spiritual alive and growing is the fact that it has been sent around the world by good voices that thoroughly and fiercely believed in what it said.

Leontyne Price has also engaged in spiritual adaptation. On her programs a few years ago was a "Cantata Sacré" in five parts, each based on a spiritual. The spirituals used were "Peter, Go Ring Dem Bells," "Sometimes I Feel Like a Motherless Child," "Let Us Break Bread Together," "Ride On, King Jesus," and "Were You There?" The composer of this unusual adaptation was John Carter. Although it was not unanimously well received, many critics and audiences enjoyed it. One critic called it a breathtaking tour de force.

With her voice and her temperament Miss Price could sing any spiritual superlatively well. Those that she seems to have sung most in recent years are "Ezekiel Saw the Wheel," "He's Got The Whole World in His Hands," "His Name So Sweet," "Lord, I Just Can't Keep from Cryin'," "My Soul's Been Anchored," "On Ma Journey," "Sometimes I Feel Like a Motherless Child," "Swing Low, Sweet Chariot," and "You Can Tell the World." Within her range of spirituals her favorite arrangers are Margaret Bonds, Harry T. Burleigh, Hall Johnson, Edward Boatner, and Florence Price.

As long as there is a Leontyne Price or someone of her stature—if that is always possible—the Afro-American spiritual will be floated into the air with the sincerity, the sweetness, the depth, the color, and the magnificence with which it was endowed by its creators.

OTHER ARTISTS AND PERFORMERS

To this list of outstanding contributors to the development of the spiritual as a phenomenon, one could add a list of several hundred more moderate contributors. This second list would include all kinds of performers and composers, individuals as well as groups. Among the individuals would be performers as diverse as Joan Baez, Jules Bledsoe, the Georgia Peach, Marie Knight, and Sister Rosetta Tharpe. Among the groups would be an equally great diversity in the Golden Gates, the Sabbath Glee Club, Thrasher Wonders, the Weavers, and the Williams Colored Singers.

In spite of the pressures of space, a handful of Afro-American composers require at least modest mention. These are George Ballanta Taylor, Edward Boatner, Will Marion Cook, Carl Diton, W. C. Handy, Marylou I. Jackson, Mary Grissom, Eva Jessye, and Margaret Bonds. Besides arranging spirituals, most of these directed choirs or accompanied soloists or otherwise introduced spirituals into some broad sphere of public enjoyment and appreciation.

Carl Diton, formerly a pupil of Constantin Sternberg, was an organizer of the National Association of Negro Musicians, an association dedicated to resisting the desecration of spirituals into ragtime. He was pianist, organist, composer, arranger. One of his articles was entitled "The Struggle of the Negro Musician." He was the first composer to employ a spiritual as thematic material for organ composition. He was also the first to employ spirituals in art-song form a la Schumann and Brahms.

OTHER COMPOSERS MOTIVATED BY SPIRITUALS

Below is a selected list of American composers, and their works, who were inspired by the Afro-American spiritual or who used spirituals or spiritual motifs in their compositions. These composers are given in alphabetical order by last name.

Composer	Works
Harold Arlen and Ted Koehler	*Americanegro Suite* (1941): four spirituals, a dream, and a lullaby
Maurice Arnold (Strothotte)	*Plantation Dances* (1894)
Cecil Burleigh (1885–)	*Plantation Sketches, Op. 36*
John Alden Carpenter	
George W. Chadwick (1854–1931)	*Second Symphony*
Aaron Copland	Eleventh of *Twelve Poems to Emily Dickinson* (1949–50); second of *Old American-Songs* (Second Set, 1954: "Zion's Walls")
Richard Donovan	*Fantasy on American Folk Ballads* (1941)
Frank Erickson	*Deep River Suite* (1953) published in series, *American Classics for Band;* uses "Swing Low," "Deep River," and "Joshua Fit de Battle ob Jericho"
Arthur Farwell	*Plantation Melody* (ca. 1905) in *From Mesa to Plain; Folk-Songs of the West and South* (1905); *Two Negro Spirituals* (1905)
Henry Franklin Gilbert	*Negro Episode* (1897); *American Humoresque* (1897); *Negro Rhapsody* (1913); *The Dance in Place Congo, Comedy Overture on Negro Themes* (called by Olin Downes the most promising sign of American musical independence yet). Gilbert also projected an opera on Uncle Remus.
Louis Gruenberg (1884–)	The opera *Emperor Jones:* "Standin' in the Need of Prayer" used with modification; *Negro Spirituals* (1926)
Henry Hadley	"South" in his *Symphony in D Minor, No. 4,* "North, East, South and West" (1911)
William J. Henderson (1855–1937)	
Walter Kramer	*Rhapsodie*
Ernest R. Kroeger (1862–1934)	*Ten American Sketches, Op. 53; Caprice Negu; Dance Negu*
George Lynn	*Ain' Go'n' to Study War No Mo'* (1964) dedicated to Hall Johnson
Edward MacDowell (1861–1908)	*Woodland Sketches; Uncle Remus*
Harl McDonald (1899–1955)	*Suite for Strings on American Negro Themes* (1933)

George McKay   *Port Royal* (1861), folksong suite for
                                orchestra, songs used: "Hold Your Light
                                on Canaan Shore," "Go Down in Lone-
                                some Valley," "Heaven Shall Be My
                                Home"
Daniel Gregory Mason   *String Quartet in G Minor on Negro
                                Theme*s (1930), uses "Deep River"
John Powell (1882–)   *Rapsodie Nègre;* "Elégie Nègre" in *Suite
                                Sudiste; Humoresque Negre No. 2* (1906)
William Reddick (1890–)   *Rapsodie Nègre* for orchestra and piano
                                (1921, 1922)
Henry Schoenfeld (1857–1936)   *The Sunny South; Rural Symphony;
                                Sonata for Piano and Violin*

❨ *Forms Influenced by the Spiritual*

ADAPTATIONS

A part of the fame of the spiritual has arisen through the numerous, and often curious, ways it has been imitated, adapted, and distorted. Tim Dennison, Sr., lists the following as some of the by-products of the spiritual: work songs, play songs, animal songs, mother songs, and minstrel. For minstrel he cites as prime imitators Stephen Foster and James Bland. The foreword to the Oak Publications 1965 edition of *Slave Songs in the United States* says that in the spiritual are the roots of jazz, swing, rhythm and blues, rock and roll, and modern gospel songs. On the research of Gerald Haslam we learn that the steps from the spiritual (Afro-American oral tradition through blues, jazz, gospel, and freedom songs) to "folk rock" are direct. The emphasis, he says, is on spoken or sung poetry set to a basically African rhythmic mode.

During the 1930s and 1940s adapting and arranging spirituals was a regular business sponsored by music publishers. Among the adapters were Al Johns, Chris Smith, Sam Lucas, Roberta Martin, Robert Anderson, Myrtle Jackson, Kenneth Morris, and James Sands. The arrangers included Wellington Adams "Wyneberry Boyd," W. Arthur Calhoun, William C. Elkins, Purnell F. Hall, E. Aldama Jackson, Yolande Maddox, Kaye Parker, Jean Stor (pseudonym of W. Astor Morgan), Wen Talbert, A. Jack Thomas, Carlette C. Thomas, LaSalle J. Williams, and Noah Francis Ryder.

Some of the adaptations were extremely interesting. Among these were Oliver Wendell Holmes's poem, "To Canaan (A Song of the Six Hundred Thousand)," which contained parallels to such spirituals as "Joshua Fit the Battle of Jericho" and "I Am Bound for the Promised Land" (this poem was published in the *Boston Evening Transcript*, August 12, 1862, and became quite popular); "Swing Low, Sweet Chariot," a spiritual in the form of an art-song, by Carl Diton; and "Troubled in Mind," arranged and adapted by Will Marion Cook, with lyrics by his son, Mercer Cook. George Lynn's *Ain' Go'n' to Study War No Mo'* was announced as a spiritual paraphrase.

Another adaptation was a harmonization of a Hollis Dann arrangement of "On Canaan Shore" by Harvey Worthington Loomis. Presented by a cappella chorus, it showed up in a concert of the Chicago Symphony Orchestra in 1931. This was not the first time for spirituals in that element. The orchestra had played them "in their primitive form," Dett says, in 1918.

An adaptation located by Beatrice Landeck is found in her *Git on Board*, a collection of folk songs arranged for mixed chorus. It goes,

> Lincoln set the Negro free,
> Why is he still in slavery? (repeat)
> Jim Crow!

Carl Van Vechten called some of the adaptations unbearable. One of these he accused of very bad taste was Price's operatic ending to "My Soul's Been Anchored in the Lord." Generally speaking, he said, it is utterly impossible for white people to comprehend the Negro's point of view in spirituals or in other things Negro; and so the final word on the spiritual had to be spoken by Negroes. Even so, he declared that some of the worst arrangements of spirituals were done by Negroes.

In 1963, *Trumpets of the Lord*, an adaptation of several James Weldon Johnson pieces, was professionally produced. It contained a Noah medley, a funeral suite, and a freedom suite. Altogether, it used sixteen spirituals.

MINSTREL SONGS

Since Stephen Foster's songs are often confused with spirituals, even in the minds of well-meaning people, it is necessary to try to dispel the confusion. Stephen Foster made one trip to the South before manhood; he saw Augusta and Louisville; he never knew plantation life, although his entire life (1826–64) was lived before the end of the Civil War. He got some "South" from the boat crews on the Ohio River.

His family, in western Pennsylvania, were ardent Democrats and hated Abolitionists. They had a "bound boy," Thomas Hunter and a "bound girl," Olivia Pise, called Lieve. By Lieve, Stephen was introduced to spirituals. She was a devout Christian in a shouting Negro church. Once Stephen had heard the spirituals, he not only demanded that Lieve keep singing them for him, but insisted on going to church with her where he could hear more and hear them in their fullness. Lieve took him to her church. "Here," says Stephen's biographer, John Tasker Howard and his son, Morrison Foster, "he stored up in his mind 'many a gem of purest ray serene,' drawn from these caves of Negro melody." A number of strains he heard there, he considered too good to lose, and so he preserved them in his songs.

Thus, Edward Lueders did not exaggerate when he said of this writer for Christy's minstrels, "The source, the color, and the native appeal of Foster's songs came from the unstudied melodic style and rhythm of the music developed by the American Negro." Nor is N. Clifford Page inaccurate when he writes, "His natural leaning to the music of the South was directed and intensified by attendance at various Negro camp-meetings, and resulted in the characteristic folk-songs, *My Old Kentucky Home, Massa's in the Cold, Cold Ground, Old Folks at Home,* and others." In addition, C. Coons (in *As America Sang*) says flatly that Foster's song style is based on the Negro spiritual. Lueders, Page, and Coons represent the trend of scholarship which opposes George Pullen Jackson, who says Foster was indebted to white song.

To establish that the most famous of the minstrel composers took his material directly from the Afro-American spirituals is the best way to open debate on the full relationship between spirituals and minstrel. In 1908, W. L. Hubbard, the music historian, had declared that the inspirations of the minstrel "were derived from negro sources." In 1931 Isaac Goldberg had expressed the debt of the minstrel to the spiritual and ragtime.

As early as 1868 John Mason Brown had declared that Negro minstrelsy was not reflective of the Negro slave; that Christy, Bryant, and Newcomb were not true interpreters of the Negro; and further, that no genuine Negro song ever betrayed straining after vowel endings, and few of them used triple time.

The Cavalcade of the American Negro ties important minstrel developments to entertainment provided by free Negroes. The success and popularity of free Negro entertainers in Philadelphia in 1732 led Major Dumbleton to organize his African Serenaders, later a famous minstrel troupe. The same idea resulted in other such minstrel organizations.

Hans Nathan in *Dan Emmett and the Rise of Negro Minstrelsy* says that the influence of Negro hymns on Negro minstrelsy is slight. He seems to have forgotten all about Stephen Foster. He does find some relationship between the Negro "shout" and the minstrel "walk-around" and between a hymn in a Negro prayer meeting in New York City and the minstrel routine of "Old K.Y. Ky." He mentions three Negro spirituals which the minstrels transposed, "O'er the Crossing," "I'm in Trouble," and "The Lonesome Valley." He also speaks of expressions from the workaday reality of slave life. One of these, "joining the union," appears in numerous spirituals in various forms.

Nathan's dismissal of the spiritual as an influence upon minstrelsy is far from conclusive. He seems to have avoided a thorough examination of the question for fear of finding an influence.

Constance Rourke speaks in praise of the minstrel and downgrades the spiritual. Rayford Logan comments on the minstrel's habit, for laughter's sake, of developing the Negro ludicrously. When commenting upon the Fisk Jubilee Singers in 1873, the *Glasgow Herald* said, "Nothing in common with spurious negroes who, as 'Christy's Minstrels,' profess to sing the melodies of the plantation." And Sigmund Spaeth speaks of the Negro spiritual as the real thing in comparison with minstrelsy. Chirgwin says simply that minstrels are a poor imitation of the spiritual. In the *Encyclopaedia Britannica* (1964 ed.), Claude L. Shaver says that the minstrel show was based upon the singing and dancing of Negro slaves; that in its early forms it often adhered somewhat closely to Southern Negro types, but departed from this closeness in its later forms.

The examples of Foster and Bland show clearly that the spiritual did influence the minstrel, at least in the later years of the nineteenth century. Far more than the three songs mentioned by Nathan are spiritual adaptations. W. F. Shaw in *Popular Songs and Ballads No. 1* shows the reliance of "The Great Jubilee Song," sung by Tedding Minstrels, upon the spiritual, "Dar's One More Ribber to Cross." A thorough search would undoubtedly reveal dozens, maybe hundreds, of such borrowings. The scope of this influence needs to be worked out by minstrel experts with a passion for, and no fear of, the full truth.

In *Negro Minstrel Melodies*, edited by Harry T. Burleigh, are several spiritual adaptations and other songs based on spiritual motifs. A few examples are, H. T. Bryant's "Balm of Gilead"; James A. Bland's "Oh! Dem Golden Slippers!"; and Henry C. Work's "Wake Nicodemus."

JAZZ

A great debate has also raged around the influence of the spiritual upon jazz. To scholars the influence is reasonably clear: All the major bibliographies and study lists on jazz, from Europe as well as America, carry a healthy number of items about spirituals. This shows that the influence of the spiritual on jazz is taken for granted. Wolfgang Suppan's "Die seit 1945 erschienene deutschsprachige Literatur zum Jazz," for example, has sixty-one spiritual items in its jazz bibliography. Paul Breman, a Dutch writer on the Afro-American spiritual (now living in London), says that everybody interested in jazz looks at spirituals. In *Das Jazzbuch* (1953), Joachim Ernst Berendt, the outstanding German expert on jazz, says that jazz emerges so directly from the spiritual that it is almost impossible to tell where the spiritual stops and jazz begins.

In 1923, when jazz was less than half a century old, Samuel Chotzinoff, a musician and a music critic, wrote for *Vanity Fair* an article called "Jazz: A Brief History." In this article he said unequivocally that the Negro spiritual, with its remarkable sheer musical quality, formed the basis and salient peculiarity of present-day jazz. He offered in evidence two characteristics of the spiritual: its insistent and lively 2–4 rhythm and its physical effect on the listener. The Negro, he concluded, erected a structure of entertainment "on the vital and living rhythm of his folk-tune." A year later, writing for the *Etude*, A. Garbet, relying upon some of Chotzinoff's evidence and adding some of his own, traced the origin of jazz to Negro spirituals.

In 1926 Ballanta Taylor (who was born in Africa) was quoted in an interview in the *New York Times* as saying that the basic principle of jazz, its rhythm, was African, but that its harmony and synchronization were not. He did declare that, if African music had never come to this country, there would have been no jazz. Another African, W. E. Ward, writing in the *Gold Coast Review* in 1927, called American jazz a false and feeble imitation of a mixture of African and European music. He indicated certain characteristics of the spiritual that are found in jazz.

In 1931 Norman and Tom Sargant, writing on "Negro-American Music or The Origin of Jazz" for the *Musical Times* of London, expressed the hope that jazz would regain the nobility of the Negro spiritual from which it sprang and leave off its present degradation. Three years later, another Englishman, Sir Richard R. Terry, declared quite emphatically that jazz was certainly not the creation of Negroes; clearly that of white men.

In 1944 the *Harvard Dictionary of Music* was published, edited by Willi Apel. The article on "Jazz" was done by Lloyd Hibberd. In this article the influence of the spiritual on ragtime, blues, and jazz in general was specifically traced. The next year, S. I. Hayakawa called jazz a hybrid, its ultimate source being Negro folk music, including work songs, dances, shouts, religious songs and chants, dance rhythms brought over from Africa, and field songs. Dan G. Hoffman, also in 1945, called jazz a lineal descendant of Negro folk music.

Also in 1944 Ernest Borneman pointed out that the spiritual, among other early Negro folk music, provided suitable material for jazz improvisation, mainly because it represented the direct ancestry of the jazz idiom. He added, "When ragtime gave way to jazz, jazz turned to the spiritual for inspiration as ragtime had done half a century before."

Louis Harap, writing on "The Case for Hot Jazz" in 1947, declares that "hot jazz" drew heavily upon the primitive features in the music of the American Negro, clearly indicating the spiritual.

Charles Edward Smith wrote in 1950 for the *Saturday Review of Literature* a scholarly article with the title "Folk Music, and Roots of Jazz." Dating the arrival of jazz about 1890, and the location of birth "around New Orleans," he states quite flatly that the Negro spiritual and other folk music are root music that fed the melodic and rhythmic style of jazz. Not quite so positive, but leaning in the same direction, was Rudi Blesh in his *Shining Trumpets* (1953): Jazz, he says, emerged from a fusion of all Negro musics about 1880—work songs, spirituals, ragtime, blues.

In *Before the Mayflower* (1966) Lerone Bennett, Jr., after describing African music and Afro-American slave music, credits the spiritual with having produced prison music, jazz, and blues. And John F. Szwed, in 1968, declares that the earliest jazz musicians drew from brass marching bands, Spanish dances, English religious songs, romantic piano music, Negro folk songs and spirituals, and West Indian religious cult music.

Thus, of the sixteen students of music, writing over a period of forty years, nine flatly credit the spiritual as the prime force in the founding of jazz and five others give the spiritual partial credit. It is not merely the preponderance of individuals that is impressive; it is, rather, the evidence they offer in support of their views. Furthermore, it is a well-known fact that, regardless of the origins of jazz, jazz musicians and jazz composers have relied heavily on spirituals for material and inspirational ideas. They still do. As Marshall W. Stearns says in *The Story of Jazz,* "The religious music of the Negro continues to furnish a reservoir of inspiration to the entire jazz tradition."

BLUES

As to the influence of the spirituals on the blues, Stearns quotes Rudi Blesh to the effect that "How Long Blues" is derived from the spiritual, and that "Precious Lord Hold My Hand" and "Nobody's Fault but Mine" are essentially mixtures of spirituals and blues. Borneman shows how beats by voice, hands, and feet passed from spirituals to blues and to other secondary elements. Paul Oliver indicates the relationship between the spiritual "Poor Rosy, Poor Gal" and Red Nelson's "Crying Mother Blues." It has been shown above that Lerone Bennett, Jr., traced the influence of spirituals upon blues. Norman and Tom Sargant have demonstrated that the melancholy outlook of the spiritual gave rise to blues and that many spirituals are distinctly blues. They cite in evidence "I'm Goin' to Tell God All o' My Troubles."

If you turn back to "Appreciation of Things Going Wrong and of Riddles in the World" in Chapter 19, you will find several spirituals which have all the fundamental character of blues. Take this one, for example,

> One day, Lord, one day, Lord,
> Walkin' long, Lord, Wid hung down head, Lord!
> Chillun:— an achin' heart, Lord!

Or this one:

> Sometimes I feel like a moanin' dove
> Sometimes I feel like a moanin' dove
> Wring my han's an' cry, cry, cry,
> Wring my han's an' cry, cry.

And this one, the most famous "blue" spiritual of them all,

> Sometimes I feel like a motherless child,
> Sometimes I feel like a motherless child,
> Sometimes I feel like a motherless child,
> A long ways from ho-o-o-ome,
> A long ways from home.

> Sometimes I feel like I'm almost gone,
> Sometimes I feel like I'm almost gone,
> Sometimes I feel like I'm almost gone,
> A long ways from home,
> A long ways from home.

There are dozens more spirituals like these, closely akin to full blues.

The Reverend Gary Davis specializes in what he calls "holy blues." In his book *The Holy Blues* (1970) are eighty songs. Sixteen of these are full and admitted spirituals. Most of the others are spiritual adaptations.

Garland in *The Sound of Soul* cites a 1931 radio broadcast in which W. C. Handy, sometimes called the "father of the blues," says that his blues compositions were inspired by spirituals. Handy is also quoted as saying that the blues take the pathetic melody of the spirituals. Garland also quotes John Lee Hooker as saying that not only blues, but all other Negro music derive from spirituals.

Several writers have demurred from agreeing with the influence of spirituals on blues by insisting that the spiritual was created for group singing and the blues for individual singing. This is a very dubious distinction. Although an artistic device, the pronoun *I* appears as the lead element in hundreds of spirituals. The *I* of the blues frankly enlists the support of a sympathizing group. Since, regardless of their authorship, both are obviously folk songs, such a distinction can never stand.

In Paul Oliver's *Blues Fell This Morning*, the foreword by Richard Wright clearly describes the folk community of the spiritual, which later created the blues. The blues are like the spiritual in recognizing the stern realities of life but in maintaining through them a durable fortitude. As Wright puts it,

> Yet the most astonishing aspect of the blues is that, though replete with a sense of defeat and downheartedness, they are not intrinsically pessimistic. . . . No matter how repressive was the American environment, the Negro never lost faith in or doubted his deeply endemic capacity to live. All blues are a lusty, lyrical realism charged with taut sensibility.

To sum things up, Shirley and Driggs, in their *Book of the Blues*, write,

> As far as can be determined, blues developed in the rural South, out of a variety of sources, including work songs and field hollers and spirituals of slaves and ex-slaves.

On the preponderance of the evidence, the blues are a child of the spiritual.

RAGTIME

What is true of jazz and the blues is equally true of the intermediate development known as ragtime. We have already quoted several writers on this parentage. Besides these, Walter Goldstein in "The Natural Harmonic and Rhythmic Sense of the Negro" has called ragtime "the debased offspring" of Negro song. Oscar Seagle says specifically that ragtime comes from the spiritual; he then adds that this is not damnation but proof of appeal. Ten years before the first ragtime was published, says Borneman, the spiritual had ragtime accompaniments in piano transcriptions. He cites as evidence Roy Carew's sheet music, in 1883, of "Good Lord'll Help Me on My Way." Other writers have shown direct borrowings in ragtime from the spiritual.

The so-called coon song belongs in the same category. While conceding that the coon shout is of ancient origin and present in many countries, John J. Niles insists that sacred shouts are unknown elsewhere than in North America. He shows direct influence of the spiritual upon coon shouts in the United States. One of his examples of coon shouters is Ophelia "Black Alfalfa" Simpson, wife of Henry "Dead Dog" Simpson.

COUNTRY MUSIC

In *Country Music U.S.A.*, Bill Malone is unequivocal. Although the most "pure white" of all American musical forms, he says, country music has borrowed heavily from black spirituals and other black music. He cites several country music singers who have sung or still sing spirituals, as, for example, Clyde "Red" Foley and his rendition of "Steal Away." He also credits blues as having developed from work songs and spirituals.

POPULAR SONGS

Many popular songs are derived from spirituals. In their *Anglo-American Folksong Style* Roger D. Abrahams and George Foss indicate this fact. They say that "Careless Love" shows strong Negro influence and may be of Negro origin. In *A History of Popular Music in America* Sigmund Spaeth says that "Wagon Wheels," the extremely popular song of the 1930s, stems in part from "Swing Low, Sweet Chariot."

NEOSPIRITUALS

A number of amateurs have tried to create spirituals or neospirituals and have gotten their offerings published. Louise Ayres Garnett published three such items in the *Outlook* for April, 1922, "Gwine up ter Heab'n," "Ev'ywhars Dat Anybody Knows," and "Slow en Easy." Zora Neale Hurston did an article on "Spirituals and Neo-Spirituals" for Nancy Cunard's *Negro Anthology* (1934). In the same book appeared Harry Miller's "Cotton Fields," which he called an old spiritual never before printed. In *Bandanna Ballads* a Miss Howard Weeden published eight poems with spiritual connotations. A similar exercise is found in *Plantation Songs* by Eli Shepperd (pseudonym for Martha Young). Shaemas O'Sheel published "Two Spirituals" in the *Commonweal*, but his adaptations have very little of the spirit of the original songs. In two different issues of the *Catholic World*, John Richard Moreland brought out "Doomsday" and "De Promise Lan'," both of which he dared to compare with spirituals. Something close to the real thing is found in Genevieve Taggard's "Two Poems" in *The Crisis*, the first of which was based on "My Way's Cloudy"; the second commemorated Marian Anderson's singing on the steps of the Lincoln Memorial in Washington.

Carrying the game of neospirituals a step farther, David W. Guion brought out *Five Imaginary Early Louisiana Songs of Slavery*.

RING-GAME SONGS

Many poems in imitation of spirituals have served as songs for ring games. Some of these have appeared in the *Journal of American Folklore*. One of them was called "A Ring Game from North Carolina: Granddaddy is Dead." Another, sung by black children in Georgia a half century ago, is reminiscent of the call and response technique in such a spiritual as "Certainly, Lord,"

> "Did you go to the lynchin'?"
> "Yes, ma'am!"
> "Did they lynch that man?"
> "Yes, ma'am!"
> "Did the man cry?"
> "Yes, ma'am!"
> "How did he cry?"
> "Baa, baa!"
> (repeat).

SPIRITUAL BURLESQUES

In his *Negro Poetry and Drama* and in articles in *Phylon*, Sterling Brown writes of secular songs which grew up side by side with spirituals. Some of the seculars are burlesques of the spirituals, as for example, "God's got your number; He knows where you live," "Death's got a warrant for you,"

> I don't want to ride in no golden chariot,
> I don't want to wear no golden crown,
> I want to stay down here and be
> Just as I am without one plea,

and

> I seen Solomon and Moses
> Playing ring around de roses. . . .
> I seen King Pharaoh's daughter
> Seeking Moses on de water. . . .
> Seen ole Jonah swallowin' de whale
> And I pulled de lion's tail;
> I've sailed all over Canaan on a log.

The famous spiritual "Live A-Humble" became "Live-A-Humbug."

SWING

John Sebastian offers a concert given at Carnegie Hall on December 23, 1938, as proof of the patrimony of swing from spirituals. At this concert three thousand listeners were held spellbound. Mitchell's Christian Singers, a male quartet of Kinston, North Carolina, uniquely sang "While He's Passing By," "You Rise Up," and "My Mother Died Shouting." Sister Rosetta Tharpe sang Holy Roller hymns, such as "Rock Me" and "I Can't Sit Down."

"Spirituals to Swing" concerts were held several times in New York City in the late 1930s. One of the most memorable at Carnegie Hall was held on December 24, 1939. It featured Count Basie and his band, Ida Cox as singer, and Sterling Brown as master of ceremonies.

GOSPEL SONGS

What is called *gospel music* is hardly anything more than an effort to give the spiritual a modernity in form, content, and beat. Whereas the spiritual was created and disseminated by the folk, the gospel hymn is written by well-known individuals and swept into the religious community on a tide of evangelical fervor. As Gerald Haslam puts it, the spiritual has a modern counterpart in the gospel song. Two interesting articles have described its origin and early development: Arna Bontemps, "Rock, Church, Rock!" in *Common Ground* for Autumn 1942 and John W. Work, "Changing Patterns in Negro Folk Songs," in the *Journal of American Folklore* for April–June 1949.

For the transition from spiritual to gospel, Work credits chiefly the Primitive Baptist churches of the South. Bontemps gives the credit to a Methodist minister in Philadelphia, the Reverend Charles A. Tindley. Reverend Tindley's productive period was 1901 to 1906. Two of his favorite songs were "Stand by Me" and "Nothing Between." He made no secret of his having leaned heavily on the Afro-American spiritual.

In the estimation of John W. Work, rhythmic variations play a very big role in the transition. The rhythmic piano of the Reverend Zema Hill, a

Primitive Baptist minister of Nashville, Tennessee, caused an influx of young people to his church. It was imitated by other churches, some of which organized choirs around it. Still other churches borrowed the rhythmic piano and added guitar, saxophone, trombone, violin, and tambourines. The principal percussion was provided by handclapping off the beat. Work observes that three or four hundred pairs of hands can produce an astounding rhythmic impact. In the Holiness churches, the chief touch of gospel was traditional spirituals distorted by rhythmic accompaniment.

Bontemps and Work agree that the chief force in the development of gospel music was Thomas A. Dorsey. His first gospel song was "I Do, Don't You" in 1921. According to Bontemps, Dorsey has added tabernacle song material and blues touches to the spiritual. Dorsey unabashedly names Reverend Tindley as the originator of the gospel style.

Gospel songs with close kinship to spirituals are Thomas Dorsey, "Precious Lord, Take My Hand"; Kenneth Morris, "One Day, When I Was Lost in Gloom"; and Roberta Martin, "Didn't It Rain?" Bontemps says that the last of the three is miles ahead of the spiritual of the same name.

"Precious Lord, Take My Hand" is not only one of the most famous gospel songs; it is one of the most popular songs now being sung by black congregations. It combines two elements that were foremost in the creation of the spiritual: intense religious devotion and reaction to realism. Dorsey says it was written after a day of bitter tragedy.

In writing of "Gospel Hymns of a Negro Church in Chicago," Richard Alan Waterman makes the following comment, "Many Africans came over to this side of the world and they did not forget their cultural background. This has been proved in other fields, time and time again."

John F. Szwed illustrates gospel singing by reference to a group from the Church of God in Christ, organized in 1895 in Mississippi. This group is noted for "exuberant shouting songs (called 'gospel,' for they were said to be the 'truth'), songs always accompanied by instruments alien to the European religious tradition: guitar, piano, trumpet, and drums." Szwed says that this gospel singing is strongly rhythmic and heavy with melisma (single syllable with more than one note).

Gospel singers, Langston Hughes said, do not rehearse songs. They listen and absorb; then they improvise. There is certainly no doubt that gospel singing has expanded into innumerable methods and styles since the start of the 1960s.

OTHER SPIRITUAL ADAPTATIONS

John J. Niles, a white Kentuckian, believed that his having been brought up in a neighborhood where he heard spirituals regularly entitled him to make some very unusual adaptations. His first group of such adaptations he called *Impressions of a Negro Camp Meeting*. He says that the melodies are based on traditional tunes, but are not spirituals. His words, however, are very definitely the words of spirituals, "Live humble, humble," "Pharaoh's army drownded in the sea," and "John's come down from de mountain," to mention only three. His second group he called *Seven Negro Exaltations*. In his preface to the exaltations he wrote that Negro music lasts because (like all folk music) it sprang from a vital need; it was the outburst of a suppressed soul.

Clarence Joseph Rivers is responsible for an "American Mass Program" in the style of the Negro spiritual." Although there are no words, the styling includes entrance hymn, acclamation, offertory, Sanctus, communion, and recessional.

Occasionally a very original singer develops a style of singing spirituals which amounts to an adaptation. Leadbelly was such a singer. His treatment of spirituals is quite different from anyone else's. His general background and prison experience added to his natural talents produced a whole new world of spirituals. The fact that he also sang other Negro folk songs enables the listener to make interesting comparisons between them and the spiritual.

Books advertising themselves as special arrangements for spiritual and various unorthodox instruments have been on the market for many years. Some of these instruments are the banjo, the ukelele, and the "fiddle."

Spirituals sung by white groups, both amateur and professional, have been reported for almost a hundred years. Back in 1872, W. A. Barret said that "sperichils" had been adopted by many white congregations and when sung with spirit and swaying produced "indescribable" results. Verses were variable, changing with the whim of the singer or with new circumstances. It should be clearly noted that Barret was talking about Negro spirituals, not the white kind.

One of the most remarkable of the white groups singing Negro spirituals was the Society for the Preservation of Spirituals of Charleston, South Carolina. This society was founded about 1923 by fifteen or twenty Charlestonians, all whites. Its purposes were to sing spirituals, to preserve them, to educate the rising generation in their character and rendition, and to maintain "a social organization for the pleasure of the members." The last item of purpose effectively and permanently excluded Negro members. Even the whites had to belong to ancient South Carolina families, such as the Hutsons, the Pinckneys, the Rutledges, the Warings, and the Heywards.

In 1931 the Society published the *Carolina Low-Country*. In this somewhat remarkable book were articles by Augustine T. Smythe, Herbert Ravenal Sass, Alfred Huger, Thomas R. Waring, Archibald Rutledge, DuBose Heyward, and Robert W. Gordon. While the other articles dealt with the background and character of the South Carolina settlements, Gordon's dealt with the spiritual itself.

A part of the remarkableness was found in the flight from reality. Sass, for example, said that in the Negro slave cabins were contentment, abundant rations, and the sound of banjos and singing. "With all its faults . . . it is an age and a land of courage, integrity, and beauty." He said that prosperity arose from white man's brain and black man's sinews.

Heyward justified the use of the lash by recalling that it was used at the time in the United States Navy and the New England public whipping post. He spoke tenderly of the Negro's genius for forming happy relationships—"something beautiful and tender and enriching to both black and white in the master-servant relationship."

Gordon told how the spiritual was used by boatmen, field workers, women at household tasks, and for lullaby and dancing ("holy dance" or "shout"). The inability of the slave to read and write was never a block to the dissemination of the songs. The spiritual grew outside of the church because of restrictions. It is obvious that Gordon's section is the most accurate and believable.

The rest of the book—104 of the 327 pages—consists of a large collection of spirituals, words and music. Arrangements were made by Katherine C. Hutson, Josephine Pinckney, and Caroline Pinckney Rutledge. Both in the printed songs and in the regular songfests, a strong attempt was made to reproduce the dialect and the singing methods of the South Carolina slave.

When one closes one's eyes and reconstructs in one's mind the actual conditions under which this Society operated, he is overwhelmed by the impact of the slave spiritual upon so elegant a group of untouchable palefaces. Maude Barragan, describing their antics for the *Etude*, says that they sang in semicircle, clapping their hands and stamping their feet. Their singing, they believed, was authentic to the last degree. They did painstaking research to reconstruct the slave settings as background for their songs.

SOUL MUSIC

Although hard to define, soul music is pretty generally understood. Arnold Shaw's *World of Soul* (1969) gives the spiritual a great deal of credit. First, he says that the spirituals had a larger part in the blues than any other type of song. Then, he shows that soul musicians—Solomon Burke, Wilson Pickett, and others—got started by singing or recording spirituals. (He might have added Aretha Franklin, Nina Simone, and many other more famous names.) Third, he comes out flatly (p. 238) and says that soul music had its beginning in the dark days of the black spiritual.

When Shaw opens his Part Three, in which he addresses himself directly and finally to soul singing, he quotes a famous spiritual:

> My Lord, he calls me,
> He calls me by the thunder!
> The trumpet sounds within-a my soul.

And there he stops—on a most significant word.

⟦ *Development Through Publications*

COLLECTIONS AND INTRODUCTIONS

If the word *collection* means a book with one or more spirituals published for reasons of preservation, then this author has found almost five hundred spiritual collections in more than a dozen languages. One collection has 187 spirituals; the average is 10 to 15. Most collections have prefaces, forewords, introductions, or notes. These books tell the reader things the collector thinks he ought to know to understand, appreciate, sing, or play the songs properly, according to the collector's views. Sometimes, especially in foreign countries, they make a display of those fragments of the history of American Negroes or of American Negro music which the author deems necessary. You can tell by reading only a short distance what sources the collector is relying on. One collector and interpreter lists more than five hundred sources.

These collections are a testimony both to the popularity and to the manysidedness of spirituals. They reflect what people, particularly foreigners, think of American Negroes, and many of the ideas are quaint. In some instances they provide curious people in a given locality with cultural information and insights. About half of them publish the music with the words, and are thus aids to singing or instrumentalizing.

No other folk song has commanded such great attention for so long a period in so many parts of the world. As Robert Gordon said back in 1927, the Negro spiritual is the most extensive and varied body of folk song still alive and growing in any civilized country. When, to the books and articles and comments on the spiritual itself, are added those on the forms derived from the spiritual, the body of works is truly phenomenal.

Field collecting and recording of spirituals has abated in the last few years—the number of original singers has just about been exhausted—but it went on at a rapid rate for thirty or forty years. In 1926 Carl Engel, editor of the *Musical Quarterly*, reported in his magazine that the collecting and recording of Negro melodies had made great strides in recent years. For a number of years Marion Kerby specialized in collections from the Mississippi Delta. For a much greater number of years the *Journal of American Folklore* and other state and regional folklore journals made a special effort to publish songs collected by their correspondents all over the South, and in a few Northern areas. Robert Gordon said that he recorded 350 spirituals on the Georgia coast between Brunswick and Savannah within three months. John Lomax and Dorothy Scarborough scoured the South and the Southwest for these songs, with admirable results. In *On the Trail of Negro Folk-Songs* Dorothy Scarborough wrote that she wanted "Swing Low, Sweet Chariot" sung at her funeral. In *Can't Get a Red Bird* she came up with some very original spirituals, like this one,

Oh, it's g-l-o-r-y to know I'm s-a-v-e-d!
I'm h-a-p-p-y to tell I'm f-r-double e!
Once I was b-o-u-n-d In the chains of s-i-n.
It's v-i-c-t-o-r-y To know I've Christ with-in!

Collections of spirituals have been published for young readers, for old darkies, for firesides, for the American spirit, from the hickory and the cotton, to name only a very few occasions. Songs have been taken from prisons and hospitals, and from shrimp and oyster houses. It is notable that during the heyday of collecting spirituals, most of the work was done by whites; but not all of it. Dett and Work in the Hampton and Fisk neighborhoods respectively have already been mentioned for their spiritual hunts.

In the January 1931 issue of the *Musical Digest* is a double portrait of two very ardent collectors of spirituals and other American folk songs—Marion Kerby and John Niles. (Marian Anderson refers to Marion Kerby in her autobiography.) The portrait maker recalls Miss Kerby's times at places like the Stovall Plantations in the Mississippi Delta. Down there she was in and out of Negro cabins, prayer meetings, and other gatherings where songs were likely to be sung. She listened to itinerant preachers, cotton growers, mill hands. She learned the command of the Southern Negro over the spiritual, its croon, lament, exhortation. Also, she received the evidence for how "Steal Away" and other songs were used as secret meeting and runaway songs, a code not understood by white overseers. Some black preachers, she found out, knew the Bible from cover to cover, although they were unable to read. One of these was Charles Haeffer, a blind preacher and ballad singer. At that time Kerby and Niles had 250 songs in their concert repertory. Niles's interest in black song was just beginning.

More recently, other bright minds have been brought into the search. Byron Arnold, who published a collection called *Folk Songs of Alabama*, which contains thirty-four spirituals, was born in the North. He went south to teach music and was literally transformed by black music. Collecting songs from all over Alabama, he specialized in a place called Gees Bend, near Montgomery. In Southern California, where he now teaches, he still plays for his friends and visitors records he made in Gees Bend, records of "I'm Going to Stand There Anyhow" and " 'Zekiel Saw the Wheel." They are pure music, unexampled, utterly original, and lovely.

Another very remarkable collector is James Leisy, president of the Wadsworth Publishing Company. He was fascinated by folk songs, especially black ones, at an early age. By 15, he knew lots of songs; from then on, he learned new ones all the time. As the son of a famous English teacher in Texas, he met many folk experts—Dobie, the Lomaxes, Sandburg, Niles. So adept was he in music that he had the choice between being a professional musician or a book publisher. Among his publications of folk song collections are *Abingdon Song Kit, Folk Song Fest, Let's All Sing, Hootenanny Tonight, Songs for Pickin' and Singin', Songs for Swinging House-*

mothers, and *The Folk Song Abecedary*. In the last three are a total of sixty-eight spirituals.

Under the Federal Music Project, as reported by William F. MacDonald, the state of Mississippi yielded up a vast collection of spirituals, work songs, play songs, river songs, hillbilly songs, and fiddler's tunes. After being mimeographed and bound, these songs were supplied to state colleges, county libraries, and other educational institutions.

Outside of the singing colleges, the number of black collectors has been small. J. Mason Brewer has been one of these, and his work has been outstanding. As long ago as 1946 he organized the South Carolina Negro Folklore Guild. The aim of this organization was to collect Negro folk material and to use it in a statewide movement in intercultural education. Since moving to Texas, he has been diligent in encouraging the preservation and publication of Negro folklore of all kinds.

The concern on a broad scale by American Negroes about the need for preserving their treasures in song goes back at least to 1890 with the founding of the Society for the Collection of Negro Folk Lore. At the Hampton Conference of 1899 there was much talk on the above subject. It was finally agreed that ragtime and coon songs should be discouraged, but that "the beautiful plantation melodies should be preserved." The Reverend Ernest Lyon (minister to Liberia, 1903–11) said at this meeting, "The plantation songs are our own; . . . they were born out of our sufferings, and express deep things. Never let them go." A fuller story of this whole interest and action is found in August Meier's *Negro Thought in America, 1880–1915*.

INTERPRETATIONS

It has already been shown that a large number of the collections carried sections on interpretation, but there are, in addition, hundreds of books, articles, and comments which deal with interpretations alone. Comparatively few of these interpretations are based on research in available documents. Most of them are "inspirations" apparently derived from hearing or reading the songs, and whipped into being through some light thinking.

Some are flat, honest opinions by people who make no pretense at musical or anthropological backgrounds. These are sometimes quite refreshing. Heywood Broun, for example, says that the Negro spiritual "rose up out of a swirl when two civilizations wholly dissimilar met head on." The men of Africa, he went on, were children of a lost tribe—their meeting with the Bible was a homecoming. Moses had in mind the slaves of the Carolinas when he told Pharaoh to let his people go. He ends his sketch by praising "Crucifixion" ("Were You There When They Crucified My Lord?"). He also says at the end that one of Lawrence Brown's arrangements of "Joshua Fit de Battle of Jericho" is "the most exciting song ever composed."

In nearly a dozen commentaries for the *New York Herald Tribune*, for

Opportunity, for *Theatre Magazine*, for *Vanity Fair*, Carl Van Vechten, who was knowledgeable in music, gave vent to a variety of original opinions about these songs. In spite of his much writing, he constantly insisted that white people could not really interpret the songs. At the end of one article he wrote, "If any race boasts a more interesting folklore than the American Negro I do not know what that race is." In another article he said that the Negroes could rescue the dying concert business if they would develop concerts based on authoritatively sung, authentically performed Negro spirituals. In another, he says that spirituals are inferior to blues, but that no folk poetry has deeper feeling or more imaginative imagery. In reviewing Kennedy's *Mellows*, he says Kennedy has perverted the spirituals; he nevertheless recommends a few of Kennedy's songs, such as "If You Can't Come, Send One Angel Down."

One of the most interesting practices of interpreters has been their use of the songs as headpieces for chapters in books. In T. J. Woofter, Jr.'s *Black Yeomanry*, about life on St. Helena Island, an Afro-American spiritual opens each chapter. The theme of the spiritual is a guide to the chapter's development.

The convictions of serious writers that have led to methods of interpretation are one of the most interesting sets of things in the study of the Afro-American spiritual. Apparently, a writer, guided by his individualistic or professional background or by what he conceives to be a fresh (and much needed) interpretation, turns to the songs with a new vital concern. Because the songs are so flexible in philosophical twists and turns, they readily cooperate. The result is a whole new approach, or what the convinced writer believes to be wholly new. The critical literature of the spiritual is spread over so wide a territory—general magazines and newspapers, theological papers, musical and ethnomusical journals, folklore documents, literary, historical, sociological, philosophical, and psychological periodicals, anthropological studies, travel books, biographies and autobiographies, books of fiction, drama, poetry, books by publishers with various editorial slants—that sometimes what is new in one world is not new in another. As a searcher in all these worlds, however, I can testify that very rarely have any of these hundreds of books and articles of spiritual interpretation been utterly worthless or uninteresting.

The scope is too great for the mention here of every such approach. A few of the approaches are indispensable. First, there is the field of theological criticism and Bible analysis. Although these two overlap, emphasis may be stronger in one phase than in the other. Hugh Henry Proctor's "The Theology of the Songs of the Southern Slave" has already been summarized. A similar treatment had been done in 1891 by C. J. Ryder in *The Theology of the Plantation Songs*, published by the American Missionary Association. A far more extensive and intensive treatment of the theological approach has been done in Theo Lehmann's *Negro Spirituals: Geschichte und Theologie,* but this book has not been translated into English. A summary of its contents and conclusions will be given a little later in Part Three, in the discussion of German treatments of the spiritual.

Three writers have been more specific about the use of the Bible by spirituals. In 1947 Father L. M. Friedel, of the Society of the Divine Word, published a booklet entitled *The Bible and the Negro Spirituals.* His booklet was obviously directed toward encouraging more Negroes to become Catholics. It opens with a quotation from the Bible (Psalms 118:54) which he has translated, "Thy laws are become my song in the place of my pilgrimage." The Negro race, he declares, can truly say this with the psalmist.

Father Friedel notes that, even in this period, St. Augustine scholastics were allowed to sing a few well-selected spirituals on festive occasions: "I Couldn't Hear Nobody Pray," "We Are Climbing Jacob's Ladder," "Hold Out Yo' Light, You Heab'nboun' Sojer," and "Go Tell It on de Mountain, Dat Jesus Christ Is Born." He notes also that the use of "sweet" for the chariot in "Swing Low, Sweet Chariot" is similar to the imagery in Proverbs 25:11, which refers to "apples of gold on beds of silver."

His use of Biblical passages is limited, but he makes a very intensive analysis of the Biblical ideas he selects. For example, he shows that Jordan in the spiritual rarely refers to the river described in the Apocalypse, but it does so in "Roll, Jordan, Roll." He insists, however, that the spirituals are rooted in the Bible, and indicates that they follow the King James version instead of Douay. He cites the following Biblical texts as illustrative: Isaiah 60:1, Exodus 6:11, Psalms 139:5, II Timothy 4:6, II Corinthians 5:1, and Psalms 60:3.

Spirituals, he says, can be classified in three groups, according to their Biblical inspiration, (1) celebrating Biblical heroes; (2) depicting the Bible-inspired Christian life; (3) exemplifying the Bible-born Christian hope. Under the first he cites as leading characters Adam, Noah, Abraham, Jacob, Moses, Joshua, Gideon, David, Elias, Isaiah, Jeremiah, Ezekiel, Daniel, Jonah, Peter, Paul, Silas, John, Mary, Martha, and Jesus, as the greatest heroes. He says that the passion and death of Jesus are profoundly expressed in the spiritual.

Under the second he notes the deep interest in Elias and Ezekiel and the reap-what-you-sow passages from Paul, especially Galatians 6:8. Under the third he lists as inspirations I Thessalonians 4:13, Philemon 3:20–21, James 5:13, and Acts 16 (the Paul and Silas jail story). He is impressed by the fact that the spirituals had so much hope. The jubilee (freedom) songs he traces to Leviticus 25:41.

Although the makers of the spiritual were not Catholics, Father Friedel states that few of their songs are objectionable to Catholics. Catholic Negro slaves did not compose spirituals, according to Father Friedel, because they lacked their own priests and the occasion to use the songs at religious services. In his estimation the songs were created for church singing.

Father Friedel also notes the absence of some very likely Biblical candidates for spirituals: Tobias, Judith, and Maccabeus. But he has already stated, and quite correctly, that the creator of the spirituals used the King James Bible. In the King James, these inspiring characters do not appear.

Within its limitations this booklet makes interesting analyses. Its limitations are sometimes severe: Father Friedel admits that he bases his arguments on only five to six hundred songs; he obviously has not studied African sources or, very deeply, the life of the slave; he ignores the fact that some spirituals he mentions have no religious connotation whatsoever. Even so, his approach is valid and valuable to the comprehensive student of the spirituals.

Another analyst of the Biblical background of the spirituals is Jeremiah Wright, who did a master's thesis under the supervision of the present writer on the subject "The Treatment of Biblical Passages in Negro Spirituals" (1969). Wright's Part One deals with definitions, essential backgrounds, purposes, and methods. It includes creative reactions to the slave's religion, his use of the Bible, and his originality.

In Part Two Wright demonstrates the uses made of the Old Testament. His main subtopics are the Creation, the Fall of Man, Noah, Abraham, Isaac, Jacob, Moses, the Ten Commandments, Joshua, Samson, Samuel, David, Hezekiah, the Psalms, Daniel, and Jonah.

Wright's Part Three takes up the New Testament in the spiritual. His main subjects are the birth, childhood, ministry of Christ and Christ's life beyond his ministry, the democratization of Christianity, the death and resurrection of Christ, the Pauline problem, the Apocalyptic spirituals, and Prophecy and Apocalypse. In his Appendix he gives Biblical sources of the songs both in Biblical order and in alphabetical order. His analysis is based on about three hundred spirituals, but his reading before selection was far more extensive.

Although not specifically theological analysis, the sermons in Martin Luther King's *Strength to Love* are exegeses by a justly famous theologian. One of them is called "A Knock at Midnight." Having established that it is midnight in the social order, Dr. King inquires as to the proper behavior of men at such a time. In one of his inquiries he speaks of ineffective Negro churches. "If the choir sings a Negro spiritual," he says of a church freezing with classism, "the members claim an affront to their class status." "This type of church," Dr. King continues, "tragically fails to recognize that worship at its best is a social experience in which people from all levels of life come together to affirm their oneness and unity under God."

Later in the sermon, Dr. King strikes further, deeper, and more specifically into the unifying character of spirituals,

Midnight is a confusing hour when it is difficult to be faithful. The most inspiring word that the church may speak is that no midnight long remains. The weary traveler by midnight who asks for bread is really seeking the dawn. Our eternal message of hope is that dawn will come. Our slave foreparents realized this. They were never unmindful of the fact of midnight, for always there was the rawhide whip of the overseer and the auction block where families were torn asunder to remind them of its reality. When they thought of the agonizing darkness of midnight, they sang:

> Oh, nobody knows de trouble I've seen;
> Glory Hallelujah!
>
> Sometimes I'm up, sometimes I'm down,
> Oh, yes, Lord,
> Sometimes I'm almost to de groun',
> Oh, yes, Lord,
>
> Oh, nobody knows de trouble I've seen,
> Glory Hallelujah!

Encompassed by a staggering midnight but believing that morning would come, they sang:

> I'm so glad trouble don't last alway.
> O my Lord, O my Lord, what shall I do?

Their positive belief in the dawn was the growing edge of hope that kept the slaves faithful amid the most barren and tragic circumstances.

Faith in the dawn arises from the faith that God is good and just. When one believes this, he knows that the contradications of life are neither final nor ultimate. . . . Even the most starless midnight may herald the dawn of some great fulfillment.

Perhaps the most intensive study of Biblical influences in the spiritual is found in Christa Dixon's *Wesen und Wandel geistlicher Volkslieder Negro Spirituals.* This book will also be discussed under the German treatment. It is appropriate to mention here, however, that Dr. Dixon has analyzed three hundred spirituals under fifty-seven headings. Her analyses are not only deeply intensive but quite creative.

From the standpoint of folk variations, two writers have set the spiritual within the broad framework of folk traditions. In *American Folk Music* (1939) Annabel Morris Buchanan has devoted a section to "American Negro Folk Music" and a subsection to "American Negro Songs and Spirituals." In view of the fact that she treats in the same work Anglo-American, Indian, Creole, Canadian, Mexican, Spanish, German, Norwegian, Hungarian, and Portuguese phases with reference to America, the relationship of the Afro-American spiritual in the American folk family is depicted.

Not all of Miss Buchanan's propositions with reference to the Afro-American spiritual stand the test of the known facts. But she has done some very useful things. She has broken down, for example, the songs and spirituals into groups—solo, choral, instrumental. Under instrumental, she discusses spirituals prepared for piano, two pianos, organ, chamber music, orchestra, and brass ensemble or band. It should be noted that from the standpoint of straight bibliography, Charles Haywood has similar breakdowns in his *Bibliography of North American Folklore and Folksong* (1: 453–90, 2d rev. ed.). In 1962, the Detroit Public Library issued a news release on the latest addition to its anthem catalog series: one hundred spirituals in anthem form.

To illustrate the scope of variation in the production of spirituals for use, the present author selected (January, 1971) from the file box of the Music Division of the Library of Congress all the cards on publication of spirituals which, over a four year span, he had never seen. The number came to 44, of which all but twelve were dated 1960 or later. The breakdown was as follows (publication identified by last name of arranger, composer, or publisher):

Spirituals arranged for instruments

organ	piano	guitar	flute	or-chestra	march
Bock	Franklin-Pike	Duarte	Johnson	Davye	Davis
Hancock	León	Johnson		Elliott	
Kendall	Southern Music	Krupp			
Rapley	Nevin	Southern Music	*bass*		
Warner	Petersen	Petersen			
	Radzik		Petersen		
	Tolson				

Spirituals arranged for voices

student exercise	choir	clarinet choir	cantata	anthem	madrigal
	Koster		De Cormier-	Hadler	Busch
Ehret-Gardner	Hogar del libro	Tamiami	McKayle	Rasley	
Gardner	Otterström				
Gardner				*hymn*	
				Ford	

Foreign countries as places of publication were represented as follows:

England: Franklin-Pike, Hattey, Southern Music, Rapley
France: Geoffray
Germany: Kaufmann, Koster, Krupp, Petersen
Poland: Radzik
Spain: Hogar del libro   Mexico: Ortiz   Cuba: León

The place of the spiritual in the folklore of the American Negro has been set by J. Mason Brewer in *American Negro Folklore* (1968). In this book one can catch interrelationships between the spiritual and folk blues, slave seculars, work songs, ballads, proverbs, rhymes, riddles, and other samples of black folklore. There is also an interesting chapter on "The Negro's Religion." Although Professor Brewer, a hard worker and dedicated folklorist, leaves considerable room for disagreement here and there, he has done an excellent coordination. His approach to the interpretation of spirituals is valid in the highest degree.

We have already mentioned Albert Sidney Beckham and his psychological approach. It may be added here that Beckham submits interesting conclusions on the basis of his statistical study. He observes, for example, that the spirituals are erroneously called "sorrow songs." He finds a preponderance of songs given over to elation, joy, and hope, and a good many in which sorrow and joy are intermingled. He deplores the spirituals which stress fear, mainly because he believes that these will lead to a feeling of inferiority among Negro children.

The ethnomusicological approach has been on the rise in recent years. Back in 1919, Nathaniel Dett was hailing an early invasion of ethnological research into the field of the spiritual. He was praising the determination of Natalie Curtis Burlin to study Negro songs and anticipated the same brilliance she had shown in her book on Amerindian folk songs. He deplored the fact that, with reference to the spiritual, the art of ethnological research took second place to that of artistic creation.

Mrs. Burlin, he said, would advocate a native manner of harmonization. In all collections so far, Dett declared, except the one by Emily Hallowell of the *Calhoun Plantation Songs,* conventional harmony had been spoiled by transcribers.

The popularity of the ethnomusicological approach to the study of spirituals is demonstrated in the international bibliography of dissertations and theses, produced in 1966 by Frank Gillis and Alan P. Merriam, entitled *Ethnomusicology and Folk Music.* Of the 873 listings found in this volume, 90 touch upon the Afro-American spiritual. Half of the ninety touch rather strongly, and a dozen or more deal entirely with the spiritual.

One of those listed is a master's thesis by Nancy Gertrude Merritt, done also under the supervision of the present writer, and entitled "Negro Spirituals in American Collections" (1940).* Besides an evaluation of collections and of the problems of collecting, this handbook outlines such literary problems of the spiritual as those of slavish imitation, communal or individual origin, models, social origin, and the spiritual as poetry. It also discusses the spiritual as an American institution.

* Miss Merritt's thesis, like Mr. Wright's and all other theses done at Howard University, is available through the Negro Collection of the Founders Library at the University.

The main service of Miss Merritt's book is an alphabetical listing of seventeen hundred spirituals on the basis of eighty collections. She indicates that a spiritual can be found in as many as ten different collections. Though done a number of years ago, this checklist is still the most comprehensive available.

An eclectic interpretive approach is followed by William E. Guy in *The Message of the Negro Spiritual* (1946). Within this variety, meanings for seventeen spirituals are offered.

A purely artistic approach to spiritual interpretation is quite common, and not always successful. The main trouble is that the poetry of the spiritual is generally too rich in hidden meaning for the superficial examination of the quick essay. Another big trouble is that the background of the songs cannot be "sopped up" in a few hours. Of course, each person is entitled to his own views about the meaning of any poem. It just happens that, with deep and colorful poetry, the view of the careful thinker is likely to be more fulfilling than that of the fly-by-night, however brilliant or clever.

One very interesting artistic approach is found in A. L. Morton's "Promise of Victory: A Note on the Negro Spiritual" (published in *Language of Men*, 1945). Taking "I Stood by de Ribber of Jordan," for example, he inquires if the subject is death, freedom, or freedom in death. He concludes that it is all three. The poem has been written on three planes, and the three planes have given it its richness and depth. Death is not only a friend but a triumph over the oppressor. Nothing holds back the singer from the struggle for life. Thus, death is life.

A special approach for this chapter will be that one based on social implications. Back in 1939, the present writer published in the *Journal of Negro Education* an article on "The Social Implications of the Negro Spiritual." This article indicated, for the first time in a coordinated way, the manner in which the slave's inner personal and group drives were expressed in his songs. This social emphasis was pursued in a more recent article, "Reflections on the Origins of the Negro Spiritual," in the Fall 1969 issue of *Negro American Literature Forum*.

This social emphasis was picked up by the late, and deeply revered, Bernard Katz in his *Social Implications of Early Negro Music in the United States* (1969). Besides a lively introduction, Mr. Katz republishes the standard essays on the spiritual and related songs by W. E. B. Du Bois, W. F. Allen, James Weldon Johnson, R. Nathaniel Dett, James Miller McKim, H. G. Spaulding, Lucy McKim Garrison, T. W. Higginson, John Mason Brown, George W. Cable, H. C. Wood, William E. Barton, Marion A. Haskell, John Lovell, Jr., and J. Rosamund Johnson. In the course of such publication it reprints 150 songs, most of them with the appropriate music.

In reviewing Mr. Katz's book, Russell Roth of the *Minneapolis Star* used the headline, " 'Escapism' theory of Negro music wrong—it's stout poetry." He notes that some of the out-of-print documents revived by the book have long been craved by students of black music today. The argument for social justice in the songs, expressed by Lovell, he calls "prophetic and would seem self-evident today."

Landon Dowdey's *Journey to Freedom* (1969), a casebook with music, shows how spirituals fulfill important principles of life. One by one Dowdey demonstrates the individual's address to the following by using appropriate spirituals: mystery, fear, courage, love, sorrow, change, struggle, help, suffering, creation, and the kingdom. He also has chapters on "Sing to the Lord a New Song" and "Spirituals for City People."

In *Phylon* for 1963, Wayman B. McLaughlin chooses to attack the problem of "Symbolism and Mysticism in the Spirituals." Emphasizing that he is making a new approach and not trying to rule out others, he finds much symbolism and a great deal of mysticism. As one would expect from a professor of philosophy, he laces his arguments with much allusion to many philosophers and philosophical concepts.

Black Music in Our Culture (1970) reflects an effort on the part of the Black Music Committee of Indiana University (Dominique-René de Lerma, chairman) to locate and exploit curricular ideas on the subjects, materials, and problems of black music. The publication, summarizing discussions of experts and other interested parties, has fourteen references to spirituals.

A JURY OF INTERPRETERS

Because the careful interpretation of the Afro-American spiritual involves many problems that have become fraught with confusion, it was decided to invite a jury of knowledgeable people to deal with some basic problems. The jury was asked to ignore basic information. It was requested to give "judgments, opinions, and reactions growing out of your personal experience, thinking, and imagination."

The main justification of this jury is the inherent nature of folk song and the peculiar career of Afro-American folk song in America. As a live consideration, folk song is, generally speaking, two things: It is what the folk meant when they created it and it is what people outside the folk get when they hear it sung or study it or note its reaction upon others. Since this is true, the full effects of a folk song cannot be delivered until the second phase is explored. And since the position and attitude and intelligence of the explorer are essential factors to the exploration, they cannot be overlooked.

The Afro-American folk song has caused as much controversy and variety of opinion as any folk song anywhere. The fact that in outward appearance it is a purely religious song involves it in the vagaries of American religious history and in hit-and-miss theological discussion. The fact that it was created by slaves and that very few interpreters have carefully studied American slavery or made a serious effort to think and feel like American slaves, has worn an enormous hole into which many interpreters have fallen. The energy with which a handful of white Southerners have presented an inconclusive case about its origins and the widespread acceptance of this case without careful examination of its obvious inconclusiveness, have been another major problem. The failure to recognize mask and irony in the Afro-American spiritual, as in all folk song, is still another. And there are many, many other such problems in this whole big field of interpretation.

But interpretation of the Afro-American spiritual has proceeded now for over a hundred years and has spread to many parts of the world. Considering the limited evidence available to the interpreter, it has been, on the whole, deeply sincere and incisive. If every new interpreter could have read, or would have read, all the interpretation up to his time, some good might have ensued. But interpretation has been so widely spread, and interpreters have not always been comprehensive scholars, so this has been impossible.

The variety in viewpoints has been both help and hindrance. A sociologist like Frazier, an anthropologist like Herskovits or Bastide, a psychologist like Beckham tend to ignore the musical and literary qualities. Paying back the compliment, the musicians and literary analysts have paid small attention to the historical and anthropological elements. Some interpreters have stationed themselves at the crossroads, but often with a "crossroads bias."

The purpose of the present statement is not to belittle or to criticize adversely. It is to state the scope and complexity of the problem of interpretation. Within such a complexity, any honest interpreter may find himself beleaguered. But it is better to have the views of intelligent men and women who have studied the spiritual more than casually on some of the basic problems than to leave the matter wide open for speculation. Perhaps the reader will be inspired to examine all the evidence and create therefrom a whole new, wise, and beautiful interpretation.

The jury was impaneled by writing letters to a large number of scholars, critics, and writers and asking them to fill out a questionnaire. This method has obvious drawbacks, but it seems to be the best all-around. Twenty-eight replies have been received to the scholars' questionnaire and one to the artists' questionnaire.

Of the twenty-eight, all have at some time written an article or a book on the Afro-American spiritual or on some phase of its background. Seven are or have been university professors; five are presently editors or directors of research institutions; one is a music historian and one a music librarian; one is the president of a publishing company; one is a practicing Methodist minister; one is a Catholic priest; one is dean of the chapel of a Midwestern college; one is managing editor of a magazine of very large circulation; one is a railroad official very active in the cultural life of his community; and the others are what might be called regular professional writers. The respondent to the artists' questionnaire is a composer. The fact that people of such diverse training and interests have been magnetized into the world of the spiritual is a tremendous asset to a broad and significant interpretation.

The geographical distribution of the jury is equally inspiring. The American scholar, creative writer, historian, and folklorist have naturally treated the spiritual as a home product; their foreign counterparts are expected to be more objective. Often, however, they share the same general facts and their insights are indistinguishable. The freshness in viewpoint may arise from either side of the ocean. When the European interpreter looks at the spiritual through eyes disciplined by comparison with his home folk products or enriched by personal experiences in America, he is likely to produce interesting new slants. This, of course, does not cancel out the fact that some of the most rigorous scholarship and keen analyses have been carried out by Americans.

In any case, the geographical origins of the members of the jury are as follows: U.S.A., twelve; West Germany, five; England and France, three each; Belgium, East Germany, Mexico, the Netherlands, and South Africa, one each.

Twelve of the members have been engaged in personal conversation by the present writer. This conversation has tended to clarify the questions on the questionnaire. In addition, it resulted in suggestions and ideas which have been used in other parts of the book, with proper ascription of source.

The twenty-nine members of the jury, in alphabetical order, may now be introduced, along with their occupations and home locations.

Scholars

Ames, David W.
Professor of Anthropology
San Francisco State College
San Francisco, California

Ames, Russell
Author
Oaxaca, Mexico

Aptheker, Herbert
Director, The American Institute
    for Marxist Studies
New York, New York

Arvey, Verna
Author
Los Angeles, California

Bernard, Kenneth A.
Professor of History

Boston University
Boston, Massachusetts

Chase, Gilbert
Music Historian
Chapel Hill, North Carolina

Epstein, Dena J.
Assistant Music Librarian
The University of Chicago
Chicago, Illinois

Hansen, Kurt H.
Author
Hamburg, West Germany

Haslam, Gerald W.
Assistant Professor of English
Sonoma State College
Rohnert Park, California

Jahn, Janheinz
Author
Messel, West Germany

Knesebeck, Paridam von dem
Author
Bremke, West Germany

Lehmann, Theo
Teacher and Theologian
Karl-Marx-Stadt, East Germany

Leisy, James F.
President, Wadsworth Publishing
  Company
Belmont, California

Nettl, Bruno
Chairman, Division of Musicology
University of Illinois
Urbana, Illinois

Oliver, Paul
Head, Department of Arts and
  History
Architectural Association School
  of Architecture
London, England

Pool, Rosey E.
Author
London, England

Rookmaaker, H. R.
Professor of Art
Free University
Amsterdam, The Netherlands

Schlein, Irving
Author
New York, New York

Schmidt-Joos, Siegfried
Editor, *Der Spiegel* (magazine)
Hamburg, West Germany

Serrand, Father A. V.
Catholic Priest
Les Riceys, France

Smith, Peter D.
Methodist Minister
Sheffield, England

Suppan, Wolfgang
Konservator (Curator)
Deutsches Volksliedarchiv
Freiburg, West Germany

Tate, Thad W.
Editor, *William and Mary
  Quarterly*
College of William and Mary
Williamsburg, Virginia

Tracey, Hugh
Director, International Library of
  African Music
Transvaal, South Africa

Wagner, Jean
Professor of English
University of Grenoble
Grenoble, France

Washington, Joseph R., Jr.
Dean, Edward Dwight Eaton
  Chapel
Beloit College
Beloit, Wisconsin

Waterschoot, Hector
Railroad Official
St.-Niklaas, Belgium

Yourcenar, Marguerite
Author
France (visiting in Northeast
  Harbor, Maine)

Artist

Still, William Grant
Composer
Los Angeles, California

THE QUESTIONS

The questions have naturally been phrased as provocatively as possible. They deal with topics which have proved highly controversial, in the literature, evoking wide differences of opinion, often contradictory, even from the most reputable scholars. In this style of phrasing, the purpose has been to elicit the sharpest possible answers and rejoinders. The significant thing is the reliance the writer places upon a deep-seated belief or a point of view, not the facts involved. The prevailing attitude toward the spiritual has been based upon such reliances rather than upon cold facts.

SCHOLARS' QUESTIONNAIRE

Question 1

What is your private opinion on the origins of the Afro-American spiritual, which has been proved to exist both on the North American continent and in the West Indies well before 1800? How much African element would you say it contains? If the white and black spiritual merely grew up side by side, what determines the borrowing from white to black, particularly in view of the richer and older African tradition in music and folk expression?

The thing most stressed in the answers on origins was the need of the creative singer. The primary need seemed to be for musical and rhythmic self-expression; but there was the need for escape from inhuman treatment; the deeply psychological need of people in search for security after having been torn from their traditional environment; the need to make meaningful responses; the need for overcoming the depth of alienation and for learning new cultural patterns for long-rooted feelings, beliefs, hopes, and understandings.

One writer said that the matter was one for the statement of evidence not for statement of opinion. But the fact is that for a hundred years, the keenest writers have been stating the evidence and drawing from the evidence they state an enormous variety of opinions. The opinions of the trend of the evidence from such a jury as this will certainly be valuable in helping to dispel the confusion.

Five writers believed that the black spiritual originated in some form of whiteness, melodic line, white harmony, elements characteristic of the great awakening and of the traditional songs of America, white church music and white Protestant Christianity, the black musical way of expressing the white hymn, the teachings of English, Scottish, and Irish preachers. Others credited an interlocking relationship of white and black. One said that the slave singer accepted some modes and views of the whites, but only in the sense of conquering the conqueror. One writer mentioned that the depth of the slave's despair was the thing which touched the searing beauty of his song with fire.

The amount and quality of African element was treated in both specific and general terms. Some writers employed such phrases as "origins essentially African," "structure evidence of West African oral tradition," "the slaves' own tradition of folkmusic, folksong, and folkdance," and significant African retentions. A long list of African characteristics was spelled out, including, rhythm (referred to seven times), melisma, overlapping, leader-chorus technique (referred to three times), melodies, use of voice, ideas, attitudes, beliefs, cadence, imagery, handclapping, possession idea, speaking in tongues, verse-response, style of delivery, chant, choral polyphony, repetition, spontaneity, distinctive modality, pitch, numerology, euphony, onomatopoeia, and contrast. One writer quoted Herbert Spinden to the effect that repetition has the effect of rhyming thoughts rather than words. In the estimation of one critic, the richness of the African tradition has remained unrecognized and underestimated because of the European way of analyzing music, with tune more important than performance practice. For one writer, the intangible musicality of the African was unwittingly applied.

As to borrowing, four main theories were developed. The theories and the number of supporters for each are as follows:

Both ways (black to white and white to black)	4
Mainly white to black	6
Mainly black to white	3
No appreciable white to black	1

Several critics felt that, since the white man was entrenched, the borrowing had to be from him. One varied this theme by saying that the oppressed always borrows from the oppressor; another, that the weaker always takes from the stronger. Two suggested that the elaborate arguments of George Pullen Jackson had either gone overboard or were discredited. One said that the growing influence of Christianity accounted for the flow from white to black.

Question 2

If these slaves were contented with their earthly lot, why did they sing so much of the land beyond the grave? Do these songs prove that they swallowed the white man's religion whole? Do you read the songs as containing evidence of criticism or dissatisfaction concerning the life or the religion imposed upon the singing slave? Is there a difference between the everyday slave and the one who sang?

Thirteen of the respondents said that the songs prove discontent, but in various ways. Two said that "contentment" was either not the main thing or not the appropriate word. For one, all folk songs are songs of protest; for another, these songs are definitely songs of protest, disguised or in camouflage, and this feature is one of the sources of their power. As one writer puts it, the songs are one of many evidences of deep discontent.

By implication, several of the commentators indicate that the main evidence of discontent is in the determination to look for something better in a different life. This different life was either the land beyond the grave or the free North. If it was the free North, then the songs show discontent by becoming freedom songs. For one writer, the discontented slave looks to his home in Africa; for another, since Africa is out of the question, he looks beyond the grave. One other writer calls them "truly sorrow songs" and still another refers to the subtle use of dual meanings. For two, the songs are definitely rebellious; for one more, they show religious and secular motives simultaneously.

For one interpreter, the act of singing is more and more the content. In the same vein, one says that the songs themselves represent a certain adaptation to slavery. In the songs, says one, is concern for an unknown future and hope for a better world.

Whatever the lyrics say, it is suggested, the songs bespeak the cultural heritage of the singers. On the other hand, it appears that the slaves found in the white man's religion a means of deliverance to a happier existence just as the white man did. Adaptation and natural acculturation are pointed out, as well as the seeking of assurances of security. To one pair of eyes there is a mixture of rebelliousness, determination to escape to the North, resignation to the inevitable, and reliance on the land beyond the grave.

Criticism and dissatisfaction are seen by at least four respondents. "Nobody Knows the Trouble I See" is offered as one illustration of both. On the other hand, there is seen in the songs a mysticism growing out of Wesleyan or Baptist evangelicism.

As to swallowing the white man's religion whole, two of our answerers believed that the slaves did, and two believed that they definitely did not. The remaining writers are somewhere in between. One goes so far as to say that the religion was not imposed upon the slaves; they accepted it freely and gladly identified with Jesus and the Israelites. Another says that this whole question is bound up in African psychology. One stresses the point that the spirituals show the slave to have had the vitality of early Christians.

Most of the jury do not believe that there is a difference between the everyday slave and the slave who sang. The point of the spiritual, say two, is its collective character. Three said that the slave sang every day without reservation, and one other that he sang when inspired. One declared that the singing slave was probably more artistic, creative, rhythmic, flexible, and a greater lover of life. Some extraordinary individuals, says one thinker, may often have served as the genesis of these songs, but general singing altered them. A deeper and sadder question, he believes, is that of how men sensitive enough to create spirituals could have endured slavery. He is thankful that some of these people, at least, did not become inured to their condition, for without them we would not have had the spirituals.

Question 3

Folk songs traditionally employ mask and symbol; is there any to speak of in the Negro spiritual, in your estimation?

Fifteen of the respondents said without qualification that the Afro-American spiritual employs both mask and symbol; one said that mask was probable and symbol definite; another, that all have symbol but some have mask. One underlined the fact that the folk song always uses language that is masked and masking at the same time, full of symbols which are comprehensible in the respective relevant traditions and groups. Five insisted that there is symbol but no mask. Examples of songs using both were "Didn't My Lord Deliver Daniel, And Why Not Every Man?" "Steal Away," "Wade in the Water," "Follow the Drinking Gourd," "Joshua Fit the Battle of Jericho," "Good News," and "All God's Chillun Got Shoes." One writer perceptively noted that scholars find more symbol than the creators of the songs probably did. Several agreed that the spirituals are steeped in symbols, Biblical and otherwise (that is, such things as objects and happenings). One compared spirituals and blues, saying that both are full of symbols. One said that mask and symbol enabled the slave to cloak his desire for freedom. Two or three others commented on the range of significations in the symbols used.

Question 4

How do you account for the wide dissemination of these black songs over all these years and throughout the world (e.g., spiritual festivals in Germany in the late 1960s, recent use of spirituals by the Czechs and the Poles, French Catholic choirs singing these songs on regular tours, South African Negroes preparing and publishing 120 songs at one time for use among Bantu peoples, recent articles on the spiritual in Indian publications, etc.)? If the white spiritual was the lead song in this category, why did it not achieve respect, popularity, and vigorous life in America and in other countries?

Most of the answers to the reasons for the wide dissemination dealt with the following propositions: profound feelings and observations coupled with consummate artistry; universal expression of suffering and hope; eloquent creative statements of oppressed peoples; the most lively religious feelings of our time; the rhythm and the other means of musical interpretation; the popularizing methods of the Abolitionist movement and of the Jubilee Singers; a genuine dislike for slavery, oppression, and injustice by European countries; quality; true art; the unparalleled power of expression exhibited by the songs; their novelty; their adaptability to the communications media—movies, radio, records, etc.; their being a valid and moving expression of a particular culture; their congeniality to the universal spirit of freedom; their wild spontaneity; their combination of great simplicity, attractive melodic line, and arresting rhythmic impulse; their sentimentality, especially of a Schubertized, Westernized variety; their pure, simple, honest, and accurate expression, full of pathos and throbbing reality; a worldwide interest in the Negro's social and economic plight; and the wider diffusion of anthropological and ethnological techniques. In addition, there was mentioned the ineluctable influence of the spiritual upon the American music which followed it and the great power of African-derived music.

As to the white spiritual, seven respondents said specifically that it had no influence upon the black; one said it did influence the black; one said it was influenced by the black. Most respondents agreed that it was an inferior type of song, written for a narrow clientele, and incapable of projecting a great appeal. One writer said that it was equally valid with the black and sometimes almost as moving, but speaking for a particular variant of Anglo-American culture that is simply not so widely understood or widely appealing.

Question 5

In your estimation is the spiritual a purely religious song or is it a universal expression with outer religious manifestations? Is it primarily expression, primarily communication, or both? Will you please briefly elucidate your answers.

Counting those who had reservations or who based their answers on limited definitions, eight respondents said the spiritual was purely religious; but four of these said that its being so did not prevent its being universal also. One said it was universal because it was purely religious. Another said that it was impurely religious, political, and otherwise. Several insisted on the blending of the religious and the secular. One underscored the fact that, although couched in religious form, it was a deeply psychological phenomenon.

One writer said that the spiritual was implanted and well accepted at first as religious manifestation. It was soon used, however, to portray general human (or more exactly, inhuman) conditions of life.

One critic noted that the spiritual exploited the pragmatic and universal parts of religion. Another said it was religious in the sense of *religio*, which covered more than church functions, which, in fact, covered all really communicative activity. Still another said it was protest and agony, couched in religious color.

As to the question of expression and communication, fourteen said it was both; of the fourteen, two said it was primarily expression, two said that expression and communication were intertwined, and one suggested a happy meeting point of the two. One defined *expression* as "art" and *communication* as "tool." Spirituals, he said, had been used as tools but in too transient, utilitarian, and demeaning ways for them to be identified as such.

Question 6

Do you accept the view that the spiritual influenced (and influences) minstrel, Stephen Foster-ism, jazz, ragtime, swing, blues, country music, gospel, etc.? Why?

Nineteen answers were a flat yes. Several pointed out the difficulty of tracing such influences. Several also emphasized the mutual influences between the spiritual and the other forms, and among the various forms. One was not sure of the influence of the spiritual over gospel; one saw very small influence of the spiritual over ragtime. One excluded the works of Stephen Foster from the list of spiritual influences. To one the relationship between the spiritual and the blues was more of a cousinhood than a parental thing, such as with gospel. While one stressed the overall tremendous effects of Afro-American music, another warned that some of the influences referred to were direct and powerful and others were diluted. One writer referred, insightfully, to the influences which happen subtly through the experience of individuals as they grow up.

Question 7

Do you have evidence that the folk community that originally produced these songs is still in existence? Is it still making songs? If not in songs, is it making known its feelings and attitudes in other ways?

With a number of reservations, because of more or less radical changes that have taken place, nine of the respondents answered the first question yes. Some pointed to the still strong influences from Africa; one mentioned the ghetto as a modern variation of the slave community. One said that the concept of folk community in the sense implied was too vague to identify. But two declared the gospel song as today's spiritual, from the same general community. Six writers said that the folk community in question was still making songs.

There were also nine who said that the folk community which created the spiritual had passed off the stage, although one of these said that the spirit of the original community was still alive. One said that the community had changed through natural, sociological transformation, the influence of musical phenomena, and the spread of mass media. Beyond the song today there are other possibilities of expression, such as letting oneself be manipulated (gaining a feeling of happiness) by the mass media.

Question 8

In your view is the spiritual a *group song* and the blues an *individual song?*

Eleven answered yes to both questions, although three or four had reservations. One critic said that the spiritual was both, but the blues was just an individual song. Another insisted that every song created by an individual was taken up by the group. Each, said another, sings group experiences largely because the group is made up of individuals. Most spirituals, said still another, are group songs, but many are intensely personal. One declared that both were mainly group songs. And one, finally, stated that the distinction was artificial and on the whole untenable.

One of the interpreters had a highly coordinated answer. Most spirituals, he said, are group songs, although patterns often suggest the individualistic. The majority fall into two categories, (1) a really collective group song, and (2) a locomotive pulling the group—verse and response. The leaders felt responsibility for keeping the group moving in a certain way. The blues started as an individual song; the spiritual is primarily a collective one.

Another interpreter points out that blues is not solely an individual song, not for the past forty years anyway. He recalls that blues bands and groups have been characteristic of cities from Memphis to Chicago and Detroit. He concedes, however, that, creatively speaking, blues are most successfully sung solo.

Still another interpreter notes that the blues is a very personal art form, but that it has a universal meaning. It expresses the feelings not only of an individual but of a group. The spiritual, on the other hand, can be sung by a group and by an individual. In each case, therefore, the question of group song or individual song is only a question of practical interpretation.

One writer says that instrumental influences play a larger part in the blues than they do in the spiritual.

Question 9

What is your opinion on the barbarism of the slaves brought from Africa to America? Were these slaves taken from an area of savages? Did the slave brokers choose the lowest element in the area?

Only one of the respondents expressed the idea that there was any barbarism in the background of the slave singers or that the slaves in question came from an area of savages. Several objected even to the use of the terms.

Several pointed out that the background culture of the slaves was comparable to the agricultural civilization of the East or of Europe at the time. One stated that the slaves were no more savage than the Europeans in America who slaughtered Indians. Two others suggested barbaric traits among the whites.

Six of the respondents said that the brokers took what they could get in the African homelands. Seven seemed to think that strong physical qualities were stressed by the slave brokers. The consensus was that the slaves were representative of the various levels of African society, from average citizens to kings and courtiers. The following groups were mentioned as among those most likely to have been taken from Africa and brought to America: whole communities, the most gifted people available, the high culture, the young and strong, the politically and militarily weak.

Question 10

You will probably agree that folk songs generally reflect the life of the people: do these songs suggest a mild slavery with close interrelationship between master and slave? Do they suggest that the masters as a general rule taught religion to their slaves and gave them free opportunity to practice Christianity?

In the first place, not every respondent agreed that folk songs generally reflected the life of the people. One said that as a historian he could not bring himself to extrapolate social conditions from songs. Another questioned the premise on the ground that folk songs in England stressed a curious glamor about knights and ladies, lords and mistresses, and popular heroes (like Robin Hood). Folk songs give color to the life of the people and only sometimes reflect it. Still another respondent says that the questions raised cannot be answered by the songs.

Even so, one respondent said that the songs suggest a mild slavery and ten others said that they did not. Eight said that the songs definitely did not show a close interrelationship between master and slave; one said that they did. Eight also said that the songs show that masters taught their slaves Christianity and allowed them to practice it; eight said just the reverse.

Aside from these more specific answers, there were a number of answers with qualifications. Some Christian opportunities were granted, said one writer, providing there was no damage to the whites. Christianity was used as a form of oppression, said another, and the Christian slave was not rebellious. One writer noted that allusions to masters were generally uncomplimentary, such as "No More Auction Block for Me" and "Try My Best For to Serve No Master." Another reviewer reminded the student to be sure to study the psychology of the Africans in the background in trying to answer such questions.

In answering the artists' questionnaire, Mr. Still said that his approach was purely musical with deep respect for the unlettered folk artists who created the songs. He declined to make comparisons between or among songs, believing all impressive in one way or another. He accounts for the popularity of the spirituals because they are beautiful, ingratiating, and memorable. The composer finds that audiences everywhere are appreciative of spirituals with no distinction on this score between Americans and foreigners.

As to their religious quotient, Mr. Still declares that the spirituals are predominantly religious expressions even when they are rhythmic. He is aware of the fusion of African musical impulses with those of peoples all over the Western Hemisphere and of the differences in outward character. He believes that the various folk forms have influenced each other only broadly. When asked what methods he uses to adapt the songs for various purposes, he says that he lets the character of each song dictate its own treatment.

The overall answers of these twenty-nine experts demonstrate the tremendous scope and variety of the problems affecting the interpretation of the spirituals. One should remember that a folk song is not just its music but also all the effects it produces. On this basis our jury has revealed the great range of the songs. Since the songs are still being sung and interpreted all over the world, it will probably be years before these songs reach a maturity of production.

Besides a deep vote of thanks, the jury deserves a special commendation. Each has shown a rich and unusual point of view. They have explored these vital questions not only comprehensively but intensively. They have given the reader the benefit of wide reading and vigorous, original thinking. If the whole of their answers could have been displayed, the reader would have seen ingenious elaboration, illustration, and distinctive styles.

Considering that every singer, professional or amateur, every listener, and every reader about spirituals is an interpreter, for himself and for others, interpretation becomes an unbelievably great activity. Our jury, we are sure, has let the light shine in a most valuable way.

SPECIAL INDIVIDUAL INTERPRETATIONS

Frederick Douglass

As a former slave, Frederick Douglass had great respect and admiration for the spirituals. In his *Autobiography*, especially in the early versions called *My Bondage and My Freedom*, he mentions the slave's secular songs too, but he had a special place in his heart for the spirituals. His earliest reference to singing is in the fact that slaves were expected to sing as well as work. "A silent slave is not liked by masters or overseers. '*Make a noise,*' '*make a noise,*' and '*bear a hand*' are the words usually addressed to the slaves when there is silence among them." Teamsters, said Douglass, sang to let overseers know where they were and that they were getting on with the work. He felt that to let spiritual-minded men and women just hear the slaves sing would be more impressive than to have them read volumes about physical cruelties; the songs "speak to the heart and to the soul of the thoughtful."

Douglass's account of the songs as "breathing the prayer and complaint of souls boiling over with the bitterest anguish" is well known. "Every tone," he reiterates,

> was a testimony against slavery, and a prayer to God for deliverance from chains. . . . These songs still follow me, to deepen my hatred of slavery, and quicken my sympathies for my brethren in bonds. If any one wishes to be impressed with a sense of the soul-killing power of slavery, let him go to Col. Lloyd's plantation, and, on allowance day, place himself in the deep, pine woods, and there let him, in silence, thoughtfully analyze the sounds that shall pass through the chambers of his soul, and if he is not thus impressed, it will only be because "there is no flesh in his obdurate heart."

In writing about the effects of holidays, Douglass describes the hand-clapping and rhythms that accompanied the singing and the irony and overt criticism in the songs themselves. Although these were not spirituals, they illustrate the methods by which a number of spirituals were delivered.

In a later section, which he heads "Hymns with a Double Meaning," Douglass writes,

A keen observer might have detected in our repeated singing of

> O Canaan, sweet Canaan,
> I am bound for the land of Canaan,

something more than a hope of reaching heaven. We meant to reach the *north*—and the north was our Canaan.

> I thought I heard them say,
> There were lions in the way,
> I don't expect to stay
> Much longer here.
> Run to Jesus—shun the danger—
> I don't expect to stay
> Much longer here,

was a favorite air, and had a double meaning. In the lips of some, it meant the expectation of a speedy summons to a world of spirits; but, in the lips of our company, it simply meant, a speedy pilgrimage toward a free state, and deliverance from all the evils and dangers of slavery.

Booker T. Washington

Although considered a conservative in his attitude toward Southern whites, Booker T. Washington was no conservative where spirituals were concerned. His reference to freedom singing under the guise of religious singing has already been given. He believed firmly in the fact that the spiritual emphasized freedom of the body in this world.

In his introduction to Samuel Coleridge-Taylor's *Twenty-Four Negro Melodies* (the introduction was written in 1904; the book was published in 1905), Booker Washington reviews some pungent facts in the background of American Negro folk music. He begins by deploring the fact that, at that moment, interest in the plantation songs seemed to be dying out with the generation that gave them birth. He deplored also the fact that the spirituals were in too many minds associated with "rag" music and the more reprehensible "coon" song.

Then he turns for a few brief paragraphs to the history of these folk songs. Their predominant characteristic, he says, is their essential spontaneity. In Africa, music had sprung into life at the war dance, at funerals, at marriage festivals. Upon this African foundation, the American plantation song was built. According to the testimony of African students at Tuskegee, there are native African melodies that reveal the close relationship between the two.

But the imagery and the sentiments, he declares, are an American product. He states specifically, "Wherever companies of Negroes were working together, in the cotton fields and tobacco factories, on the levees and steamboats, on sugar plantations, and chiefly in the fervor of religious gatherings, these melodies sprang into life."

He says, further, that often a person with an exceptional voice was paid to lead the singing on the theory that such singing increased the amount of labor. Whatever the reason and the process, the songs which have come forth remind the race of the "rock whence it was hewn." They foster race pride. In slavery days, they "furnished an outlet for the anguish of smitten hearts."

No race, he continues, "has ever sung so sweetly or with such perfect charity, while looking forward to the 'year of Jubilee.' " He recalls also the great number of scriptural allusions and the unique interpretations of standard hymns.

He expresses the view that the songs from Virginia and the more northern slave states, because of the milder slavery, are more bright and joyous than those from the Gulf states. He asserts that the songs breathe a childlike faith in a personal Father, "and glow with the hope that the children of bondage will ultimately pass out of the wilderness of slavery into the land of freedom." He then presents a very striking picture,

> In singing of a deliverance which they believed would surely come, with bodies swaying, with the enthusiasm born of a common experience and of a common hope, they lost sight for the moment of the auction-block, of the separation of mother and child, of sister and brother. There is in the plantation songs a pathos and a beauty that appeals to a wide range of tastes, and their harmony makes abiding impression upon persons of the highest culture. The music of these songs goes to the heart because it comes from the heart.

As to the perpetuation of the songs, he mentions both the slowing down of singing among black people in the large city churches and the fervent continuation among people in the smaller towns and country districts, where most of the black people live. He mentions also the preservation work carried on by the colleges, especially Fisk, Hampton, and Tuskegee.

His admiration for Coleridge-Taylor and the work he is doing in developing these songs along with other African-born melodies is extremely high:

> It is, I repeat, a cause for special gratitude that the foremost musician of his race, a man in the zenith of his powers, should seek to chronicle, and thus perpetuate, the old melodies that are so rapidly passing away.

He praises the composer, also, for giving the melodies "an art form fully imbued with their essential spirit."

At the close of his introduction, Booker Washington reminds his reader of the plea by Thomas P. Fenner (the Hampton conductor and composer) that the people retain and nurture this wonderful music. Fenner hopes that the great musical sense of the race will, as the race matures, call forth a composer "who would bring the music of the future out of this music of the past." "May we not," concludes Booker Washington, "look to Samuel Coleridge-Taylor for a fulfillment of this prophecy?"

As president of Tuskegee he insisted on singing of the songs by students. Every student sang spirituals two or three times a week. Booker Washington encouraged the playing of spirituals by N. Clark Smith and the Tuskegee band. Conductor Smith brought out several volumes based on this singing and playing. Among these were *New Plantation Melodies* (1906) as sung by the Tuskegee Institute Quartette; *New Jubilee Songs for Quartette, Choir or Chorus, Concert, Church & Home* (1906); and *Favorite Folk-Melodies* (1913), as sung by Tuskegee students, directed by Mrs. Jennie C. Lee, compiled and arranged by N. Clark Smith.

Some people at Tuskegee will tell you that Booker T. Washington's last written expression to the world was an article about spirituals. They are doubtless referring to "Plantation Melodies, Their Value," published in the *Musical Courier* for December 23, 1915, a few weeks after Dr. Washington's death. In an editor's note we learn that the article had been written in September, 1915, at the behest of Albert A. Van de Mark, a music manager of Lockport, New York.

In this short article, Dr. Washington states that the gift of song, brought from Africa by the Negro slave, was his most precious possession in America. It served him as comfort and solace when everything else failed. Although many of his songs are sad, many, too, are joyous, following his naturally happy and cheerful character. He reiterates the fact that everywhere in the world they have been sung, these songs touch "the common heart of man."

He admits that for a while after the Civil War the black man turned away from his traditional music. He is glad that the change in him has caused him to renew his pride in these his great folk songs and to desire to preserve them and their memories.

Colonel Thomas Wentworth Higginson

Colonel Higginson's article, "Negro Spirituals," in the *Atlantic Monthly* for June 1867, was almost as important in the history of the spirituals as *Slave Songs of the United States*. The editors of the latter volume included in their foreword a strong acknowledgment to Higginson. They were indebted, they said, for his "friendly encouragement and for direct and indirect contributions to their original stock of songs." They thanked him for suggesting names of persons likely to have information for them and for improving every opportunity to procure them material.

Higginson's article has been referred to several times in this book for its information and insights. There are other interpretations of his, however, which have not been mentioned. He said that in the songs sometimes the present predominates, sometimes the future, but that the combination of the two was always implied. The songs, he declared, were a stimulus to the slave's courage. There was no parallel instance, he declared, of an oppressed race sustained by religious sentiment alone. In his article he gives the words of thirty-eight songs and enlightening notes on many of them.

W. E. B. Du Bois

In 1903, W. E. B. Du Bois published a book of essays called *The Souls of Black Folk*. As a piece of writing and as an expression of Du Bois's basic philosophy, it is sometimes called the greatest of many this grand patriarch wrote during his ninety-five years. The last essay of the book was a scholarly and poetic treatment of the spirituals, entitled "Of the Sorrow Songs."

Thirty-one years later, Zora Neale Hurston contradicted Du Bois. She said that the spirituals were not primarily songs of sorrow but songs of happy release. But Du Bois's emphasis upon the sorrow element is legitimate. He uses sorrow more in the sense of "imaginatively serious" than in the sense of "sad." In a way he was following the emphasis of Frederick Douglass.

"Of the Sorrow Songs" is a truly great piece of writing. It opens by quoting several lines from the spiritual,

> I walk through the churchyard
> To lay this body down.

He tells how the songs came to him one by one, unknown yet an intimate part of his experience. Commenting on America's concentration on vigor and ingenuity rather than beauty, he calls these songs "the most beautiful expression of human experience born this side the seas." He also calls them the greatest gift of the Negro people.

He pays due credit to Lucy McKim Garrison, Thomas Wentworth Higginson, and George L. White in seeing that the songs got a hearing. He shows the relationship of these Afro-American expressions to primitive African music. For example, he quotes from "Do bana coba, gene me, gene me!" which he says came to him from his great, great grandmother, and ties it in with

> You may bury me in the East,
> You may bury me in the West,
> But I'll hear the trumpet sound in that morning.

He says that "Nobody Knows the Trouble I've Seen" was sung by freedmen horribly disappointed at the refusal of the United States to give them land on which to grow. He explains the constant appearance of thunder in the songs by the awe felt by the slaves for the sudden wild thunderstorms of the South.

He does not omit reference to the love songs and the songs of death; like other writers he mentions the lack of the fear of death among the slaves. Here is how he speaks of the hope that runs through the spirituals,

Through all the sorrow of the Sorrow Songs there breathes a hope—a faith in the ultimate justice of things. The minor cadences of despair change often to triumph and calm confidence. Sometimes it is faith in life, sometimes faith in death, sometimes assurance of boundless justice in some fair world beyond. But whichever it is, the meaning is always clear: that sometime, somewhere, men will judge men by their souls and not by their skins. Is such a hope justified? Do the Sorrow Songs sing true?

He ends his brilliant essay on a note of challenge to America,

Your country? How came it yours? Before the Pilgrims landed we were here. Here we have brought our three gifts and mingled them with yours: a gift of story and song . . . the gift of sweat and brawn to beat back the wilderness, conquer the soil, and lay the foundations of this vast economic empire two hundred years earlier than your weak hands could have done it; the third, a gift of the Spirit. . . . Actively we have woven ourselves with the very warp and woof of this nation,—we fought their battles, shared their sorrow, mingled our blood with theirs, and generation after generation have pleaded with a headstrong, careless people to despise not Justice, Mercy, and Truth, lest the nation be smitten with a curse. Our song, our toil, our cheer, and warning have been given to this nation in blood-brotherhood. Are not these gifts worth the giving? Is not this work and striving? Would America have been America without her Negro people?

Written nearly seventy years ago, "Of the Sorrow Songs" has not always kept pace with recent scholarship. But no interpretation of the spiritual is more clear-eyed and deep.

Mark Twain

One would hardly expect Mark Twain (Samuel Langhorne Clemens) to be among the enthusiastic interpreters of the spiritual, but there he is. He sang spirituals to his children, Susy and Clara. He acted them out, not only for his children but for grown-ups, too. In Hartford he went to the church of a Mr. Twitchell to hear the Hampton Singers sing these songs which he loved; he sang under his breath with them.

When the Fisk Jubilee Singers first went to Europe, Mark Twain wrote letters to his friends and publishers in England on their behalf. Deploring the "negro minstrels" who had misrepresented plantation music, he urged his correspondents not to fail to hear these great and true singers. "I do not know when anything has so moved me" as their plaintive melodies, he wrote.

One of his biographers reports that he suddenly began singing spirituals at the home of the Warners one night. With both eyes shut, he sang low and sweet, his two hands up to his head, "just as though the sorrow of them negroes was upon him." He sang "Nobody Knows the Trouble I Seen, Nobody Knows but Jesus." When he came to the "Glory Hallelujah!" he gave a great shout. Listeners said they would never forget it.

In Florence, Italy, Mark sang spirituals for a sick Mrs. Clemens. She loved the songs as he did. It made her happy to hear him singing them again.

His real interpretation of the spirituals, however, is found in a letter he wrote to the Reverend Mr. Twitchell on August 22, 1897. The letter was written in Lucerne, Switzerland. He begins by telling of having entertained six of the Fisk Jubilee Singers in his home a few nights before. One of them he had met in London twenty-four years ago. Three of the six were born in slavery, and the other three were the children of slaves. Yet, says Twain, "How charming they were—in spirit, manner, language, pronunciation, enunciation, grammar, phrasing, matter, carriage, clothes—in every detail that goes to make the real lady and gentleman, and welcome guest."

He then goes on to describe the concert at the village hotel. The "Jubilees" placed a spell upon the German and Swiss men and women grouped around the tables with beer mugs in front of them. They wiped out all indifference. "It was a triumph," Mark Twain said. "It reminded me of Launcelot riding in Sir Kay's armor and astonishing complacent Knights who thought they had struck a soft thing."

He went on to say that the "Jubilees" sang a lot of pieces.

> Arduous and painstaking cultivation has not diminished or artificialized their music, but on the contrary—to my surprise—has mightily reinforced its eloquence and beauty. Away back in the beginning—to my mind—their music made all other vocal music cheap; and that early notion is emphasized now. It is utterly beautiful to me; and it moves me infinitely more than any other music can. I think in the Jubilees and their songs America has produced the perfectest flower of the ages; and I wish it were a foreign product, so that she would worship it and lavish money on it and go properly crazy over it.

He ends by saying that the German music critics praised the concert and that one of the Jubilee men was a son of General Joe Johnson, "and was educated by him after the war."

Carl Van Vechten

Excerpts from the interpretive criticism of Carl Van Vechten have already been referred to. His comments on the spiritual spread over a period of twenty-five years, from the early 1920s to the late 1940s. He commented on books, singers, composers, and individual songs. He did not hesitate to give his current views, although at times they contradicted what he had previously said on a given subject.

In his review of Roland Hayes's *My Songs* he recalled that Hayes had almost single-handedly introduced the spirituals to the concert-going public. He said that Harry T. Burleigh was his only serious rival in this regard. Roland Hayes had pointed out that there was no one way to present the songs, so long as the singer preserved the original mood and the serious purpose.

In "Moanin' Wid a Sword in Ma Han' " (an ironical takeoff on a famous spiritual), Van Vechten complains of the reluctance of the Negro to develop and exploit his racial gifts. He says that only Roland Hayes and Paul Robeson, by constantly singing spirituals, were taking their responsibilities seriously. He ended on the note that the great Negro always climbed to the top on the basis of his Negro heritage.

He congratulated Guinzberg and Oppenheimer for inaugurating their new publishing house, the Viking Press, with the Johnsons' *Book of American Negro Spirituals*. Again and again he said that the spirituals were the richest heritage of the Negro race. In loud tones he called for a discography on the spiritual. He said that J. Rosamund Johnson's *Rolling Along in Song* "should please any one who likes to whistle 'Little David' in the bathtub, and who is there who doesn't?" In his sketchbook called *In the Garret* (1920) he made scattered comments on spirituals.

H. L. Mencken

Several times already H. L. Mencken has been quoted in forthright statements about the spiritual. In Part One, speaking of the South, Mencken is quoted as having said that "its only native music it owes to the despised negro." Several other of his pithy remarks have been incorporated as the book has moved along.

Mencken's concept of the spiritual was of a song developed by talented individual Negro creators during the camp meeting tradition. In fact, he calls the spiritual the best of the survivors of that tradition. Since Methodist hymns lack rhythm, Mencken says, the spiritual improved on Methodist hymns both as to rhythm and harmony. He said that it was mulatto rather than Negro.

Like many people of his time, he felt that the Negro had natural musical gifts. Any crowd of Negroes, he declared, can give any tune new dignity and interest with strange and entrancing harmonies. "In the midst of harsh discords, they produce effects of extraordinary beauty." His cry of hope for discovering the authors of the spiritual was indeed plaintive.

James Weldon Johnson

In Ellen Tarry's *Young Jim* (a story of the early years of James Weldon Johnson) is described his grandmother's expectation that he was going to be a preacher because of his constant church attendance and his remembering large sections of the Bible. There is also a sketch about a church service at Hampton in which spirituals, especially "No Hidin' Place down There" and "Swing Low," played a considerable part. Then Miss Tarry tells of the young James singing spirituals in New England with the Atlanta University quartet.

As everyone knows, young Jim did not develop into a preacher, but he became one of the best interpreters of the traditional Negro preacher in his excellent collection of "Seven Negro Sermons in Verse" called *God's Trombones*. This book was created out of the stuff of spirituals.

Ernest Cater Tate in his doctoral thesis, "The Social Implications of the Writings and the Career of James Weldon Johnson" (New York University, 1959), says Johnson was one of the first to call attention to the folk songs of the Afro-American as evidence of his contribution to American civilization. Also, says Tate, he explained the true meaning of the spirituals and set the Negro to looking at them in a new light. Most of the way, Tate's statement is quite accurate.

In 1912 James Weldon Johnson published the first edition of *The Autobiography of an Ex-Colored Man* (in later editions *Ex-Coloured* replaced *Ex-Colored*), in which he told of a fair Negro who left the black community and went over into the white. While still a black man, the protagonist of the story was aware of four things which refuted the oft advanced theory of the Negro's inferiority and his lack of originality and artistic skill: the Uncle Remus stories, the jubilee songs, ragtime music, and the cakewalk. Also in his early career, the protagonist was impressed by the preaching of the Reverend John Brown and the singing of "Singing Johnson." Johnson used all of these references in later books.

After the colored man had become an ex-colored man, he attended a Carnegie Hall meeting in the interest of Hampton Institute. His hearing the Hampton students sing awakened memories which left him sad.

Johnson's later evaluations of the spiritual were much more direct. They are found mainly in a number of magazine articles and in the prefaces to two collections, *The Book of American Negro Poetry* and *The Books of American Negro Spirituals*. In one article he speaks of the criticizing of Roland Hayes for including English, French, German, and Italian songs in his programs: "Why doesn't he confine himself to the Spirituals?" asked the critics. This was true in spite of the fact that no tenor on the American concert stage could surpass Roland Hayes in the singing of French and German songs. The theme of the article was the dilemma of Negro artists.

In another article he wrote of a change in the attitude of American whites with regard to their evaluation of spirituals. Formerly, he said, the spiritual caused people to have sympathy and pity for the "poor Negro." Now (1928), there is admiration for the race's creative genius. The spiritual has caused people to look at the other folk art creations of the Negro. He predicted that sooner or later composers will take spirituals as material. Almost as he spoke, his predictions started coming true (as the evidence on pages 457–58 demonstrates). In a third sample article he reiterated that the bulk of spirituals were African style.

In the foreword to his *Book of American Negro Poetry*, he pointed out that the best of the black poets had relied at least in part upon traditional Negro material. In his preface to *The Books of American Negro Spirituals* he gave a condensed but perceptive history of the spirituals up to that time (1925–26), a sketch of the meaning of the songs, a projection of the way they were created, and an estimate of their value.

Alain Locke

Most of the spiritual commentaries by Alain Locke are found in six places: his article, "The Negro Spirituals" in *The New Negro: An Interpretation* (1925); "The Technical Study of the Spirituals: A Review," in *Opportunity: Journal of Negro Life* for November 1925; "Negro Contributions to America" in *The World Tomorrow* for June 1929; "Toward a Critique of Negro Music," in *Opportunity* for November and December 1934; *The Negro and His Music* (1936); and "Spirituals" for *Commemoration of the Seventy-Fifth Anniversary of the Proclamation of the Thirteenth Amendment to the Constitution of the United States*, December 18, 1940.

As has been said earlier, Alain Locke believed that Christianity was the power motif behind the spirituals. Like James Weldon Johnson, he credited much of the talk about spirituals in the 1920s to artistic appreciation; later, he said, these songs will be shown to be profound and capable of a spiritual dynamic of great force. The Negro, he insisted, had developed a special discipline and a spiritual heritage which may make him a protagonist in our culture of spiritual and mystical values.

In "Toward a Critique of Negro Music," Professor Locke was most unhappy. Things Negro, he began, were the victim of uncritical praise or calculated disparagement. Most writing about Negro music was "platitudinous piffle, repetitious bosh," praise more damaging than disparagement. Negro music needed, he thought, a bitter tonic of criticism. Negro musicians in vital touch with their folk traditions were in slavery to Tin Pan Alley.

He would rescue from the flames, he went on, only the following critiques of Negro music: W. F. Allen's comments on slave songs; Higginson's essay; Krehbiel's book; a few paragraphs from James Weldon Johnson; the essay in *The New Negro;* W. C. Handy and Abbe Niles on Negro folk music; Carl Van Vechten's writings; Langston Hughes's expressions on the blues; Dorothy Scarborough's writings; a few pages from *Tin Pan Alley;* R. D. Darrell on Duke Ellington; some of Olin Downes's essays; jazz notes from Irving Schwerké and Robert Goffin; sketches by Henry Cowell and Theodore Chandler. The most original and pioneering use of Negro themes had been done, he said, by Dvořák, Copland, Alden Carpenter, George

Gershwin, Paul Whiteman, and Sesana. Much of Burleigh, Rosamund Johnson, and Dett, he added, was sophisticated or diluted.

Only a revolutionary originality and innovation, he declared, can transform the situation. Vocal music offered promise because of the gift of Negro singing. But the Negro spiritual not in the barbershop and stage straitjacket had been developed in a line false to its native choral nature. Only Eva Jessye and Hall Johnson had been consistently good. While his article was in the press, William Dawson's *Negro Folk Symphony* blossomed forth. This, Locke said, was definitely on the right track.

Sterling Brown

A close friend and collaborator of Locke, Sterling Brown developed into one of the major authorities on the spiritual and on other Afro-American folk contributions. In 1937 he brought out *Negro Poetry and Drama* in which Chapter 2 was devoted to "Negro Folk Poetry." In 1941 he was the senior editor of *The Negro Caravan*, which had a large section on "Folk Literature," of which nine pages were given to "Spirituals." And in the 1950s Professor Brown did several articles for *Phylon* on "Negro Folk Expression."

In the article in *Negro Poetry and Drama* Professor Brown corrects an impression left by Mencken about the inability of the folk to create songs:

> It is likely that although lines, couplets, or even entire songs may have originated with individuals, the folk were the court of final resort. They approved or rejected, changed lines that they did not understand, inserted stanzas from many different sources wherever they pleased, sometimes sang a choral response unrelated to the leader's line, e.g.,
>
> Leader: You never can tell what a hypocrite will do
> Chorus: Way in de middle of de air. . . .
>
> and kept them in the storehouse of their memory, for oral transmission to the next generation or for circulation in their wanderings to other, sometimes remote sections. The spirituals are folk products.

Brown was quite direct in his evaluation of the writings of those who tried to overthrow the "originality" of the spirituals. He showed that the parallels of white spirituals offered as models of the Afro-American variety were far from the finished Afro-American product. He conceded that the "romantic theory of completely African origin for the spirituals" had been disproved. But he also pointed out that camp meeting models for the best Negro spirituals remain to be presented. And he added that those who thought the slave was talking about "freedom from sin" when he sang of freedom were propounding a theory "convincing only to those who must defend slavery at all costs."

Brown's article in *The Negro Caravan* is a review of the spiritual's development up to 1941. He evaluates the various conflicting theories and makes reasonable disposition of them, particularly those of George Pullen Jackson, Guy Johnson, and Newman White on one side and Krehbiel, Dett, and Ballanta Taylor on the other. Once again he emphasizes the Afro-American folk, saying that from the folk storehouse came ideas, vocabulary, idioms, and images.

Miles Mark Fisher

The Reverend Doctor Miles Mark Fisher, formerly pastor of the White Rock Baptist Church in Durham, North Carolina, submitted at the University of Chicago in 1945, a doctoral thesis, *Negro Slave Songs in the United States*. The thesis was published in 1953 from a fund contributed to the American Historical Association by the Carnegie Corporation of New York. It is an admirable piece of scholarship and an indispensable study for anyone wishing to know about spirituals.

In spite of its excellence as scholarship and sheer good writing, it fails to demonstrate its thesis—that the spirituals were written by slaves who wanted to go back to Africa. There is little doubt that some slaves wanted to go back to Africa, and that some actually did. One might also concede that some spirituals were written for that purpose. But the evidence Dr. Fisher presents does not prove that spirituals as a whole concerned themselves with a return to Africa. Furthermore, to believe in this proposition, one would have to have very strong evidence that most slaves were ready to go back to Africa; as has been shown in this book (on pages 112–113), the evidence proves quite the contrary. The slaves did not begin to exhaust even the chances given them to go to Africa. On the other hand, many thousands risked their lives to go to the northern sections of the United States and to Canada when Africa was available to thousands of manumitted slaves or to slaves eligible for manumission for their mere agreement.

Even so, Dr. Fisher's argument is extremely interesting reading. His bibliography of twenty pages is most valuable. He has accumulated much enlightening and revealing detail throughout his book. His final chapter, "Understanding Spirituals," is a masterpiece of revelations.

Howard Thurman

Howard Thurman is a distinguished American preacher and lecturer. He is a man of keen insights and of unusual ability in expressing himself. For merly dean of the chapel at Howard University, he recently retired as dean of the chapel at Boston University. He has been in demand for many years as a speaker in every part of the United States and in other parts of the world. He has often used spirituals for his speaking inspirations.

Howard Thurman told this writer that he had sung spirituals in church from his earliest days as a child. He said that his sister used to lead them and often invented new verses. As a student at Morehouse College, he ran into student resentment of spirituals. The Morehouse students refused to sing spirituals for white outsiders; they sang them only for themselves.

This resentment caused Howard Thurman to begin investigating spirituals. About 1929, he says he began writing to correct false attitudes and to show the Negro the value of his songs. He has used spirituals, he says, in sermons, talks, and in all kinds of ways. He finds their imagination, variety, and depth of great value.

In 1939, in the American magazine *Christendom* (there was a magazine of the same name published in England at the same time), Thurman wrote an article which he called "Religious Ideas in Negro Spirituals." He announced right away that he was not going to discuss music or poetry, but the inspired expressions of people removed from their familiar environment and from emotional security. A man without a home, the slave became a traditional Christian, a fact amazing and ironical. The slave, says Thurman, adapted a religion which his master and his master's society had disgraced. On this basis they believed, with their preacher, that they were no longer slaves, or niggers, but God's children.

The substance of the remainder of this article is found in the two books Thurman wrote on spirituals, which we are about to describe. It is important to note, however, that his opening gun, fired in this article, represented a most unusual approach to the interpretation of these songs.

One of his books is called *Deep River* (1945), and it is subtitled *Reflections on the Religious Insight of Certain of the Negro Spirituals*. In seven chapters (the first chapter deals with backgrounds) Dr. Thurman gives his unique interpretations of six spirituals: "The Blind Man Stood on the Road and Cried," "Heaven! Heaven!," "There Is a Balm in Gilead," "Deep River," "We Are Climbing Jacob's Ladder," and "Wade in the Water, Children." Although he sticks to a somewhat orthodox religious formula, his insights and coordinations are quite remarkable.

In 1947 Dr. Thurman was invited by Harvard University to give the Ingersoll Lecture on the Immortality of Man. The result was *The Negro Spiritual Speaks of Life and Death*, which was published in 1947. Early in the lecture he borrows from *Deep River* his list of sources of the raw materials of the spiritual, three in number: the world of nature, the stuff of experience, and the Bible, the sacred book of those who had enslaved the makers of the spirituals.

He then reveals what the spiritual has to say about death. The slave, he reminds his listeners, faced always the imminent threat of death. Spirituals like "Oh Freedom!" were his declaration that there were things in life worse than death. The slave's contact with the dead was immediate, inescapable, and dramatic, as many spirituals show. And yet his songs of death were songs of assurance since he believed in a power stronger than death.

As to life, he sang of the solitariness of the human spirit as, for example, in "I Got to Walk My Lonesome Valley." He also expressed personal reaction to the vindictiveness and cruelty of his fellows without indicating a like vindictiveness and cruelty. He thought of life, says Dr. Thurman, as a pilgrimage or sojourn to his true home, with God. The pilgrimage was starkly rugged ("It's a Mighty Rocky Road"), but the slave evinced a great commitment in carrying on ("Stay in the Field"). In his songs he reflected a sense of the deep intimacy between the soul and God. He was curiously concerned with the Judgment Day; he demonstrated a belief in a personal immortality and in a moral order in which men participate, limitless in creativity and design. Through all these expressions he turned a worthless life into a life worth living.

In "The Meaning of Spirituals," Thurman reiterates the way in which the songs elevate the slaves to high position. They underscored their belief that they were not slaves or "niggers," but God's children.

If one is to credit Dr. Thurman, the slave was pure Christian, through and through. In his interpretation, also, is very little irony and symbol. He writes as though the songs were prose statements of "literal truth." In spite of these doubtful elements, his interpretations of the spirituals hold together under a unified philosophy and are full of excitement and beauty.

John A. and Alan Lomax

Following a commission from several distinguished members of the faculty of Harvard University, John Avery Lomax went on a search for American folk songs. As a Sheldon Fellow at Harvard he had advertised in the *Dallas* (Texas) *News* of May 29, 1912 for "typical Negro songs." His announcement was supported by such Harvard luminaries as Barrett Wendell, G. L. Kittredge, F. N. Robinson, and L. B. R. Briggs. Before he entered the lists, the American folk song was not considered a respectable form of literature. As the result of his indefatigable and successful searches, researches, editing, and publishing, folk song in America was ushered into the temple of literature.

In 1934, with his son, Alan, John A. Lomax published *American Ballads and Folk Songs*. This book contained twenty-three spirituals and a great deal about the backgrounds of the spiritual. John A. and Alan had made a special effort to collect and record Afro-American songs. Both of them contributed greatly to the development of the Archive of American Folk Song, which had been established in the Library of Congress in 1928 by Carl Engel, chief of the Music Division of the Library. The Archive is now the greatest center for spirituals, words, music, and discography.

In 1936 John A. published a book of folk songs as sung by Leadbelly, a longtime convict in the penitentiaries of Texas and Louisiana. Besides actual spirituals which Leadbelly sang, this book contained many folk songs obviously derived from spirituals.

In 1947 John A. brought out his *Adventures of a Ballad Hunter*. It was the result of his searching for folk songs on the Texas Gulf Coast, between the Colorado and the Brazos rivers, "where Negroes are thicker than mustang grapes." He found folk singers in their most natural surroundings, in the easy sociability of homes, churches, schools, fields, woodyards. He had one meeting with seven hundred Negro teachers in the Music Hall at Prairie View College. He recorded such flavorsome statements as "Borned of the Holy Spearmint!" and "And splunged Him in the side."

In this most interesting book, he gives the backgrounds and at least some of the texts for twenty-nine spirituals. Some of them are quite well known; others are variants of well-known spirituals; others are originals. Some notable lines are "I want to meet Death smilin'," "Three stars in the East, three stars in the West," "Bless Jesus! Dat's my bread!" "Dem little slippers dat my Lord give me," "Jes' so de tree fall, jes' so it lie," "If you give God a dime, why you want a saucer cream? How is that? Oh, you don't love God," and "Angel flew from the bottom of the pit."

Alan Lomax has not only carried forward his father's work but has greatly extended the range. In 1959 he published in the *American Anthropologist* an article, "Folk Song Style," in which he shows clear relationship between musical style on the one hand and social context and life style on the other. The findings in this article served as the background for his "cantometrics" and "choreometrics" projects conducted at Columbia University. So far, the outstanding achievement of these projects has been *Folk Song Style and Culture*, published by the American Association for the Advancement of Science in 1968. In this book he and his staff demonstrate the supremacy of African musical styles, particularly in the use of overlap, polyphony, polyrhythm, and group singing; the solid relationship between the African and the Afro-American styles of singing and instrumentalizing; and the influence of social factors upon the development of music in Africa and in other parts of the world.

Also in 1959, Alan Lomax published *The Rainbow Sign: A Southern Documentary*. Among other comments is the following:

> The Southern Negro folk singer stands at the creative center of American popular culture. He absorbed the British folk-song tradition and learned Western European harmony, yet he never gave up the basic musical approach of his African ancestors. . . . His spirituals, work songs, ballads, and blues are the most distinctive American folk songs.

In 1966, by invitation, Alan Lomax delivered before the Division of Psychology and the Arts of the American Psychological Association a lecture on "The Good and the Beautiful in Folksong" (published in the *Journal of American Folklore*, 1967). In this lecture are quite a few statements significant to the study of folk songs, such as the following,

> Singing is an act of communication and therefore can be studied as behavior. Since a folksong is transmitted orally by all or most members of a

culture, generation after generation, it represents an extremely high consensus about patterns of meaning and behavior of cultural rather than individual significance.

This rule can certainly be applied to the Afro-American folk community,
down to the present day, with reference to the spread and influence of the
spiritual.

One of Alan Lomax's most impressive statements about folk backgrounds
of the Afro-American is found in his lecture, "Black Musical Style." The
advice in this statement is so good that I have requested—and been granted
—permission to print it here:

> Of the survival of African musical style in the Americas, there can be
> no doubt. It is the passionate area of our cultural life. The young people
> devote themselves to black dancing; their favorite songs are at present
> mostly blues. If today I offer further proof of this survival, it is only to
> open the way to a discussion of its significance—especially for black Ameri-
> cans. Most of you are black by culture and inheritance—and us others are
> at least black by allegiance. For us, then, the survival of this music is not
> merely the rattle of the bones of ancestors, but the flowing in us of a river
> whose living water sustains us, whose source and whose destination we
> must know. When we mark the strength of African musical style in the
> New World, I believe we assert the existence of a black culture style that
> shapes our lives. But this discussion cannot be conducted with the con-
> ventional tools of Western European musicology and history. If you play
> the European poker game, you are bound to go to the cleaners. For ex-
> ample, Europeans have been specially concerned with print, philosophy,
> drawing utensils, the meticulous arts of the lamp; Africans have been busy
> with the sociable arts—dance, song, proverb, ritual, oratory, music. Each
> one of these arts is a communications system through which a culture can
> transmit its value set, its point of view. Therefore we must not look down
> upon our own—the sociable arts—or downgrade them as inferior commu-
> nicators of culture and civilization, simply because the North European
> has downgraded them, being too shy, too withdrawn to be an accomplished
> singer, dancer, orator. We will find in song, in music, in dance, as solid,
> as sure a record of history and witness of cultural integrity as in the stones
> of the Egyptians or the piled-up libraries of Europe. If, as black historians
> you turn away from the arts of your people and play history like Euro-
> peans, you will lose the game, for the dice are loaded against you.

LeRoi Jones

A very modern, and up-to-date, interpreter of the Afro-American spiritual is LeRoi Jones. He seems to have no regular book devoted entirely to
the spiritual, but his two books on music and black society, *Blues People*
(1963) and *Black Music* (1967), and his essay on "The Myth of a Negro
Literature" abound in spiritual references. They also show wide reading in

backgrounds and deep thought. Best of all, they relate the spiritual to other forms of the music of the black man in America in many interesting ways.

In the essay mentioned above, Jones notes that only in music has the American Negro made a significantly profound contribution. Negro music alone, says Jones, drawing its strengths and beauties out of the depths of the black man's soul, and especially from the lower classes, has been able to survive the constant and willful dilutions of the black middle class.

Blues People has a great deal to say about slaves and their motivations. It insists, quite wisely, that the first slaves did not believe that they would be in America forever. They thought of themselves as captives in a foreign land. As human beings are supposed to do, they reacted quite sharply to the lack of human relationship.

Jones frankly accepts the view of Herskovits that most attitudes, customs, and cultural characteristics of the American Negro are traceable directly or indirectly to Africa. Even though the African was perpetually developing some of the most complex and complicated ideas of the world imaginable, he was, in America, forced into an alien world without cultural references or familiar human attitudes.

At this point Jones makes an observation which is at the heart of the understanding of Afro-American music. It is that black men are the only descendants of people in America who were not happy to come here. Regardless of his displacement and alienation, his music, dance, and religion, the nonmaterial aspects of his African culture, were impossible to eradicate.

Moving to the slave's religious backgrounds, Jones declares that Christianity was adopted by the slave long before the missionaries and evangelists set out to convert him. One reason for this was that in his African setting, religion was a totality. When he moved into this new setting, and his home religions were taken from him, he had to find as quickly as possible a viable substitute. Also, his growing social awareness caused the slave to adopt Christianity somewhat speedily. According to Jones, masses of Negro slaves entered the Christian church.

Christianity, then, was a movement away from Africa for the slave. But in his particular brand of Christianity, the slave kept many Africanisms. One of these was emphasis on spirit possession. Another was the use of music. Jones quotes an old African dictum, "The spirit will not descend without song."

Jones declares that both the blues and the religious songs of the slaves stem from the Afro-American/American work songs which had originated in West Africa. Both, he says, began in slavery. Even the subject matter and content of the first Afro-church music comes from work songs. No aspect of Negro song is complete without the shout, he states, if only as a matter of style.

Before going further, let us look back and examine. There is no question about the validity of Jones's point of view or about the demonstrability of

most of his facts. There is equally no question about the depth of his insights or his ability to make coordinations intelligently. There is considerable question about two things: his theories of the origins of the spirituals
and the blues and his declarations that great masses of black slaves adopted
Christianity. Jones himself speaks of the totality of the African religion.
This undoubtedly means that religion encompassed all types of activity
and motivated work, play, daily action, and even social, economic, and
political policy. This point of view was retained by the African in America.
If these things are true, how could the Afro-American folk song have
stemmed from anything other than a religious song? Even the work song
in Africa was basically religious; and many spirituals, as we have shown,
are essentially work songs.

As to the great hordes of black slaves falling over each other to adopt
Christianity, this could hardly be true because of the obstacles which we
have reviewed. Most slaves never got the chance to adopt the religion of
their masters. Many who got the chance were repelled by the wide
discrepancy between the theory and the practice. The best that can be
said is that the everyday slave borrowed certain ideas and essences of Christianity, as we have shown, and fitted out his own new religion to take the
place of that of which he had been deprived. When Jones says that the
black church was the only place where the Negro could be emotionally
free, he is probably speaking of a postslavery time. In their hearts, the
great majority of slaves were always free. Their job was to bring this inner
feeling to reality. Their songs helped them to realize this apparently impossible task.

Jones recognizes the unique nature of the slave's Christianity when he
states that the slave's practice of this religion was totally strange to the
West. Within this practice was his religious music. According to Jones,
the superficial forms of this music were European and American, but there
the imitation ended. The lyrics, rhythms, and harmonies were essentially
African. The Negro's religious music was his own creation. This includes
spirituals, church marches, ring and shuffle shouts, chants, "sankeys," camp
or meeting songs, hymns, "ballits," and everything else. Nothing could
be more true.

Jones says that it is quite simple for an African melody to be used as a
Christian song. He says also that almost all parts of the black Christian
church had to do with music. When preacher and congregation reached
their peak, their music rivaled any of the more formal Afro-American
musics in intensity and beauty. No matter how much the spiritual might
resemble the white hymn superficially, when it was sung, there was no
doubt that it was black song. The incredibly beautiful Jesus of the spiritual
is a grand man of flesh and blood, whether he is sung by church women or
by women who left the church to sing devil songs.

The above set of comments is rich in truth and full of deep insights. So is Jones's description of the God of the black slave. The God spoken about in the black songs, he says, is not the same as the one in the white songs. The God the slaves worshipped (except the pure white God of the toms) had to be willing to free them somehow, someway, one sweet day. The land changed with this God in charge. Slaves and freedmen in the churches wanted to be identified with this God, on earth as well as in heaven. The closer the church to Africa, the blacker the God (the blacker the spirit); the closer to the will and meaning of the West, the whiter the God. This, says Jones, is still so.

In Jones's view, the church no longer provides refuge for black people. Even the poorest and blackest have drifted away. The world has opened up, but the church has not. But, says Jones, the emotionalism and spirit of the church will always demand the animating life of the black man.

His comments on the influence of religious music among black people are interesting and vital. He notes, for example, that black music has always had an element of protest; freedom couched in the metaphorical language of the Bible, substituting Jews for themselves, to escape massa's understanding. He restates the old cliché that if you just change the lyrics of the spiritual, you have rhythm and blues songs. This, he says, is true, by and large. He asserts also that "black religious roots are still held on to conspicuously in the most moving of music." The preacher-congregation/leader-chorus style of music, he declares, is the oldest and still the most common jazz form as well. Religious and secular black music have always cross-fertilized each other.

Jones hopes that the future will bring a "Unity Music"—black music which is jazz, blues, religious, and secular.

If one really wants a full story of the interpretation of spirituals, these two books of Jones's are indispensable. First, they bring the interpretive mind and heart almost down to the present moment. Second, they evaluate the spiritual in terms of its total background in song and religion. Third, they are the product of a truly incisive and poetically aware writer.

POETS AND THE SPIRITUAL

Earlier in Part Three it has been shown that poets, amateur and professional, have written poems based on spirituals, produced neospirituals, or written in imitation of spirituals. It remains to be said that such poets have helped to produce the phenomenon of the spiritual through their allegiance to the model. Arthur Palmer Hudson, for example, recalls that Whittier's "Songs of the Slaves in the Desert" suggests the old spirituals, especially in the refrain, "Where are we going, Rubee?"

James Weldon Johnson is a good example. His *God's Trombones* are sermons practically inspired by spirituals and the language of spirituals. His "O Black and Unknown Bards" is a eulogy to the makers of spirituals.

In a number of poems he throws in a line or two reminiscent of or referring to spirituals. In "The Black Mammy," for example, he speaks of "thy sweet croon, so plaintive and so wild."

The same thing is true of Paul Laurence Dunbar. Besides writing a number of poems and stories of the experiences of slaves on the plantation, he often employs phrases from actual spirituals. One of his poems is called "A Spiritual." Charles Eaton Burch has interpreted this poem in the light of Dunbar's general interest in the plantation slave. He credits Dunbar with having given a true record of the black men toiling and singing day and night. He says that "A Spiritual" contains all the emotion and enthusiasm "characteristic of these zealous souls." More than any other poet, Burch declares, Dunbar has given us the poetry of the black man on the plantation.

In *Negro Poets and Their Poems*, a volume dedicated to the writers of spirituals, Robert T. Kerlin, the editor, reminds the reader that many poems in his volume are reminiscent of the spirituals. This fact is clearly one of the reasons for his dedication.

J. A. Macon brought out in 1883 *Uncle Gabe Tucker; or, Reflection, Song, and Sentiment in the Quarters*. Uncle Gabe Tucker is apparently a second Uncle Remus. His songs are adaptations of Afro-American spirituals, and some of them are quite effective. Nearly all are basic in the sense that the spiritual is a basic representation of the life of the slave.

In his "The Congo: A Study of the Negro Race" (1914), Vachel Lindsay shows that he has saturated himself in the spirituals. In one stanza he reproduces a shout session which with some alteration might easily have been one of the secret meetings where spirituals were created and first taught to a group,

III. THE HOPE OF THEIR RELIGION

A good old negro in the slums of the town
Preached at a sister for her velvet gown.
Howled at a brother for his low-down ways,
His prawling, guzzling, sneak-thief days.
Beat on the Bible till he wore it out
Starting the jubilee revival shout.
And some had visions, as they stood on chairs,
And sang of Jacob, and the golden stairs,
And they all repented, thousand strong
From the stupor and savagery and sin and wrong
And slammed their hymn books till they shook the room
With "glory, glory, glory,
And Boom, boom, Boom."

Poetry Magazine published in its October 1917 issue Lindsay's Negro sermon, "How Samson Bore away the Gates of Gaza." In December

1917, it published Natalie Curtis's (Burlin) commentary on the Lindsay sermon. Miss Curtis said that Lindsay had told the Samson story with the artless familiarity of the true folk singer. She said that Lindsay's lines were reminiscent of such spirituals as "Gawd's A-Gwine t' Move All de Troubles Away" and "Ride on, Jesus." She called attention to the endless verses of "Ride on, Jesus," bringing in, separately, father, brother, sister, deacon, preacher, etc. She concluded that the sudden flashes of imagery proclaimed the ingenious Negro folk singer a true poet.

Waverley T. Carmichael published poems in the vein of spirituals in his book of songs, *From the Heart of a Folk* (1918). His volume carried an introduction by a famous English professor, James Holly Hanford.

In the "Lento Grave" section of his *Dark Symphony*, Melvin B. Tolson, an Afro-American poet, has written,

> The centuries-old pathos in our voices
> Saddens the great white world,
> And the wizardry of our dusky rhythms,
> Conjures up shadow-shapes of ante-bellum years:

> Black slaves singing *One More River to Cross*
> In the torture tombs of slave ships,
> Black slaves singing *Steal Away to Jesus*
> In jungle swamps,
> Black slaves singing *The Crucifixion*
> In slave-pens at midnight,
> Black slaves singing *Swing Low, Sweet Chariot*
> In cabins of death,
> Black slaves singing *Go Down, Moses*
> In the canebrakes of the Southern Pharaohs.

Sterling Brown's book of poems, *Southern Road*, has many echoes of the spiritual. One poem is called "When De Saints Go Ma'ching Home": it contains a number of good tradition-bred lines. In one of his most powerful poems, the one called "Strong Men," Sterling Brown wrote,

> They dragged you from homeland,
> They chained you in coffles,
> They huddled you spoon-fashion in filthy hatches,
> They sold you to give a few gentlemen ease.

> They broke you in like oxen,
> They scourged you,
> They branded you,
> They made your women breeders,
> They swelled your numbers with bastards . . .
> They taught you the religion they disgraced.

> You sang:
> > Keep a-inchin' along
> > Lak a po' inch worm . . .

You sang:
> Bye and bye
> I'm gonna lay down dis heaby load . . .

You sang:
> Walk togedder, chillen,
> Dontcha git weary . . .

> *The strong men keep a-comin' on*
> *The strong men git stronger.*

Not using actual songs, but reflecting on the manner of their creation, Lance Jeffers, another Afro-American poet, has written "On Listening to Spirituals,"

> When the master lived a king and I a starving hutted slave beneath the lash, and
>
> when my five-year-old son was driven at dawn to cottonfield to pick until he could no longer see the sun, and
>
> when master called my wife to the big house when mistress was gone, took her against her will and gave her a dollar to be still, and when she turned upon her pride and cleavered it, cursed her dignity and stamped on it, came back to me with his evil on her thighs, hung her head when I condemned her with my eyes,
>
> what broken mettle of my soul wept steel, cracked teeth in self-contempt upon my flesh, crept underground to seek new roots and secret breathing place?
>
> When all the hatred of my bones was buried in a forgotten county of my soul,
> then from beauty muscled from the degradation of my oaken bread,
> I stroked on slavery soil the mighty colors of my song; a passionate heaven rose no God in heaven could create!

In a personal letter Jeffers has told how he happened to write the above poem:

I was giving a poetry reading at Elizabeth City State Teachers College, in the summer of 1962. I had asked that spirituals be played during the reading. It was a long time since I had heard them—and listening to them, I saw —as I often used to see then—the black people of that time: I had a vision of the black people of that time, and of their greatness: saw that they were the greatest black people, the greatest people of any kind, that this country has produced. I understood vaguely their grief, saw myself among them, picking cotton, saw their hangups, their neuroses, their attempts to adjust, their overwhelming anger and hatred, which they somehow sublimated, saw, perhaps above all, their godliness as a people—as we have seen it in our own day in Malcolm and Martin—saw their sublimation of their anger and rage and hatred in the poetry of song that is unsurpassed in the world for its grandeur and for its beauty. I've written other poems about the slaves. They are in *Nine Black Poets*, published by Moore, in Durham, and in *Burning Spear*, published by the Howard poets in 1963.

One very unusual poem, almost a spiritual but perhaps not quite, is reported by E. C. L. Adams in the *Southern Workman*. Adams calls the poem "A South Carolina Folk Song." In reality, it is a funeral sermon by a plantation Negro. Of this poetic effort Adams says,

> This evidence of the dramatic, unique, and roaring imagination of the Negro seems worthy of special note. . . . Starting in a speaking voice he went on for about half an hour gradually working up into a shout and being joined, first by one or two voices in the congregation, then by a few more, and at last by the whole number.

A fragment of the poem goes,

Main Poet	Other Voices
Our brother is dead	
He rests from the labor	He sleeps, oh, he sleeps
Wey de tall pines grow	On the banks of a river
On the banks of a river	On the banks of a river
He trouble is done	
He's left dis world	On the wings of glory
On the wings of glory	On the wings of glory
	On the wings of glory
Out of life's storm	
Out of life's darkness	
He sails in the light	
Away from his troubles	
Away from the night	
He is gone to the kingdom of love	
In the raiment of angels	In the raiment
To the region above	In the raiment of angels
An' he sleeps	
Wey de tall pines grow	
On the banks of a river	
An' he soul's in flight	
With the starry-crowned angels	
To the golden height	Ah yes, my Jesus! Jesus
	With the starry-crowned angels
An' he sleeps	On the banks of a river
Wey de tall pines grow	
On the banks of a river	
The flowers is bloomin'	
And the birds is singin'	
Wey de wind blows soft	
As the breath of an angel	
An' he sleeps wey de tall pines grow	An' he sleeps
	Wey de tall pines grow
	On the banks of a river

On the banks of a river
An' his sperrit is guarded
By a flaming-faced angel

> Yes, Jesus, by a flaming-faced angel
> On the banks of a river

Standin' on mountains of rest
An' he sleeps wey de tall pines grow
On the banks of a river

> He sleeps! Oh, he sleeps!

FICTION WRITERS AND THE SPIRITUAL

Special uses of the spiritual by fiction writers, dramatists, motion pictures, radio, and television have been, over the years, quite numerous and extremely varied. A few samples will, therefore, be given just to illustrate some of the trends.

White fiction writers, especially Southerners, have employed the spiritual quite extensively. DuBose Heyward, mentioned earlier as a member of the Charleston Society for the Preservation of Spirituals, used many spirituals in *Porgy* and *Mamba's Daughters*. In the former book he featured "Death, Ain't Yuh Gots No Shame?" "Leanin' on My Lord," and "Home in de Rock." In the latter book he skillfully employs "Light in de Grabeyard Outshine de Sun" and "Honour de Lamb."

William Faulkner was constantly bringing spirituals into his stories. One of his most famous stories is the great "Go Down, Moses."

"Go Down, Moses" is a subtle, but powerful, dramatization of Mollie Worsham Beauchamp. An old black woman with a keen sense of freedom, justice, and dignity, she insists that her grandson Butch (Samuel Worsham Beauchamp), whom she "brought up," has been sold to Pharaoh by the owner of the Mississippi farm on which she lived, Roth (Carothers) Edmonds. She goes in to Jefferson to get Gavin Stevens, the lawyer, to be her Moses and get her child back.

It turns out that Butch is being electrocuted that night in Joliet, Illinois. While backing numbers in Chicago, he had found it necessary to shoot a policeman in the back. Without giving Mollie the full story, Gavin sees that Butch's body is brought home. Mollie, her white friend and relative Miss Worsham, Gavin, and the editor of the paper ride in great dignity in the funeral procession that takes Butch to a quiet grave after a stormy life. Pharaoh has again been defeated. Mollie wants the whole story spread in the paper.

In the *Sewanee Review* for July–September 1936, Arthur Palmer Hudson presented "The Singing South." It was the result of a study of folk song in recent fiction describing Southern life. It included forty-seven pieces by thirty-one different writers.

Mary Johnston, for example, said that she used snatches of Negro spirituals and invents them if she has no line ready to hand. "Some are genuine —perhaps the most—but others ground into me." "There's One More River to Cross" appears as one of the songs sung by soldiers coming home from the Creek War in John Trotwood Moore's *Hearts of Hickory: A Study of Andrew Jackson.* In the same novel, Old Sam Williams, General Jackson's bugler, is credited with having composed the following spiritual:

> Ole Gabri'l wuz standin' by the gate,
> An' a-watchin' down below-ah,
> Dah's jes' one minute fur to wait
> To heah dat bugle below-ah.

Nineteen of twenty-two short stories selected had Afro-American spirituals among other folk songs. Wilbur Daniel Steele's "Satan am a Snake" is based on the following spiritual:

> Satan am a snake
> An' he lay in de grass,
> An' always wait
> Whar de Christian pass.

Steele also used the related spirituals "Satan am a liah, An' a conjur too," and "Satan am mad, An' I am glad,/He done los' a soul He thought he had."

In the terrifically famous and popular *Gone with the Wind* (1936) Margaret Mitchell several times uses or refers to spirituals. Since her story is set in Georgia and often makes slaves into front characters, she could hardly avoid doing so. Her most spectacular usage is her having Big Sam (six and a half feet tall and ebony black) sing:

> Go do-ow, Moses! Waaa-ay do-own in Eee-jup laa-an!
> An' te-el O'le Faa-ro-o
> Ter let mah pee-pul go!

Since Miss Mitchell undoubtedly knew this song to have been proscribed by state and local authorities, she was obviously projecting the rebellious blood of some of her slave characters.

As one of the outstanding searchers for and appreciators of spirituals, Dorothy Scarborough would be expected to use them in her novels. So she does. In *The Wind* (1925) she has a leading white character, Letty, think of a spiritual her black friend, Aunt Charity, used to sing:

> I run to de rock for to hide my face,
> But de rock cry out, "No hiding-place,
> No hiding-place here!"

Later in the story, Letty hums softly an old spiritual she had learned from her black mammy in Virginia:

> Lord, I don't want to die in a storm, in a storm! . . .
> When de wind blows east, an' de wind blows west,
> Lord, I don't want to die in a storm!

A few pages later, Letty sings the song openly.

In a novel entitled *Here Come Joe Mungin* (1942), Chalmers S. Murray uses spirituals effectively to produce atmosphere and flavor. Two of these are quite striking,

> Honey in the rock for to feed God chillun . . .
> Robe in the rock for to feed God chillun . . .
> Crown in the rock for to feed God chillun,

and

> Three white horses side by side,
> One of them horses Jesus ride.
> Yes He did, yes He did.

The idea known to every slave of escaping slavery by following the Big Dipper of the stars, and expanded in several popular spirituals, has been developed in Frances Gaither's novel, *Follow the Drinking Gourd.*

The spiritual has been a great favorite with Afro-American fiction writers. In J. Saunders Redding's *No Day of Triumph* (1942), which is autobiography in fictional form, there are only four chapters and the title and theme of each are taken from spirituals: "Troubled in Mind," "Don't Be Weary, Traveler," "Poor Wayfarin' Stranger," and "There Is a Balm."

John Killens in *Youngblood* (1954) has spirituals as lead poems for each of his four parts,

Lead poem for Part One:
> "Didn't my Lord deliver Daniel
> And why not every man?"

Lead poem for Part Two:
> "No Hiding Place"
> > "I went to the rock to hide my face
> > The rock cried out—'No hiding place.' "

Lead poem for Part Three:
> "Jubilee"
> > "One of these morning about five o'clock
> > This old world's gonna reel and rock
> > Pharaoh's Army got drownded."

Lead poem for Part Four:
> "And before I'd be a slave
> I'd be buried in my grave
> And go home to my Lord
> And be free."

This particular freedom theme had previously appeared in "Fire and Cloud," one of the novelettes of Richard Wright's *Uncle Tom's Children.* The Negro preacher, Reverend Taylor, who gave his life trying to organize his people and correct their problems, developed the overpowering concept, "Freedom belongs t' the strong!"

Many years later, Richard Wright published in *White Man, Listen!* (1957) an essay entitled "The Literature of the Negro in the United States." In showing how far the spiritual is from Phillis Wheatley, he writes, "We are now dealing with people who have lost their individuality, whose reactions are fiercely elemental, whose shattered lives are burdened by impulses they cannot master or control."

He also shows how spirituals covered a wide range of feeling in these people:

Pathos: "Sometimes I Feel Like a Motherless Child"

Nostalgia: "Swing Low, Sweet Chariot"

Paradoxical note of triumphant defeat: "Steal Away"

Militancy disguised in religious imagery: "Joshua Fit de Battle of Jericho"

Outright rebellion couched in Biblical symbols; the Negro a Negro even in his religion, consciousness of being a rejected American:
"If I had-a my way,
I'd tear this building down"

In conclusion of this section he declares that authorless utterances from the lips of slaves are the single most significant contribution of folk and religious songs to our national culture.

More than any other fiction writer in a single novel Margaret Walker used spirituals in *Jubilee* (1966). In private conversation she has said that she intended the spirituals to be not only indicative but thematic. It is obvious that the spirituals reflect the motives and poetic attitudes in the life of Vyvy Ware and the other characters better than any other words could. By chapters they appear as follows:

Chapter	Spiritual
1	"Swing low, sweet chariot, Coming for to carry me home"
	"Soon one morning, Death come knocking at my door. (repeat twice) Oh, my Lord, Oh, my Lord, What shall I do?"
2	"When Israel was in Egypt's land— Let my people go.

Oppressed so hard they could not stand—
Let my people go."

4   "I am a poor way-faring stranger,
I'm tossed in this wide world alone.
No hope have I for tomorrow,
I'm trying to make heaven my home.
Sometimes I am tossed and driven, Lord,
Sometimes I don't know where to roam.
I've heard of a city called heaven,
I've started to make it my home."

6   "I'm gwine sit at the welcome table,
Some of these days"

"I been buked and I been scorned, Lord, (repeat)
I been talked about sho's you borned."

"But I ain't gwine a-lay my religion down, Lord, (repeat)
I ain't gwine lay my religion down
Untell I wears a heavenly crown."

"Before this time another year,
I may be dead and gone.
Be in some lonesome graveyard bed,
O, Lord have mercy, Lord, how long?"

7   "No more auction block for me!"

12   "Deep River
My home is over Jordan.
Deep River, Lord,
I want to cross over into Campground."

14   "There's a star in the East on Christmas morn,
Rise up shepherds and foller,
It'll lead to the place where the Savior's born,
Rise up shepherds and foller."

"Oh, Mary, what you going to name your newborn baby?
What you going to name that pretty little boy?"

15   "Oh, Freedom, Oh, Freedom,
Oh, Freedom over me,
And before I'll be a slave
I'll be buried in my grave
And go home to my Lawd and be free."

16   "My way's cloudy,
Lawdy, my way's cloudy."

"I want to die easy, when I die (repeat)
I want to die easy, when I die
Shout salvation as I fly
I want to die easy, when I die"

17   "In that great gitting-up morning
Fare you well, fare you well (repeat)

There's a better day a-coming
Fare you well, fare you well" (repeat)

29   "One of these mornings bright and fair
I'm gwine take my wings and try the air"

41   "I am bound for the promised land, (repeat)
Oh, who will come and go with me?
I am bound for the promised land"

"I'll be dar, I'll be dar
When de muster roll am calling, I'll be dar sure's yer born
Oh, come you sinners, go wid me
Oh, I'll be dar."

43   "I'm gwineta lay down my sword and shield,
Down by the riverside, (repeat twice)
And study war no more!"

"Forty days, forty nights, when de rain kepta falling
De wicked climb the trees and for help kepta calling
Didn't it rain?"

"God told Noah by the rainbow sign
No more water, but the fire next time."

45   "Oh, brother, I'm working in the high ground,
Gwine to git to heaven by and by."

46   "I'm a-rolling, I'm a-rolling,
I'm a-rolling through an unfriendly world." (repeat)

"Tell me how you feel when you come out the wilderness?
Come out the wilderness,
Come out the wilderness,
Tell me how you feel when you come out the wilderness,
Leaning on the Lawd?"

50   "Children grumbled on the way:
Ah wisht ah hadda died in Egypt's land.
Children they forgot to pray:
Ah wisht ah hadda died in Egypt's land."

51   "Great Day!
Great Day, the Righteous marching.
Great Day!
God's gonna build up Zion's walls."

52   "Now ain't them hard trials
And great tribulations?
Ain't them hard trials?
I'm bound to leave this land."

54   "I got a home in that rock, (repeat)
Don't you see?
I got a home in that rock,
Debbil in hell can't bother me,
Don't you see?"

55   "Come by heah, Lawd,
         Come by heah!"

57   "Lawd, ah doan feel no-ways tired,
         Oh, glory hallelujah!
         For I hope to shout glory when this world is on fire
         Oh, glory hallelujah!"

58   "Oh, come and go with me (repeat twice)
         To my father's house,
         There is joy, joy, joy!"

Reflecting the philosophical strength and the colorful language of the spirituals, a number of novelists have chosen spiritual fragments as the titles for major fiction. In many cases the spiritual idea goes far deeper than the title, often pervading the whole work. Some of the outstanding selections are as follows:

Alston Anderson, *All God's Children* (1965)
James Baldwin, *Go Tell It on the Mountain* (1953)
James Baldwin, *Tell Me How Long the Train's Been Gone* (1968); though not a novel, Baldwin's *The Fire Next Time* (1963) is worthy of note, as being written by a famous novelist.
Arna Bontemps, *Chariot in the Sky* (1951)
Richard Coleman, *Don't You Weep . . . Don't You Moan* (1935)
Herbert Hill, ed., *Soon, One Morning* (1963), short stories, poems, etc. by American Negroes
Rudolph Fisher, *The Walls of Jericho* (1928)
William Faulkner, *Go Down, Moses and Other Stories* (1942)
Welbourn Kelley, *Inchin' Along* (1932)
Kathryn Johnston Noyes, *Jacob's Ladder* (1965)
Edwin A. Peeples, *Swing Low* (1945)
Margaret Walker, *Jubilee* (1966)
Chancellor Williams, *Have You Been to the River?* (1952)
Lillian E. Wood, *"Let My People Go"* (n.d.)

Baldwin's *Go Tell It on the Mountain* employs fourteen spirituals with great force and imagination. In this novel, singing is not an adjunct; it is the motive power of characters and action, it is the most natural thing any character does. Baldwin's facility with spirituals clearly shows that he was brought up on them. They are to him like food and drink. Even when his people are not singing, spiritual phrases run through his prose.

DRAMATISTS AND THE SPIRITUAL

On the American stage, and on other stages, dramatists have used spirituals thousands of times. In her book on *The Negro in the American Theatre*, Edith J. R. Isaacs states that the Negro spiritual has made effective scenes in many plays. She also observes that the spiritual is constantly imitated in the drama. And she adds, "Nor is it too much to say that the response of large audiences to the pure quality of this Negro folk music has stimulated the interest in other American folk songs—until recently living largely neglected in the hills and on the plains." For range of use of spirituals and spiritual adaptations in musical drama, one can go all the way from *Shuffle Along* in 1921 to *Finian's Rainbow* in 1946. Eugene O'Neill's *All God's Children Got Wings* (1924)—the title from one of the most famous of spirituals—is almost the beginning of a new dramatic epoch.

Of "Ol' Man River," the memorable song in *Show Boat* (1927), by Jerome Kern and Oscar Hammerstein II, David Ewen (*Complete Book of the American Musical Theater*, New York, Henry Holt, 1958), says:

> Perhaps most famous of all the songs [in *Show Boat*] is Joe's immortal hymn to the Mississippi, "Ol' Man River," so remarkable in catching the personality and overtones of the Negro spiritual that it is now sometimes described as an American folk song.

Some time before 1930, a musical religious pageant called *Heaven Bound* was evolved. It has been played by church choirs over the country literally thousands of times. Many observers have described and analyzed it, perhaps none better than Redding S. Sugg, Jr., in the December 1963 issue (Vol. XXVII) of the *Southern Folklore Quarterly*. Such a folk drama has naturally assumed a variety of forms, but in nearly every form it has invigorated its story with about twenty spirituals. The choir of the Big Bethel A.M.E. Church of Atlanta, says Sugg, performed *Heaven Bound* 644 times between 1930 and 1963, including a signal production in 1931 at the Atlanta Municipal Auditorium for the World Ecumenical Conference.

DuBose Heyward made a strike on Broadway with spirituals in his *Porgy* (1927). In a summary article, "Tragedy and Spirituals in the Black Belt," the *Literary Digest* sums up the reaction of the Broadway community to the play. The consensus was that the spirituals made the play come alive. An excerpt from Alan Dale's review is typical:

> To hear the "spirituals" sung as they were sung last night is worth twice the price of a seat at the Guild Theater.
> At the close of one of the scenes this singing of one particular spiritual aroused the effervescent enthusiasm of the audience. It was marvelously well done. There were the fervor, the hysteria, the emotionalism and the curious abandon that must accompany such outbursts.

We have already mentioned the effective role of spirituals in Heyward's novels, *Porgy* and *Mamba's Daughters* (1939). The first production of *Porgy* ran for 217 performances and that of *Mamba's Daughters* for 162.

Mamba's Daughters was enlivened by the singing and playing of Ethel Waters in the leading role of Hagar. Where the novel of the same name had only two spirituals, the drama had eight, and Miss Waters had full opportunity to display her enormous talents and skills. It was her first significant opportunity as a dramatic actress (she had recently played in the Guthrie McClintic production of *Androcles and the Lion*), and McClintic was her director. According to Mrs. Isaacs, her performance established her "in a position which no other Negro actress had yet achieved." For Mrs. Isaacs the reason for her success was obvious: "What made Ethel Waters' success the more remarkable was that, with all her long experience, she had never lost the haunting folk quality that distinguished both her acting and her singing from the beginning."

When Gershwin was ready to transform Heyward's *Porgy* into the great American opera, *Porgy and Bess* (1935), he went to Charleston to meet the Heywards. He told his biographer, Isaac Goldberg, that he did his opera on the Negroes instead of the Indians because he felt strong ties to the Negroes. For weeks he regaled himself by listening to the singing of spirituals at the nearby Hendersonville church. Acting as an expert, Heyward described for Gershwin the technique of the shouting accompaniment of the spirituals. On February 26, 1934, Gershwin wrote Heyward that he was composing *Porgy and Bess*, doing the songs and the spirituals first. From June to August of 1934, Gershwin was with the Gullahs on a small island ten miles from Charleston, listening to their singing and speaking, and feeling, says Goldberg, more like being on a homecoming instead of an exploration.

With Todd Duncan and Anne Brown singing the great leading roles, *Porgy and Bess*, its spirituals and spiritual-derived songs aglow, hit the world like an earthquake on October 10, 1935. Generally credited with being the first American folk opera, it became an immediate and phenomenal success. It remained impressively in the public eye for more than twenty years, accounting for much of the early popularity of Leontyne Price and William Warfield. This later version of *Porgy and Bess* opened on March 10, 1953, and held the boards in its initial run for 305 performances. Along with many other famous musical Americans, after majestic treatment throughout the United States, the play toured Latin America and the Soviet Union to unstinted applause.

Through a generous use of spirituals and of the folk community that produced them, Charleston has contributed many dramas and musicals to the professional and amateur theaters. In 1937, Virginia C. Tupper reported in the *Etude* the annual folk music drama in Charleston's Gullah districts. The drama had grown up on the "Fairlawn Plantation" of Wadmalaw Island. Even during the depression, Negro field hands had met here every Tuesday and sung spirituals and found solace. Gershwin had listened to fifty of them sing. The music drama had featured three moods of the colorful life of the Negro population: religious meetings, burial service, and barn dance. At least six spirituals, some very rare, were generally included.

In April 1940 Frederick H. Koch, the founder and director of the Carolina Playmakers, had introduced a new Gullah drama in the pages of the *Southern Literary Messenger*. He wrote to present and to praise Caroline Hart Crum's *Got No Sorrow*. Next to his introduction is the text of the play. Within introduction and text are some striking lines from spirituals:

> Everybuddy who is libbin'
> Gut to die, gut to die
> De lawyer, de *prea*-cher
> Can' git away,
> We all gut to die on dat jedgement day
>
> Tribe of Israel, choice of God
> Cross de ribber on dry sod
>
> Cain and Abel had a fight
> Cain knocked Abel out ob sight
>
> Ober de heels een Zi—
> Een Zion lan'
> An' den he say he gwine shake 'em my—
> My righteous han'.

Another play under Professor Koch's direction and published with an introduction by him was *Three Links of Chain* (1940) by Kate Porter Lewis. It was based on the famous spiritual, "Sister Mary Had Three Links of Chain." Still another was Rietta Bailey, *Washed in de Blood* (1938), called a ritualistic Negro drama of rural Georgia. Although using spirituals and neospirituals, it lacks the natural sting of the black folk.

Earl Robinson and Millard Lampell wrote in 1943 a cantata called *The Lonesome Train*. Its Alabama church section is rooted in spirituals. In production, it was further invigorated through remarkable performances and singing by Richard Huey.

The Denmark Vesey story was dramatically retold by Dorothy Heyward (wife of DuBose) and produced on Broadway with an excellent cast, opening on November 3, 1948. Entitled *Set My People Free*, it featured two spirituals. Ten years later, Alex and Michel (called the Drinking Gourds) brought out at Town Hall *Let My People Go!*, a slave cycle. The two producers used songs from their library of slave songs, which they said exceeded thirty-five hundred. In *A Land Beyond the River* (1963) (concerning the struggle for equal education), Loften Mitchell employs two spirituals. A white Princeton professor, Martin B. Duberman, wrote, in 1964, a controversial drama called *In White America*. In this play are six spirituals, several of which are reprised more than once.

Throughout his vast output, Langston Hughes employed spirituals by direct quotation, by indirect reference, and by implication of meaning. In one of his plays, *Tambourines to Glory*, there are a number of outright traditional songs as well as a number of songs adapted from spirituals. Among the former are "When the Saints Go Marching In," "What He's Done for Me," "Who'll Be a Witness?" and "Children, We Shall All Be Free." Among the latter, copyrighted by Langston Hughes and Jobe Huntley, are "Upon This Rock," "As I Go," "I'm Gonna Testify," "Home to God," "God's Got a Way," "Let the Church Say Amen," and "Tambourines to Glory."

In *A List of Negro Plays* (1938) published by the National Service Bureau, Federal Theatre Project, WPA, edited by John D. Silvera, several of the plays have spirituals in them. James P. Johnson's *Yamekraw* (1927), expressing the religious fervor and happy moods of a Negro settlement on the outskirts of Savannah, Georgia, is based on spiritual and blues melodies. One of the University of Michigan plays of 1932 is Adolph Levy's *Go Down, Moses.*

Spirituals invaded some widely scattered dramatic types during the 1920s. Ransom Rideout's *Deep River* received a notable production by the Community Players at Berkeley Playhouse. And again spirituals were both background and foreground in the Provincetown Players' production of Paul Green's *In Abraham's Bosom* (1926). *In Abraham's Bosom*, starring Frank Wilson, Rose McClendon, and Abbie Mitchell, went on to win the Pulitzer Prize for drama for that season.

No doubt, the most famous and highly respected Broadway drama in which spirituals occupy a very large role was Marc Connelly's *The Green Pastures: A Fable* (1930). In private conversation Marc Connelly said that he wrote this play to present people with genuine faith. In an era of unbelievers and misbelievers he discovered in Roark Bradford's Southern sketches, *Ol' Man Adam an' His Chillun* (1929), a large group of people who really believed in something. After inspecting the group personally, he was further inspired to do the drama.

The spirituals were sung by a choir under the direction of Hall Johnson. In the printed versions of the play, Marc Connelly expressed thanks to Alma Lillie Hubbard of New Orleans for assisting him in the selection of the spirituals. His debt of gratitude to Mrs. Hubbard is underlined in *Voices Offstage: A Book of Memoirs* (1968). She was the pianist of the black church in New Orleans, in Jackson Square, where he several times attended services. She taught him "jump-ups" like "Rise, Shine, Give God the Glory."

The spirituals of *The Green Pastures* in the order in which they were sung were as follows: "Rise, Shine, Give God the Glory"; "When the Saints Come Marching In"; "Certainly, Lawd"; "So High You Can't Get over It"; "Bright Mansions Above"; "Turn You Round"; "Run, Sinner, Run"; "You Better Mind"; "Dere's No Hidin' Place"; "Feastin' Table"; "I Want to Be Ready"; "Dey Ol' Ark's A-Movering"; "A City Called Heaven"; "My Lord's A-Writin' All de Time"; "Go Down, Moses"; "Mary, Don't You Weep"; "I'm Noways Weary and I'm Noways Tired";

"Joshua Fit de Battle of Jericho"; "Cain't Stay Away"; "Death's Gwinter Lay His Cold Icy Hands on Me"; "A Blind Man Stood in de Middle of de Road"; "March On"; "Hallelujah, King Jesus."

A remarkable scene, involving a famous spiritual, was omitted from *The Green Pastures* even after rehearsals had begun. One of the directors, says Connelly, was greatly distressed by this omission since he considered the scene the best in the play. Connelly ruled it out because it did not blend well into the developing action.

When the scene was published in the September 1930 issue of *Hearst's International and Cosmopolitan Magazine* and in book form in 1937, it was called "Little David." It retold the story of the most famous of shepherd boys and of the killer of Goliath in the mood and spirit of the faithful and imaginative Louisiana blacks. It used "Little David, Play on Yo' Hawp" to keen advantage.

James Baldwin's *Amen Corner*, based on his successful novel, *Go Tell It on the Mountain*, finally reached Broadway in 1968. Though containing only six major spirituals, it was swept by spiritual and gospel atmosphere throughout. The main character was based on Baldwin's own father, who had been a lively evangelist.

In recent years no one has turned spirituals to more dramatic account than Alvin Ailey. Ailey is primarily a dance director and a choreographer, but much of his success in dance drama has been due to his maturity and versatility as an actor. The spirituals have particularly inspired him. In them he finds a broad spread of creative opportunities that speak to dancers and audiences of the present day. In Lindsay Patterson's *Anthology of the American Negro in the Theatre* (New York, Publishers Company, 1967) is an expressive picture of the Alvin Ailey Dance Company performing "Revelations," a dance suite based on spirituals.

MOTION PICTURES AND THE SPIRITUAL

Spirituals have occurred in motion pictures almost since the founding of the medium. They are brought in through innumerable channels. Occasionally, a big Broadway spectacle like *The Green Pastures* (filmed 1936) is transferred bodily to the films. On the other hand, a single song may be used, or phrases from a song. The spiritual is used for atmosphere, action, and large production numbers.

In 1936, the spiritual choir of Hall Johnson, which had participated in the remarkable success of *The Green Pastures*, was employed in three other pictures: *Dimples*, *Banjo on My Knee*, and *Rainbow on the River*. Spirituals also played a large part in the appeal of King Vidor's *Hallelujah* in 1929.

In 1963 Sidney Poitier, an Afro-American actor, won an Academy Award for best actor for his leading role in *Lilies of the Field*. Strongly assisting him in this recognition was a spiritual, "Amen," which was the musical leitmotiv throughout the play. Although an established spiritual, "Amen" was given new and colorful clothes through an arrangement by Jester Hairston. Hairston's voice was also used.

The work of Jester Hairston, in motion pictures and elsewhere, has already been reviewed. It might be added that he has been a motion picture choral director since 1935, and most of his considerable artistry and training ability has been devoted to the building of spiritual choirs.

RADIO AND THE SPIRITUAL

Spirituals have held forth on the air for half a century and for a while dominated certain portions of radio. The Fisk, Hampton, Tuskegee, and other college choirs were signed, at various times, to regular programs on national networks. Such professional singers as Wings Over Jordan and the Southernaires also held regular spots on network radio for years. Other singing groups and individual singers have poured millions of spirituals and thousands of versions of established spirituals through network and local radio stations.

In an article published in *Better Homes and Gardens* for July 1932, entitled "Negro Spirituals at our own Firesides," Avis Carlson calls attention to the large audience for the appreciation of spirituals brought in by radio. In 1947 the editor and historian Edith J. R. Isaacs recorded, "There is now hardly a day that goes by without Spirituals on the radio."

TELEVISION AND THE SPIRITUAL

Like the other mass media, television has greatly contributed to the continued appreciation of the spirituals and to their introduction to younger and younger generations. Visiting singers on regular shows—soloists, quartets, and choruses, amateurs and professionals—often address the viewer-listener's sight and hearing with their version of some spiritual. Sketches and dramas using spirituals have been presented for many years and are still a part of television fare. In June 1970 a Dutch choir on international television sang "Go Down, Moses" as part of the protest of Dutch Catholics against requiring priests to be celibates. Occasionally, there is some very large and important presentation of these songs, such as in the periods when Marian Anderson and Leontyne Price sang for the Telephone Hour.

RECORDS AND THE SPIRITUAL

The recording of the spirituals has been going on now for well over half a century, both by scholarly folklorists and other collectors and by commercial firms presenting established or promising singers or singing groups.

The Archive of Folk Song has thousands of these records on file and has made arrangements for interested listeners to hear them. We hereby submit a statement from the Archive describing its holdings and designating them by number. The statement was prepared by the Reference Librarian, Joseph C. Hickerson.

PRINCIPAL COLLECTIONS OF FIELD RECORDINGS IN THE
ARCHIVE OF FOLK SONG WHICH CONTAIN NEGRO SPIRITUALS

Robert W. Gordon cylinder collection. Includes Negro religious songs recorded in Georgia in the late 1920s.

AFS 1–286; 309–535; 663–743; 829–876; 878–944; 1001–1054; 1299–1339; 2589–2728; 3942–4087. 1089 disc recordings of folk music from Southern states, made by John A. and Alan Lomax 1933–1940. Includes Negro religious songs from Virginia, North and South Carolina, Florida, Georgia, Alabama, Mississippi, Louisiana, Arkansas, Texas, and the Bahamas.

AFS 2735–3153. 419 disc recordings of folklore from Southern states made by Herbert Halpert in 1939. Includes Negro religious songs from Mississippi.

AFS 4706–4708. 3 disc recordings made ca. 1940 by John Rosser, Jr., at College Station, Texas, of the singing of two Negro gospel groups.

AFS 4709–4731. 23 disc recordings made 1941 in Maryland and Delaware by Jerome Weisner, Joseph Liss, and Glenn Gildersleeve, including Negro religious songs.

AFS 4757–4786; 5147–5167; 6604–6673; 6678–6690; 6734–6740. 141 disc recordings made in cooperation with Fisk University of Negro religious and secular folklore in Mississippi, Tennessee, Alabama, and Georgia. Recorded 1939–1942 by Alan Lomax, John Work, and Lewis Jones.

AFS 5035–5098. 64 disc recordings of Negro secular and religious music made 1941 in Alabama by Robert Sonkin.

AFS 5168–5214; 5436–5510. 122 disc recordings of Negro religious services made 1941 in Texas by John Henry Faulk.

AFS 5586–5592. 7 disc recordings of a Negro Baptist church service made ca. 1940 in Nashville, Tennessee, by John Vincent.

AFS 6178. Disc recording of Negro spirituals made 1945 in Philadelphia by Laura E. Ross.

AFS 6986–6993; 7039–7053. 23 disc recordings of Negro folk music made 1943 in Georgia by Willis L. James and Lewis Jones.

AFS 7057–7059; 7600–7601. 5 disc recordings of David Prior of the Bahamas made 1943 and 1944 in Washington, D.C., by B. A. Botkin.

AFS 8222–8321. 100 disc recordings of Negro folk music and narrative made in late 1930s and early 1940s in Virginia by Roscoe Lewis of Hampton Institute.

AFS 8968. 1 disc recording of Willie Wilkerson of North Carolina, made 1947 in Washington, D.C.

AFS 9988–9997. 10 7"-reels tape of Negro religious services and songs made 1950 in North Carolina by Cyrus B. Koonce.

AFS 10,081. 1 10"-reel tape of a Negro church service made ca. 1950 in North Carolina by Nelson S. Barker.

AFS 10,749; 10,757–10,762. 7 7"-reels tape of Negro prison songs recorded 1951 in Texas by Pete Seeger and John Lomax, Jr.

AFS 10,899; 11,303–304. 3 10"-reels tape of Negro religious songs and services recorded mid-1950s in South Carolina by Penn Community Services.

AFS 11,306. 1 10"-reel of Pennsylvania folklore recorded 1956 by Frank Hoffmann. Includes Negro religious songs recorded at a migrant workers' camp.

AFS 11,330–332. 3 10"-reels tape of Southern Ohio folklore recorded mid-1950s by Bruce Buckley and John Ball. Includes Negro religious songs.

AFS 11,475. 1 10"-reel tape of Gullah tales, Negro spirituals, and street cries from South Carolina, from material loaned by Harold S. Reeves and Russell Wood.

AFS 12,027–12,029. 3 10"-reels tape of Mississippi John Hurt, recorded 1963 in Washington, D.C., by Joseph C. Hickerson and Richard K. Spottswood.

AFS 12,032. 1 10"-reel tape of Negro religious songs sung by Rev. Robert Wilkins of Memphis, Tennessee. Recorded 1964 in Washington, D.C., by Joseph C. Hickerson and Richard K. Spottswood.

AFS 12,296; 12,319. 2 reels tape of Negro religious songs sung by Maggie F. Gomillion of South Carolina. Recorded 1964 and 1965 in Silver Spring, Md., and Washington, D.C., by Mrs. Samuel H. Horne and Mrs. Rae Korson.

AFS 12,318; 13,042–13,047. 7 reels tape Negro religious and secular folklore recorded 1964–1966 in Texas prisons by Bruce Jackson.

AFS 12,346–12,349. 4 disc recordings of a 1936 WEAF broadcast featuring the Society for the Preservation of the Negro Spiritual of Charleston, South Carolina.

AFS 12,575–12,596. 22 7"-reels tape of Louisiana, Mississippi, and Iowa folklore recorded 1957–1966 by Harry Oster. Includes Negro religious songs and services from Louisiana and Mississippi.

AFS 14,079–14,082. 4 10"-reels tape of Tennessee church services recorded 1968–1969 by Eleanor Dickinson. Includes some Negro services and songs.

AFS 14,083–14,086. 4 10"-reels tape of North and South Carolina folklore recorded 1949 by B. A. Botkin. Includes Negro church services and songs recorded from radio broadcasts.

AFS 14,169. 1 7"-reel tape of Negro folksinger Mable Hillary at Brunswick, Georgia, 1968. Gift of Kirby Rogers.

AFS 14,204–14,216. 13 10"-reels tape from the unissued collections of Folk Legacy Records, Inc., Sharon, Conn. Includes Negro religious songs recorded in North Carolina 1962–1963 by Sandy Paton, Lee B. Haggerty, and Henry Felt.

AFS 14,234–14,240. 7 10"-reels tape. Negro folktales and church services recorded in Rappahannock Co., Virginia, 1969–1970 by Chuck Perdue.

AFS 14,292–14,297. 6 10"-reels tape. North Carolina folk music recorded by Alan Jabbour 1966–1968, including Negro church services.

Charles Haywood has seven closely packed double-columned pages of spiritual discography in his *Bibliography of North American Folklore* (1951, 1961). His discography is one of the indications that discography of the spiritual is rapidly approaching published bibliography.

As far back as May 1916 there was an article on the recording of spirituals in the *Literary Digest*. George A. Miller was reported in this article as trying to get down songs he had heard on his father's plantation. Two of the recorded songs were reproduced: "Trouble Gwine ter War'y Me Down" and "Somebody Buried in de Graveyard." The latter song, according to the report, was sung by three cotton hoers as they went up and down the long cotton rows, keeping time with their hoes. Its words were as follows,

> Somebody buried in de graveyard,
> Somebody buried in de sea;
> Gwine ter git up in de mornin' shoutin'
> Gwine ter sound de jubilee.
> If you git dare befo' I do,
> You run an' tell de Lord,
> I'm er comin' on too—Oh!
> Somebody dyin' in de mount'in'
> Somebody dyin' in de baid,
> Gwine ter git up in de mornin' shoutin'
> Gwine ter rise up from de daid.
> If you git dare befo' I do,
> You run an' tell de Lord,
> I'm er comin' on too.

In 1939–40, the State Department of the United States published the report of the Committee of the Conference on Inter-American Relations in the Field of Music. Twenty pages of this report, compiled by Alan Lomax, are devoted to American folk songs on commercial records, and spirituals are included.

Morton Gould's memorable "Spirituals for Strings" was recorded for RCA Victor in 1961 and published in book form in 1964. It reproduces nine spirituals in the distinctive Gould fashion, without words.

Of the many records from Afro-American searchers and recorders, the following two are mentioned: "Bayard Rustin Sings," released by Fellowship Publications in New York City and "Historical Interpretations of Negro Spirituals" and "Lift Every Voice and Sing," released by Mrs. Dorothy Conley Elam of Berlin, New Jersey.

(Civil Rights Expression and the Spiritual

If anyone has the impression that down through the years since Emancipation spirituals have been sung almost always by religious groups, he should immediately disabuse himself of this notion. In this book it has been shown that the secret meetings at which many, if not most, of the songs were created were community gatherings rather than predominantly religious meetings. Often the religious motif was introduced, but keeping the community tight and together was the prime purpose. It has also been shown that spirituals have been sung for a great many purposes, not just in churches. One of the primary uses of the spiritual, and one of its great reasons for expansion, has been civil rights expression.

As early as 1868 John Mason Brown had indicated the change taking place in the new freedman. He was, said Brown, different from the slave, more reflective, cautious, shrewd; more taciturn, more keenly alive to such practical issues as labor and compensation; more grave and sober. Another white Southerner, James Bond, writing in the *Louisville Courier-Journal* in 1921, had noted also the continuing change. He said that Negro singing was changing because a new Negro was developing in the South; the race was passing from a state of childhood and settling down to serious tasks as demanded by the new age and the complex civilization in which it was living. The Negro, Bond said, was hanging his harp on the willow in order to spend more time with buying homes, educating his children, launching commercial enterprises, and learning to recognize his rights. He was not giving up his song. He would return later with a new and more appropriate song.

As everyone knows, the political consciousness of the Afro-American burgeoned greatly during the span of years between these two articles. The sense of rights and the determination to fight for them were the two strongest manifestations of this burgeoning. Many spirituals were ready-made for such developments; and they were heavily used for these purposes.

Emancipation ceremonies, usually held on January first each year, were often key times for renewing the faith and resharpening the determination. Lincoln has already been introduced as a singer of spirituals in a group of contrabands (all Afro-Americans). On the very first Emancipation Day (1863), Lincoln had a White House reception. Right after the reception, without further ceremony, Lincoln signed the Emancipation Proclamation. At a contrabands' meeting that day in Washington, as Bernard records, an elderly man sang "I'm a Free Man Now"; an aged woman sang "Go Down, Moses"; another sang "There Will Be No More Taskmasters." Four thousand Negroes paraded in Norfolk. The black citizens of Portland, Maine, held an "Emancipation Levee." The *New York Tribune* of December 31, 1862, and January 1, 1863, report the widespread singing of "The Song of the Contrabands" and "Oh! Let My People Go," a variant of "Go Down, Moses."

John E. Washington reports that memorable December 31 (Watch Night) in his *They Knew Lincoln*. He says that when the bells of New York rang after the Watch Night meetings, many of the crowd yelled such things as, "Praise God . . . Freed at last . . . I'm so glad . . . I'm freed at last . . . Before I'd be a slave I'll be carried to my grave."

The Singing Sixties (1960), a book by Willard A. and Porter W. Heaps, describes similar singing activity in their chapter on "The Negro and the

Contraband." Natalie Curtis Burlin, writing in 1913, states that Negro music had improved the understanding between whites and blacks. She referred particularly to the great chorus at Carnegie Hall on Lincoln's Birthday, 1913, singing "O Freedom."

Five years later, Mrs. Burlin's own "Hymn to Freedom" began to fill the air. It was based on freedom spirituals in general, but set to the music of a single spiritual, "O Ride on, Jesus." In it are references to "martyred Belgium," "wounded France," "struggling Russia," "the starving Pole," "bowed Roumania," and "the stricken Serb." Like the freedom spirituals, it calls on freedom to march and ride. It was first sung at the Penn Normal and Agricultural Institute at St. Helena Island, South Carolina, in July 1918. The occasion was a farewell to the eighteen Island men called up in the draft for World War I, the war to make the world safe for democracy.

The publication of *The Negro Spiritualist Hymnal*, edited by the Reverend Silas W. Brister in 1963, was offered as a share in the Centennial Jubilee of the Emancipation Proclamation.

In more recent years spirituals have played a large part in labor singing and in general freedom singing. Issues of *People's Songs* and *Sing Out!* have rarely been without some spiritual which in its original form or in some adaptation is advancing the causes of labor freedom or of general freedom. B. A. Botkin noted in 1947 that these songs and their adaptations made freedom more than a word. It is a call to action, an act of liberating or being liberated from bondage or oppression. By nature democratic, these folk songs belong to the group and perfectly express group attitudes.

In 1964 Perry Friedman published in Berlin, Germany, *Hör zu, Mister Bilbo*, which he advertised as "Lieder aus der amerikanischen Arbeiterbewegung, 1860–1950" (Songs of the American labor movement, 1860–1950). In the introduction to the book Sidney Gordon makes reference to the birth of the Negro spiritual out of slavery and the war against slavery. A spiritual, "Gospel Train," has been adapted to "Der Gerwerkschaftszug" (union train). The union songs that fill the book are printed with German and English texts opposite. Three other spirituals are given in their original versions: "No More Auction Block for Me" (Nie mehr Sklavenmarkt); "I'm on My Way" (Ich kenn der Weg)—a reference to Harriet Tubman and the Underground Railroad; and "Down by the Riverside" (Dort an dem grossen Fluss).

Also published in Berlin was *And Why Not Every Man* (1961), an anthology edited by Herbert Aptheker. Aptheker calls his book "The Story of the Fight Against Negro Slavery." Twenty-two spirituals help Aptheker tell his story.

A recent new edition of *Slave Songs of the United States* refers to the fact that songs of the freedom movement are heard today in churches and on the highways of the South, and that the spirituals being republished are, therefore, an inspiration and memory "of the living heart of history." John

Greenway and Russell Ames have written about the spiritual as protest song—Greenway in *American Folksongs of Protest* and Ames in several very perceptive articles in the *Journal of American Folklore* and *Science and Society*.

Indeed the end of the 1950s and the beginning of the 1960s were a peak period for spirituals in civil rights. Martin Luther King, Jr., had turned many spirituals into freedom songs, including "We Shall Overcome," presumably adapted from an early spiritual. In speaking of spirituals as morale builders and sources of spiritual support, Joseph R. Washington, Jr., calls attention to the singing of "Lord, I Want to Be a Christian" by students in jail in the earliest sit-ins.

Guy and Candie Carawan have contributed a great deal to the business of providing songs and atmosphere for the freedom movement in America. In *We Shall Overcome* (1963) the subtitle is *Songs of the Southern Freedom Movement*. It included actual spirituals and spiritual adaptations to cover freedom rides, Albany, Georgia, voter registration, Greenwood, Birmingham, and the like. Along similar lines *Ain't You Got a Right to the Tree of Life?*, with Robert Yellen as photographer, was published in 1966. In 1968 came *Freedom Is a Constant Struggle*, containing songs of the freedom movement with documentary photographs. The introduction announces that these songs have evolved since the 1963 march on Washington, continuing the work of *We Shall Overcome* which does the same thing for the period before 1963.

Not only do the spirituals adapt beautifully as freedom and labor songs, but there are also good books describing the process. De Turk and Poulin's *The American Folk Scene* gives the "dimensions of the folksong revival." It consists of a number of articles by well-known writers in the field. In their introductory statement the editors declare that traditional freedom songs (spirituals) not only articulate the Negro's longing for liberation; they also give voice to any man's bid for freedom.

In *The American Folk Scene*, Pete Seeger asks, "How many white people have rediscovered their own humanity through the singing of American Negro songs?" Ironically, Kenneth Keating declares "Gonna lay down my sword and shield" a sinister folk plot for disarmament. Describing picketing Negroes in Marion, North Carolina, Robert Sherman tells how they chanted rewritten black spirituals across the darkness to inspire faith and courage. He also gives a new version of the origin of "We Shall Overcome"; he says it was taken from Charles A. Tindley's "I'll Overcome Some Day" (1901), which in turn derived from Galatians 6:9; "And let us not be weary in well doing: for in due season we shall reap, if we faint not." He tells how Negro members of the Food and Tobacco Workers Association sang it on the picket lines in 1946 and how Zilphia Horton taught it to her students at the Highlander Folk School in Tennessee.

Summing up the influence of the spiritual in these movements, the editors declare that all the characteristics of the freedom song have had their place in the freedom movement of America's Negroes. Many articles in *Sing Out!* prove the spiritual a guide to freedom thinking for whites and blacks too. One in 1966, "Watering the Roots," urges loving research into the basic forms of Negro expression.

Josh Dunson's *Freedom in the Air* (1965), song movements of the sixties, has a very long list of adaptations from spirituals. At the outset he notes that adaptations of Afro-American songs like "Oh Freedom" and "We Are Soldiers" brought hundreds into mass meetings with the first note because the songs were known and needed only the change of a word or two to make them freedom songs. He told how Carawan with his Nashville Quartet led rally after rally in the North and throughout the South. They used "Hold On," "Sit at the Welcome Table," and many other spirituals.

Dunson also describes the initiation of the Albany movement by two field secretaries of the Student Nonviolent Coordinating Committee, Charles Sherrod and Cordell Reason, from Albany State College in Georgia. "This Little Light of Mine," "We Shall Not Be Moved," and "Oh, Freedom" were some of the songs that developed magic during the Albany movement. Dunson says that the movement brought only the best singing and gave many new songs, based on spirituals, to the freedom drive. These songs gave the Negro and his helpers community pride, purpose, and unity.

"This Little Light of Mine" underwent variations from at least eight leaders. Some of the lines used were,

> Up and down this street, Lord, I'm going
>   to let it shine, . . .
> Every time I'm bleeding, . . .
> Voting for my Freedom.

"Go Tell It on the Mountain" also made many good adaptations, of which one was,

> I wouldn't be Governor Wallace,
> I'll tell you the reason why,
> I'd be afraid He might call me
> And I wouldn't be ready to die.

The freedom movement in general was proud of the fact that it had tapped a strong and militant Afro-American heritage. The adapters were also proud. Of the spirituals, the Reverend Andrew Young said, "We all know you can't trust a Negro on the negotiating committee who doesn't like his people's music. We learned that in Birmingham!"

Shelton and Gahr in *The Face of Folk Music* continue the story of the effective use of spiritual adaptations. One of the transformations they recall is,

Go down, Kennedy,
'Way down in Georgia land.
Tell old Pritchett
To let my people go.

(Pritchett was the chief of police of Albany.)

The story of the arrival of Negroes into Southern politics by Pat Watters and Reese Cleghorn, published 1967, was called *Climbing Jacob's Ladder*. The famous spiritual is quoted near the beginning to point direction.

In the May 1, 1970, issue of the *Washington Post*, Michael Kernan wrote about some new activities of the famous balladeer, Joe Glazer. At this stage Joe was working for the government, as a labor educator in USIA. His film, "Songs and Stories of Labor," was scheduled for premiere that night. Joe was speaking of the great songs which had come out of the South, and the spirituals were high on his list. One of the memorable adaptations that he sings was "We Are Building a Strong Union," based on the spiritual "We Are Climbing Jacob's Ladder." In Joe's *Songs of Peace, Freedom, and Protest* (1970) are sixteen very live spirituals.

Joe says that he recorded "We Shall Overcome" in 1949 at Charleston, South Carolina. It grew, he says, out of "I Will Be All Right."

Students at Howard University adapted a spiritual during their takeover of the administration building on the campus in 1968. To the tune of "Study War No More," they sang,

We ain't going to shuffle no more,
We ain't going to shuffle no more,
We ain't going to shuffle no god-dam more.

❲ *The Spiritual and Other Folk Songs in America and Elsewhere*

One of the things which has kept the spiritual alive and growing and which has boosted its stock in national and world markets is the constant comparison with other folk songs. Back in 1894 Arthur Weld said that American music was nonexistent and unlikely to develop because America had no race or nationality, no distinctive blood, no characteristic talent, no reliable system of music education, and no composers who did not produce German music (Chadwick, Paine, MacDowell, Foote, Parker, Whiting, etc.).

Undiscouraged, a number of writers have been tracing the strands of basically American music. One of these, Don Yoder, is an enthusiast of Pennsylvania (Dutchified) spirituals. In one of his books he wrote of "The Spiritual Tradition in America." Placing the Negro spiritual in the camp meeting tradition, he cleared the road for the Pennsylvania spiritual as a truly American product.

When Willi Apel and Ralph Daniel came to the word "Spirituals" in their *Harvard Brief Dictionary of Music* (1960), they found only one spiritual, "religious songs of the American Negro." They somehow failed to recognize the "white spiritual" of George Pullen Jackson and the "Dutchified" spiritual of Don Yoder. This was an especial disservice to George Pullen Jackson, who spent more than twenty years and many books and articles proving that the "white spiritual of the Southern upland" was *the* American spiritual, from which all others derived. The fact that this white spiritual is known only to scholars and a few Southern church people, whereas the Afro-American spiritual is known, respected, sung, and loved around the world, makes little difference to him and the few scholars he has managed to convince.

The Afro-American spiritual has been compared to songs of very early vintage. Joseph Hutchinson Smith showed similarities between it and ancient ballads in music, oral tradition, principle of incremental repetition, and community composing. Thomas Garnett wrote a bachelor of divinity thesis entitled "A Comparative Study of Ancient Hebrew and American Negro Folk-Songs."

A number of writers have compared the Afro-American spiritual with the English and Scottish popular ballads. Benjamin Brawley, for example, says that it is more affected by nature than the English and Scottish ballads. Sister Mary Hilarion says that the creators of the spiritual must have had contact with the English and Scottish songs. Writing on "The Negro and the Ballad," C. Alphonso Smith cites a Negro variant of one of Professor Child's ballads, taken from Montgomery, Alabama, in 1897. The Child ballad in question was "Sir Hugh, or, The Jew's Daughter." And John A. Lomax during his *Adventures of a Ballad Hunter*, searching for spirituals in Texas, found a Negro singer of English ballads.

The spiritual can be and has been compared to folk songs in other lands. In personal conversation, Dr. J. H. Nketia has compared it with the folk songs of Ghana, about which he was written in a most scholarly manner. The late Albert Luthuli of South Africa, Nobel prize winner, used a phrase from an Afro-American spiritual as the title of his book in 1962, *Let My People Go*. In the book he quotes an African folk song which seems distantly related to the spiritual. In 1951, Alexander Sandilands published in South Africa *A Hundred and Twenty Negro Spirituals*. He said in his introduction that he wished to provide for African teachers, pupils, ministers, people. The music of the Afro-American spiritual, he said, retained the African idiom and struck a chord in true African hearts. Even far-removed Bantu music had strong similarities with West African Negro music, which helped to produce the spiritual. As one would expect, spirituals are an impressive segment in Mellinger E. Henry's *Bibliography for the Study of American Folk-Songs with Many Titles of Folk-Songs (and Titles That Have to Do with Folk-Songs from Other Lands)*.

Many writers have pointed to parallels, sources, borrowings, and other relationships between the spiritual and various types of West Indian music. Rogie Clark and Edric Connor have done these things for Trinidad, Connor going so far as to publish fifteen West Indian Negro spirituals. Several of them, "De Virgin Mary Had a Baby Boy," "When Joshua Walk Roun' Jericho," "Weary Travellers," "Safe in de Promise' Land," are startlingly close to their North American counterparts. Sir Hans Sloane, Walter Jekyll, Helen Roberts, and Haynes Trebor have done similarly for Jamaica. True, some of Trebor's information is faulty, but he has written nevertheless. Sir Hans (who wrote in 1707) included reference to slave music of other West Indian islands also. Joseph Hutchinson Smith also wrote about the West Indies as a whole; he referred to Monk Lewis, *Journal of a Residence among the Negroes in the West Indies*, dating back to 1795.

A great many writers have tied the spiritual in with American songs of many types and kinds. The Federal Writers Project anthology, *American Stuff*, has related it to convict songs; Grace Cleveland Porter to folk games; John Greenway and Lawrence Gellert to songs of protest; Florence H. Botsford and Rogie Clark to varied folk songs; the Progressive Book Company of Chicago to college songs and songs of fraternities and sororities; Ruth Crawford Seeger and Herbert H. Wernecke to Christmas songs; the Womans Press to "Songs, Rounds, and Carols"; David Ewen and Sigmund Spaeth to popular music in America; and Albert E. Wier to "A Thousand Songs." In five volumes of their *World in Tune*, the Krones (Beatrice and Max) have as many spirituals. Here, spirituals qualify as descants, easy basses, and "great songs of faith."

The spiritual has been shown to have its share of kinship with American sections. Through Arthur Farwell, it becomes a song of the West and South. Fifty of the two hundred songs in Albert E. Wier's *Songs of the Sunny South* are spirituals. It is included by Carl Holliday in *Three Centuries of Southern Poetry, 1607–1907* (nine spirituals). Hazel Kinscella's *History Sings* has spirituals in its section "Along Southern Borders." It is referred to indirectly by Emma Bell Miles in her article on the singing of the Kentucky, Tennessee, and Carolina mountains, called "Some Real American Music." Vance Randolph mentions it in his two books on folk songs of the Ozarks. Hundreds of spirituals and spiritual-derived songs are set down in Bruce A. Rosenberg's checklist of WPA holdings called *The Folksongs of Virginia*. Sixty-five are recorded by Belden and Hudson in "Folk Songs from North Carolina" of *The Frank C. Brown Collection of North Carolina Folklore*.

It naturally takes a position near the front when American folklore in general is being discussed. Chapter 5 of Richard M. Dorson's *American Folklore* deals with "The Negro." The spiritual and its related songs occupy almost half of César Saerchinger's "The Folk Element in American

Music." It is referred to by Stith Thompson in his "American Folklore after Fifty Years." It is well treated in Frank Luther's *Americans and Their Songs;* in John Anthony Scott's *The Ballad of America;* and in Pete Seeger's *American Favorite Ballads.* At least one spiritual appears in each of the following colorful American compilations: Carl Carmer, *America Sings;* Grafman and Manning, *Folk Music USA;* and Alan Lomax, *Hard-Hitting Songs for Hard-Hit People.*

Paul F. Laubenstein in "An Apocalyptic Reincarnation" (*Journal of Biblical Literature* for 1932) has pointed up the parallels between the Jewish and the African folk traditions, using the spirituals as his key to the African and the Bible as key to the Jewish. The struggle of oppressed Jews in re the spirituals is also discussed in *Sing Out!* for December 1951 under the heading "Heritage: U.S.A."

There are, as one would expect, many comparisons between the spirituals and Amerindian songs, by Harvey Gaul, by George Herzog, by Charles Hofmann, and others.

Sometimes the relationship of the spiritual is indirect and subtle. In *American Folksong* Woody Guthrie tells how, born to Texas parents, he grew up in the midst of music. All around him were songs of all kinds, not just Scottish and Irish and Mexican and Spanish but "many made up by the Negroes of the South." His father, he tells, sang "in his Indian and Negro half chant" as he rode down the road or called horses.

Solomon Jones and Paul Tanner, in a 1970 article in the *Music Journal,* complain because no one has told of the "black moans." While the spiritual, they say, expressed the evilness of slavery, the black moans told of an imminent freedom, "a black-initiated liberation." These moans were a common foundation for worship, they declare. They encouraged and counseled direct rebellion to potential runaways. Accepting the black moan as a folk form, one should remind these authors that the spiritual did all things they claim for the moans; and more; and earlier; and longer.

As a crowning touch the spiritual has appeared in a number of anthologies and interpretive works whose titles bespeak their elegance:

Title	Number of Spirituals
Charles Haywood, *A Bibliography of North American Folklore and Folksong*	Hundreds listed by title
Julius Mattfeld, *The Folk Music of the Western Hemisphere*	
Bruno Nettl, *Folk and Traditional Music of the Western Continents*	
Alan Lomax and Svatara Jakobsonova, *Freedom Songs of the United Nations*	2

❨ The Spiritual and Art

In 1930, as we have reported (page 410), Ramsay MacDonald, the Prime Minister of England, told the Hampton Singers of a painting then hanging in the Royal Academy exhibition. Done by Mark Symon, it represented a modern conception of Christ crucified. It was named, said the Prime Minister, for a very famous spiritual, "Were You There When They Crucified My Lord?"

In the Salles Gaveau, an art gallery in Paris, there stood for many years a sculpture of Roland Hayes in the act of singing "Steal Away." In 1932 William Arms Fisher reports that, at that time, there was hanging in the Anderson Gallery, Richmond, a remarkable painting in color of an old Negro woman. This painting was done by Marjorie Wintermute, born in San Francisco. In Miss Wintermute's picture, the features of the woman represent the sentiments of "Swing Low, Sweet Chariot." By 1940 there was in the home of Mr. and Mrs. Lawrence Tibbett a mural painted by William Yarrow. This mural was designated "Phases of Music in America." Pictures and legends in the mural relate to various spirituals and indicate that the spiritual is the father of jazz.

These are samples of art work growing out of the spirituals. Perhaps the most striking examples, however, come from the art pieces of Allan Rohan Crite. In 1944 he published *Were You There When They Crucified My Lord?* There are no words, only pictures to portray the event. In 1948 he did a similar representation which he called *Three Spirituals from Earth to Heaven*. Roland Hayes wrote the introduction to the book. Of Crite's work, the art critic of the *New York Herald Tribune* wrote, "Among the most moving documents of religious art that have come from America in recent years are the brush-and-ink setting of Negro spirituals made by this distinguished American artist."

The three spirituals Crite depicts are "Nobody Knows the Trouble I See"—the figure clad in overalls represents the melody; "Swing Low, Sweet Chariot"—again the motif is an overall-clad figure, and Jordan is a swiftly running stream; "Heaven"—which has three motifs, robes, harps, and wings; the beatific vision is the final goal of man.

The reproduction of John McCrady's painting, "Swing Low, Sweet Chariot," hangs in the Collection of the City Art Museum of St. Louis, Missouri. A large oil painting of the original Jubilee Singers, done by the Court artist of England at the suggestion of Queen Victoria, hangs in Fisk Memorial Chapel.

⟮ *The Spiritual and the Folk Community*

The spiritual was, of course, created by an Afro-American folk community. In general terms its creation was completed by 1870. After it became known to the public, however, it began to develop its own folk community, black and white. Its appeal has been broad enough to attract a considerable and devoted following. Most of these people find it impossible to get their musical satisfactions or to fulfill their musical needs except through the spiritual. Many of them sing spirituals as the original singers did—out of a deep and crying need.

The attraction of whites into the spiritual folk community is not surprising. They are, after all, human beings with human ears, a sense of human predicament and destiny, and human hearts; they, therefore, find the spirituals as irresistible as their equally human black brothers. The fact that white singers often find it difficult to get all of the music out of the songs is beside the point. When one adopts a song, he does so in his own way, and one of the factors of his own way is his own singing equipment. Although he fails to compete with the best spiritual singers, his heart and his mind are served, and that is his reason for singing a particular song.

For many years the Afro-American spiritual has been acknowledged as a regular and important branch of folklore. The recurrence of "discovery reports" on these songs in the *Journal of American Folklore* is prime evidence. Added to these reports are many references in *Abstracts of Folklore Studies*.

William Augustus Logan of Birmingham, Alabama, is an interesting white member of the spiritual folk community. Born in Murfreesboro, Arkansas, he learned to love the music during his childhood. He set it down from members of Negro churches in Arkansas. By 1939 he had become a regular collector of spirituals. He wrote an article for the *Musician* on "Song Gleaning among the Cabins." He told of the "delights of discovery which are the reward of persistence." In 1955, with Allen M. Garrett, he published *Road to Heaven*, a collection of twenty-eight spirituals. He had acquired them from the following states: Alabama, one; Arkansas, ten; Georgia, three; Kentucky, one; Mississippi, three; North Carolina, five; South Carolina, one; Virginia, four. By publishing so excellent a collection, he lays the foundation for other people to become members of the spiritual folk community.

The white and black contrasts in the spiritual folk community since 1870 are most revelatory. Much of the "plantation tradition" literature, though often misguided and maudlin, attempted to show a warm understanding between the master and the slave class. An example is Mrs. James H. Dooley's *Dem Good Old Times*, brought out by a New York publisher in 1906. On the one hand Grandaddy, an old black slave, points up differences, "But white folks ligion nuver did gree wid cullured folks, un dey did'n have much use fur it less'n dey wuz mighty sick un bout to die."

On the other hand there is the anticipated union of the black Mammy and her good white folks in the nether land. Grandaddy continues, "Den dey always want Miss, un she hope [helped] many a poor soul cross dem stormy waters over to de shinin sho." But Mammy herself, suspended between earth and heaven, was even more dramatic. To herself she sang,

> Swing low, Sweet Chariot, come fur to carry me home;
> Swing low, Sweet Chariot, come fur to carry me home.

At that she looked up and said, "Yes, Mistress, I's comin', I's comin'," "un wid a smile on her face, she went to de promis lan."

Long before she died, Mammy had been a font of wisdom and blessed advice to the white folks. A sample of her poetry is very close to the spirituals which stressed the hard fairness of the just universe,

> Ef you ceive, you bleege to grieve;
> Ef you lie, you sho to die.

These contrasts are continued on a more scientific basis, although without the reference to spirituals, in the cultural discussions of Henry Glassie in a book called *Pattern in the Material: Folk Culture of the Eastern United States* (1968). Using evidence from Ralph Ellison and C. Keil and his own observations, Glassie shows likenesses and differences of Southern whites and Negroes in much the same way as is shown by their respective reactions to spirituals. Pursuing the fancy that they know the blacks better than anyone else, Southern whites have developed (since Emancipation) a great and warm appreciation for spirituals. They go into black communities and ask that the songs be sung for them. When a singing aggregation that specializes in spirituals comes their way, they flock to hear it. But as they listen, they reconstruct in their minds their own sweet version of the plantation. This version, in most respects, is far from what the slave creators intended. It is just as far from the proved facts of the matter.

The black community is also often mistaken about the import of the songs. They have swallowed the white propaganda that the slaves accepted the white religion whole, and in the songs gave up on this earth and staked all their hopes on a world beyond death. Not having much African background, they take the slave's religion to be the superficial, wishy-washy thing the white man's was, and often is. Thus, they turn against the spirituals as having the wrong slant for the progressive black in America yesterday, today, and tomorrow. They do not seem to realize that the moral fiber, the sheer guts, the courage, the nobly rebellious spirit, the resiliency, the drive, the total religion, the sense of unity, the faith and undiscouragibility under pressure, the ironic tone, and the artistic genius of the slave creator of these songs would stand the present black man in mighty good stead if he could only recover them.

As an incisive Negro psychologist discussing spirituals, Albert Sidney Beckham, has already been mentioned. His frankness in showing the good points and weak points of the songs, psychologically, has been an asset. Occasionally, his evaluations are dubious. He says, for instance, that it is unfortunate that some spirituals are songs of fear. To sing such songs leads to a feeling of inferiority among Negro children. Fear songs, he declares, were constantly sung during the labors of the day. Of course, there are songs of doubt and struggle; and songs which recognize overwhelming odds against the slave. But songs of pure, unalloyed fear, or songs of fear unaccompanied by a spirit of resistance, do not occur among the six thousand or so this writer has seen. Dr. Beckham cites none.

Quite varied is the reaction of black and white preachers within the post-Emancipation spiritual community. The contempt for the spirituals expressed and indicated by Bishop Henry McNeal Turner, of the A.M.E. Church, has already been demonstrated. Turner was commissioned a bishop in 1868, just three years after the conclusion of the Civil War. The first edition of his *Hymn Book,* from which he rigorously excluded all spirituals, was just five years later. Considering the political tone of his times, one might excuse Bishop Turner for not wanting to do anything that would seem to be turning back the clock. One could have wished, however, that a man of his intelligence and influence had penetrated more deeply into the true significance of the songs.

Though lacking in formal education, John Jasper was stoutly in the spiritual tradition. A preacher of unexampled eloquence and power, he used songs naturally, both regular spirituals and songs which he created in the spiritual mode. One of his biographers, a white man, says that his songs were mellow and tender, and reminiscent of the laboring and suffering Negro. Wherever he went, the Anglo-Saxon (who invited him in) waived racial prejudice and drank truth as it poured in crystal streams from his lips.

He was a great funeral preacher and a great depicter of heaven. Two spirituals he used were "Ev'Budy Got ter Rise ter Meet King Jesus in de Mornin' " and "My Soul Will Mount Higher in a Chariot of Fire." One song he created from the Book of Revelation was called "I Beheld and Lo." The Reverend John Jasper prolonged the philosophical and lyric traditions of the spiritual up to the twentieth century.

Many white ministers have employed spirituals in oral and published sermons. Sometimes the deep and broad connotations of a single spiritual will serve for a series of sermons. An example is found in sermons for Lent and Easter by the Reverend Erich H. Heintzen (then of Champaign, Illinois) in a book called *Were You There?* (1958). The development of the "Were You There?" theme proceeds as follows,

> When He Gave the Holy Supper?
> When He Was Betrayed?
> When He Was Denied?
> When He Was Accused?
> When He Was Condemned?
> When He Was Crowned with Thorns?
> When He Was Crucified?
> When He Was Laid in the Tomb?
> When He Rose from the Grave?

Although it should have been unnecessary, Negro musicians have sought to encourage the appreciation of spirituals among the black community. In the *Southern Workman* for 1918, Nathaniel Dett asks why Negro musicians have not done much for their own music. He urges the black musician to train himself in his own traditions, to turn out appropriate music, and to circulate this music through the ranks. He also requests the government to aid Negro musicians who will keep up their folk traditions.

The National Association of Negro Musicians has already been introduced. In its seventh annual convention, held in Indianapolis in July 1925, it stressed two points: dedication to the highest and best in music and appreciation and support of Negro music and musicians. It complimented itself that, during the seven years of its existence, it had already increased respect for Negro music. At the convention meeting, in several programs, spirituals were sung by trained groups, in community groups, and in the presentation of new talent. In 1947, the association's president, Clarence H. Wilson, announced to the press that he would ask the heads of the broadcasting chains to bar spirituals from the networks unless they were played in a reverent manner.

It is quite impossible to show the breadth and depth of the spiritual folk community during the past hundred years, or even for the present day. One would have to include by the millions homes, schools, churches, sit-ins, parades, marches, union meetings, and hundreds of other places. When Booker T. Washington was buried, and again when he was memorialized by Tuskegee students, these very spirituals were devotionally sung. On the occasion of the funeral services for Dr. Martin Luther King, Jr., both at the church and at the college, spirituals constituted major parts of the programs. The fact of spiritual singing and the choice of spirituals were both a measure of the specific section of the folk community to which Drs. Washington and King belonged.

The collections of spirituals are often a fair indication of the demand and of the nature of the folk community. Helen Diamond Benedict brought out in 1924 *Belair Plantation Melodies*, songs from the Belair sugar plantation in Louisiana. She said in her foreword that these songs had been sung for many generations, at baptizings, weddings, funerals, and revivals, the women keeping up an accompaniment with their feet. Robert Gordon adds shrimp and oyster houses to the places where the songs are sung. Harvey B. Gaul notes that spirituals (in 1918) were generally sung by most Negro workers since they preferred religious songs while working. Some of the singers included longshoremen in Baltimore, Savannah, and New Orleans; workers on the Philadelphia wharves, Harrisburg back streets, and in the Westinghouse plant in Pittsburgh. Alice Graham writes of the rare privilege of hearing seventy-five cotton field workers sing plantation melodies (at one time they were called "plantations") as part of the one hundredth anniversary of Columbus, Mississippi. Lafcadio Hearn reflects the influence of spirituals upon levee workers in *Children of the Levee*.

Titles of other collections reveal the groups of the folk community who are the targets: James F. Leisy, *Songs for Pickin' and Singin'* (1962); W. H. Sherwood, *Soothing Songs* (1891); the Weavers, *The Caroler's Songbook* (1952); Frank Lynn, *Songs for Swinging Housemothers* (1961); and Robert Silverman, *Swingin' Spirituals* (1962). Far back in 1889, a San Francisco music publisher had presented Frederick G. Carnes, *Kentucky Jubilee Singers' Scottische*, including three spirituals among other music.

Home and fireside collections were brought out by Florence H. Botsford and Margaret Bradford Boni in 1937 and 1947, respectively. Children's collections and bibliographies include Helen Grant Cushing's *Children's Song Index* (1936) (listing twenty-two spirituals); Charlemae Rollins's *We Build Together* (1948); and Beatrice Landeck's *Songs To Grow On* (1950).

Girls get special consideration. Pitts, Glenn, Watters, and Wersen, *The Girls Book* came out in 1959, with three spirituals in it. Janet E. Tobitt, Music Consultant to the Girl Scouts of the U.S.A., published *A Book of Negro Songs* (n.d.).

Women are also singled out. Through the Womans Press Sue Bailey Thurman wrote instructions for "Worship Moods in Negro Spirituals." The Womans Press also brought out *Songs, Rounds, and Carols*, with seven spirituals. And Marion Cuthbert published *We Sing America*, with four spirituals in it.

Hootenanny means a gathering of folk singers (and sometimes also dancers) for a public sing in which the audience is often invited to join. The *Hootenanny Song Book*, compiled and edited by Irwin Silber, carried eighteen spirituals in its 1963 edition. Stressing "the traditional spirit of the hoot," James F. Leisy projects six spirituals in his *Hootenanny Tonight!* (1964). In Ruth A. Barnes, *I Hear America Singing* (1937), are two spirituals; but in *Hear America Singing* (1967) by the Afro-American novelist,

William Attaway, is a section entitled "Of African Descent" that presents eight spirituals. *Songs of Many Nations* was published in 1941; its eleventh edition appeared in 1958. It is a songbook created for the use of the United Church of Christ. Its eleventh edition had eleven spirituals.

An unusual school incorporated by the Regents of the University of the State of New York, called "The Music School Settlement for Colored People," addressed itself to Negro folk song in 1913. Over two thousand children received instruction in the singing of these songs. Concerts at Carnegie Hall by the Clef Club, composed of leading Negro musicians, helped to raise funds for this unique school. The Randolph Field (Texas) Tuesday Musical Club, an Air Force organization, devoted a meeting to the singing and discussion of spirituals in 1936.

Beloved and favorite spirituals have exhausted a great deal of printer's ink. A few samples are as follows: *Jack Snyder's Collection of Favorite American Negro Spirituals* (1926); William Stickles, *Fifteen Favorite Spirituals* (1952); Virginia C. Thomas, *Old Time Spirituals* (five favorite spirituals) (1953); Smith and Peterson, *Favorite Spirituals* (1961); Ernest J. Ford, *Book of Favorite Hymns* (contains nine spirituals) (1962); Alfred B. Smith, *Favorite Spirituals* (1963); and Willie Webb, *Most Beloved Spirituals* (1963).

The reasons why people sing at all are probably more numerous than the number of songs, especially since there are far more singers than songs and more than one reason per singer. An inkling of the reasons why people sing spirituals can be gained from the auspices of their preparation and presentation.

In 1924, W. D. Weatherford noted that there was a time just after the Civil War when Negroes would not sing spirituals (he probably should have said some Negroes). He adds, however, that such a time is now gone. He gives partial credit for the change to the Southern white man who begged the Negroes to sing their songs for him. Three years after Weatherford wrote, Alberta Williams insisted that the Negro must sing, and sing spontaneously, if his wonderful songs were to survive. The whites, she said, try to sing them, but their efforts lack the beauty of the black singer, especially one from the rural areas.

In the *New York World* for December 28, 1871, is described a tense occasion when spirituals were sung. Frank Mays, a Negro of Grenada, Mississippi, had murdered his wife. Although taking little pain to deny his crime, he expected to escape punishment, and later to get a light punishment, because of his political connections in reconstruction Mississippi. It turned out that he had overestimated his political strength; the date of his execution by hanging arrived. As he continued to look grimly and vainly for rescue, his friends and acquaintances at the hanging station began to sing spirituals. The reporter on the scene wrote, "As all joined in the simple melody the effect was grand."

World Wars I and II gave great boosts to spiritual singing. During the former, as reported in the *Musical Courier,* the Selma (Alabama) Jubilee Corps presented concerts of spirituals as Red Cross benefits. Soldiers and others heard "Swing Low," "Standing in the Need of Prayer," "Daniel in the Lion's Den," and "Old Time Religion," along with "The Star Spangled Banner." Also, in World War I, Natalie Burlin cites the singing of spirituals in the camps and the encouragement of this singing by Emmett J. Scott of the War Department, and by other executives. "Negro Spirituals in France" was the subject of an essay in the *Southwestern Christian Advocate* by a Y.M.C.A. worker, associated with soldiers "over there." In World War II, black GI's were reported enlivening army camps by singing spirituals, both straight and in swing tempo. Minna Lederman of the *New York Times* declared (after describing their singing of other songs): "It is with spirituals, however, that Negro troops really go to town."

By some evaluators of the spirituals, their being reduced to the concert stage has been deplored. The theory is that the original flavor of the songs is thereby washed away. For audiences this theory is highly untenable. Thousands of listeners have gone out of concert halls after hearing a program of spirituals greatly uplifted and humming the songs to themselves. Some have gone from these halls to bookstores and music shops to purchase volumes of spirituals for home use. In any case, the concert audience, composed of uncounted tens of thousands of listeners, has been one of the great contributors to the spiritual folk community.

As a sample of concert successes in this field are four reports in the *Southern Workman* during the 1920s. In the first of these, Negro folk music is said to have received a flattering reception in Carnegie Hall at Christmas time under the baton of Dr. Frank Damrosch. Two Christmas spirituals, arranged by Natalie Burlin, were featured. A glowing record of the occasion was spread on the pages of the *New York Tribune* by Henry Edward Krehbiel, the famous music critic.

In the second, similar concerts were reported a few months later at the Brooklyn Academy of Music by the Choral Art Club of Brooklyn and by a combination of choral societies of Columbia University. The third told of a Music Festival in the Fifth Regiment Armory of Baltimore, in an auditorium with a seating capacity of more than twenty thousand. According to the Baltimore daily papers, the climax of the festival was the presentation of two spiritual arrangements of Harry T. Burleigh, "Deep River" and "Dig My Grave." The fourth commemorated a Town Hall recital in New York City of J. Rosamund Johnson and Taylor Gordon. One *Times* reporter said that this "renaissance of the spiritual is only one phase of the new sense of social consciousness on the part of the Negro. . . . At all events, here is music stamped with distinctive genius and glowing with fire struck from the inner granite of the soul."

The folk community has been enlarged in both America and other parts of the world through the employment of spirituals in the regular educational institutions. Back in 1901 Bessie Cleaveland informed her readers that the spiritual was no longer for the favored few; it was now being taught in public schools. She was happy over the fact that these songs learned by children at school reached out to influence their parents. Book publishers in the field were cooperating. She gave instructions for the training of students in this music.

> These songs are fondly cherished as a rich inheritance by our students, who can do much to extend the knowledge of and love for them in the hearts of Negro children throughout the South by having them sung daily in their schools wherever they may teach. . . . The singing of plantation songs is a regular and much loved feature of the Sunday evening chapel service; a few of these melodies are also sung by the choir each Sunday afternoon at the close of service.

Beatrice Landeck, in *People's Songs* for February–March 1947, has also discussed the subject in "Use of Folk Music in Schools."

Nathaniel Dett gave high praise to this kind of public school effort in his article "As the Negro School Sings." Deploring the commercialization of spirituals, he declared that the school was the right place to preserve them properly. Pupils should be taught the significance of the spirituals; they should be given the opportunity, in singing them, to produce the effect of beauty and naturalness. He found the school superior to the church for this purpose because of a more intelligent direction of affairs. In conclusion he declared that unless the Negro school could intelligently handle this native art, there was little hope for the future of Negro music.

Ruth Tooze and Beatrice Krone included the spiritual in their book on *Literature and Music as Resources for Social Studies*. And Kenneth Westerman refers to spirituals (under the heading of "Negro Folk Songs") when in *Emergent Voice* he gives instructions on how the voice is developed as a practical and artistic instrument.

In 1924 Mabel Travis Wood described the Community Service Recreation Programs for Negroes in forty-seven cities. She told how George L. Johnson had been devoting the past two years to helping black community groups develop choirs. Through choirs and choruses, she said, the spirituals and plantation songs had been kept before the people at their finest.

Under such auspices a concert in a public park of Fort Wayne, Indiana, had drawn three thousand citizens, both black and white. The Community Chorus program of Parsons, Kansas, was hailed as the most worthwhile ever given by a local group. Other such highly distinguished concerts were given in New Haven, Connecticut; Augusta, Georgia; Hickory, North Carolina; Richmond, Indiana; Rockford, Illinois; and Dayton, Ohio.

Throughout the nation these community choruses among the black communities had proceeded through one or both of two types of singing: the singing of spirituals according to tradition and without printed music, and the performance of various arrangements of spirituals and of original works for choruses. Choruses, particularly the younger members, were educated in both the religious spirit and the musical feeling of the spirituals.

That spirituals qualify as songs for the peace movement is attested by Agnes Friesen in "Singing on the Peace Walk" (see *Sing Out!* for Summer 1962).

⟨ *The Spiritual and the Catholics*

Since the spirituals are decidedly Protestant in their surface theology and since Catholic music, especially before Vatican II, has been decidedly restricted, it is interesting to examine the Catholic attitude toward the spirituals. For most of the century during which the spiritual has been known to the general public, Catholic magazines, like the *Catholic World,* and Catholic writers have been among its most enthusiastic appreciators. Father Edward F. Murphy (in 1930) and Sister Mary Hilarion (in 1936) wrote articles on the spiritual that were keenly perceptive. In 1962 the Reverend Frederick McManus, professor of Canon Law at Catholic University, called it likely that spirituals would be adapted for evening services in Catholic churches.

We have already seen the analyses and conclusions of Father L. M. Friedel in his Catholic-oriented work, *The Bible and the Negro Spirituals.* In his point of view as well as in his details, Father Friedel reflects a clear theological position as well as a genuine understanding of literature and music. Despite the shortcomings of his book, the canon of spiritual criticism would be much poorer without it. His book is, without doubt, the fullest statement of the songs set against the background of the Catholic faith.

In Europe the attitude of the Catholics toward the spiritual has been even more striking. For more than twenty years Louis Achille has trained choirs composed of young French students in and around Lyons to sing spirituals in English. Achille was born in Martinique, educated in Paris, and spent a number of years teaching in the United States. Not only has he developed spiritual choirs; he has translated spirituals into French and written about them most appreciatively in French and in English. One of his articles has been published in a German magazine. He reports that the spiritual has revolutionized Catholic music in France: since Vatican II much of the new French church music has been influenced by it, directly or indirectly.

Father A. Z. Serrand, a Dominican priest, for ten years stationed in Les Riceys, France, has published two books of spirituals and is working on another. He selects his songs with a special eye toward his own community and his functions as a priest with them. He read many books about spirituals at American Cultural Centers and all the time found that these books were in great demand. He says that he worked on the spirituals to supply a real need in French singing. He believes that the rhythm of the spiritual is best expressed by body movement. The first spiritual he heard was "Good News"; as sounds and words, it was most impressive to him. Since he believes spirituals are freedom songs, he encourages his people to believe the same. Everyone wants to be free, he says, but not everyone can give vent to his desire for freedom. The Negro spiritual motivates this expression.

Although stationed in Paris, Father Guy de Fatto travels over the world. His job is to stimulate young people to work in the Church. He goes where he is needed and he uses spirituals as his strongest weapon. For ten years a jazz musician, he is still a great believer in the power of rhythm. He adapts spirituals for singing; he makes records of them; he teaches them to groups; he expounds upon their meanings. He says that his work is now so heavy that he will ask French musicians to help him adapt these songs. In his gospel nights, he uses individual singers, choirs, and instruments. Although at first he had trouble with his lively methods, now, he says, bishops encourage him.

Thus, the Roman Catholic, in America and abroad, is enlightened to the spiritual and uses it for a great variety of purposes. He finds it inspiring for church work and just for singing. He finds it easily adaptable to Catholic ways.

❨ The Spiritual and Jewish Philosophy

A number of our writers have traced from the spirituals parallels between the Biblical Jews and the American slaves. Some, Jews and non-Jews, have gone beneath the surface to show that there was more than a casual use of Jewish personalities and events. At least one has spoken of the influence of the moral fiber and majesty of the Hebrew prophets. Only one has made a comparison in depth between the Afro-American spiritual and the Jewish way of life.

That one is Paul F. Laubenstein, writing in the *Journal of Biblical Literature* for 1932 on "An Apocalyptic Reincarnation." Laubenstein opens his memorable article by quoting Edward Steiner to the effect that the influence of the spirituals made *The Green Pastures* more distinctive than the passion play which he saw in Oberammergau in 1930.

He then turns to a basic issue. The spirituals, he says, strike a note of confidence in an age with "futilitarian" leanings. They prove life not unfriendly to the realization of the highest human values. Showing trust in a not-too-far-off vindication of righteousness, they stress an outlook basic in Jewish and Christian circles from 200 B.C. to 150 A.D.

Laubenstein believes the parallel between this Jewish-Christian apocalyptic (e.g. Daniel, the Revelations, and other areas of the Bible) and the

Aframerican psalmody to be one of the most striking in religious and literary history. The black originators, he says, derived their material from the Scriptures but made it their very own "with a wholehearted appreciation that entitles their work to rank as an authentic manifestation of the type—a reincarnation in ebony."

Laubenstein notes, quite rightly, that the spiritual writers were not attracted to all parts of the Bible. They used very little of its legislation, wisdom literature, advanced ethics, and theology. But they adapted a great deal of the history, narrative, and apocalyptic. Laubenstein sets down three good reasons for the choice:

(1) The African perceptual consciousness, as illustrated in the native tendency to "think" in pictures, sounds, motion, and emotion rather than in the abstract. He offers the following examples:

Visual: "I looked over Jordan, What did I see?"
Auditory: "My Lord . . . calls me by the thunder;
The trumpet sounds within-a my soul"
Kinesthetic: "Gonna walk all over God's heaven"
Affective: "Sometimes I feel like a motherless child"

(2) The slave's attraction to the apocalyptic. This is in line with his immediate needs and social situation. These are similar to those of Israel in Egypt and Babylonia.

(3) The Jewish-Christian apocalyptic which is close to African ideas and practices. In proof, Laubenstein offers similarities between Semitic and Bantu dialects. He also demonstrates that the Aframerican usage was no mere borrowing; the spiritual singer omitted, added, freely adapted.

Eventually, Laubenstein goes to work to specify the similarities between the Jewish-Christian apocalyptic and the Aframerican approach found in the spirituals:

(1) Literature of affliction
(2) Feeling of being God's man
Seen especially in the comparison between the Hebrew Jehovah and the Bantu one creator God, Mawu, the heavenly coverer. If one is God's property, he is assured of care. Note the concept of the Jewish "chosen people."
(3) Idea of divine favoritism
This led to an optimism about the future and an apocalyptic faith and compensatory utility. These characteristics appear in both the Jewish and the Aframerican worlds.
(4) Great Day fully expected and prepared for
(5) Final judgment scene
Neither resurrection of the body nor a place for the departed was foreign to Africa. Like the Jewish people, the spiritual singer appreciated both the terror and the sublimity of the occasion. Both were also impressed with the Divine Bookkeeper.

(6) The part of terror inspired by natural cataclysms
(7) The resultant awful delight
(8) The appearance of the Messiah
(9) Anonymity and composite authorship
     Characteristic of both Jewish and Negro creators, also characteristic are
     the uncomplimentary and veiled allusions to ruling personages. But there
     are no pseudonyms in the Negro as there are in the Jewish.
(10) Cryptic use of words
     Use of words and expressions with double esoteric meaning is a known
     African trait. In both Jewish and Christian there are also mystic num-
     bers.

In showing differences between the Jewish and the Aframerican, Laubenstein mentions form; the tendency of the Jewish to engage in loud and
frequent maledictions as opposed to the lack of bitterness in the spiritual;
the tendency of the Jewish to be more worldwide at the outset as opposed
to the more personal, "more I," practices of the Negro. The spiritual, he
says, "is 'heart's blood made lyric.' "

Laubenstein notes that both predict. He indicates also that in the Negro
song is a pious hilarity (a sense of humor) that rarely appears in the Jewish.
After completing his comparison, Laubenstein concludes, "The Negro
slave actually gave to the world a new and distinctive body of apocalyptic
literature."

In their *Man and His Music: The Story of Musical Experience in the
West* Harman, Milner, and Mellers write of Aaron Copland's use of Negro
themes. Mellers particularly declares that Copland is reflecting the fact that
both Negro and Jew are dispossessed peoples who become for Copland
symbolic of urban man's uprootedness.

As a climax for these Jewish-Negro musical parallels we can review a
notable fact. When George L. White named his Colored Christian Singers
the Jubilee Singers, he did so in memory of the Jewish year of jubilee.

❰ The Afro-American Spiritual in Foreign Lands

There is no continent on earth (and few countries) where the Afro-
American spiritual has not been sung. Traveling choirs, individual concert
artists, members of the Armed Forces, diplomats, convention delegates, and
visitors who are rank amateurs have carried it around the globe many times
over. In hundreds of books prepared for the foreign trade the songs have
been made ready for natives of every description to sing them in their own
way. At the behest of many countries experts in the spiritual have traveled
around to teach the people on five continents how to sing them. Some natives have been taught by Afro-American wives (or husbands) who have
married into foreign families. No matter how far from the original the

singing gets, the spiritual has brought millions of people over the world their own special brand of freedom feeling, joy, compassion, religious faith, human identification, and sweet sorrow.

Since the Fisk Jubilee Singers aroused the world to the magic of these songs in the 1870s, they have been wafted in the air like a very beneficent fallout. Besides being sung, they have been incessantly talked about and written about. When the talk dies down, always a new concert singer, or blues and gospel singer, appears to dress the spiritual in new clothes for the avid foreigner. The tendency of foreigners is to want the songs for their very own.

Thus, the world has seen a profusion of translations. As a sample here is a snatch from "Go Down, Moses" in six languages, besides English:

French:
From Louis T. Achille, "Negro Spirituals," in *Esprit 19* (May 1951): 710.

> Descends, Moïse,
> Jusqu'au fond de la terre d'Egypte
> Et dis au grand Pharaon
> Qu'il libere mon peuple

German:
From Joachim Ernest Berendt and Paridam von dem Knesebeck, *Spirituals* (Munich: Nymphenburger Verlagshandlung, 1955), p. 25.

> Geh hin, Moses,
> Hinab ins Agypterland,
> Sag alt Pharao
> Er soll mein Volk ziehen lassen.

Czechoslovakian:
From Zbyněk Kožnar; *Černošské Spiritualy* (Prague: Státní Hudební Vydavatelství, 1961), p. 8.

> At jde Moj-zis,
>   do zeme egyptské
> a dí Farao,
>   hned narod propust' muj!

Hungarian:
From Miklos Forrai, *Zúgj Hullám* (Deep river) (Budapest: Zenemükiadó Vállalat, 1965), p. 8.

> Jojj el Mózes
> Rad vár a siró nep,
> oldd meg láncat
> Lesze szabad meg!

Polish:
From Witold Rudziński, *Negro Spirituals* (Krakow: Polskie Wydawn, Muzyezne, 1961), p. 9.

> Ruszyl Moj-zesz,
> Szli znim zEgiptu pól
> Powiedz wladcy
> Chce iść naród moj.

Spanish:
From J. M. Fonollosa and Alfredo Papo, *Breve Antologia de Los Cantos Spirituals Negros* (Barcelona: Cobalto, 1951), p. 17.

> Baja, Moisés
> a la tierra de Egipto.
> Di al viejo Faraón
> que liberte a mi pueble.

Original English: Go down, Moses,
Way down in Egypt's land.
Tell old Pharaoh
To let my people go!

Already in this book we have shown the incursion of the spiritual into many countries. To tell a reasonably complete story would require a separate book of some size, which some day we hope to write. Our present purpose is to show some of the more remarkable aspects of this conquest, to trace very lightly the scope and depth, the powerful and curious impact of this phenomenal song in countries outside the land of its birth. In a few cases we rely upon evidence garnered through personal interview.

We have listed the countries in alphabetical order. Germany is the only country where the story is told in some depth, partly because the German has outdistanced other countries in his demonstration of appreciation. But nowhere has there been time to tell a full story.

AFRICA

Since in a very real sense the songs derive in large part from Africa, it is notable that their return to a kind of homeland has been full of appreciation. Alikija, Ballanta Taylor, Senghor, and other Africans have noted on many occasions the fact that identical melodies and sometimes identical sentiments of the Afro-American spiritual have existed, and still exist, among the African folk. Afro-American singers of spirituals, as individual artists and as groups, have been and still are well received in Africa. Spiritual records sell well in some of the cities.

The most notable volume of collected spirituals in Africa is Alexander Sandilands, *A Hundred and Twenty Negro Spirituals* (Morija, Basutoland, South Africa, 1951). Sandilands says these songs were selected with a view to their being used by Africans in Africa, especially African teachers, pupils, ministers, and congregations. These songs, he says, strike a chord in true African hearts.

Although he did not collect spirituals for his home country, Ballanta Taylor of Sierra Leone contributed much to the understanding of spirituals in America. In his home country he lectured on the spirituals. Fela Sowande of Lagos, Nigeria, has arranged many spirituals and published them in the United States. Chappell and Company of New York brought out his *Six Negro Spirituals* and both Chappell and G. Ricordi published his individual arrangements, about a dozen of them, in the late 1950s.

Many singers have sung spirituals in African concert halls. Todd Duncan, one of these, wrote "South African Songs and Negro Spirituals" for the *Music Journal* (May–June 1950). A recent such singer is Mrs. Cathy Mbathi, formerly of Nairobi, Kenya, now of Mombasa. Born in Detroit, she attended Piney Woods and graduated from Barrington College. She married a young man from Kenya and went to Africa with him. Besides doing concerts, she has done a record entitled, "Introducing Cathy Mbathi Singing Your Favorite Negro Spirituals."

We may recall from Part One that spirituals were sung in the festival competition in Nairobi. Spirituals were sung enthusiastically when Jester Hairston came to Africa to teach them. He organized choirs and produced concerts in Mali, Ivory Coast, Ghana, Nigeria, the Cameroons, and Senegal.

Interpretations of spirituals have been done by Léopold Sédar Senghor, president of Senegal, in an essay, "La Poésie Négro-Américaine," in his *Liberté I: Négritude et Humanisme* (1964); by Anne Kenny in *The Negro Spiritual and Other Essays* (1943), published in Cairo; by Rupert Van Gogh in "The Evolution of Jazz" for the *West African Review* (March 1935); and by W. E. Ward in "Music in the Gold Coast" for the *Gold Coast Review* (July–December 1927). Though not claiming to be an authority on the spiritual, Hugh M. Tracey of Roodepoort, South Africa, has interesting thoughts about these songs as his appearance on the jury described earlier in Part Three shows.

AUSTRALIA

We have already noted that one of the early editions of the story of the Jubilee Singers was published in Melbourne in 1886, with the copyright covering New Zealand and Tasmania. Many American concert singers—Marian Anderson, Todd Duncan, Lawrence Winters, and others—have sung spirituals in concerts in the Australian cities.

AUSTRIA

Austria was a European country inviting Fisk Jubilee Singers for years before 1930. In the fall season 1923 Roland Hayes had sung to enthusiastic audiences in Vienna and Graz. Austria was also one of the countries where Jester Hairston organized spiritual choirs. In Vienna, in 1926, Louis Gruenberg published his *Negro Spirituals*, containing twenty spirituals with music and German and English texts, and an introduction.

BELGIUM

In Louvain in 1940 Pierre de Bézoard published *Les Négro Spirituals*—nine songs with exciting notes. In 1938, Verna Arvey and William Grant Still wrote for *La Revue Internationale de Musique* of Brussels an article on "Negro Music in the Americas." In 1969 *Dimanche* in Brussels published a story about the American-born spiritual singer of France, John Littleton. It was entitled "Que pensez-vous des 'messes de jeunes'?"

The outstanding writer on the subject of spirituals in Belgium is Hector Waterschoot. He has written keenly on the spiritual and has presented spirituals for his readers to read and to sing. Not a college graduate, Waterschoot is a railroad official. His considerable knowledge of his two fields of publication, modern art and American Negro song, he has gained through sheer personal application. He has spent his whole life in St. Niklaas, about ten miles from the border of the Netherlands. As a stout member of the Flemish community, he publishes in the Dutch language.

His first acquaintance with spirituals (jazz and blues also) came through broadcasts he heard from Brussels when he was about sixteen. He has published two books on spirituals and is at work upon his third. His first book, *De Poezie der Negro-Spirituals* (1960) was published for the cultural organization to which he belongs. It was primarily historical and descriptive, containing an interesting chapter on spirituals as the expression of profane feelings. When the demand for his book far exceeded expectations, his publisher in Antwerp persuaded him to work on broader lines. In *Negers Zingen Spirituals en Blues* (1964) he presented forty spirituals with music and full notes. The first edition of three thousand sold out. The publisher now wants something even more extensive. In 1966 for *Kultuur Leven,* a magazine in Louvain, Belgium, Waterschoot did an article, "Negers bidden zingend" (Negroes praying and singing).

The introduction of *Negers Zingen Spirituals en Blues* is a most interesting document. Besides some interesting parallels between past and present, Waterschoot writes a sturdy historical background for the songs. He refers to the Negro musical elements in the works of Ravel, Stravinsky, and Darius Milhaud. He notes the strong African influence behind the songs, especially as seen in the power of the community. He develops the main themes of the songs, Old Testament figures and incidents, Jesus, the Promised Land, and the personal concerns of the slaves. He establishes the spirituals as the foundation for the blues and for other profane Afro-American songs.

CANADA

For Canada the situation is quite similar to that in the United States—concerts, small groups, individual singers, congregations, collections, books and articles of interpretation, television, records, and the like. But for Canada we have something special.

At the Archives of Traditional Music, Folklore Institute, Indiana University, to which I was introduced by Professor Richard Dorson, 68–246–F refers to an unusual series of tapes. They are the recordings of the music sung at a wake in honor of the late Maggie Pleasant, held in the Maritime Provinces of Nova Scotia in 1967. Among other songs unobtrusively done (in many verses each) by the holders of the wake are fourteen Afro-American spirituals. These include "Steal Away," "Gettin' Ready for That Great Day," "When the Saints Go Marchin' In," "We Shall Walk Through the Valley," "Swing Low, Sweet Chariot," and "You Gonna Reap Just What You Sow."

The *Journal of the International Folk Music Council* often dispenses information about Afro-American spirituals. It is at present published in Canada.

The *Catalogue of Canadian Composers* (1952) lists the following composers and works: Ernest H. Dainty, "Deep River," for piano, harp, tympany, and chimes; Clarence Vernon Frayn, "Weary Chilluns" (which the composer calls a spiritual), for voice; Graham George, "Ride On!" for choir; and Leonard Henry Leacock, "A Negro Melody," for violin and piano.

CZECHOSLOVAKIA

The deep interest of Antonín Dvořák, the great Bohemian composer and director-teacher in New York, in Afro-American spirituals has several times been reviewed. In 1958 Lubomír Dorůžka published in Prague *Hudba Amerických Černochů* (The music of the American Negro). A brief summary of this book follows.

Lubomír Dorůžka essays to establish Christianity as the decisive force in the cultural life of the plantation slaves. He writes with critical appreciation, however, of the hypocritical role of the slave owner and the Christian "missionaries" of the South. He is aware of the revolutionary role played by Christian allegories in slave rebellions. In summarizing the music, he ties together the white and black elements. He brings in the handclapping and the ecstasy. He is contaminated by George Pullen Jackson's theories of blacks borrowing from white liturgical music. He reviews the successes of the Fisk Jubilee Singers and of concert artists like Robeson. From Borio Asafyev, he takes material to establish parallels between Russian folk songs and Afro-American singing. From the Johnsons' *Books of American Negro Spirituals* he spells out details of actual songs.

Three years later, Zbyněk Kožnar brought out *Černošské Spiritualy* (Negro spirituals). It contained thirty-four spirituals with music and text in Czechoslovakian and English. There was also a brief introduction.

The famous Czechoslovakian Orientalist J. Stanislav has paid his respects to the Afro-American spiritual in a speech delivered in April 1961. The title of the speech was "Some Remarks on the Development of Musical Creation among African Peoples." He compares Congo funeral chants and religious songs from Dahomey with Afro-American spirituals and finds impressive parallels. His speech has been published in William K. Archer, editor, *The Preservation of Traditional Forms of the Learned and Popular Music of the Orient and the Occident* (1964).

In 1923, Roland Hayes sang spirituals in Karlovy Váry (Karlsbad) and Prague.

DENMARK

Among other connections with the subject, the Danes heard the early Fisk Jubilee Singers and have heard thousands of singers do spirituals since. They were so impressed that they invited Jester Hairston to teach them to sing spirituals for themselves.

In 1951, in *Dansk Musiktidsskrift* of Copenhagen, there appeared William Grant Still's "Negrene i Amerikansk Musik."

ENGLAND

In England the Afro-American spiritual is as much at home as it is in America. The English heard the original Fisk Jubilee Singers. They have heard and sung spirituals ever since. To Roland Hayes, Marian Anderson, and Paul Robeson, as the royalty of spiritual singers, the English have been almost idolatrous. In quantity, their production of books and articles concerning the songs is second only to that of the Americans.

Collections of spirituals or of music based on spirituals have been published in England by the following: Eric Ball, Sir Granville Bantock, Sebastian Brown, Harry T. Burleigh, Herbert A. Chambers, Edric Connor, Frederick Delius, John Foulds, Eleanor Franklin-Pike, Philip Hattey, the *News-Chronicle* (songbook), Ernest Newton, Felton Rapley, R. W. Saar, Peter Smith, Southern Music Publishing Company, Phyllis Tate, and Edna Thomas.

Books or articles about the spiritual or containing interpretive items have been written by the following for English publishers: Thomas Ashe; Ernest Borneman; Thomas Cooper; Nancy Cunard; Samuel Davies; Amelia Defries; Clare Delius; William Faux; Alec Harman, Anthony Milner, and Wilfrid Mellers; Mellinger Henry; Frances Anne Kemble; Constant Lambert; Frances Butler Leigh; W. J. Linton; Alan Lomax; Sir Charles Lyell, the Reverend William Wyndham Malet, J. B. T. Marsh and associates; A. L. Morton; Peter Noble; Alma Norman; Paul Oliver; Rosey Pool and Eric Walrond; Grace Porter and Henry W. Loomis; Henry Russell; W. C. Berwick Sayers; Marie Seton; Sir Richard R. Terry; Douglas H. Varley; Richard Wallaschek; and Diedrich Westermann.

For articles on the spiritual one may peruse the following magazines: the *Chesterian, Good Words,* the *International Review of Missions, Journal of the Folk-Song Society, Journal of the International Folk Music Council, Keynote, Music and Letters, Musical News and Herald,* the *Musical Stand-*

ard, the *Musical Times and New Music Review*. Add to these two giant music encyclopedias: *Grove's Dictionary of Music and Musicians* and the *New Oxford History of Music*.

We interviewed in their homes two extremely interesting lovers of the spiritual. Paul Oliver, who lives in Highgate, London, generally writes on the blues but is a great spiritual fancier. He first heard Negro singing at Stoke Montclair when American servicemen were just coming into England during World War II. From that first time he says he was hooked. But since the age of ten he has been collecting folk records.

In his *Blues Fell This Morning* (1960), the foreword is written by Richard Wright. Wright describes the folk community of the spiritual which later created the blues. In Oliver's *Story of the Blues* (1969), he has an introduction, "Long Hot Summer Days," in which there is a great deal about the backgrounds of the spiritual.

Peter Smith is a young Methodist minister who lives in Sheffield, England. His guitar goes with him wherever he goes; he plays it well, and sings well too. Before settling down to the ministry, he traveled in the United States, playing folk music—guitars, bass, washboards.

To the Reverend Peter Smith, the spiritual is a live, not a bookish, thing. He also believes that a revival in folk music in general would be an invigorating thing for institutional religion and for the people at large. That is why he published his folk volumes, *Faith, Folk & Clarity* and *Faith, Folk & Festivity*, both 1969. With such songs as these, Christians can communicate their faith in contemporary terms in church, radio, television, and wherever people meet.

Faith, Folk & Clarity has fifteen spirituals. Peter Smith sings all folk songs, including spirituals, as a celebration of life. His comments on the songs reflect his deep concern not only in faith and worship but in all the people's problems: freedom and prejudice, war and peace, world need, social concerns.

FINLAND

To Finland, also, at the request of the people, Jester Hairston came and trained choirs to sing spirituals.

FRANCE

With England and Germany, France ranks high in appreciation of the Afro-American spiritual. In all the usual ways it has been in the spiritual whirl for the past hundred years. As a matter of fact it heard an excess of spirituals when the black doughboys were in France during World Wars I and II. It has entertained thousands of American performers of the spiritual, including the Hall Johnson choirs.

In John Littleton it has its own American spiritual singer. Born in Tallulah, Louisiana, he was in the occupation as a soldier. In Vichy, in 1963, he was asked to sing for young people. He sang a few spirituals. Eventually, the demand was great, he sang more than sixty. From that beginning he is now an established singer, popular with all ages, a hit in records and television. He now sings in France, Germany, Spain, Belgium, and Italy. He believes that his singing helps with the problems of the young. As he sings, he talks to the people, gets them to understand the songs, has them sing along with him. The effect is electrifying.

Louis Thomas Achille, who now teaches in Lyons, was born in Martinique. His schoolmates in Paris at Louis Le Grand were President Senghor and Prime Minister Pompidou. He first heard spirituals as a very young man. Later, in Paris, he heard Roland Hayes and the Fisk Jubilee Singers. For twenty-two years he has been teaching spirituals, in English, to the young men of his school in Lyons. He makes his own arrangements. He has composed songs similar to spirituals. His Park Glee Club sings spirituals in concerts and makes records. As a devout Roman Catholic, he has introduced spirituals into all types of religious exercises.

His articles on the spiritual have appeared in American, English, French, and German journals. A few of them are as follows: "Negro Spirituals," *Esprit*, May 1951; "Les Négro-spirituals et l'expansion de la culture noire," *Présence Africaine*, November 1956; "Résonances Spirituelles," *Rythmes du Monde;* "Les Négro Spirituals, musique populaire sacrée," *Rythmes du Monde*, 1958; "Amérique du Nord," *Le Monde Noir*, 1950; "L'artiste noir et son peuple," *Présence Africaine*, October–November 1957; "Verbe Noir," *Aspects de la Culture Noire*, 1958; "La 'confidence' du professeur ACHILLE sur les Negro Spirituals" (a confession), *La République* (Toulon), December 31, 1969.

In 1963, Jean Wagner received his doctorate from the University of Paris after writing his major thesis on *Les Poètes Nègres des Etats-Unis*. Seven pages of this masterful book are devoted to the spirituals, and spirituals are mentioned in other sections. He warns against being carried away with the African element since many things called African are just human. He is now professor of English at the University of Grenoble.

In 1964 Marguerite Yourcenar published an unusual spiritual collection, *Fleuve Profond, Sombre Rivière* (Deep river, somber river). With spirituals and related poems, she presented a hundred songs. She also wrote an elaborate introduction (forty-four pages). Her book is one of the best foreign collections of spirituals.

Simon J. Copans, American-born, is director of the Institut d'Etudes Américaines in Paris. In 1947, when he was French representative of the Voice of America, he was asked by the program director of the French Broadcasting System to do weekly programs on American music—jazz, folk songs, spirituals, and the like. His program, which started with the title

"Deep River," is still going on. Hundreds of thousands of French, Swiss, Belgians, and Dutch have learned to love spirituals through this program. Many young French singers, particularly one Protestant group, began singing spirituals all over France after being inspired by the program.

In 1964 Copans published a book on American history as seen through folk songs for French readers. Chapter 4 of this book, "Let My People Go," dealt with spirituals and their meaning. His paper on "The African Heritage: The Music of the American Negro" was read at the First World Festival of Negro Arts, which convened in Dakar, Senegal, April 1966. It was published in *Présence Africaine* in 1968.

Copans also lectures on the spirituals in Paris. On the basis of his wide experience he says that the French people, Catholics, Protestants, nonbelievers, intellectuals, professional men, manufacturers, workers, old people, middle-aged people, adolescents, and children, love the spirituals.

Books about the spiritual and its backgrounds have been published in France by Roger Bastide, Stephen Chauvet, André Coeuroy and André Schaeffner, Oscar Comettant, Alfred D'Almbert, Xavier Eyma, Frederic Pohl, Julien Tiersot, and Léonie Villard. Individual spirituals and spiritual collections have been brought out by Père Guy de Fatto, César Claude Goeffray, Eugène Jolas, Jacques Poterat, Father A. Z. Serrand, and Marguerite Yourcenar. An article on the spiritual can be found in the *Encyclopédie de la Musique et Dictionnaire du Conservatoire*.

Magazines which have published articles on the spiritual are *Journal de la Société des Américanistes, Les Langues Modernes, Le Ménestrel, Présence Africaine, Recherches et Débats des Centre, Catholique des Intellectuels,* and *La Vie Spirituelle*.

GERMANY

No country, not even the United States of America, has in recent years maintained a livelier interest in the Afro-American spiritual than Germany. The statement is almost as true for East Germany as for West Germany. The popularity of Robeson, the exacting publication of analyses and appreciations of the spiritual in East Germany stamp it as a highly appreciative country. But not quite so appreciative as West Germany.

Various troupes of the Fisk Jubilee Singers performed in Germany from the mid-1870s on. Besides the Hall Johnson Choir and Jester Hairston, the Stars of Faith of Black Nativity, the annual Spiritual Festivals in Frankfurt, there are literally hundreds of other manifestations. Even the German publishers, Hans Gerig-Polyphon, Nymphenburger, Burckhardthaus, Fischer Bücherei, Furche Verlag H. Rennebach KG, and others, are profoundly interested in spiritual publication. Polyphon publishes spirituals as textbooks for use in schools. Francis C. Charles, a native of Trinidad, who operates a record store in downtown Berlin, assured me that spiritual records sell steadily and often rise to best sellers. In Berlin, also, I was told by a resident that the Stars of Faith of Black Nativity, an American group of spiritual singers, filled a large auditorium in the city three times in a single year.

German congregations try hard to sing these songs. Most of the published collections of spirituals carry the music to encourage singing; most of them also carry the German text.

Four doctoral theses dealing with the spiritual have appeared in print within the past twenty years; three of these deal exclusively with spirituals. These theses are Hermine Barz (Mainz, 1951), *The Development of the Poetry of the Negro in North America;* Christa Dixon (Bonn, 1965), *Wesen und Wandel geistlicher Volkslieder Negro Spirituals;* Theo Lehmann (Halle, 1962), *Negro Spirituals: Geschichte und Theologie;* and Margaret Ley (Munich, 1954), *Spirituals: Ein Beitrag zur Analyse der religiösen Liedschöpfung bei den nord-amerikanischen Negern.*

Books by and about the spirituals and their backgrounds, involving mountains of research, have come from the following hands: Ernst Bartsch, Joachim Ernst Berendt, Klaus Buhé, Alfons M. Dauer, Perry Friedman, Wolfgang Fürster, Victor Gorochow, Janheinz Jahn, Paridam von dem Knesebeck, Theo Lehmann, Karl-Heinz Schönfelder and Ingebert Hucke, and Father Lothar Zenetti.

From the following have come many collections of spirituals, often with elaborate notes: Carlo Bohländer, Heinz Cammin, Victor Gorochow, Kurt Heinrich Hansen, Fred Harz, Frederick Hefmann, Janheinz Jahn, Otto Kaufmann, Ernst Koster, Karlheinz Krupp, Bishop Hans Lilje, Ralf Petersen, H. Sallman, Siegfried Schmidt-Joos, Johannes C. Schimmel, Karl-Heinz Schönfelder and Ingebert Hucke, and Karl Wiedenfeld (pen name Michael Cord).

Many magazines have contributed spiritual literature. Among these are *Africa Heute, Jahrbuch für musikalische Volks-u. Volkerkunde, Melos, Musica, Musik und Altar, Musik und Gesellschaft, Musik und Kirche, Theologische Zeitschrift, Wort und Warheit, Zeitschrift für Ethnologie,* and *Zeitwende: Die Neue Furche.* Add two large encyclopedias: *Die Musik in Geschichte und Gegenwart* and *Jahrbuch für Volksliedforschung.*

The following personalities and their works are hereby presented as a fair sample of the German contribution to the phenomenon of the Afro-American spiritual.

Spirituals: Religious Songs of the American Negro was published by Joachim Ernst Berendt and Paridam von dem Knesebeck in Munich in 1955. It had thirty-eight spirituals with music and with English text followed by German text. The "Epilogue" (pp. 79–85) was a critique of the songs. The critique begins with a historical statement. It contains the authors' explanations of how the slave singers developed their words and music. In the estimation of the authors the spiritual is a mixture of European and African parts. They find in it a great deal of religious underpinning. They also state that the Negro is incapable of separating the physical from the spiritual, the material from matters of soul, the worldly from the religious in matters of art. They develop the relationship between the motives that produced the spiritual and those which produced gospel songs and jazz. As of 1955, they say that the black power of expression and testimony is felt by white artists not only as an enrichment, but also as motivation.

Berendt is an outstanding German authority on the spiritual and other Afro-American folk stuff. Besides the present volume he has written about spirituals in the following: *Das Jazzbuch* (1953); *Jazzlife* (1961) with William Claxton; *Schwarzer Gesang II*; and "Jazz und Alte Musik" in *Prisma der Gegenwärtigen Musik*. (This book is based on lectures given all over Germany in the mid-1950s.) He has also published editions of individual spirituals such as his "Oh Jesus, My Jesus" in *Zeitwende: Die Neue Furche* for July 1963.

Knesebeck has also been a steady writer on the spirituals. In a letter to the present writer he says that his interest in the subject dates from his hearing black soldiers sing spirituals in Munich about three years after the war. He read *The Negro Caravan* and began a collaboration with Eva Hesse O'Donnell and with Joachim Berendt. He also developed a correspondence with Langston Hughes and published Hughes's autobiography after translating it into German. In his estimation the recording industry played the greatest role in the dissemination of spirituals throughout Germany. He says, however, that the writings of Mrs. O'Donnell, Janheinz Jahn, Bishop Lilje, Heinrich Hansen, and Knesebeck opened up the way. Perhaps Knesebeck's most significant publication on the subject was in 1961 when he brought out *Schwarzer Gesang I: Spirituals English-Deutsch*, containing fifty spirituals.

Alfons Michael Dauer has been quoted in Part One of this book. As head of the anthropological and musicological departments of the Institute for Scientific Cinematology in Göttingen, he has done a great deal of research and publishing in the foregrounds and backgrounds of the spiritual. His scholarship is impeccable and his insights are full of value. In his conclusions he relies upon chains of evidence fully tested by field research, consultation, and extremely careful thinking.

Besides the articles referred to earlier ("Kinesis und Katharsis," "Lieder der Gonja," "Musik-Landschaften in Afrika," and "Stil und Technik in afrikanischen Tanz"), Professor Dauer is author of two books most valuable to any serious researcher in the spiritual. In one of these, *Der Jazz* (1958) (which he says he worked on for ten years), he gives backgrounds for the spiritual and its relationship to other Afro-American musical impulses. In another *Jazz: Die Magische Musik* (1961), he devotes eleven pages ("Gottesverehrung und Gottesbeschwörung") to a discussion of the spiritual and its elemental character.

In February 1965, the faculty of philosophy at Friedrich-Wilhelm University, Bonn, conferred upon Christa Dixon the degree of doctor of philosophy. Her thesis for this degree was *Wesen und Wandel geistlicher Volkslieder Negro Spirituals*. (Being and change in religious folksongs ...). This thesis was published at Wuppertal in 1967. In her first chapter of Part One she gives remarks basic to the understanding of the spirituals; Chapter 2 discusses the link with Biblical expression; Chapter 3, the display of Biblical declarations; Chapter 4, the vivification of Biblical utterances; and Chapter 5, the shaping of Biblical utterances. In Part Two she gives the full texts of fifty-seven spirituals in the center column, the references from the Bible in the left column and the exact language of the references in the right column. Part Two is entirely in English.

Dr. Dixon's thesis is full and methodical. She has gone to the deepest ground roots of the points she has raised. Her book deserves translation in English if for no other reason than an examination of her methods. Her bibliography is well chosen. She also includes a "Bibelstellen register" in which she lists each relevant book of the Bible and each relevant chapter opposite the page number where the relevant spiritual may be found. Much of her research was done in the United States, and she had advice from American experts.

In my personal conversation with her, I learned that she first became acquainted with spirituals in school. She said that her class sang them in English when she was in the equivalent of American high school. Her choir director at Düsseldorf composed songs based on spirituals. She observes that even atheists are able to project their own feelings into the songs. She says she did her thesis from a folklore standpoint. For the textual criticism, she borrowed methods from German theology and German criticism in language and literature.

Rochus Hagen of Cologne published his "Abriss der Geschichte der Spiritualforschung" (Outline history of spiritual research) in *Jahrbuch für musikalische Volks-u. Volkerkunde* (1968). He traces the first mention of the spiritual to the article "Songs of the Blacks," which he says appeared in the November 15, 1856, issue of *Dwight's Journal of Music*. (Actually, this article first appeared in the *Evangelist* and was reprinted by Dwight.) He also refers to the following commentators: Thomas Jefferson, 1803; J. Miller McKim, 1862; Lucy McKim [Garrison], 1862; H. G. Spaulding, 1863; Thomas Wentworth Higginson, 1867. He devotes much space to what he calls the most important collections, beginning with *Slave Songs of the United States* (1867). He discusses Dvořák and his influence, George Pullen Jackson and his influence, Cable, Courlander, and Chase. Near the end of his dissertation, he offers comparisons between the North American spiritual and African-type songs farther south in the Western Hemisphere. He ends with a brief discussion of scientific spiritual research. His bibliography (eight pages) is also a valuable document.

Rochus Hagen wrote " 'Deutsche Spirituals' und Jazzmesse" (German spirituals and jazz mass) for *Musik und Kirche* (March–April 1966). This article is an investigation of the use of Afro-American music in Catholic church services. A controversy on this subject has been going on for some time. It was recently heightened by the release of the RCA record, "Jazz Suite on the Mass Texts," composed by Lalo Schifrin, a young Argentinian. Hagen asks if jazz belongs in the church. He notes that jazz masses are being celebrated in many parts of the world, partly because they are said to bring believer and priest closer together. He notes also that Germans have experimented with spirituals in many ways since their introduction to Germany in 1877. In the official Catholic opinion, however, Europeans cannot sing spirituals in the true Negro manner. The European lacks the basic quality of spontaneity. There are also problems in religious ecstasy and fascination. The official conclusion is that Europeans cannot feel the ecstasy and should not try to imitate it.

"Negro Spirituals in Kirchenchor" (Negro spirituals in the church choir) appeared in *Musik und Kirche*, in the September–October issue for 1967. Written by Rochus Hagen, it sets the total number of spirituals at nine hundred. The songs, Hagen says, relate experiences of personal conversion. The modern American black rarely sings spirituals, he continues. The songs are sung only in a few rural areas in the South. For most American blacks gospel songs have supplanted spirituals. The gospel song, though, is far inferior to the spiritual; it is bombastic and shallow; it reveals no clear line of thought; it deals entirely with a chain of inconsequential, subjective emotion. The spiritual, although possessing a simple and striking melody, is not sung in church services because it deals with the religious experiences of the individual rather than with God. Rather than being sung in its original rhythm it should be sung strictly metrically and in a slightly accentuated manner. Doing away with the complicated Negro rhythms would, of course, rob the spiritual of its exotic effects for Europeans.

Musik und Kirche published in November–December 1966 Rochus Hagen's review of Theo Lehmann's *Negro Spirituals: Geschichte und Theologie*. Hagen hailed this book as the first attempt at a systematic clarification of the spiritual in Germany. Hagen says that Lehmann traces the songs back to white Protestantism. He pays little regard to the music. He goes heavily into the subject of the psychology of the spiritual. He accepts the white spiritual thesis without discussing the problems associated with it. According to Hagen, Lehmann gives an excellent portrayal of the historical background of the spiritual, but fails to mention Barton's *Old Plantation Hymns*, although Barton was interested in spiritual theology.

Also in *Musik und Kirche* (for March–April 1969) appeared Hagen's review of Christa Dixon's *Wesen und Wandel geistlicher Volkslieder Negro Spirituals*. He calls Dr. Dixon's book one of the most interesting on religious folklore. In contrast to Lehmann's book, says Hagen, Dr. Dixon makes a thorough examination of the theological background and avoids high-flying theories. He praises her for presenting the Bible texts from which the spirituals are taken.

In *Musica* for March–April 1967 Rochus M. Hagen wrote on "Das Spiritual: Versuche zu seiner Enforschung" (The spiritual: an investigatory essay). He begins with a historical sketch tracing the spirituals in Germany from their first appearance—the Fisk Jubilee Singers—in 1877. He discusses evaluations by Elcho, Wallaschek, Jeannette Robinson Murphy, Emily Hallowell, Natalie Curtis Burlin, William Arms Fisher, George Pullen Jackson, and Percival Kirby. To Krehbiel in 1914 he gives credit for the real beginning of scientific spiritual research. He then evaluates the contributions of Newman White, Guy B. Johnson, Richard A. Waterman, and Miles Mark Fisher. He notes that analysis of the texts has been far greater than analysis of the music. He says that the controversy over the origin of the songs arises mainly because both sides put too great an emphasis upon originality. A reconsideration of the methodical basis of the problem, in his estimation, draws both groups closer together. He urges more scientific probing into spiritual research.

Kurt Heinrich Hansen of Hamburg joined with the late Lawrence Winters, black concert and dramatic singer of America, to disseminate Afro-American spirituals in Germany. By this time Winters, after a long and brilliant career in America and in other parts of the world, had settled down in Hamburg. He and Dr. Hansen did concerts, radio broadcasts, records, and tapes celebrating the spirituals. Winters's records and the scripts of the broadcasts are available. Thirty-three spirituals are covered. References are to *The Book of Spirituals and Gospel Songs*, edited by Bishop Hans Lilje, Hansen, and Siegfried Schmidt-Joos. Occasionally, for comparisons, Winters sang the songs in English; usually he sang the spirituals in German translations made by Hansen.

Hansen's discussions are usually linguistic. He shows how Low German is closer to the "slang" in which the spirituals were created than High German. He also discusses the historical settings, referring, for example, to Harriet Tubman as Moses. When he hears that there is a plan to introduce spirituals into the religious services of Europe, he wonders how they will be sung.

Dr. Hansen told this writer that one reason for the spread of the spirituals in Germany was the kindness of black soldiers to Germans after the War. Without patronizing, the black soldier accepted the German as a fellow underdog. He said also that the spiritual creators were great artists because they did not know they were. The songs enabled the slave to survive. They were not invented. They grew up out of people with a common fate and human compassion.

No one outside the United States has written more on, and more authoritatively about, African and Afro-American literature, including folk literature, than Janheinz Jahn, of Messel (near Frankfurt). Though most of his books are written originally in German, they are translated into other languages regularly—English, Swedish, Italian, French, Norwegian, Spanish (for South America), Dutch. Occasionally, as in *Neo-African Literature: A History of Black Writing* (1968), he writes in English. A bibliography of his works in 1968 listed forty-six items, not counting translations. He has added to the list since. He normally spends a month in Africa each year doing research. In 1962 he published *Negro Spirituals*, giving both English and German texts for seventy-nine spirituals.

In a personal interview Jahn made several pungent observations. He says the spirituals are related more to a group than to a race; that discrimination of the Afro-American has intensified the inner natural (African) tendencies; that some songs may have been produced by several original creators, each doing a different verse; and that moving slaves caused new songs to be brought into various districts.

His *Neo-African Literature* is an excellent piece of organization and good writing. After Part One, which is introductory, he turns to "The African Scene" in Part Two and "The American Scene" in Part Three. He includes the literature of the West Indies and South America. His comments on the literature of North American Negroes (which he brings down to the present day) are based on the reading of six hundred writers.

Chapter 9 of Part Two is entitled "The Negro Spiritual." He notes that the African in America lost his native languages but retained his philosophy, religious practice, poetry, song, and dance. All this the white American overlooked. The words of the spirituals show slavery to be an initiation stage—an initiation toward rebirth, as of a new personality. The slaves invoked a religious magic; for example, they called on the Lord again and again without their drums. Dauer is witness to the fact that the earlier spirituals were danced. The African philosophy of *magara* (complete and happy life) is fully maintained. Jahn discounts both the theory of white origin and that of solid protest; we are dealing, he says, "not with hope of salvation but with real salvation; . . . not with real rebellion but with magical liberation." Although much has been written about spirituals, Jahn observes that so far there is no full analysis of them in their relationship to Africa.

In *Muntu* (London, 1961), Jahn records that dancing became dearer and more sacred to the slaves the more the slaveowners suppressed it and punished the dancers. This fact is relevant to the dancing movements by which most spirituals were accompanied in their creation and perpetuation. Jahn also incisively states that "On the basis of African philosophy there can be no strict separation of sacred and profane. Everything sacred has a secular counterpart, and everything secular a relevance to religion." This view supports our previous demonstration that among slave songs the spiritual and the non-spiritual (work song, secular song, etc.) are so close together that there is little justification for thinking of them in separate classifications.

In the matter of the African's lack of writing, *Muntu* calls attention to the fact that drums are superior to writing in conveying information. He is impressed by the African's word-sense regardless of a written language. In Africa, he reiterates, the word produces, commands, conjures, speaks in imperatives. The word is there before the image. Jahn is also impressed by the fact that African poetry convinces through fascination rather than logic. African poetry and prose, old and new, he says, are determined by responsibility.

From the discussion of drum-language and the other creative factors, one becomes aware that the African suffered little through a paucity of writing. He obviously believed that his communicative and educational systems had no need for a limited device such as writing. If they had required writing, Africans would have had no difficulty in establishing it.

At length *Muntu* declares that the true folk spiritual is residual African folk art. Jahn deplores the purification of "ugly and unlovely Africanisms" by the Fisk Jubilee Singers. He also believes that the Christian influences have been considerably exaggerated.

Wolfgang Laade wrote for *Musik und Kirche* (March–April 1969 issue) a review of John Littleton's record of spirituals. Laade says that Littleton is in the "middle class" compared to Mahalia Jackson. He nevertheless reached a high point with "Go Tell It on the Mountain." In spite of some lack of enthusiasm Laade at length declares that the more he listened to the record, the more he grew to like Littleton's voice.

Theo Lehmann is a minister who lives in Karl-Marx-Stadt in East Germany. After publishing a volume of fifty spirituals in a book called *Nobody Knows . . .* (1961), he brought out in 1965 *Negro Spirituals: Geschichte und Theologie* (History and theology). This latter book (after some revision) had been his doctoral thesis at the university in Halle, East Germany. Lehmann's thesis was in two parts. Part One dealt first with historical backgrounds. In its second section it discussed the introduction of the American Negro to Christianity. In its third section it describes the origin of the spirituals, which he calls a mixture of two cultures although he leans heavily in the direction of the white background. Part Two deals with the following topics: the essential testimonies of faith in the Negro spirituals; the eschatology of the Negro spirituals; and the entirety of the Negro spirituals.

Lehmann's subsections on "Death," "The Holy Ghost," "The Jordan-Symbol," "The Resurrection," "The Return of Christ and the Judgment," "The Image of God," "The Image of Christ" (including the question, "Is Christ black-skinned?"), "Hell and the Devil," "Baptism," and "Rebirth" are full of detail he has patiently culled from spiritual texts and spiritual scholarship. But his views on these subjects come through. They reflect more intellectual analysis of the evidence than a personal knowledge of the folk group creating the songs. In Lehmann the scholar swallows up the human approach. Even so, his book is a masterful study which cannot be overlooked by any analyst seeking to know the full meaning and effects of the songs.

The bibliography of *Negro Spirituals: Geschichte und Theologie* contains 515 items from references published in Africa, America, Austria, England, France, Germany, and Switzerland. Six of these are articles by Lehmann himself, published in various journals.

In *Nobody Knows . . .* (1961), Theo Lehmann presents fifty spirituals, German and English text. It was published four years before his doctoral thesis, *Negro Spirituals: Geschichte und Theologie.* His selection of songs covers the range of spirituals from several standpoints, such as types, moods, tempos, and the like.

No doubt the largest and most beautiful publication of spirituals in Germany has been *Das Buch der Spirituals und Gospel Songs* (1961). Its editors are three of Germany's most distinguished scholars and personalities: Bishop Hans Lilje, Kurt Heinrich Hansen, and Siegfried Schmidt-Joos. It contains 102 spirituals in German and English texts.

It also presents several extremely well-written analyses: (1) "The Religious Song of the Negro" by Bishop Lilje; (2) "The Spirituals and Gospel Songs" by Kurt Hansen; and (3) "The Story of the Music" by Siegfried Schmidt-Joos. At the end of the large book is a discography and a bibliography.

A sketch of Dr. Hansen has already been presented. In his office in Hannover Bishop Lilje answered a number of questions about his life with spirituals. He talked of the interest of young people in the songs because, in the midst of intellectual difficulties, spirituals spoke in a voice they could understand. The Christian faith these songs express has no vague generalities, it is the "real stuff." He first heard spirituals sung in 1928, by Julia Derricotte, an American, at a meeting in Mysore, India. He learned to sing them and has done so many times with great satisfaction. He uses them in his sermons. The longing they express points to distant goals for all human beings. As to the future, he believes the songs are part of the classical basis of every future development of faith. Since we will have to look for ways not to be overcome by sharp divisions, the spirit of the spirituals will help. They will suggest new elements by their undisputed quality.

The third editor is one of the most important journalists in Germany. As editor of *Der Spiegel* (roughly equivalent to *Time* and *Life* in Germany), Siegfried Schmidt-Joos writes with authority and originality. In tracing the development of spirituals in Germany, he called the Jubilee Singers part of an exotic period; during the twenties and thirties the songs were more of a gimmick; they became a matter of serious concern in the forties. He believes that much of the interest in spirituals today arises from jazz.

He recalls that *Das Buch Der Spirituals und Gospel Songs*, even at a price of $12.50, sold out its first printing of four thousand copies within six months. The first spiritual festival took place in 1964; since then, they have happened all over Europe. Concerts rather than church services have carried the spiritual to popularity. What is needed is a specific kind of interpretation for these and other good melodies.

Margaret Ley earned a doctorate in 1954 from the University of Munich with a thesis entitled *Spirituals*. Her subtitle was *A Contribution to the Analysis of the Religious Songs of the North American Negroes during the Time of Slavery*. In her introduction (Part One) she did a survey of the historical basis, the linguistic basis, and the musical basis of the songs. In Part Two she studied the tone material, form, rhythm, and linguistic peculiarities of the texts (including verse construction and dialect). Spirituals, she says, are the Negro's own folk songs. They are the impulsive creations of a group of people excluded from the civilization process of their time. The artistic heritage of Africa flourished in America in a new form. The Negro's special kind of musical conscience was responsible for their creation. Dr. Ley also refers to the lack of separation between sacred and secular songs and to the uses of spirituals for church services, work songs, and "secret language." Improvisation is the very essence of the spirituals, she declares. The emphasis on rhythm in Negro music reflects the relationship in African music between music and dance.

In his article, "Die Kirchenmusik in den USA" (in *Musik und Kirche* for November–December 1967), Karl Ferdinand Müller devotes several pages to the spiritual. He calls the spiritual a special event in the development of American church music. He notes the mutual influences of spirituals upon jazz and jazz upon spirituals. The spiritual, Müller says, exerted strong influence upon the whole of American music and especially upon the music of the church. The language of the spiritual is taken from the vernacular. The fascinating thing about them, Müller says, is the simple, completely existential character of the texts with their strong dramatic and lyric accents. The same spiritual sung in the church is sung in the concert hall.

One of the earliest Germans to develop a serious interest in Afro-American literature and to introduce this literature to the German reading public was Eva Hesse O'Donnell. In 1950 she was translating the poetry of Langston Hughes, Waring Cuney, Richard V. Durham, and others and publishing it in German newspapers (e.g. *Die Neue Zeitung* of Munich). In 1953 she and Paridam von dem Knesebeck published *Meine dunklen Hände* (My dark hands), a collection of translated modern American Negro lyrics. This volume had great influence. In fact, when several of the present writers about the spiritual were asked to name one person who most influenced them to search in the field, they all named Eva Hesse O'Donnell. Besides her publications she encouraged writers through conversation and correspondence. Without her it is probable that the great interest in the spiritual, now found in all parts of Germany, would have been delayed.

In the March–April 1966 issue of *Musik und Kirche*, Gottfried Schweizer describes and evaluates the 1966 spiritual and gospel festival. Some of the groups appearing on the program were the Harmonizing Four, the Gospelairs, and the Dorothy Norwood Singers. The author found the program stimulating mainly because of the enthusiasm of the performers and the direct relationship of the song texts to God's word. For his taste there was not overmuch of aesthetic value. The Harmonizing Four, he felt, employed an embarrassingly sentimental harmony. Bishop Samuel Kelsey and the Reverend John I. Little really preached sermons to the accompaniment of the guitar and the recitative of the choir. The Gospelairs were the most modern. In their heavily rhythmic approach he found strong influence of show business. They encouraged the audience to clap hands and respond vocally (which the audience enthusiastically did) without paying much attention to the religious text.

According to Berendt a leading group singing spirituals in Germany is Spiritual Studio, Düsseldorf, under the supervision of H. Texter and K. H. Lyrmann.

In 1963 Father Lothar Zenetti published *Peitsche und Psalm* (Whip and psalm). He called this book history and faith, spirituals and gospel songs of the North American Negro. After four chapters dealing with American and African backgrounds, Father Zenetti turns to the origin of the spirituals, which he says took place within the revival movement. He does say that it is strange how little the whites were able to capture the being or the nature of the blacks. Sorrow, for instance, in the black man is a philosophical thing; when the white man is troubled, he (being a spoiled child) becomes neurotic. Father Zenetti lists the various types of feelings and subjects rendered into song. He says that the spirituals gained popularity in Europe because Europeans mistook concert arrangements for genuine folklore. In America, the lower class and rural Negro continued to sing and develop the spiritual. Through changed social conditions, the spiritual evolved into the gospel song.

HUNGARY

When Paul Robeson sang "Deep River" in Budapest, it was said that he glorified the Danube. When Frigyes Sandor published *Musical Education in Hungary* he recommended the study of folk songs by children as needful for the center of musical education for children in school and kindergarten. He did not mention spirituals, but he did imply them.

In 1965, Miklos Forrai published *Zúgj Hullám*, a collection of a dozen spirituals for voice and piano. His preface was in Hungarian and English. In it he celebrated these beautiful melodies which signified "the doom of slavery, the longing for freedom, the craving for happiness and eternal peace."

Janos Gonda in his book on *Jazz* (1965) has included elaborate background studies in Afro-American music and more than one reference to spirituals. Much of his analysis is scientifically musical. He relates the Afro-American music of South America and the West Indies to that of North America. In an implicit reply to those who have said that slavery in North America wiped out all African tradition, he demonstrates the durability of the Afro-American musical instinct and the highly developed musicality. He mentions specifically the substitution of handclapping for drums, and the rhythmic body movement. Quoting Joachim Berendt, he establishes the fanatical faith with which the black man sings and plays. From Margaret Butcher he sets down the six geographical centers in Afro-American music. He points up the links between spiritual and blues, jazz, work song, and other folk musical expression. He credits the wandering preacher and the gospel and street singer with dissemination of the spiritual. Illustratively, he offers intimate discussion of such spirituals as "Man of Calvary," "When the Saints Go Marching In," "Ain't No Grave Can Hold My Body Down," and "The New Burying Ground." He insists that the spiritual was western-ized through concert singing. Under the influence of jazz, he says, spiritual singing changed. He also says that the older chorus type spirituals have been changed into today's gospel songs.

The Hungarians have heard spirituals beautifully sung at least since 1923 when Roland Hayes, at his peak, sang in Budapest.

INDIA

We have already told of a memorable concert of the Fisk Jubilee Singers at the Taj Mahal. At that time it was noted that "all good Mahomedans reverence the name of Jesus." In *Folkmusic and Folklore* (*1*, 1967), Swami Parampanthi wrote on "Negro Spiritual in American Folksongs and Folk-lore." The article appeared in an issue which described a great variety of Indian folk songs and which contained excerpts from Tagore's pronounce-ments on folk music and folklore.

IRELAND

William Bartram's *Travels* . . . , which briefly describe the singing of slaves in the American South, was published in Dublin in 1793.

During the several years of recurrent visits from the Fisk Jubilee Singers in the 1870s and 1880s, Irish periodicals made constant reference to the singers and their songs. In a sample review, found in the *Daily Courier* (Dublin) for January 31, 1876, it was remarked that no entertainment had ever drawn together in Dublin such an enormous audience as the Jubilee Singers drew to the Round Round of the Rotunda. The reviewer men-tioned the originality of the melodies and the strange beauty generated by the simplicity of the words and the fervor with which they were sung. He also described the compliments paid by Mr. Loudin (the director of the singers) to "warm and true" Irish hearts.

ITALY

In 1906, Felica Ferrero published in *Rivista Musicale Italiana* an article entitled "La Musica dei Negri Americani." He begins by reflecting upon the fact that the spiritual became a well-defined art, comparable to the musical folklore of other nations. As it develops, he says, it is sung both by Negro peasants and by whites who do not know its origin—a curious tribute, he calls this, that the American, so backward in musical resources of every type, pays unconsciously to his former slaves. He notes that city Negroes, ashamed of the songs, do not sing them. From here he proceeds to a description of the various types of Afro-American music, concluding that the Negro folklore is all in religious songs. In the course of his ultimate review, he quotes from and elaborates upon twenty spirituals. "Gideon's Band," he says, developed when a stall at a fair in the South showed Gideon on a white horse attacking the camp of the Midianites. He refers to "In Dat Great Gittin' Up Mornin'" and "Bright Sparkles in de Churchyard" as *cantilena*. He also ties in the work of the Fisk and Hampton singers, especially the books stemming from them. To Booker Washington and Robert Moton he gives credit for having helped him collect his material.

In 1961 Roberto Leydi published in Milan *La Musica dei Primitivi*. Chapter 7 deals with the Negro style in Africa and Chapter 8 with the Negro style in America.

Most of the autumn season of 1927 Roland Hayes was in Italy; Siena and Florence were particularly gracious to him.

LIECHTENSTEIN

In 1969 Janheinz Jahn brought out his book, *The Black Experience*, dealing with four hundred years of black literature from Africa to America, in Liechtenstein.

THE NETHERLANDS

In Paul Breman's *Spirituals* (1958) is a long and intricate historical background. He goes deeply into African and American religious backgrounds. From the camp meeting and the Bible he derives the chief impetus for the black spiritual. He says that northern whites interfered with the music of the Negro, particularly his religious music, especially since they knew nothing of the existence of white folk songs. Conceding that some of the most touching spirituals are in all probability of Negro origin, he deplores the fact that the influence of poor whites upon this Negro music has been played down. In the main section of his book he presents thirty-five spirituals, words and music, with summaries, notes, and comments. He also presents a bibliography of sources.

In a personal interview in London (where Breman has lived since 1959) he said that his interest in Negro authors and folklore goes back to the mid-1940s. He expects soon to do translations of some of Berendt's works and is planning a series of paperbacks on Afro-American stuff, with his Dutch publishers. He has written a book on the blues, which, he says, sells only half as well as his book on spirituals. He says that his correspondence shows that Catholics in Holland use his spiritual book for choral society, school choir, and the like. He admitted that in his book he had overemphasized the white development. He would like people to know more about the realistic life of the slaves who produced the songs. Everybody interested in jazz, says Paul Breman, looks at spirituals.

In their *Ik Zag Hoe Zwart Ik Was* (I saw how black I was) (1958), Rosey E. Pool and Paul Breman discuss the position of the Afro-American in America. It is not only the pigmentation, they say, which gives the Negroes a place apart, even among minority groups. It is also the mental resilience that created the spirituals, the respect-for-nothing irony and sharp self-criticism that comes through the blues, and the sense of collectivity that comes to expression in New Orleans jazz. The spirituals, they continue, were a normal reaction to the closing of other doors for black expression (denial of education, social and political restrictions, etc.). Spiritual texts are often literary documents. In discussing "Free at Last" (given both in melody and verse, in Dutch and English), they refer to the fact that religious meetings were the only opportunity for the slaves to express their collective longing for freedom. They insist, however, that the talk of deliverance is a clear ambiguity. "Study War No More" they say, started out as a song of the struggle for freedom; after the Civil War, it was translated into a peace song for people who were fed up with fighting.

Seven years after *Ik Zag Hoe Zwart Ik Was*, Rosey Pool brought out *Ik Ben De Nieuwe Neger* (I am the new Negro). In several references she stresses the symbolism and the social meaning of the spirituals. The reference to shoes in "Heaven," for example, goes back to the barefooted status of slaves, or the need to wear some one else's cast-off slippers. As soon as we interpret the "Heavenly Land," she says, as the land of freedom, the spiritual becomes a song of resistance. She mentions Harriet Tubman's use of spirituals as code songs. She shows how spirituals in the 1950s found wide use as freedom songs. She gives original interpretations to "Certainly, Lord!" and "Balm in Gilead." A memorable part of her book is her apostrophe to Mahalia Jackson.

Like her countryman Paul Breman, Rosey Pool now lives in London (in

Highgate). She has traveled and taught a great deal in the United States. Her interest in all kinds of freedom songs dates back quite far. In Holland, she says, in the wars with Spain going back to the sixteenth century, the people sang freedom songs under the mask of religious songs. The militancy of the Afro-American, according to Rosey Pool, began in the spiritual.

The most touching part of a long interview with her concerned her recital of her experiences in a Dutch jail under the Nazis during World War II. Every morning the call came for some members of the group to be carried off to the kitchens where they would be burned to ashes. Miss Pool taught her fellow members the Afro-American spirituals; their singing brought them courage and built their resistance. After escaping from the Nazi jail, she worked with the Dutch underground, using the code name Harriet.

H. R. Rookmaaker is a professor of art in the Free University of Amsterdam. He began collecting records for his gramophone when he was sixteen; he now has an enormous collection, and much of it is spirituals and gospel songs. After World War II (he had been a prisoner of war in Germany), he developed an interest in the spiritual.

In 1960, at the request of his publisher, he did a book entitled *Jazz, Blues, Spirituals*. Shortly after this book came out, he came to America "to check on what he had written." He believes that the spiritual is an improvisation based on white music. Even so, he thinks the Negro talent in the matter had real quality and depth.

In Dutch youth camps, he says, they sing mostly English songs, an occasional spiritual. The Afro-American spiritual, he believes, must be sung like Mahalia Jackson sings, not in the Schubertized, concertized manner of the Fisk Jubilee Singers and Marian Anderson.

In 1966 he published in the *Gordon Review* an article on "Let's Sing the Old Dr. Watts: A Chapter in the History of Negro Spirituals." Since then he has made a tape, playing ninety minutes, in which he delivers a lecture entitled "The Development of Negro Spirituals." During the lecture he plays spiritual records.

Another Netherlander, Gerard Hengeveld, has published *Twenty American Songs and Negro Spirituals* (n.d.). Ten of the songs are spirituals. Also, Will G. Gilbert and C. Poustochkine published *Jazzmuziek* in The Hague in 1952. It was advertised as an introduction to the folk music of the North American Negro.

NORWAY

In 1963 the Norwegians invited Jester Hairston to come over and teach them to sing spirituals. Under the auspices of the State Department of the United States of America, he did so.

POLAND

Marian Radzik has a collection, *Ten Negro Spirituals, na fortepian,* brought out in Krakow (Polskie Wydawn, Muzyezne) in 1960.

Witold Rudziński's *Negro Spirituals* (1961) presents ten songs translated into Polish. The literal translations of the songs are a revelation of the way the spiritual is read and felt by this Polish musician. "Deep River," for example, comes out this way,

THE RIVER IS ROARING

The river is roaring,
My home is on the Jordan.
The river's current is roaring.
Oh, Lord! I want to go back to the camp.

Lord, to Thee again I report,
Lord, to Thee again I report,
Put me back again
In my camp.
I implore Thee, Lord!

"Swing Low, Sweet Chariot" comes out "Rush, roll my chariot/Carrying me to my holy land." "Let My People Go" becomes "My People Want to Go." And "Sometimes I Feel Like a Motherless Child" is read,

Sometimes, here, in these alien parts,
I feel like an orphan without strength. . . .

My home is far from here, . . .

Long is the way to it.

Sometimes here, in these alien parts,
I feel like a wandering dog. . . .

My home is far from here, . . .

Long is the way to it.

SCOTLAND

We have already mentioned some of the Scottish reviews of the various performances of the Fisk Jubilee Singers, especially one by William C. Chambers. Other such reviews appeared in the *Edinburgh Daily Mail,* the *Scotsman,* the *Glasgow Herald,* and many other Scottish publications.

Ella Sheppard, one of the original Fisk Jubilee Singers, writes particularly of Edinburgh and Glasgow. They sang, she said, in those places at 6 A.M. breakfasts to thousands of poor; at 9 A.M. Sunday schools; in the afternoon to working people; later to outcasts, often in Guild Halls, where people stood shoulder to shoulder; women one hour, men the next. They sang in the open air to thousands; they sang in hospitals, prisons, and beside sick beds.

On their fourth visit to Scotland (season 1899–1900), the Fisk Jubilee Singers sang two concerts a day, running through the week. That way they sang to twenty-five thousand people; hundreds were turned away.

One of the earliest and most influential foreign articles on the spiritual was A. M. Chirgwin, "The Vogue of the Negro Spiritual," in the *Edinburgh Review* for January, 1928.

SOVIET UNION

We have already remarked the adulation accorded the Fisk Jubilee Singers by the Czarevich and Czarevna of Russia and the eminent successes of two spiritual singers in the Soviet Union, Marian Anderson and Paul Robeson. As early as 1930, Edward F. Murphy wrote that Fisk bands were in demand in Scandinavia and the Soviet Union. Dr. A. Craig has reported that some of the songs of the early Fisk group were translated into Russian and Lettish. Landon Dowdey in *Journey to Freedom* (1969) says that spirituals have bridged all cultural, ideological, and political barriers to become the rage of the Soviet Union.

Concerning Roland Hayes and his singing, including his spirituals, in 1928, the music reviewer of *Pravda* had written: "Out of every song with its deeply musical mood was born a feeling of wonder reaching such a high point in technique that we can speak of it only in highest praise." Hayes had sung spirituals and other songs not only in Moscow (at two large concerts), but also in Leningrad, Kiev, Kharkov, and Rostov.

V. Konen published in 1965 his musical summary of America entitled *Puti Amerikanskoi Muzyki* (The pathways of American music). Besides a separate chapter on the spirituals, the book contains references to spirituals in many places. It seems to have avoided overt political indoctrination in the presentation of material.

Konen begins by discussing the influence of *Slave Songs* in 1867. He then brings in George White and the Fisk Jubilee Singers. Noting that interest in the spirituals has not weakened in a century, he attempts to account for the fact in the nature of the music, especially the words, the fresh unusual harmonies and the fine rhythmic nuances. The fact that nothing like this had ever happened before he cites as a factor.

Crediting Krehbiel with inventing the term *Afro-American music*, he records Krehbiel's great reliance on the superiority of African folk consciousness in the songs. He shows how the spirituals graduated from simple "songs of the blacks" to America's only folk music, in the 1930s. He describes the spiritual war between Negrophiles (stressing original and African elements) and Negrophobes (stressing Anglo-American elements). He brings in Dvořák and his influence.

Later, he goes into the socioeconomic and religious backgrounds of the songs. He traces their use by composers like Gershwin and Jerome Kern. He states his belief that the music is superior to the words and develops the melodic design. Stressing improvisation, he demonstrates perpetually new variations. The features of African performing style give the songs, he says, a vivid primordiality, as in the free and ecstatic jubilations. In his view the rhythmic virtuosity of the songs is not known to European music. He demonstrates also vestiges of African polyphony.

As to the texts, he records that the highly gifted Negro people have created works of a vast generalized force. From the spiritual wealth and beauty of an oppressed people over two centuries have come expressions of suffering, faith, and protest "with staggering drama and deep emotion." Their vivid artistic novelty has attained classical generalization of expression. "In the ordinary force of influence, in the ideological and emotional depth, in the artistic uniqueness lies the true and nontransient significance of these Afro-American songs."

Dmitri Shostakovich, the composer, published in *Sovetskaja Muzyka* for 1953 an article on Negro music entitled "Pesni gneva i bor'by." Although not dealing directly with spirituals, it has some bearing on the subject.

SPAIN

Early in Part Three we told of William L. Dawson's teaching spirituals in Spain. On the testimony of the natives, his success was remarkable.

Roland Hayes first visited Madrid in 1925. He spent six weeks in Barcelona in 1926.

Through a translation of eighteen spirituals and notes, J. M. Fonollosa and Alfreda Papo brought out in Barcelona in 1951 their *Breve Antologia de los Cantos Spirituals Negros*. They give both words and music for the songs selected. In their introduction is a passionate statement of the circumstances under which the spirituals were produced. In historical terms they show how the singing slaves were " 'buked and scorned." They show also how white America eventually realized that these beings they had despised had forged an artistic world so varied, so intense, and so profoundly emotional as no one had ever imagined. These blacks had introduced, say these editors, something new and different into the universal sense of beauty, not only in music but also in poetry. This great accomplishment has invigorated the world through melodious performance in concert halls and in a multitude of records. In the spirituals are songs of painful yearnings, songs of joy, Biblical reminiscence, allusions to death and eternal life, and exhortations to penance. Their aim in the volume is to arouse among their readers that same enthusiasm that their entry into this admirable field of Negro lyrics aroused in them.

As late as 1927, Hogar del libro published a volume of spirituals with the cover title "Espirituals negres." The volume was illustrated by J. Giménez. Words were in Catalan.

SWEDEN

As he did in other Scandinavian countries in 1963, Jester Hairston taught the singing of spirituals in Sweden.

In *A New Song* (1969) Jan Arvid Hellström has developed a plan for study involving ten meetings on Negro spirituals and Swedish church songs. This plan will give participants in his circle a deeper understanding of Bible texts. It includes making concrete the historical situation in which the songs were written and demonstrating the methods by which Bible texts inspired creative song writers. Hellström uses Theo Lehmann's *Negro Spirituals* as a basic text. He also traces the social backgrounds of the spirituals in the United States and examines such questions as their musical rhythm. He notes that spiritual music is not yet allowed in churches, but is informally sung outside. The topic for his third meeting is "The Deep River." With these songs he pursues Jesus on earth and the effects of his ministry.

In *Musikrevy* (1960), published in Stockholm, Ake Runmark wrote on "Negrospiritualens rötter" (Negro spiritual troupes).

SWITZERLAND

The following books, dealing in whole or in part with the foreground or background of Afro-American spirituals, have been published in Switzerland: Ernst Ferand, *Improvisation in der Musik*, Zurich, 1938; Bruno Knobel, *Jazzfibel*, Solothurn, 1960; Jean Améry, *Im Banne des Jazz*, Zurich, 1961; Hall Johnson, *Thirty Negro Spirituals*, Zurich, 1965 (originally New York, 1949).

WESTERN HEMISPHERE

South America and the West Indies have often heard spiritual singers from the North, including bands of college students, such as those from Howard and Dillard universities. Occasional references to spirituals are found in the literature of the South, especially in Brazil and Mexico.

Spirituals, very similar and sometimes identical to those sung by the North American blacks, are sung, and have been sung for years, in the Bahamas, Jamaica, and Trinidad.

The following articles are a sample of the literature describing the Afro-

American spiritual in books and journals of the Western Hemisphere (not including the United States of America): Enrique Andreu, "Los 'Spirituals Negro Songs' y su Acción étnico-social," *Estudios Afrocubanos* (1937); Melville J. Herskovits, "El estudio de la música negra en el hemisferio occidental," *Boletin Latino-Americano de Música* (October 1941); Nestor R. Ortiz Oderigo, *Panorama de la Música Afroamericana* (Buenos Aires, 1944).

In *Revista Musical Chilena* for October–November 1948 (published in Chile) was an interesting story. Written by Eugenio Pereira Salas, the article was entitled "El Rincón de la Historia: La llegada de los 'Negro Spirituals' a Chile." The article essayed to describe the introduction of Negro spirituals into Chile. It says that spirituals came to Valparaiso in 1859 and to Santiago in 1860. The songs described, however, turned out to belong to the minstrel tradition. The fact that Negro spirituals were advertised is highly significant.

YUGOSLAVIA

Paul Robeson sang spirituals to appreciative audiences in Yugoslavia. Jester Hairston taught spiritual choirs there to sing the songs for themselves.

❖◆

CHAPTER TWENTY-SIX

The Flame Burns Brightly

. .
.

W
HEN looking back over the record, it is interesting to compare the songs themselves with the great fire they have set burning throughout the world. Most of the fire is the work of a handful of songs. Never have folk songs burned so brightly or for so long a time. Never have folk songs given birth to so many live and growing children. And the flames with their unexpected colors continue!

A list of all the accomplishments of the Afro-American spiritual, as recorded by willing and knowing evaluators, would be a book in itself, and one of considerable size. What has been done in this book is to borrow a few sentences from a relatively few of the evaluations. At the close it might be helpful to make some lists that sum up the major reactions. These phrases are taken from musicians, anthropologists, historians, musicologists, scholars, newspaper reporters, poets, folklorists, philosophers, even a mathematician, and a few others from various walks of life. Where a figure appears in parentheses, the view expressed is held by more than one person.

Things the Spiritual Has Done

Provided expression for inarticulate masses
Helped to supply a national music (3)
Contributed to world music
Improved understanding between the races (3)
Produced good dance music (by fathering jazz)
Created enthusiasm among musicians
Achieved popularity by reaction of minds of those almost driven to distraction by American complexities
Developed human brotherhood (2)
Challenged the concept of Nordic superiority

Interested and aroused the white man through innate eloquence
Showed black pioneers at work
Produced remarkable physical effects
Told of universal striving and weariness
Went straight to the heart
Helped people to the simple faith which higher education left faltering
Reflected the four freedoms
Cast a potent spell that revivifies the past

THINGS THE SPIRITUAL IS

Inspiration and memory "of the living heart of history"
America's greatest artistic achievement
Music of the highest aesthetic quality
Most extensive and varied body of folk songs now alive and growing
An international, universal language (2)
Most beautiful body of folk music in the world
Loveliest sounds
Most exquisite
Ecstatic
At once the admiration and despair of educated musicians
Source of inspiration for world's musical experience
One of the greatest gifts of black man to human family
Most vital area in United States folk music
"Perfectest flower of the ages"
Universally popular in the United States
Sign of nobility
Unique and inimitable
Song of the Negro soul
Groping of an uprooted African people among alien words, alien customs, and heartbreaking readjustments
Proof of what the Negro can be
Hope of our musical future
"Gold-dusty from tumbling amidst the stars"
The race's richest treasure
Lively leaven in American way of life
More thrilling than any concert song
Most significant contribution of folk and religious songs to our national culture
Best moaning music in the world
Its beauty "beyond the limitations of language, arts and time"

THINGS THE SPIRITUAL IS NOT

Not lament, but exaltation
Seldom grotesque
Not relic of degradation

THINGS THE SPIRITUAL SHOULD DO

Call forth white sympathy and cooperation
Tie North and South together

Occasionally, the evaluation climbs to high superlatives. W. C. Handy, "the father of the blues," said on a radio broadcast that he was always inspired by spirituals; and, further, that the spirituals did more for the Negro's emancipation than all the guns of the Civil War.

Not all the evaluations, however, have been complimentary. In the midst of the controversy over Dvořák's recommendation that spirituals and Indian songs should be used as a basis for American national music, one writer insisted that neither the spiritual nor any other song truly expressed America. Another writer rejected the spiritual as a basis for national music with a long argument which ended with the sentence, "We are Caucasians."

Robert R. Moton, who followed Booker T. Washington as president at Tuskegee, was not sanguine about the spirituals when he first went to school at Hampton. He enjoyed the Hampton singing, but was disappointed that these songs were sung in an educational institution. He had come to school to learn to do things differently: If there was to be music, why not profound church music or classical songs? He especially resented black students revealing their religious and emotional depths to whites. On the other hand, he complained because minstrel shows had caused the Afro-American to despise his own songs.

Moton felt that the whites were making fun, not only of Negro songs, but of the color and religion of the blacks. He urged his people to "use every opportunity to dignify the music . . . not merely encouraging the Negro to sing his folk songs in their truly beautiful primitive form, but also by encouraging him to show their possibilities for use as themes for anthems, oratorios, and even operas."

Their value, he believed, was more than inspirational. In the most realistic sense it was also practical. He declared that "in these songs the Negro has an instrument with which to batter down the walls of opposition and prejudices stronger than all the logic, all the resentment, all the hatred that could be brought against them." These songs, he concluded, were a message of good will to all the world.

Kelly Miller, another Afro-American philosopher, spoke of the shame the spirituals aroused in the breasts of sensitive Negroes and of the many Negroes who believed the songs a badge of slavery. A white writer joined this view in a 1922 article by indicating that the elite among Negroes had discarded the spirituals because they had no striking meaning for the forward-looking and intelligent Negro. Another white writer said that the songs had been discredited by Negro teachers.

In the late 1920s Carl Van Vechten wrote of the reluctance of the Negro to develop and exploit his racial gifts. He was happy, though, that the spir-

itual had stayed alive despite the determined opposition of the Negroes.
J. W. Work, an Afro-American musician, agreed with him that the Negro
was slowly overcoming his resentment of the spiritual. Jeannette Murphy
feared that the spirituals were going to be lost through a failure of appreciation. In 1940, for example, in a Statewide Recreation Program on "The
Negro Sings" in Florida, there was no spiritual sung, and apparently no
mention of spirituals.

Fearing, like Jeannette Murphy, the loss of the songs through malappre-
ciation, Dorothy Scarborough urged methods for their preservation. She
often praised their dignity and value. She paid her real respects by insisting
that someone sing "Swing Low" at her funeral. "Swing Low" and "Deep
River" actually were played over the ashes of Irvin S. Cobb, the famous
humorist, in 1944. His family remembered that they were his favorite spirituals and his favorite music.

But today as the Afro-American studies his own history, which he has
been doing on a large scale for only a very short while, and comes to know
that the spiritual was not slavish, always spoke to the self-respect of the
slave as a man, and was often downright revolutionary, the tide among
Afro-Americans has turned in favor of these songs. Except for a small segment who still think of the songs as wholly religious and who deplore religion and another small segment who have not taken the trouble to discover
what the songs really mean, the Afro-American is proud of his great musical creation. He adapts many of the songs to the present scene. He sings
them with gusto for a great variety of occasions.

And there, before you, is the Afro-American spiritual. It was Afro-
American in three senses: strongly African, strongly American, and a
curious and magnificent mixture of the two. No matter where it got its
materials, like Shakespeare it was original in every fundamental way. It
sang primarily of the life and aspirations of slaves. It was deeply realistic
and, without paradox, full of irony and symbol. It was the expression of
a folk community that had been singing its way through lives for at least
two millenniums. It was religious in the total sense, not in the sense of the
American white man. There was very little of camp meeting or Methodist
hymn in it—very few slaves knew anything about camp meetings or Methodist hymn. There was very little of return to Africa. Besides the realism,
there was the deep sorrow (occasioned by the contemplation of the human
condition), the deep understanding of the human struggle (not just of the
slave's struggle), and the deep joy of knowing that real manhood and faith
could overcome *any* bad human condition. There was no revenge, although
plenty of recognition of the grounds for revenge; no hopelessness, although
plenty of recognition of great trouble in the world; and no inconsolable
pain. There was no fear of death. There was humor and heartache, and the
future was a mighty revolutionary dream, sure to come true.

Arthur Morton says that these songs are a new *Pilgrim's Progress* composed in the universal language of song. They appeal to many people who have no religion and no religious philosophy. They are "proof of the indestructible goodness and power to survive and conquer which exists not only in the Negro people but in all people everywhere. They give us a promise of victory in which we know we can have absolute trust."

Herein is the spiritual's prime greatness. These slaves did not stop with writing about the human soul on its journey to the stars. They brought in their personal experiences, but they did not sing for themselves alone. They sang faith and hope and truth for all mankind. They sang the triumph, however long it took, of freedom and justice. They sang the right of every man to his exalted portion of the tree of life.

And for these reasons, wherever they touch the world's people, who perpetually need to rebelieve in freedom and justice and man's individual greatness, the world's people sing! We all sing together:

> Den my little soul's a-goin' t' shine, shine,
> Yes, my little soul's a-goin' t' shine.

❀❖❀❖❀❖❀❖❀❖❀❖❖❖❀❖❀❖❀❖❀❖❀❖❀❖❀❖❀❖❀❖❀❖❀❖❀❖❀❖❀❖

Source Notes

.   .
.

PART I

Chapter 2

Blacking, John, "The Role of Music in the Culture of the Venda of the Northern Transvaal," *Studies in Ethnomusicology*, II (1965).

Blok, Aleksandr, *The Spirit of Music*. London, Lindsay Drummond, Ltd., 1946.

Boughton, Rutland, *The Reality of Music*. London, Kegan Paul, Trench, Trubner & Co., Ltd., 1934.

Bowra, C. M., *Primitive Song*. Cleveland, The World Publishing Co., 1962.

Burlin, Natalie Curtis, "Again the Negro," *Poetry*, XI (1917).

Combs, Josiah, "Dialect of the Folk-Song," *Dialect Notes*, IV (1916).

Davidson, Basil, *The African Genius*. Boston, Little, Brown and Co., 1969.

Dvořák, Antonín, "Music in America," *Harper's New Monthly Magazine*, XC (1895).

Dwight, John S., "The Spiritual Worth of Music," *Dwight's Journal of Music*, XI (Sep 19, 1857).

Goldron, Romain, *Ancient and Oriental Music*. New York, Doubleday & Co., Inc., 1968.

Grainger, Percy, "The Impress of Personality in Unwritten Music," *The Musical Quarterly*, I (1915).

Hanson, Howard, "The Creative Attitude," *Proceedings of the Music Teachers National Association*, 29th Ser., 1935.

Lomax, Alan, *The Rainbow Sign: A Southern Documentary*. New York, Duell, Sloan and Pearce, 1959.

Merriam: quotations from pp. 190, 204, 205. Evanston, Northwestern University Press, 1964.

Nketia, J. H. Kwabena, "The Music of Africa," *Journal of Human Relations*, VIII (1960).

Sachs, Curt, *The Rise of Music in the Ancient World—East and West*. New York, W. W. Norton & Co., Inc., 1943.

Siegmeister, Elie, *Music and Society*. New York, Critics Group Press, 1938.

Tagore, Rabindranath, from *The Religion of Man* (Hibbert Lectures at Oxford, 1930), *Folkmusic and Folklore* (India), I (1967).

Tracey, Hugh: quoted in Lystad, Robert A., *The African World*. New York, Frederick A. Praeger, 1965.

Chapter 3

Greenway, John, *Literature Among the Primitives*. Hatboro, Pa., Folklore Associates, 1964.

Hoffman, Dan G., "The Folk Art of Jazz," *The Antioch Review*, V (Mar 1945).

Hofmann, Charles, *American Indians Sing*. New York, The John Day Co., 1967.

Krehbiel, Henry Edward, *Afro-American Folksongs: A Study in Racial and National Music*. New York, G. Schirmer, 1914. Contains quotation from Grimm.

Nettl, Bruno, *Folk and Traditional Music of the Western Continents*. Englewood Cliffs, N.J., Prentice-Hall, Inc., 1965.

Nketia, J. H. K., *Folk Songs of Ghana*. Legon, University of Ghana, 1963.

Schuller, Gunther, *Early Jazz: Its Roots and Musical Development*. New York, Oxford University Press, 1968.

Sharp, Cecil J., *English Folk Song: Some Conclusions*. 4th ed., London, Simpkin, Marshall, Hamilton, Kent & Co., Ltd., 1907; Belmont, Cal., Wadsworth Publishing Co., Inc., 1965. Contains definition of folk music.

Tremearne, A. J. N., *Hausa Superstitions and Customs*. London, John Bale, Sons & Danielsson, Ltd., 1913.

Utley: in Coffin, Tristram Potter, ed., *Our Living Traditions*. New York, Basic Books, Inc., 1968.

Vaughan Williams, Ralph, *National Music*. London, Oxford University Press, 1934.

Westermann, Diedrich, *The African Today and Tomorrow*. London, Oxford University Press, 1949.

Chapter 4

Jackson, George Pullen, *White and Negro Spirituals*. New York, J. J. Augustin, 1943.

Johnsons' books of spirituals: New York, Viking Press.

Turner, Lucile Price, "Negro Spirituals in the Making," *The Musical Quarterly*, XVII (Oct 1931).

Chapter 5

von Hornbostel, Erich M., "American Negro Songs," *The International Review of Missions*, XV (Oct 1926).

Mencken, H. L., *A Book of Prefaces*. New York, Alfred A. Knopf, 1917.

Stefan-Gruenfeldt, Paul, *Anton Dvořák*. New York, The Greystone Press, 1941.

"Songs of the Blacks," *The Evangelist*, XXVII (Oct 23, 1856).

Chapter 6

Afolabi Ojo, G. J., *Yoruba Culture*. London, University of Ife and University of London Press, Ltd., 1966.

Alakija, Oluwole, "Is the African Musical?" In Cunard, Nancy, *Negro Anthology*. London, Wishart & Co., 1934.

Amistad 1, ed. John A. Williams and Charles F. Harris. New York, Random House, 1970.

Andrée: quoted by Du Bois, *Black Folk Then and Now* (q.v.).

Arvey, Verna, and Still, William Grant, "Negro Music in the Americas," *La Revue Internationale de Musique* (Bruxelles), II (May–June 1938).

Ballanta Taylor, "American Jazz Is Not African" (Interview of Nicholas George Julius Ballanta Taylor), *New York Times*, Sep 19, 1926.

Barz, Hermine, *The Development of the Poetry of the Negro in North America*. Mainz (Germany) (doctoral thesis), 1951.

Bauer, Marion, and Peyser, Ethel, *Music Through the Ages*. New York, G. P. Putnam's Sons, 1932, 1946, 1967.

Beals: quoted by Du Bois, *Black Folk Then and Now* (q.v.).

Benezet, Anthony, *A Caution and Warning to Great Britain and Her Colonies*. Philadelphia, Henry Miller, 1766.

Blacking, "The Role of Music in the Culture of the Venda of the Northern Transvaal."

Boas: quoted by Du Bois, *Black Folk Then and Now* (q.v.).

Borneman, Ernest, "The Anthropologist Looks at Jazz," *The Record Changer*, III (Aug 1944). Same information found in *A Critic Looks at Jazz*. London, Jazz Music Books, 1946.

Bradford, Perry, *Born With the Blues*. New York, Oak Publications, 1965.

Brandel, Rose, "Music of the Giants and the Pygmies of the Belgian Congo," *Journal of the American Musicological Society*, V (1952).

Brawley, Benjamin, *The Negro in Literature and Art*. New York, Duffield & Co., 1930.

Bremer, Fredrika, *The Homes of the New World; Impressions of America*. New York, Harper and Brothers, 1853.

Bryce, Lord: quoted by Burlin, Natalie Curtis, *Songs and Tales of the Dark Continent* (q.v.).

Burleigh, Harry T., *I Stood On De Ribber Ob Jerdon*. London, G. Ricordi & Co., 1918.

Burlin, Natalie Curtis, *Songs and Tales of the Dark Continent*. New York, G. Schirmer, 1920.

Cadornega: found in Davidson, Basil, ed., *The African Past* (q.v.).

Chase, Gilbert, *America's Music: From the Pilgrims to the Present*. New York, McGraw-Hill Book Co., 1966.

Chirgwin, A. M., "The Vogue of the Negro Spiritual," *The Edinburgh Review*, CCXLVII (Jan 1928).

Clark, Desmond: found in Davidson, Basil, ed., *The African Past* (q.v.).

Conneau, Théophile, *Captain Canot; or, Twenty Years of an African Slaver*. New York, D. Appleton & Co., 1854.

Curtin, Philip D., ed., *Africa Remembered: Narratives by West Africans from the Era of the Slave Trade.* Madison, The University of Wisconsin Press, 1967.

Curtin, Philip D., *The Atlantic Slave Trade: A Census.* Madison, The University of Wisconsin Press, 1969.

Dauer, Alfons M., "Kinesis und Katharsis," *Africa Heute* (Oct 1969).

Dauer, Alfons M., "Stil und Technik im afrikanischen Tanz," *Africa Heute* (Dec 1967).

Davidson, Basil, *The African Genius.* Boston, Little, Brown and Co., 1969.

Davidson, Basil, ed., *The African Past.* Boston, Little, Brown and Co., 1964.

Davies, Samuel, *et al., Letters from the Rev. Samuel Davies, Etc. Shewing the State of Religion (Particularly Among the Negroes) in Virginia.* London, n.p., 1757.

Deerr: summarized in Curtin, *The Atlantic Slave Trade.*

Delafosse, Maurice, *The Negroes in Africa: History and Culture.* Washington, The Associated Publishers, 1931.

Donnan, Elizabeth, *Documents Illustrative of the History of the Slave Trade To America.* New York, Octagon Books, Inc., 1965.

Dow, George Francis, *Slave Ships and Sailing.* Salem, Mass., Marine Research Society, 1927.

Dowd, Jerome, *The Negro in American Life.* New York, The Century Co., 1926.

Du Bois, W. E. B., *Black Folk Then and Now.* New York, Henry Holt and Co., 1939.

Du Bois, W. E. B., "The Enforcement of the Slave-Trade Laws," *Annual Report of the American Historical Association for the Year 1891.* Washington, Government Printing Office, 1892.

Du Bois, W. E. B., *The Negro.* New York, Henry Holt and Co., 1915.

Du Bois, W. E. B., *The Suppression of the African Slave-Trade to the United States of America, 1638–1870.* New York, Longmans, Green, and Co., 1896.

Du Chaillu, Paul, *Adventures in the Great Forest of Equatorial Africa and the Country of the Dwarfs.* New York, Harper and Brothers, 1890.

Edwards, Charles L., *Bahama Songs and Stories.* Boston (for the American Folk-Lore Society), Houghton Mifflin and Co., 1895.

Ellis, George W., *Negro Culture in West Africa.* New York, The Neale Publishing Co., 1914.

Equiano, Olaudah (Gustavus Vassa), *Equiano's Travels.* New York, Frederick A. Praeger, 1967.

Equiano, Olaudah, *The Interesting Narrative of the Life of Olaudah Equiano, or Gustavus Vassa, the African.* London, published by the author, 1789.

Finkelstein, Sidney, "The Music of Africa," *Sing Out!* V (1955).

Finnegan, Ruth, *Limba Stories and Story-Telling.* Oxford, Clarendon Press, 1967.

Fisher, William Arms, " 'Swing Low, Sweet Chariot': The Romance of a Famous Spiritual," *The Etude,* L (Aug 1932).

Ford, Theodore P., *God Wills the Negro.* Chicago, The Geographical Institute Press, 1939.

von Franzius: quoted in Du Bois, *The Negro* (q.v.).

Frazier: for Professor Frazier's estimates see pp. 89–91.

"French observers" (p. 41)—Coeuroy, André and Schaeffner, André, *Le Jazz: La Musique Moderne*. Paris, Éditions Claude Aveline, 1926.

Frobenius: quoted in Du Bois, *Black Folk Then and Now* (q.v.).

Funkhouser, Myrtle, "Folk-Lore of the American Negro: A Bibliography," *Bulletin of Bibliography and Dramatic Index*, XVI (Sep 1936 to Dec 1939).

Gaskin, L. J. P., *A Select Bibliography of Music in Africa*. London, International African Institute, 1965.

Gobineau: quoted in Parrish, Lydia, "The Plantation Songs of Our Old Negro Slaves," *Country Life*, LXIX (Dec 1935).

Gonzales, Ambrose, *The Black Border*. Columbia, S.C., The State Company, 1922.

Gonzales, Ambrose, *With Aesop Along the Black Border*. Columbia, S.C., The State Company, 1924.

Gorer, Geoffrey, *Africa Dances*. New York, Alfred A. Knopf, 1935.

Henri Gregoire's book was republished by the McGrath Publishing Company in College Park, Maryland, in 1967.

Guillaume, Paul, and Munro, Thomas, *La Sculpture Nègre Primitive*. Paris, Les Éditions G. Crès et Cie., 1929.

Hall, Frederick, "The Negro Spiritual," *The Midwest Journal*, I (1949).

Hanna, Judith Lynne, "African Dance as Education," *Impulse 1965: Dance and Education Now*.

Hare, Maud Cuney, "Afro-American Folk-Song Contribution," *The Musical Observer*, XV (Feb 1917).

Haywood, Charles, *A Bibliography of North American Folklore and Folksong*. New York, Greenberg, 1951; 2nd ed., 1961.

Herskovits, Melville J., *Patterns of Negro Music*. Springfield, Ill., Illinois State Academy of Sciences, 1941.

Herskovits, Melville J., "The Study of African Oral Art," in Dorson, Richard M., ed., *Folklore Research around the World: A North American Point of View*. Bloomington, Indiana University Press, 1961.

Hichens, William, "Music: A Triumph of African Art," *Art and Archaeology*, XXIII (Jan–Feb 1932).

Hoffman, "The Folk Art of Jazz."

Hubbard, W. L., ed., *History of American Music*. Toledo, Irving Squire, 1908.

"Informed observer" (p. 28): Miss Kingsley, referred to for her *West African Studies* by Du Bois, *Black Folk Then and Now* (q.v.).

Jobson, Richard, *The Golden Trade*. London, Nicholas Okes, 1623; The Penguin Press, 1932.

Kennedy, R. Emmet, "The Poetic and Melodic Gifts of the Negro," *The Etude*, XLI (Mar 1923).

Kerlin, Robert T., *Negro Poets and Their Poems*. Washington, Associated Publishers, Inc., 1923.

Kirby, Percival, "A Study of Negro Harmony," *The Musical Quarterly*, XVI (Jul 1930).

Kyagambiddwa, Joseph, *African Music from the Source of the Nile*. New York, Frederick A. Praeger, 1955.

Leakey, L. S. B.: quoted in Davidson, *The African Genius* (q.v.).

Lenz and Du Chaillu: quoted in Du Bois, *The Negro* (q.v.).

Livingstone: quoted in Du Bois, *Black Folk Then and Now* (q.v.).

Lomax, Alan, "Africanisms in New World Music," in *Papers of the Conference on Research and Resources of Haiti, Research Institute for the Study of Man*. New York, Columbia University, 1969.

Lomax, Alan, *Folk Song Style and Culture*. Washington, American Association for the Advancement of Science, 1968.

Lugard, Lady: quoted in Ellis, *Negro Culture in West Africa* (q.v.).

von Luschan, *Verhandlungen der berliner Gesellschaft für Anthropologie:* quoted in Du Bois, *The Negro* (q.v.).

McGinty, Doris Evans, "African Tribal Music: A Study of Transition," *Journal of Human Relations*, VIII (1960).

McKinney, Howard, *Music and Man*. Chicago, American Book Co., 1948.

Mommsen: quoted in Du Bois, *Black Folk Then and Now* (q.v.).

de Mortillet, Gabriel: quoted in Du Bois, *Black Folk Then and Now* (q.v.).

Murdock, George Peter, *Africa: Its Peoples and Their Culture History*. New York, McGraw-Hill Book Co., 1959.

Nketia, "The Music of Africa."

Osifekunde of Ijebu: found in Curtin, *Africa Remembered* (q.v.).

"One writer" (p. 63): Clark, F. A., *The Black Music Master*. Philadelphia, published by the author, 1923.

Parampanthi, Swami, "Negro Spiritual in American Folksong and Folklore," *Folkmusic and Folklore* (India), I (1967).

Park, Mungo, *Travels in the Interior Districts of Africa*. Philadelphia, James Humphreys, 1800.

Park: quoted in Du Bois, *Black Folk Then and Now* (q.v.).

Quaque, Philip: found in Curtin, *Africa Remembered* (q.v.).

Ratzel: quoted in Du Bois, *Black Folk Then and Now* (q.v.).

Rhodes, Willard, "Music as an Agent of Political Expression," *Sing Out!* XIII (Feb–Mar 1963).

Rublowsky, John, *Music in America*. New York, Crowell-Collier Press, 1967.

Sandilands, Alexander, *A Hundred and Twenty Negro Spirituals*. Morija (Basutoland), Morija Sesuto Book Depot, 1951.

Scarborough, Dorothy, *On the Trail of Negro Folk-Songs*. Cambridge, Harvard University Press, 1925.

Seagle, Oscar, "The Negro Spiritual," *Musical Courier*, LXXIV (May 1917).

Siegmeister, *Music and Society*.

Smith, M. G., "The African Heritage in the Caribbean," in Rubin, Vera, *Caribbean Studies: A Symposium*. University College of the West Indies (Jamaica), 1957.

Stanislav, J., "Some Remarks on the Development of Musical Creation Among African Peoples," in Archer, William K., ed., *The Preservation of Traditional Forms of the Learned and Popular Music of the Orient and the Occident*. Urbana, Institute of Communications Research, 1964.

Starkey, Marion L., *Striving to Make It My Home*. New York, W. W. Norton & Co., 1964.

Stearns, Marshall, "West African Music and American Popular Culture," in

Alberts, Arthur S., *Tribal, Folk and Cafe Music of West Africa.* New York, Field Recordings, 1950.

Still, William Grant: see Arvey, Verna.

Suppan, Wolfgang, "Die Seit 1945 erschienene deutschsprachige Literatur zum Jazz," *Jahrbuch Für Volksliedforschung,* XII (1967). Contains 61 items on the spiritual.

Sweeney, James Johnson, ed., *African Negro Art.* New York, The Museum of Modern Art, 1935.

Tannenbaum, Frank, *Slave and Citizen: The Negro in the Americas.* New York, Alfred A. Knopf, 1947.

(Tennyson, Alfred), *A Chronological List of the Works of Alfred Lord Tennyson.* n.p., n.d.

Tennyson, Alfred, *The Complete Poetical Works.* Boston, James R. Osgood and Co., 1871. The poem "Timbuctoo," pp. 400–403.

Tennyson, Alfred, *The Poetic and Dramatic Works of Alfred Lord Tennyson.* Boston, Houghton Mifflin Co., 1898. Notes on "Timbuctoo," p. 778.

Thieme, Darius L., *African Music: A Briefly Annotated Bibliography.* Washington, Library of Congress: Music Division, 1964.

Thieme, Darius L., "Negro Folksong Scholarship in the United States," *African Music: Journal of the African Music Society,* II (1960).

Tillinghast, Joseph Alexander, *The Negro in Africa and America.* New York, Published for the American Economic Association by The Macmillan Co., 1902.

Tracey, Hugh T., *et al., Codification of African Music and Textbook Project.* Roodepoort (South Africa), The International Library of African Music, 1969.

Turner, Lorenzo D., "African Survivals in the New World with Special Emphasis on the Arts," in *Africa Seen by Negroes.* Dijon (France), Published for *Présence Africaine* by Imprimerie Bourguignonne, 1958.

Varley, Douglas H., *African Native Music* (an annotated bibliography). London, The Royal Empire Society, 1936.

Weman, Henry, *African Music and the Church in Africa.* Uppsala (Sweden), Svenska Institutet För Missionforskning, 1960.

Willett, Frank, "Two Thousand Years of Sculpture," in Davidson, Basil, ed., *The African Past* (q.v.).

Woodson, Carter G., *The African Background Outlined.* Washington, The Association for the Study of Negro Life and History, Inc., 1936.

Chapter 7

Allen, William Francis, Ware, Charles Pickard, and Garrison, Lucy McKim, *Slave Songs of the United States.* New York, Peter Smith, 1867.

Barrett, Harris, "Negro Folk Songs," *The Southern Workman,* XLI (Apr 1912).

Benson, Louis F., *The English Hymn.* Richmond, John Knox Press, 1962.

Borneman, "The Anthropologist Looks at Jazz."

Epstein, Dena J., "Slave Music in the United States Before 1860: A Survey of Sources," *Music Library Association Notes,* 2nd. Ser., XX (1963).

Faux, William, *Memorable Days in America.* London, W. Simpkin and R. Marshall, 1823.

For Professor Frazier's opinions, see pp. 89–91.

Gillum, Ruth H., "The Negro Folksong in the American Culture," *The Journal of Negro Education,* XII (1943).

Herskovits has negated these assumptions in many places, but particularly in *The Myth of the Negro Past.* Boston, Beacon Press, 1958.

von Hornbostel, "American Negro Songs."

Jackson, Bruce, "The Glory Songs of the Land," in Potter, ed., *Our Living Traditions.*

Lomax, Alan, particularly in *Folk Song Style and Culture.*

Trollope, Frances M., *Domestic Manners of the Americans.* New York, Howard Wilford Bell, 1904.

Turner, "African Survivals in the New World with Special Emphasis on the Arts."

Chapter 8

Kemble, Frances Anne, *Journal of a Residence on a Georgian Plantation in 1838–1839.* London, Longman and Co.; New York, Harper and Brothers, 1863.

Mencken, H. L., "Negroes' Contribution to Music Condensed in a Book of Spirituals," *The World* (New York), Nov 15, 1925.

Niles, John Jacob, "White Pioneers and Black," *The Musical Quarterly,* XVIII (Jan 1932).

The Sacred Harp: quoted by George Pullen Jackson in *White Spirituals in the Southern Uplands.* Chapel Hill, The University of North Carolina Press, 1933.

"Songs of the Blacks," *The Evangelist,* XXVII (Oct 23, 1856).

Chapter 9

Cleveland, Catharine C., *The Great Revival in the West, 1797–1805.* Chicago, The University of Chicago Press, 1916.

Eaton, Clement, "The Ebb of the Great Revival," *The North Carolina Historical Review,* XXIII (Jan 1946).

Fisher, Miles Mark, *Negro Slave Songs in the United States.* New York, The Citadel Press, 1953.

Gaul, Harvey B., "Negro Spirituals," *New Music Review,* XVII (Apr 1918).

Hitchcock, H. Wiley, *Music in the United States: A Historical Introduction.* Englewood Cliffs, N.J., Prentice-Hall, 1969.

Johnson, Charles A., "The Frontier Camp Meeting: Contemporary and Historical Appraisals, 1805–1840," *The Mississippi Valley Historical Review,* XXXVII (Jun 1950).

Johnson, Charles A., *The Frontier Camp Meeting: Religion's Harvest Time.* Dallas, Southern Methodist University Press, 1955.

Lakin, Benjamin: quoted in Johnson, *The Frontier Camp Meeting.*

Long, John D.: quoted in Johnson, *The Frontier Camp Meeting.*

McGee, John, "Commencement of the Great Revival of Religion in Kentucky and Tennessee, in 1799," *The Methodist Magazine,* IV (May 1821).

McGready, James, "A Short Narrative of the Revival of Religion in Logan County," *The New-York Missionary Magazine and Repository of Religious Intelligence*, IV (Jan, Apr, May, and Jun 1803).

Nottingham, Elizabeth, *Methodism and the Frontier: Indiana Proving Ground*. New York, Columbia University Press, 1941.

Shurter, Robert L., "The Camp Meeting in the Early Life and Literature of the Mid-West," *The East Tennessee Historical Society's Publications*, No. 5 (Jan 1933).

Trollope, *Domestic Manners of the Americans*.

Watson, John Fanning: Watson's *Methodist Error, Or, Friendly, Christian Advice, To those Methodists, Who indulge in extravagant religious emotions and bodily exercises* (Trenton, 1819): quoted in Johnson, "The Frontier Camp Meeting." Also discussed in Yoder, Don, *Pennsylvania Spirituals*. Lancaster, Pennsylvania Folklife Society, 1961.

Chapter 10

Arvey and Still, "Negro Music in the Americas."

Bass, Robert Duncan, "Negro Songs from the Pedee Country," *The Journal of American Folklore*, XLIV (Oct–Dec 1931).

Botkin, B. A., "Self-Portraiture and Social Criticism in Negro Folk-Song," *Opportunity*, V (Feb 1927).

Bastide, Roger, *Les Amériques Noires*. Paris, Payot, 1967.

Brand, Oscar, *The Ballad Mongers*. New York, Funk & Wagnalls Co., Inc., 1962.

Brown, John Mason, "Songs of the Slave," *Lippincott's Magazine*, II (Dec 1868).

Chambers, Herbert A., *The Treasury of Negro Spirituals*. London, Blandford, 1953.

Conley, Dorothy L., "Origin of the Negro Spirituals," *The Negro History Bulletin*, XXV (May 1962).

Du Bois, W. E. B., "Black America," in Ringel, Fred J., ed., *America As Americans See It*. New York, The Literary Guild, 1932.

Finkelstein, Sidney, *Composer and Nation: The Folk Heritage of Music*. New York, International Publishers, 1960.

Gilchrist, Anne G., "The Folk Element in Early Revival Hymns and Tunes," *Journal of the Folk-Song Society*, VIII (Dec 1928).

Grew, Sydney, "National Music and the Folk-Song," *The Musical Quarterly*, VII (Apr 1921).

Howard, Joseph, *Drums in the Americas*. New York, Oak Publications, 1967.

Lavat, Père: his *Nouveau Voyage aux isles de l'Amérique* quoted by Nettel, Reginald, *A Social History of Traditional Song*. New York, Augustus M. Kelley, 1969.

Mencken, H. L., "Songs of the American Negro," *The World Review*, I (Feb 8, 1926).

Oliver, Paul, *The Story of the Blues*. Philadelphia, Chilton Book Co., 1969.

Owen, May West, "Negro Spirituals: Their Origin, Development and Place in American Folk Song," *The Musical Observer*, XIX (Dec 1920).

Peterkin, Julia, *Roll, Jordan, Roll*. New York, Robert O. Ballou, 1933.

"Slave Songs of the United States": review of book of the same title by Allen et al., in *The Nation*, V (Nov 21, 1867).

Tonsor, Johann, "Negro Music," *Music* (Chicago), III (Dec 1892).

Woofter, T. J., Jr., *Black Yeomanry: Life on St. Helena Island*. New York, Henry Holt and Co., 1930.

Yoder, *Pennsylvania Spirituals*.

Chapter 11

Bartram, William, *Travels through North and South Carolina, Georgia, East and West Florida, the Cherokee Country, etc.* Dublin, J. Moore, W. Jones, 1793.

Barz, *The Development of the Poetry of the Negro in North America*.

Benedict, Ruth: definition of "Folklore" in *Encyclopedia of the Social Sciences*.

Chase, *America's Music*.

Davies, *Letters*.

Epstein, Dena J., *"Folk Culture on St. Helena Island, South Carolina:* by Guy B. Johnson," a review in *Notes* (quarterly journal of the Music Library Association), XXV (Mar 1969).

Epstein, "Slave Music in the United States Before 1860."

Fauset, Arthur Huff, *Black Gods of the Metropolis*. Philadelphia, Publications of the Philadelphia Anthropological Society, 1944.

Finkelstein, *Composer and Nation*.

Fisher, *Negro Slave Songs in the United States*.

Frazier, E. Franklin, *The Negro Church in America*. New York, Shocken Books, 1963.

Frazier, E. Franklin, *The Negro Family in the United States*. Chicago, The University of Chicago Press, 1939.

Frazier, E. Franklin, "The Negro Slave Family," *Journal of Negro History*, XV (1930).

Gaul, "Negro Spirituals."

Gilchrist, Anne G., and Broadwood, Lucy: as reported by Buchanan, Annabel Morris in "Folk Music in America," *International Cyclopedia of Music and Musicians*. New York, Dodd, Mead and Co., 1964.

Johnson, Guy B., *Folk Culture on St. Helena Island, South Carolina*. Chapel Hill, The University of North Carolina Press, 1930.

Jones, Raymond Julius, *A Comparative Study of Religious Cult Behavior among Negroes with Special Reference to Emotional Group Conditioning Factors*. Washington, Howard University Studies in the Social Sciences, 1939.

Primitive Music, published by Longmans, Green, and Co.

Schneider, "Primitive Music."

Smith, Joseph Hutchinson, "Folk-Songs of the American Negro," *The Sewanee Review*, XXXII (Apr 1924).

Waterman, "African Patterns in Trinidad Negro Music."

Chapter 12

Alakija, "Is the African Musical?"

Allen, Richard, *A Collection of Hymns & Spiritual Songs from Various Authors*. Philadelphia, T. L. Plowman, 1801.

Arrowood, Mary Dickson, and Hamilton, Thomas Hoffman, "Nine Negro Spirituals from Lower South Carolina," *The Journal of American Folklore*, XLI (Oct–Dec 1928).

Arvey, Verna, "W.G.S.–Creator of Indigenous American Music," *The Chesterian*, XX (May–Jun 1939). (Sketch of William Grant Still.)

Barret, W. A., "Negro Hymnology," *The Musical Times* (London), XV (Aug 1, 1872).

Barry, Phillips, "Negro Folk-Songs from Maine," *Bulletin of the Folk-Song Society of the Northeast* (1934 and 1935).

Barz, *The Development of the Poetry of the Negro in North America*.

Bremer, *The Homes of the New World*.

Brown, William Wells, *Narrative of William W. Brown, A Fugitive Slave*. Boston, Anti-Slavery Office, 1847.

Buermeyer, Laurence, "The Negro Spirituals and American Art," *Opportunity*, IV (May 1926).

Burlin, Natalie Curtis, "Black Singers and Players," *The Musical Quarterly*, V (Oct 1919).

Chirgwin, "The Vogue of the Negro Spiritual."

Cooper, Thomas, *The African Pilgrim's Hymns*. London, J. Bertrand, 1820.

Dett, R. N., *The Dett Collection of Negro Spirituals*. Chicago, Hall & McCreary, 1936.

Franklin, John Hope, *From Slavery to Freedom*. New York, Alfred A. Knopf, 1967.

Gaul, "Negro Spirituals."

Goldstein, Walter, "The Natural Harmonic and Rhythmic Sense of the Negro." *Papers and Proceedings of the Music Teachers National Association* (1917).

Greenway, John, *American Folksongs of Protest*. Philadelphia, University of Pennsylvania Press, 1953.

Harris, Joel Chandler, *Uncle Remus, His Songs and His Sayings*. New York, D. Appleton and Co., 1881.

Herskovits, *The Myth of the Negro Past*.

Hilarion, Sister Mary, "The Negro Spiritual," *The Catholic World*, CXLIII (Apr 1, 1936).

Kirby, "A Study of Negro Harmony."

Krehbiel, *Afro-American Folksongs*.

Landeck, Beatrice, *Echoes of Africa in Folk Songs of the Americas*. New York, David McKay Co., Inc., 1961.

Laubenstein, Paul Fritz, "Race Values in Aframerican Music," *The Musical Quarterly*, XVI (Jul 1930).

Lomax, *The Rainbow Sign*.

Mencken, "Negroes' Contribution to Music Condensed in a Book of Spirituals."

Moderwell, Hiram Kelly, "The Epic of the Black Man," *The New Republic*, XII (Sep 8, 1917).

Murphy, Jeannette Robinson, "Survival of African Music in America," *Appletons' Popular Science Monthly*, LV (Sep 1899).

Niles, "White Pioneers and Black."

Olmsted, Frederick Law, *A Journey in the Seaboard Slave States*. New York, Dix and Edwards, 1856.

Parrish, "The Plantation Songs of Our Old Negro Slaves."

Phillips, Waldo B., "Negro Spirituals in Retrospect," *The Negro History Bulletin*, XXII (Dec 1958).

Puckett, Newbell Niles, *Folk Beliefs of the Southern Negro*. Chapel Hill, The University of North Carolina Press, 1926.

Redpath, James, *The Roving Editor: Or, Talks with Slaves in the Southern States*. New York, A. B. Burdick, 1859.

Russell, Henry, *Cheer, Boys, Cheer!* London, John Macqueen, 1895.

Shillito, Edward, "The Poet and the Race Problem," *The Christian Century*, XLVI (Jul 17, 1929).

Silber, Irwin, "Review of John Greenway's *American Folk Songs of Protest*," *Sing Out!* III (Jun 1953).

Szwed, John F., "Negro Music: Urban Renewal," in Coffin, *Our Living Traditions*.

Tonsor, "Negro Music."

Towne, Laura M., *Letters and Diary of Laura M. Towne*. Cambridge, The Riverside Press, 1912.

Van Vechten, Carl, "Don't Let Dis Harves' Pass," *The New York Herald Tribune Books*, Oct 31, 1926.

Van Vechten, Carl, "The Songs of the Negro," *The New York Herald Tribune Books*, Oct 25, 1925.

Ward, W. E., "Music in the Gold Coast," *The Gold Coast Review*, III (Jul–Dec 1927).

Waterman, Richard A., "'Hot' Rhythm in Negro Music," *Journal of the American Musicological Society*, I (1948).

Chapter 13

Barz, *The Development of the Poetry of the Negro in North America*.

Beckham, Albert Sidney, "The Psychology of Negro Spirituals," *The Southern Workman*, LX (Sep 1931).

Billington, Ray: see Introduction to Fisher, *Negro Slave Songs in the United States*.

Borneman, "The Anthropologist Looks at Jazz."

Bremer, *The Homes of the New World*.

Brown, Sterling, "Negro Folk Expression: Spirituals, Seculars, Ballads and Work Songs," *Phylon*, XIV (1953).

Brown, Sterling, "Spirituals," in Brown, Sterling, Davis, Arthur P., and Lee, Ulysses, eds., *The Negro Caravan*. New York, The Dryden Press, 1941.

Cable, George W., "Creole Slave Songs," *The Century Magazine*, XXXI (Apr 1886).

Chase, *America's Music*.

Cresswell, Nicholas, *The Journal of Nicholas Cresswell, 1774–1777*. New York, The Dial Press, 1924.

Davies, *Letters.*

Davis, Allison, "What Does Negro Youth Think of Present-Day Negro Leaders?" *The Southern Workman,* LVII (Feb 1928).

Dett, R. Nathaniel, "Understanding the Spiritual," in *The Dett Collection of Negro Spirituals.*

Faux, *Memorable Days in America.*

Finkelstein, *Composer and Nation.*

Fisher, *Negro Slave Songs in the United States.*

(Garrison) McKim, Lucy, "Songs of the Port Royal 'Contrabands,'" *Dwight's Journal of Music,* XXI (Nov 8, 1862).

Haslam, Gerald W., "Black and Unknown Bards: American Slavery and Its Literary Tradition," *ETC.: A Review of General Semantics,* XXV (Dec 1968).

Hayakawa, S. I., "Popular Songs vs. the Facts of Life," in Hayakawa, S. I., ed., *The Use and Misuse of Language.* Greenwich, Fawcett Publications, 1964.

Hayes, Roland, *My Songs.* Boston, Little, Brown and Co., 1948.

Hughes, Langston, ed., *An African Treasury.* New York, Crown Publishers, Inc., 1960.

Katz, William Loren, *Eyewitness: The Negro in American History.* New York, Pitman Publishing Corp., 1967.

Kemble, *Journal of a Residence on a Georgian Plantation in 1838–1839.*

Kenny, Anne, *The Negro Spiritual and Other Essays.* Cairo (Egypt), R. Schindler, 1943.

Lomax, Louis E., *The Negro Revolt.* New York, Harper and Brothers, 1962.

Lorenz, Edmund S., *Church Music.* New York, Fleming H. Revell, 1923.

Miller, Kelly, "The Artistic Gifts of the Negro," *The Voice of the Negro,* III (Apr 1906).

Moderwell, "The Epic of the Black Man."

Morse, Jim, ed., *The Dell Book of Great American Folk Songs.* New York, Dell Publishing Co., 1963.

Murphy, "Survival of African Music in America."

The Negro in Virginia. New York, Hastings House, 1940.

New Inverness Petition: see McCall, Capt. Hugh, *The History of Georgia.* Savannah, Seymour & Williams, 1811. The Petition is also discussed in Caroline Couper Lovell, *The Golden Isles of Georgia.* Boston, Little, Brown, and Co., 1932.

Peterkin, *Roll, Jordan, Roll.*

Porter, Dorothy B., "Early American Negro Writings: A Bibliographical Study," *The Papers of the Bibliographical Society of America,* XXXIX (1945).

Reuter, Edward Byron, *The American Race Problem.* New York, Thomas Y. Crowell Co., 1927, 1938.

Smith, "Folk-Songs of the American Negro."

Staudenraus, P. J., *The African Colonization Movement, 1816–1865.* New York, Columbia University Press, 1961.

Stroyer, Jacob, *My Life in the South.* Salem, Salem Observer Book and Job Print, 1879, 1889.

Talbot, Edith, "True Religion in Negro Hymns," *The Southern Workman,* LI (May, Jun, Jul 1922).

Thomas, W. H., "Some Current Folk-Songs of the Negro," *Rainbow in the Morning, Publications of the Texas Folklore Society,* V (1926).

Tubman, Harriet: Conrad expanded his *Etude* article into a book, *Harriet Tubman.* Washington, The Associated Publishers, Inc., 1943. He and other writers on the fabulous little lady confess great obligation to Sarah Elizabeth Hopkins Bradford's researches, beginning with *Scenes in the Life of Harriet Tubman* (Auburn, N.Y., W. J. Moses, printer, 1869) and continuing with *Harriet, the Moses of Her People* (New York, published for the author by George R. Lockwood and Son, 1869, 1897, 1901). *Harriet Tubman, the Moses of Her People* (published in 1961 by Corinth Books, New York) is merely a reprint of the second work.

Washington, Booker T., *Up From Slavery.* Garden City, N.Y., The Sun Dial Press, 1901.

Washington, Joseph R., Jr., *Black Religion.* Boston, Beacon Press, 1964.

Weatherford, W. D., *The Negro from Africa to America.* New York, George H. Doran Co., 1924.

Wesley, Charles H., "The Negro Has Always Wanted the Four Freedoms," in Logan, Rayford W., *What the Negro Wants.* Chapel Hill, The University of North Carolina Press, 1944.

Wesley, John, *The Letters of the Rev. John Wesley, A. M.,* ed. by John Telford, Vol. VIII, "Letters to William Wilberforce." London, The Epworth Press, 1931.

White, Clarence Cameron, "The Story of the Negro Spiritual 'Nobody Knows the Trouble I've Seen,' " *The Musical Observer,* XXIII (Jun 1924).

Williams, Alberta, "A Race History Told in Songs," *The World Review,* IV (Feb 14, 1927).

Woodson, Carter G., *Negro Orators and Their Orations.* Washington, The Associated Publishers, Inc., 1925.

Work, Frederick J., *Folk Songs of the American Negro.* Nashville, Work Brothers & Hart Co., 1907.

PART II

The legal references to slavery are interspersed throughout Part II. They are concentrated somewhat heavily in the section in Chapter 15 called "Recognition of Legal Hypocrisy." In many respects they are the strongest evidence of the mind of the slaveholder and of the strategic position of the slave. Unless specifically accounted for, they are taken from one or more of the following sources (see Source Notes for full bibliographical reference): Catterall, Helen Tunnicliff, *Judicial Cases Concerning American Slavery and the Negro;* Cobb, Thomas R. R., *An Inquiry into the Law of Negro Slavery in the United States of America;* Guild, June Purcell, *Black Laws of Virginia.* Henry, Howell M., *The Police Control of the Slave in South Carolina;* Hurd, John Codman, *The Law of Freedom and Bondage in the United States;* Johnston, Sir Harry, *The Negro in the New World;* Sydnor, Charles Sackett, *Slavery in Mississippi.*

For many of the topics of Part II, and for some of those in Parts I and III, the researcher will find a valuable resource in the doctoral thesis (New York University) of Zelma Watson George. It is called "A Guide to Negro Music" and a large part of it is "an annotated bibliography of Negro folk music." Available in microfilm (Ann Arbor, Mich., University Microfilms, 1954), it has also been substantially reproduced in Volume II of the *American Negro Reference Book*, edited by John Preston Davis, under the heading, "Negro Music in American Life." The Moorland Collection of Howard University also contains a "Bibliographical Index to Negro Music," compiled by Dr. George. The *American Negro Reference Book*, part of the *Negro Heritage Library*, was published by Educational Heritage (Yonkers, N.Y.) in 1966.

Chapter 14

Ames, Russell, "Protest and Irony in Negro Folksong," *Science and Society*, XIV (1950).

Appomatiox: *Richmond* (Va.) *Enquirer*, Oct 21, 1831.

Conrad, Joseph, "Author's Note," *The New Review*, XVII (Dec 1897).

Downes, Olin and Siegmeister, Elie, *A Treasury of American Song*. New York, Alfred A. Knopf, 1943.

Nettl, *Folk and Traditional Music of the Western Continents*.

Nketia's comment (p. 132) was given in personal interview.

Tagore, *From the Religion of Man*. Excerpts.

Chapter 15

Achille, Louis T., "L'Artiste Noir et Son Peuple," *Présence Africaine* No. 16 (Oct–Nov 1957).

Achille, Louis T., "Verbe Noir," *Aspects de la Culture Noire* in *Recherches et Débats de Centre Catholique des Intellectuels Français* (Sep 1958).

African Negro culture by recorded evidence goes back 5000 years (p. 136), McKinney, *Music and Man*.

The Alabama State Sentinel (Selma, Alabama, daily).

Allen, *et al.*, *Slave Songs of the United States*.

American Slavery As It Is. New York, The American Anti-Slavery Society, 1839.

American Slavery. Report of a Public Meeting Held at Finsbury Chapel, Moorfields, to Receive Frederick Douglass, the American Slave, on Friday, May 22, 1846. London, Christopher B. Christian and Co., 1846.

Ames, Russell, *The Story of American Folk Song*. New York, Grosset & Dunlap, 1960.

Aptheker, Herbert, *Negro Slave Revolts in the United States, 1526–1860*. New York, International Publishers, 1939.

Aptheker, Herbert, ed., *One Continual Cry* (David Walker's Appeal). New York, Humanities Press, 1965.

Armstrong, Orland Kay, *Old Massa's People*. Indianapolis, The Bobbs-Merrill Co., 1931.

Arrowood and Hamilton, "Nine Negro Spirituals from Lower South Carolina."

Asbury and Wesley: quoted by Matlack, *The History of American Slavery and Methodism, from 1790 to 1849*.

Ashe, Thomas, *Travels in America*. London, Richard Phillips, 1808.

". . . at least 2000 years" (reference to age of African culture, p. 136): Personal letter from Alan Lomax, dated November 5, 1969.

Avirett, James Battle, *The Old Plantation*. New York, F. Tennyson Neely Co., 1901.

Ball, Charles, *Slavery in the United States: A Narrative of the Life and Adventures of Charles Ball, a Black Man*. Lewistown, Pa., John W. Shugert, 1836.

Ballanta Taylor: "American Jazz Is Not African."

Bancroft, Frederic, *Slave Trading in the Old South*. Baltimore, J. H. Furst Co., 1931.

Barry, Phillips, "American Folk Music," *Southern Folklore Quarterly*, I (Jun 1937).

Barton, William E., "Old Plantation Hymns," *The New England Magazine*, N.S. XIX (Dec 1898).

Barton, William E., *Old Plantation Hymns*. Boston, Lamson, Wolffe and Co., 1899.

Bartram, *Travels*.

Bauer, Raymond A., and Alice H., "Day by Day Resistance to Slavery," *The Journal of Negro History*, XXVII (Oct 1942).

Bernard, Kenneth A., *Lincoln and the Music of the Civil War*. Caldwell, Idaho, The Caxton Printers, Ltd., 1966.

Borneman, "The Anthropologist Looks at Jazz."

Botkin, B. A., "The Folk-Say of Freedom Songs," *New Masses*, LXV (Oct 21, 1947).

Bradford, *Born with the Blues*.

Brand, Oscar, *The Ballad Mongers*.

Bremer, *The Homes of the New World*.

Brent, Linda, *Incidents in the Life of a Slave Girl*. Boston, published by the author, 1861.

Brooks, Walter H., *The Silver Bluff Church*. Washington, Press of R. H. Pendleton, 1910.

Browning, James Blackwell, "The Free Negro in Ante-Bellum North Carolina," *The North Carolina Historical Review*, XV (Jan 1938).

Bruner, C. V., *An Abstract of the Religious Instruction of the Slaves in the Antebellum South*. Nashville, George Peabody College for Teachers, 1933.

Buckmaster, Henrietta, *Let My People Go*. New York, Harper and Brothers, 1941.

Bureau of the Census, *Historical Statistics of the United States, Colonial Times to 1957*. Washington, Government Printing Office, 1960.

Bureau of the Census, *Negro Population, 1790–1915*. Washington, Government Printing Office, 1918.

Burlin, Natalie Curtis, "Negro Music at Birth," *The Musical Quarterly*, V (Jan 1919).

Burns, Sir Alan, *History of the British West Indies*. London, George Allen & Unwin, Ltd., 1954.

Carroll, Joseph Cephas, *Slave Insurrections in the United States, 1800–1865*. Boston, Chapman & Grimes, Inc., 1938.

Catterall, Helen Tunnicliff, *Judicial Cases Concerning American Slavery and the Negro*. Washington, Carnegie Institution of Washington, 1926–1937.

Cavalcade of the American Negro. Chicago, Diamond Jubilee Exposition Authority, 1940.

Chase, *America's Music*.

Chirgwin, A. M., "The Vogue of the Negro Spiritual."

Christensen, Abigail M. H., "Spirituals and 'Shouts' of Southern Negroes," *The Journal of American Folk-Lore*, VII (Jan–Mar 1894).

Clark, Edgar Rogie, "Folk Music Confusion," *The Music Journal*, VII (Jul–Aug 1949).

Clark, Elmer T., *The Negro and His Religion*. Nashville, The Cokesbury Press, 1924.

Clarke, The Honorable J. G.: From *Reports of Cases Adjudged in the Supreme Court of Mississippi*, ed. by R. J. Walker. Natchez, Courier and Journal Office, 1834.

Clergyman of the Protestant Episcopal Church, *Bishop Hopkins' Letter on Slavery Ripped Up and his misuse of the Sacred Scriptures exposed*. New York, John F. Trow, 1863.

Cobb, Thomas R. R., *An Inquiry into the Law of Negro Slavery in the United States of America*. Philadelphia, T. & J. W. Johnson & Co., 1858.

Coleman, Satis N., and Bregman, Adolph, *Songs of American Folks*. New York, The John Day Co., 1942.

Combs, Josiah H., *Folk-Songs of the Southern United States*. Austin, The University of Texas Press, 1967.

The Congressional Globe, 1st Session, 1849–1850: Vol. XIX. Washington, John C. Rives, 1850.

Conley, Dorothy L., "Origin of the Negro Spirituals."

Couch, W. T., *Culture in the South*. Chapel Hill, The University of North Carolina Press, 1934.

Dabney, Wendell P., "Slave Risings and Race Riots," in Cunard, Nancy, *Negro Anthology*.

David story (p. 176): *The Nashville Republican and State Gazette*, Nov 26, 1831.

Davies, *Letters*.

Davis, Allison, "What Does Negro Youth Think of Present-Day Negro Leaders?"

Dawson, William L., "Interpretation of the Religious Folk-Songs of the American Negro," *The Etude*, LXXIII (Mar 1955).

DeBow's Review, quotation from (p. 154): Henry, Howell M., *The Police Control of the Slave in South Carolina* (q.v.).

Dickson, A. F., *Plantation Sermons*. Philadelphia, Presbyterian Board of Publication, 1856.

Diton, Carl, collector & harmonizer, *Thirty-Six South Carolina Spirituals*. New York, G. Schirmer, 1928.

Douglass, Frederick, *My Bondage and My Freedom*. New York and Auburn, Miller, Oston & Mulligan, 1855.

Downes, Olin, and Siegmeister, Elie, *A Treasury of American Song*. New York, Alfred A. Knopf, 1943.

Drew, Benjamin, *The Refugee: or The Narratives of Fugitive Slaves in Canada, Related by Themselves*. Boston, Jewett, Proctor and Worthington, 1856.

Du Bois, *The Negro*. (ref: "running away the only effective revolt.")

Du Bois, W. E. B., *The Souls of Black Folk*. Chicago, A. C. McClurg and Co., 1903; New York, Fawcett Publications, 1961.

Earnest, Joseph B., Jr., *The Religious Development of the Negro in Virginia*. Charlottesville, The Michie Company, 1914.

"Eighteenth Century Slaves as Advertised by Their Masters," *The Journal of Negro History*, I (Apr 1916).

Elizabeth, *Elizabeth, A Colored Minister of the Gospel, Born in Slavery*. Philadelphia, Philadelphia Tract Association of Friends, 1899.

Elkins, Stanley M., *Slavery: A Problem in American Institutional and Intellectual Life*. Chicago, The University of Chicago Press, 1959.

Elzy, Ruby, "The Spirit of the Spirituals," *The Etude*, LXI (Aug 1943).

Emerson, "The Rhodora."

Epstein, Dena J., "Slave Music in the United States Before 1860."

Famous Episcopal Bishop from Vermont: Hopkins, John H. (q.v.).

Faux, William, *Memorable Days in America*.

Fenner, Thomas P., arr., *Cabin and Plantation Songs*. New York, G. P. Putnam's Sons, 1878.

Finkelstein, Sidney, *Composer and Nation*.

Fisher, *Negro Slave Songs in the United States*.

Fletcher, Tom, *One Hundred Years of the Negro in Show Business*. New York, Burdge & Co., Ltd., 1954.

Flint, Timothy, *Recollections of the Last Ten Years*, New York, Alfred A. Knopf, 1932 (originally published Boston, Cummings, Hilliard, and Co., 1826).

C. F.-Forten, Charlotte, "Letter from St. Helena's Island, Beaufort, S.C.," *The Liberator*, XXXII (Dec 12, 1862).

Franklin, *From Slavery to Freedom*.

Fry, Gladys M., "The System of Psychological Control," *Negro American Literature Forum*, III (1969).

Gara, Larry, *The Liberty Line: The Legend of the Underground Railroad*. Lexington, The University of Kentucky Press, 1961.

Garland, Phyl, *The Sound of Soul*. Chicago, Henry Regnery Co., 1969.

Gayarré, Charles, *History of Louisiana*. New York, William J. Widdleton, 1866.

Gilman, Caroline, *Recollections of a Southern Matron*. New York, Harper & Brothers, 1838.

God Struck Me Dead. Nashville, Social Science Institute of Fisk University, 1945.

Gray, Lewis C., *History of Agriculture in the Southern United States to 1860*. Washington, The Carnegie Institution of Washington, 1933.

Gregoire, *An Enquiry Concerning the Intellectual and Moral Faculties and Literature of Negroes*.

Guild, June Purcell, *Black Laws of Virginia*. Richmond, Whittet & Shepperson, 1936.

Haskell, Marion Alexander, "Negro 'Spirituals,'" *The Century Magazine*, LVIII (Aug 1899).

Haslam, "Black and Unknown Bards."

Hatcher, William E., *John Jasper*. New York, Fleming H. Revell Co., 1908.

Henry, Howell M., *The Police Control of the Slave in South Carolina*. Emory, Va., n.p., 1914.

Herskovits, *The Myth of the Negro Past*.

(Hildreth, Richard) "Author of 'Archy Moore,' " *Despotism in America*. Boston, Whipple and Damrell, 1840.

Hobson, Anne, *In Old Alabama*. New York, Doubleday, Page & Company, 1903. (36 spirituals)

Hopkins, John H. (Bishop), *Letter from the Right Rev. John H. Hopkins, D.D., LL.D. . . . on the Bible View of Slavery*. New York, W. F. Kost, 1861.

Hopkins, John H., *A Scriptural, Ecclesiastical, and Historical View of Slavery*, New York, W. I. Pooley & Co., 1864.

Hubbard, W. L., ed., *History of American Music*.

Hubbell, Jay B., "Negro Boatman's Songs," *Southern Folklore Quarterly*, XVIII (Dec 1954).

Hurd, John Codman, *The Law of Freedom and Bondage in the United States*. Boston, Little, Brown and Co., 1858, 1862.

"Instruction of the Colored Population," *The Evangelist*, XXIX (May 27, 1858).

James, C. L. R., "The Atlantic Slave Trade and Slavery: Some Interpretations of Their Significance in the Development of the United States and the Western World," in *Amistad 1*, ed. by John A. Williams and Charles F. Harris. New York, Random House, 1970.

Johnson, James Weldon, *God's Trombones*. New York, The Viking Press, 1927.

Johnson, James Weldon, and Johnson, J. Rosamund, *The Book of American Negro Spirituals*. New York, The Viking Press, 1925.

Johnson's "O Black and Unknown Bards" appeared first in *St. Peter Relates an Incident*. New York, The Viking Press, 1917.

Johnston, Sir Harry, *The Negro in the New World*, London, Methuen & Co., Ltd., 1910.

Jones, Charles Colcock, *The Religious Instruction of the Negroes*. Princeton, N.J., D'Hart & Connolly, 1832.

Katz, William Loren, *Eyewitness*.

Kaufmann, Helen, *From Jehovah to Jazz*. New York, Dodd, Mead, and Co., 1937.

Kemble, *Journal of a Residence on a Georgian Plantation*.

Kerlin, Robert T., "Canticles of Love and Woe: Negro Spirituals," *The Southern Workman*, L (Feb 1921).

Kerlin, Robert T., *Negro Poets and Their Poems*. Washington, Associated Publishers, Inc., 1923.

Kilham, Elizabeth, "Sketches in Color. Fourth," *Putnam's Magazine*, V (Mar 1870).

Landeck, Beatrice, *Echoes of Africa in Folk Songs of the Americas*. New York, David McKay Company, Inc., 1961.

Laws, G. Malcolm, *Native American Balladry*. Philadelphia, The American Folklore Society, 1964.

Lehmann, Theo, *Negro Spirituals: Geschichte und Theologie*. Berlin, Eckart-Verlag, 1965.

Lemmerman, Karl, "Improvised Negro Songs," *The New Republic*, XIII (Dec 22, 1917).

Lester, Julius, *To Be a Slave*. New York, The Dial Press, 1968.

Locke, Alain, "Negro Contributions to America," *The World Tomorrow*, XII (Jun 1929).

Locke, Alain, "Spirituals," in *Commemoration* (by Library of Congress) *of the Seventy-Fifth Anniversary of the Proclamation of the Thirteenth Amendment to the Constitution of the United States, December 18, 1940.* Washington, Government Printing Office, 1943.

Long, John Dixon, *Pictures of Slavery in Church and State*. Philadelphia, published by the author, 1857.

Lovell, Caroline Couper, *The Golden Isles of Georgia*. Boston, Little, Brown and Co., 1932.

Lumpkin, J.: quoted in Catterall, Helen Tunnicliff, *Judicial Cases Concerning American Slavery and the Negro*.

Lyell, Sir Charles, *A Second Visit to the United States of North America*. London, John Murray, 1849.

McAdams, Nettie Fitzgerald, "Folk-songs of the American Negro." M.A. thesis, University of California, Berkeley, 1923.

McKim, James Miller, "Negro Songs," *Dwight's Journal of Music*, XXI (Aug 9, 1862).

MacTaggart, Esther, "I Saw a Spiritual Born," *The Etude*, LVIII (Apr 1940).

Malet, the Reverend William Wyndham, *An Errand to the South in the Summer of 1862*. London, Richard Bentley, 1863.

Mallard, R. Q., *Plantation Life Before Emancipation*. Richmond, Whittet & Shepperson, 1892.

Mather, Cotton, *Rules for the Society of Negroes*. 1693. n.p. (Reproduced by George H. Moore, Lenox Library, New York).

Matlock, Lucius C., *The History of American Slavery and Methodism, from 1780 to 1849* . . . New York, 5 Spruce Street, 1849.

Mays, Benjamin, *The Negro's God as Reflected in His Literature*. Boston, Chapman & Grimes, Inc., 1938.

Mencken, H. L., "Negroes' Contribution to Music Condensed in a Book of Spirituals."

Mencken, H. L., "Songs of the American Negro," *The World Review*, I (Feb 8, 1926).

Murphy, Edward F., "Black Music," *The Catholic World*, CXXX (Mar 1930).

Murphy, "Survival of African Music in America."

Negro preacher (p. 183): as reported by G. W. S. in "Negro Sermons," *Good Words*, VIII (Mar 1, 1867).

Nettel, *A Social History of Traditional Song*.

Nettl, *Folk and Traditional Music of the Western Continents*.

Nichols, Roy F., "The Progress of the American Negro in Slavery," *The American Negro, The Annals* (The American Academy of Political and Social Science), CXXXX (Nov 1928).

Park, *Travels in the Interior Districts of Africa*.

Parker, William, "The Freedman's Story," *The Atlantic Monthly*, XVII (Feb and Mar 1866).

Patterson, Lindsay, ed., *The Negro in Music and Art*. New York, Publishers Company, Inc., 1967.

Petersburg (Va.) *Intelligencer:* writer reprinted in *The Nashville* (Tenn.) *Republican and State Gazette*, Dec 15, 1831.

Phillips, Ulrich Bonnell, *Life and Labor in the Old South*. Boston, Little, Brown and Co., 1929.

Pickard, Kate E. R., *The Kidnapped and the Ransomed*. Syracuse, William T. Hamilton, 1856.

Poem in *Atlantic Monthly* (1891): quoted in Jackson, Bruce, *The Negro and His Folklore in Nineteenth-Century Periodicals*. Austin and London, University of Texas Press, 1967.

(Pollard, Edward A.), *Southern Spy, or Curiosities of Negro Slavery in the South*. Reprinted as *Black Diamonds Gathered in the Darkey Homes of the South*. Washington, Henry Polkinhorn, 1859.

Preston, Denis and McCarthy, Albert, "Poetry of Afro-American Folk Song," *Folk*, Part One (Feb 1945).

Prideau, Peter: see Henry, *The Police Control of the Slave in South Carolina*.

Pringle, Elizabeth W. Allston, *Chronicles of Chicora Wood* (New York, Charles Scribner's Sons, 1922) and *A Woman Rice Planter* (New York, The Macmillan Co., 1913).

Proctor, Hugh Henry, "The Theology of the Songs of the Southern Slave," in *Between Black and White*. Boston, Pilgrim Press, 1925.

Rankin, John, *Letters on American Slavery*. Boston, Garrison & Knapp, 1833.

Ravenel, Henry William, "Recollections of Southern Plantation Life," *The Yale Review* (1936).

Read, Allen W., "The Speech of Negroes in Colonial America," *The Journal of Negro History*, XXIV (Jul 1939).

Robb, Bernard, *Welcum Hinges*. New York, E. P. Dutton and Co., Inc. 1942.

Rutledge, Archibald, *Deep River* (Columbia, S.C., The R. L. Bryan Co., 1960); *God's Children* (Indianapolis, The Bobbs-Merrill Co., 1947); and *It Will Be Daybreak Soon* (New York, Fleming H. Revell Company, 1938).

Sandburg, Carl, *Abraham Lincoln: The Prairie Years*. New York, Harcourt, Brace & Co., 1926.

San Francisco Herald, Nov 28, 1851.

Scarborough, *On the Trail of Negro Folk-Songs*.

Seagle, "The Negro Spiritual."

Senghor, President: personal interview.

Siebert, William H., *The Underground Railroad from Slavery to Freedom*. New York, The Macmillan Co., 1898.

Simkins, Francis Butler, *A History of the South*. New York, Alfred A. Knopf, 1963.

Singers unfit to be slaves (p. 200)—C. W. D., "Contraband Singing," *Dwight's Journal of Music*, XIX (Sep 7, 1861).

"Slave Songs of the United States," review in *The Nation*, V (Nov 21, 1867).

"Slave Narratives" (typed copy). Washington, Library of Congress, 1941.

Smith, "Folk-Songs of the American Negro."

Smith, C. Alphonso, "The Negro and the Ballad," *University of Virginia Alumni Bulletin*, VI (Jan 1913).

Spaulding, H. G., "Under the Palmetto," *The Continental Monthly*, IV (Aug 1863).

Spiro, Melford E., "Religious Systems as Culturally Constituted Defense Mechanisms," in *Context and Meaning in Cultural Anthropology*. New York, The Free Press, 1965.

Stampp, Kenneth M., *The Peculiar Institution*. New York, Alfred A. Knopf, 1965.

Starkey, *Striving to Make It My Home*.

Statistical View of the United States, ed. J. D. B. DeBow. Washington, Beverley Tucker, 1854.

Sterling, Philip and Logan, Rayford, *Four Took Freedom*. Garden City, N.Y., Doubleday & Co., 1967.

Steward, T. G., "Negro Imagery," *The New Republic*, XII (Sep 29, 1917).

Still, William, *The Underground Railroad*. Philadelphia, Porter and Coats, 1812.

Stoddard, Albert H., "Origin, Dialect, Beliefs, and Characteristics of the Negroes of the South Carolina and Georgia Coasts," *The Georgia Historical Quarterly*, XXVIII (Sep 1944).

Stroyer, *My Life in the South*.

Sydnor, Charles Sackett, *Slavery in Mississippi*. New York, D. Appleton-Century Company, Inc., 1933.

Tannenbaum, *Slave and Citizen*.

Turner, "Negro Spirituals in the Making."

Turner, Nat: reports based on news stories and editorial comments from the following newspapers: *The Nashville* (Tenn.) *Republican and State Gazette*, Nov and Dec 1831; *Richmond* (Va.) *Enquirer*, Oct and Nov 1831; *Star, and North Carolina State Gazette* (Raleigh, N.C.), Sep–Nov 1831.

Vesey's conspiracy and religious fanaticism (p. 179): Hamilton, James, Jr., *Negro Plot*. Boston, Joseph W. Ingraham, 1822.

Vesey's use of the Bible to uphold the fight for personal freedom (p. 189): *The Trial Record of Denmark Vesey*, with introduction by John Oliver Killens. Boston, Beacon Press, 1970.

Walker, David, *David Walker's Appeal*, ed. by Charles M. Wiltse. New York, Hill and Wang, 1965; originally published 1929. Also see Aptheker, Herbert, ed., *One Continual Cry* (David Walker's Appeal). New York, Humanities Press, 1965.

Walker, Margaret, *Jubilee*. Boston, Houghton Mifflin and Co., 1966.

Washington, Joseph R., Jr., *Black Religion*. Boston, Beacon Press, 1964.

Wesley, John: see Asbury.

Whaley, Marcellus S., *The Old Types Pass*. Boston, The Christopher Publishing House, 1925.

Wheeler, Mary, *Steamboatin' Days*. Baton Rouge, La., State University Press, 1944.

Whipple, T. K., *Study Out the Land*. Berkeley and Los Angeles, University of California Press, 1943.

White, Clarence Cameron, "Negro Music a Contribution to the National Music of America," *The Musical Observer*, XVIII, XIX, XX (1919–1920).

Wilson, G. R., "The Religion of the American Negro Slave: His Attitude Toward Life and Death," *The Journal of Negro History*, VIII (Jan 1923).

Wish, Harvey, "American Slave Insurrections Before 1861," *The Journal of Negro History*, XXII (Jul 1937).

Woodson, Carter G., *The Education of the Negro Prior to 1861*. Washington, The Associated Publishers, Inc., 1919.

Woodson, *Negro Orators and Their Orations*.

Woolman, John, *The Works of John Woolman*. Philadelphia, Joseph Crukshank, 1774.

Besides the general references listed above, the section called "The Fugitive and Insurrectionary Spirit" deserves a special brief bibliography. The following works have been selected:

Addington, Wendell G., "Slave Insurrections in Texas," *The Journal of Negro History*, XXXV (Oct 1950).

Cheek, William F., *Black Resistance Before the Civil War*. Beverly Hills, California, Glencoe Press, 1970.

Fredrickson, George M. and Lasch, Christopher, "Resistance to Slavery," *Civil War History*, XIII (Dec 1967).

Lofton, John, *Insurrection in South Carolina: The Turbulent World of Denmark Vesey*. Yellow Springs, Ohio, The Antioch Press, 1964.

Genovese, Eugene D., "Rebelliousness and Docility in the Negro Slave: A Critique of the Elkins Thesis," *Civil War History*, XIII (Dec 1967).

Kilson, Marion D. de B., "Towards Freedom: An Analysis of Slave Revolts in the United States," *Phylon*, XXV (Summer 1964).

McKibben, Davidson Burns, "Negro Slave Insurrections in Mississippi, 1800–1865," *The Journal of Negro History*, XXXIV (Jan 1949).

Mannix, Daniel P. (in collaboration with Cowley, Malcolm), *Black Cargoes: A History of the Atlantic Slave Trade, 1518–1865*. New York, The Viking Press, 1962.

Mullin, Gerald Wallace, "Patterns of Slave Behavior in Eighteenth-Century Virginia" (Ph.D. thesis, History, University of California at Berkeley, 1968).

Nichols, Charles H., *Many Thousand Gone*. Leiden, E. J. Brill, 1963.

Porter, Kenneth Wiggins, "Negroes and the Seminole War, 1835–1842," *The Journal of Southern History*, XXX (Nov 1964).

Powdermaker, Hortense, "The Channeling of Negro Aggression by the Cultural Process," in Levine, Lawrence W. and Middlekauf, Robert, eds., *The National Temper: Readings in American History*. New York, Harcourt, Brace & World, Inc., 1968.

Russell, Marion J., "American Slave Discontent in Records of the High Courts," *The Journal of Negro History*, XXXI (Jul 1946).

Steward, Austin, *Twenty-two Years a Slave, and Forty Years a Freeman*. Rochester, N.Y., William Alling, 1857.

Wax, Darold D., "Negro Resistance to the Early American Slave Trade," *The Journal of Negro History*, LI (Jan 1966).

Wolfe, Bernard, "Uncle Remus and the Malevolent Rabbit," *Commentary*, VIII (Jul 1949); also in Levine and Middlekauf, *The National Temper*.

Chapter 16

Laws, *Native American Balladry*.

Chapter 17

Douglass, *My Bondage and My Freedom*.

Chapter 18

Baldwin, James, *Tell Me How Long the Train's Been Gone*. New York, The Dial Press, 1968.
Jackson, G. P., *White and Negro Spirituals*. New York, J. J. Augustin, 1943.

Chapter 19

Douglass, *My Bondage and My Freedom*.
Du Bois, *The Souls of Black Folk*.
McKim, J. N.: quoted by Downes and Siegmeister, *A Treasury of American Song*.
Quaque, Philip: excerpts from *Letters* in Curtin, *Africa Remembered*.

Chapter 20

Beckham, "The Psychology of Negro Spirituals."
Botkin, "The Folk-Say of Freedom Songs."
Botkin, "Self-Portraiture and Social Criticism in Negro Folk-Song."
Douglass, *My Bondage and My Freedom*.
Downes and Siegmeister, *A Treasury of American Song*.
Finkelstein, *Composer and Nation*.
Haslam, "Black and Unknown Bards."
Higginson, Thomas Wentworth, "Negro Spirituals," *Atlantic Monthly*, XIX (Jun 1867); also Chapter IX in Higginson's *Army Life in a Black Regiment*. Boston, Fields, Osgood & Co., 1870.
Johnson, J. W., and Johnson, J. R., *The Book of American Negro Spirituals:* see Preface.
Lomax, John A., "Self-Pity in Negro Folk-Songs," *The Nation*, CV (Aug 9, 1917).
Mitchell, Margaret, *Gone With the Wind*. New York, The Macmillan Co., 1936.
Siebert, *The Underground Railroad from Slavery to Freedom*.
Still, William, *The Underground Railroad*.
Work, John W., *American Negro Songs*. New York, Howell, Soskin & Co., 1940.

Chapter 21

Allen, *et al.*, *Slave Songs of the United States:* foreword by Irving Schlein. New York, Oak Publications, 1965.
Botkin, "The Folk-Say of Freedom Songs."
"Christmas Carols from Georgia" (submitted by Emma M. Backus), *The Journal of American Folk-Lore*, XII (Jul–Sep 1899).

McAdams, Nettie Fitzgerald, "Folk-songs of the American Negro."
"Negro Hymn of the Judgment Day," *The Journal of American Folk-Lore*, IX (Jul–Sep 1896).
Rosenberg, Bruce A., *The Art of the American Folk Preacher*. New York, Oxford University Press, 1970.
Scarborough, *On the Trail of Negro Folk-Songs*.

Chapter 22

Ames, Russell, "Implications of Negro Folk Song," *Science and Society*, XV (1951).
Botkin, B. A., "Tradition Challenges the Negro," *Negro Digest*, IV (Jun 1946).
Broderick, Francis L. and Meier, August, *Negro Protest Thought in the Twentieth Century*. Indianapolis, The Bobbs-Merrill Company, 1965.
Hampton Negro Conference, Number III, Jul 1899: "Music, Literature, and the Drama."
Haslam, Gerald W., "Two Traditions in Afro-American Literature," *Research Studies*, XXXVII (Sep 1969).
Johnston, *The Negro in the New World*.
Miller, "The Artistic Gifts of the Negro."

PART III

Chapter 23

Baud-Bovey, Samuel, "The Problems of the Preservation of Traditional Forms," in Archer, ed., *The Preservation of Traditional Forms of the Learned and Popular Music of the Orient and Occident*.
Beckham, "The Psychology of Negro Spirituals."
Botkin, "Self-Portraiture and Social Criticism in Negro Folk-Song."
Blesh, Rudi, and Janis, Harriet, *They All Played Ragtime*. New York, Oak Publications, 1966.
Downes and Siegmeister, *A Treasury of American Song*.

Chapter 24

Allen, *et al.*, *Slave Songs of the United States*.
Epstein, Dena J., "Lucy McKim Garrison, American Musician," *Bulletin of the New York Public Library*, LXVII (Oct 1963).
Higginson, "Negro Spirituals."
Parrish, "The Plantation Songs of Our Old Negro Slaves."
Tracey, Hugh, "The Development of Music," *African Music*, III (1963).
Work, *American Negro Songs*.

Chapter 25

Many of the facts about the origin and early development of the Fisk Jubilee Singers have been garnered or substantiated from original sources in the Negro Collection of the Fisk University Library. For the Hampton Singers, the lead source has been original sources in the Peabody Collection of Hampton Institute, especially the early issues of the *Southern Workman*. These original sources include hundreds of newspaper clippings, letters, holograph diaries, contracts, financial records, programs, personal memoranda, hand-written reports, and the like. Similar original materials have been provided by Tuskegee Institute and the Piney Woods Country Life School.

Abrahams, Roger D. and Foss, George, *Anglo-American Folksong Style*. Englewood Cliffs, N.J., Prentice-Hall, Inc., 1968.

Achille, Louis T., "L'Artiste Noir et Son Peuple."

Achille, Louis T., translator, "Negro Spirituals," *Esprit 19* (May 1951).

Achille, Louis T., "Les Négro spirituals," *Le Monde Religieux*, XXVIII (1960–1961).

Achille, Louis T., "Die 'Negro Spirituals' Als Geistliche Volksmusik," *Musik und Altar*, XI (Oct 1958).

Achille, Louis T., "Les Négro-spirituals et l'expansion de la culture noire," *Présence Africaine* (Nov 1956).

Achille, Louis T., "Les Négro Spirituals, musique populaire sacrée," *Rythmes du Monde*, N.S. VI (1958).

Achille, Louis T., "Résonances Spirituelles," *Rythmes du Monde*, No. 1 (1948).

Achille, Louis T., "Verbe Noir," *Aspects de la Culture Noire* in *Recherches et Débats de Centre Catholique des Intellectuels Français*, No. 24 (Sep 1958).

Re Achille, Louis T.: P. F., "A L'Amicale Antillaise: La 'confidence' du professeur ACHILLE sur les Negro Spirituals," *La République* (Toulon), Dec 31, 1969.

Ades, Hawley, arr., *A Spiritual Festival*. Delaware Water Gap, Pa., Shawnee Press, 1967.

Allen *et al.*, *Slave Songs of the United States*.

American Folklore Society, *Abstract of Folklore Studies*. Lafayette, Ind. and Philadelphia, Pa., The American Folklore Society, 1963–.

"An American said . . ." (p. 413): Cuyler of the *New York Tribune*, as reported by R. Nathaniel Dett in "The Emancipation of Negro Music," *Southern Workman*, XLVII (Apr 1918).

American Stuff. New York, The Viking Press, 1937.

Ames, Russell, "Art in Negro Folksong," *Journal of American Folklore*, LVI (Oct–Dec 1943).

Ames, "Implications of Negro Folk Song."

Ames, "Protest and Irony in Negro Folk Song."

Anderson, Marian, *My Lord, What a Morning* (autobiography). New York, The Viking Press, 1956.

"Another reviewer" (p. 411): *Cincinnati Daily Gazette*, Oct 17, 1871.

"Another reviewer" (p. 413): *Portland* (Maine) *Daily Advertiser*, Apr 23, 1872.

Aptheker, Herbert, ed., *And Why Not Every Man?* Berlin, Seven Seas Publishers, 1961.

Arnold, Byron, *Folk Songs of Alabama*. University, The University of Alabama Press, 1950.

Arvey and Still, "Negro Music in the Americas." (Note on Hall Johnson.)

"Association of Negro Musicians," *Southern Workman*, LIV (Sep 1925).

Attaway, William, *Hear America Singing*. New York, The Lion Press, 1967.

Bailey, Rietta, "Washed in de Blood," in Seldon, Samuel, ed., *International Folk Plays*. Chapel Hill, The University of North Carolina Press, 1949.

Baldwin, James, *The Amen Corner*. New York, The Dial Press, 1968.

Baldwin, James, *Go Tell It on the Mountain*. New York, The Dial Press, 1952.

Baldwin, James, *Tell Me How Long the Train's Been Gone*.

Ball, Eric, comp., *2nd Rhapsody on Negro Spirituals for Brass Band*. London, Besson and Co., Ltd., 1954.

Ballanta Taylor: "American Jazz Is Not African."

Ballanta Taylor, Nicholas George Julius, *Saint Helena Island Spirituals*. New York, G. Schirmer, 1925.

Bantock, Sir Granville, *Ten Negro Spirituals*. London, Novello & Co., Ltd., 1932.

Barnes, Ruth A., *I Hear America Singing*. Chicago, The John C. Winston Co., 1937.

Barragan, Maude, "Putting the Spirit in Spirituals" (*re* Charleston Society for the Preservation of Negro Spirituals), *The Etude*, XLIX (Feb 1931).

Barret, "Negro Hymnology."

Barry, "Negro Folk-Songs from Maine."

Bartsch, Ernst, *Neger, Jazz und Tiefer Süden*. Leipzig, F. A. Brockhaus, 1956.

Barz, *The Development of the Poetry of the Negro in North America*.

Beckham, "The Psychology of Negro Spirituals."

"Beecher's Negro Minstrels," *New York Herald*, Dec 28, 1871.

Belafonte, Harry, *Songs Belafonte Sings*. New York, Duell, Sloan and Pearce, 1962.

Belden, Henry M. and Hudson, Arthur Palmer, *The Frank C. Brown Collection of North Carolina Folklore*. Durham, Duke University Press, 1952.

Benedict, Helen Diamond, *Belair Plantation Melodies*. New Orleans, published by the author, 1924.

Bennett, Lerone, Jr., *Before the Mayflower*. Chicago, Johnson Publishing Company, 1966.

Berendt, Joachim Ernst, *Das Jazzbuch*. Frankfurt, Fischer Bücherei, 1953.

Berendt, Joachim Ernst, "Oh Jesus, My Jesus . . . ," *Zeitwende: Die Neue Furche*, XXXIV (Jul 1963).

Berendt, Joachim Ernst (p. 571): personal letter.

Berendt, Joachim Ernst, *Schwarzer Gesang II*. Munich, Nymphenburger Verlagshandlung, 1962.

Berendt, Joachim Ernst and Claxton, William, *Jazzlife*. Baden Baden, Burda Druck and Verlag GMBH Ottenburg, 1961.

Berendt, Joachim Ernst and Knesebeck, Paridam von dem, *Spirituals: Geistliche lieder der Neger Amerikas. Originaltexte—Melodien und Übertragungen*. Munich, Nymphenburger Verlagshandlung, 1955.

Berendt, Joachim Ernst and Tröller, Josef, "Jazz und Alte Musik," *Prisma der Gegenwärtigen Musik*. Hamburg, Furche Verlag, 1959.

Bernard, Kenneth A., *Lincoln and the Music of the Civil War*. Caldwell, Idaho, The Caxton Printers, Ltd., 1966.

Best, Dick and Beth, eds., *Song Fest*. New York, Crown Publishers, 1948, 1955.

Bézoard, Pierre de, *Les Negro Spirituals*. Louvain, Belgium, Xaveriana, 1940.

Black and Unknown Bards (poems selected by Eric Walrond and Rosey Pool). Aldington, Kent, England, The Hand and Flower Press, 1958.

Black Music in Our Culture. Kent, O., Kent State University Press, 1970.

Blesh, Rudi, *et al.*, *O Susanna*. New York & London, Grove Press, Inc., 1960. (This is an English version of a picture-book describing blues, ballads, spirituals, and jazz, with pictures by Horst Geldmacher, text by Günter Grass, musical scores by Herman Wilson, and epilogue by Joachim Ernst Berendt—published in German, in Frankfurt, Vienna, and Zurich, by Büchergilde Gutenberg, in 1959.)

Blesh, Rudi, *Shining Trumpets*. New York, Alfred A. Knopf, 1953.

Bock, Fred, comp., *Wade in the Water and Other Popular Spirituals* (arranged for all organs). Waco, Texas, Sacred Songs, 1967.

Bond, James, "The Hushed Negro Singing," *The Courier-Journal* (Louisville, Ky.), Sep 29, 1921.

Boni, Margaret Bradford, *Fireside Book of Folk Songs*. New York, Simon and Schuster, 1947.

Bontemps, Arna, *Chariot in the Sky*. Philadelphia, The John C. Winston Co., 1951.

Bontemps, Arna, "Rock, Church, Rock!" *Common Ground*, III (1942).

Borneman, "The Anthropologist Looks at Jazz."

Boston reviewer (p. 414): *Boston Daily Globe*, Apr 18, 1872.

Botkin, "The Folk-Say of Freedom Songs."

Botsford, Florence H., *Folk Songs of Many Peoples*. New York, The Womans Press, 1921–1922.

Botsford, Florence H., *The Universal Songster for Home, School and Community*. New York, G. Schirmer, 1937.

Bowen, Stirling: excerpt from Announcement for Spring Concert Tour, Tuskegee Institute Choir, Apr–May 1936.

Brand, *The Ballad Mongers*.

Brant, Leroy V., "Delius in America," *The Etude*, LXVIII (Aug 1950).

Brawley, *The Negro in Literature and Art*.

Breman, Paul: comment on jazz made in personal interview.

Breman, Paul, *Spirituals*. The Hague, The Netherlands, N.V. Servire, 1958.

Brewer, J. Mason, *American Negro Folklore*. Chicago, Quadrangle Books, 1968.

Brewer, J. Mason, "South Carolina Negro Folklore Guild," *Journal of American Folklore*, LIX (Oct–Dec 1946).

Brister, Silas W., Sr., *The Negro Spiritualist Hymnal*. n.p., 1963.

Broun, Heywood on Roland Hayes: quoted from *Boston Globe* in "Hampton and Roland Hayes," *Southern Workman*, LIII (Feb 1924).

Brown, "Negro Folk Expression."

Brown, Sebastian H., *Eight Negro Spirituals*. London, Oxford University Press, 1963.

Brown, "Songs of the Slave."

Brown, Sterling, *Negro Poetry and Drama*. Washington, Associates in Negro Folk Education, 1937.

Brown, Sterling, "Roland Hayes," *Opportunity*, III (Jun 1925).

Brown, Sterling, *Southern Road*. New York, Harcourt, Brace and Co., 1932.

Brown, Sterling, Davis, Arthur P., Lee, Ulysses, *The Negro Caravan*. New York, The Dryden Press, 1941.

Buchanan, Annabel Morris, *American Folk Music*. Ithaca, New York, National Federation Publications, 1939.

Buhé, Klaus, *Deep River*. London, Schott & Co., Ltd., 1963.

Buhé, Klaus, *Spirituals and Folksongs*. London, Schott & Co., Ltd., 1964.

Burch, Charles Eaton, "The Plantation Negro in Dunbar's Poetry," *The Southern Workman*, L (May 1921).

Burleigh, Harry T., *Negro Minstrel Melodies*. New York, G. Schirmer, Inc., 1909.

Burlin, Natalie Curtis, "Hymn of Freedom," *Southern Workman*, XLVII (Oct 1918).

Burlin report on spirituals during World War I: "The Hymns in the Camps," *Southern Workman*, XLVII (Oct 1918).

Busch, Adolf Georg Wilhelm, *Seven Madrigals on Negro Spirituals*. New York, Independent Music Publishers, 1942.

Cambridge (England) *Express and Eastern Counties Weekly News*, Feb 14, 1874.

Cammin, Heinz, comp., *Spirituals and Songs*. Mainz, B. Schott's Sönne, 1969.

"Canning Negro Melodies," *The Literary Digest*, LII (May 27, 1916).

Carawan, Guy and Candie, *Ain't You Got a Right to the Tree of Life?* New York, Simon and Schuster, 1966.

Carawan, Guy and Candie, comps. and eds., *Freedom Is a Constant Struggle*. New York, Oak Publications, 1968.

Carawan, Guy and Candie, comps., *We Shall Overcome!* New York, Oak Publications, 1963.

Carmer, Carl, *America Sings*. New York, Alfred A. Knopf, 1942.

Carmichael, Waverley Turner, *From the Heart of a Folk*. Boston, The Cornhill Co., 1918.

Carnes, Frederick G., *Kentucky Jubilee Singers' Scottische*. San Francisco, L. Budd Rosenberg Music Publishing House, 1889.

Catalogue of Canadian Composers, ed. Kallman, Helmut. Toronto, Canadian Broadcasting Corp., 1952.

Cavalcade of the American Negro. Prepared by Workers of the Writers' Program of the Work Projects Administration in the State of Illinois. Chicago, Diamond Jubilee Exposition Authority, 1940.

Chambers, *The Treasury of Negro Spirituals*.

(Chambers, William) W.C., "The Jubilee Singers," *Chambers's Journal of Popular Literature, Science, and Art* (Edinburgh), LV (Jan 12, 1878).

Chauvet, Stephen, *Musique Nègre*. Paris, Société d'Éditions Géographiques, Maritimes et Coloniales, 1929.

Cheatham, Frederic C., *Twelve Negro Spirituals*. Richmond, Radio Station WRVA, 1932.

Chirgwin, "The Vogue of the Negro Spiritual."

Chotzinoff, Samuel, "Jazz: A Brief History," *Vanity Fair*, XX (Jun 1923).

Cincinnati reviewer (p. 415): *Cincinnati Daily Gazette*, Oct 9, 1871.

Cincinnati reviewer (p. 415): *Cincinnati Daily Gazette*, Oct 18, 1871.

Clark, Rogie, *Copper Sun*. Bryn Mawr, Theodore Presser Co., 1957. Includes Trinidadian folk songs.

Cleaveland, Bessie, "Music in Public Schools," *Southern Workman*, XXX (Apr 1901).

Clemens, Samuel Langhorne (Mark Twain), letter on behalf of Jubilee Singers: see Pike, Gustavus D., *The Singing Campaign for Ten Thousand Pounds; or, the Jubilee Singers in Great Britain*. New York, American Missionary Association, 1875.

Clemens, Samuel Langhorne (Mark Twain), *Mark Twain's Letters*. New York, Harper & Brothers, 1917. Volume II.

Coleridge-Taylor, Samuel, *Twenty-Four Negro Melodies Transcribed for the Piano*. Boston, Oliver Ditson Company, 1905.

Comettant, Oscar, *Trois Ans Aux États-Unis*. Paris, Pagnerre Libraire-Éditeur, 1857.

Comettant, Oscar, *Voyage Pittoresque et Anecdotique Dans Le Nord et Le Sud Des États-Unis D'Amérique*. Paris, A. Laplace, 1866.

Connelly, Marc, *Little David*. New York, Dramatists Play Service, 1937.

Connelly, Marc, *The Green Pastures*. New York, Farrar & Rinehart, Inc., 1929.

Connelly, Marc, *Voices Offstage: A Book of Memoirs*. Chicago, Holt, Rinehart & Winston, Inc., 1968.

Connor, Edric, coll. & ed., *Songs from Trinidad*. London, Oxford University Press, 1958.

Cooke, Charles L., arr., *Robbins Choral Collection—Negro Spirituals*. New York, Robbins Music Corporation, 1942.

Coons, C., *As America Sang*. Chicago, Rubank, Inc., 1942.

Cooper, *The African Pilgrim's Hymns*.

Copans, Simon J., "Let My People Go," *Les Langues Modernes* (Association des Professeurs de Langues Vivantes de L'Enseignment Public). Paris, n.d.

Copans, Simon J.: personal letters and reports.

Cord, Michael, *Spirituals in Slow and March*. Cologne, Edition Melodia Hans Gerig, 1961.

Cord, Michael, *Spirituals in Swing*. Cologne, Edition Melodia Hans Gerig, 1961.

Crite, Allan Rohan, *Three Spirituals from Earth to Heaven*. Cambridge, Harvard University Press, 1948.

Crite, Allan Rohan, *Were You There When They Crucified My Lord*. Cambridge, Harvard University Press, 1944.

Crite: review of *Three Spirituals from Earth to Heaven*, *New York Herald Tribune*, Jan 16, 1949.

Cushing, Helen Grant, comp., *Children's Song Index*. New York, H. W. Wilson Co., 1936.

Cuthbert, Marion, *We Sing America*. New York, Friendship Press, 1936.

D'Almbert, Alfred, *Flanerie Parisienne Aux États-Unis*. Paris, Librairie Théatrale, 1856.

Dann, Hollis, ed., *Fifty-Eight Spirituals for Choral Use*. Boston, C. C. Birchard & Co., 1924.

Dauer, Alfons M., *Der Jazz*. Kassel, Im Erich Röth-Verlag, 1958.

Dauer, Alfons M., *Jazz: Der Magische Musik*. Bremen, Carl Schünemann Verlag, 1961.

Davis, Albert Oliver, *Spirituals on Parade* (arr. for march). Cleveland, Ludwig Music Publishing Co., 1952.

Davis, Rev. Gary, *The Holy Blues*. New York, Robbins Music Corporation and Chandos Music Company, 1970.

Davye, John J., *Spirituals, for orchestra*. n.p., 1957.

Dawson, William L., "Interpretation of the Religious Folk-Songs of the American Negro," *The Etude*, LXXIII (Mar 1955).

Dawson, William L., *Negro Folk Symphony*. Delaware Water Gap, Pa., Shawnee Press, 1965.

Dawson, William L.: personal interview.

De Cormier, Robert and McKayle, Donald, *They Called Her Moses*. New York, Lawson-Gould Music Publishers, 1969.

Defries, Amelia, *The Fortunate Islands*. London, Cecil Palmer, 1929.

Delius, Clare, *Frederick Delius*. London, Ivor Nicholson & Watson, 1935.

Delius, Frederick, *Appalachia: Variations on an Old Slave Song with Final Chorus*. London, Boosey and Hawkes, 1927.

Delius: Kruse, Paul, "Florida in the Life and Works of Frederick Delius." Paper read before the Jacksonville Historical Society. Jacksonville, The Society, 1942.

Dennison, Tim, Sr., *The American Negro and His Amazing Music*. New York, Vantage, 1963.

Dett, R. Nathaniel, "As the Negro School Sings," *Southern Workman*, LVI (Jul 1927).

Dett, R. Nathaniel, "Ethnologist Aids Composer to Draw Inspiration from Heart of People," *Musical America*, XXX (May 31, 1919).

Dett, R. Nathaniel, "Negro Music of the Present," *Southern Workman*, XLVII (May 1918).

De Turk, David A. and Poulin, A., Jr., *The American Folk Scene*. New York, Dell Publishing Co., 1967. (Contains articles by Pete Seeger, Kenneth Keating, and Robert Sherman.)

Deutsch, Leonhard, coll. and arr., *A Treasury of the World's Finest Folk Song*. New York, Crown Publishers, Inc., 1942, 1967.

Diton, Carl, "The Struggle of the Negro Musician," *The Etude*, XLVIII (Feb 1930).

Dixon, Christa, *Wesen und Wandel Geistlicher Volkslieder Negro Spirituals*. Wuppertal (Germany), Jugenddeinst-Verlag, 1967.

Dooley, Mrs. James H., *Dem Good Old Times*. New York, Doubleday, Page & Co., 1906.

Dorson, Richard M., *American Folklore*. Chicago, University of Chicago Press, 1959.

Dorůžka, Lubomír, *Hudba Amerických Černochů* (The music of the American Negro). Prague, Ustřední Dúm Lidové Tvořivosti, 1958.

Douglass, *My Bondage and My Freedom*.

Dowdey, Landon Gerald, *Journey to Freedom*. Chicago, The Swallow Press, Inc., 1969.

Downes, Olin, *Olin Downes on Music*. New York, Simon and Schuster, 1957.

Drake, St. Clair and Cayton, Horace, *Black Metropolis*. New York, Harper and Row, 1962.

Duarte, John W., comp., *Sing Negro Spirituals* (guitar accompaniments). New York, Associated Music Publishers, 1968.

Duberman, Martin B., *In White America*. Boston, Houghton Mifflin Co., 1964.

Du Bois, *The Souls of Black Folk*.

Dunbar, Paul Laurence, *The Complete Poems of Paul Laurence Dunbar*. New York, Dodd, Mead and Co., 1920.

Duncan, Madam A. E., arr., *Happy Songster for Revivals, Churches and Sunday Schools*. Americus, Gammage Print Shop, n.d.

Duncan, Todd, "South African Songs and Negro Spirituals," *The Music Journal*, VIII (May–Jun 1950).

Dunson, Josh, *Freedom in the Air*. New York, International Publishers, 1965.

Dvořák, Antonín, *Sinfonia IX Mi Minore*. Prague, Artia, 1954.

Edinburgh Courant (re Fisk Jubilee Singers): Oct 15, 1873.

Ehret, Walter and Gardner, Maurice, *Three in Song*. Great Neck, N.Y., Staff Music Publishing Co., 1958.

Elliott, Delwyn, arr., *Three Spirituals, for orchestra*. Berkeley, Cal., Wynn Music, 1963.

Engel, Carl, "Views and Reviews," *The Musical Quarterly*, XII (Apr 1926).

English reviewer (p. 413): *The Birmingham Daily Mail*, Apr 10, 1874.

One Englishman (p. 413): *The Daily Post* (Liverpool), Jan 16, 1874.

Ewen, David, *Panorama of American Popular Music*. Englewood Cliffs, N.J., Prentice-Hall, Inc., 1957.

Eyma, Louis Xavier, *Les Peaux Noires*. Paris, Michel Levy Frères, 1857.

Farwell, Arthur, *Folk-Songs of the West and South*. Newton Centre, Mass., The Wa-Wan Press, 1905.

Faulkner, William, *Go Down, Moses and Other Stories*. New York, Random House, 1942.

Fenner: referred to in Booker T. Washington's Introduction to Samuel Coleridge-Taylor's *Twenty-Four Negro Melodies Transcribed for the Piano*. (q.v.)

Ferrero, Felica, "La Musica dei Negri Americani," *Rivista Musicale Italiana*, XIII (1906).

Fisher, *Negro Slave Songs in the United States*.

Fisher, William Arms, *Goin' Home*. Boston, Oliver Ditson Co., 1922.

Fisher, " 'Swing Low, Sweet Chariot': The Romance of a Famous Spiritual."

Fisk Jubilee Singers in London, 1873: except where specific sources are quoted, details of this trip have been assembled from clippings, programs, scrapbooks, notes, testimonials, and dozens of other relics in the G. D. Pike Envelope in the special Jubilee collection of Fisk University. Most of the clippings are dated in the spring and summer of 1873.

Fisk Jubilee Singers in London, 1873—newspaper accounts:
"Coloured Jubilee Singers at Willis's Rooms," *The Daily News*, May 7, 1873;
"Emancipated Slaves," *The Globe*, May 7, 1873;

"The Jubilee Singers," *The Daily Telegraph,* May 8, 1873;

"The Jubilee Singers," *The Standard,* May 7, 1873;

"The Jubilee Singers," *The Times,* May 7, 1873;

"Our Representative Man: After a Visit to the Jubilee Singers and La Fille de Madame Angot, he reports to the Editor," *Punch, or the London Charivari,* LXIV (June 7, 1873).

"The Fisk Jubilee Singers" (letter to Editor of the *New York Times* by Eva Gauthier), the *New York Times,* Nov 1, 1925.

Fonollosa, J. M., and Papo, Alfreda, *Breve Antologia de Los Cantos Spirituals Negros.* Barcelona (Spain), Cobalto, 1951.

Ford, Ernest J., *Book of Favorite Hymns.* Englewood Cliffs, N.J., Prentice-Hall, Inc., 1962.

Forrai, Miklos, ed., *Zúgj Hullám* (Deep River). Budapest, Zenemükiadó Vállalat, 1965.

Foster, Stephen C., *Twenty Songs,* ed. by N. Clifford Page. Boston, Oliver Ditson, 1906.

Foulds, John, *Fantasie of Negro Spirituals.* London, Bosworth and Co., Ltd., 1932.

Franklin-Pike, Eleanor, comp. and arr., *The Easiest Tune Book of Negro Spirituals, and American Plantation Songs.* London, E. Ashdown, 1966.

Friedel, Father L. M., *The Bible and the Negro Spirituals.* Bay St. Louis, Miss., n.p., 1947.

Friedman, Perry, coll., *Hör zu, Mister Bilbo.* Berlin, Rütten & Loenig, 1964 (?).

Fürster, Wolfgang, *Spirituals: Geistliche Negerlieder.* n.p., n.d.

Gaither, Frances, *Follow the Drinking Gourd.* New York, The Macmillan Co., 1940.

Garbet, A., "The Musical Scrapbook," *The Etude,* XLII (Oct 1924).

Gardner, Maurice, comp. and arr., *Tunes for Three or Four.* Great Neck, N.Y., Staff Music Publishing Co., 1964.

Gardner, Maurice, arr., *Tunes for Two or Three.* Great Neck, N.Y., Staff Music Publishing Co., 1961.

Garland, *The Sound of Soul.*

Garnett, Louise Ayres, "Spirituals," *Outlook,* CXXX (Apr 12, 1922).

Garnett, Thomas: thesis written at School of Religion, Howard University, 1937.

Gaul, "Negro Spirituals."

Gellert, Lawrence, coll., *Negro Songs of Protest.* New York, American Music League, 1936.

Gellert, Lawrence, "Negro Songs of Protest in America," *Music Vanguard,* I (Mar–Apr 1935).

Gershwin, George, *Porgy and Bess.* New York, Gershwin Publishing Corp., 1958.

Gilbert, Will G., and Poustochkine, C., *Jazzmuziek.* The Hague, Kruseman, 1952.

Gillis, Frank, and Merriam, Alan P., *Ethnomusicology and Folk Music.* Middletown, Conn., Wesleyan University Press, 1966.

Gladstone, William Ewart, Prime Minister of England: quoted in Chambers, William, "The Jubilee Singers" (q.v.)

Glassie, Henry, *Pattern in the Material: Folk Culture of the Eastern United States*. Philadelphia, University of Pennsylvania Press, 1968.

Goldberg, Isaac, *George Gershwin*. New York, Simon and Schuster, 1931.

Goldberg, Isaac, *Tin Pan Alley*. New York, Frederick Ungar Publishing Co., 1930, 1961.

Goldstein, "The Natural Harmonic and Rhythmic Sense of the Negro."

Gonda, János, *Jazz*. Budapest, Zenemükiadó, 1965.

Gonzáles de la Peña, Antonio, *Report*. American Embassy, Madrid, Spain. (mimeograph copy) (Concerns William L. Dawson.)

Gordon, Philip, "America in American Music," *Common Ground*, VII (1947).

Gordon, Robert Winslow, *Folk-Songs of America*. New York, National Service Bureau, 1938.

Gorochow, Victor, *Ich Singe Amerika* (Ein Lebensbild Paul Robesons). Berlin, Verlag Neues Leben, 1955.

Grafman, Howard and Manning, B. T., *Folk Music USA*. New York, The Citadel Press, 1962.

Graham, Alice, "Original Plantation Melodies as One Rarely Hears Them," *The Etude*, XL (Nov 1922).

Green, Paul, *The Field God, and In Abraham's Bosom*. New York, R. M. McBride & Co., 1927.

Greenway, *American Folksongs of Protest*.

Grissom, Mary Allen, *The Negro Sings a New Heaven*. Chapel Hill, The University of North Carolina Press, 1930.

Gruenberg, Louis, *Negro Spirituals*. Vienna, Universal-Edition A. G., 1926.

Guion, David, *Five Imaginary Early Louisiana Songs of Slavery*. New York, G. Schirmer, Inc., 1929.

Guthrie, Woody, *American Folksong*. New York, Oak Publications, 1961.

Guy, William E., *The Message of the Negro Spiritual*. St. Paul, The Williamson Press, 1946.

Hadler, Rosemary, comp., *The Junior Anthem Book of Spirituals*. Dayton, O., Lorenz Publishing Co., 1969.

Hallowell, Emily, coll. and ed., *Calhoun Plantation Songs*. Boston, C. W. Thompson & Co., 1901. Also *Supplement to Calhoun Plantation Songs* ... 1905.

Hampton—"brave little band of singers": "The Hampton Singers and Endowments," *Southern Workman*, IV (Apr 1875).

Hampton Negro Conference, No. 3, Jul 1899: "Music, Literature, and the Drama."

Hampton Singers (original group): From its first issue—in January, 1872—*The Southern Workman* carried monthly accounts of the preparations, travels, and experiences of these singers. The visits of the singers to the home of Longfellow and to the grave of Sumner are told in Vol. III (Sep 1874).

Hancock, Eugene W., *An Organ Book of Spirituals*. Dayton, O., Lorenz Publishing Co., 1966.

Hansen, Kurt Heinrich, "Spirituals auf Deutsch." Notes to accompany recorded spirituals by Lawrence Winters. Typewritten manuscript.

Harap, Louis, "The Case for Hot Jazz," in De Toledano, Ralph, *Frontiers of Jazz*. New York, Oliver Durrell, Inc., 1947.

Harman, Alec, Milner, Anthony, and Mellers, Wilfrid, *Man and His Music: The Story of Musical Experience in the West.* New York, Oxford University Press, 1962.

Harz, Fred, *Negro Spirituals, für Gitarre.* Cologne, Hans Gerig, 1962.

Haslam, "Black and Unknown Bards."

Haslam, Gerald W., "Two Traditions in Afro-American Literature," *Research Studies,* XXXVII (Sep 1969). (Note on gospel song.)

Hattey, Philip, arr., *Three Spirituals.* London, Oxford University Press, 1962.

Haverhill (Conn.) *Bulletin* on Hampton Singers: quoted in *Southern Workman,* II (Jun 1873).

Hawkins, Floyd W., *Hallelujah; Unique Gospel Songs and Spirituals.* Kansas City, Mo., Lillenas Publishing Co., 1958.

Hayakawa, S. I., "35th and State: Reflections on the History of Jazz." Pamphlet based on lecture in Poetry Magazine Modern Arts Series, Mar 17, 1945, Arts Club, Chicago.

Hayes, *My Songs.*

Hayes, Roland

    For Deems Taylor quotation: *The World* (New York), Nov 29, 1924.

    Brawley, Benjamin, *The Negro Genius.* New York, Dodd, Mead & Co., Inc., 1937.

    Helm, MacKinley, *Angel Mo' and Her Son, Roland Hayes.* Boston, Little, Brown and Co., 1945.

    Henderson, W. J., "The Rise of Roland Hayes," *The Mentor,* XIV (May 1926).

    "A Negro Artist in Song," *The Literary Digest,* LXXX (Jan 5, 1924).

    "A Performer of Vocal Miracles," *Current Opinion,* LXXVI (Apr 1924).

    "A Son of Slaves Who Sings to Kings," *The Literary Digest,* LXXXVI (Jul 25, 1925).

    Straus, Henrietta, "Music: Roland Hayes," *The Nation,* CXVII (Dec 19, 1923).

    See also *Olin Downes on Music.*

Heaps, Willard, and Porter, W., *The Singing Sixties.* Norman, University of Oklahoma Press, 1960.

Hearn, Lafcadio, *Children of the Levee,* ed. by O. W. Frost. Lexington, The University of Kentucky Press, 1957.

Hefmann, Frederick, *Amerika Singt.* Frankfurt am Main, Europäische Verlagsanstalt, 1966.

Heintzen, Erich H., *Were You There?* St. Louis, Concordia Publishing House, 1958.

Hellström, Jan Arvid, *En Ny Sång.* Stockholm (Sweden), A-B Tryckmans, 1969.

Hengeveld, Gerard, arr., *20 American Songs and Negro Spirituals.* Amsterdam, Uitgave Broekmans en Van Poppel, n.d.

Mellinger Henry's *Bibliography* was published in London, n.d.

"Heritage: U.S.A.," *Sing Out!* II (Dec 1951).

Herzog, George, "African Influences in North American Indian Music," *Papers Read at the International Congress of Musicology* (held at New York, Sep 11–16, 1939).

Heyward, Dorothy, *Set My People Free*. Master copy—manuscript.

Heyward, Du Bose, *Mamba's Daughters* (novel). Garden City, N.Y., Doubleday, Doran & Co., 1929.

Heyward, Du Bose, *Porgy* (novel). New York, George H. Doran, 1925.

Heyward, Dorothy and Du Bose, *Mamba's Daughters* (play). New York, Farrar and Rinehart, 1939.

Heyward, Dorothy and Du Bose, *Porgy, a play in four acts*. Garden City, N.Y., Doubleday, Doran & Co., 1928.

Higginson, "Negro Spirituals."

Hilarion, Sister Mary, "The Negro Spiritual."

Hoffman, "The Folk Art of Jazz."

Hofmann, Charles, *American Indians Sing*. New York, The John Day Co., 1967.

Holliday, Carl, *Three Centuries of Southern Poetry, 1607–1907*. Nashville, Publishing House of the M. E. Church South, 1908.

Howard, John Tasker, *Stephen Foster, America's Troubadour*. New York, Thomas Y. Crowell Co., 1953. (Contains quotations from Morrison Foster, son of Stephen, and from Morrison Foster's *Biography, Songs and Musical Compositions of Stephen C. Foster*.)

Howard University Latin American Tour, 1960: "Latin American Relations Get Boost from Triumphant Tour by Howard Choir," *The Howard University Magazine*, III (Jan 1961); Logan, Rayford W., *Howard University: The First Hundred Years, 1867–1967*. New York, New York University Press, 1969.

Howard University student rebellion, 1909:

"Balk at Folk Songs: Howard University Students Threaten to Revolt," *The Washington Post*, Dec 19, 1909;

"Comment at Howard: Sentiment Divided on Subject of Negro Folk Songs," *The Washington Post*, Dec 20, 1909;

"A Just Rebellion" (editorial), *The Sun* (New York), Dec 21, 1909;

Locke, B. H., "Folk Songs at Howard," *Howard University Journal*, Dec 17, 1909;

Miller, Kelly, "The Spirit of Howard University," (letter to the editor), *The Sun* (New York), Dec 24, 1909.

Hubbard, ed., *History of American Music*.

Hudson, Arthur Palmer, "The Singing South," *The Sewanee Review*, XLIV (Jul–Sep 1936).

Hughes, Langston, "Gospel Singing: When the Spirit Really Moves," *New York: The Sunday Herald Tribune Magazine*, Oct 27, 1963.

Hughes, Langston, *Tambourines to Glory*. In Hughes, *Five Plays*. Bloomington, Indiana University Press, 1963.

Hunt, Arthur Billings, arr. and comp., *Southland Spirituals and Jubilees*. Wheaton, Ill., Van Kampen Press, 1951.

Hurston, Zora Neale, "Spirituals and Neo-Spirituals," in Cunard, *Negro Anthology*.

The Hymn Book of the African Methodist Episcopal Church. Philadelphia, Publication Department of the A. M. E. Church, 1873.

Isaacs, Edith J. R., *The Negro in the American Theatre*. New York, Theatre Arts, Inc., 1947.

Jackson, George Pullen, "Stephen Foster's Debt to American Folk-Song," *The Musical Quarterly*, XXII (Apr 1936).

Jackson, Mahalia (with Evan McLeod Wylie), *Movin' On Up*. New York, Hawthorn Books, Inc., 1966.

Jackson, Mahalia: for special note on Newport (p. 453), see Blesh *et al., O Susanna.*

Jahn, Janheinz, *The Black Experience: 400 Years of Black Literature from Africa and the Americas*. Nendeln, Liechtenstein, Kraus Reprint, 1969.

Jahn, Janheinz, *Muntu*. London, Faber and Faber, 1961.

Jahn, Janheinz, *Neo-African Literature*. New York, Grove Press, Inc., 1968.

Jahn, Janheinz, *Negro Spirituals*. Frankfurt am Main, Fischer Bücherei, 1962.

Jeffers, Lance, "On Listening to Spirituals," in Chapman, Abraham, ed., *Black Voices*. New York and Toronto, The New American Library, 1968.

Jekyll, Walter, *Jamaican Song and Story*. London, for the Folklore Society by David Nutt, 1907; New York, Dover Publications, Inc., 1966.

Johnson, David N., comp. and arr., *Twelve Folksongs and Spirituals* (for voices, flute, and guitar accompaniment). Minneapolis, Augsburg Publishing House, 1968.

Johnson, *God's Trombones*.

Johnson, Hall, note on: see Arvey and Still.

Johnson, James P., *Yamekraw*. New York, Perry Bradford, Inc., 1927.

(Johnson, James Weldon) Anon., *The Autobiography of an Ex-Colored Man*. Boston, Sherman, French & Co., 1912.

Johnson, James Weldon, *The Autobiography of an Ex-Coloured Man*. New York, Alfred A. Knopf, 1928.

Johnson, James Weldon, *The Book of American Negro Poetry*. New York, Harcourt, Brace and Co., 1922, 1931.

Johnson, James Weldon, "Race Prejudice and the Negro Artist," *Harper's Magazine*, CLVII (Nov 1928).

Johnson, James Weldon, and Johnson, J. Rosamund, *The Books of American Negro Spirituals*. New York, The Viking Press, 1925, 1926, 1940.

Johnson, J. Rosamund, *Rolling Along in Song*. New York, The Viking Press, 1937.

Johnson, J. Rosamund, *Sixteen Negro Spirituals*. New York, Handy Brothers Music Co., Inc., 1939.

Jolas, Eugène, *Le Nègre Qui Chante*. Paris, Cahiers Libres, 1928.

Jones, LeRoi, *Black Music*. New York, William Morrow and Co., 1967.

Jones, LeRoi, *Blues People*. New York, William Morrow and Co., 1963.

Jones, LeRoi, "The Myth of a Negro Literature," in *Home: Social Essays*. London, MacGibbon & Kee, Ltd., 1968.

Jones, Solomon, and Tanner, Paul, "Afro-American Music: Black Moans," *Music Journal*, XXVIII (Mar 1970).

"The Jubilee Singers," *Illustrated Christian Weekly*, II (May 4, 1872).

"The 'Jubilee Singers,'" *New-York Daily Tribune*, Dec 28, 1871.

"The Jubilee Singers," *The World: New York*, Dec 29, 1871.

"The Jubilee Singers of America at Castle Wemyss," *Glasgow* (Scotland) *Herald*, Aug 18, 1873.

Katz, Bernard, ed., *The Social Implications of Early Negro Music in the United States*. New York, Arno Press and the *New York Times*, 1969.

Kaufmann, Otto, arr., *Sieben Spirituals.* Wolfenbüttel, Möseler Verlag, 1963.

Keating, Kenneth B., "Mine Enemy, The Folksinger," *Sing Out!* XIII (Dec 1963–Jan 1964). Reprinted in De Turk and Poulin, eds., *The American Folk Scene.*

Kendall, Ben, arr., *34 Spirituals* (for . . . organs). New York, Charling Music Corp., 1963.

Kenny, *The Negro Spiritual and Other Essays.*

Kerby, Marion, "A Warning Against Over-Refinement of the Negro Spiritual," *The Musician,* XXXIII (Jul 1928).

Kerlin, *Negro Poets and Their Poems.*

Kernan, Michael, "Glazer's Songs Still Work for Labor," *The Washington Post,* May 1, 1970.

Killens, John O., *Youngblood.* New York, The Dial Press, Inc., 1954.

King, Martin Luther, Jr., *Strength to Love.* New York, Harper and Row, 1963.

Kinscella, Hazel Gertrude, *History Sings.* Lincoln, The University Publishing Co., 1948.

Knesebeck, Paridam von dem, *Schwarzer Gesang I: Spirituals English-Deutsch.* Munich, Nymphenburger Verlagshandlung, 1961.

Koch, Frederick H., "A Gullah Negro Drama," *The Southern Literary Messenger,* II (Apr 1940).

Konen, V., *Puti Amerikanskoi Muzyki.* Moscow, Soviet Union, Musika, 1965.

Koster, Ernst, *Kleine Schwarze Passion.* Mainz, B. Schott's Söhne, 1958.

Kožnar, Zbyněk, *Černošské Spritualy.* Praha, Státní Hudební Vydavatelství, 1961.

Krone, Beatrice and Max, *Descants and Easy Basses* (1950); *From Descants to Trios* (1944); *Great Songs of Faith* (1944); *Intermediate Descants* (1954); *More Descants & Easy Basses* (1951): all published Chicago, Neil A. Kjos.

Krupp, Karlheinz, comp., *Down By the Riverside.* Mainz, B. Schott's Söhne, 1969.

Lambert, Constant, *Music Ho!* London, Faber, 1934.

Landeck, Beatrice, comp. and ed., *"Git on Board."* New York, Edward B. Marks Music Corp., 1944.

Landeck, Beatrice, *Songs to Grow On.* New York, Edward B. Marks Music Corp., 1950.

Laubenstein, Paul F., "An Apocalyptic Reincarnation," *Journal of Biblical Literature,* LI (1932).

Lawton, Mary for Leary, Katy, "A Lifetime with Mark Twain," *Pictorial Review,* XXVI (Apr, May, Jun, Jul, Aug, Sep 1925). Republished in Lawton, Mary, *A Lifetime with Mark Twain.* New York, Harcourt, Brace and Co., 1925.

Leavitt, Helen Sewall, Killduff, Helen Bonney, and Freeman, Warren S., *Adventures in Singing.* Boston, C. C. Birchard & Co., 1952, 1953.

Lederman, Minna, "Negro GI's Set War to Swing Tempo," *New York Times,* Mar 19, 1944.

Lehmann, *Negro Spirituals: Geschichte und Theologie.*

Lehmann, Theo, *Nobody Knows. . . .* Leipzig, Koehler & Amelang, 1961.

Leigh, Frances Butler, *Ten Years on a Georgia Plantation Since the War.* London, Richard Bentley & Son, 1883.

Leisy, James F., *Abingdon Song Kit.* Nashville, Abingdon Press, 1957.

Leisy, James F., *The Folk Song Abecedary*. New York, Hawthorn Books, Inc., 1966.

Leisy, James F., *Folk Song Fest*. New York, Sam Fox Publishing Co., Inc., 1964.

Leisy, James F., *Hootenanny Tonight!* Greenwich, Fawcett Publications, Inc., 1964.

Leisy, James F., *Let's All Sing*. Nashville, Abingdon Press, 1959.

Leisy, James F., *Songs for Pickin' and Singin'*. Greenwich, Fawcett Publications, Inc., 1962.

León, Argeliers, *Akorín; cantos negros para piano*. La Habana, Ediciones del Departamento de Música de la Biblioteca Nacional, J. Marti, 1962.

Let My People Go! (slave cycle) with Alex and Michel, produced at Town Hall, New York, Sep 28, 1958. Program.

Levy, Adolph, "Go Down, Moses," in Rowe, Kenneth Thorpe, ed., *University of Michigan Plays*. Ann Arbor, George Wahr, 1932.

Lewis, Kate Porter, *Alabama Folk Plays*. Chapel Hill, The University of North Carolina Press, 1943.

Ley, Margaret, *Spirituals: Ein Beitrag zur Analyse der religiösen Liedschöpfung bei den nordamerikanischen Negern*. Microfilm copy of doctoral dissertation from the University of Munich, Munich, Germany.

Leydi, Roberto, *La Musica dei Primitivi*. Milano, Il Saggiatore, 1961.

Lilje, Bishop Hans, Hansen, Kurt Heinrich, and Schmidt-Joos, Siegfried, *Das Buch der Spirituals und Gospel Songs*. Hamburg, Furche Verlag H. Rennebach KG, 1961.

Lindsay, Vachel, *The Congo and Other Poems*. New York, The Macmillan Co., 1914.

Lindsay, Vachel, "How Samson Bore Away the Gates of Gaza," *Poetry*, XI (Oct 1917).

Linton, W. J., *The Poetry of America*. London, George Bell & Sons, 1878.

A List of Negro Plays. New York, National Service Bureau, Federal Theatre Project, WPA, 1938.

Re Littleton, John: "Que pensez-vous des 'messes de jeunes,'" *Dimanche* (Brussels), Aug 24, 1969.

Liverpool reviewer (p. 413): *The Daily Post* (Liverpool, England), Jan 16, 1874.

Locke, Alain, "The Technical Study of the Spirituals—A Review," *Opportunity*, III (Nov 1925).

Locke, Alain, "Toward a Critique of Negro Music," *Opportunity*, XII (Nov and Dec 1934).

Locke, Alain, ed., *The New Negro: An Interpretation*. New York, Albert & Charles Boni, 1925.

Locke, "Negro Contributions to America."

Locke, "Spirituals."

Logan, Rayford, *The Negro in American Life and Thought: The Nadir 1877–1901*. New York, The Dial Press, Inc., 1954.

Logan, William A., "Song Gleanings Among the Cabins," *The Musician*, XLIV (Jul 1939).

Logan, William A., coll. and Garrett, Allen M., ed., *Road to Heaven*. University, University of Alabama Press, 1955.

Lomax, *Folk Song Style and Culture*.

Lomax, *The Rainbow Sign.*

Lomax, Alan, *Hard-Hitting Songs for Hard-Hit People.* New York, Oak Publications, 1967.

Lomax, Alan, "Folk Song Style," *American Anthropologist,* LXI (Dec 1959).

Lomax, Alan, *The Folk Songs of North America in the English Language.* London, Cassell and Co., Ltd., 1960.

Lomax, Alan, "The Good and the Beautiful in Folksong," *Journal of American Folklore,* LXXX (Jul–Sep 1967).

Lomax, Alan, comp., *The Penguin Book of American Folk Songs.* London, Lowe & Brydone, Ltd., 1964.

Lomax, Alan, and Jakobsonova, Svatara, *Freedom Songs of the United Nations.* Washington, D.C., 1943. (Bound typescript.)

Lomax, John A., *Adventures of a Ballad Hunter.* New York, The Macmillan Co., 1947.

Lomax, John A., *Negro Folk Songs as Sung by Leadbelly.* . . . New York, The Macmillan Co., 1936.

Lomax, John A. and Alan, *American Ballads and Folk Songs.* New York, The Macmillan Co., 1934.

Look Away; 56 Negro Folk Songs. Delaware, O., Cooperative Recreation Service, 1960.

Loudin Company Jubilee Singers at Taj Mahal: reported from *Delhi Gazette* by *Fisk Herald,* VII (Apr 1890).

Lovell, John, Jr., "Reflections on the Origins of the Negro Spiritual," *Negro American Literature Forum,* III (1969).

Lovell, John, Jr., "The Social Implications of the Negro Spiritual," *Journal of Negro Education,* VIII (Oct 1939).

Luboff, Norman, and Stracke, Win, comps., *Songs of Man.* Englewood Cliffs, N.J., Prentice-Hall, Inc., 1965.

Lueders, Edward, *Carl Van Vechten and the Twenties.* Albuquerque, University of New Mexico, 1955.

Luther, Frank, *Americans and Their Songs.* New York, Harper and Brothers, 1942.

Luthuli, Albert, *Let My People Go.* New York, McGraw-Hill Book Co., 1962.

Lyell, *A Second Visit to the United States of North America.*

Lynn, Frank, ed. (pseud. for Leisy, James F.), *Songs for Swinging Housemothers.* San Francisco, Fearon Publishers, 1961, 1963.

McDonald, William F., *Federal Relief Administration and the Arts.* Columbus, Ohio State University Press, 1969.

McLaughlin, Wayman B., "Symbolism and Mysticism in the Spirituals," *Phylon,* XXIV (1963).

McManus, Rev. Frederick, "Spirituals Studied for Catholic Rites," *Detroit Free Press,* Oct 25, 1962.

Macon, J. A., *Uncle Gabe Tucker.* Philadelphia, J. B. Lippincott Co., 1883.

Malet, *An Errand to the South in the Summer of 1862.*

Malone, Bill C., *Country Music U.S.A.* Austin, University of Texas Press, 1968.

Marsh, J. B. T., *The Story of the Jubilee Singers; with their songs.* London, Hodder and Stoughton, 1877. Also *The Story of the Jubilee Singers Including Their Songs.* London, Hodder and Stoughton, 1903.

Mattfeld, Julius, comp., *The Folk Music of the Western Hemisphere*. New York, New York Public Library, 1925.

Mays, Benjamin Elijah, and Nicholson, Joseph William, *The Negro's Church*. New York, Russell and Russell, 1933.

Mbathi, Mrs. Cathy: personal interview in Nairobi.

Meier, August, *Negro Thought in America, 1880–1915*. Ann Arbor, The University of Michigan Press, 1963.

Mencken's note on sale of Reverend Pike's editions of jubilee songs: Mencken, "Negroes' Contribution to Music Condensed in a Book of Spirituals."

Mencken's "Songs of the American Negro" and his "Negroes' Contributions to Music Condensed in a Book of Spirituals" contain the core of his ideas on the spirituals.

Mignone, Francisco, *Canto de Negros*. New York, Edward B. Marks Music Corp., 1943.

Miles, Emma Bell, "Some Real American Music," *Harper's Monthly Magazine*, CIX (Jun 1904).

Milkey, Edward Talbert, *34 Spirituals*. New York, Mayfair Music Corp., 1961.

Miller, "The Artistic Gifts of the Negro."

Mitchell, *Gone with the Wind*.

Mitchell, Loften, *A Land Beyond the River*. Cody, Wyo., Pioneer Drama Service, 1963.

Mize, J. T. H., ed., *Who Is Who in Music*. Chicago, Who is Who in Music, Inc., Ltd., 1951.

Moreland, John Richard, "Doomsday," *The Catholic World*, CXXX (Jan 1930).

Moreland, John Richard, "De Promise Lan'," *The Catholic World*, CXXXIII (Jul 1931).

Morris, Homer *et al.*, *Jubilee Songs*. Dallas, Stamps-Baxter Music & Print Co., 1945.

Morton, A. L., *Language of Men*. London, Cobbett Press, 1945.

Moton, Robert R. (p. 415), "Negro Folk Music," *Southern Workman*, XLIV (Jun 1915).

Murphy, "Black Music."

Murphy, "Survival of African Music in America."

Murray, Chalmers S., *Here Come Joe Mungin*. New York, G. P. Putnam's Sons, 1942.

Murray, Charlotte W., "The Story of Harry T. Burleigh," *The Hymn*, XVII (Oct 1966).

Report of Music School Settlement for Colored People: Martin, David I., "The Attitude of the Negro Toward the Folk Song of His Race." New York, 1913.

Nathan, Hans, *Dan Emmett and the Rise of Negro Minstrelsy*. Norman, University of Oklahoma Press, 1962.

"A Negro Spiritual Contest in Columbus (Georgia)," *The Playground*, XX (Apr 1926).

"Negro Spirituals in France," *Southern Workman*, XLVII (Nov 1918).

Negro Spirituals (for song, piano & guitar). London, Southern Music Publishing Co., 1963.

Negro-spirituals; seleccionats per l'equip Telstar-33. Barcelona, Hogar del libro, 1967.

Nevin, Mark, arr., *Sacred Songs and Spirituals for the Young Pianist*. New York, B. F. Wood Music Co., 1965.

Newton, Ernest, *Twelve Negro Spiritual Songs*. London, F. Pitman Hart & Co., Ltd., 1925.

One New York reviewer (p. 415): Cuyler of the *New York Tribune* quoted by R. Nathaniel Dett in "The Emancipation of Negro Music," *Southern Workman*, XLVII (Apr 1918).

New York Weekly Review on Hampton Singers: quoted in *Southern Workman*, II (May 1873).

Niles, John J., *Impressions of a Negro Camp Meeting*. Boston, Carl Fischer, Inc., 1925.

Niles, John J., coll. and arr., *Seven Negro Exaltations*. New York, G. Schirmer, 1929.

Niles, John J., "Shout, Coon, Shout," *The Musical Quarterly*, XVI (Oct 1930).

Noble, Peter, *The Negro in Films*. London, Skelton Robinson, 1948.

Norman, Alma, *Ballads of Jamaica*. London, Longmans, Green and Co., Ltd., 1967.

(O'Donnell), Eva Hesse and Knesebeck, Paridam von dem, *Meine dunklen Hände*. Munich, Nymphenburger Verlagshandlung, 1953.

Okun, Milton, *The Personal Choices of America's Folk Singers*. New York, The Macmillan Co., 1968.

Oliver, Paul, *Blues Fell This Morning*. London, Cassell & Co., Ltd., 1960.

Oliver, *The Story of the Blues*.

One Hundred and One Gospel and Spiritual Songs. New York, General Music Publishing Co., 1963.

Ortiz, Adalberto, *Tierra, son y tambor; cantares negros y mulatos*. México, D. F., Ediciones La Cigarra, 1945.

O'Sheel, Sheamas, "Two Spirituals," *The Commonweal*, IX (Feb 27, 1929).

Otterström, Thorvald, *Songs of the American Negro* (harmonized and arranged for mixed chorus). Milwaukee, n.p., 1943.

Page, N. Clifford, "Stephen C. Foster," (introductory note) in Foster, Stephen C., *Twenty Songs*, ed. by N. Clifford Page. Boston, Oliver Ditson, 1906.

Petersen, Ralf, comp., *Spirituals for All* (mixed choir, piano, guitar, bass). Mainz, B. Schott's Söhne, 1968.

Pike, Gustavus D., *The Jubilee Singers and Their Campaign for Twenty Thousand Dollars*. Boston, Lee and Shepard, 1873.

Pike, Gustavus D., *The Singing Campaign for Ten Thousand Pounds; or, The Jubilee Singers in Great Britain*.

Pitts, L. B., Glenn, M., Watters, L. E., Werson, L. G., *The Girls Book*. Boston, Ginn and Co., 1959.

Pohl, Frederic, *Chansons Sur Des Poemes Nègres*. Lyons, France, Éditions Beal, 1943.

Pool, Rosey E., *Beyond the Blues*. Lympne, Kent, England, The Hand & Flower Press, 1962.

Pool, Rosey E., *Ik Ben De Nieuwe Neger*. The Hague, The Netherlands, Bert Bakker, 1965.

Pool, Rosey E. and Breman, Paul, *Ik Zag Hoe Zwart Ik Was*. The Hague, The Netherlands, Bert Bakker, 1958.

Porter, Grave Cleveland, *Negro Folk Singing Games and Folk Games of the Habitants*. London, J. Curwen & Sons, 1914.

Portland, Maine reviewer (p. 413): *Portland Daily Advertiser*, Apr 23, 1872.

Poterat, Jacques, and Salabert, Francis, arrs., *Les Plus Célèbres Negro Spirituals*. Paris, Éditions Salabert, 1945, 1946.

Pravda review of Roland Hayes (1928): reprinted in Brawley, Benjamin, *The Negro Genius*. New York, Dodd, Mead & Co., Inc., 1937.

Price, Leontyne, evaluations and information:

> George, Collins, "Soprano Gives Flawless Recital," *Detroit Free Press*, Mar 15, 1960;
>
> Hume, Paul, "Versatile Artistry Displayed by Soprano Leontyne Price," *The Washington Post and Times Herald*, Apr 6, 1959;
>
> Mossman, Josef, "Top Artistry Shown by Leontyne Price," *Detroit News*, Mar 19, 1960;
>
> "A Voice Like a Banner Flying," *Time*, LXXVII (Mar 10, 1961); condensed in *Reader's Digest*, LXXVIII (Jun 1961).

Programme of Negro Poetry, "Black and Unknown Bards," produced by Gordon Heath at Royal Court Theatre, Oct 5, 1958. London, Press of Villiers Publications, Ltd., 1958.

Radzik, Marian, arr., *Ten Negro Spirituals, na fortepian*. Krakow, Polskie Wydawn, Muzyczne, 1960.

Ramsey, William, "Jester Hairston—Afro-American Ambassador," *Music Journal*, XXVIII (Oct 1970).

Randolph, Vance, ed., *Ozark Folksongs*. Columbia, State Historical Society of Missouri, 1948.

Randolph, Vance, *The Ozarks*. New York, The Vanguard Press, 1931.

Rapley, Felton, comp., *Negro Spirituals, for all organs*. London, Chappell, 1969.

Ratcliff, T. P., *News-Chronicle Song Book*. London, *News-Chronicle* Publications Dept., 1921.

Redding, J. Saunders, *No Day of Triumph*. New York, Harper & Brothers, 1942.

Reviewer on p. 413: "To one," *Cincinnati Daily Gazette*, Oct 9, 1871.

"A Ring Game from North Carolina: Granddaddy is Dead," in Coffin, Tristram P., and Cohen, Hennig, eds., *Folklore in America* (selections from the *Journal of American Folklore*). New York, Doubleday & Co., 1966.

Rivers, Clarence Joseph, *American Mass Program*. Cincinnati, World Library of Sacred Music, 1964.

Roberts, Helen H., "Possible Survivals of African Song in Jamaica," *The Musical Quarterly*, XII (Jul 1926).

Robinson, Earl, and Lampell, Millard, *The Lonesome Train* (a cantata). New York, Sun Music Co., 1945.

Rollins, Charlemae, *We Build Together*. Chicago, The National Council of Teachers of English, 1948.

Rookmaaker, H. R., *Jazz, Blues, Spirituals*. Leiden, The Netherlands, N. V. Gebr. Zomer & Keunings Uitgeversmaatschappij Wageningen, 1960.

Rookmaaker, H. R., "Let's Sing the Old Dr. Watts: A Chapter in the History of Negro Spirituals," *The Gordon Review*, IX (1966).

Rookmaaker: personal interview.

Rosenberg, Bruce A., *The Folksongs of Virginia*. Charlottesville, The University Press of Virginia, 1969.

Roth, Russell, reviewer, " 'Escapism' theory of Negro music wrong—it's stout poetry," *Minneapolis Star*, Feb 11, 1970.

Rourke, Constance, *The Roots of American Culture and Other Essays*. New York, Harcourt, Brace and Co., 1942.

Rudziński, Witold, *Negro Spirituals*. Krakow, Polskie Wydawn, Muzycne, 1961.

Ryder, C. J., *The Theology of the Plantation Songs*. New York, American Missionary Association, Bible House, 1891.

Saar, R. W., arr., *Twelve Negro Spirituals*. London, W. Paxton & Co., Ltd., 1927.

Saerchinger, César, "The Folk Element in American Music," in *The Art of Music*. New York, The National Society of Music, 1916.

Sallman, H., *De Gospel Ship* (Der Schiff der Frohen Botschaft). Bad-Godesberg, Voggenreiter Verlag, 1963.

Sandor, Frigyes, ed., *Musical Education in Hungary*. London, Boosey & Hawkes, 1969.

Sargent, Norman and Tom, "Negro-American Music or The Origin of Jazz," *The Musical Times* (London), LXXII (Jul, Aug, Sep 1931).

Sayers, W. C. Berwick, *Samuel Coleridge-Taylor, Musician*. London, Augener Ltd., 1927.

Scarborough, Dorothy, *Can't Get a Red Bird*. New York, Harper & Brothers, 1929.

(Scarborough, Dorothy) Anon., *The Wind*. New York, Harper & Brothers, 1925.

Schimmel, Johannes C., *Spirituals and Gospel Songs*. Berlin, Burckhardthaus, 1963.

Schönfelder, Karl-Heinz and Hucke, Ingeberg, *Schwarzer Bruder: Lyrik amerikanischer Neger*. Leipzig, Philipp Reclam, Jr., 1966.

Scott, John Anthony, *The Ballad of America*. New York, Bantam Books, Inc., 1966.

Seagle, "The Negro Spiritual."

Sebastian, John, "From Spirituals to Swing," *New Masses*, XX (Jan 3, 1939).

Seeger, Pete, *American Favorite Ballads*. New York, Oak Publications, 1961.

Seeger, Ruth, *American Folk Songs for Christmas*. Garden City, N.Y., Doubleday and Co., Inc., 1953.

Selma Jubilee Corps: reported in *Musical Courier*, LXXV (Aug 23, 1917).

Senghor, Léopold Sédar (President of Senegal), "La Poésie Négro-Américaine," in *Liberté I: Négritude et Humanisme*. Paris, Éditions du Seuil, 1964.

Serrand, A. Z., "Une Bible en Noir et Rouge," *La Vie Spirituelle*, No. 544 (Nov 1968).

Serrand, A. Z., *Hallelujah*. Paris, Les Éditions du Cerf, 1957.

Serrand, A. Z., *Spirituals*. Paris, Les Éditions du Cerf, n.d.

Seton, Marie, *Paul Robeson*. London, Dennis Dobson, 1958.

Shaftesbury, Earl of: speech reported in article entitled "The Jubilee Singers at Castle Wemyss," *Glasgow Herald*, Aug 18, 1873.

Shaver, Claude L., "Minstrel Show," *Encyclopaedia Britannica*. Chicago, Encyclopaedia Britannica, Inc., 1964.

Shaw, Arnold, *The World of Soul*. New York, Cowles Book Co., Inc., 1970.

Shaw, W. F., *Popular Songs and Ballads*. Burlington, Vt., n.p., 1882.

Shelton, Robert, and Gahr, David, *The Face of Folk Music*. New York, The Citadel Press, 1968.

(Moore) Sheppard, Ella (one of original Fisk Jubilee Singers), "Historical Sketch of the Jubilee Singers," *Fisk University News* (After Forty Years Number), II (Oct 1911).

Shepperd, Eli (pseud. for Martha Young), *Plantation Songs*. New York, R. H. Russell, 1931.

Sherwood, W. H., *Soothing Songs*. Kansas City, Kansas City Presse Print, 1891.

Shirley, Kay and Driggs, Frank, *The Book of the Blues*. New York, Crown Publishers, Inc., 1963.

Shostakovich, D., "Pesni gneva i bor'by," *Sovetskaja Muzyka*, VI (1953).

Silber, Irwin, comp. & ed., *Hootenanny Song Book*. New York, Consolidated Music Publishers, Inc., 1963.

Silverman, Robert, *Swingin' Spirituals*. New York, Edward B. Marks Music Corp., 1962.

Sloane, Sir Hans, *A Voyage to the Islands Madera, Barbados, Nieves, S. Christophers and Jamaica.* . . . London, published by the author, 1707.

Smith, Alfred Barnerd, *Favorite Spirituals*. Grand Rapids, Mich., Singspiration, Inc., 1961, 1963.

Smith, Charles Edward, "Folk Music, the Roots of Jazz," *The Saturday Review of Literature*, XXXIII (Jul 29, 1950).

Smith, "Folk-Songs of the American Negro."

Smith, "The Negro and the Ballad."

Smith, N. Clark, *Favorite Folk-Melodies*. Chicago, N. C. Smith, 1913.

Smith, N. Clark, *New Jubilee Songs for Quartette, Choir or Chorus, Concert, Church & Home*. Chicago, Jubilee Music Co., 1906.

Smith, N. Clark, *New Plantation Melodies*. Chicago, Smith Jubilee Music Co., 1906.

Smith, Peter, comp., *Faith, Folk & Clarity*. Norfolk, England, Galliard Ltd., 1969; New York, Galaxy Music Corp., 1969.

Snyder, Jack, *Jack Snyder's Collection of Favorite American Negro Spirituals*. New York, Jack Snyder Publishing Co., Inc., 1926.

Society for the Preservation of Spirituals, *The Carolina Low-Country*. New York, The Macmillan Co., 1931.

Songs and Spirituals of Negro Composition. Chicago, Progressive Book Co., 1928.

Songs of Many Nations. Delaware, O., Cooperative Recreation Service, Inc., 1941, 1958.

Songs, Rounds, and Carols. New York, The Womans Press, 1940.

"A South Carolina Folk Song" (recorded by E. C. L. Adams), *Southern Workman*, LIV (Dec 1925).

Southern Workman reports:

Briscoe, Joseph R., "The Baltimore Music Festival," LIII (Feb 1924);
Davis, J. E., "Negro Music," XLIX (May 1920);
Davis, J. E., "Recognition of Negro Music," XLIX (Jan 1920);
"Popularity of the Spirituals," LV (Apr 1926).

Sowande, Fela, *Sheet Music:* "All I Do," "Goin' to Set Down," "Couldn't Hear Nobody Pray," "De Angels Are Watchin'," "Heav'n Bells Are Ringin'," "Nobody Knows de Trouble I See," "Wheel, oh Wheel," "Stan' Still, Jordan," "Wid a Sword in Ma Han' "—New York, G. Ricordi, 1958 and other years.

Sowande, Fela, *Six Negro Spirituals*. New York, Chappell and Co., Ltd., 1955.

Spaeth, Sigmund, *A History of Popular Music in America*. New York, Random House, 1948.

Stearns, Marshall W., *The Story of Jazz*. New York, Oxford University Press, 1956.

Stefan-Gruenfeldt, *Anton Dvořák*.

Stickles, William, *Fifteen Favorite Spirituals*. New York, Charles H. Hansen Music Co., 1952.

Still, W. G., "Negrene i Amerikansk Musik," *Dansk Musiktidsskrift* (Copenhagen), XXVI (1951).

Still, William Grant (pp. 451-52): see Arvey, Verna, "W. G. S.—Creator of Indigenous American Music."

Still, William Grant, *Twelve Negro Spirituals*. New York, Handy Brothers Music Co., Inc., 1937.

Straight Texas, ed. Dobie and Boatright. Austin, Texas Folklore Society, 1937.

Szwed, "Negro Music: Urban Renewal."

Tamiami, Cory, *Four Early American Spirituals* (for clarinet choir). Avant Music, 1961.

Tate, Phyllis, *Four Negro Spirituals*. London, Oxford University Press, 1957.

Taylor, Marshall W., *A Collection of Revival Hymns and Plantation Melodies*. Cincinnati, M. W. T. & W. C. Echols, 1883.

Terry, Richard R., *Voodooism in Music and Other Essays*. London, Burns Oates & Washbourne, Ltd., 1934.

Thomas, Edna, *Negro Spirituals*. London, Keith Prowse & Co., Ltd., 1924.

Thomas, Virginia C., *Old Time Spirituals*. New York, Mills Music, Inc., 1953.

Thompson, Stith, "American Folklore After Fifty Years," *The Journal of American Folklore*, LI (Jan–Mar 1938).

Thurman, Howard, *Deep River*. New York, Harper & Brothers, 1945, 1955.

Thurman, Howard, "The Meaning of Spirituals," in Patterson, Lindsay, *The Negro in Music and Art*.

Thurman, Howard, *The Negro Spiritual Speaks of Life and Death*. New York, Harper & Brothers, 1947.

Thurman, Howard, "Religious Ideas in Negro Spirituals," *Christendom*, IV (1939).

Thurman, Sue Bailey, "Worship Moods in Negro Spirituals," *The Womans Press*, XXV (Jan 1931).

Tibbett mural reported in McKinney, Howard D. and Anderson, W. R., *Music in History*. New York, American Book Co., 1940.

Tiersot, Julien, *La Musique chez les peuples indigènes de l'Amérique du Nord (États-Unis et Canada)*. Paris, Librairie Fischbacher, 1910.

Tobitt, Janet E., *A Book of Negro Songs*. Pleasantville, N.Y., n.p., n.d.

Tolson, Melvin B., *Rendezvous with America*. New York, Dodd, Mead & Co., 1944.

Tolson, Peggy, comp., *Spirituals at the Piano*. Kansas City, Mo., Lillenas Publishing Co., 1969.

Tooze, Ruth and Krone, Beatrice, *Literature and Music as Resources for Social Studies*. Englewood Cliffs, N.J., Prentice-Hall, Inc., 1955.

Townsend, Leroy Clifford, *Thunder an' Lightnin' Britches*. St. Petersburg, Fla., Blue Peninsular Sanctuary, 1942.

"Tragedy and Spirituals in the Black Belt," *The Literary Digest*, XCV (Nov 5, 1927): contains quotation from Alan Dale.

Trebor, Haynes, "Ethnography of Jazz," *New York Times*, Apr 17, 1927. Written from Port Antonio, Jamaica.

Tupper, Virginia, "Plantation Echoes," *The Etude*, LV (Mar 1937).

Utica Jubilee Singers Spirituals. Boston, Oliver Ditson Co., 1930.

Van Gogh, Rupert, "The Evolution of Jazz," *The West African Review*, VI (Mar 1935).

Sample Van Vechten articles are as follows:

"All God's Chillun Got Songs," *Theatre Magazine*, XLII (Aug 1925);

"Don't Let Dis Harves' Pass," *The New York Herald Tribune Books*, Oct 31, 1926;

"The Folksongs of the American Negro," *Vanity Fair*, XXIV (Jul 1925);

"Religious Folk Songs of the American Negro—A Review," *Opportunity*, III (Nov 1925);

"Moanin' Wid A Sword In Ma Han'," *Vanity Fair*, XXV (Feb 1926);

"Some Cakewalks and Blues and Spirituals," *The New York Herald Tribune Books*, May 30, 1937;

"Soul of a People Lifted in Song," *New York Herald Tribune Weekly Book Review*, XXV (Nov 21, 1948).

Van Vechten, Carl, *In the Garret*. New York, Alfred A. Knopf, 1920.

Villard, Léonie, *La Poésie américaine*. Paris, Bardas Frères: Les Éditions Françaises Nouvelles, 1945.

Wagner, Jean, *Les Poètes Nègres des États-Unis*. Paris, Librairie Istra, 1963.

Wagner, Jean: personal interview.

Walker, *Jubilee*.

Ward, W. E., "Music in the Gold Coast," *The Gold Coast Review*, III (Jul–Dec 1927).

Warner, Richard, arr., *Five Spirituals, for organ*. Delaware Water Gap, Pa., Shawnee Press, 1967.

Washington, *Black Religion*.

Washington, Booker T., Introduction in Coleridge-Taylor, *Twenty-Four Negro Melodies Transcribed for the Piano*.

Washington, Booker T., "Plantation Melodies, Their Value," *Musical Courier*, LXXI (Dec 23, 1915).

Washington, John E., *They Knew Lincoln*. New York, E. P. Dutton & Co., Inc., 1942.

"Watering the Roots," *Sing Out!* XV (Jan 1966).

Waterman, Richard Alan, "Gospel Hymns of a Negro Church in Chicago," *Journal of the International Folk Music Council,* III (1951).

Waterschoot, Hector, "Negers bidden zingend," *Kultuur Leven,* XXXIII (May 1966).

Waterschoot, Hector, *Negers Zingen Spirituals en Blues.* Antwerp, n.v. Standaard-Boekhandel, 1964.

Waterschoot, Hector. *De Poezie der Negro-Spirituals.* Antwerp, n.v. Standaard-Boekhandel, 1960.

Watters, Pat and Cleghorn, Reese, *Climbing Jacob's Ladder.* New York, Harcourt, Brace and World, Inc., 1967.

Weatherford, W. D., *The Negro from Africa to America.* New York, George H. Doran Co., 1924.

The Weavers, *The Caroler's Songbook.* New York, Folkways Music Publishers, Inc., 1952.

Webb, Willie, *Most Beloved Spirituals.* New York, Chappell & Co., Inc., 1963.

Weeden, (Miss) Howard, "Bandanna Ballads," *The Ladies Home Journal,* XVII (Apr 1900); as a book: New York, Doubleday & McClure Co., 1899.

Weld, Arthur, "A Contribution to the Discussion of 'Americanism' in Music," *Music,* V (Apr 1894).

Wernecke, Herbert H., *Christmas Songs and Their Stories.* Philadelphia, The Westminster Press, 1957.

Westerman, Kenneth N., *Emergent Voice.* Ann Arbor, Mich., n.p., 1946.

Westermann, *The African Today and Tomorrow.*

White, George: as quoted in *The Cincinnati Commercial,* Oct 9, 1871.

Wiedenfeld, Karl, *Spirituals.* Cologne, Edition Melodia Hans Gerig, 1960.

Wier, Albert E., ed., *The Book of a Thousand Songs.* New York, World Syndicate Co., Inc., 1918.

Wier, Albert E., *Songs of the Sunny South.* New York, D. Appleton and Co., 1929.

Williams, "A Race History Told in Songs."

Wilson, J. Dover: quoted in Robeson, Paul, *Here I Stand.* New York, Othello Associates, 1958.

Wings Over Jordan information, except that from Townsend, *Thunder an' Lightnin' Britches* (q.v.): taken from Robbins, Jhan and June, "Negro Choir (Wings Over Jordan) Fights Prejudice," *The Washington Post,* Nov 21, 1948.

Wood, Mabel Travis, "Community Preservation of Negro Music," *The Southern Workman,* LIII (Feb 1924).

Woofter, T. J., Jr., *Black Yeomanry.* New York, Henry Holt and Co., 1930.

Work, Frederick J., *Folk Songs of the American Negro.* Nashville, Work Brothers & Hart Co., 1907.

Work, John W., *American Negro Songs.*

Work, John W., "Changing Patterns in Negro Folk Songs," *The Journal of American Folk-lore,* LXII (Apr–Jun 1949).

Work, John W., *Folk Song of the American Negro.* Nashville, Fisk University Press, 1915.

Work, John W., *Jubilee.* New York, Holt, Rinehart and Winston, Inc., 1962.

Work, John W., *Ten Spirituals*. New York, Ethel Smith Music Corp., 1952.

Wright, Richard, *Uncle Tom's Children*. New York, Harper and Brothers, 1938.

Wright, Richard, *White Man, Listen!* New York, Doubleday & Co., Inc., 1957.

Young, Andrew: quoted in Dunson, *Freedom in the Air*.

Yourcenar, Marguerite, *Fleuve Profound, Sombre Rivière*. Paris, Éditions Galli-
mard, 1964.

Zenetti, Lothar, *Peitsche und Psalm*. Munich, Verlag J. Pfeiffer, 1963.

Zimmerman, Heinz Werner, *Three Spirituals*. Minneapolis, Augsburg Publishing House, 1969.

Chapter 26

"Another white writer" (p. 583): Parrish, "The Plantation Songs of Our Old
Negro Slaves."

"Another writer" (p. 583): Van Cleve, John S., "Americanism in Musical Art,"
Music, XV (Dec 1898).

Cobb, Irvin S. funeral: "Negro Spirituals Requiem for Cobb," *New York Times*,
Mar 14, 1944.

Handy, W. C.: quoted in Garland, *The Sound of Soul*.

Miller, "The Artistic Gifts of the Negro."

Moton, Robert R., *Finding A Way Out* (autobiography). Garden City, N.Y.,
Doubleday, Page & Co., 1920.

Moton, Robert R., "Negro Folk Music," *The Southern Workman*, XLIV (Jun
1915).

Murphy, "Survival of African Music in America."

Scarborough, *On the Trail of Negro Folk-Songs*.

Statewide Recreation Project (Florida), *The Negro Sings*. Jacksonville, Statewide Recreation Project, 1940.

Van Vechten, "Moanin' Wid A Sword in Ma Han'" and "The Songs of the
Negro."

"White writer" (p. 583): Perkins, A. E., "Negro Spirituals from the Far South,"
Journal of American Folk-lore, XXXV (Jan–Mar 1922).

Work, John W., Introduction in Work, F. J., *Folk Songs of the American
Negro*.

Index to Spirituals

. .
.

This book is based upon the meanings and flavor of more than 6,000 Afro-American spirituals that were found in the course of the investigation. Only about 500 of these are specifically referred to in the text and indexed here, but they are adequate to show the basic lights radiated by the total group.

The indexing is an accounting of lines, stanzas, and references in the text. If the entry in the text is (or begins with a line that is) the same as the title of the song, then only the title is given. If it is different, the entry is followed by the title in parentheses and italics. If the entry is a first line and not a title, its basic words are capitalized; otherwise they are set down as they appear in the text.

No effort is made here to list all the songs in which a given line may appear; only the song from which it was taken by the author is listed. In the few instances in which spiritual fragments are taken from collectors who give no title or first line, an arbitrary title (closely connected with the fragment) has been assigned.

Just as the songs—following normal pathways of oral tradition—vary their lines without losing their identities, so the titles vary from collector to collector. The titles used here are the most common ones. Occasionally, where other titles are well known, they are listed with a cross reference to the title used.

The spelling generally follows that of the sources. No apologies need be made for spelling the same word in several different ways because these ways are a reflection of what skilled collectors actually heard. To maintain the relation to songs in the text, however, variant spellings and deliveries are recorded in brackets where they are needed.

[637]

Index